Handbook of
Clinical Health Psychology

Handbook of
Clinical Health Psychology

Edited by

Susan Llewelyn
Course Director
Oxford Doctoral Course in Clinical Psychology
University of Oxford, UK

and

Paul Kennedy
Reader in Clinical Psychology and Academic Director
Oxford Doctoral Course in Clinical Psychology
University of Oxford, UK

WILEY

Other Wiley Editorial Offices

John Wiley & Sons Inc., 111 River Street, Hoboken, NJ 07030, USA

Jossey-Bass, 989 Market Street, San Francisco, CA 94103-1741, USA

Wiley-VCH Verlag GmbH, Boschstr. 12, D-69469 Weinheim, Germany

John Wiley & Sons Australia Ltd, 33 Park Road, Milton, Queensland 4064, Australia

John Wiley & Sons (Asia) Pte Ltd, 2 Clementi Loop #02-01, Jin Xing Distripark, Singapore 129809

John Wiley & Sons Canada Ltd, 22 Worcester Road, Etobicoke, Ontario, Canada M9W 1L1

Wiley also publishes its books in a variety of electronic formats. Some content that appears
in print may not be available in electronic books.

Library of Congress Cataloging-in-Publication Data

Handbook of clinical health psychology / edited by Susan Llewelyn and
Paul Kennedy.
p.   cm.
Includes bibliographical references and index.
ISBN 0-471-48544-6
1. Clinical health psychology—Handbooks, manuals, etc.   I. Llewelyn,
Susan P.   II. Kennedy, Paul, 1959–

R726.7.H3542   2003
616′.001′9—dc21   2002156596

British Library Cataloguing in Publication Data

A catalogue record for this book is available from the British Library

ISBN 0-471-48544-6

Typeset in 10/12pt Times by TechBooks Electronic Services, New Delhi, India
Printed and bound in Great Britain by Biddles Ltd, Guildford and King's Lynn
This book is printed on acid-free paper responsibly manufactured from sustainable forestry
in which at least two trees are planted for each one used for paper production.

To my mother Joan, who will be fascinated by the book, and my late father Derek. Also to Guy and our children, Josie and James, who made it all worthwhile.

To Oonagh for her love and support, and our children, Julia and Dermot, for their joy. Also to my late mother Teresa for her humour and enthusiasm, and my father George.

Contents

About the Editors

Susan Llewelyn, PhD, FBPsS

Dr Susan Llewelyn is a Chartered Clinical Psychologist and Fellow of the British Psychological Society. She is currently Course Director on the Oxford Doctoral Course in Clinical Psychology and Honorary Senior Lecturer in Clinical Psychology at the University of Oxford. Dr Llewelyn is also Supernumerary Fellow at Harris Manchester College, University of Oxford. She has held posts as an Academic Psychologist in four UK universities, and has also worked as a Clinical Psychologist in the UK National Health Service for over 20 years.

She has published widely in academic and professional journals, having authored over 90 articles, books, book chapters or papers, and has edited professional journals, as well as a previous text in Health Psychology. She has a particular interest in training and in the promotion of clinical psychology, especially in health care. She has recently held the post of UK Chair of the Committee for Training in Clinical Psychology, and was a member of the Mental Health Act Commission.

Paul Kennedy, DPhil, MSc, FBPsS, CPsychol

Dr Paul Kennedy is Reader in Clinical Psychology at the University of Oxford, Academic Director on the Oxford Doctoral Course in Clinical Psychology, and Head of Clinical Psychology at the National Spinal Injuries Centre, Stoke Mandeville Hospital. He studied at the University of Ulster and Queens University, Belfast, and has worked in clinical health psychology since graduating from his clinical training in 1984. He has established clinical health psychology services in a number of areas.

Dr Kennedy has published over 70 scientific papers for peer-reviewed journals and has been a contributor to a number of book chapters. He is an active researcher with a broad portfolio of research on adjustment, coping and rehabilitation. He serves on the editorial board of the Journal of Clinical Psychology in Medical Settings. He was elected a Fellow of the British Psychological Society in 1999, served on the Committee of the Division of Health Psychology and was made a Supernumerary Fellow of Harris Manchester College, University of Oxford, in 2001. He is founding Chair of the Multidisciplinary Association of Spinal Cord Injury Professionals. In 2002 he was awarded the Distinguished Service Award by the American Association of Spinal Cord Injury Psychologists and Social Workers.

List of Contributors

Beth Alder, PhD, CPsychol, FBPsS, *Director of Research, Faculty of Health and Life Sciences, Napier University, 74 Canaan Lane, Edinburgh EH9 2TB, Scotland*

Gerhard Andersson, PhD, *Associate Professor, Departments of Psychology and Audiology, Uppsala University, Box 1225, SE-751 42 Uppsalla, Sweden*

David Mark Baguley, BSc, MSc, MBA, SRCS, *Head of Audiology, Audiology (94), Addenbrooke's Hospital, Hills Road, Cambridge CB2 2QQ, UK*

Cynthia Belar, PhD, *Executive Director, Education Directorate, American Psychological Association, 750 First Street, NE, Washington, DC 20002-4242, USA*

Paul Bennett, PhD, *Bristol Doctorate in Clinical Psychology, St Matthias Campus, University of the West of England, Bristol BS16 2JP, UK*

Suzanne Bennett Johnson, PhD, *Professor and Chair, Department of Medical Humanities and Social Sciences, Florida State University College of Medicine, Tallahassee, FL 32306-4300, USA*

Joyce A. Corsica, PhD, *Assistant Professor, Director of Outpatient Psychotherapy, Rush-Presbyterian St Luke's Medical Center, Chicago, IL 60612-3833, USA*

Jane Duff, BSc Hons, DClinPsychol, *Principal Psychologist, National Spinal Injuries Centre, Stoke Mandeville Hospital NHS Trust, Mandeville Road, Aylesbury, Bucks HP21 8AL, UK*

Patricia E. Durning, PhD, *Postdoctoral Associate, Department of Clinical and Health Psychology, University of Florida, PO Box 100165, 1600 SW Archer Road, Gainesville, FL 32610-0165, USA*

Timothy R. Elliott, PhD, ABPP, *Associate Professor and Psychologist, Department of Physical Medicine and Rehabilitation, 1717 6th Avenue South, University of Alabama at Birmingham, Birmingham, AL 35233, USA*

Janet E. Farmer, PhD, *Associate Professor, Department of Physical Medicine and Rehabilitation, University of Missouri Health Science Center, One Hospital Drive DC046.00, Columbia, MO 65212, USA*

Robert G. Frank, PhD, *Dean and Professor of Clinical and Health Psychology, College of Health Professions, PO Box 100185, Gainesville, FL 32610-0165, USA*

Mary Gilhooly, PhD, *Professor of Gerontology and Health Studies and Director, Centre of Gerontology and Health Studies, University of Paisley, High Street, Paisley, PA1 2BE, Scotland*

Robert L. Glueckauf, PhD, *Professor and Director, Center for Research on Telehealth and Healthcare Communications, Department of Clinical and Health Psychology, University of Florida, PO Box 100165, 1600 SW Archer Road, Gainesville, FL 32610-0165, USA*

Barbara Hedge, PhD, Professor, *Director of Clinical Psychology Training, Department of Psychology, University of Waikato, Private Bag 3105, Hamilton, New Zealand*

Adrian A. Kaptein, PhD, *Medical Psychology, Leiden University Medical Center, PO Box 9555, 2300 RB Lieden, The Netherlands*

Paul Kennedy, DPhil, MSc, FBPsS, CPsychol, *Reader in Clinical Psychology, University of Oxford and Academic Director, Oxford Doctoral Course in Clinical Psychology, Isis Education Centre, Warneford Hospital, Headington, Oxford OX3 7JX, UK*

Gerry Kent, PhD, *Senior Lecturer in Clinical Psychology, The University of Sheffield, Clinical Psychology Unit, Department of Psychology, Western Bank, Sheffield S10 2TP, UK*

Timothy U. Ketterson, *Center for Research on Telehealth and Healthcare Communications, Department of Clinical and Health Psychology, University of Florida, PO Box 100165, 1600 SW Archer Road, Gainesville, FL 32610-0165, USA*

Kristin M. Kilbourn, PhD, MPH, *Assistant Professor, Department of Psychology, Northern Arizona University, PO Box 15106, Flagstaff, AZ 86011-5106, USA*

Joshua C. Klapow, PhD, *Associate Professor, Department of Psychology, University of Alabama at Birmingham, 1665 University Blvd, RPHB 330, Birmingham, AL 35294, USA*

Gary Latchford, PhD, *Lecturer in Clinical Psychology, Academic Unit of Psychiatry, University of Leeds, 15 Hyde Terrace, Leeds LS2 9LT, UK and Consultant Clinical Psychologist, Department of Clinical and Health Psychology, St James's University Hospital, Beckett Street, Leeds, UK*

Wolfgang Linden, PhD, *Professor of Clinical Psychology, University of British Columbia, Psychology Department, 2136 West Mall, Vancouver, BC V6T 1Z4, Canada*

Susan Llewelyn, PhD, MSc, BA(Hons), FBPsS, CPsychol, *Oxford Doctoral Course in Clinical Psychology, Isis Education Centre, Warneford Hospital, Headington, Oxford OX3 7JX, UK*

Jeffrey S. Loomis, BS, *Director of Operations, Center for Research on Telehealth and Healthcare Communications, Department of Clinical and Health Psychology,*

University of Florida, PO Box 100165, 1600 SW Archer Road, Gainesville, FL 32610-0165, USA

Eileen McDonach, *Research Assistant, Centre of Gerontology and Health Studies, University of Paisley, High Street, Paisley, PA1 2BE, Scotland*

Laurence McKenna, MClinPsychol, PhD, *Consultant Clinical Psychologist, Audiology Centre, Royal National Throat, Nose and Ear Hospital, Grays Inn Road, London WC1X 8DA, UK*

Susan Michie, CHealthPsychol, MPhil, DPhil, *Reader in Clinical Health Psychology, Department of Psychology, University College London, 1–19 Torrington Place, London WC1E 7HR, UK*

Elena S. Monarch, PhD, *Post-doctoral Fellow, Department of Anesthesiology, Box 356540, University of Washington, Seattle, WA 98195, USA*

Jeri Morris, PhD, ABPN, *Assistant Professor, Northwestern University Medical School, Chicago II, 401, East Illinois, Suite 320, Chicago, IL 60611, USA*

Dawn Newman Carlson, *Center for Pediatric Psychology and Family Studies, Department of Clinical and Health Psychology, University of Florida Health Sciences Center, PO Box 100165, Gainesville, FL 32610-0165, USA*

David W. Nickelson, PsyD, JD, *Special Assistant to the Executive Director, Practice Directorate, American Psychological Association, 750 First Street, NE, Washington, DC 20002-4242, USA*

Richard Glynn Owens, PhD, *Professor, Department of Psychology, Tamaki Campus, University of Auckland, Private Bag 92019, Auckland, New Zealand. Currently at School of Psychology, University of Wales, Bangor, Gwynedd, LL57 2AS, UK*

Michael G. Perri, PhD, ABPP, *Professor, Department of Clinical and Health Psychology, University of Florida, PO Box 100165, 1600 SW Archer Road, Gainesville, FL 32610-0165, USA*

Treven C. Pickett, PsyD, *Post-doctoral Associate, Brain Rehabilitation Research Center (151A), Malcolm Randall VA Medical Center, 1601 SW Archer Road, Gainesville, FL 32608-1197, USA*

Patricia Rivera, PhD, *Project Coordinator, Project FOCUS, Department of Physical Medicine and Rehabilitation, 1717 6th Avenue South, University of Alabama at Birmingham, Birmingham, AL 35233, USA*

James R. Rodrigue, PhD, *Professor and Director, Center for Behavioral Health Research on Organ Transplantation and Donation* and *Professor, Departments of Clinical and Health Psychology, Surgery and Pediatrics, PO Box 100165, 1600 SW Archer Road, Gainesville, FL 32610-0165, USA*

Margreet Scharloo, PhD, *Medical Psychology, Leiden University Medical Center, PO Box 9555, 2300 RB Lieden, The Netherlands*

Michael Sharpe, MA, MD, MRCP, MRCPsych, *Reader in Psychological Medicine, University of Edinburgh, Royal Edinburgh Hospital, Edinburgh EH10 5HF, Scotland*

Pauline Slade, PhD, *Professor of Clinical Psychology/Consultant Clinical Psychologist, Clinical Psychology Unit, Department of Psychology, University of Sheffield, Western Bank, Sheffield S10 2TN, UK*

William B. Stiles, PhD, *Professor, Department of Psychology, Miami University, Oxford, Ohio 45045, USA*

Dennis C. Turk, PhD, *John and Emma Bonica Professor of Anesthesiology and Pain Research, Department of Anesthesiology, Box 356540, University of Washington, Seattle, WA 98195, USA*

Michelle R. Widows, PhD, *Visiting Assistant Professor, Department of Clinical and Health Psychology, University of Florida, PO Box 100165, 1600 SW Archer Road, Gainesville, FL 32610-0165, USA*

Barbara Wren, CHealthPsychol, MSc, *Occupational Health Psychologist, Occupational Health and Safety Unit, Royal Free Hampstead NHS Trust, Pond Street, London NW3 2QG, UK*

Preface

[T]here are only things perceiving, and things perceived.
(George Berkeley (1713), *Dialogues 3*, p. 235)

All the knowledge we have in agriculture, gardening, chemistry and medicine is built upon the same foundation. And if ever our philosophy concerning the human mind is carried so far as to deserve the name of science, which ought never to be despaired of, it must be by observing facts, reducing them to general rules, and drawing just conclusions from them.
(Thomas Reid (1764), p. 113, *An Inquiry into the Human Mind on the Principles of Common Sense*)

Clinical health psychology and non-clinical health psychology share the aim of using the methods, models, and interventions of psychology to achieve better scientific understanding and more effective interventions in health problems and health care.
(Johnston & Johnston, 1998)

There has been a considerable growth in science, practice and acceptance of the psychological factors associated with health in the past 20 years. The premise is not new but the integration of psychological models, interventions and empirical findings place clinical health psychology at the vanguard of health expansion, so much so that Belar (1997) considers "clinical health psychology as a specialty for the 21st century, if not *the* specialty for the professional practice of psychology in health care". It uses the theories and techniques of psychology, and focuses on an understanding of the aetiology, maintenance and consequences of mental and physical health and disability for individuals, their families and carers. As the discipline of psychology changes and matures, so does the discipline of clinical health psychology, so that both the field of enquiry, and the methods of investigation, have developed enormously in scope and complexity in recent years. The number of practising clinical health psychologists has burgeoned, as has the number of dedicated training courses. Opportunities now exist for the practice of clinical health psychology in a wide range of health care settings, as applied to almost every presentation of health-related distress. It was within this context that we identified the need for a current Handbook, which highlights existing thinking and applications in this growing field of enquiry and practice.

The origins of this Handbook lie in the editors' conviction that clinical health psychology has a vital role to play in the provision of health care, and hence in important aspects of most people's everyday experience of their lives. This is a concern for all of us as, in addition to the need for scholarship and understanding, we are all likely (through our own experience or those close to us) to have first-hand experience of chronic conditions, disability and/or trauma. The findings and applications of clinical health psychology that are presented here will, we hope, increase our understanding of, generate solutions to, and review priorities of the factors that can enhance the quality of people's lives.

As clinical health psychologists in the early part of the twenty-first century, we are aware of the contribution of researchers, theoreticians and clinicians who have seen clearly before us that the body and the mind cannot be separated, and who first set out on the demanding journey to discover how the embodied self is experienced in sickness and in health. Our methods are those of the scientist-practitioner, so for the most part we have chosen, as contributing authors, a range of clinical practitioners who practise what they preach—that is, those who use scientific procedures to investigate their subject, but who, as clinicians, also understand what they are reporting from a very practical point of view. However, we are not only scientist-practitioners, we also have a strong belief in the ethical stance of clinical health psychology, that is, that all people have worth, and that we are interested in making a difference to people whose life is altered through disease and disability. This not only refers to people who experience adverse health difficulties but those involved in treatment, care and the planning of health services.

We know there is still a long way to go, but hope that this volume will assist in the process of understanding the complexities of the human condition.

Susan Llewelyn
Paul Kennedy
Oxford, October 2002

REFERENCES

Belar, C.D. (1997). Clinical health psychology: a specialty for the 21st century. *Health Psychology*, **16**, 411–416.

Johnston, D.W. & Johnston, M. (1998). Editors of Volume 8: *Health Psychology*. In Alan Bellack & Michel Hersen, *Comprehensive Clinical Psychology*. New York: Pergamon.

Acknowledgements

We have been encouraged in this venture by many people and would like to acknowledge the considerable support we have received. We would like to thank Michael Coombs, then commissioning editor for Wiley, who recognised the need for an up-to-date account of clinical health psychology, seeing it as an exciting field that has much to offer both the consumers and providers of health care. We would also like to thank Vivien Ward, Publisher, Lesley Valerio and all at John Wiley & Sons for their support, as well as the many librarians for their indispensable assistance. Thanks are also due to all our chapter authors for their willingness to contribute, the quality of their work and for submitting their articles on time. We are also indebted to Mrs Linda Hall for her excellent coordination and organisational skills, effective liaison with our contributors and manuscript preparation.

We are grateful to many of our teachers and mentors for their education and endorsement, specifically Marie Johnston and David Smail, who have encouraged us to think critically, recognise the integration of the mind, body and social context, and how the scientist-practitioner approach can illuminate and progress our work. We have also learned from those psychologists who have demonstrated how many of the factors that influence our health are outside individual control, such as the nature of the environment, global wealth distribution and social and cultural inequalities. Our clinical colleagues and service users have also encouraged us by contributing directly and indirectly to our commitment, enthusiasm, comprehension and empathy.

PART I

Psychological Models and the Experience of Health Care

CHAPTER 1

Introduction and Overview

Susan Llewelyn
and
Paul Kennedy
University of Oxford, UK

The science and practice of clinical health psychology represents one of the most successful expansions in the discipline of psychology in the past 20 years. Clinical health psychology is becoming a success story. It is now recognised that psychological issues play a crucial role in almost every health care condition, and that addressing these issues will increase well-being and quality of life. From centres specialising in cancer and heart disease to those working with dermatology and trauma, clinical health psychologists have become part of the health care team in many parts of developed health economies. They have contributed to the increasing range of treatments offered to patients and to the growing sophistication of interventions available, and have increased awareness of the need for both evidence-based practice and research. Despite this, however, there is still a very long way to go until psychological input is available to all patients and all staff in health care. Provision of clinical heath psychology services remains patchy outside the larger centres, particularly those outside the economically developed world. This volume documents much of what has been achieved so far, and indicates what is still to be achieved.

The twenty-first century has already seen a range of astounding developments in the provision of health care, primarily but not only in the more economically advantaged countries, and will undoubtedly see many more. Advances in biotechnology, genetics and knowledge management systems have already resulted in profound changes in what is seen as possible and desirable in health, and this explosion in knowledge and application will almost certainly continue. Central to these changes are psychological issues which impact on and are impacted by the changing nature of health care. This volume, published near the start of the century, provides an overview of what we know now about clinical health psychology, and how current knowledge is put into practice. Written mainly by authors who are both academics and clinical practitioners, each chapter also raises questions for the future, as the discipline comes to elaborate its understanding and the range of possible applications.

As editors of this volume we think it is important to open with a brief consideration of some of the key issues in health care, even if many of these facts are by now reasonably well known. These issues not only provide a context for the practice of clinical health psychology,

Handbook of Clinical Health Psychology. Edited by S. Llewelyn and P. Kennedy.

but also demonstrate the need for it. The list is not comprehensive but is illustrative of the inseparability of health care from wider social and demographic developments.

- Eight out of ten of the top causes of death in the developed world have psychosocial components in their aetiology and/or maintenance. Forty-five per cent of all causes of death are cardiovascular in nature (see Chapter 6).
- About half of all the people who have ever lived to be 65 or older are alive today (see Chapter 22).
- Sixteen out of 20 of the most frequently diagnosed conditions in primary care have some behavioural component which could be amenable to intervention by clinical health psychologists.
- Approximately 5% of the health care budget is spent on prevention, and disproportionate expenditure is spent in the last two weeks of people's lives.
- In the USA, for example, 19% of the population over the age of five have some form of disability. Of those over 65 years, 42% are disabled.
- Approximately three million people world-wide die each year from a tobacco-related disease. Ninety per cent of COPD is caused by smoking (see Chapter 9).
- Also, the growing diseases of civilisation (cancer, coronary heart disease) are mediated by social isolation, obesity and substance abuse.
- Chronic, but not acute, conditions are the main focus of health care, at least in the developed world.

All this suggests that psychological issues must play an increasingly central role in the provision of health care in all types of setting, from primary care to specialist centres. An ageing population in developed countries means that probably the major issues presented to health care providers are the problems of living with chronic conditions and disability, such that quality of life issues become prominent (68% of health care costs are spent on management of chronic conditions (see Chapter 5)). Health care providers need to become adept at helping people to manage the consequences of disability and ill health, in order to help them to increase their functional abilities, and to develop a wide range of methods of ensuring social and vocational engagement and support. Associated with this are issues of choice and rationing, given that it is unlikely that it will prove possible for most nations to manage to fund the spiralling costs resulting from developments in research in biogenetics and pharmacology. Societies will also need to develop ways of helping people to deal with predictive information and resulting choices. We need to help people to behave in healthier ways, given that we know that many illnesses or disabilities could have been prevented. For the discipline of clinical health psychology, all this means that we need more parsimonious and predictive models of health behaviour, together with research that develops the evidence base. We also need to ensure that research in this area is resourced. We need to demonstrate that psychological and rehabilitative issues are just as important to health care as medical or pharmacological intervention. Most crucially, we need to put these models and this evidence into practice, so that patients and health care providers can benefit from what we know.

Another way of putting this is that, as health care providers, we all need to be aware of ethical, moral and emotional issues in health care, not just the technical aspects (Crossley, 2001). Patients are people before they are patients, and so are health care providers.

THIS VOLUME: OVERVIEW

This volume aims to provide an overview of what we know about clinical health psychology, and how to apply that knowledge. Putting together any Handbook is inevitably an ambitious venture. Its intention is to provide a comprehensive overview of the practice of clinical health psychology in the twenty-first century for practitioners, researchers, academics and students in clinical psychology, health psychology, psychiatry, nursing and other therapeutic professions. It aims primarily to be a well-referenced but practical resource which provides an authoritative, up-to-date guide to empirically validated interventions in the psychology of health care. It is intended to be used frequently by practitioners, trainees and others who will use the resource when approaching work in a particular area of clinical health psychology. Strategic issues are discussed throughout the book, together with a consideration of some of the research issues which limit or explain the evidence that is presented. This should allow practitioners of clinical health psychology to judge what may be helpful for their own particular area of practice or research, and to learn from the endeavours of others.

Although it is a Handbook, we hope that this volume is not used as a "cookbook", whereby specific approaches are taken off the shelf for use in all situations. Instead we hope that it will help practitioners to ensure that their practice is informed by concepts, models and evidence that are "state of the art". Full references are provided to key texts, although the text does not aspire to be encyclopaedic. Given the vast and ever-expanding range of knowledge in clinical psychology, the Handbook cannot hope to be comprehensive, and it would be quite easy for any reader to spot areas that have had to be omitted. Having said that, we hope that all the major conceptual and service delivery issues have been introduced, such that a reasonably comprehensive overview of today's clinical health psychology can be obtained by a dedicated reader.

The book has been structured to allow the systematic presentation of conceptual, process, content and contextual issues in the practice of clinical health psychology. Prior to the main body of the Handbook—i.e. in the introductory five chapters—the book considers contextual issues and the importance of topics including communication, technology, ageism and power, all of which have an impact on how clinical health psychology is delivered by practitioners and experienced by recipients of services.

Chapter 2 by Belar looks at the importance of underlying models for the effective practice of health psychology, with an emphasis on the biopsychosocial model. Chapter 3 by Kennedy and Llewelyn, Chapter 4 by Michie and Wren, and Chapter 5 by Elliott and Rivera provide summaries of evidence concerning patients', staff's and families' experience of crucial aspects of the delivery of care, such as communication, adherence and stress.

Making up the main body of the text, Chapters 6 to 22 are written by established practitioners, each of whom has been asked to provide a well-supported account of knowledge in key areas of application in clinical health psychology. Each contributor has written a conceptual synthesis of the area, and has demonstrated how key models are related to formulation, service delivery and research. Areas covered include heart disease, oncology, diabetes, spinal cord injury, gynaecology, reproductive health, pain, chronic fatigue, trauma, dermatology, transplants, health problems of older adults, COPD, obesity, cognitive impairment and HIV. There are other areas that could have been included, but we hope to have captured a reasonable cross-section of present practice. We have not tried to impose a consistent style onto authors, but to allow contributors to present their area in as informative a way as possible. Nonetheless, each chapter provides information on:

- the condition and the effective psychological input that can be or has been provided;
- the theoretical perspectives that underpin theory and practice of health psychology in the area;
- the methods that have been used to research the area, and the limitations of application;
- the agenda for future research and policy in the area.

Each chapter should thus constitute an authoritative account of the main areas of practice within clinical health psychology, following the structure noted above. Although most of the evidence discussed concerns work with adults, some of the chapters do discuss the practice of clinical psychology with children. Naturally, children and families are often affected by the conditions discussed, even if they are not the patients. It is the case, however, that the bulk of this text does not specifically consider the issues raised by working with children. We understand that the publishers are planning a subsequent volume concerning clinical health psychology with children.

After the main body of the text, the concluding six chapters provide, first, a consideration of the adequacy and scope of research methodology in clinical health psychology, and, second, on account of the wider context within which clinical health psychology is delivered. The authors are all concerned in different ways with what a clinical health psychologist can contribute in terms of knowledge, research and theory. Chapter 23 by Owens explores the use of research themes in clinical health psychology, including consideration of the particular demands of doing quantitative research in applied, clinical settings, while Chapter 24 by Stiles looks at the growth of qualitative methodology, and ways of ensuring reliability and validity. Chapter 25 by Bennett considers the social context of health, the impact of poverty, and reduced access to resources by substantial numbers of patients in most health care systems in the world. New developments in the delivery of clinical health psychology are considered in Chapter 26 by Glueckauf and his colleagues, in which there is discussion of current information-based societies, with particular emphasis on telemedicine. Chapter 27 by Frank and his colleagues explores policy issues, while Chapter 28 provides an overall account of the practice of clinical health psychology and its likely future development. Chapter 28 also considers implications for professional development, as well as training, and concludes by looking at ways forward in clinical health psychology in responding to the challenges raised in all the chapters.

Throughout the Handbook, the biopsychosocial model is the major theoretical model underpinning all contributions, but use is also made of other models. In particular, the cognitive model is advocated for most of the interventions, given the strength of the evidence base for this approach. Overall, it is intended that the book will act as an informative guide to the delivery of effective interventions in a changing and challenging health care context.

REFERENCE

Crossley, M. (2001). Do we need to rethink health psychology? *Psychology, Health and Medicine*, **6**, 243–255.

CHAPTER 2

Models and Concepts

Cynthia Belar
University of Florida and
American Psychological Association, USA

The following archival definition was recorded in 1997 when the American Psychological Association formally recognized clinical health psychology as a specialty in the professional practice of psychology.

> Clinical Health Psychology applies scientific knowledge of the interrelationships among behavioral, emotional, cognitive, social and biological components in health and disease to the promotion and maintenance of health; the prevention, treatment and rehabilitation of illness and disability; and the improvement of the health care system. The distinct focus of Clinical Health Psychology is on physical health problems. The specialty is dedicated to the development of knowledge regarding the interface between behavior and health, and to the delivery of high quality services based on that knowledge to individuals, families, and health care systems. (APA, 1997)

Yet this recognition by organized psychology did not mark its beginning. Instead, this recognition marked the culmination of decades of international development in the scientific knowledge base for practice, relevant education and training opportunities, and mechanisms for credentialing. In exploring models and concepts in clinical health psychology, this chapter[*] will focus on its key features and describe the breadth of its applications in terms of problems addressed and populations served.

KEY FEATURES OF CLINICAL HEALTH PSYCHOLOGY

A key feature of clinical health psychology is its breadth. Although individual psychologists focus specific areas for their work, the field itself comprises a very broad area of research and practice. Another key feature is the biopsychosocial model—the underlying model for the entire field. Other features include the focus on prevention and health promotion, the need for collaborative work with other health care disciplines and a commitment to life-long learning. In addition, an emphasis on cost-effectiveness and medical cost offset has permeated the growth of clinical health psychology, probably more so than other areas of

---

[*] This chapter was prepared by Cynthia Belar, PhD, in her personal capacity and does not reflect the views or opinions of the Education Directorate or any other component or governance group of the American Psychological Association.

Handbook of Clinical Health Psychology. Edited by S. Llewelyn and P. Kennedy.
© 2003 John Wiley & Sons, Ltd.

psychological practice. Each of these key features is briefly described below, and references are provided for further study.

The Biopsychosocial Model of Health and Illness

In addition to its foundations in psychological science, clinical health psychology has roots in other health and social sciences.

> Biological, cognitive, affective, social and psychological bases of health and disease are bodies of knowledge that, when integrated with knowledge of biological cognitive-affective, social and psychological bases of behavior, constitute the distinctive knowledge base of Clinical Health Psychology. This includes broad understanding of biology, pharmacology, anatomy, human physiology and pathophysiology, and psychoneuroimmunology. Clinical Health psychologists also have knowledge of how learning, memory, perception, cognition, and motivation influence health behaviors, are affected by physical illness/injury/disability, and can affect response to illness/injury/disability. Knowledge of the impact of social support, culture, physician–patient relationships, health policy and the organization of health care delivery systems on health and help-seeking is also fundamental, as is knowledge of diversity and minority health issues, individual differences in coping, emotional and behavioral risk factors for disease/injury/disability, human development issues in health and illness, and the impact of psychopathology on disease, injury, disability and treatment. (APA, 1997)

A core aspect of this description is the focus on the *integration* of biological, psychological and sociocultural bodies of knowledge as related to health. This focus on integration in a biopsychosocial model reflects a unitary view of mind–body relationships—a view that actually predominated in human history until the Middle Ages when medical views of illness emerged in the West along with beliefs that mind and body were distinct entities. With the separation of church and state, the church claimed the mind; the state claimed the body. Descartes' proposal that explanations for bodily processes were found in the body itself further de-emphasized the role of emotions in health following the Renaissance. The dualistic approach to health care in Western civilization was consolidated with the development of physical medicine.

Attention to the role of psychological factors in health revived in the nineteenth century and became more formalized in the study of psychosomatic medicine in the early twentieth century. As unitary concepts of health received renewed attention, empirical research in psychophysiology and the effects of stress on disease flourished. It was also recognized that illness was a part of life, and that coping with illness was a complex psychological process that could affect health itself. Thus coping became a focus for theory and research, and the basis for the development of numerous psychological interventions. By the late 1970s the evidence for the relationships between behavior and health were so compelling in the United States that the Institute of Medicine (IOM) commissioned the landmark report that documented that 50% of mortality from the ten leading causes of death could be traced to behavior (Institute of Medicine, 1982). Over the past 25 years there has been worldwide interest in the interrelationships among biological, psychological and sociocultural aspects of health and illness, yet despite the explosion in the knowledge, the exact mechanisms of interplay among these factors remains a challenge for the field. A number of concepts have received considerable attention by researchers and clinicians, some of which are listed below.

- Coping (Zeidner & Endler, 1996)
- Culture and health (Landrine & Klonoff, 2001)
- Hardiness, resilience, optimism (Ouellette & DiPlacido, 2001)
- Health and illness beliefs (Fishbein et al., 2001)
- Patient control/perceived control (Auerbach, 2000; Wallston, 2001)
- Psychoneuroimmunology (Cohen & Herbert, 1996; Miller & Cohen, 2001)
- Psychophysiological self-regulation/visceral learning (Engel, 2001; Gatchel & Blanchard, 1993)
- Quality of life (Kaplan, 2000)
- Self-efficacy (Bandura, 1997)
- Social cognition models (Suls & Martin, 2001)
- Social support (Uchino, Cacioppo & Kiecolt-Glaser, 1996)
- Stress (Dougall & Baum, 2001).

In examining the conceptual and research underpinnings of clinical health psychology, it soon becomes obvious that the field grew out of the interplay between research and practice. Since its more formal beginnings it has been closely tied with the scientist-practitioner model in clinical psychology. Historically, however, there were not the demands for clinical services that facilitated the growth of clinical psychology after World War II—namely, the mental health needs of returning veterans. This does not mean that there were no public needs for the services of clinical health psychologists. Rather, these needs were not well recognized by the public, other disciplines, or policy-makers. Yet "clinical health psychologists were often on the frontiers of professional practice, creating and disseminating knowledge in new terrains, and in developing new and different service delivery models that took root and spread (e.g., Wilbert Fordyce's contributions to the understanding of chronic pain syndromes and subsequent development of roles for psychologists in pain clinics)" (Belar, 1995, p. 1). Developments in the field actually created the markets for practice.

A Focus on Health Promotion and Prevention

Another key feature of clinical health psychology is that its focus is not solely on disease or deficit. There is also a significant emphasis on health, which, as emphasized in the World Health Organization's definition, is not the mere absence of disease or symptoms. Clinical health psychologists are concerned with health promotion, such as promoting healthy behavior (e.g., exercise) and issues relevant to healthy work settings, communities, and environments. They are also concerned with "normal" conditions related to health, such as childbirth, aging, and end-of-life-issues. Moreover, within the past decade there has been a re-emergence of interest in positive psychology, with a focus on its implications for health (Snyder & Lopez, 2002).

By definition, clinical health psychology also has a significant focus on prevention. Kaplan (2000) articulates the important difference between primary and secondary prevention. Secondary prevention is most often based on a traditional biomedical disease model that focuses on early identification and treatment of existing disease. Behavioral factors are clearly important in screening procedures for problems such as breast cancer and prostate cancer, and psychologists do have significant roles to play in research and practice. However, primary prevention requires interventions that reduce the probability that a health problem will develop and is almost always based on a behavioral model, e.g., smoking prevention and cessation. Kaplan argues that primary prevention may be actually more cost-effective in promoting population health than secondary prevention, and calls for increased resource allocation for primary prevention that is distinct from the delivery of health care services in the current health care system.

Cost-effectiveness and Clinical Health Psychology

Themes of cost-effectiveness and medical cost offset have permeated clinical health psychology from the outset. Although current health care reform has driven emphases on evidence-based and cost-effective care in general, the emphasis in clinical health psychology goes back to some of the earliest empirical work in the field that examined the relationship between psychological factors and surgical outcome (and differences in inpatient days). One might hypothesize that, early on, psychologists recognized that improvement in health outcomes would not be a sufficient argument for including psychological services in a system dominated by medical procedures and controlled by the profession of medicine. In considering this possibility it is interesting to note that some of the seminal medical cost offset data came from a capitated care system in which incentives for both physicians and psychologists were aligned (e.g., Cummings & Follette, 1968).

It is important to note that the concept of cost-effectiveness is related to both the prevention and the treatment of disease, and that assessment of each requires that different variables be addressed. Friedman et al. (1995) provide an excellent overview of clinical health psychology and cost offset by reviewing six pathways by which psychological services can both maximize clinical care and have economic benefits: (1) empowering patients in appropriate self-care; (2) modification of psychophysiological pathways; (3) modification of overt behaviors impacting health; (4) provision of social support; (5) identification of undiagnosed psychiatric problems; and (6) screening and intervention for somatization disorder.

The Need for Interprofessional Care

Another key feature of clinical health psychology is collaboration with other health care professionals in a variety of health care settings. Whereas clinical psychology tended to foster collaborations primarily with psychiatrists and psychiatric social workers in mental health settings, clinical health psychologists work with an array of other medical specialties and health professionals. In fact, interdisciplinary work is viewed as fundamental to research and practice, and thus is a core component in graduate education and training.

McDaniel, Campbell and Seaburn (1995) have described a series of principles of collaboration that have guided their work in primary care settings, that are useful for a variety of interprofessional collaborations in health care. Among these are the importance of healing the mind–body split, making families a part of the health care team, developing a common mission with other providers, avoiding professional ethnocentrism, respecting cultural differences, promoting a community of caring, and attending to development of good relationships.

Clinical health psychologists interact with a diversity of other health professions; the kinds of disciplines are determined by the psychologist's focused area of research or practice. For example, when working in women's health, contact with internal medicine, nurse practitioners, and obstetrician–gynecologists is frequent. If working with children, contact with pediatricians and pediatric specialists is more common. Psychologists working with organ transplant patients interact with a variety of different medical specialties, plus nursing and medical social work staff. A psychologist working in the area of pain management may interact with anesthesiologists, dentists, oncologists, psychiatrists, rheumatologists, orthopedic surgeons, neurosurgeons, physical therapists, and occupational therapists among others.

The setting in which the clinical health psychologist works plays a role in the nature of contacts with other health professions. If working in independent practice with outpatients, contact is often via telephone or through written reports. If working in group practices, clinics, or hospital settings, contact is also through side-by-side patient contact, team functioning, clinical rounds, and "curbside" consultation. Effective clinical health psychologists appreciate that health care settings differ with respect to their sociocultural and political issues, and realize the importance of learning how to function effectively within them.

In addition to independent and group practices, a sample of more specific settings in which clinical health psychologists provide services are: (1) ambulatory care, including primary care (e.g., family practice and internal medicine, pediatric care, college counseling clinics, school health clinics); (2) urgent care (e.g., emergency areas, walk-in clinics); (3) specialty care (e.g., pain clinics, arthritis clinics, oncology clinics, neurology clinics, surgery clinics, dental clinics, pulmonary clinics); (4) hospice (residential and home care); (5) hospital/residential-based care, including medical–surgical wards, consultation–liaison units, intensive care units (e.g., burn, coronary care); (6) rehabilitation units (e.g., spinal cord, cardiac, head injury, pain, pulmonary, stroke); (7) nursing home care; (8) industrial and other worksite settings; and (9) public health agencies.

The Breadth of Clinical Health Psychology

The breadth of clinical health psychology is demonstrated not only by the settings in which psychologists work, but by the problems addressed in research and practice, the populations served, and the services provided.

Problems Addressed

There are at least nine categories of problems addressed in clinical health psychology research and practice (Belar, 1980, 1997; Belar & Deardorff, 1995). These are briefly described below, with some examples noted. This listing is clearly not exhaustive, but illustrates the breadth of the field.

1. *Psychological factors secondary to disease/injury/disability.* Many health problems are associated with psychological sequelae that can range from normal adjustment reactions

to major depression in the individual or family members. As examples, there are often body image concerns following disfiguring burns, amputation, and other surgeries; there are posttraumatic stress disorders subsequent to accidents and violent crimes; and there are family issues related to injury, chronic illness, and death. Moreover, psychological factors can complicate recovery from illness, e.g., depression post-myocardial infarction.

2. *Somatic presentations of psychological dysfunction.* Some mental health problems present with primarily somatic symptoms. For example, many patients who seek emergency services for chest pain are subsequently diagnosed as having had a panic attack. Somatization disorders are also commonly addressed in clinical health psychology.

3. *Psychophysiological disorders.* A number of health problems have significant psychophysiological components that are addressed in basic and applied research as well as practice, e.g., tension and migraine headache, irritable bowel syndrome.

4. *Physical symptoms/conditions responsive to behavioral interventions.* There are a number of conditions that, regardless of etiology, can be responsive to psychological interventions. Examples include urinary and fecal incontinence, pain, and anticipatory nausea associated with chemotherapy.

5. *Somatic complications associated with behavioral factors.* Some health problems are exacerbated by behavioral factors. A diabetic's failure to self-manage insulin dosage properly can result in poor outcome; inappropriate weight bearing on sprained ankles can delay healing; and failure to take immunosuppressives can result in organ transplant rejection. In general, behavioral compliance with medical regimens is a significant factor in health and an area of significant research and practice in clinical health psychology.

6. *Psychological presentation of organic disease/problems.* Although some mental health problems present with physical symptoms, clinical health psychologists must also be knowledgeable about medical problems that present with psychological symptoms. For example, depression can be a presenting symptom in hypothyroidism and some cancers. Moreover, there are a number of medical regimens with known psychological side-effects, e.g., depression with interferon treatment for hepatitis C, steroid-induced psychoses.

7. *Psychological and behavioral aspects of stressful medical procedures.* Many medical procedures can be stressful for patients, e.g., wound debridement. Moreover, advances in health care have presented new psychological challenges for patients. For example, earlier magnetic resonance imaging equipment was associated with a high rate of claustrophobic reactions that prevented its use for some patients. Advances in assisted reproductive technology have presented new challenges to couples in coping and decision-making. Psychological preparation for and management of stressful medical procedures has a long history in the field, with some of the earliest empirical work being in preparation for surgery.

8. *Behavioral risk factors for disease/injury/disability.* It is well accepted that there are significant behavioral risk factors for many health problems. Smoking, weight, exercise, and substance abuse are all extensively addressed in research and practice. In addition, behaviors such as risk-taking, seat belt and helmet usage, and storage of toxic materials are also related to health problems and of importance in the field.

9. *Problems of health care providers and health care systems.* Clinical health psychology is not just patient-centered, but relevant to health care providers and the design of health care systems themselves. For example, the provider–patient relationship is associated

with patient satisfaction (and adherence) and thus of interest to both health care systems and individual providers. Moreover, clinical health psychology addresses problems of burnout in the health care professions, and stress in intensive care settings such as burn units and hospice. They also participate in program development and evaluation, the development of clinical pathways, and quality assurance activities for health care systems.

Populations Served

Clinical health psychology serves populations through the entire life span, prenatal to end-of-life, with the full range of identified health problems. The international system for classification of health problems is provided by the World Health Organization (WHO), whose Tenth Revision of the *International Statistical Classification of Diseases and Related Health Problems* (ICD-10) is the most recent in a series begun in 1893 (WHO, 1992). The ICD-10 is used for general epidemiological purposes, coding for insurance benefits, and the evaluation of health care. The system also provides a useful framework for examining psychology's role in health care.

There are 16 disease categories in the ICD-10 as listed in Table 2.1. Inspection of these categories reveals that each and every category contains patient populations served by clinical health psychology through research or practice. When we consider issues of prevention, it quickly becomes apparent that the entire general population can also be served.

It is also noteworthy that mental disorders represent only one category of health problems in the ICD-10. Whereas historically much of clinical psychology has had mental disorders as its primary focus, clinical health psychology addresses the full range of health problems as described in this classification system. In fact, during the past decade professional psychology has been experiencing a figure ground reversal phenomenon in viewing itself as a health profession versus, primarily, a mental health profession. What was once its major

Table 2.1   International classification of diseases

I	Infectious and parasitic diseases
II	Neoplasms
III	Endocrine, nutritional and metabolic diseases
IV	Diseases of the blood and blood-forming organs
V	Mental disorders
VI	Diseases of the nervous system and sense organs
VII	Diseases of the circulatory system
VIII	Diseases of the respiratory system
IX	Diseases of the digestive system
X	Diseases of the genito-urinary system
XI	Complications of pregnancy, childbirth, and the puerperium
XII	Diseases of the skin and subcutaneous tissue
XIII	Diseases of the musculoskeletal system and connective tissue
XIV	Congenital anomalies
XV	Certain conditions originating in the perinatal period
XVI	Injury and poisoning

Source: World Health Organization (1992). *International Classification of Diseases and Related Health Problems, Tenth Revision* (ICD-10). Geneva, Switzerland: Author.

focus is now but one, albeit very important, subset in the domain of health research and practice activities related to health that psychology has to offer.

In considering populations served, it is especially important to note that patients are not the only focus in clinical health psychology. As important are the family and social environment, health care providers, and aspects of the health care system itself. Consultation to other providers, organizations, and policy-makers are by no means uncommon.

Services Provided

Another parameter for understanding clinical health psychology is through a description of the variety of services offered. Clinical health psychologists engage in a heterogeneous set of teaching, research, assessment, intervention, consultation, and public policy activities in a variety of settings as noted above. With respect to teaching, it is important to note that many are involved in the education and training of other health professionals, and not just future psychologists. Such efforts are critical to a more full integration of health and behavior research and practice.

Clinical health psychology services (assessment, intervention, and consultation) can have multiple foci: the patient, the patient's family, the health care providers, or other aspects of the patient's environment, including the health care system. Services involve a biopsychosocial approach as described above, and are often multidimensional, targeting physiological, affective, cognitive, and behavioral features of the individual and his or her environment. For example, interventions might target muscle tension levels via biofeedback, or depression via cognitive-behavioral therapy, or health beliefs through cognitive therapy, or treatment adherence through a self-monitoring program. Consultation can be patient-centered, or staff- or systems-centered, e.g., helping staff to deal with angry feelings toward a patient refusing additional treatment, promoting the use of prompts in intensive care units to foster orientation, participation in rehabilitation planning, design of health care communications and service delivery systems, or involvement in health policy development.

Combining a model for clinical services developed by Belar and Deardorff (1995) and a model related to psychological services in health care developed by the APA Workgroup on the Expanding Role of Psychology in Health Care (1998), a three-dimensional model of clinical health psychology can be portrayed that captures the breadth in the field. As shown in Figure 2.1, psychologists provide a range of clinical services at a variety of levels across the wide spectrum of health problems. A fourth dimension, could it be portrayed, is the timing of the service, whether it be for primary prevention, secondary prevention, or tertiary prevention. This further illustrates the range of contributions of clinical health psychology.

The implications of this breadth in clinical health psychology is clear: no one psychologist can be expert in each and every area of research and practice. Individual psychologists are more focused in their work, although many remain generalists as in primary care psychology. Yet all recognize that another key theme in the field is the emphasis on lifelong learning.

The Necessity for Lifelong Learning

Given the breadth of the field, the explosion of knowledge, and the need to keep abreast of rapid advances in health care, clinical health psychologists must maintain a commitment to lifelong learning. Although formal continuing education requirements exist in some

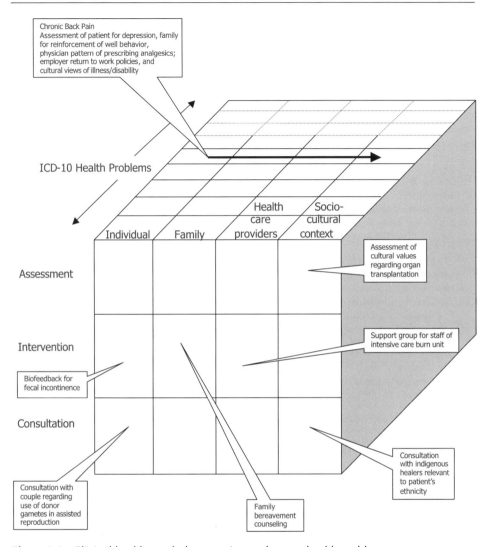

Figure 2.1 Clinical health psychology services × focus × health problems

credentialing systems, the predominant focus of the discipline and profession has been upon self-directed learning for postgraduate professional development. Obviously, self-directed learning requires an accurate self-assessment of one's knowledge and skills, thus an important aspect of graduate education is the development of an attitude that not only values lifelong learning, but also promotes skills in self-assessment and self-directed study. Belar and colleagues proposed a model for self-assessment in clinical health psychology that can be used to promote ethical expansion of practice by those in the field (Belar et al., 2001). Table 2.2 lists specific questions that can used by psychologists to gauge their expertise in core domains of requisite knowledge and skills. Where deficits are identified, psychologists can then design self-study programs using handbooks such as this one as a core reference and seek appropriate consultation.

Table 2.2 Template for self-assessment in clinical health psychology[a]

1. Do I have knowledge of the biological bases of health and disease as related to this problem? How is this related to the biological bases of behavior?
2. Do I have knowledge of the cognitive-affective bases of health and disease as related to this problem? How is this related to the cognitive-affective bases of behavior?
3. Do I have knowledge of the social bases of health and disease as related to this problem? How is this related to the social bases of behavior?
4. Do I have knowledge of the developmental and individual bases of health and disease as related to this problem? How is this related to developmental and individual bases of behavior?
5. Do I have knowledge of the interactions among biological, affective, cognitive, social, and developmental components (e.g., psychophysiological aspects)? Do I understand the relationships between this problem and the patient and his or her environment (including family, health care system, and sociocultural environment)?
6. Do I have knowledge and skills of the empirically supported clinical assessment methods for this problem and how assessment might be affected by information in areas described by Questions 1–5?
7. Do I have knowledge of, and skill in implementing, the empirically supported interventions relevant to this problem? Do I have knowledge of how the proposed psychological intervention might impact physiological processes and vice versa?
8. Do I have knowledge of the roles and functions of other health care professionals relevant to this patient's problem? Do I have skills to communicate and collaborate with them?
9. Do I understand the sociopolitical features of the health care delivery system that can impact this problem?
10. Am I aware of the health policy issues relevant to this problem?
11. Am I aware of the distinctive ethical issues related to practice with this problem?
12. Am I aware of the distinctive legal issues related to practice with this problem?
13. Am I aware of the special professional issues associated with practice with this problem?

[a] From Belar et al. (2001). Self-assessment in clinical health psychology: a model for ethical expansion of practice. *Professional Psychology: Research and Practice*, **32**, 137. (Copyright © 2001 by the American Psychological Association. Reprinted with permission.)

FUTURE DIRECTIONS

There are a number of reasons why clinical health psychology has and will continue to prosper, many of which have been noted in the past but are as relevant today (Gentry, 1984).

1. *Deficiencies in the biomedical model.* There has been increasing recognition of the limitations of the traditional medical model to adequately explain health and illness, whereas research support for the biopsychosocial model has mounted.
2. *Maturation of behavioral science research and practice.* With advances in theory and methods, there has been an increased body of knowledge linking behavior and health, e.g., multivariate methods such as path analysis, the application of learning theory to disease, psychoneuroimmunology.
3. *Shift from infectious to chronic disease.* As patterns of mortality and morbidity have changed, and the importance of chronic diseases to world health have been noted, there has been increased recognition of the influence of behavioral factors in chronic disease.

4. *Focus on prevention.* As health care assumes a population perspective, more attention is drawn to prevention and the role of health risk behaviors and individual self-management in the promotion of health and prevention of illness.

5. *Increased cost of health care.* As health care costs escalate without sufficient access to or demonstrations of improved health status, alternatives to traditional medical care are sought and marketplace shifts drive changes in services available.

6. *Increased concern with quality of life.* With advances in technology and increased costs, questions are raised as to quality of life, not just length of life.

These reasons also remain relevant to the growth of clinical health psychology in the future, although some aspects of the field are likely to undergo more rapid change than others. In March 2000, the APA Division of Health Psychology hosted a conference to examine the future of health psychology. The conference addressed the evolution of the biopsychosocial model, advances in medicine, changes in population demographics, health care economics, and the health psychology marketplace; needs and advances in primary prevention, and developments in psychological interventions. Some of the recommendations most relevant to clinical health psychology were for more attention to genetics; organ and tissue transplantation; pharmacology; telehealth; health informatics; primary care; and issues of diversity in health care. Advances in medicine and technology were also identified as having significant ramifications for health psychology. For example, advances in health care assessment and treatment often increase complexity in decision-making for providers as well as for patients and their families. Moreover, there can be physical and psychosocial adverse iatrogenic effects of procedures that make patient selection and preparation increasingly complex. New ethical, legal, and economic issues are raised, and there are increased needs to tailor new advances for individual differences and diverse populations.

A look toward the future must also acknowledge the impact of globalization. Oldenburg (2002) highlights the need for a broadened scope of research and practice given the increased understanding of global influences on health (e.g., war, changes in the natural environment). Since transportation, communications, and industrialization will only increase the interconnectedness between developed and developing nations, an international view of health issues is needed "to include a more 'upstream' focus on economic, social and environmental determinants of health" (Oldenburg, 2002, p. 13).

Perhaps the most fundamental issue for the future of the field is the need to maintain an ongoing commitment to the scientific bases of practice and the development of an accumulated knowledge base. Historically much of the outcome literature has been noncumulative; replications are not frequently published even though replication is valued as a cornerstone of science. There is little doubt that it will be cumulative knowledge that will have the greatest potential for impact on health policy, which in turn will affect the fate of clinical health psychology.

REFERENCES

APA (1997). *Archival Description of Clinical Health Psychology as a Specialty in Professional Psychology.* Minutes of the Council of Representatives Meeting, August 1997. Washington, DC: American Psychological Association.

APA (1998). *Report of the Workgroup on the Expanding Role of Psychology in Healthcare.* Washington, DC: American Psychological Association.

Auerbach, S.M. (2000). Should patients have control over their own health care? Empirical evidence and research issues. *Annals of Behavioral Medicine*, **22**, 246–259.

Bandura, A. (1997). *Self-efficacy: The Exercise of Control*. New York: Freeman.

Belar, C.D. (1980). Training the clinical psychology student in behavioral medicine. *Professional Psychology*, **11**, 620–627.

Belar, C.D. (1995). Presidential Column. *The Health Psychologist*, December, p. 1.

Belar, C.D. (1997). Clinical health psychology: a specialty for the 21st century. *Health Psychology*, **16**, 411–416.

Belar, C.D. & Deardorff, W. (1995). *Clinical Health Psychology in Medical Settings: A Practitioner's Guidebook*. Washington, DC: American Psychological Association.

Belar, C.D., Brown, R.A., Hersch, L.E., Hornyak, L.M., Rozensky, R.H., Sheridan, E.P., Brown, R.T. & Reed, G.W. (2001). Self-assessment in clinical health psychology: a model for ethical expansion of practice. *Professional Psychology: Research and Practice*, **32**, 135–141.

Cohen, S. & Herbert, T.B. (1996). Health psychology: psychological factors and physical disease from the perspective of human psychoneuroimmunology. *Annual Review of Psychology*, **47**, 113–142.

Cummings, N.A. & Follette, W.T. (1968). Psychiatric services and medical utilization in a prepaid health plan setting: Part II. *Medical Care*, **6**, 31–41.

Dougall, A.L. & Baum, A. (2001). Stress, health, and illness. In A. Baum, T.A. Revenson & J.E. Singer (Eds), *Handbook of Health Psychology* (pp. 321–337). Mahwah, NJ: Lawrence Erlbaum Associates.

Engel, B.T. (2001). Visceral learning. In A. Baum, T.A. Revenson & J.E. Singer (Eds), *Handbook of Health Psychology* (pp. 85–94). Mahwah, NJ: Lawrence Erlbaum Associates.

Fishbein, M., Triandis, H.C., Kanfer, F.H., Becker, M., Middlestadt, S.E. & Eichler, A. (2001). Factors influencing behavior and behavior change. In A. Baum, T.A. Revenson & J.E. Singer (Eds), *Handbook of Health Psychology* (pp. 3–17). Mahwah, NJ: Lawrence Erlbaum Associates.

Friedman, R., Sobel, D., Myers, P., Caudill, M. & Benson, H. (1995). Behavioral medicine, clinical health psychology, and cost offset. *Health Psychology*, **14**, 509–518.

Gatchel, R.J. & Blanchard, E.B. (Eds) (1993). *Psychophysiological Disorders: Research and Clinical Applications*. Washington, DC: American Psychological Association.

Gentry, W.D. (Ed.) (1984). *Handbook of Behavioral Medicine*. New York: Guilford Press.

Institute of Medicine (1982). *Health and Behavior: Frontiers of Research in the Biobehavioral Sciences*. Report of a study by committee of the Institute of Medicine, Division of Mental Health and Behavioral Medicine. National Academy Press, 384. NTIS Accession No. PB 82 260–068.

Kaplan, R.M. (2000). Two pathways to prevention. *American Psychologist*, **55**, 382–396.

Landrine, H. & Klonoff, E.A. (2001). Cultural diversity and health psychology. In A. Baum, T.A. Revenson & J.E. Singer (Eds), *Handbook of Health Psychology* (pp. 851–891). Mahwah, NJ: Lawrence Erlbaum Associates.

McDaniel, S., Campbell, T. & Seaburn, D. (1995). *Families, Systems and Health*, **14**, 283–298.

Miller, G.E. & Cohen, S. (2001). Psychological interventions and the immune system: a meta-analytic review and critique. *Health Psychology*, **20**, 47–63.

Oldenburg, B. (2002). Preventing chronic disease and improving health: broadening the scope of behavioral medicine research and practice. *International Journal of Behavioral Medicine*, **9**, 1–16.

Ouellette, S.C. & DiPlacido, J. (2001). Personality's role in the protection and enhancement of health. In A. Baum, T.A. Revenson & J.E. Singer (Eds), *Handbook of Health Psychology* (pp. 175–193). Mahwah, NJ: Lawrence Erlbaum Associates.

Snyder, C.R. & Lopez, S.J. (Eds) (2002). *Handbook of Positive Psychology*. London: Oxford University Press.

Suls, J. & Martin, R. (2001). Social comparison processes in the physical health domain. In A. Baum, T.A. Revenson & J.E. Singer (Eds), *Handbook of Health Psychology* (pp. 195–208). Mahwah, NJ: Lawrence Erlbaum Associates.

Uchino, B.N., Cacioppo, J.T. & Kiecolt-Glaser, J.K. (1996). The relationship between social support and physiological processes: a review with emphasis on underlying mechanisms and implications for health. *Psychological Bulletin*, **119**, 488–531.

Wallston, K.A. (2001). Conceptualization and operationalization of perceived control. In A. Baum, T.A. Revenson & J.E. Singer (Eds), *Handbook of Health Psychology* (pp. 49–58). Mahwah, NJ: Lawrence Erlbaum Associates.

WHO (1992). *International Classification of Diseases and Related Health Problems, Tenth Revision* (ICD-10). Geneva, Switzerland: World Health Organization.

Zeidner, M. & Endler, N. (Eds) (1996). *Handbook of Coping: Theory, Research, Applications*. New York: John Wiley & Sons.

CHAPTER 3

The Person's Experience of Health Care

Paul Kennedy
and
Susan Llewelyn
University of Oxford, UK

INTRODUCTION

In this chapter we will focus on the individual's experience of the health care system. This experience is influenced by many factors that include historical, cultural and economic developments. In the early part of the nineteenth century, it was only the worthy "poor" who were hospitalised, with the wealthy being attended in their homes by doctors and nurses. Technology and specialised services increased during the twentieth century, especially in the areas of acute care, and hospitals grew in their influence and dominance in health care provision. Now, at the beginning of the twenty-first century, there has been another technological and conceptual shift, this time from hospitals to primary care, and length of hospitalisation has been greatly reduced. Although medical doctors continue to be the key coordinators of the interface between the patient's experience of illness and provision of treatment, it is increasingly being recognised that psychological issues, particularly concerning communication, are central to this experience.

We will begin this chapter by examining factors associated with doctor–patient communication; we will then explore patient participation in decision-making, and review critical aspects of adherence. With the growth of chronic conditions, adherence has become an even greater issue and challenge to health care systems. It does not matter how extensive the evidence base is for the treatment and intervention; if the patient does not take the "medicine", the treatment will have little or no effect. There is then a section looking at the expert patient, self-management and self-help issues, and a concluding section concerning the patient's experience of, and communication about, bad news.

Handbook of Clinical Health Psychology. Edited by S. Llewelyn and P. Kennedy.
© 2003 John Wiley & Sons, Ltd.

DOCTOR–PATIENT COMMUNICATION

Patient Satisfaction

In recent decades, the communication process during medical consultation has been under review, largely as a result of the high level of dissatisfaction with this process reported by patients. Ley (1988) reviewed studies of hospital patients and general practice patients and found that 41% were dissatisfied with communication about their treatment in hospital while 28% were dissatisfied with communication in general practice. Over the years, the proportion of dissatisfied patients has remained stable (Ong et al., 1995; Steptoe et al., 1991). A number of studies have also shown an association between poor communication and malpractice claims. The communication problems most frequently identified are inadequate explanations for diagnosis or treatment, feeling ignored, devaluing patient and family views, and patients feeling rushed (Beckman et al., 1994; Hickson et al., 1992; Vincent, Young & Phillips, 1994). Ley (1989) has placed satisfaction as a key outcome of patient understanding and memory, which in turn predicts compliance. Ley and others have concluded that satisfaction is determined by the content of the consultation and that patients want as much communication as possible, even if it is bad news (see later in this chapter).

In a recent review, Williams, Weinman and Dale (1998) examined the components of patient satisfaction and doctor–patient communication, in particular the information provision and the information-seeking behaviours of doctors and patients, and found that relationship and affective factors during medical encounters were associated with both patient satisfaction and the communication style of the doctor. Many of the studies reviewed in their paper utilised the Interaction Analysis System (IAS). This is an observational instrument that allows researchers to identify, categorise and quantify features of medical encounters. Papers by Bales (1950), Roter (1977) and Stiles et al. (1979) are examples of studies using the most commonly applied IAS systems. The system normally uses audio- or video-recorded doctor–patient interactions which are then broken into segments and coded, using categories such as: shows solidarity; agrees; gives suggestions; gives opinions; shows tension. Roter, Hall and Katz (1988), for example, identified six broad communication variables which include information-giving, information-seeking, social conversation, positive talk, negative talk and partnership building. From their review, Williams, Weinman and Dale (1998) concluded that doctors' general information provision during consultations is positively related to patient satisfaction. Patient information to doctors was also positively related to satisfaction, with the exception of excessive talking. Generally, time spent on examination, giving information and listening were all associated with increased satisfaction. Nevertheless, this review also highlighted some of the contradictory findings in the relationship between information provision and patient satisfaction. For example, time spent on talking about the patient's history was found to be both negatively and positively related to patient satisfaction, while increased question-asking by patients was negatively associated with patient satisfaction. A more recent study, however, found no significant negative effects of increased question-asking by patients.

The manner in which information is provided is also of critical concern. Williams, Weinman and Dale (1998) reviewed the relationship between doctor and patient (for example, the degree of friendliness) and the feelings expressed in terms of positive and negative affect (for example, tension in tone) and concluded that there was evidence that doctor–patient relationship and the expression of affect during consultations were important factors in patient satisfaction. Doctors' friendliness, courteous behaviour, social conversation, encouraging and empathic behaviours, partnership building and patients' liking of the doctor as a person, and faith in doctors in general, were all positively related to patient satisfaction. However, doctor anger or disagreement and the expression of negative tones by both patients and doctors were negatively related to patient satisfaction. Paradoxically, negative doctor affect has also been found to be related to increased patient satisfaction. Hall, Roter and Rand (1981), in a review of the audio-tapes of 50 consultations, concluded that negative physician affect expressed in tone of voice, with positive affect communicated through words, is interpreted by patients as positive since this may reflect the seriousness and concern on the part of the physician.

How the communication is conveyed, and who conveys it, is also important. Bensing (1991) found that only 7% of the emotional communication is conveyed verbally, 22% is transferred by voice tone, but 55% is transferred by visual cues such as eye contact and body positioning. Few studies have, however, used a systematic approach to the coding of non-verbal interaction. Smith, Polis and Hadac (1981) found that close physical proximity increased patient understanding, whereas more touching led to lower scores in understanding the information given. A number of studies have identified gender differences in doctors' communication styles. Female doctors were generally found to adopt a more patient-centred communication style, whereas male doctors tended to be more directive and controlling (West, 1990). Coupland, Robinson and Coupland (1994) examined relationships between medical and socio-relational relations of doctor–patient discourse, and found that consultations were initiated by some form of socio-relational talk, before moving on to a more medically framed talk.

Many communication researchers agree that there is an important distinction between patient-centred and doctor-centred behaviours (Molleman et al., 1984; Ong et al., 1995; Williams, Weinman & Dale, 1998). The patient-centred style consists of more affective behaviours (empathy, openness and reassurance) and is thought to be more egalitarian with greater patient involvement in the decision-making process. The doctor-centred style (or disease-centred approach) is one where the physician is task-focused, concentrates on his or her own agenda and seeks to reach a clear diagnosis of the problem through a textbook style description. Stewart (1984) defined patient-centred interactions as "those in which the patient's point of view is actively sought by the physicians. This implies that the physician behaves in a manner that facilitates the patient expressing him or herself and that for his or her part, the patient speaks openly and asks questions." Williams, Weinman and Dale (1998), in their review of communication style and patient satisfaction, found that higher patient-centredness and empathy during consultations were associated with increased patient satisfaction. However, for patients presenting with a physical problem, a directing style from the doctor was also found to be associated with higher satisfaction, higher than for those who received a sharing style.

Communication of course involves both patient and physician. Studies of patient behaviour suggest that patients are often reluctant to ask questions. Roter (1989) found that only 6% of the interaction involved patients asking questions. Older adults, patients with existing communication difficulties and learning disabilities, as well as children (Tates & Meeuwesen, 2001), are all less actively involved in doctor–patient interactions. Bennett (2000) reported that between half and three-quarters of patients who want more information during a medical consultation do not ask for it. McKinley and Middleton (1999) conducted a content analysis of written agenda forms completed by 819 patients who consulted 46 randomly selected general practitioners and found that almost all patients had requests they wished to make of their doctor, 60% had their own ideas about what was wrong, and 38% had considered explanations about why they were unwell. They concluded that most patients came to a consultation with a particular agenda. Yet medical staff may not always succeed in encouraging patients to ask questions, or in providing enough time for the full expression of patient concerns. Marvel et al. (1999) found that only 28% of physicians elicited their patients' complete agenda. In all other cases, patients were "redirected" or "interrupted" before they could finish voicing their concerns. Beckman and Frankel (1984) found that patients were interrupted, on average, 18 seconds after beginning the description of their symptoms, and only 23% of patients felt able to complete their statement after the doctor's interruption. Not surprisingly, many patients feel their diagnosis is incomplete (Stimson, 1974).

Recall and Understanding

It is also clear from a number of studies that there are many difficulties with recall and understanding and, further, that patients with a limited understanding of the information provided, and those with poor recall, may remain dissatisfied. Ley (1998) suggests that up to 53% of people report not having fully understood the information they were given. Boyle (1970) examined patients' definitions of different illnesses and reported that, when given a checklist, many patients had a poor understanding of the terminology used. Sarriff et al. (1992) found that many patients have difficulty understanding prescription instructions. Ley (1998) identified a linear relationship between the amount of information given and the percentage recalled. Seventy-five per cent of information given in four statements is likely to be retained, while only 50% of information given in 10 statements will be recalled. Interestingly, some of these confusions may also exist among staff: Hadlow and Pitts (1991) examined the understanding of common health terms by doctors, nurses and patients. The results of their survey showed that clear differences of understanding of common medical and psychological terms exist. The level of correct understanding was highest for physicians (70%) and lowest for patients (36%).

Implications of Low Satisfaction, Recall and Understanding

The above review of studies has demonstrated links between recall, understanding and satisfaction. In turn, high levels of dissatisfaction have significant implications for the physical and emotional well-being of patients. Parle, Jones and Maguire (1996) examined maladaptive coping and affective disorders in 600 newly diagnosed cancer patients. They found that one of the strongest predictors of later anxiety and depression was the number and severity of patients' unresolved concerns. Molleman et al. (1984) concluded that dissatisfaction with communication resulted in poorer coping with cancer, and Ley (1982) concluded that it resulted in non-compliance with medical advice (see below). One response to this has been to encourage a greater degree of patients' involvement in decision-making about their own treatment, which will now be considered.

PATIENT PARTICIPATION IN DECISION-MAKING

Those with an interest in medical ethics have by and large accepted the principle that autonomy (what the patient wants) trumps beneficence (what the doctor thinks is best for the patient) in all but the most extreme circumstances (Balint & Shelton, 1996). The American College of Physicians (1984) declared that the patient has a right to self-determination, while the World Health Organisation has stated that patient involvement in care is not only desirable but is a social, economic and technical necessity (Waterworth & Luker, 1990). Some observers have suggested that medicine is facing a general crisis of confidence because of its failure to share knowledge (Charles, Gafni & Whelan, 1997) while the public is becoming increasingly more aware and sceptical of physicians. Furthermore, the Internet has become a powerful medium for patients to obtain information about medical problems and treatments (Strum, 1997), and in many instances patients have access to this information without having recourse to their physicians.

All of this has raised the question of patient participation in decision-making. Guadagnoli and Ward (1998) reviewed the research which provides evidence both for and against patient participation in decision-making, and concluded that (a) patients want to be informed of treatment alternatives, (b) they, in general, want to be involved in treatment decisions when more than one treatment alternative exists, although (c) the benefits of participation have not yet been clearly demonstrated in research studies. For example, Beaver et al. (1996) reviewed 150 women diagnosed with breast cancer and found that 20% wanted an active role in deciding their treatment, 28% preferred a joint decision and 52% wanted their surgeon to decide for them. Deber, Kraetschmer and Irvine (1996) distinguished between problem-solving and decision-making. They found that most patients want physicians to do the problem-solving, but they wanted to be involved in treatment decisions. Also, Deber, Kraetschmer and Irvine's survey of 285 patients scheduled for an angiogram showed that, in general, patients wanted physicians to make the diagnosis and identify the treatment, while having a strong preference for their own involvement in decisions such as treatment choice. Mazur and Hickam (1997) concluded that 68% of their participants indicated a preference for decision-making when faced with a possibility of an invasive medical procedure such as surgery.

Significantly, Kaplan (1991) suggested that the issue is one of distinguishing between treatment outcomes, the choice of which should be in the control of the patient, and the means for achieving these outcomes, which should depend on the advice from the physician. Frosch and Kaplan (1999) reviewed research on shared decision-making and concluded that the benefits depend on the type of problem and the patient. They suggested that shared decision-making is more appropriate when there is medical uncertainty, and when the patient is both younger and better educated. They also suggested that patients do want to be consulted about the impact of treatment, as quite clearly different issues will be important for different patients.

Although it is not conclusive, there is some evidence that the expanding involvement of patients in health care produces better health outcomes, providing an empirical rationale for what may have been an inevitable shift in power and social control (Kaplan, Greenfield & Ware, 1989). Guadagnoli and Ward (1998) conclude in their review that patients' involvement in their care leads to improved medical outcomes such as reduced pain and anxiety, quicker recovery and increased compliance. Devine and Cook's (1983) meta-analysis on the positive impact of psycho-education on length of hospital stay is also suggestive of the benefits of patient involvement. Other studies, however, do not show this; for example,

Morris and Royle (1987) found no difference between breast cancer patients who chose their treatment and those who did not. As a possible explanation for this mixed set of findings, it is worth noting that many studies have been conducted with small samples and inadequate follow-up, and that much more research is needed. Guadagnoli and Ward conclude that patient participation is justified on moral grounds, as well as any evidence on effectiveness. Similar points are made by patients' organisations and pressure groups, who are increasingly unwilling to leave decisions to medical experts.

Turning to medical staff themselves, despite the increasing shift towards patient-centred medicine in recent years, Frosch and Kaplan (1999) were unable to locate studies that directly surveyed large samples of physicians regarding their views on shared decision-making, and suggest that the acceptability of shared decision-making is mixed, and may be linked to level of communication skills of individual clinicians. Eraker and Politser (1982) reported that physicians were reluctant to disclose information relevant to making uncertain choices, especially when these choices involved trade-offs among risks, disability and death. There does appear to be a discrepancy here between the views of staff and patients. For example, Sullivan, Menapace and White (2001) reported that the vast majority of patients in an acute-care facility in the USA (99%) wanted to know about their condition, and would want to be told if they had a life-threatening illness. Most (62%) wanted to be told all the details, but this contrasted with nurses and physicians, of whom only 29% and 39% respectively thought all details should be given.

Although evidence on the impact of patient involvement in decision-making is unclear, evidence is reasonably consistent concerning views on communication about decisions. Dowsett et al. (2000), for example, examined patients' and their relatives' preferences for, and satisfaction with, patient-centred and doctor-centred consulting styles. One hundred and thirteen women who had been treated for breast cancer and 48 of their relatives or friends watched video-tape scenarios of an oncology consultation. Using professional actors, viewers were randomly allocated to either a good prognosis or poor prognosis video, and segments were presented in both styles to enable viewers to directly compare and contrast patient-centred and doctor-centred approaches. Both patients and their relatives or friends significantly preferred a patient-centred consulting style across all aspects of the consultation. This was particularly so when the patient had a poor prognosis.

Encouraging Participation

Based on the view that patient participation should be encouraged, Greenfield, Kaplan and Ware (1985) have designed an intervention to facilitate participation in decision-making. Participants were randomised into one of two conditions. In the experimental condition participants were taught how to elicit more information, to recognise medical decisions and to negotiate these decisions with physicians. Participants allocated to the control group received didactic information regarding their condition. Results showed that the experimental patients were more involved with their medical encounters and were more assertive with their physicians and elicited more information. The experimental group also showed an improvement in subjective well-being, even though levels of pain were rated the same across the two groups at follow-up.

An alternative approach is to set up technological systems to improve involvement. Shared decision-making programmes are video programmes presented in an interactive format using a videodisc player and computer (Kasper & Fowler, 1993). They contain information about medical conditions and descriptions of the benefits and risks of treatment alternatives. Decision boards work on a similar but simpler basis (Levine et al., 1992). The decision board separates making a choice into three components: (1) treatment choices, (2) chance of outcome and (3) outcome. Most patients report that the decision board helped them make decisions. Decision boards present a viable alternative method for facilitating shared decision-making, especially if one considers the estimated costs of a shared decision-making programme video, which was estimated to be $750 000 by the authors (Kasper et al., 1992).

ADHERENCE

As noted above, Ley (1988) and others have suggested that there is a close link between satisfaction, understanding, recall and adherence. Adherence to treatment plans is considered a critical indicator of the effectiveness of doctor–patient communication. Adherence may involve behavioural change or completion of prescribed medication, and is a major problem for both acute and chronic health conditions. Many health practitioners remain unaware of the extent of the problem. Establishing the efficacy of a therapeutic intervention requires considerable resources. This is undermined if many, or even most, patients fail to follow their treatment sufficiently to obtain therapeutic benefit.

We will now examine the issues associated with adherence and include a review of the extent of the problem; the assessment of adherence; the factors associated with poor adherence; and the strategies for maximising adherence. It is also important to acknowledge that health practitioners often fail to adhere to health recommendations themselves.

Extent of Problem

It is estimated that overall, 40% of patients fail to adhere to any given treatment regime. Seventy-eight per cent adhere to acute plans and 54% adhere to the treatment programme in chronic conditions (DiMatteo, 1995; Ley, 1979). Haynes (1976) estimated that adhering to appointment times was about 50%, while adhering to the drug treatments prescribed ranged from 42 to 62%. Fiedler (1982) estimated that about one-third of patients always comply, one-third of patients sometimes comply and one-third never comply. The rates of adherence among people with hypertension tend to average about 64% (Dunbar-Jacobs, Dwyer & Dunning, 1991). Bartlett et al. (2002) highlight how adherence levels of greater than or equal to 95% are required to maintain virologic suppression in the treatment of HIV. However, most studies show that between 40 and 60% or less than 90% of patients are adherent. Kane et al. (2001) reported an adherence level of 40% in people with ulcerative colitis, and concluded that non-adherence is associated with taking multiple medications. Adherence is also a problem with children. Hazzard, Hutchinson and Krawiecki (1990) report an adherence rate of 44% with children on anti-convulsant therapy. Perkins and Epstein (1988) suggested that as behavioural requirements are greater than the requirements of drug-taking, adherence rates for exercise programmes are even lower than those for other medical interventions. Carmody, Matarazzo and Istvan (1987) reviewed the literature promoting adherence for healthy heart diets, including the reduction of fat, cholesterol and sodium, and found a range of adherence from 13 to 76%. Overall, Rodgers and Ruffin (1998) concluded that, in the USA, poor adherence is a highly significant problem leading to excessive morbidity, mortality and medical costs.

Poor adherence and non-adherence to practice guidelines by staff are also important aspects of the problem. Halm et al. (2000) found that 43% of physicians were non-adherent with clinical practice guidelines in the treatment of pneumonia. Furthermore, they found that those physicians with more experience of pneumonia were less likely than those less experienced to follow guidelines. Ley (1988) found that between 12 and 76% of medical practitioners failed to prescribe antibiotics appropriately. Yeo et al. (1994) found that general practitioners adhered poorly to recommendations for prescribing tranquillisers despite being provided with well-constructed educational protocols. Health professionals not only fail to adhere to professional guidelines, but they often base their treatment decisions on inaccurate information. Ross (1991), comparing general practitioners, district nurses and patients' perceptions of medication regimes, found that for only 5% of patients was there complete agreement in the number and type of medications used by the patients. In addition, 44% of patients were taking medications that were not recorded.

The Assessment of Compliance

To evaluate adherence to treatment programmes, it is critical that we have transparent, accurate and standardised assessments. Dunbar-Jacobs, Burke and Puczynski (1995) concluded that errors in measurement of adherence are generally biased towards an overestimate. For example, Gordis, Markowitz and Lilienfeld (1969) highlighted the inaccuracy in using interviews to estimate patient reliability in taking antibiotics, and found that 83% of parents claimed that their children were taking the medication although 92% of the children's urine samples showed no sign of the children having taken the drug. Adherence assessment techniques include self-report measures (interviews; diet and activity questionnaires; daily diaries), electronic monitoring (physiological measurement during track exercise; electronic indicators of medication use; event by event data collection), pill counts, recording of pharmacy refills, and physiological markers (measures of metabolites in the serum; assessment of sodium and cholesterol levels). These measures are not without their difficulties as some are unreliable, such as pill counts (Rudd et al., 1990), or are expensive and cumbersome, such as assessing drug metabolites over a lengthy period of time. Other techniques, such as regular telephone check-ups, may risk damaging the doctor–patient relationship if the patient feels distrusted by the medical team. Nonetheless, Dunbar-Jacobs, Burke and Puczynski (1995) emphasised the need for measures of patient behaviour that are more accurate than those relying simply on self-report. Recently electronic medication monitors have enabled longitudinal assessment of discrete dosing episodes, permit the dose-by-dose determination of adherence, and are useful in highlighting discrepancies between self-report and actual adherence. Moulding (1999) suggests that such monitors may enhance directly observed therapies rather than replace them.

Factors Associated with Poor Adherence

Factors contributing to poor adherence include characteristics of patients, the nature of the disease and the treatment itself, as well as social and cultural factors.

Table 3.1 Patient characteristics most relevant in adherence[a]

1. Whether or not the patient knows what she or he has to do
2. How well the patient was able to adhere to treatment in the past
3. Self-efficacy expectations
4. Biased implementation of the regime
5. Social support
6. Satisfaction with medical care
7. Avoidance coping

[a] While some of these may seem counter-intuitive (e.g. avoidance coping), most are potentially modifiable and amenable to change.

Patient Characteristics

Early studies tended to identify the demographic and personality determinants of adherence. Sackett and Haynes (1976), in a systematic review of 185 studies, found no clear relationship between race, gender, educational experience, intelligence, marital status, occupational status, income and ethnic or cultural background and adherent behaviours. Kane et al. (2001) reported that non-adherence is associated with taking multiple medications, being single and being male. Meichenbaum and Turk (1987) suggested that extremes of age may be one of the few consistent findings, in that the very young are more adverse to bad-tasting medicine, and the very old are more susceptible to forgetfulness, hence both groups are less likely to be adherent. However, younger adults may also be less adherent (Bosley, Fosbury & Cochrane, 1995; Lorenc & Branthwaite, 1993) for a host of other reasons, including disagreement about the diagnosis, holding a different model of illness or circumstantial difficulties.

There is little evidence that personality characteristics predict adherence behaviours (Bosley, Fosbury & Cochrane, 1995; Mischel, 1968). Social cognitive models that describe the beliefs associated with adherence have been proposed, but their predictive value has generally been poor. Dunbar-Jacobs, Burke and Puczynski (1995) have suggested a number of patient characteristics to be the most relevant in predicting adherent behaviour. These are summarised in Table 3.1.

Disease and Treatment Characteristics

Marks et al. (2000) suggest that the most frequently mentioned disease characteristics linked to poor adherence are the severity of the disease, and the visibility of the symptoms. When the symptoms are obvious and unwanted, the person is more likely to comply with treatment which offers a promise of removing them. However, when the prognosis is poor, there is evidence that the rate of compliance is reduced. Dolgin et al. (1986) found compliance lower in those cancer patients whose survival prospects were poor. Meichenbaum and Turk (1987) identified four factors associated with non-adherence: preparation for treatment (waiting times, cohesiveness of treatment delivery and convenience); immediate nature of treatment (complexity of treatment regime, duration of treatment regime and degree of behavioural change needed); administration of treatment (adequacy of supervision, continuity of care and parental involvement); and consequences of treatment (medication and social side-effects).

Many patients get confused with complicated treatment protocols—for example, those required by antiretrotherapy for HIV. Bartlett et al. (2002) and Ley (1979) found that patients forget at least one-third of the information given by their physician. This situation is exacerbated further if their treatment programme includes multiple factors such as dietary changes, an increase in exercise, as well as drug intervention. Adherence also tends to decline over time, with long-term therapy declining to approximately 50% irrespective of illness or setting (Sackett & Snow, 1979). Furthermore, drugs with greater physical side-effects are associated with poorer adherence. Social side-effects are additionally particularly difficult.

We have discussed earlier in this chapter how practitioners who adopt a more patient-centred or affiliate style of interaction can enhance adherence. DiMatteo and DiNicola (1982) suggested that patients were more compliant if the physician was warm, caring, friendly and interested. In behavioural terms, this means smiling, effective eye contact and leaning towards the patient. Squier (1990) concluded that there is strong evidence that the affective quality of the doctor–patient relationship is a key determinant of patient satisfaction and hence adherence to treatment. In particular, warmth, caring, positive regard, lack of tension and non-verbal expressiveness appeared to be the most important elements in establishing and maintaining a good working relationship, and in encouraging adherence.

In a two-year longitudinal study, DiMatteo et al. (1993) examined the role of the medical system itself in patient adherence. They found no significant effect of personal characteristics of doctors, but that physician specialty did appear to be related to adherence. Practice characteristics were also found to be important, such that having a busier practice, more definite plans for follow-up appointments, and the perceived willingness of the physician to answer questions for patients all enhanced adherence to medication. Other factors that enhanced adherence in this study included the number of tests being ordered by the physician and physician's global job satisfaction ratings.

Social and Cultural Factors

Choosing whether or not to adhere to a treatment regime will also depend on a person's social and cultural context. For example, decisions whether or not to behave in healthy ways such as practising safe sex, or following a low-fat diet, is likely to depend in part on the meaning ascribed to these behaviours within specific cultural groups, and most crucially on what the individual thinks that his or her significant others will think of them for wanting to behave in a particular way (see Conner & Sparks, 1996; Godin & Kok, 1996, for a review of the use of the Theory of Planned Behaviour in relation to health). Different cultural groups may ascribe different meanings to both symptoms and appropriate treatment regimes, meaning that take-up of treatment will vary. For example, in a study of over 17 000 women who received follow-up recommendations following screening mammography, non-white women were less likely to adhere to the recommendations than white women. Ethnicity also appeared to interact with age, education, health insurance and family history of breast cancer to influence the probability of adherence (Strzelczyk & Dignan, 2002). Social support has been shown to play a role: a study by Catz et al. (2000) of 72 patients undergoing antiretroviral therapy found that perceived self-efficacy and social support were related to adherence. It is also likely that factors such as accessibility of transport, availability of childcare and the costs involved in taking time off work will also have an impact on adherence to treatment regimes.

Improving Adherence

Much of the research on adherence is focused on determinants, predictors and associated factors. Less attention has been devoted to intervention studies designed to improve adherence. In a recent systematic review, Haynes et al. (2001) found that just 19 intervention studies were published in the past four decades which used a randomised-controlled design, with both adherence and clinical outcome measured with a six-month or longer follow-up. Only one-half of these studies reported a positive impact on adherence. Initial adherence, perhaps not surprisingly, is a major predictor of long-term adherence. Morrell et al. (1997) investigated the medication-taking behaviours of 48 adults diagnosed with hypertension, and found that initial adherence was one of the factors that consistently predicted higher levels of adherence. Therefore, the initial engagement in initiating the treatment regime appears critical in maintaining subsequent adherence.

In a systematic review of interventions for promoting adherence to tuberculosis management, Volmink and Garner (2000) found that a combination package of monetary incentives and health education, and greater supervision by tuberculosis clinic staff, increased the number of people completing tuberculosis treatment. Direct observation by clinic nurses of people swallowing their tuberculosis drugs did not, however, increase the likelihood of treatment success. Hegel et al. (1992), in a study comparing the efficacy of behavioural and cognitive strategies to enhance adherence in a small sample of haemodialysis patients, found that behavioural strategies (positive reinforcement, shaping and self-monitoring) were more effective than cognitive strategies (modification of health beliefs). Smith et al. (1997) assessed the contribution of motivational interviewing strategies to behavioural obesity intervention programmes. Obese women were randomly assigned into a standard 16-week behavioural weight control programme that provided instruction in diet, exercise and behavioural modification. All participants were allocated to the same group of the behavioural programme, with three individualised motivational interviewing sessions added. The motivational group attended significantly more group meetings, completed significantly more food diaries and recorded blood glucose significantly more often than the standard intervention group. The authors suggest that standard behavioural programmes could be augmented with motivational interviewing.

Most interventions reviewed used a variety of behavioural strategies, which have emphasised self-monitoring, goal-setting, behavioural-contracting, and reinforcement. Other approaches have involved organisational changes. Renders et al. (2001), for example, systematically studied interventions aiming to improve the management of diabetes mellitus in a primary care outpatient and community setting. They reviewed 41 studies, which involved more than 200 practices and 48 000 patients, 27 of which were randomised-controlled trials. The authors concluded that multifaceted professional interventions could enhance the performance of health care professionals in managing patients with diabetes. They also reported the helpfulness of organisational interventions in improving regular prompted recall and review of patients (such as central computerised tracking systems or nurses who regularly contact a patient), and also in improving overall diabetes management. They concluded both that the addition of patient-oriented interventions can lead to improved patient health outcomes, and that nurses can play an important role in patient-oriented interventions through patient education or facilitating adherence to treatment.

Ley (1998) comprehensively reviewed the giving of information and its effect on adherence, and concluded that a combination of written and verbal information produces the highest level of knowledge and adherence. He suggested, for example, that in 1986, the use of written materials concerning ten frequently prescribed drugs could have saved over $228 million. Annesi (1998), in a controlled study, utilised computer feedback to significantly increase attendance and adherence to an exercise treatment regime, and produced significantly fewer dropouts in a community exercise setting.

COLLABORATIVE MANAGEMENT/EXPERT PATIENT

Having reviewed the importance of communication and its effects on the individual's experience of health care and adherence, we now turn to an approach which attempts to improve satisfaction and effective health care, by involving patients as closely as possible in their own health management. Von Korff et al. (1997) suggest that collaborative management is care that strengthens and supports self-care, in the context of other medical, nursing and rehabilitation interventions. It includes core services across a range of conditions, and involves:

- collaborative definition of the problem, whereby patients' understandings are included in diagnosis
- targeting, goal-setting and planning focused on a specific problem, with realistic goals and action plans to achieve those goals
- creation of a range of support services and self-management strategies
- active follow-up.

Von Korff et al. review evidence suggesting that these programmes reduce mortality and disability and reduce costs in the long term. For example, patients suffering from heart disease who receive a collaborative psychosocial rehabilitation package reported significantly fewer problems and incurred much lower health care costs. Patients with diabetes who received a combination of education and support in self-management significantly reduced their weight and also risk of further complications. Arthritis sufferers who participated in self-help programmes reported less pain and a greater ability to manage their own conditions. Asthma patients who learned self-management reported fewer hospital visits and reduced heath care costs.

Working collaboratively may demand new skills from staff. As noted above, Guadagnoli and Ward (1998) suggest that evidence shows that patients do want to be informed of treatment alternatives and to participate in decisions about alternatives, although it is important for staff to be able to assess patients' level of "readiness" to participate. They suggest that the model developed by Prochaska, Velicier and Rossi (1994) could be adopted here, whereby clinicians could estimate patients' ability to participate, and act accordingly. That is, staff should assess the extent to which patients are willing and able to take on responsibilities for aspects of their own health care. Johnson and Meischke (1991), among others, have reported that most oncology patients want diagnostic and prognostic information; and similarly for many Alzheimer's disease patients (Johnson, Bouman & Pinner, 2001). There may be a link with age, and levels of education, and there also seem to be cultural differences. Younge et al. (1997), for example, suggest that the proportion of people who want to receive full information is lower in non-English speaking countries. There may also be ethnic differences concerning who should be told first, and the need to consult relatives.

Clearly staff will need to be able to assess these factors as well as the expressed views of the individual.

Seeing the patient as an expert is as much an economic, practical and social issue as it is a medical or even moral issue. In the UK and the USA, for example, there is an increasing emphasis on the importance of patients in the management of their own health conditions in recognition of the changing presentation of illness, and awareness of the predominance of chronic rather than acute disease. "When acute disease was the primary cause of illness, patients were generally inexperienced and passive recipients of medical care. Now that chronic disease has become the principal medical problem, the patient must become a co-partner in the process" (Holman & Lorig, 2000, p. 526). Seeing the patient as a partner or expert does not mean either instructing the patient or handing over total responsibility to the patient, but developing patients' confidence and motivation to use their own skills to take effective control of their lives with chronic illness or disability (Department of Health, 2001). The UK has recently adopted an eight-point plan to develop patient self-management training programmes, which includes:

- Promotion of an expectation that patients have expertise about their own conditions.
- Identification of barriers to effective self-management.
- Training staff to work collaboratively, and to value the importance of user-led self-management.
- Integration of self-management into existing provision.
- Development of courses concerning self-management skills for patients, to encourage patients' confidence in how to manage their condition better.

In all of these initiatives, there is an attempt to help individuals to recognise and respond appropriately to their own symptoms, and to make the most effective use of medication and services. Hence individuals can effectively access social and medical services when needed, and learn to manage episodes of exacerbation. The aim is to enable people to achieve a good quality of life despite having a chronic condition. The skills needed to do this include problem-solving, formation of a patient–professional partnership, and most importantly the development of confidence and self-belief that individuals can indeed take control of their own lives despite their illness or disability (Department of Health, 2001).

BREAKING BAD NEWS

The final issue to be considered in this chapter about the person's experience of health care concerns the giving and receiving of bad news. This is also discussed in Chapter 4 (Wren & Michie). Bad news can be seen as information which negatively affects people's views of themselves and their future (Buckman, 1984). The experience of most clinicians suggests that the way in which bad news is given can have a powerful impact on how the patient copes. For example, using euphemisms can cause uncertainty and delay understanding, as well as building up future communication problems. Being abrupt can lead to a catastrophic reaction from the patient, while being intolerant of emotional reactions may damage the patient's ability to respond appropriately, and may delay the process of coming to terms with (processing) the information. Giving bad news is not easy and clinicians do not always receive appropriate training in how to communicate effectively (Campbell, 1994). Clinical health psychologists may be in the position of breaking bad news or helping a team of colleagues to do so effectively. There are, however, few controlled studies of how best to give bad news, and those that have been carried out are not conclusive (Walsh, Girgis & Sanson-Fisher, 1998).

Given this, a number of practice guidelines have been developed. In Australia, for example, guidelines are based on a critical review of existing literature, and a further review by consensus panels of medical staff, nursing staff, social workers, lay people, clergy and cancer patients (Girgis & Sanson-Fischer, 1995). These guidelines recommend that the team must be agreed about what should be communicated, that only one person should actually be responsible for the communication, and that cultural sensitivity is needed given that different cultural groups may have different attitudes towards who should receive what type of information. The telephone should not be used, unless there are exceptional circumstances, and the information given should be documented in the patient's notes.

Girgis and Sanson-Fischer's guidelines include 13 components:

- Give bad news in private.
- Provide enough time for preparation, discussion and questions.
- Assess the patient's level of understanding.
- Provide information truthfully, using simple language.
- Encourage emotional expression.
- Respond empathically.
- Provide a broad time frame for the patient.
- Reassure the patient that support will be available.
- Arrange a review (ideally within 24 hours).
- Discuss options and ensure that the patient has as much control as possible.
- Discuss family involvement and sharing information.
- Discuss the support available.
- Provide concise and consistent written or audio-taped information.

In order to make this easier for staff to use in practice, Baile et al. (1999) have suggested a six-step protocol for breaking bad news—SPIKES:

- **S**ettings must be right, including privacy and comfort, with **S**ufficient time.
- **P**atients' own **P**erceptions of the illness must be elicited.
- **I**nvitations should be given to patients to say how much **I**nformation is wanted.
- **K**nowledge and education about the condition should be provided after warning the patient that bad news is coming—in simple language, frequently checking understanding and avoiding the use of blunt language. Breaking bad news too suddenly can cause patients to deny or cause psychological disorganisation, hence a gradual disclosure is important.
- **E**motions should be responded to with **E**mpathy, maybe using touch if appropriate, and an expression of awareness of what the patient may be feeling.
- **S**ummaries should be provided together with a **S**trategy for what to do next, including recommendations about support services, and an offer to answer questions at a later date.

Baile et al. suggest that patients are greatly helped if they perceive that medical staff have genuine concern for them and for their quality of life. Nowhere is this more important than when discussing palliative care, when a common fear is of abandonment, as well as a fear of being a burden to others. Baile et al. have also described a number of key communication skills in giving bad news which they have developed in oncology, although it also applies in other settings. These include:

- Using direct, open-ended questions, such as "tell me what is worrying you".
- Making an alliance with the patient (using "we" statements and emphasising working together cooperatively).
- Making hopeful or encouraging statements, since there is usually something that can be done to ameliorate the situation, even if it is to offer the possibility of better pain control. However the encouragement of false hope is very unhelpful.
- Showing empathy.
- Identifying other worries, particularly about the patient's family, or feelings of anger, guilt and depression.

Most authors also recommend the use of audio-taped or written information which should help with the gradual assimilation of the information. Ley (1988) and Ley and Llewelyn (1994) review evidence concerning the best way in which to structure such information, both verbal and written, including the use of short sentences, choosing specific rather than general statements, using explicit categorisation and repetition, and checking understanding.

FUTURE DIRECTIONS

This chapter has reviewed evidence concerning the person's experience of health care, and has covered communication, satisfaction and adherence with treatment, and the breaking of bad news. Failure to adhere to treatment recommendations results in increased morbidity, mortality and increased costs. Much research has examined this important area in the past 40 years. Future directions for research include the need to focus on improving methods of assessing adherence and developing strategies for improving adherence. It is possible that newer technologies may enhance our capacity to measure, assess and intervene. In addition to increasing our involvement in methodologically sound intervention studies, we also need to promote within the health care domain a greater awareness of these problems. In this chapter we have reviewed a more collaborative approach to the issue, which is for the health care provider to get alongside the patient and to make maximum use of the patient's expertise. It seems very likely, given escalating costs of health care and growing levels of consumer awareness, that this approach will grow quickly, and will have a major impact on the provision of health care during the next few decades. Lastly, we examined the question of giving bad news, and how this is best accomplished. There is ample scope for more sensitively conducted research in this area, which must inevitably concern all professionals and their patients sooner or later.

REFERENCES

American College of Physicians (1984). *Ethics Manual*. Part I: History of medical ethics, the physician and the patient, the physician's relationship to other physicians, the physician and society. Ad Hoc Committee on Medical Ethics, American College of Physicians. *Annals of International Medicine*, **101** (1), 129–137.

Annesi, J.J. (1998). Effects of computer feedback on adherence to exercise. *Perceptual and Motor Skills*, **87** (2), 723–730.

Baile, W.F., Glober, G.A., Lenzi, R., Beale, E.A. & Kudelka, A.P. (1999). Discussing disease progression and end-of life decisions. *Oncology*, **13**, 1021–1031.

Bales, R.F. (1950). *Interaction Process Analysis: A Method for the Study of Small Groups*. Cambridge, MA: Addison-Wesley.

Balint, J. & Shelton, W. (1996). Regaining the initiative. Forging a new model of the patient–physician relationship. *Journal of the American Medical Association*, **275** (11), 887–891.

Bartlett, S.J., Lukk, P., Butz, A., Lampros-Klein, F. & Rand, C.S. (2002). Enhancing medication adherence among inner-city children with asthma: results from pilot studies. *Journal of Asthma*, **39** (1), 47–54.

Beaver, K., Luker, K.A., Owens, R.G., Leinster, S.J., Degner, L.F. & Sloan, J.A. (1996). Treatment decision making in women newly diagnosed with breast cancer. *Cancer Nursing*, **19** (1), 8–19.

Beckman, H.B. & Frankel, R.M. (1984). The effect of physician behavior on the collection of data. *Annals of Internal Medicine*, **101**, 692–696.

Beckman, H.B., Markakis, K.M., Suchman, A.L. & Frankel, R.M. (1994). The doctor–patient relationship and malpractice: lessons form plaintiff depositions. *Archives of International Medicine*, **154**, 1365–1370.

Bennett, A.H. (2000). Finding success in a capitated environment. *Family Practice Management*, **7** (7), 49–53.

Bensing, J.M. (1991). Doctor–patient communication and the quality of care. *Social Medicine*, **32**, 1301.

Bosley, C.M., Fosbury, J.A. & Cochrane, G.M. (1995). The psychological factors associated with poor compliance with treatment in asthma. *European Respiratory Journal*, **8**, 899–904.

Boyle, C.M. (1970). Differences in patients' and doctors' interpretation of some common medical terms. *British Medical Journal*, **2**, 286–289.

Buckman, R. (1984). Breaking bad news: why is it still so difficult? *British Medical Journal*, **288**, 1597–1599.

Campbell, M.L. (1994). Breaking bad news to patients. *Journal of the American Medical* Association, **271**, 1052.

Carmody, T.P., Matarazzo, J.D. & Istvan, J.A. (1987). Promoting adherence to heart-healthy diets: a review of the literature. *Journal of Compliance in Health Care*, **2**, 105–124.

Catz, S.L., Kelly, J.A., Bogart, L.M., Benotsch, E.G. & McAuliffe, T.L. (2000). Patterns, correlates, and barriers to medical adherence among persons prescribed new treatments for HIV disease. *Health Psychology*, **19** (2), 124–133.

Charles, C., Gafni, A. & Whelan, T. (1997). Shared decision-making in the medical encounter: what does it mean? (or it takes at least two to tango). *Social Science and Medicine*, **44** (5), 681–692.

Conner, M. & Sparks, P. (1996). The theory of planned behaviour and health behaviours. In M. Conner & P. Norman (Eds), *Predicting Health Behaviour* (pp. 121–162). Buckingham, UK: Open University Press.

Coupland, J., Robinson, J.D. & Coupland, N. (1994). Frame negotiation in doctor–elderly consultations. *Discourse and Society*, **5**, 89–124.

Deber, R.B., Kraetschmer, N. & Irvine, J. (1996). What role do patients wish to play in treatment decision making? *Archives of Internal Medicine*, **156** (13), 1414–1420.

Department of Health (2001). *The Expert Patient: A New Approach to Chromic Disease Management for the 21st Century*. London: UK.

Devine, E.C. & Cook, T.D. (1983). A meta-analytic analysis of effects of psycho-educational interventions on length of post surgical hospital stay. *Nursing Research*, **32**, 267–274.

DiMatteo, M.R. (1995). Patient adherence to pharmacotherapy: the importance of effective communication. *Formulary*, **30** (10), 596–598.

DiMatteo, M.R. & DiNicola, D.D. (1982). *Achieving Patient Compliance*. New York: Pergamon.

DiMatteo, M.R., Sherbourne, C.D., Hays, R.D., Ordway, L., Kravitz, R.L., McGynn, E.A., Kaplan, S. & Rogers, W.H. (1993). Physicians' characteristics influence patients' adherence to medical treatment: results from the Medical Outcomes Study. *Health Psychology*, **12** (2), 93–102.

Dolgin, M.J., Katz, E.R., Doctors, S.R. & Seigel, S.E. (1986). Caregivers' perceptions of medical compliance in adolescents with cancer. *Journal of Adolescent Health Care*, **7**, 22–27.

Dowsett, S.M., Saul, J.L., Butow, P.N., Dunn, S.M., Boyer, M.J., Findlow, R. & Dunsmore, J. (2000). Communication styles in the cancer consultation: preferences for a patient-centred approach. *Psycho-Oncology*, **9**, 147–156.

Dunbar-Jacobs, J., Burke, L.E. & Puczynski, S. (1995). Clinical assessment and management of adherence to medical regimens. In P.M. Nicassio & T.W. Smith (Eds), *Managing Chronic Illness: A Biopsychosocial Perspective*. Washington, DC: American Psychological Association.

Dunbar-Jacobs, J., Dwyer, K. & Dunning, E.J. (1991). Compliance with anti-hypertensive regimens: a review of the research in the 1980's. *Annals of Behavioural Medicine*, **13**, 32–39.

Eraker, S.A. & Politser, P. (1982). How decisions are reached: physician and patient. *Annals of Internal Medicine*, **97** (2), 262–268.

Fiedler, D.O. (1982). Managing medication and compliance: physician–pharmacist–patient interaction. *Journal of the American Geriatrics Society*, **30**, S113–S117.

Frosch, D.L. & Kaplan, R.M. (1999). Shared decision making in clinical medicine: past research and future directions. *American Journal of Preventative Medicine*, **17**, 285–294.

Girgis, A. & Sanson-Fischer, R.W. (1995). Breaking bad news: consensus guidelines for medical practitioners. *Journal of Clinical Oncology*, **13**, 2449–2456.

Godin, C. & Kok, G. (1996). The theory of planned behavior: a review of its applications on health-related behaviors. *American Journal of Health Promotion*, **11**, 87–98.

Gordis, L., Markowitz, M. & Lilienfeld, A.M. (1969). Why patients don't follow medical advice: a study of children on long-term anti-streptococcal prophylaxis. *Journal of Paediatrics*, **75**, 957–968.

Greenfield, S., Kaplan, S. & Ware, J.E. (1985). Expanding patient involvement in care—effects on patient outcomes. *Annals of International Medicine*, **102**, 520–528.

Guadagnoli, E. & Ward, P. (1998). Patients participation in decision making. *Social Science and Medicine*, **47** (3), 329–339.

Hadlow, J. & Pitts, M. (1991). The understanding of common health terms by doctors, nurses and patients. *Social Science and Medicine*, **32**, 193–196.

Hall, J.A., Roter, D.L. & Rand, C.S. (1981). Communication of affect between patient and physician. *Journal of Health and Social Behaviour*, **22**, 18–30.

Halm, E.A., Atlas, S.J., Borowsky, L.H., Benzer, T.I., Metlay, J.P., Chang, Y.C. & Singer, D.E. (2000). Understanding physician adherence with a pneumonia practice guideline: effects of patient, system and physician factors. *Archives of International Medicine*, **160** (1), 98–104.

Haynes, R.B. (1976). A critical review of the determinants of patient compliance with therapeutic regimens. In D.L. Sackett & R.B. Haynes (Eds), *Compliance with Therapeutic Regimens*. London: Johns Hopkins University Press.

Haynes, R.B., Montague, P., Oliver, T., McKibbon, K.A., Brouwers, M.C. & Kanini, R. (2001). Interventions for helping patients to follow prescriptions for medications [Systematic Review]. *Cochrane Database of Systematic Reviews*. York, UK: Cochrane Consumers & Communication Goup.

Hazzard, A., Hutchinson, S.J. & Krawiecki, N. (1990). Factors related to adherence to medical regimens in paediatric seizure patients. *Journal of Paediatric Psychology*, **15**, 543–555.

Hegel, M.T., Ayllon, T., Thiel, G. & Oulton, B. (1992). Improving adherence to fluid restrictions in male hemodialysis patients: a comparison of cognitive and behavioral approaches. *Health Psychology*, **11** (5), 324–330.

Hickson, G.B., Clayton, E.W., Githens, P.B. & Sloan, F.A. (1992). Factors that prompted families to file medical malpractice claims following perinatal injuries. *Journal of the American Medical Association*, **272** (20), 1583–1587.

Holman, H.R. & Lorig, K.R. (2000). Patients as partners in managing chronic disease: partnership is a prerequisite for effective and efficient health care. *British Medical Journal*, **320**, 526–527.

Johnson, H., Bouman, W.P. & Pinner, G. (2001). On telling the truth in Alzheimer's disease. *International Psychogeriatrics*, **12**, 221–229.

Johnson, J. & Meischke, H. (1991). Women's preferences for cancer information from specific communication channels. *American Behavioural Scientist*, **34**, 742–755.

Kane, S.V., Cohen, R.D., Aikens, J.E. & Hanauer, S.B. (2001). Prevalence of nonadherence with maintenance mesalamine in quiescent ulcerative colitis. *American Journal of Gastroenterology*, **96** (10), 2929–2933.

Kaplan, R.M. (1991). Health-related quality of life in-patient decision making. *Journal of Social Issues*, **47** (4), 69–90.

Kaplan, S.H., Greenfield, S. & Ware, J.E. (1989). Assessing the effects of physician–patient interactions on the outcomes of chronic disease. *Medical Care*, **27** (3), S110–S127.

Kasper, J.F. & Fowler, F.J. (1993). Responding to the challenge. A status report on shared decision-making programs. *HMO Practice*, **7** (4), 176–181.

Kasper, J.F., Mulley, A.G. Jr, Wennberg, J.E. & Wennberg, E. (1992). Developing shared decision-making programs to improve the quality of health care. *Quality Review Bulletin*, **18** (6), 183–190.

Levine, M.N., Gafni, A., Markham, B. & MacFarlane, D. (1992). A bedside decision instrument to elicit a patient's preference concerning adjuvant chemotherapy for breast cancer. *Annals of Internal Medicine*, **117** (1), 53–58.

Ley, P. (1979). Memory for medical information. *British Journal of Social and Clinical Psychology*, **18**, 245–256.

Ley, P. (1982). Satisfaction, compliance, and communication. *British Journal of Clinical Psychology*, **21**, 241–254.

Ley, P. (1988). *Communicating with patients. Improving communication, satisfaction and compliance.* London: Chapman & Hall.

Ley, P. (1989). Improving patients' understanding, recall, satisfaction and compliance. In A.K. Broome (Ed.), *Health Psychology: Processes and Applications* (pp. 74–102). London: Chapman & Hall.

Ley, P. (1998). The use and improvement of written communication in mental health care and promotion. *Psychology Health and Medicine*, **3** (1), 19–53. Carfax Publishing Ltd, USA.

Ley, P. & Llewelyn, S.P. (1994). Improving patients' understanding, recall, satisfaction and compliance. In A. Broome & S.P. Llewelyn (Eds), *Health Psychology* (pp. 75–98). London: Chapman & Hall.

Lorenc, L. & Branthwaite, A. (1993). Are older adults less compliant with prescribed medication than younger adults? *British Journal of Clinical Psychology*, **32**, 485–492.

Marks, D.F., Murray, M., Evans, B. & Willig, C. (2000). *Health Psychology: Theory, Research and Practice.* London: Sage.

Marvel, M.K., Epstein, R.M., Flowers, K. & Beckman, H.B. (1999). Soliciting the patient's agenda: have we improved? *Journal of the American Medical Association*, **281** (3), 283–287.

Mazur, D.J. & Hickam, D.H. (1997). Patients' preferences for risk disclosure and role in decision making for invasive medical procedures. *Journal of General Internal Medicine*, **12** (2), 114–117.

McKinley, R.K. & Middleton, J.F. (1999). What do patients want from doctors? Content analysis of written patient agendas for the consultation. *British Journal of General Practice*, **49**, 796–800.

Meichenbaum, D. & Turk, D.C. (1987). *Facilitating Treatment Adherence: A Practitioners Guidebook.* New York: Plenum Press.

Mischel, W. (1968). *Personality and Assessment.* New York: John Wiley & Sons.

Molleman, E., Krabbendan, P.J., Annyas, A.A., Koops, H.S., Sleijfer, D.T. & Vermay, A. (1984). The significance of the doctor–patient relationship in coping with cancer. *Social Science and Medicine*, **18**, 475–480.

Morrell, R.W., Park, D.C., Kidder, D.P. & Martin, M. (1997). Adherence to antihypertensive medications across the life span. *Gerontologist*, **37** (5), 609–619.

Morris, J. & Royle, G.T. (1987). Choice of surgery for early breast cancer. *British Journal of Surgery*, **74**, 1017–1019.

Moulding, T.S. (1999). Medication monitors to treat tuberculosis. A supplement to directly observed therapy [Journal Article]. *American Journal of Respiratory and Critical Care Medicine*, **159** (3), 989–991.

Ong, L.M.L., deHaes, J.C.J.M., Hoos, A.M. & Lammes, F.B. (1995). Doctor–patient communication: a review of the literature. *Social Science and Medicine*, **40**, 903–918.

Parle, M., Jones, B. & Maguire, P. (1996). Maladaptive coping and affective disorders among cancer patients. *Psychological Medicine*, **26** (4), 735–744.

Perkins, K.A. & Epstein, L.H. (1988). In R.K. Dishman (Ed.), *Exercise Adherence: Its Impact on Public Health* (pp. 399–416). Champaign, IL: Human Kinetics Books.

Prochaska, J.O., Velicier, W.F. & Rossi, J.S. (1994). Stages of change and decisional balance for 12 problem behaviors. *Health Psychology*, **13**, 1–8.

Renders, C.M., Valk, G.D., Griffin, S.J., Wagner, E.H., Eijk Van, J.T. & Assendelft, W.J. (2001). Interventions to improve the management of diabetes in primary care, outpatient, and community settings: a systematic review. *Diabetes Care*, **24** (10), 1821–1833.

Rodgers, P. & Ruffin, D.M. (1998). Medication nonadherence—Part 1: Health and Humanistic Consequences. *Managed Care Interface*, August, pp. 58–60.

Ross, F.M. (1991). Patient compliance: whose responsibility? *Social Science and Medicine*, **32**, 89–94.

Roter, D.L. (1977). Patient-participation in the patient–provider relationship: the effects of patient question-asking on the quality of interaction, satisfaction and compliance. *Health Education Monographs*, **5**, 281–330.

Roter, D.L. (1989). Which facets of communication have strong effects on outcome—a meta-analysis. In M. Stewart & D. Roter (Eds), *Communicating with Medical Patients*. London: Sage.

Roter, D.L., Hall, J.A. & Katz, N.R. (1988). Patient–physician communication: a descriptive summary of the literature. *Patient Education and Counselling*, **12**, 99–119.

Rudd, P., Ahmed, S., Zachary, V., Barton, C. & Bonduelle, D. (1990). Improved compliance measures: applications in an ambulatory hypertensive drug trial. *Clinical Pharmacology and Therapeutics*, **48**, 676–685.

Sackett, D.L. & Haynes, R.B. (1976). *Compliance with Therapeutic Regimens*. London: Johns Hopkins University Press.

Sackett, D.L. & Snow, J.C. (1979). The magnitude of compliance and non-compliance. In R.B. Haynes, D.L. Sackett & D.W. Taylor (Eds), *Compliance in Health Care* (pp. 11–22). Baltimore, MD: Johns Hopkins University Press.

Sarriff, A., Aziz, N.A., Hassan, Y., Ibrahim, P. & Darwis, Y. (1992). A study of patients' self-interpretation of prescription instructions. *Journal of Clinical Pharmacy and Therapeutics*, **17** (2), 125–128.

Smith, C.K., Polis, E. & Hadac, R.R. (1981). Characteristics of the initial medical interview associated with patient satisfaction and understanding. *Journal of Family Practice*, **12**, 283.

Smith, D.E., Heckemeyer, C.M., Kratt, P.P. & Mason, D.A. (1997). Motivational interviewing to improve adherence to a behavioral weight-control program for older obese women with NIDDM. A pilot study. *Diabetes Care*, **20** (1), 52–54.

Squier, R.W. (1990). A model of empathic understanding and adherence to treatment regimens in practitioner–patient relationships. *Social Science and Medicine*, **30**, 325–339.

Steptoe, A., Sutcliffe, I., Allen, B. & Coombes, C. (1991). Satisfaction with communication, medical knowledge, and coping style in patients with metastatic cancer. *Social Science and Medicine*, **32**, 627.

Stewart, M.A. (1984). What is a successful doctor-patient interview? A study of interactions and outcomes. *Social Science and Medicine*, **19**, 167–175.

Stiles, W.B., Putnam, S.M., Wolf, M.H. & James, S.A. (1979). Interaction exchange structure and patient satisfaction with medical interviews. *Medical Care*, **17** (6), 667–681.

Stimson, G.V. (1974). Obeying doctor's orders: a view from the other side. *Social Science and Medicine*, **8**, 97–104.

Strum, S. (1997). Consultation and patient information on the Internet: the patients' forum. *British Journal of Urology*, **80** (Suppl. 3), 22–26.

Strzelczyk, J.J. & Dignan, M.B. (2002). Disparities in adherence to recommended follow-up on screening mammography: interaction of sociodemographic factors. *Ethnicity and Disease*, **12** (1), 77–86.

Sullivan, R.J., Menapace, L.W. & White, R.M. (2001). Truth-telling and patient diagnoses. *Journal of Medical Ethics*, **27**, 192–197.

Tates, K. & Meeuwesen, L. (2001). Doctor–parent–child communication. A (re)view of the literature. *Social Science and Medicine*, **52**, 839–851.

Vincent, C., Young, M. & Phillips, A. (1994). Why do people sue doctors? A study of patients and relatives taking legal action. *Lancet*, **343** (8913), 1609–1613.

Volmink, J. & Garner, P. (2000). Interventions for promoting adherence to tuberculosis management. *Cochrane Database of Systematic Review*, (2), CD000010.

Von Korff, M., Gruman, J., Schaefer, J., Curry, S.J. & Wagner, E.H. (1997). Collaborative management of chronic illness. *Annals of Internal Medicine*, **127**, 1097–1102.

Walsh, R.A., Girgis, A. & Sanson-Fisher, R.W. (1998). Breaking bad news 2: what evidence is available to guide clinicians? *Behavioral Medicine*, **24**, 61–72.

Waterworth, S. & Luker, K.A. (1990). Reluctant collaborators: do patients want to be involved in decisions concerning care? *Journal of Advanced Nursing*, **15** (8), 971–976.

West, C. (1990). Not just doctors' orders: directive–response sequences in patients' visits to women and men physicians. *Discourse and Society*, **1**, 85–113.

Williams, S., Weinman, J. & Dale, J. (1998). Doctor–patient communication and patient satisfaction: a review. *Family Practice*, **15** (5), 480–492.

Yeo, G.T., de-Burgh, S.P., Letton, T., Shaw, J., Donnelly, N., Swinburn, M.E., Phillips, S., Bridges-Webb, C. & Mant, A. (1994). Educational visiting and hypnosedative prescribing in general practice. *Family Practice*, **11**, 57–61.

Younge, D., Moreau, P., Ezzat, A. & Gray, A. (1997). Communicating with cancer patients in Saudi Arabia. *Annals of the New York Academy of Sciences*, **809**, 309–316.

CHAPTER 4

Staff Experience of the Health Care System

Barbara Wren
Royal Free Hampstead NHS Trust, London, UK
and
Susan Michie
University College, London, UK

INTRODUCTION

This chapter provides an overview of the psychological aspects of working in health care systems. Topics covered include the relationship between effects of work and staff health, sources of pressure at work and the changes needed to support staff and protect their health.

THE CHANGING CONTEXT OF HEALTH CARE

Health care systems in the developed world pose particular challenges to the staff that work in them. This results from:

- years of large-scale organisational change
- increasing pressures to contain costs
- rapid technological advances and rising expectations of patients
- an increase in the levels of accountability that are expected of staff
- the nature of the work, which involves responsibility for people's lives and dealing regularly with distressing illness and death.

Health services in countries with developed economies face the following problems, which influence the shape of services and the demands on staff:

- increasing chronicity and disability in health service users as people live longer
- heightened expectations and demands
- cost escalation and budgetary pressures.

Handbook of Clinical Health Psychology. Edited by S. Llewelyn and P. Kennedy.
© 2003 John Wiley & Sons, Ltd.

During the past decade, providers of health care services have shifted their emphasis from treatment of illness to interventions aimed at promoting well-being. The increasing emphasis on providing evidence-based health care (Lin, 2001) has produced demands for greater knowledge of the evidence on which their practice is based.

There are additional changes which influence the demands experienced by health care staff, including reductions in the average length of stay in hospital and growth in day surgery. Job insecurity has been heightened by changed structures, the abolition in some cases of levels and categories of jobs, and amended contracts of employment. This has led to concern among some health care professionals about the disappearance of traditional career structures and professional roles. These fears are likely to be increased by proposals to merge roles, adjust boundaries and flatten structures.

Health services in developed countries also face problems with retaining skilled staff. In the UK National Health Service (NHS), for example, levels of staff turnover and early retirement continue to increase (Secombe & Smith, 1997), and this impacts on services in a number of ways. The shortages of staff are a drain to resources, both human and financial, and lead to increased pressure on remaining staff who must deliver services with depleted numbers. The high turnover means that there is a loss of skills and of the investment that has been made in training and developing staff. Costs are also incurred in training new staff and in managing ongoing staff shortages. Staff sickness and absence are other major costs to health care systems, with recent figures in the UK suggesting that sickness absence rates of 5% and more are costing the NHS more than £700 million a year (Williams, Michie & Pattani, 1999).

In summary, the context in which health care staff are working is constantly changing in ways that increase the level of work demands and, in many cases, reduce the support and job security available to staff. Both of these factors are known to contribute to ill health at work.

ILL HEALTH IN HEALTH CARE STAFF

There is a large body of evidence that health care staff experience greater levels of both physical and psychological ill health than the population in general. For example, in the UK, 27% of health care staff report high levels of psychological disturbance in comparison to 18% of the population in general (Wall, Bolden & Borrill, 1997).

Doctors

The evidence suggests that doctors suffer higher levels of stress, depression and alcohol abuse than the general population (Baldwin et al., 1997). Doctors experience significant levels of stress, comparatively high rates of suicide and varying degrees of morbidity and early retirement (Agius et al., 1996). Symptoms of stress and depression have been shown to be high in junior doctors both in the UK (Firth-Cozens, 1987) and in the USA (Hsu & Marshall, 1987; Hurwitz et al., 1987). The long hours worked, high workload, pressure of work and the impact of these on personal life have been shown to be associated with psychological disturbance. In female doctors, psychological disturbance is also associated with sexual harassment at work, discrimination, and lack of senior role models. For junior doctors, relationships with consultants and other staff are associated with psychological difficulties whereas in consultants, low job satisfaction because of inadequate resources, high levels of responsibility and conflict, and lack of management training contributed to psychological difficulties (Williams, Michie & Pattani, 1999).

Doctors are also reluctant to seek help for their own problems, are more likely to self-medicate, and to continue working if they are ill. In one study (Baldwin et al., 1997) 52% of doctors had never taken time off when they were ill and 33% had only taken time off once. In addition, 66% of doctors said that they prescribed for themselves when they were ill and 34% were not registered with a GP.

Nurses

The aspects of work associated with ill health for nurses include high workload, workload pressures and their effect on personal life, unpredictable staffing and staff shortages and lack of time to provide emotional support to patients. Management style has also been shown to impact on both levels of ill health and absenteeism in nurses (Firth & Britton, 1989; Gray-Toft & Anderson, 1985).

Managers

Stress among managers in health care is also high. A number of studies in the UK have demonstrated that stress in NHS managers is much higher than managers in other employment sectors, both public and private (Borrill et al., 1998). The major factors contributing to the stress of managers are levels of demand, levels of influence, role conflict, lack of feedback and lack of autonomy, support and control.

It can be seen that stress is a significant feature of health care work associated with aspects of work and rates of staff ill health. Due to its contribution to the experience of health care work, stress will be considered in more detail below.

STRESS IN HEALTH CARE WORK

Psychological Models

Stress can be caused by a number of factors related to both the content and the context of the work. Models of stress provide a framework for assessing and intervening at an individual and organisational level to reduce work-related stress in health care settings. Two widely used models will be described.

The Transactional Model of Stress

The transactional model of stress (Lazarus & Folkman, 1984) emphasises the importance of people's perceptions of not only the stress to which they are exposed but also of their own coping resources. The model proposes that the ability of people to prevent or reduce stress is determined by their appraisal of

- the threat within a situation (primary appraisal) and
- their coping skills to deal with that threat (secondary appraisal).

The process of primary and secondary appraisal is informed and influenced by previous experiences and the sense that is made of them by an individual. In encountering a stressor the individual is making an ongoing assessment of the challenge being posed and his or her resources to respond to this challenge. These appraisals have been shaped by past experiences of confronting stress and, in turn, influence future behaviour and appraisals. Thus, the process of appraisal, behaviour and stress is a continuous cycle. Managing stress can result from changing the way the situation is appraised (cognitive techniques) and responded to (behavioural or cognitive techniques). This model suggests a number of areas for intervention which include addressing the actual level of demands and threats to which people are exposed, their resources and skills to cope with them, and their perceptions of the situations in which they find themselves.

The Demands–Control–Support Model

The demands–support–control model (Karasek, 1979) outlines the conditions of work that are likely to lead to stress and outcomes such as poor health and sickness absence. According to this model, work-related strain and risks to health are most likely to arise when high job demands are coupled with low decision latitude (i.e. low personal control over work and limited opportunities to develop skills). On the other hand, high job demands with high decision latitude facilitates motivation to learn, active learning and a sense of accomplishment. Of the two, decision latitude has been found to have more impact than demand. This model has been extended to include social support at work as a predictor of job strain (Johnson & Hall, 1988). Social support at work (from managers, supervisors or colleagues) can help to reduce the effects of stressful job conditions. Karasek's model has received sufficient empirical support for it to provide a useful framework for planning and implementing organisational interventions in health care settings (Karasek, 1979).

Consequences of Stress: Burnout

One of the consequences of stress may be burnout. This refers to emotional exhaustion, depersonalisation and a feeling of reduced accomplishment, which can occur among individuals who work with people in some capacity (Maslach, 1982). Since the term was first coined (Freudenberger, 1974) it has come to be seen as a "wearing out" from the stress of work (Miller et al., 1990). Burnout is often seen as the end stage in a breakdown of adaptation that results from the long-term imbalance of demands and resources. Maslach (1982) has identified three dimensions of burnout:

- Loss of energy and a generalised fatigue
- Depersonalisation, which involves negative perceptions of others particularly of patients in a health care setting
- Negative attitudes towards oneself and a low sense of personal accomplishment.

Certain characteristics of (i) individuals and (ii) work conditions increase the likelihood of burnout.

Individuals

- Those who enter their profession with high goals and expectations
- Younger employees
- Those with less "hardy" personalities. Hardy personalities have been defined as people who approach demands with a sense of commitment, control and challenge (Kobasa, Maddi & Kahn, 1982).

Work Conditions

- Situations where there is role conflict or ambiguity
- Lack of social support, particularly from supervisors
- Lack of feedback
- Poor participation in decision-making
- Lack of autonomy.

Participation in decision-making, support from supervisors and support from coworkers can all serve to reduce the perception of stressors in the workplace, to decrease the likelihood of the experience of burnout and increase the experience of positive outcomes such as satisfaction and commitment (Miller et al., 1990).

ASPECTS OF WORK ASSOCIATED WITH ILL HEALTH

The majority of health care occupations cope with high workloads in the context of the need for few errors while working often in difficult and chaotic conditions. There are a number of aspects of this work which can impact on staff health, such as organisational aspects, including the way in which it is designed and structured, and levels of involvement and control. In addition, staff may be exposed to violence at work, have to break bad news to patients, and may feel threatened by the possibility of making mistakes, and of subsequent litigation.

Organisational Aspects of Health Care Work

Work Overload and Pressure of Work

Recent changes in the provision and use of health services have led to overwork for many health care staff. This takes the form of an increase in the number of hours worked (work-load) and an increased amount of work expected of staff within their working hours (work pressure). For example, in the last ten years in the UK, NHS expenditure has increased by 16% while activity has increased by 32% (Williams, Michie & Pattani, 1999). Bridging this gap has led to an increased pressure on staff, and one of the reasons for this increased pressure is that patients now have shorter stays in hospitals and need more intensive care in hospital and at follow-up when they are discharged.

Lack of Control over Work and Lack of Participation in Decision-making

There is consistent evidence that low levels of control over work are associated with high levels of stress-related outcomes including anxiety, psychological distress, burnout, irritability, psychosomatic health complaints and alcohol consumption (Terry & Jimmieson, 1999). A number of studies have identified an association between the lack of control over work and the lack of participation in decision-making and health problems in health care staff (Karasek, 1990; Johnson et al., 1996). The physical health problems associated with these aspects of work include cardiovascular mortality and back and joint pain (Johnson, Hall & Ford, 1995). In addition there is an association between these features of work and sickness absence (Williams, Michie & Pattani, 1999).

Poor Social Support at Work

The quality of relationships at work has been shown to be associated with health risk. Poor social support at work has been associated with increased risk of coronary heart disease and impaired mental health (Stansfield et al., 1997).

Unclear Management and Work Role

Unclear work roles and unclear management are associated with health problems in health care staff (Arsenault, Dolan & Van Ameringen, 1991; Martin, 1984).

Conflict between Work and Family Demands

A recent review has highlighted the serious consequences of conflict between work and family demands (Allen et al., 2000; Thomas & Gangster, 1995). A new national initiative in the UK, for example, is providing resources to help health care workers to achieve a healthy home/life balance (Department of Health, 2000).

Some Specific Demands of Health Care Work

Violence to Staff

In recent years there has been a growing concern about the increasing frequency of violence at work and a recognition that health care staff are at risk in their working environment (Cox & Leather, 1994; Health Service Advisory Committee, 1987; Schnieden, 1993). There are also indications that violence towards health care staff is underreported (Schnieden, 1993) and growing evidence of its psychological, physical, social and economic costs (Wykes & Mezey, 1994). In the USA, health care assaults are most common in psychiatric hospitals, then in accident and emergency departments and, thirdly, in intensive care units (Drummond, Sparr & Gordon, 1989). In the UK, the pattern is slightly different, with violence occurring most frequently in accident and emergency departments, then in community health and psychiatric care settings (Health Service Advisory Committee, 1987).

Research has demonstrated that staff who are in closest contact with patients, such as junior nurses, are most at risk (Rix & Seymour, 1988) and that most assaults are directed towards either nurses or other patients (Noble & Roger, 1989). The psychological effects of workplace assaults on nurses have been documented in a number of studies and includes increased anxiety, ruminations, intrusive thoughts about the incident, muscle tenseness, fatigue and the onset of post-traumatic stress (Lanza, 1983; Whittington & Wykes, 1989). Nurses who have been assaulted also increase their level of alcohol, nicotine and food intake in the hours and days after the incident. Sleep disturbances become increasingly common as time goes on. Many victims describe few opportunities to talk about how they felt about the incident.

In one study of 5000 US public sector staff, those who had been assaulted were 55% more likely to be depressed than those not assaulted, 82% more likely to report symptoms associated with anxiety, and 53% more likely to report low job satisfaction (Driscoll, Worthington & Hurrell, 1995). Those who had been assaulted and had little social support had higher levels of depression than those with strong social support. Those who had been assaulted benefited from the support and understanding of their coworkers and from jobs where they were able to have control over the level of work demands. The study concluded that providing support and personal control over work are important elements of programmes for treating post-traumatic stress disorder following workplace assault.

Staffing levels and the amount of work pressure may affect physical and verbal violence. An association has been shown between violence and agency staff levels in psychiatric hospitals (Fineberg, James & Shah, 1988). Adequate provision of well-trained staff is thought to be important in the prevention of violence (Brailsford & Stevenson, 1973). Effective training includes aggression and anger control (Infantino & Musingo, 1985; Whittington & Wykes, 1989). Adequate resources, training and support can help to reduce the likelihood of violence occurring and reduce its impact on staff.

Breaking Bad News

Bad news is "any news that drastically and negatively alters the patient's view of his or her future" (Buckman, 1988). Giving bad news is among the most challenging tasks faced by health professionals and there is evidence that the way in which it is given affects those receiving such news. However, many health care professionals find it difficult to give such news. In the past this has resulted in doctors not telling patients the whole truth, although this appears to be changing. In 1951, 90% of doctors said that they did not discuss the truth with their patients, whereas 25 years later the findings were almost reversed with 90% of doctors reporting that they did discuss the truth with their patients (Novack et al., 1979).

There are a number of reasons why breaking bad news is a difficult task for health professionals. In some cases they are not sure how to do it and unclear about how it fits into their role as a health care provider (Lloyd & Bor, 1999). There may be a fear of causing upset or an unpredictable emotional reaction, fear of being blamed for the news and of being seen to fail. In addition, there may be fears of legal consequences. Changing medical practice means that it is becoming easier to attach responsibility for any medical "failure" to doctors or nurses. For some health professionals there may be what Buckman (1999) calls a "fear of the untaught", an uncertainty about what happens next and about not having the answers to some of the questions that may be asked. Breaking bad news requires an alternative to the professional detachment which many health professionals have been trained to cultivate or have developed to protect themselves emotionally. In discussing bad news they are often required to use their emotions to respond sensitively, to admit in some instances that they don't know, and to come into contact with their own feelings about illness and death.

Giving bad news effectively can help a patient to understand and maintain some hope in situations of difficulty, to maintain a positive relationship between the patient and the health professional, and to protect health professionals from possible burnout through becoming over-involved in patients' anger, distress or agitation (Lloyd & Bor, 1999).

Two general skills required for breaking bad news are:

- Divulging information in a way that is sensitive to the patient's level of knowledge and understanding, and judgement of how much the patient needs to know.
- Creating a dialogue between the patient and the professional that may provide some therapeutic benefit for the patient.

The following are key components of effective communication of bad news:

1. Identify the patient's current concerns and level of knowledge.
2. Warn of impending news.
3. Provide information at the patient's pace and in manageable chunks.
4. Allow the patient to indicate when he or she has heard enough.
5. Give space for the news to be absorbed.
6. Handle any reactions.

Key aspects of breaking bad news effectively involve eliciting the patient's own resources for coping to instil realistic hope. It is also important that health care professionals communicate with their colleagues about what a patient has been told and provide support for each other in order to reduce the emotional impact of this task (Lloyd & Bor, 1999). Further discussion of this topic is also provided in Chapter 3 of this *Handbook*.

The Impact of Mistakes, and the Threat of Litigation

The relationship between patients and health care providers has changed dramatically over the last 20 years. The role of the patient has changed from that of a recipient of health care services to that of a consumer. This is associated with patients being more informed about health matters and having higher demands of health care services. Patients today are more likely to question the skills of health care providers and less likely to be forgiving if they do not receive the outcomes they had hoped for. The increased expectations of patients cannot always be met. Patients often come to health professionals with a wish for certainty when all that can be offered is a risk estimate of the outcome of an illness (Vincent, 1999). The changing attitudes and expectations of patients have affected staff in a number of ways. First, they have increased the importance of good communication skills in health care work. The most common cause of litigation is failure in communication rather than medical negligence (Buckman, 1999). Second, they have led to raised concerns among health professionals about litigation and the impact of clinical errors. The main underlying causes of errors in medicine are communication and supervision problems, excessive workload, and deficiencies in education, training and the use of locums (Vincent, 1999).

There are many studies that demonstrate that medical accidents or adverse events are by no means rare. In one study, 50% of doctors reported that their experience of stress at work (resulting from tiredness and pressure from overwork) had resulted in a lowered standard of clinical care (Firth-Cozens, 1997). In 40% of cases doctors reported feeling irritable or angry with patients, 7.4% of doctors said that they had made a serious mistake that had not led to the death of the patient, and 2.4% said that they had made a clinical error which had led to the death of a patient.

The psychological consequences for staff involved in medical accidents and mistakes can be serious and include depression, anger, shame and loss of confidence (Charles, Wilbert & Franke, 1985). Increasing attention is being paid to ways to reduce the likelihood of errors and their consequences for patients and health care staff. The frequency and impact of medical errors on patients, staff and health care systems has been the subject of major academic studies in the USA and Australia (Kohn, Corrigan & Donaldson, 1999; Wilson et al., 1995). A recent report (Department of Health, 2000) has drawn together information from British, North American and Australian studies to make recommendations for the development of a health service culture which takes a broad approach to responding to, and learning from, the occurrence and impact of errors. This approach considers problems in the context of the whole system in which they occur and has led to the identification of a number of recommended mechanisms though which organisations can learn from failures in medical care (Department of Health, 2000):

- Have coordinated mechanisms for reporting and analysing adverse incidents.
- Promote an open culture in which errors and service failures can be reported and discussed.
- Establish systems for ensuring that, where lessons are identified, the necessary changes are put into practice.
- Develop an appreciation of the value of the systems approach to preventing, analysing and learning from error.

As well as cultural change, a number of structural changes can be made to reduce the likelihood of medical errors. Factors that contribute to the occurrence of mistakes should be addressed, for example, by increasing levels of support at work, and by ensuring that professionals are not working an excessive number of hours and are getting enough sleep (Firth-Cozens & Greenhalgh, 1997; Vincent, 1999). A number of studies have demonstrated the relationship between inadequate sleep and a tendency towards self-criticism which, when combined with lowered mood, may lead to lowered standards of care. Introducing a system designed to reduce sleep deprivation has been found to reduce medical errors (Gottlieb et al., 1991). Medication errors and legal suits have also been shown to be reduced significantly by the introduction of stress management courses (Jones et al., 1988).

In order to help health professionals to deal with the possibility of litigation, they should be provided with:

- information about medical law and the legal process
- access to formal support and counselling
- communication skills training.

It has also been recommended that departments and teams develop policies on openness with injured patients in the event of medical errors.

INTERVENTIONS

There is a considerable body of literature on interventions aimed at improving staff experiences at work and reducing the health risks to which staff are exposed (Williams, Michie & Pattani, 1999). The three dimensions of the demand–control–support model (Karasek, 1979) have been shown to be effective in interventions (Bond & Bunce, 2001).

Interventions can focus on individual or on organisational change or, in some cases, such as training programmes, on both. Interventions aiming to eliminate or reduce stressful job characteristics and working conditions to improve employee well-being can be categorised into primary, secondary or tertiary level interventions.

Primary Interventions

Primary interventions aim to remove or reduce stress at work. They include clarifying roles and relationships at work, increasing autonomy, reducing excessive workload and changing work design. An example of a primary intervention is one carried out in a rural hospital that targeted the patient care delivery system. A project team of representatives from all nursing levels and shifts (Murphy et al., 1994) met weekly with an outside facilitator and analysed the current patient care delivery system in order to develop a new service delivery model. This intervention led to a reduction in levels of stress and staff turnover and an increase in satisfaction at work. The commitment of senior nursing management to the intervention and staff participation in decision-making were seen as key factors contributing to its success.

Developing effective team working is another example of a primary intervention. Effective teams are those which have clear group and individual objectives, meet regularly, and value the skills of individual members (Carter & West, 1999; Guzzo & Shea, 1992). Teams can address factors necessary to promote the well-being of team members, such as ensuring that work is distributed evenly, giving practical and emotional support, and developing a team culture of early recognition of stress so that problems can be tackled sooner rather than later. In the USA primary care teamworking has been shown to improve staff motivation and health care delivery (Wood, Farrow & Elliott, 1994).

Primary interventions may also target the development of skills for health care work such as communication skills. The ability to communicate effectively and sensitively is a key skill in health care and there is a body of evidence to demonstrate that good communication leads to accurate history-taking and diagnosis, patient adherence to treatment plans, and patient satisfaction with the care that they receive. There is a wealth of publications on communication in medicine, with increasing attention paid to training health professionals in communication skills (e.g., see Davis & Fallowfield, 1991; Ley, 1988; Tuckett et al.,

1985). Good communication throughout health care organisations is beneficial to staff health and staff productivity (Williams, Michie & Pattani, 1999).

Secondary Interventions

Secondary interventions seek to improve people's resources and skills in tackling sources and consequences of stress. Examples are those that aim to improve coping skills, strategies for managing time and priorities, and assertiveness skills. Training is a common form of secondary intervention. One study trained staff about the importance of support at work in order to improve their coping resources (Heaney, Price & Rafferty, 1995). This intervention involved educating staff about participatory problem-solving approaches and providing them with skills to implement these approaches in the work setting. The study found significant effects on personal social support, group problem-solving, job satisfaction and employee mental health.

Another evaluation of training in coping skills included developing new strategies and tactics to reduce the excessive demands of work by changing work objectives, working methods and work relationships (Murphy, 1999). This intervention was found to be effective for those with the ability to implement changes when they return to their own workplace.

Tertiary Interventions

Tertiary interventions aim to help workers who have already developed stress-related problems. Examples are the provision of counselling and psychotherapy services for work-related problems and the establishment of employee assistance programmes (EAPs). They also include the provision of consultancy services aiming to help the organisation to address and respond to teams and departments in difficulty.

Research on workplace counselling provides some evidence for its benefits, although many evaluation studies are methodologically flawed (Berridge & Cooper, 1993; Reynolds & Shapiro, 1991). Many do not have control groups and there is a great variety in the outcomes assessed with measures that are not always reliable and valid. Some studies have shown that counselling has benefits for employees' psychological well-being (e.g. Reynolds, 1997) and has saved money in terms of absenteeism and work productivity (Maiden, 1988). This US study of 2500 staff who were counselled over 30 months demonstrated that for every dollar spent on counselling, about seven dollars was saved. Work-related counselling has also been shown to increase people's feelings of competence and control (Firth-Cozens & Hardy, 1992).

Summary

There are a number of features which predict the success of organisational interventions at each of the levels described above (Murphy, 1999).

- *Staff Involvement*. The participation of workers in organisational interventions is associated with job satisfaction, feeling in control and organisational effectiveness.

- *Management Commitment.* Management commitment is a key determinant of the success or failure of organisational change projects.
- *Supportive Organisational Culture.* A culture that is supportive of change and demonstrates commitment to change at all levels of the organisations is an important predictor of the likelihood of success of organisational interventions.

ORGANISATIONAL INTERVENTIONS WITH HEALTH CARE STAFF: THE EVIDENCE BASE

A study from the UK provides an example of an evidence-based programme of action to increase physical and psychological health, work attendance and organisational efficiency in health care staff (Williams, Michie & Pattani, 1999). It is based on a systematic review of ill health in health care staff and the evidence of effectiveness of interventions with these staff to improve health and associated sickness absence in Europe, the USA and Australia.

The study's researchers identified only 13 methodologically acceptable intervention studies. Seven of these targeted physical health and psychological problems (Gronningsaeter, Hytten & Skauli, 1992; Heaney, Price & Rafferty, 1995; Jones et al., 1988; Kagan, Kagan & Watson, 1995; Lokk & Arnetz, 1997; Malcolm, Harrison & Forster, 1993; Ratti & Piling, 1997). The remainder were concerned specifically with musculoskeletal problems (Donaldson et al. 1993; Haig, Linton & McIntosh, 1990; McGrail, Tsai & Bernacki, 1995; Ratti & Piling, 1997; Van Poppel, Roes & Smid, 1997; Wiesel, Boden & Feffer, 1994).

Successful interventions used training and organisational approaches to increase participation in decision-making and problem-solving, increase support and feedback and improve communication (Gronningsaeter, Hytten & Skauli, 1992; Heaney, Price & Rafferty, 1995; Kagan, Kagan & Watson, 1995; Lokk & Arnetz, 1997; Malcolm, Harrison & Forster, 1993; Smoot & Gonzales, 1995). These studies found that:

- Those participants taught skills to mobilise support at work and to participate in problem-solving and decision-making reported more supportive feedback, feeling more able to cope and better team functioning and work climate. Among those most at risk of leaving, those undergoing the training reported reduced depression (Heaney, Price & Rafferty, 1995).
- Staff facing organisational change who were taught skills of stress management, how to participate in, and control, their work showed a decrease of stress hormone levels (Lokk & Arnetz, 1997).
- Staff taught verbal and non-verbal communication and empathy skills demonstrated reduced staff resignations and sick leave (Smoot & Gonzales, 1995).
- Physically inactive employees undergoing stress management training improved their perceived coping ability, and those undergoing aerobic exercise improved their feelings of well-being and decreased their complaints of muscle pain, but also reported reduced job satisfaction (Gronningsaeter, Hytten & Skauli, 1992).
- Employees undergoing one of seven training programmes emphasising one or more aspects of stress management—physiological processes, coping with people or interpersonal awareness processes—showed reductions in depression, anxiety, psychological

strain and emotional exhaustion immediately after the programme. There was a further reduction in psychological strain and emotional exhaustion at 9–16 months' follow-up (Kagan, Kagan & Watson, 1995).

- Those on long-term sickness absence who were referred early to the Occupational Health Department (within two or three months' absence) reduced their sickness absence from 40 to 25 weeks before resumption of work, and from 72 to 53 weeks before leaving employment for medical reasons, leading to large financial savings (Malcolm, Harrison & Forster, 1993).

The study made a number of recommendations of ways to improve the work experience of health care staff drawn from the evidence it reviewed. The following is a summary of the key recommendations:

- Develop interventions to provide training and support to health service managers given that the study demonstrated the impact of management culture and management style and skills on staff health.
- Increase staff sense of control over work and their participation in decision-making.
- Ensure that there are opportunities for staff views to be expressed and included in policies and practices, and ensure that all staff participate in management activities and in problem-solving and decision-making.
- Develop a culture in which staff are valued, receive positive feedback and problems are identified and addressed as early as possible.
- Facilitate two-way communication at all levels of health care organisations. Provide clear leadership and clear definition of staff roles.
- Develop ways to provide support in the workplace, for example through clinical super-vision, mentoring, workplace counselling.
- Develop employment practices to ensure that workloads are manageable, and that there is job security and flexibility to achieve a healthy work life balance.
- Adopt a risk management approach to staff health which includes policies and action on bullying, harassment, racial and sexual discrimination and violence to staff.
- Ensure that structures and systems are in place to support and encourage career and staff development.
- Develop pilot schemes to implement and evaluate these recommendations.

Those interventions that were effective in improving general health were organisational programmes that included both staff and management training. The authors highlighted gaps in the evidence base and the need for further studies to refine our understanding of the relationship between aspects of work and health outcomes, and to establish evidence for the effectiveness of different interventions.

AN OCCUPATIONAL HEALTH PSYCHOLOGY INTERVENTION TO IMPROVE STAFF HEALTH

A recent project established a psychology post in the Occupational Health and Safety unit of a London hospital (Wren, 2000). The aim of the post is to develop organisational and individual interventions to reduce stress and sickness absence in NHS staff and to evaluate specific interventions. The psychologist is a trained occupational and health psychologist. The service has four components (Wren & Michie, 2000).

Staff Consultancy Service

Managers are offered structured sessions to review and develop their management and communication skills and methods for supporting staff under stress. Managers are offered a one-off session or a number of meetings depending on their need. A systems perspective is used to help managers review problems and develop their problem-solving skills. This includes helping them to deal with staff who are stressed or who may be returning to work after a period of sickness absence due to a mental health problem, exploring ways to manage a "difficult" member of the team, and reviewing ways for managers to develop their own roles or services.

Training

Training aims to improve people's ability to manage their work and other activities, time and stress levels. Skills of problem-solving, communication and negotiation are taught using a systems framework. Training packages are developed in response to departmental requests for input or offered on a hospital-wide basis. An example of the training offered includes the development of an intervention to support managers and promote the development of their problem-solving skills.

This intervention introduced managers to a systemic framework for thinking about team and organisational problems. In this way it was hoped to develop managers' skills in assessing problems as symptoms of organisational issues and begin to develop new approaches to addressing them rather than just referring them on. Managers were encouraged to consider a range of potential levels of intervention and to shift their focus from thinking about "difficult" individuals and situations to considering solutions in the wider context of teams, departments or the organisation as a whole. The training aimed to:

- provide a framework for understanding problems and the way in which they may reflect team, departmental or organisational issues (systems perspective);
- help managers to review the impact of problems on them individually;
- understand the influence of context on approaches to problem-solving;
- provide managers with a framework for problem-solving and skills practice;
- facilitate joint-working and skill-sharing in a group of managers at similar levels in the organisation.

The training is delivered as two half-day workshops called "Problem Solving under Pressure" and, to date, 50 managers have been trained.

Stress Counselling for Staff

A brief stress counselling service is offered to members of staff who are referred by or through the occupational health team. Staff are normally seen for between one and six sessions and helped to review current sources of stress and their coping skills. Where appropriate, referrals are made to other services. If relevant, managers are involved in continuing the support and stress management work begun with the psychologist. Many of the problems have an organisational component and these issues are fed back to the project steering group, which is composed of senior managers.

Organisational Interventions

Organisational interventions are developed following a process of consultancy and needs assessment with relevant managers and staff. One intervention which aimed to reduce sickness absence levels among cleaning staff by increasing staff control and support at work used the framework provided by the Karasek model (Karasek, 1979) to assess the work characteristics of this staff group. Components of the intervention included the establishment of a system of reporting in and out of work to reduce social isolation, increasing staff contact with each other and enabling supervisors and managers to give support, listen to any problems and give helpful and positive feedback. In addition, the coffee break was extended from 15 to 30 minutes to allow staff time to leave their work areas for breaks in order to use the recreation room and meet other domestic staff.

Monthly sickness absence rates for both staff groups were collected over one year before and after the intervention and demonstrated that the mean sickness absence rates in the domestic service fell by 3.93% in the six-month period following the intervention. Further intervention is required to maintain the original sickness absence rate reductions that were achieved.

CONCLUSION

This chapter has described a range of factors influencing staff experience of working in health care settings and staff health. The evidence to date demonstrates an association between long hours and pressure of work, and management style, with psychological ill health and sickness absence (Williams, Michie & Pattani, 1999). Specific areas of management style are the extent to which staff are able to have a sense of control over their work environment, openly express their views and participate in management, joint problem-solving and decision-making. The picture appears to be similar across the UK, Europe and the USA. Organisational interventions aimed at changing some of these have been found to be effective in reducing psychological ill health.

However, it is clear that there are at present a number of limitations in our evidence base (Michie & Williams, 2003). Studies have been limited in the questions addressed and in the study designs used. Since most studies are cross-sectional, causal relationships cannot be demonstrated. It may be that the associations found reflect a tendency for more sensitive and vulnerable people to choose work in caring roles. Longitudinal studies and randomised-controlled trials are needed to investigate the causal relationships between work factors and health. Also needed are economic evaluations of interventions and studies of the relationship between staff health and job outcome, for example, quality of patient care.

The evidence that does exist highlights changes in both employment practices and management style as likely determinants of improved health. The most important factors associated with psychological ill health are workload and pressure (Williams, Michie & Pattani, 1999). This suggests that reviews of task allocation should be carried out and additional support staff recruited where necessary. An organisational climate in which working excessive hours is discouraged should be created, with managers (including doctors) setting good examples and encouraging uptake of work break and annual and study leave entitlement.

Employment practices that enhance a sense of control at work include job security, permanent contracts and flexibility, for example, allowing staff to meet family commitments. Other helpful measures are good career and staff development strategies and acting on policies to prevent bullying, harassment and violence (Williams, Michie & Pattani, 1999). Managers should facilitate more employee control and participation in decision-making at work by encouraging staff to express their views openly, by incorporating these into policies and practices, and by encouraging all staff, including clinicians, to participate in management, joint problem-solving and decision-making.

Support at work can be increased through induction programmes, regular positive feedback from managers, two-way communication and early, sensitive addressing of problems. Other supportive measures are giving clear leadership and definitions to staff roles at work, developing team-working and promoting both formal and informal social support at work. Employers should provide staff with stress management services that include organisational interventions, training and individual counselling.

Health care work is demanding and stressful as well as potentially rewarding, and people are drawn to it for a number of reasons, many of them altruistic and idealistic. These initial motivations may make staff more vulnerable to work pressure. The changes that have taken place in health care organisations, particularly over the last decade, have added to staff stress by increasing levels of demand and limiting resources and support at work. In addition, the reduction in the number of people available to work in health care due to demographic changes is an additional pressure on already stretched services, and the protection of staff health involves attending to these organisational pressures.

There is a need to support a culture shift in health care from one in which the stress of this type of work is borne by the individual, to one in which it is seen as the responsibility of the employer (Michie & Williams, 2003), and a barrier to the delivery of cost-effective, quality care (Firth-Cozens, 1999). In order to improve the experiences of health care staff, work needs to be designed in a way that protects staff health, and acknowledges the high level of psychological demands created by doing this type of work in cost-conscious organisations, with limited resources.

REFERENCES

Agius, R.M., Blenkin, H., Deary, I.J., Zealley, H.E. & Wood, R.A. (1996). Survey of perceived stress and work demands of consultant doctors. *Occupational and Environmental Medicine*, **53**, 217–224.

Allen, T.D., Herst, D.E.L., Bruck, C.S. & Sutton, M. (2000). Consequences associated with work to family conflict: a review and agenda for future research. *Journal of Occupational Health Psychology*, **5** (2), 278–308.

Arsenault, A., Dolan, S.L. & Van Ameringen, M.R. (1991). Stress and mental strain in hospital work: exploring the relationship beyond personality. *Journal of Organisational Behaviour*, **12**, 483–493.

Baldwin, P.J., Newton, R.W., Buckley, G., Roberts, M.A. & Dodd, M. (1997). Senior house officers in medicine: postal study of training and work experience. *British Medical Journal*, **314**, 740–743.

Berridge, J. & Cooper, C. (1993). Stress and coping in US organisations: the role of employee assistance programmes. *Work and Stress*, **7**, 89–102.

Bond, F.W. & Bunce, D. (2001). Job control mediates change in a work reorganisation intervention for stress reduction. *Journal of Occupational Health Psychology*, **6** (4), 290–302.

Borrill, C.S., Wall, T.D., West, M.A., Hardy, G.E., Carter, A.J., Haynes, C.E., Shapiro, D.A., Stride, C. & Wood, D. (1998). *Stress among NHS Staff: Final Report*. Institute of Work Psychology: Sheffield University.

Brailsford, D.S. & Stevenson, J. (1973). Factors related to violent and unpredictable behaviour in psychiatric hospitals. *Journal of Nervous and Mental Disease*, **18**, 9–11.

Briner, R. (1999). Absence from work. In D. Snashall (Ed.), *ABC of Work Related Disorders*. BMJ Publishing Group.

Buckman, R. (1988). Breaking bad news—why is it still so difficult? *British Medical Journal*, **288**, 1597–1599.

Buckman, R. (1999). *How to Break Bad News*. New York: Macmillan.

Carter, A.J. & West, M. (1999). Sharing the burden: teamwork in healthcare settings. In *Stress in Health Professionals: Psychological and Organisational Causes and Interventions*. Chichester: John Wiley & Sons.

Charles, S.C., Wilbert, J.R. & Franke, K.J. (1985). Sued and non-sued physician's self-reported reactions to malpractice litigation. *American Journal of Psychiatry*, **192** (4), 437–440.

Cox, T. & Leather, P. (1994). The prevention of violence at work: application of a cognitive behavioural theory. In C.L. Cooper & I.T. Robertson (Eds), *International Review of Industrial and Organisational Psychology* (vol. 9, pp. 213–245). New York: John Wiley & Sons.

Davis, M. & Fallowfield, L. (1991). *Counselling and Communication in Healthcare*. Chichester: John Wiley & Sons.

Department of Health (2000). *Improving Working Lives*. London: HMSO.

Donaldson, C.S., Stanger, L.M., Donaldson, M.W., Cram, J. & Skubick, D. (1993). A randomised crossover investigation of a back pain and disability prevention programme: possible mechanisms of change. *Journal of Occupational Rehabilitation*, **3**, 83–94.

Driscoll, R.J., Worthington, K.A. & Hurrell, J.J. (1995). Workplace assault: an emerging job stressor. *Consulting Psychology Journal: Practice and Research*, **47** (4), 205–212.

Drummond, D.J., Sparr, L.E. & Gordon, G.H. (1989). Hospital violence reduction among high risk patients. *Journal of American Medical Association*, **26** (17), 2531–2534.

Fineberg, N.A., James, D.V. & Shah, A.K. (1988). Agency nurses and violence in a psychiatric ward. *Lancet*, **I**, 474.

Firth, H. & Britton, P. (1989). Burnout, absence and turnover amongst British nursing staff. *Journal of Occupational Psychology*, **62**, 55–59.

Firth-Cozens, J. (1987). Emotional distress in junior house officers. *British Medical Journal*, **295**, 533–536.

Firth-Cozens, J. (1997). *Stress in Health Professionals: Report on Current Research*. Report to the NHS Executive R&D Division.

Firth-Cozens, J. (1999). Preface to *Stress in Health Professionals: Psychological and Organisational Causes and Interventions*. Chichester: John Wiley & Sons.

Firth-Cozens, J. & Greenhalgh, J. (1997). Doctors' perceptions of the links between stress and lowered clinical care. *Social Science and Medicine*, **44**, 1017–1022.

Firth-Cozens, J. & Hardy, G. (1992). Occupational stress, clinical treatment and changes in job perceptions. *Journal of Occupational and Organisational Psychology*, **65**, 61–75.

Freudenberger, H.J. (1974). Staff burnout. *Journal of Social Issues*, **30**, 159–165.

Gottlieb, D.J., Parenti, C.M., Peterson, C.A. & Logfren, R.P. (1991). Effect of change in house staff work schedules on resource utilisation and patient care. *Archives of Internal Medicine*, **151**, 2065–2070.

Gray-Toft, P.A. & Anderson, J.G. (1985). Organisational stress in the hospital: development of a model for diagnosis and prediction. *Health Services Research*, **19**, 753–774.

Gronningsaeter, H., Hytten, K. & Skauli, G. (1992). Improved health and coping by physical exercise or cognitive behavioural stress management training in a work environment. *Psychology and Health*, **7**, 147–163.

Guzzo, R.A. & Shea, G.P. (1992). Group performance and intergroup relations. In M.D. Dunnette & L.M. Hough (Eds), *Handbook of Industrial and Organisational Psychology* (pp. 269–313). Palo Alto, CA: Consulting Psychologists Press.

Haig, A.J., Linton, P. & McIntosh, M. (1990). Aggressive early management by a specialist in physical medicine and rehabilitation: effect lost time due to injuries in hospital employees. *Journal of Occupational Medicine*, **32**, 241–242.

Health Service Advisory Committee (1987). *Violence to Staff: DHSS Advisory Committee on Violence to Staff Report*. London: HMSO.

Heaney, C.A., Price, R.M. & Rafferty, J. (1995). Increasing coping resources at work: a field experiment to increase social support, improve work team functioning and enhance employee mental health. *Journal of Organisational Behaviour*, **16**, 335–352.

Hsu, K. & Marshall, V. (1987). Prevalence of depression and distress in a large sample of Canadian residents, interns and fellows. *American Journal of Psychiatry*, **144**, 1561–1566.

Hurwitz, T.A., Beiser, M., Nichol, H., Patrick, L. & Kozak, J. (1987). Impaired interns and residents. *Canadian Journal of Psychiatry*, **32**, 165–169.

Infantino, J.A. & Musingo, S.Y. (1985). Assaults and injuries among staff with and without training in aggression control techniques. *Hospital and Community Psychiatry*, **36**, 1312–1314.

Johnson, J.V. & Hall, E.M. (1988). Job strain, workplace social support and cardiovascular disease: a cross-sectional study of a random sample of the Swedish working population. *American Journal of Public Health*, **78**, 1336–1342.

Johnson, J.V., Hall, E.M. & Ford, D.E. (1995). The psychosocial work environment of physicians. *Journal of Occupational and Environmental Medicine*, **37** (9), 1151–1159.

Johnson, J.V., Stewart, W., Hall, E.M., Fredland, P. & Theorell, T. (1996). Long-term psychosocial work environment and cardiovascular mortality among Swedish women. *American Journal of Public Health*, **86**, 324–331.

Jones, J.W., Barge, B.N., Steffy, B.D., Fay, L.M., Kunz, L.K. & Wuebker, L.J. (1988). Stress and medical malpractice: organisational risk assessment and intervention. *Journal of Applied Psychology*, **4**, 727–735.

Kagan, N.I., Kagan, H. & Watson, M.G. (1995). Stress reduction in the workplace: the effectiveness of psycho-educational programmes. *Journal of Counselling Psychology*, **42**, 71–78.

Karasek, R.A. (1979). Job demands, job decision latitude and mental strain: implications for job redesign. *Administrative Science Quarterly*, **24**, 285–311.

Karasek, R.A. (1990). Lower health risk with increasing job control among white-collar workers. *Journal of Organisational Behaviour*, **11**, 171–185.

Kobasa, S.C., Maddi, S.R. & Kahn, S.C. (1982). Hardiness and health: a prospective study. *Journal of Personality and Social Psychology*, **42**, 168–177.

Kohn, L., Corrigan, J. & Donaldson, M. (1999). *To Err Is Human: Building a Safer Health System*. Washington, DC: Institute of Medicine.

Lanza, M. (1983). The reactions of nursing staff to physical assault by patients. *Hospital and Community Psychiatry*, **34**, 44–47.

Lazarus, R. & Folkman, S. (1984). *Stress, Appraisal and Coping*. New York: Springer.

Ley, P. (1988). *Communicating with Patients: Improving Communication, Satisfaction and Compliance*. London: Chapman & Hall.

Lin, Y.J. (2001). Effects of organisational and environmental factors on service differentiation strategy of integrated healthcare networks. *Health Service Management Research*, **14** (1), 18–26.

Lloyd, M. & Bor, R. (1999). *Communication Skills for Medicine*. UK: Churchill Livingstone.

Lokk, J. & Arnetz, B. (1997). Psychophysiological concomitants of organisational change in health care personnel: effects of a controlled intervention study. *Psychotherapy and Psychosomatic Medicine*, **66**, 74–77.

Maiden, R. (1988). EAP evaluation in a Federal Government Agency. *Employee Assistance Quarterly*, **3**, 191–203.

Malcolm, R.M., Harrison, J. & Forster, H. (1993). Effects of changing the pattern of sickness absence referrals in a local authority. *Occupational Medicine*, **43**, 211–215.

Martin, L.R. (1984). Organisational interventions. In J. Firth-Cozens & R. Payne (Eds), *Stress in Health Professionals*. Chichester: John Wiley & Sons.

Maslach, C. (1982). *Burnout: The Cost of Caring*. Englewood Cliffs, NJ: Prentice Hall.

McGrail, M.P., Tsai, S.P. & Bernacki, E.J. (1995). A comprehensive initiative to manage the incidence and cost of occupational injury and illness. *Journal of Occupational and Environmental Medicine*, **37**, 1263–1268.

Michie, S. & Williams, S. (2003). Reducing work related psychological ill health and sickness absence: a systematic literature review. *Occupational and Environmental Medicine*, **60**, 3–9.

Miller, K.I., Ellis, B.H., Zook, E.G. & Lyles, J.S. (1990). An integrated model of communication, stress and burnout in the workplace. *Communication Research*, **17** (3), 300–326.

Murphy, L.R. (1999). Organisational interventions to reduce stress in health care workers. In *Stress in Health Professionals: Psychological and Organisational Causes and Interventions*. Chichester: John Wiley & Sons.

Murphy, R., Pearlman, F., Rea, C. & Papazian-Boyce, L. (1994). Work redesign: a return to the basics. *Nursing Management*, **25**, 37–39.

Noble, P. & Roger, S. (1989). Violence by psychiatric inpatients. *British Journal of Psychiatry*, **155**, 384–390.

Novack, D.H., Plumer, R., Smith, R.L., Ochtihill, H., Morrow, G.R. & Bennett, J.M. (1979). Changes in physicians' attitudes towards telling the cancer patient. *Journal of the American Medical Association*, **241**, 897–900.

Quick, J.C. (1999). Occupational health psychology: historical roots and future directions. *Health Psychology*, **18** (1), 82–88.

Ratti, N. & Piling, K. (1997). Back pain in the workplace. *British Journal of Rheumatology*, **36**, 260–264.

Reynolds, S. (1997). Psychological wellbeing at work: is prevention better than cure? *Journal of Psychosomatic Research*, **43**, 93–102.

Reynolds, S. & Shapiro, D. (1991). Stress reduction in transition: conceptual problems in the design, implementation and evaluation of work site stress management interventions. *Human Relations*, **44**, 717–733.

Rix, G. & Seymour, D. (1988). Violent incidents on a regional secure unit. *Journal of Advanced Nursing*, **13**, 746–775.

Schnieden, V. (1993). Violence at work. *Archives of Emergency Medicine*, **10**, 79–85.

Secombe, I. & Smith, G. (1997). *Taking Part: Registered Nurses and the Labour Market in 1997*. The Institute of Employment Studies.

Smoot, S.L. & Gonzales, J.C. (1995). Cost effective communication skills training for state hospital employees. *Psychiatric Services*, **46**, 819–822.

Stansfield, S.A., North, F.M., White, I. & Marmot, M.G. (1997). Work characteristics and psychiatric disorder in civil servants in London. *Journal of Epidemiology and Community Health*, **49**, 48–53.

Terry, D.J. & Jimmieson, N.L. (1999). Work control and employee well being: a decade review. In C.L. Cooper & I.T. Robertson (Eds), *International Review of Industrial and Organisational Psychology* (pp. 95–148). Chichester: John Wiley & Sons.

Thomas, L.T. & Gangster, D.C. (1995). Impact of family supportive work variables on work family conflict and strain: a control perspective. *Journal of Applied Psychology*, **80**, 6–15.

Tuckett, D., Boulton, M., Olson, C. & Williams, A. (1985). *Meetings between Experts: An Approach to Sharing Ideas in Medical Consultations*. London: Tavistock Publications.

Van Poppel, M.N.M., Roes, B.W. & Smid, T. (1997). A systematic review of controlled trials on the prevention of back pain in industry. *Occupational and Environmental Medicine*, **54**, 841–847.

Vincent, C.A. (1999). Fallibility, uncertainty and the impact of mistakes and litigation. In J. Firth-Cozens & R. Payne (Eds), *Stress in Health Professionals*. Chichester: John Wiley & Sons.

Wall, T.D., Bolden, R.I. & Borrill, C.S. (1997). Minor psychiatric disorder in NHS Trust staff: occupational and gender differences. *British Journal of Psychiatry*, **171**, 519–523.

Whittington, R. & Wykes, T. (1989). Staff strain and social support in a psychiatric hospital following assault by a patient. *Journal of Advanced Nursing*, **17**, 480–486.

Wiesel, S.W., Boden, S.D. & Feffer, M.C. (1994). A quality based protocol for the management of musculoskeletal injuries. *Clinical Orthopaedics*, **301**, 164–176.

Williams, S., Michie, S. & Pattani, S. (1999). *Improving the Health of the NHS Workforce*. Report of the Partnership on the Health of the NHS Workforce. The Nuffield Trust.

Wilson, R.M., Runciman, W.B. & Gibberd, R.W. et al. (1995). The quality in Australian health care study. *Medical Journal of Australia*, **163**, 458–471.

Wood, N., Farrow, S. & Elliott, B. (1994). A review of primary healthcare organisations. *Journal of Clinical Nursing*, **3** (4), 243–250.

Wren, B. (2000). Occupational health psychology in an NHS Trust. *Journal of Primary Care Mental Health*, **3**, 8–12.

Wren, B. & Michie, S. (2000). *Occupational health psychology: setting up a service in an NHS Trust*. Poster presented at the British Psychological Society Division of Health Psychology Conference, Autumn 2000.

Wren, B. & Michie, S. (2001). *An occupational health psychology intervention in an NHS Trust*. Poster presented at the British Psychological Society Division of Health Psychology Conference, Autumn 2001.

Wykes, T. & Mezey, G. (1994). Counselling for victims of violence. In T. Wykes (Ed.), *Violence and Healthcare Professionals*. London: Chapman & Hall.

CHAPTER 5

The Experience of Families and their Carers in Health Care

Timothy R. Elliott

and

Patricia Rivera

University of Alabama at Birmingham, USA

INTRODUCTION

In their daily routines, families have more influence on the personal health of each member than any other individual or any health service provider. This is particularly true in the development of and adjustment to a chronic disease or disability such that any palliative effects of interactions with a health care service provider can be augmented or undermined by family members who assume pivotal roles in the ongoing health behaviors of their kin. Although these family members are typically viewed as ancillary to the delivery of health services, this chapter asserts that families are an integral and vital component of health, and that health care professionals must attend to the unique features of families in order to enhance the health of the patient. Because families living with those with disease and disability probably have more influence on their health than any single professional health care provider, it is prudent that these persons receive as equitable a degree of training and skill development as observed in the training of other health professionals (Lengnick-Hall, 1995). This approach will necessitate a collaborative—rather than an authoritarian or paternalistic—partnership with families that includes their opinions about needs and solutions in research projects and service delivery programs (Israel et al., 1998), and may also require more community-based, in-home intervention programs than typically offered by most professional psychologists.

It must be noted that families, in which individuals assume both care recipient and carer roles, vary in the degree to which they include non-blood kin ("fictive kin"); families also differ in ways in which members from older and extended generations are involved in the immediate family circle. In this chapter, we discuss the experience of individuals faced with the care of a family member with a chronic illness or disability as they attempt to navigate

Handbook of Clinical Health Psychology. Edited by S. Llewelyn and P. Kennedy.
© 2003 John Wiley & Sons, Ltd.

health care systems. We will begin with a discussion of the historical background of caregiving in the USA as an example, outline the dilemma faced by carers in the USA, then present models of caregiver stress and, finally, review current treatment approaches.

Demographic trends and changes in the health care system in the USA, as elsewhere, have focused attention on the welfare and quality of life of an increasing elderly and disabled population. In the USA there are more than four million adults aged 65 years and older living in their communities, and another 33 million persons with disabilities (US Census Bureau, 1997), who require some form of assistance with such basic needs as bathing, dressing and toileting. It is generally up to their family members to provide this care as well as emotional, physical and financial support (Alzheimer's Association & National Alliance for Caregiving, 1999; National Alliance for Caregiving & American Association of Retired Persons, 1997). It is acknowledged that the responsibility and commitment associated with the carer role can take a toll on the individual's emotional well-being and resources thus compromising the carer's productivity, mental health, and physical well-being, and increasing the possibility of abuse directed at the dependent individual (Quayhagen et al., 1997).

Factors such as the physical and psychological demands made by the care recipient, the limitations on freedom and social interactions that accompany the care recipient's need for supervision, the financial burden, and the additional roles assumed by most carers including those of wife, parent, spouse and employee, all contribute to carer distress (Alzheimer's Association & National Alliance for Caregiving, 1999; National Alliance for Caregiving & American Association of Retired Persons, 1997; National Institute on Aging & National Institute on Mental Health, 1999).

HISTORICAL BACKGROUND OF CAREGIVING

Demographic, social and economic trends including reduced health care services have all contributed to an increase in personal responsibility for the care of family members. While in the USA, for example, the Social Security Act of 1930 made provision for some services that allowed individuals to increase dependence on public and private resources for the personal care of their disabled or elderly kin (Schorr, 1980), the services and programs were neither comprehensive nor a solution to the problem of caregiving. Furthermore, decreased birth rates, increased life expectancy, increased divorce rates, and more women in the workforce have reduced the pool of available caregivers in the USA and most Western countries. Thus, for example, the millions of Americans who rely on informal care from family members have found themselves in a situation where there are many more seniors and disabled adults than there are carers (Subcommittee on Human Services of the Select Committee on Aging, 1987).

Fifty-nine per cent of American women between the ages of 45 and 54 work full time (US Department of Labor, Bureau of Labor Statistics, 1995). This segment of the population is the group in the USA most likely to assume the role of family carer to an aging parent or disabled spouse or child. While the result of this trend is a reduced pool of potential female carers in the home, today's increased acceptance of men in non-traditional roles coupled with the prohibitive costs of institutionalization and professional in-home care may actually encourage men to take a more active approach in caregiving.

The high rates of divorce have also had important ramifications. For those individuals who have not remarried, spousal support—the primary source of carer support—is not available, and their caregiving responsibilities often fall on the children (Cicirelli, 1983). In addition to overcoming resentments and family conflict issues, these carers must also struggle with providing care and supervision to individuals who may not live together. For those divorcees who do remarry, filial responsibility may actually decrease, thereby reducing the pool of available carers (Cicirelli, 1983).

Finally, the number of chronic health problems have escalated in most Western societies and health care programs often limit services to persons with these conditions, thus compelling many family members to assume carer roles during periods that are not traditionally associated with provision of care (Hoffman, Rice & Sung, 1996). The role of the family carer has intensified with dramatic cutbacks in health care services, and the emergence of managed care as the predominant health care paradigm in Western countries has had many adverse effects on families with a member who has a chronic disease or disability (Council on Scientific Affairs, American Medical Association, 1993). With these changes in health care allocation—and with increases in the incidence of chronic disease and disability—more individuals will be compelled to assume the role of primary carer for a family member who incurs chronic disease or disability. Chronic health conditions and the management of symptoms associated with them account for approximately 68% of all health care expenditures in American health care systems, for example, and this may represent the greatest single challenge facing modern health care (Frank, 1997). As the number of chronic health problems continues to increase in contemporary society, and as the number of elderly individuals increases with advances in medical care, increased pressure will be placed on families to assume responsibility for the ongoing health care and adjustment of members with these conditions.

REACTIONS TO CHANGING ROLES AND EXPECTATIONS

When an individual incurs a chronic health condition, the degree of onset can vary in impact on the family. Some problems that are commonly considered to be age-related may be perceived as developmentally *on-time* (cf. Neugarten, 1979), albeit stressful and undesirable. In contrast, conditions that occur in accidents or trauma can be more stressful to a family in that these are construed as *off-time* events, in terms of developmental expectations for the individual and the family. Many young adults who incur severe physical disability in these circumstances may have considerable difficulty living independently, and a parent or spouse may have to assume carer duties at the expense of other career goals and activities. Individuals who incur severe physical disability often have considerable life expectancy, and thus the need for assistance from a family member may exist throughout a lifetime.

The roles and responsibilities associated with caregiving for a family member with a disability are many, and may vary from simple errands to such physically and emotionally challenging tasks as feeding, transferring, bathing or toileting. Depending on the type of care required, carers may also provide assistance ranging from a few hours a day to round-the-clock care. Although the type of assistance given depends on an individual's level of disability, one basic responsibility is for the carer to provide emotional support through regular contact, company and conversation.

The emotional life of a family, however, is influenced tremendously by factors that are typically operational prior to the onset of any health condition. There is no universal response or sequence of emotional reactions that characterize a family's experience. Clinicians are often vigilant for manifestations of denial, assuming family members are unconsciously unable to accept the fact that a loved one may be permanently affected by a diagnosis. But clinicians often fail to appreciate that many people are generally unaware or uninformed about specific health problems and their concomitants, and thus may have legitimate difficulty in understanding the meaning and ramifications of a specific condition. Denial is not a single, simplistic entity: families may not deny the factual existence of a particular condition, but they may not accept the implications of the condition as promulgated by clinical staff (Lazarus, 1983). Families that maintain goals and expectations, and who express optimism in the wake of acquired disability, are often labeled by staff and treated with disregard and condescension (Elliott & Kurylo, 2000), when in fact the family is expressing little more than a difference of opinion with staff (Novack & Richards, 1991).

At times, clinicians may embrace erroneous assumptions about the healing properties of time for family members. For example, it is often assumed that family members who are compelled to accept caregiving duties following the onset of disability will become more comfortable over time with routine and familiarity. However, empirical research indicates that carers who are depressed, anxious and in ill health during the initial inpatient stay of a loved one who has incurred disability are more likely to display increases in depression, anxiety and ill health over the course of the first year of caregiving. In contrast, carers who do not report adjustment problems during the inpatient stay are more likely to adapt well over the year (Shewchuk, Richards & Elliott, 1998).

Elaborate research designs and methodologies reveal that carers are at risk for disruptions in cardiovascular and immune functioning (Vitaliano, 1997). Their psychological and physical problems can be exacerbated as carers neglect their own health and care (Burton et al., 1997). Carers often face competing demands of multiple roles such as employment, and lack time for recreational and leisure pursuits, thus compromising their personal health and opportunities for positive mood experiences (Quittner et al., 1992, 1998). The factors identified as having the greatest negative impact on carer burden and stress are time limitations on personal activities, caregiving demands, patient deterioration, and patient uncooperativeness (Alzheimer's Association & National Alliance for Caregiving, 1999; National Alliance for Caregiving & American Association of Retired Persons, 1997). Many more adults with disabilities are admitted to long-term nursing facilities because of carer burnout than from a worsening of their physical condition (National Family Caregivers Association, 1999). Evidence indicates that older carers are at risk of mortality, compared to peers who are not carers, presumably due to the combined factors of prolonged stress, physical demands of providing care, and biological vulnerabilities (Schulz & Beach, 1999).

The financial burden resulting from missed work, termination of long-term public assistance such as social security benefits, or the cost of in-home services is another source of stress faced by carers (Pavalko & Artis, 1997). For example, the typical cost for Adult Day Care in California is $40 per day, or over $4100 a year if used twice a week. The use of an in-home attendant for eight hours weekly can add another $4500 a year, bringing the cost of care to almost $9000 annually. And although many state or private agencies exist to offer respite assistance to those in need, qualification criteria frequently exclude families in greatest need such as those on assistance programs.

While researchers and clinicians usually focus on the adjustment problems experienced by families following disability and disease, some families may actually experience positive changes (Perlesz, Kinsella & Crowe, 1999). Olkin (1999) observes that acquired disability can force family members to directly confront issues of trust, mortality and values, which in turn compel members to develop deeper commitments and restructure the meaning of marriage or kinship. Some family members report a greater sense of closeness, a greater emphasis on family and personal relationships, and positive changes in shared family values (Crewe, 1993). Support from family members is associated with greater acceptance of disability and personal meaning among persons with physical disability (Li & Moore, 1998). Many studies appear to over-report or misrepresent distress experienced by siblings of children with disability, and these issues seem to be adversely slanted by methodological and theoretical approaches that perpetuate negative views and ignore positive aspects of this experience (Perlesz, Kinsella & Crowe, 1999; Summers, White & Summers, 1994).

Family carers may experience positive shifts in their values and reconsider goals that were altered in the face of disability, and these shifts are indicative of stress-related growth and subjective well-being (King & Patterson, 2000; King et al., 2000). There is evidence to suggest that older family members in particular may be likely to experience some health and emotional benefits in providing care for a loved one (Beach et al., 2000; Kramer, 1997).

CULTURAL ISSUES

It is critical to remember that all factors affecting a carer's experience must be considered within the context of the individual's cultural and interpersonal life experiences (Aranda & Knight, 1997; Ingersoll-Dayton, Morgan & Antonucci, 1997; Martire, Stephens & Atienza, 1997). Ethnicity and culture contribute to a variation in the stress and coping process because of (a) differential risks to specific diseases and disorders, (b) differences in appraisal of stressors, and (c) the differential effects of stress-mediating factors such as family and social support. For example, the impact of role change and anticipatory grief is likely to be experienced quite differently by a traditionally home-based wife who must learn to run a household effectively while simultaneously trying to maintain the dignity of her disabled husband, than by the independent working woman who finds herself challenged by the domestic tasks of caring for her aging parents (Rivera & Marlo, 1999). Additionally, other factors such as socio-economic status, familial interdependence, level of acculturation, immigration status, and fear of stigma regarding a disease or physical disability (Aranda & Knight, 1997; Sotomayor & Randolph, 1988) may influence minority group members' experiences of caregiving, and place them at a disadvantage for social and professional services, resulting in levels of distress that are much greater than those documented in samples of non-minority carers.

In order to best address the needs of minority consumers of health care services it is important to understand some of the common misconceptions which surround their utilization of psychologically based services. Errors in judgment about cultural groups are frequently based on stereotypes. Because families of color are often stereotyped as being close-knit and supportive of their kin, for example, social service agencies may not take the time to assess the actual needs of this population. This assumption may lead to less allocation of resources, manpower, and finances for outreach to those communities (Valle, 1981), which in turn may help to perpetuate the misconception that they underutilize social services because they are taken care of by their own families (Henderson & Gutierrez-Mayka, 1992).

Valle (1981) proposed that a collaborative, community-based approach is needed to meet the challenges of working with carers of minority elderly and disabled persons. Valle recommends that education occur through culturally pre-existing social networks such as churches, community link-persons or religious leaders, and family networks. Aranda (1990) has further argued that interventions that are culturally relevant and utilize bilingual/bicultural staff are likely to increase minority utilization of services, as are interventions such as classes or support groups which do not carry stigmas of mental health problems, and which facilitate empowerment and encourage personal responsibility for change. Considerably more information about the experience of caregiving for individuals of differing cultural backgrounds must be obtained, in order to adequately address service needs, delivery and utilization.

There are also *cross-cultural* issues that should be considered when studying the experience of families and health. Research has documented compelling differences between carers in American families and those in other nations. Among carers for disabled, older adults, for example, carers in American families appear to have spent less time with a care recipient before assuming the carer role than family carers in Switzerland (Karlin, O'Reilly & Williams, 1997). Another study found family carers of Alzheimer's disease (AD) patients in the USA reported more depression and anxiety than carers of AD patients in China, although coping styles and behaviors were similar between the two groups (Shaw et al., 1997). The reasons for these and other differences are unclear and they are open to further study. It is important to note, however, that study of *within-group* differences between members of a specific culture reveals that psychological characteristics often predict adjustment among family members in a theoretically consistent and interpretable manner (Chan, Lee & Lieh-Mak, 2000).

EXPERTS ON THEIR DAILY LIVES

Qualitative research designs provide valuable insights into the family experience. But many theorists and researchers make assumptions about families and their reactions, needs and problems following the onset of disease and disability, and take a "top-down" approach to the development of services and programs that does not take into account the opinions and perspectives of individuals who live daily with chronic health conditions (Shewchuk & Elliott, 2000). It is preferable to regard families who have a member with health problem as experts on the "realities of their daily lives" (Mechanic, 1998, p. 284).

Severe physical disabilities that necessitate both changes and assistance in basic self-care and activities of daily living compel families to deal with a range of unique problems. Typically, professionals assume these problems constitute the sources of burden on families, however, in a focus group of carers for persons with spinal cord injury (SCI), carers ranked problems concerning interpersonal and familial stress higher than instrumental activities associated with self-care regimens (Elliott & Shewchuk, 2002). Specifically, carers ranked the following as problematic: "hateful attitudes of the care recipients", "carer feelings of guilt", "lack of appreciation", "care recipient is demanding and bossy", "finding challenging activities for the care recipient", "not enough time in the day", and "sense of obligation to keep care recipient busy". Out of 18 problems ranked by these carers, only one specifically concerned self-care activities. In contrast, a self-report study in Hong Kong found that spouses of persons with SCI reported a health- or disability-related problem as the primary source of stress in their lives; family interactions and relationship issues were the second most frequently nominated problem (Chan, 2000).

Neurological disabilities that primarily affect brain-related functions can have substantial cognitive sequelae in addition to occasional physical impairments. This can result in substantive changes in behavioral expression, memory and self-regulation. In another focus group study, husbands of women with traumatic brain injury (TBI) identified specific problems with their wives' loss of autonomy, mood swings, insecurities, overprotectiveness, reluctance to leave home, and change in lifestyle as particularly stressful (Willer et al., 1991). Wives of men with TBI reported specific problems with husbands' personality changes, memory loss, lack of insight, lack of acceptance, reduction in financial resources, loss of emotional support, and feeling unable to meet children's needs. Other qualitative studies have found that family carers have many concerns about interpersonal relationships, quality of life, and emotional commitments (Chwalisz & Stark-Wroblewski, 1996; Long, Glueckauf & Rasmussen, 1998).

There is some evidence that family members may have more ongoing concerns about management and adherence issues when a member has a chronic disease like diabetes. These carers report great concern about their loved one "driving alone", the disease progression, and the adherence to insulin dosing schedules and dietary habits (Miller et al., 2000). It appears that chronic disease imposes fewer interpersonal and familial disruptions than mobility-related impairments (e.g., SCI) or neurological disabilities (e.g., TBI). Once a family manages the instrumental tasks associated with disability, the quality of interpersonal relationships may then be of chief concern to those in committed, ongoing relationships. The ambiguity of disease management and progression, however, may be salient to family carers who assist a member with a chronic disease.

SOCIAL AND FAMILY SUPPORT

Families are often considered an extension—if not an embodiment—of social support. Indeed, individuals who have incurred spinal cord injury report that partners and family members are more useful than friends and professional staff in helping them to cope during the first year of disability (Rogers & Kennedy, 2000). Dakof and Taylor (1990) found that patients with chronic health problems identified practical assistance from spouses and other family members to be especially supportive, and lower levels of family support have been associated with a greater mortality rate among hemodialysis patients (Christensen et al., 1994). Effective family support has also been associated with improved social adjustment and less psychological distress among bone marrow transplant survivors in Europe (Molassiotis, Van Den Akker & Boughton, 1997).

Specific characteristics of these supportive networks that have been identified as crucial include the amount of support available, the adequacy of the support, and overall satisfaction with the support received (Mittleman et al., 1994). Alternatively, unmet needs and negative interactions with others are two additional characteristics of social support that have been reported to contribute to psychological distress in carers (MaloneBeach & Zarit, 1995; Redinbaugh, MacCallum & Kiecolt-Glaser, 1995; Rivera et al., 1991). People who are married reported greater life satisfaction in the first year of disability than persons who are single or divorced (Putzke, Elliott & Richards, 2001), but spousal partners can be a source of considerable stress (Coyne & DeLongis, 1986). In some cases, family members offer less support in reaction to the emotional distress of the care recipient, which can burden and alienate family members (Bolger et al., 1996), and induce expressions of anger

(Lane & Hobfoll, 1992). Family interaction patterns have stronger associations with self-reported health behavior among cardiac patients than other social support variables (Franks, Campbell & Shields, 1992).

Marital quality and satisfaction may be directly related to patient adjustment following the onset of disease and disability (Coyne & Smith, 1991). The care recipient may at times encounter expressions of hostility, which exacerbates their distress (Fiske, Coyne & Smith, 1991). Spousal criticism, in particular, has been predictive of greater patient distress and maladaptive coping behaviors (Manne & Zautra, 1989), with patient health-compromising behaviors (Franks, Campbell & Shields, 1992), and with increased primary care utilization of cardiac patients (Fiscella, Franks & Shields, 1997). In other situations, family members may overprotect the care recipient from potentially stressful situations that might inadvertently compromise the emotional adjustment of both carer and care recipient (Coyne & Smith, 1991; Suls et al., 1997). Care recipients who place a high premium on functional independence prior to their debilitating condition may have the greatest difficulty accepting support from a spouse (Martire et al., 2002).

PARENTING AND GENDER ROLES

Women are more likely to assume the role of carer for an ill family member. Much of the extant literature has understandably focused on mothers, wives and daughters in these roles (Moen, Robison & Dempster-McClain, 1995). Although women report more distress than men in caregiving roles, these differences might be due to the willingness of women to report distress (Gallagher-Thompson et al., 1998). Gender differences in adjustment may cloud our understanding of how spousal and parental carers react differently to the health of a family member. Wives of patients with heart failure report more distress than husbands of women with this condition, and the distress reported by the women in the carer role is directly associated with their perceptions of marital quality (Rohrbaugh et al., 2002). Rose et al. (1996) found that while husbands increased household activity after a wife experienced a myocardial infarction, the recovering wives still took on as many household duties as the husbands. One explanation for this finding might be that the resumption of the homemaker role of these women was critical to their well-being and recovery.

Children's adjustment is often associated with the mother's adjustment, but maternal carer adjustment is influenced more by stress, family support, and personal resources than the severity of the condition or functional abilities of the child (Wallander & Varni, 1989; Wallander, Pitt & Mellins, 1990; Wallander et al., 1988, 1989a, 1989b). Mothers often encounter social isolation as they care for a child with a chronic disease or disability, while fathers encounter strains associated with financial obligations and work-related activities that may affect the care and well-being of the child (Frank et al., 2001; Holmbeck et al., 1997). Although the impact of fathers on child adjustment has been largely overlooked in past research, accumulating evidence now demonstrates that fathers have a considerable impact on the adjustment of a child with a chronic health condition, even when the father does operate as the family carer, per se. For example, father's drinking problems and parental strain were predictive of child adjustment over a four-year period (Timko et al., 1993). Chaney et al. (1997) found child adjustment over a year was directly related to increases in fathers' distress, and not the mothers' distress. A decline in fathers' adjustment was inversely related to mothers' adjustment.

Parents can model effective coping skills for their ill children, who in turn may utilize similar strategies with beneficial results (Kliewer & Lewis, 1995) in their self-care regimens (Chaney & Peterson, 1989). Behavioral problems and health complaints of adolescents with chronic disease are more likely in families lower in family competence (Kell et al., 1998) and in those marriages characterized by poor adjustment and interactional strain between husbands and wives (Clay et al., 1995; Frank et al., 1998).

THEORETICAL EXPLANATIONS OF FAMILY EXPERIENCE FOLLOWING DISABILITY

Several important models have tried to explain family dynamics in the wake of a chronic health condition in a member. Notable among these is Minuchin's conceptualization of rigid, over-protective, and enmeshed family interaction patterns that contribute to the development and exacerbation of psychosomatic illnesses in children (Minuchin et al., 1975). Subsequent research has not supported the basic tenets of this model (Coyne & Anderson, 1989). Recent evidence indicates that some of these interactive patterns in which a child's input is recruited into dyadic discussions may be related to marital quality, and be useful in long-term coping, monitoring, and management of a chronic condition (Northey, Griffin & Krainz, 1998). Increased family cohesion and the high quality of mother–child interactions are predictive of positive growth in socialization, daily living skills, and communication among young children with Down's syndrome (Hauser-Cram et al., 1999).

In contrast, research has supported models of family behavior that posit that well-intentioned efforts by a spouse to allay the pain and suffering expressed by a partner may inadvertently reinforce "disabled" behavior and reward the patient for emitting these behaviors (Fordyce, 1976). Spouses of chronic pain patients tend to be more solicitous than spouses of persons without pain (Flor, Kerns & Turk, 1987; Romano et al., 1992). Furthermore, parents who have more effective written and verbal problem-solving skills have been found to be more adherent with complex self-care regimens for their children than parents of children noted for poor compliance (Fehrenbach & Peterson, 1989), and may exhibit less distress with long-lasting benefits that can be observed up to three years later (Rivara et al., 1996). These skills may be a major determinant of patient behavioral outcomes in the first year of injury (Kinsella et al., 1999).

Effective social problem-solving abilities are associated with optimal adjustment among people in general (D'Zurilla & Nezu, 1999) and are predictive of carer depression, anxiety and ill health in the first year of caring for a family member with a disability (Elliott, Shewchuk & Richards, 2001). Other data indicate that problem-solving abilities are predictably associated with carer adjustment across the life span, including mothers of disabled children (Noojin & Wallander, 1997) and spouses of persons who have experienced a stroke (Grant et al., 2001a).

The ability of the carer to solve problems associated with life in general, and those associated with caregiving may be directly related to the adjustment and health of the care recipient. Carer tendencies to carelessly and impulsively solve problems have been associated with lower acceptance of disability among persons with SCI at discharge from a rehabilitation hospital. Moreover, carer impulsive and careless problem-solving styles—assessed at discharge—correctly classified the majority of care recipients who developed pressure sores a year later (Elliott, Shewchuk & Richards, 1999). A problem-solving model is attractive because it features a logical framework with testable hypotheses, a supportive literature base, a psychometrically sound measure, and clear directions for interventions (D'Zurilla & Nezu, 1999). Cognitive-behavioral perspectives appear to have considerable potential in understanding and conceptualizing family dynamics following disability.

PSYCHOLOGICAL INTERVENTIONS

There is an urgent need for programs that help family carers to address the routines and tasks "...essential to maintaining family functioning" (Altman, Cooper & Cunningham, 1999, p. 67). Psychologists can have an immense impact in developing, evaluating and delivering interventions that address the everyday needs of carers and their care recipients. Intervention research in family health psychology indicates that psychoeducational strategies are consistently more effective than other modalities, presumably because these approaches address the specific needs of family members and often actively involve family members (Burman & Margolin, 1992; Campbell & Patterson, 1995). Psychoeducational interventions can be conducted in inpatient, outpatient, community and home settings; they can be effectively adapted to serve culturally diverse populations (e.g., in Spanish; Gallagher-Thompson et al., 2001). Programs that address the specific needs of families may be more likely to succeed (Burman & Margolin, 1992).

Interventions that include spouses as part of patient treatment, without any clear goals specific for the spouse, do not seem to be particularly effective (Moore & Chaney, 1985). However, programs that educate the spouse about a health condition and skills in self-care and coping, and that instill a greater understanding of the patient experience, are more promising (Moore, 1989). Others maintain that family therapies are still better for families that have a member presenting symptoms sensitive to family distress and interaction patterns (e.g., asthma, diabetes; Campbell & Patterson, 1995).

It is vital to consider the multiple systems that directly impinge not only on the delivery of needed services to families, but the availability and access to health care in contemporary society. Theory-based interventions can be delivered in community settings by low-cost personnel (e.g., problem-solving training for family carers: Elliott & Shewchuk, 2002; Houts et al., 1996). Problem-solving principles can be incorporated seamlessly into family education programs (Bucher et al., 1999). Program evaluation research and predictive models that take into account unique patient/family subgroups will help us to identify individuals who require more intensive therapeutic interventions from skilled staff and who are most likely to benefit from these high-cost services (Shewchuk & Elliott, 2000).

Effective interventions will address the problems *as experienced* by families (Elliott & Shewchuk, 2000). These interventions should help families to become more active and expert in their self-management and to operate competently as extensions of the formal health care system (Wagner, Austin & Von Korff, 1996). Recent programs that emphasize "partnerships" with family carers recognize their needs for education, support and counseling in the home environment (Grant et al., 2001b). These programs circumvent problems with mobility and transportation restrictions, and work within the time constraints that many carers experience. Evidence indicates that family carers and care recipients benefit from problem-solving-based interventions provided in telephone interactions (Grant et al., 2002; Roberts et al., 1995). Distance education for family carers using telephone sessions may be as effective as support groups in alleviating burden and promoting family interactions (Brown et al., 1999). Other programs have relied on home visits to provide on-site assessment and training for family carers in the first year of acquired disability (Kurylo, Elliott & Shewchuk, 2001). Computer-based technologies can be used to conduct family counseling sessions, and these modalities have been used successfully with families that have a teenage child with seizure disorders (Hufford, Glueckauf & Webb, 1999). Home-based video counseling and speaker phone counseling, and face-to-face office-based counseling appear to be equally effective in reducing problems severity experienced by families and pre-adolescents with epilepsy; moreover, these respondents preferred the two home-based modalities over the traditional office visit (Glueckauf et al., 2002).

FUTURE DIRECTIONS FOR PROGRAM AND POLICY DEVELOPMENT

The numerous creative approaches to managing carer distress and their variability in results have led to the need to identify mechanisms of action, or reasons for the efficacy of particular treatments. Identifying the "how" and "why" a treatment does what it is intended to do is a basic tenet in clinical trials and can be used in a similar fashion in examining the effectiveness of carer interventions (Gitlin et al., 2000).

Carer interventions generally cluster within four categories: family, individual, behavior management, or home-modification. While the underpinning theoretical frameworks of each imply a mechanism of action, they do not necessarily explain *how* burden or distress is reduced or eliminated. Theory refinement is an unquestionable and ongoing process in science that attempts to answer the question of *how*. Lichstein, Riedel and Grieve (1994) have proposed treatment fidelity as an approach to explaining *why* a particular procedure works. Through the careful measurement and documentation of (a) treatment delivery, (b) treatment dosage, and (c) treatment implementation by participants, critical characteristics of the intervention process can be identified. Furthermore, such systematic assessment will allow comparisons between differing treatment modalities, with the goal of identifying the mechanisms of action and the conditions necessary for optimal efficacy.

Empirical research that is embedded within a sound conceptual framework and incorporates cultural and individual differences can efficiently contribute to policy reform. Under conditions that include sufficient data, proof of cost-effectiveness, and endorsement from a consensus group, interventions can become a "standard of care" (Mahoney, Burns & Harrow, 2000), benefiting not only the consumers, but also service providers. As persons living with a chronic disease or disability have more influence on outcome than any single health provider, scientists and practitioners must form partnerships with these consumers in serving their needs and finding solutions in a manner that effects positive change at individual, systemic and programmatic levels.

ACKNOWLEDGMENT

This chapter was supported in part by the National Institute on Disability and Rehabilitation Research Grant #H133B980016A, and by Grant #R49/CCR403641, USDHHS, Centers for Disease Control and Prevention, National Center for Injury Prevention and Control to the

University of Alabama at Birmingham. Its contents are solely the responsibility of the authors and do not necessarily represent the official views of the funding agencies.

Correspondence concerning this article should be addressed to Timothy R. Elliott, Department of Physical Medicine and Rehabilitation, 1717 6th Avenue South, University of Alabama at Birmingham, Birmingham, AL 35233-7330. Electronic mail may be sent to telliott@uab.edu.

REFERENCES

Altman, B.A., Cooper, P.F. & Cunningham, P.J. (1999). The case of disability in the family: impact on health care utilization and expenditures for nondisabled members. *The Milbank Quarterly*, **77**, 39–73.

Alzheimer's Association & National Alliance for Caregiving (1999). *Who Cares? Families Caring for Persons with Alzheimer's Disease*. Washington, DC: Alzheimer's Association.

Aranda, M.P. (1990). Culture-friendly services for Latino elders. *Generations*, **14**, 55–57.

Aranda, M.P. & Knight, B.G. (1997). The influence of ethnicity and culture on the caregiver stress and coping process: a socio-cultural review and analysis. *The Gerontologist*, **37** (3), 342–354.

Beach, S.R., Schulz, R., Yee, J. & Jackson, S. (2000). Negative and positive health effects of caring for a disabled spouse: longitudinal findings from the carer health effects study. *Psychology and Aging*, **15**, 259–271.

Bolger, N., Foster, M., Vinokur, A.D. & Ng, R. (1996). Close relationships and adjustment to a life crises: the case of breast cancer. *Journal of Personality and Social Psychology*, **70**, 295–309.

Brown, R., Pain, K., Berwald, C., Hirschi, P., Delehanty, R. & Miller, H. (1999). Distance education and caregiver support groups: comparison of traditional and telephone groups. *Journal of Head Trauma Rehabilitation*, **14**, 257–268.

Bucher, J.A., Houts, P., Nezu, C.M. & Nezu, A. (1999). Improving problem-solving skills of family caregivers through group education. *Journal of Psychosocial Oncology*, **16** (3–4), 73–84.

Burman, B. & Margolin, G. (1992). Analysis of the association between marital relationships and health problems: an interactional perspective. *Psychological Bulletin*, **112**, 39–63.

Burton, L.C., Newsom, J.T., Schulz, R., Hirsch, C. & German, P.S. (1997). Preventive health behaviors among spousal carers. *Preventive Medicine*, **26**, 162–169.

Campbell, T.L. & Patterson, J.M. (1995). The effectiveness of family interventions in the treatment of physical illness. *Journal of Marital and Family Therapy*, **21**, 545–583.

Chan, C.K. (2000). Stress and coping in spouses of persons with spinal cord injuries. *Clinical Rehabilitation*, **14**, 137–144.

Chan, C.K., Lee, P. & Lieh-Mak, F. (2000). Coping with spinal cord injury: personal and marital adjustment in the Hong Kong chinese setting. *Spinal Cord*, **38**, 687–696.

Chaney, J. & Peterson, L. (1989). Family variables and disease management in juvenile rheumatoid arthritis. *Journal of Pediatric Psychology*, **14**, 389–403.

Chaney, J., Mullins, L.L., Frank, R.G. & Peterson, L. (1997). Transactional patterns of child, mother, and father adjustment in insulin-dependent diabetes mellitus: a prospective study. *Journal of Pediatric Psychology*, **22**, 229–244.

Christensen, A.J., Wiebe, J., Smith, T. & Turner, C. (1994). Predictors of survival among hemodialysis patients: effect of perceived family support. *Health Psychology*, **13**, 521–525.

Chwalisz, K. & Stark-Wroblewski, K. (1996). The subjective experiences of spouse carers of persons with brain injuries: a qualitative analysis. *Applied Neuropsychology*, **3**, 28–40.

Cicirelli, V.G. (1983). A comparison of helping behavior to elderly parents of adult children with intact and disrupted marriages. *The Gerontologist*, **23**, 619–625.

Clay, D., Wood, P.K., Frank, R.G., Hagglund, K. & Johnson, J. (1995). Examining systematic differences in adaptation to chronic illness: a growth modeling approach. *Rehabilitation Psychology*, **40**, 61–70.

Council on Scientific Affairs, American Medical Association (1993). Physicians and family carers: a model for partnership. *Journal of the American Medical Association*, **269**, 1282–1284.

Coyne, J.C. & Anderson, B.J. (1989). The "psychosomatic family" reconsidered II: recalling a defective model and looking ahead. *Journal of Marital and Family Therapy*, **15**, 139–148.

Coyne, J.C. & DeLongis. A. (1986). Going beyond social support: the role of social relationships in adaptation. *Journal of Consulting and Clinical Psychology*, **54**, 454–460.

Coyne, J.C. & Smith, D.A. (1991). Couples coping with a myocardial infarction: a contextual perspective on wives' distress. *Journal of Personality and Social Psychology*, **61**, 404–412.

Crewe, N. (1993). Spousal relationships and disability. In F.P. Haseltine, S. Cole & D. Gray (Eds), *Reproductive Issues for Persons with Physical Disabilities* (pp. 141–151). Baltimore, MD: Paul H. Brookes Publishing.

Dakof, G.A. & Taylor, S.E. (1990). Victim's perceptions of social support: what is helpful for whom? *Journal of Personality and Social Psychology*, **58**, 80–89.

D'Zurilla, T.J. & Nezu, A. (1999). *Problem-Solving Therapy: A Social Competence Approach to Clinical Intervention*. New York: Springer.

Elliott, T. & Kurylo, M. (2000). Hope over disability: lessons from one young woman's triumph. In C.R. Snyder (Ed.), *The Handbook of Hope: Theory, Measures, and Applications* (pp. 373–386). New York: Academic Press.

Elliott, T. & Shewchuk, R. (2000). Problem solving therapy for family caregivers of persons with severe physical disabilities. In C. Radnitz (Ed.), *Cognitive-Behavioral Interventions for Persons with Disabilities* (pp. 309–327). New York: Jason Aronson, Inc.

Elliott, T. & Shewchuk, R. (2002). Using the nominal group technique to identify the problems experienced by persons living with severe physical disabilities. *Journal of Clinical Psychology in Medical Settings*, **9**, 65–76.

Elliott, T., Shewchuk, R. & Richards, J.S. (1999). Caregiver social problem-solving abilities and family member adjustment to recent-onset physical disability. *Rehabilitation Psychology*, **44**, 104–123.

Elliott, T., Shewchuk, R. & Richards, J.S. (2001). Family caregiver problem solving abilities and adjustment during the initial year of the caregiving role. *Journal of Counseling Psychology*, **48**, 223–232.

Fehrenbach, A.M. & Peterson, L. (1989). Parental problem-solving skills, stress, and dietary compliance in phenylketonuria. *Journal of Consulting and Clinical Psychology*, **57**, 237–241.

Fiscella, K., Franks, P. & Shields, C.G. (1997). Perceived family criticism and primary care utilization: psychosocial and biomedical pathways. *Family Process*, **36**, 25–41.

Fiske, V., Coyne, J. & Smith, D.A. (1991). Couples coping with myocardial infarction: an empirical reconsideration of the role of overprotectiveness. *Journal of Family Psychology*, **5**, 4–20.

Flor, H., Kerns, R.D. & Turk, D. (1987). The role of spouse reinforcement, perceived pain, and activity levels of chronic pain patients. *Journal of Psychosomatic Research*, **31**, 251–259.

Fordyce, W.E. (1976). *Behavioral Methods in Chronic Pain and Illness*. St Louis, MO: Mosby.

Frank, N.C., Brown, R.T., Blount, R.L. & Burke, V. (2001). Predictors of affective responses of mothers and fathers of children with cancer. *Psycho-oncology*, **10**, 293–304.

Frank, R.G. (1997). Lessons from the great battle: health care reform 1992–1994. *Archives of Physical Medicine and Rehabilitation*, **78**, 120–124.

Frank, R.G., Thayer, J., Hagglund, K., Veith, A., Schopp, L., Beck, N., Kashani, J., Goldstein, D., Cassidy, J.T., Clay, D., Chaney, J., Hewett, J. & Johnson, J. (1998). Trajectories of adaptation in pediatric chronic illness: the importance of the individual. *Journal of Consulting and Clinical Psychology*, **66**, 521–532.

Franks, P., Campbell, T.L. & Shields, C.G. (1992). Social relationships and health: the relative roles of family functioning and social support. *Social Science and Medicine*, **34**, 779–788.

Gallagher-Thompson, D., Arean, P., Rivera, P. & Thompson, L. (2001). A psychoeducational intervention to reduce stress in Hispanic caregivers. *Clinical Gerontologist*, **23** (1–2), 17–32.

Gallagher-Thompson, D., Coon, D.W., Rivera, P., Powers, D. & Zeiss, A. (1998). Family caregiving: stress, coping and intervention. In M. Hersen & V.B. Van Hasselt (Eds), *Handbook of Clinical Geropsychology* (pp. 469–493). New York: Plenum Press.

Gitlin, L.N., Corcoran, M., Martindale-Adams, J., Malone, C., Stevens, A. & Winter, L. (2000). Identifying mechanisms of action: why and how does intervention work? In R. Schulz (Ed.), *Handbook on Dementia Caregiving: Evidenced-based Interventions in Family Caregiving* (pp. 225–248). New York: Springer Publishing Co., Inc.

Glueckauf, R.L., Fritz, S., Ecklund-Johnson, E., Liss, H., Dages, P. & Carney, P. (2002). Videoconferencing-based family counseling for rural teenagers with epilepsy: Phase 1 findings. *Rehabilitation Psychology*, **47**, 49–72.

Grant, J.S., Elliott, T., Giger, J. & Bartolucci, A. (2001a). Social problem-solving abilities, social support, and adjustment among family carers of individuals with a stroke. *Rehabilitation Psychology*, **46**, 44–57.

Grant, J.S., Elliott, T., Giger, J. & Bartolucci, A. (2001b). Social problem-solving telephone partnerships with family caregivers of persons with stroke. *International Journal of Rehabilitation Research*, **24** (3), 181–189.

Grant, J.S., Elliott, T., Weaver, M., Bartolucci, A. & Giger, J. (2002). A telephone intervention with family caregivers of stroke survivors after hospital rehabilitation. *Stroke*, **33**, 2060–2065.

Hauser-Cram, P., Warfield, M., Shonkoff, J., Krauss, M., Upshur, C. & Sayer, A. (1999). Family influences on adaptive development in young children with Down's syndrome. *Child Development*, **70**, 979–989.

Henderson, J.N. & Gutierrez-Mayka, M. (1992). Ethnocultural themes in caregiving to Alzheimer's Disease patients in Hispanic families. *Clinical Gerontologist*, **11** (3/4), 59–74.

Hoffman, C., Rice, D. & Sung, H. (1996). Persons with chronic conditions: their prevalence and costs. *Journal of the American Medical Association*, **276**, 1473–1479.

Holmbeck, G.N., Corey-Ferguson, L., Hudson, T., Seefeldt, T., Shapera, W., Turner, T. & Uhler, J. (1997). Maternal, paternal, and marital functioning in families of preadolescents with spina bifida. *Journal of Pediatric Psychology*, **22**, 167–181.

Houts, P.S., Nezu, A.M., Nezu, C.M. & Bucher, J.A. (1996). The prepared family carer: a problem-solving approach to family carer education. *Patient Education and Counseling*, **27**, 63–73.

Hufford, B.J., Glueckauf, R.L. & Webb, P.M. (1999). Home-base, interactive videoconferencing for adolescents with epilepsy and their families. *Rehabilitation Psychology*, **44**, 176–193.

Ingersoll-Dayton, B., Morgan, D. & Antonucci, T. (1997). The effects of positive and negative social exchanges on aging adults. *Journal of Gerontology*, **52B** (4), S190–S199.

Israel, B.A., Schulz, A.J., Parker, E.A. & Becker, A.B. (1998). Review of community-based research: assessing partnership approaches to improve public health. *Annual Review of Public Health*, **19**, 173–202.

Karlin, N.J., O'Reilly, B.K. & Williams, S. (1997). Cross-cultural differences between Swiss and American caregivers of alzheimer's disease family members. *Journal of Clinical Geropsychology*, **3**, 257–265.

Kell, R.S., Kliewer, W., Erickson, M.T. & Ohene-Frempong, K. (1998). Psychological adjustment of adolescents with sickle cell disease: relations with demographic, medical and family competence variables. *Journal of Pediatric Psychology*, **23**, 301–312.

King, L.A. & Patterson, C. (2000). Reconstructing life goals after the birth of a child with Down's syndrome: finding happiness and growing. *International Journal of Rehabilitation and Health*, **5**, 17–30.

King, L.A., Scollon, C., Ramsey, C. & Williams, T. (2000). Stories of life transition: subjective well-being and ego development in parents of children with Down's syndrome. *Journal of Research in Personality*, **34**, 509–536.

Kinsella, G., Ong, B., Murtagh, D., Prior, M. & Sawyer, M. (1999). The role of the family for behavioral outcome in children and adolescents following traumatic brain injury. *Journal of Consulting and Clinical Psychology*, **67**, 116–123.

Kliewer, W. & Lewis, H. (1995). Family influences on coping processes in children and adolescents with sickle cell disease. *Journal of Pediatric Psychology*, **20**, 511–525.

Kramer, B.J. (1997). Gain in the caregiving experience: Where are we? What next? *The Gerontologist*, **37**, 218–232.

Kurylo, M., Elliott, T. & Shewchuk, R. (2001). FOCUS on the family carer: a problem-solving training intervention. *Journal of Counseling and Development*, **79**, 275–281.

Lane, C. & Hobfoll, S.E. (1992). How loss affects anger and alienates potential supporters. *Journal of Consulting and Clinical Psychology*, **60**, 935–942.

Lazarus, R.S. (1983). The costs and benefits of denial. In S. Breznitz (Ed.), *The Denial of Stress* (pp. 1–30). New York: International Universities Press.

Lengnick-Hall, C.A. (1995). The patient as the pivot point for quality in health care delivery. *Hospital and Health Services Administration*, **40**, 25–39.

Li, L. & Moore, D. (1998). Acceptance of disability and its correlates. *Journal of Social Psychology*, **138**, 13–25.

Lichstein, K.L., Riedel, B.W. & Grieve, R. (1994). Fair tests of clinical analysis: a treatment implementation model. *Advances in Behavioral Research Therapy*, **16**, 1–29.

Long, M.P., Glueckauf, R.L. & Rasmussen, J. (1998). Developing family counseling interventions for adults with episodic neurological disabilities: presenting problems, persons involved, and problem severity. *Rehabilitation Psychology*, **43**, 101–117.

Mahoney, D.F., Burns, R. & Harrow, B. (2000). From Intervention studies to public policy: translating research into practice. In R. Schulz (Ed.), *Handbook on Dementia Caregiving: Evidenced-based Interventions in Family Caregiving* (pp. 249–281). New York: Springer.

MaloneBeach, E. & Zarit, S. (1995). Dimensions of social support and social conflicts as predictors of caregiver depression. *International Psychogeriatrics*, **7**, 25–38.

Manne, S.L. & Zautra, A.J. (1989). Spouse criticism and support: their association with coping and psychological adjustment among women with rheumatoid arthritis. *Journal of Personality and Social Psychology*, **56**, 608–617.

Martire, L.M., Stephens, M.A.P. & Atienza, A.A. (1997). The interplay of work and caregiving: relationships between role satisfaction, role involvement, and caregivers' well-being. *Journal of Gerontology*, **52B** (5), S279–S289.

Martire, L.M., Stephens, M.A.P., Druley, J. & Wojno, W. (2002). Negative reactions to received spousal care: predictors and consequences of miscarried support. *Health Psychology*, **21**, 167–176.

Mechanic, D. (1998). Public trust and initiatives for new health care partnerships. *The Milbank Quarterly*, **76**, 281–302.

Miller, D., Shewchuk, R., Elliott, T. & Richards, J.S. (2000). Nominal group technique: a process for identifying diabetes self-care issues among patients and carers. *The Diabetes Educator*, **26**, 305–314.

Minuchin, S., Baker, L., Rosman, B., Liebman, R., Milman, L. & Todd, T. (1975). A conceptual model of psychosomatic illness in children. *Archives of General Psychiatry*, **32**, 1031–1038.

Mittleman, M., Ferris, S., Shulman, E., Steinberg, G., Mackell, J. & Ambinder, A. (1994). Efficacy of mulitcomponent individualized treatment to improve the well-being of Alzheimer's caregivers. In E. Light, G. Niederhe & B.D. Lebowitz (Eds), *Stress Effects on Family Caregivers of Alzheimer's Patients: Research and Interventions* (pp. 156–184). New York: Springer.

Moen, P., Robison, J. & Dempster-McClain, D. (1995). Caregiving and women's well-being: a life course approach. *Journal of Health and Social Behavior*, **36**, 259–273.

Molassiotis, A., Van Den Akker, O. & Boughton, B. (1997). Perceived social support, family environment, and psychosocial recovery in bone marrow transplant long-term survivors. *Social Science and Medicine*, **44**, 317–325.

Moore, J.E. & Chaney, E.F. (1985). Outpatient group treatment of chronic pain: effects of spouse involvement. *Journal of Consulting and Clinical Psychology*, **53**, 326–339.

Moore, L.I. (1989). *Behavioral changes in male spinal cord injured following two types of psychosocial rehabilitation experience*. Unpublished doctoral dissertation. St Louis University.

National Alliance for Caregiving & American Association of Retired Persons (1997). *Family Caregiving in the US: Findings from a National Survey*. Bethesda, MD: National Alliance for Caregiving.

National Family Caregivers Association (1999). *Family Caregiving Statistics* [on-line]. Available at: http://www.nfcares.org/NFC1998_stats.html. Accessed September 14, 1999.

National Institute on Aging & National Institute on Mental Health (1999). *Progress Report on Alzheimer's Disease*. US Department of Health and Human Services, Washington, DC: NIH Publication No. 99-3616.

Neugarten, B.L. (1979). Time, age, and the life cycle. *American Journal of Psychiatry*, **36**, 887–894.

Noojin, A.B. & Wallander, J.L. (1997). Perceived problem-solving ability, stress, and coping in mothers of children with physical disabilities: potential cognitive influences on adjustment. *International Journal of Behavioral Medicine*, **4**, 415–432.

Northey, S., Griffin, W.A. & Krainz, S. (1998). A partial test of the psychosomatic family model: marital interaction patterns in asthma and non-asthma families. *Journal of Family Psychology*, **12**, 220–235.

Novack, T.A. & Richards, J.S. (1991). Coping with denial among family members. *Archives of Physical Medicine and Rehabilitation*, **72**, 521.

Olkin, R. (1999). *What Psychotherapists Should Know about Disability*. New York: Guilford Press.

Pavalko, E.K. & Artis, J.E. (1997). Women's caregiving and paid work: causal relationships in late midlife. *Journal of Gerontology*, **52B** (4), S170–S179.

Perlesz, A., Kinsella, G. & Crowe, S. (1999). Impact of traumatic brain injury on the family: a critical review. *Rehabilitation Psychology*, **44**, 6–35.

Putzke, J.D., Elliott, T. & Richards, J.S. (2001). Marital status and adjustment 1 year post-spinal cord injury. *Journal of Clinical Psychology in Medical Settings*, **8**, 101–107.

Quayhagen, M., Quayhagen, M.P., Patterson, T.L., Irwin, M., Hauger, R.L. & Grant, I. (1997). Coping with dementia: family caregiver burnout and abuse. *Journal of Mental Health and Aging*, **3** (3), 357–365.

Quittner, A.L., Espelage, D., Opipari, L., Carter, B., Eid, N. & Eigen, H. (1998). Role strain in couples with and without a child with a chronic illness: associations with marital satisfaction, intimacy, and daily mood. *Health Psychology*, **59**, 1266–1278.

Quittner, A.L., Opipari, L., Regoli, M., Jacobsen, J. & Eigen, H. (1992). The impact of caregiving and role strain on family life: comparisons between mothers of children with cystic fibrosis and matched controls. *Rehabilitation Psychology*, **37**, 275–290.

Redinbaugh, E.M., MacCallum, R.C. & Kiecolt-Glaser, J.K. (1995). Recurrent syndromal depression in caregivers. *Psychology and Aging*, **10**, 358–368.

Rivara, J., Jaffe, K., Polissar, N., Fay, G., Liao, S. & Martin, K. (1996). Predictors of family functioning and change 3 years after traumatic brain injury in children. *Archives of Physical Medicine and Rehabilitation*, **77**, 754–764.

Rivera, P.A. & Marlo, H. (1999). Cultural, interpersonal and psychodynamic factors in caregiving: toward a greater understanding of treatment non-compliance. *Clinical Psychology and Psychotherapy*, **6**, 63–68.

Rivera, P.A., Rose, J.M., Futterman, A., Lovett, S.B. & Gallagher-Thompson, D. (1991). Dimensions of perceived social support in clinically depressed and non-depressed female caregivers. *Psychology and Aging*, **6**, 232–237.

Roberts, J., Brown, G.B., Streiner, D., Gafni, A., Pallister, R., Hoxby, H., Drummond-Young, M., LeGris, J. & Meichenbaum, D. (1995). Problem-solving counselling or phone-call support for outpatients with chronic illness: effective for whom? *Canadian Journal of Nursing Research*, **27** (3), 111–137.

Rogers, B. & Kennedy, P. (2000). A qualitative analysis of reported coping in a community sample of people with spinal cord injuries: the first year post discharge. *SCI Psychosocial Process*, **13**, 41, 44–49, 63.

Rohrbaugh, M.J., Cranford, J., Shobam, V., Nicklas, J., Sonnega, J. & Coyne, J.C. (2002). Couples coping with congestive heart failure: role and gender differences in psychological distress. *Journal of Family Psychology*, **16**, 3–18.

Romano, J.M., Turner, J.A., Friedman, L.S., Bukcroft, R.A., Jensen, M.P., Hops, H. & Wright, S.F. (1992). Sequential analysis of chronic pain behaviors and spouse responses. *Journal of Consulting and Clinical Psychology*, **60**, 777–782.

Rose, G.L., Suls, J., Green, P.J., Lounsburg, P. & Gordon, E. (1996). Comparison of adjustment, activity, and tangible social support in men and women patients and their spouses during the six months of post-myocardial infarction. *Annals of Behavioral Medicine*, **18**, 264–272.

Schorr, A. (1980). *"Thy father and thy mother": A second look at filial responsibility and family policy*. SSA Publication No. 13-11953. US Department of Health and Human Services, Washington, DC.

Schulz, R. & Beach, S.R. (1999). Caregiving as a risk factor for mortality: the caregiver health effects study. *Journal of the American Medical Association*, **282**, 2215–2219.

Shaw, W.S., Patterson, T., Semple, S., Grant, J., Grant, I., Yu, E., Zhang, M., Hi, Y. & Wu, W. (1997). A cross-cultural validation of coping strategies and their associations with caregiving distress. *Gerontologist*, **27**, 490–504.

Shewchuk, R. & Elliott, T. (2000). Family caregiving in chronic disease and disability: implications for rehabilitation psychology. In R.G. Frank & T. Elliott (Eds), *Handbook of Rehabilitation Psychology* (pp. 553–563). Washington, DC: American Psychological Association Press.

Shewchuk, R., Richards, J.S. & Elliott, T. (1998). Dynamic processes in health outcomes among caregivers of patients with spinal cord injuries. *Health Psychology*, **17**, 125–129.

Sotomayor, M. & Randolph, S.A. (1988). Preliminary review of caregiving issues among Hispanic elderly. In M. Sotomayor & H. Curriel (Eds), *Hispanic Elderly: A Cultural Signature* (pp. 137–160). Edinburg, TX: Pan American University Press, National Hispanic Council on Aging.

Subcommittee on Human Services of the Select Committee on Aging (1987). *Exploding the Myths: Caregiving in America*. Committee Publication No. 99-611. US Government Printing Office: Washington, D.C.

Suls, J., Green, P., Rose, G., Lounsburg, P. & Gordon, E. (1997). Hiding worries from one's spouse: associations between coping via protective buffering and distress in male post-myocardial infarction patients and their wives. *Journal of Behavioral Medicine*, **20**, 333–349.

Summers, C.R., White, K.R. & Summers, M. (1994). Siblings of children with a disability: review and analysis of the empirical literature. *Journal of Social Behavior and Personality*, **9** (5), 169–184.

Timko, C., Baumgartner, M., Moos, R.H. & Miller, J.J. (1993). Parental risk and resistance factors among children with juvenile rheumatoid disease: a four-year predictive study. *Journal of Behavioral Medicine*, **16**, 571–588.

US Census Bureau (1997). "Americans With Disabilities: Household Economic Studies", by Jack McNeil. *Current Population Reports*, Series P70–73.

US Department of Labor, Bureau of Labor Statistics (1995). *Employment and Earning*, **42** (1). Washington, DC: US Government Printing Office.

Valle, R. (1981). Natural support systems, minority groups and late life dementias: implications for service delivery, research, and policy. In N.E. Miller & G.D. Cohen (Eds), *Clinical Aspects of Alzheimer's Disease and Senile Dementia* (pp. 277–154). New York: Raven Press.

Vitaliano, P.P. (Ed.) (1997). Physiological and physical concomitants of caregiving: introduction to the special issue [Special issue]. *Annals of Behavioral Medicine*, **19** (2).

Wagner, E.H., Austin, B.T. & Von Korff, M. (1996). Organizing care for patients with chronic illness. *The Milbank Quarterly*, **74**, 511–544.

Wallander, J.L. & Varni, J. (1989). Social support and adjustment in chronically ill and handicapped children. *American Journal of Community Psychology*, **17**, 185–201.

Wallander, J.L., Pitt, L.C. & Mellins, C.A. (1990). Child functional independence and maternal psychosocial stress as risk factors threatening adaptation in mothers of physically or sensorially handicapped children. *Journal of Consulting and Clinical Psychology*, **58**, 818–824.

Wallander, J.L., Varni, J., Babani, L., Banis, H. & Wilcox, K. (1988). Children with chronic physical disorders: maternal reports of their psychological adjustment. *Journal of Pediatric Psychology*, **13**, 197–212.

Wallander, J.L., Varni, J., Babani, L., Banis, H. & Wilcox, K. (1989a). Family resources as resistance factors for psychological maladjustment in chronically ill and handicapped children. *Journal of Pediatric Psychology*, **14**, 157–173.

Wallander, J.L., Varni, J., Babani, L. & DeHaan, C. (1989b). The social environment and the adaptation of mothers of physically handicapped children. *Journal of Pediatric Psychology*, **14**, 371–387.

Willer, B.S., Allen, K., Liss, M. & Zicht, M. (1991). Problems and coping strategies of individuals with traumatic brain injury and their spouses. *Archives of Physical Medicine*, **72**, 460–464.

PART II

Clinical Conditions and the Experience of Clinical Health Psychology

CHAPTER 6

Cardiac Conditions

Wolfgang Linden
University of British Columbia, Canada

INTRODUCTION

This chapter overviews the contribution of clinical health psychology to cardiac conditions and describes some major trends in internal medicine and cardiology that shape and define where psychological input is most needed. Specific rationales, methods, and outcomes for four areas of application will be described: hypertension, preparation for cardiac surgery, cardiac rehabilitation, and coping with chronic heart failure (CHF).

PLACING PSYCHOLOGY'S CONTRIBUTIONS INTO A PATHWAY MODEL

Cardiovascular disease (CVD) is a complex disease with many different expressions and an unknown etiology. Nevertheless, there is a cluster of proven risk factors including diabetes, high blood pressure (BP), lack of fitness, poor nutrition, smoking and, more recently, the addition of psychological factors such as stress and depression (Rozanski, Blumenthal & Kaplan, 1999). Similarly, there is evidence that cardiac events are often preceded by distinct psychological challenges; this has been observed for ischemic events, i.e. a temporary lack of blood supply to the heart (Mittleman et al., 1995), for acute rises in BP (Linden, Rutledge & Con, 1998), and for sudden cardiac death (Kamarck & Jennings, 1991). Kop (1999) has diligently summarized the many possible relationships between risky behaviors and predispositions and has illustrated these in an informative path diagram (Figure 6.1).

It should be noted that Kop's model is based on an extensive review of existing research and it is recommended reading for researchers and clinicians who want to gather a clear understanding of the psychophysiological rationales for interventions described here. The particular strength of this model is that (1) it gives psychological factors a role in acute, episodic, and chronic aspects, (2) risk factors and behaviors can lead to the same critical, final disease outcome but via sometimes different pathways, and (3) these pathways are at least biologically plausible, if not already well documented.

An additional consideration, not integrated into the Kop model, is that at least some cardiac conditions are now considered due to infection and inflammation and that cardiac

Handbook of Clinical Health Psychology. Edited by S. Llewelyn and P. Kennedy.
© 2003 John Wiley & Sons, Ltd.

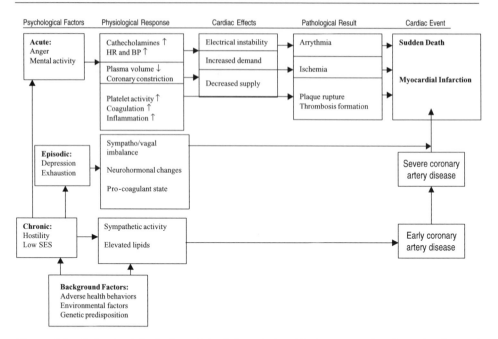

Figure 6.1 Pathophysiological model of the relationship between chronic, episodic, and acute psychological risk factors for coronary syndromes. Reproduced from W. Kop (1999) *Psychosomatic Medicine*, **61**, p. 477, with permission from Lippincott, Williams & Wilkins

disease research should integrate findings from the linkage of stress and immunomodulation (Glaser et al., 1999). Appels et al. (2000), for example, have investigated patients waiting for angioplasty and found that those patients with vital exhaustion (a combination of depressive mood and physical fatigue) also showed multiple signs of immune dysfunction that were not apparent in the psychologically non-symptomatic control sample of patients. An important issue here is the need for a sophisticated understanding of research methods, since risk factors often co-occur and interact with each other (see Ketterer, Mahr & Goldberg, 2000).

There is extensive prospective research that permits calculations and easy tracking of patients' risk probability for developing full-blown CVD; a review of tables from the Framingham study (American Heart Association, 1973) that list singular and aggregated risk probabilities show, for example, that a 50-year-old woman with five known risk factors present has a 20-fold greater risk of developing CVD over six years than has a woman without any such risk factor (the exact probabilities are 0.8% for those without risk factors versus 18.8% for those who are diabetic, smoke, have high systolic BP, high cholesterol, and enlarged hearts). Many variables, such as smoking or hypertension, have clear gradient effects such that any increase in a risk behavior translates into proportional increases of disease probability. Interestingly, almost all of these risk factors can be treated with either drugs and/or lifestyle changes, and the benefit can easily be explained as reduced risk ratios. Clinical experience suggests that patients are often quite impressed to see the benefits of successful lifestyle changes expressed in this fashion and it is worth tracking and demonstrating these risk ratio reductions to patients.

As Figure 6.1 suggests, psychological effects can be acute as well as chronic, and pathways are complex and interactive presuming many underlying mediational models. This complexity can be frustrating because many endpoints and body systems need to be studied simultaneously for a thorough understanding; we also need knowledge about how they interact cross-sectionally and prospectively. There are numerous ways whereby medical conditions may affect well-being (and vice versa). These include emotional and behavioral factors; for example, fear responses to pacemakers or depression arising in post-infarction patients. Depression in turn contributes to poor compliance with other recommended health behaviors like exercise (Ziegelstein et al., 2000), and poor compliance with medication-taking predicts higher mortality (Irvine et al., 1999). Repetitive themes that cut across various cardiac conditions are that depression, anxiety, poor anger control, social isolation, low socioeconomic status, and psychological defensiveness are likely to be contributors to disease as well as impediments in the healing process (cf. Rutledge et al., 2001; Kubzansky & Kawachi, 2000). Although the psychological variables of depression, anxiety, and defensiveness have been shown to be predictive of CVD occurrence and recurrence, they are very broad constructs and some researchers have attempted to refine and cluster the most critical features into more cardiac-specific personality patterns. One such concept is "vital exhaustion", which combines physical fatigue and depression into one construct and has been found to precede myocardial infarction (MI) (Appels, Siegrist & DeVos, 1997). It is noteworthy that vital exhaustion is not just depression and that it remains as an independent disease predictor even if other psychological risk factors like chronic workload or unreasonable need for control are taken into account (Appels, Siegrist & DeVos, 1997). Similarly, Denollet has coined the term "Type D personality", which refers to a simultaneous state of chronic negative affect paired with a habit of social withdrawal (Denollet, 1999; Denollet, Sys & Brutsaert, 1995); again, Type D personality is a particularly potent predictor of MI occurrence, and is a better predictor of acute cardiovascular stress reactivity than are many of the more traditional risk factors like depression or hostility (Habra et al., in press).

The good news about these complicated interconnected psychosomatic pathways is that successful intervention on one system may have generalized positive spillovers to other systems. A number of the studies described below will be in support of this point. A recurring theme in the rationales for psychological interventions is that psychologists effectively have to restrict themselves to working with what is controllable, namely negative affect, and inappropriate cognitions that maintain depression or that interfere, for example, with compliance. It is often frustrating to see that poverty or pervasive workplace stress are major stressors beyond control of the therapist, and that social isolation is not easily changed in the psychologist's office (Hogan, Linden & Najarian, 2002).

TRENDS IN CARDIAC CARE THAT PSYCHOLOGY NEEDS TO RESPOND TO AND PREPARE FOR

CVD mortality has decreased by 20% over the last decade (Lefkowitz & Willerson, 2001) and hypertension detection has also improved, resulting in more patients receiving better treatment. Nevertheless, CVD remains the number one killer in North America and Europe and remains a prime target for intervention because of the remaining high CVD mortality, the loss of quality of life (QOL) in surviving patients, and the high cost to society. It is striking that the speed and quality of recovery from infarction is often unrelated to disease severity, and is much more a function of perceived limitation, quality of the emotional response, as well as the subjective attractiveness of the job to which patients may consider returning (Mittag et al., 2001).

Although occluded blood vessels can be aggressively treated with angioplasty (where a balloon is directed via catheterization to a blocked site and then inflated) or a more invasive bypass surgery, one-third of patients show reocclusion within six months, and this reversal of initial medical success is poorly explained by medical factors alone.

The incidence and prevalence of CHF continues to climb at an alarming rate. In the USA, roughly 5% of the population carry this diagnosis and 550 000 new cases (i.e., roughly 2 per 1000) are diagnosed annually. The cost to the health care system associated with CHF is exorbitant and on the rise (American Heart Association, 2000). Correspondingly, this provides new challenges for psychological supports trying to manage symptoms and maximize the QOL. Once diagnosed, CHF patients have an average life expectancy of five years (McKelvie et al., 1995), and QOL is generally poor because of chronic symptoms and the known poor prognosis. In sum, cardiology advances are sometimes leading to only short-term successes without necessarily benefiting long-term prognosis; many patients develop a chronic form of the disease with associated loss of QOL. Furthermore, it is nothing less than intriguing that much of the psychological reaction to cardiac disease is largely unrelated to the actual anatomical damage and associated loss of function (Con et al., 1999), thus underscoring the need and opportunity for psychological input into cardiac disease treatments.

HYPERTENSION

Regulation of Blood Pressure

A basic understanding of the physiology of BP is necessary before a treatment plan to reduce high BP can be developed. The practitioner must understand the variables that determine BP, namely cardiac output and peripheral resistance. Cardiac output is controlled by heart rate and stroke volume which, in turn, are affected by sympathetic and parasympathetic nerve activity. Total peripheral resistance (TPR) is the resistance or impediment to the flow of blood in the arteries, arterioles, and, to a minor extent, the veins. Sympathetic activity, circulating substances in the blood, and local conditions in the tissues all influence TPR. For example, if sympathetic activity increases, arterioles constrict and present a larger resistance to the flow of blood, thereby raising BP.

Neural, kidney, and hormonal factors all control BP. The nervous system is very important in the rapid control of arterial pressure. Baroreceptors located in the walls of the heart and blood vessels are stretch receptors that monitor BP. The baroreceptors respond to distention caused by increased pressure by sending an electrical signal through nerves to the vasomotor center in the medulla of the brain. Here, groups of neurons exert control of BP. Nerve responses begin within a few seconds and can decrease pressure significantly within 5–10 seconds. The baroreceptor system is most important for short-term regulation of arterial pressure, whereas long-term regulation always requires some degree of kidney involvement. BP is expressed as systolic/diastolic in millimeters of mercury. Systolic BP (SBP) is the maximum pressure during ejection of blood from the heart, and diastolic BP (DBP) is the minimum pressure during cardiac relaxation.

Consistent with research findings that link stress to hypertension, psychological treatments are designed to reduce stress in one of two possible ways. One approach is to emphasize arousal reduction through relaxation training, meditation, and/or biofeedback, all of which are designed to improve a person's self-regulatory skills. A second approach is to conceive of stress as a multistep process involving triggers, coping behaviors, cognitions and, finally, physiological stress responses. Research using this second model tends to target deficient cognitive and behavioral stress coping skills.

Practitioners must recognize the many possible errors in routine BP assessment. The patient him/herself, the professionals, the devices, and the entire measurement situation need to be considered. Although frequently used and commonly held to be accurate, the standard mercury sphygmomanometers will soon be banned because of the risk associated with potential exposure to mercury. For professional and home use, relatively inexpensive automatic BP monitors can be purchased. They can provide reliable measures of SBP, DBP, and heart rate. It is very important to remember that office readings may falsely lead to a positive diagnosis of hypertension because of measurement apprehension (the so-called white-coat hypertension), or they can miss a substantial portion of patients who have high BP all day but present with normal readings in the clinic (white-coat normotension: Liu et al., 1999; Selenta, Hogan & Linden, 2000). These unfortunately very frequent diagnostic errors can be avoided when a 24-hour ambulatory device is used which, however, is more costly and noticeably more inconvenient for patients.

Some well-known risk factors are associated with the development of essential hypertension, such as: age, sex, heredity, race, obesity, dietary factors (alcohol, high sodium diet), lack of physical activity, psychological stress, sociocultural variables, and personality. Anxiety, anger, and depression are the primary psychological factors that have been investigated (Jorgensen et al., 1996). Scientists have consistently failed to identify a single characteristic or risk factor as the causal factor in the development or maintenance of elevated BP. Attempts have been made to describe the pathophysiology of hypertension in terms of disordered cardiac output or total peripheral resistance, or both. The hypersympathetic state of initial BP elevation depends on high cardiac output. As hypertensive disease progresses, high resistance predominates (Guyton, 1971). It is clear that the diagnosis of essential hypertension alone tells us very little about causes and psychophysiological characteristics of this heterogeneous condition. Rather, a mosaic of behavioral, psychological, and physiological factors leads to the development of chronically elevated BP.

Treating Hypertension

The Joint National Consensus Committee on Hypertension (JNC VI, 1997) placed "lifestyle modifications" (formerly called non-pharmacological therapies) as Step 1 in the algorithm for treatment of hypertension. Lifestyle modifications include sodium and alcohol restriction, physical exercise, weight control, and smoking cessation.

The first treatment stage consists of a baseline period during which the therapist repeatedly monitors and records BPs. Multiple measurements of BP can, in a portion of the hypertensive population, result in decreases in BP that are statistically and clinically significant (McGrady & Higgins, 1990). Decreases in office BP to normal levels with only monitoring do not always coincide with equal declines in home BP, so both office and home BPs should be available to the practitioner. Although the mechanism underlying the reduction in BP with monitoring is unknown, decreased anxiety or desensitization to BP measurements may be relevant factors.

Health care professionals provide various types of patient education throughout all the stages of treatment. During baseline, one may give the essential facts about hypertension, instruct the patient in the accurate measurement of BP, and give a simple explanation of the major factors affecting BP. During treatment one can provide the rationale for psychophysiological therapies as each procedure is introduced. One should also provide detailed information about each intervention, in layman's terms. Most patients can comprehend the basic biology of BP and how specific biological, chemical, and psychological factors affect their BP.

The biobehavioral therapies, including biofeedback, are useful in treating essential hypertension. They are typically described as adjuncts to standard pharmacological treatments in the moderate hypertensive patient or as an alternative to medication in the mild or borderline hypertensive patient. The JNC VI (1997) report stated that relaxation and biofeedback therapies have not been sufficiently tested to lead to firm conclusions, and that "the role of stress management techniques...is uncertain". More recently, a Canadian Consensus group (Spence et al., 1999) has concluded that individualized stress management may be an effective intervention after all. This conclusion was partly based on Linden and Chambers' (1994) argument that the classification of biofeedback and relaxation as "mere" adjuncts may be unfairly based on research protocol peculiarities in that non-drug studies typically start with much lower BPs than drug studies. This is important because Jacob et al. (1991) have shown a high positive correlation between BP at entry and subsequent degree of BP change. A corresponding adjustment for different BP levels at baseline in the Linden and Chambers meta-analysis (1994) revealed that the best non-drug treatments were as efficacious as a variety of different drug regimens. In a recent trial, using a combination of techniques including temperature biofeedback, Autogenic Training (Linden, 1990), and cognitive-behavioral therapy, the intervention reduced 24-hour means for SBP and DBP; the results were even stronger at follow-up, and the findings were replicated (Linden, Lenz & Con, 2001).

Nevertheless, there are valid criticisms of many of the published biofeedback studies because of deficiencies in design and methodology. These critiques include the absence or inadequacy of pretreatment BP monitoring, medication changes during treatment, lack of clearly defined outcome measures, questionable generalization of the decreased BP to the home or work setting, and poorly designed or absent long-term follow-up (Jacob et al., 1991).

However, close inspection of the results of even the criticized studies reveals that a percentage of participants do lower BP and/or medication significantly. The benefits of maintaining normotensive BP with reduced or no medication are noteworthy. Therefore, reviews have concluded that one can justify the psychophysiological therapies in the treatment of all levels of elevated BP.

It is likely that biofeedback and relaxation operate through different physiological mechanisms. Relaxation may have a generalized effect in reducing sympathetic nerve activity that affects heart rate and thereby decreases stroke volume. On the other hand, biofeedback may work primarily through vasomotor control, since BP could be increased and decreased (with biofeedback) without a concomitant change in heart rate. Thus, biofeedback and relaxation are complementary rather than alternative methods in BP control.

Cognitive strategies are also included in psychophysiological therapies. Development of coping skills assists patients in managing their anxiety and their reactions to stress.

Sometimes significant anxiety occurs when a patient hears the diagnosis of essential hypertension. Practitioners should consider evaluation of anxiety and cognitive strategies before the biofeedback component begins. Then, one can integrate the training of new coping skills into the biofeedback and relaxation therapies (see Linden, Lenz & Con, 2001).

Since primary hypertension is a complex, multidimensional illness (Gerin et al., 2000), it is logical to expect that people will respond with varying degrees of success to relaxation and biofeedback. As with pharmacological agents, each modality helps some individuals. Tailoring the treatment program to the person is critical to success.

With respect to biofeedback studies, information is available to predict differences in outcome (reviewed in McGrady & Linden, 2003). There have been several attempts to characterize patients for the purpose of predicting their chances of success in biofeedback programs. Patients with the best chances for success in lowering BP had higher pretreatment anxiety scores, heart rate, cortisol, plasma renin activity, and lower hand temperatures. Other work on medicated patients did not isolate similar biochemical or physiological factors but instead identified factors related to process and outcome. In a controlled comparison between thermal biofeedback and progressive relaxation, the three variables investigated were: expectancies, skill acquisition, and home practice. There were no significant differences in practice between treatment groups or between successes and failures; for thermal biofeedback, skill acquisition and expectancies were related to outcome.

While the studies described above were intended to detect technique-specific outcomes, they may underestimate the potential of multicomponent treatment packages which have been compared with a known, effective antihypertensive medication, i.e. propranolol (Kostis et al., 1992). Both treatment conditions were associated with equally large and clinically meaningful BP reductions, but the non-drug approach led to additional desirable reductions in body weight, whereas the drugs did not. Similarly, Kurz et al. (2001) offered a package of relaxation, stress management, exercise, and education to 65 patients over a six-month period. They measured BP during exercise stress which dropped from pre-follow-up to the 18-month retest from 190/84 to 184/92; resting BP did not change but antihypertensive drug use was reduced by 20–40% depending on drug class; results improved further by follow-up.

PREPARATION FOR SURGERY

The invasiveness and associated risks of any surgery, as well as the alienating environment of a busy acute care hospital, contribute to considerable apprehension, if not outright anxiety, in patients waiting for such surgery. This worsened in some countries where recent pressure on access to surgery has led to growing waiting lists which in and of themselves affect QOL and lead to deteriorating psychological health status. Two interrelated but somewhat different approaches have been considered to deal with this critical preparatory phase. In a Canadian study, 249 patients waiting for bypass surgery (not scheduled for at least ten weeks) were recruited for a pre-operative psychological treatment study (Arthur et al., 2000). The intervention consisted of education, nurse support, reinforcement, and exercise training. Compared to a no-treatment control group, the treated patients spent one day less in hospital post-surgery and had spent a smaller portion of their in-hospital stay in the expensive intensive care unit; furthermore, their QOL was superior to that of controls while waiting for surgery as well as for six months following surgery. The second approach focused on the patients' in-hospital experience in that patients waiting for bypass surgery were randomly assigned to a room-mate who already had a successful bypass versus a "control" room-mate who was also waiting for a bypass (Kulik & Mahler, 1989; Kulik, Moore & Mahler, 1993). Patients placed with a post-operative room-mate were less anxious prior to surgery, became more quickly ambulatory post-surgery, and were sent home earlier.

These two studies provide creative and clear demonstrations that attention to psychological well-being in cardiac patients waiting for hospitalization, or while in hospital, can lead to reduced distress which also translates into better recovery with associated cost-savings.

RECOVERY FROM MYOCARDIAL INFARCTION, BYPASS SURGERY, AND ANGIOPLASTY

Rationales and Targets for Behavioral Science Interventions in Rehabilitation

For many health care providers cardiac rehabilitation is synonymous with exercise-based rehabilitation, most likely due to the fact that exercise rehabilitation was typically the first component added to standard medical care. More recently, cardiac rehabilitation programs have added comprehensive dietary education and psychosocial support (Shephard & Franklin, 2001). The types of studies typically found in the non-medical cardiac rehabilitation literature can be grossly classified into either multicomponent interventions (often encompassing exercise, nutrition counseling, health education, and psychological support) versus other studies that systematically attempt to identify the added value of psychological interventions to usual care (Blumenthal & Emery, 1988). Below, these two different approaches will be discussed separately because their outcomes may vary and because they have different purposes. The former effectively tests the benefits of the best treatment package that behavioral science has to offer and is particularly important for the design of effective health service delivery models. The study of the *additional* value of psychological interventions is, of course, also relevant for program planning and service delivery but its primary purpose is to untangle what the most effective treatment components are and to feed this knowledge back to clinical researchers who want to advance theorizing as well as clinical practice.

Cardiac disease is obviously not a primarily psychological pathology although psychological factors play an important role in the recovery from a major cardiac event and may, in fact, have contributed to its development. The rehabilitation process varies greatly from one patient to another (Sotile, 1996), and this is accentuated by differences in severity of underlying disease and type of medical intervention received. A first MI hits many patients unprepared whereas bypass surgery and angioplasty are more likely to be the result of a more lengthy chain of medical investigation which, in turn, gives the patient time to prepare.

Attempting to draw conclusions about whether or not psychological interventions work is handicapped by the fact that there is no single definition for what an appropriate psychological intervention is (or should be); nor is there a clear consensus on who should be receiving this treatment. Additional variations possibly affecting outcomes are: (a) types of service provider, (b) whether treatment is group-based or individual, (c) how much treatment is available, (d) when treatment is initiated, and (e) whether treatment targets are individualized.

Non-specific treatment benefits also require study because a certain amount of distress reduction is likely to arise from good cardiology care provided by an empathic physician who provides the relevant information, checks on the patient's knowledge and corrects it where necessary, and provides stable care.

The work of a limited number of behavioral research groups has dominated the cardiac rehabilitation field and the differences in their approach serve to illustrate the possible variety of interventions. The work by Ornish and collaborators (1983, 1990 and 1998) falls in the category of multi-component programs that do not allow identification of the unique efficacy of various subcomponents. Others, namely the Recurrent Coronary Prevention Project (RCPP; Friedman et al., 1984), the Ischemic Heart Disease Life Stress Monitoring Program (IHDLSM) and M-HART study group (Frasure-Smith & Prince, 1985, 1989; Frasure-Smith et al., 1997), Jones and West (1996), Blumenthal et al. (1997), and Jan Van Dixhoorn's group (1987, 1989, 1990a, 1990b, 1998) fall into the category of research that specifically study the unique contribution of a psychological treatment. The "dominance" of these four approaches can be attributed to the good design quality of the originating studies, their sheer size, the demonstration of reversible risk via reductions in artery occlusion (as shown in Ornish's work), and the demonstration that even a brief, relatively non-specific, and inexpensive psychosocial intervention can lead to substantial and lasting reductions in mortality and cardiac event recurrences.

To the population at large, Dean Ornish may well be the best-known medical expert on comprehensive cardiac rehabilitation. In 1983, the Ornish group published a landmark paper in the prestigious medical journal *JAMA* (Ornish et al., 1983). Forty-six well-defined heart disease patients had been randomly assigned to a control group (receiving standard cardiologic care while living at home) or an experimental group. The experimental group was subjected to a rigorous three-and-a-half-week program while being housed together in a rural environment. The latter group was served a strict vegetarian, low-fat diet of 1400 kilocalories per day and was taught heart-healthy food-purchasing and preparation habits. They also learned and practiced meditation and relaxation for five hours per day. Experimental patients relative to controls demonstrated a 44% mean increase in duration of exercise, a 55% increase in total work performed on an exercycle, and other signs of improved cardiac function. Furthermore, cholesterol decreased by 20.5% and angina episodes were reduced by 91%. In a subsequent study, Ornish's group (1983) repeated the basic treatment protocol but also added angiographic measures so as to document changes in atherosclerosis severity. Twenty-eight patients were assigned to the treatment package and 20 to a usual-care control group. In the treated group, the average percentage diameter stenosis regressed by 15.5% (i.e. patients improved) whereas it worsened by 15% in the control group. These results are particularly intriguing because they suggest that lifestyle change has a direct effect on the underlying disease by reducing the narrowing of arteries. In a further breakdown of these results, these authors also showed occlusion reversal but only among those with high compliance to the nutrition and exercise recommendations, suggesting a gradient effect of lifestyle change on vessel occlusion. In response to Ornish's exciting work, critics wondered about the usefulness of this approach for large numbers of unselected cardiac patients. Many clinicians have observed that few patients are willing to subject themselves to such drastic changes, even though this does not speak against the

Ornish approach per se. The required level of motivation and persistence may apply only to a select, small group of patients, and the affordability of such a comprehensive intervention may be yet another limiting factor for mass implementation.

Another influential trial of behavioral risk factor reduction in cardiac patients was the RCPP (Friedman et al., 1984). The premise of this trial was that Type A behavior and other behavioral risk factors, i.e. nutrition, alcohol use, and exercise, required aggressive intervention. A control group of 270 patients was followed parallel with the treatment groups but it is important to note that the controls had not been randomized into the control condition. The treated group was again subdivided and randomized into either cardiac counseling (CC) (20 sessions) or CC + intensive Type A behavior counseling (for a total of 43 sessions). All interventions were provided in group format. CC consisted mostly of education about medication regimens, diet, and exercise, with occasional consultation on anxiety, depression and phobias. The CC + Type A treatment also included detailed instruction in relaxation methods, recognition of stress symptoms, and modification of stress-producing cognitions. Follow-up has now been extended up to six and a half years and, in contrast to the IHDLSM, the obtained benefits were more stable over the long follow-up. Specifically, mortality in the CC + Type A treatment was about half of that in the control group while the CC group results fell in between. Cardiac event recurrence was reduced as well in the active treatments groups. Type A behavior itself was notably reduced and this change was considered instrumental for the mortality and morbidity benefits. These results suggest that treatment effects may be proportional to the amount of intervention received.

The IHDLSM (Frasure-Smith & Prince, 1985, 1989) differs from the great majority of cardiac rehabilitation studies in that patients were randomly assigned to either a control group ($N = 224$) or a "stress monitoring" condition where nurses provided non-specific psychosocial support ($N = 229$). These nurses were not specifically trained as psychotherapists and responded to patients on an as-needed basis. More specifically, patients were contacted on a monthly basis and stress was assessed each time using a brief standardized tool. Only when stress was elevated did the nurse provide the intervention.

This approach reflects best what actually happens in clinical practice; however, it fails to allow an assessment of which intervention component had what effect. The patients from this study have now been followed for six and a half years. At one-year follow-up treated patients had only about half the mortality rate of the untreated patients but long-term follow-up indicated a gradual but steady decline of these treatment benefits.

Interestingly, Frasure-Smith (1991) later reanalyzed her data and grouped patients into two subgroups: those scoring above five on the General Health Questionnaire (GHQ), completed while still in hospital, were labeled "high stress" while the others were labeled "low stress". At five-year follow-up, it was quite apparent that the low-stress group did not benefit from intervention in that their mortality rates were relatively low anyway and indistinguishable from the control group subjects with low stress. Treated high-stress patients, however, showed only about one-third of the mortality rate over five years post-event than did their untreated, high-stress counterparts, suggesting that random assignment of all cardiac patients to psychological treatment without an assessment of actual psychological need may not be cost-efficient.

Unfortunately, Frasure-Smith et al. (1997) have shown different results in a recent replication of the IHDLSM study referred to as the M-HART study. This time the sample was even larger, included women, and was somewhat older on average (essentially due to the inclusion of female heart patients who tend to be older). The intervention was the same as in the first study. There was no treatment benefit for survival among men (2.4% vs 2.5% over

12 months) but higher mortality rates for treated women (10.3% vs 5.4%). The intervention led to only minimal reductions in anxiety and depression. These conflicting results, their meaning, and their implications for clinical practice will be discussed later in this chapter when meta-analytic study findings are compared with one another.

Van Dixhoorn's approach focuses on general arousal reduction via breathing training. This approach is based on a psychophysiological rationale, suggesting that sudden cardiac death may be triggered by unstable autonomic system activity. Specifically, this model posits that increased sympathetic arousal as well as decreased vagal control may destabilize cardiac rhythms. Support for the usefulness of breathing methods can be derived from Sakakibara's work (Sakakibara & Hayano, 1996; Sakakibara, Takeuchi & Hayano, 1994). In one study, Sakakibara and collaborators tested college students with ECG and pneumograms during 3×5 minute practice of autogenic training (AT), a relaxation method with a strong breathing component or the same length of quiet rest (a non-specific control condition). Analysis of respiration and heart rate variability data suggested that the AT practice was associated with enhanced cardiac parasympathetic tone whereas the quiet rest period was not. These findings are consistent with more basic investigations into the nervous system effects of breathing training (Sakakibara & Hayano, 1996).

Studies can also be identified by more narrowly chosen psychological targets, namely depression and hostility/Type A reduction. Depression is now considered to be a major prognostic factor for poor outcome in cardiac patients. However, the strength of this is largely based on studies published in the last decade and, not surprisingly, there has been little research so far on the cardiac outcome of depression screening and treatment in these patients. Most relevant appears to be an ongoing study by Freedland et al., from which first pilot outcome data were made public in 1996. These researchers reported on a trial with depressed cardiac patients who received cognitive-behavioral therapy (with an average of nine sessions). Twenty-three patients had been evaluated: their scores on the Beck Depression Inventory were reduced from 19.0 to 11.8 after therapy (note that a score of 10 is taken to represent the cutoff between mild depression and no depression). This area of research has already generated much interest and is likely to trigger a wave of treatment studies. Particularly noteworthy in this context is a large, multisite study completed in 2001 in the USA: the ENRICHD trial (ENRICHD Investigators, 2000) . In this study, patients are selected for high levels of depression and/or lack of social support. Depression was treated with a manualized cognitive therapy approach that is widely tested, whereas it is not clearly spelled out how the social support intervention proceeded (ENRICHD Investigators, 2000). Published results are eagerly awaited given the size and importance of this trial.

The existence of a coronary-prone personality was originally operationalized as Type A behavior and has evolved to focus on hostility, as the other components of Type A behavior did not appear to have much predictive validity for cardiac mortality. While Type A behavior reduction has been a focus in the RCPP trial (Friedman et al., 1984), there is less evidence for cardiac benefits arising from reductions in hostility, and this is an area worthy of further study.

Outcomes of Psychological Cardiac Rehabilitation

Despite known imperfections, statistical meta-analyses have greatly helped us to understand and quantify treatment outcomes. Efficacy reviews of psychological cardiac rehabilitation can be subdivided into those that are preventive in nature (i.e. targeting those at risk for heart disease) versus those patients who clearly have diagnosed heart disease. The one available meta-analysis on psychosocial interventions for the primary and secondary prevention of CAD exclusively focused on the modifiability of Type A behavior and its associated health benefits (Nunes, Frank & Kornfeld, 1987). Seven of the 18 studies reviewed by Nunes et al. represented samples with documented CAD whereas the others were samples of healthy individuals. Not surprisingly, Nunes et al. found that the size of effect went up with more intensive intervention. The effect of psychosocial treatment relative to controls (typically on medication) was evaluated for mortality and morbidity at one- and three-year follow-up. For the one-year follow-up, the effect size was $d = 0.34$ for mortality reduction (ns), $d = 0.45$ for recurrent myocardial infarction (MI) reduction (significant at $p < 0.05$), and $d = 0.57$ for combined MI recurrence and mortality (significant at $p < 0.05$). For the three-year follow-up only the combined mortality and morbidity figures suggested further enhancement of the clinical benefit with $d = 0.97$ (significant at $p < 0.001$).

In order to have a good comparison basis for the discussion of treatment effects due to behavioral interventions, a summary of a pivotal review by Lau et al. (1992) on medical and non-medical treatments may be helpful. Lau et al. reported a cumulative meta-analysis of major controlled interventions for coronary artery disease and concluded that the three most useful interventions were anticoagulants, rehabilitation regimens, and beta-blockers, each accounting for approximately 20% reduction in mortality. Treatment-specific mortality reductions of 20% are clinically significant and this figure may be considered a gold standard for judging the efficacy of other interventions.

In one meta-analysis of behavorial interventions, Oldridge et al. (1988) specifically targeted exercise and risk factor rehabilitation in their review of ten randomized clinical trials. These ten trials were carefully screened to include only studies with a high-quality methodology and included 2145 control patients and 2202 rehabilitation patients. The pooled odds-ratios suggested a 24% reduction in all-cause deaths and a 25% reduction in cardiovascular deaths for the rehabilitation groups relative to the control groups on standard medical care. While exercise was associated with a reduction in deaths, it did not have an impact on recurrence. From a quality of life and health insurance point of view, this is a disappointing finding because reduced recurrences are very important to individuals' courses of disease. Oldridge et al. (1988) further tested whether predominant emphasis on exercise or emphasis on behavioral risk factor reduction made a difference, whether treatment length affected long-term outcome, and whether time of rehabilitation initiation was associated with differential benefits. Studies were classified as being mostly exercise rehabilitation with some risk factor counseling, or mostly risk factor counseling with some exercise recommendations. Even with these different emphases, the treatments were found equally beneficial.

A meta-analysis of the associated psychological benefits of exercise treatment nicely complements the Oldridge et al. review. Kugler, Seelbach and Krueskemper (1994) identified 15 studies of exercise rehabilitation that also monitored psychological changes in patients undergoing an exercise program. These reseachers reported that exercise alone without any specific attempt at psychological intervention produced significant reductions in anxiety (effect size $d = -0.31$) and depression ($d = -0.46$).

The Oldridge et al. (1988) and the Lau et al. (1992) meta-analyses concurred in the observed benefit associated with non-drug approaches to cardiac rehabilitation, and support its routine inclusion in cardiac care. Nevertheless, in the wake of these studies there remained a lack of clarity about the specific effect that psychological interventions might have relative to nutrition and exercise interventions. Our own research group attempted to fill this gap in knowledge (Linden, Stossel & Maurice, 1996). We performed a statistical meta-analysis of 23 randomized-controlled trials that evaluated the *additional* impact of psychosocial treatment for rehabilitation from documented coronary artery disease. Mortality data were available from 12, and recurrence data from 10, of the 23 studies. Follow-up data were clustered into short (less than two years) and long (more than two years) follow-ups to allow testing of long-term benefits of interventions. The longest follow-ups included in this analysis were eight and five years. The average length of follow-up in the "less than two years" category was 12 months; the average length of follow-up in the more than two years category was 63 months (5.2 years). The results were quite consistent with those of previous reviews, both narrative and meta-analytic. The observed odds-ratio reflected a 46% reduction in recurrence for the less than two years follow-up and a 39% reduction for the longer follow-up. The analyses of the tests of psychosocial treatment on mortality (using fully randomized trial data only) revealed treatment-related mortality reductions of 41%. For follow-up greater than two years there was a continuing trend for mortality benefits (26%), although this was not statistically significant. The benefits of psychological treatment for reduced recurrence of cardiac events were very similar in magnitude and mapped onto the reductions in mortality.

With respect to psychological distress and biological risk factors, patients in the control conditions changed very little (compared to pre-test), and, if anything, they got worse. Psychological intervention, on the other hand, was associated with reductions in psychological distress ($d = -0.34$), heart rate ($d = -0.38$), cholesterol ($d = -1.54$), and systolic blood pressure ($d = -0.24$).

The reviews described above presented a rather positive set of conclusions about the impact of psychosocial treatments for cardiac patients. Interestingly, since publication of the review by Linden, Stossel and Maurice (1996), three large-scale studies have been completed and published. Together they present a rather "mixed-bag" of optimistic and pessimistic conclusions.

Jones and West (1996) reported the results from a very large trial where additional psychological intervention was contrasted with standard care in a sample of 2328 post-MI patients. A multicomponent stress management rehabilitation program had no apparent additional benefit for mortality, clinical complications, anxiety or depression. Treated patients did report less angina and less medication usage. Note that the researchers randomized all patients into one of the two treatment conditions irrespective of whether or not elevated stress, anxiety or depression were present. Curiously, the authors also reported that *all* patients suffering MI in any of six participating hospitals were randomized, hence indicating that the reported refusal rate was zero. Also of importance is the fact that the mortality rate for both groups was only 6% over the following 12 months, thus making it difficult to distinguish experimental from control treatment due to low base rates. Another very large recent trial with disappointing results was the one conducted by Frasure-Smith et al. (1997) that has already been described above.

These confusing results benefited greatly from the subsequent meta-analysis by Dusseldorp et al. (1999) who compared standard care with additional psychological treatment (as was done by Linden, Stossel & Maurice, 1996); they noted reductions in mortality odds for psychological treatment that ranged from 6 to 52% depending on the length of studied outcomes. Psychological treatment had no positive impact on short-term MI recurrence (−16%) but still showed 41% reductions in medium and long-term follow-ups. Most striking was a comparison of outcomes for those studies where psychological treatment failed to produce psychological changes with those where it succeeded. When psychological distress was not reduced by the treatment—as was true in Jones and West's study (1996)—patient mortality was higher than that of the controls (odds-ratio 0.88 : 1) and MI recurrence was not affected (odds-ratio 1.03 : 1); when, however, psychological distress was reduced, then the odds-ratios for mortality were 1.52 : 1 and for MI recurrence 1.69 : 1. The importance of demonstrating this mediational effect was also underlined by Cossette, Frasure-Smith and Lesperance (2001) who reanalyzed the disappointing M-HART results and concluded that cardiac benefits arose when psychological distress was also effectively reduced. More specifically, they found that short-term anxiety and depression reduction predicted one-year status (i.e. treatment response stability), and distress reduction was associated with reduced mortality from cardiac causes and with reduced number of readmissions.

Such findings clearly direct attention to the yet-to-be resolved question: Which patients are most likely to benefit from which treatment? Along these lines, it needs to be highlighted that the earlier rehabilitation studies tended to offer treatment almost exclusively to men who, in turn, tended to be younger than the female cardiac patients. Older patients (who more often tend to be women) benefit less from our standard treatment approaches, and therefore treatment needs to be specifically targeted to the psychosocial needs of older women. At this time, it cannot be ruled out that older female patients may actually be better off without therapy. Cardiac patients are the fortunate beneficiaries of improved cardiologic care and its associated lower post-event mortality rates, and researchers, as a consequence, need to consider trial protocols with other endpoints which are likely to change over time and which are important prognostic indicators. Such endpoints can be psychological in nature (for example, depression) or be intermediary, hard cardiac endpoints like ischemia, premature ventricular contractions, or heart period variability. This latter approach is reflected in a stress management intervention trial (Blumenthal et al., 1997) where outcomes were contrasted with those from an exercise control condition. The treatment was a small group, cognitive-behavioral intervention lasting 16 weeks with one-and-a-half-hour sessions per week; patients were not preselected for high psychological distress. During the 38-month follow-up, the stress management group had only a relative risk of 0.26 of event recurrence in comparison to the exercise controls. Ischemia was also more positively affected by stress management than by exercise. Stress management was uniquely associated with significant reductions in hostility and self-reported stress but not with any unique advantages for reducing depression or trait anxiety.

Clinical Implications and Recommendations

Psychosocial interventions deserve inclusion in cardiac rehabilitation programs in addition to drug therapy and exercise regimens. Because some interventions have failed to change psychological endpoints it is important to screen patients for actual psychological need and to demonstrate continuously that the particular intervention chosen does have an impact on psychological well-being. Observed benefits include not only targeted psychosocial endpoints like depression and anxiety but could also be demonstrated for biological risk factor reductions, and, even more importantly, for improving the odds ratios for mortality and non-fatal MI and other cardiac event recurrence. The literature on risk factor reduction with behavioral interventions is still in need of further investigation, as the small number of studies using biological measures indicates. The consistency with which psychosocial treatment generalizes to different classes of endpoints is encouraging. Nevertheless, it is unlikely that all interventions have the same effect, and the particular strengths and weaknesses of various approaches need to be individually compared for a fair assessment.

Routine provision of the same lengthy psychosocial treatment programs for all post-MI patients may not be cost-efficient. More lengthy and intensive interventions consistently produce better outcomes but more treatment is, by definition, also more expensive and there is strong reason to believe that the curve reflecting the relationships between increasing benefit with increasing cost levels off, and at some point more treatment no longer adds more benefit. However, the point at which this "levelling-off" occurs remains to be determined.

At the clinical level, patient screening and selective assignment or referral for psychological therapy appears to be more cost-efficient than giving all patients the same amount and type of intervention. Treating clinical depression in post-MI patients appears to be a particularly urgent intervention because of the known impact of depression on poor prognosis (Frasure-Smith, Lesperance & Talajic, 1995). Although it seems clinically sensible to aggressively target depression, given its associated risk for poor prognosis, there is as yet no evidence from controlled clinical trials that psychological treatment of depression improves patients' cardiac prognosis. Whether or not screening and aggressive therapy for depression could produce greater reductions in distress than is apparent in more generic cardiac rehabilitation programs, and whether or not it causally changes cardiac prognosis, is still unknown. Answering this question is, however, timely and will have great impact on sound clinical practice.

RESTENOSIS

Angioplasty has become a frequently used intervention largely because it is less invasive than bypass surgery. Unfortunately, 25–35% of vessels reocclude following angioplasty (i.e. restenosis), mostly within six months following surgery. Although severity of initial blockage and location of the vessel predict restenosis to some degree, much of the medically unexplained variance has been linked to psychological factors. In particular, the constructs of vital exhaustion and cognitive adaptation theory have been used to show the predictive power of psychological factors for explaining restenosis (Appels et al., 1997; Helgeson & Fritz, 1999). Cognitive adaptation theory describes a cluster of optimism, high self-esteem and mastery, which jointly predict lower likelihood of restenosis (Helgeson & Fritz, 1999) whereas vital exhaustion refers to a sense of lack of perceived energy, demoralization and irritability, and it predicts greater rates of restenosis. Appels et al. (1997) have developed a brief cognitive-behavioral intervention and have shown that this treatment program has potential in reducing restenosis rates in a sample of 30 patients and 65 controls. Vital exhaustion was significantly reduced and there was a corresponding 50% reduction in new coronary events over an 18-month follow-up.

COPING WITH CONGESTIVE HEART FAILURE

More incisive diagnostic procedures in cardiology, the recognition of a need for aggressive treatment, improved surgical technique and new, more potent medications have massively contributed to a longer life expectancy of cardiac patients once diagnosed. However, better management of heart disease is not equivalent to a cure, and has in fact the almost perverse consequence of creating a growing number of patients who survive their first myocardial infarction or respond well to revascularization, and who ultimately move into a condition of chronic heart failure. The psychological response to the disease and pre-existing conditions are powerful predictors of mortality and given the importance of the topic there is surprisingly little written on it in the psychological–cardiac literature to date (Profant & Dimsdale, 2000). As is the case in the rehabilitation from MI, patients with a high degree of depression, social isolation and psychological detachment are more likely to die within one year than those with high support (Califf, Krishnan & O'Connor, 2001; Murberg & Bru, 2001). Dealing effectively with depression is particularly important not only because it is a statistical predictor of mortality but also because its absolute prevalence is high with estimates ranging from 40 to 65% (Profant & Dimsdale, 2000). CHF patients account for a large portion of expensive emergency hospitalizations. A group of Swiss researchers analyzed the causes of such emergencies in 111 consecutive patients (Wagdi et al., 1993) and found that the primary cause for readmission was poor compliance with the treatment regimen (e.g. irregular use or complete refusal of medications, and excess salt and fluid intake). Other less often cited causes for the emergency were uncontrolled hypertension, insufficient diuretic therapy, angina, MI, and rhythm disturbances. With non-compliance being the most frequent reason, the researchers further investigated patient knowledge and found that a prime reason for non-adherence was a total or critical lack of knowledge about the purpose and necessary procedure for the medication regimen, insufficient follow-up by local physicians, and difficulties with adherence to the behavioral prescriptions. The conclusion was that thorough patient education and close follow-up was considered a highly cost-efficient means of managing these patients and of preventing repeated emergency hospitalizations. More recently, Fonarow et al. (1997) showed that the addition of a psychoeducational component to standard medical CHF care led to improved functional status and an 85% decrease in the hospital readmission rate for the six-month follow-up; the estimated savings for the hospital were U\$9800 per patient.

Furthermore, there is growing evidence that aggressive drug therapy for CHF will lessen the associated symptoms and enhance patients' physical functioning and, to a lesser degree, improve their subjective QOL (Dracup et al., 1992). Interestingly, the severity of the underlying disease is essentially uncorrelated with QOL, depression, or anxiety (Grady, 1993; Wagdi et al., 1993). Furthermore, the addition of behavioral change programs (nutrition, weight control) and psychological interventions leads to significant improvements in QOL (Kostis et al., 1994).

The Kostis et al. study (1994) is a high-quality example of a revealing and timely treatment study. The non-pharmacological treatment condition was added to a subsample of drug-treated patients and consisted of graduated exercise training, stress management and cognitive therapy, and dietary intervention. The additional non-pharmacological treatment was well tolerated by patients, resulting in improved exercise tolerance, and reduced body weight, depression, and anxiety. Interestingly, the placebo-controlled evaluation of digoxin treatment revealed an improvement in ejection fraction but without any corresponding change in exercise tolerance or QOL. Clearly, the take-home message from this work is that combined aggressive medical management, thorough patient education, and behavioral and psychological treatment form a potent intervention that has considerable promise, not only for patient benefit but also in terms of reduced number of emergency hospitalizations and lower health care costs.

Heart Transplantation

A subgroup of CHF patients may have the opportunity to undergo heart transplantation and, due to more experience with the transplantation surgery itself and the necessary subsequent rejection management, success rates for heart transplantation today are quite good, with ten-year survival of about 60% (Davies et al., 1996). Nevertheless, transplantation is a medically complex and emotionally difficult process and it poses particular challenges in the area of adherence. The transplant patient's QOL is typically poor while waiting for surgery; psychological interventions for anxiety, depression, and overall emotional coping are needed. Not only the pre-transplant waiting periods, but also the recovery require a very supportive social network.

An additional, largely unavoidable stressor is the fact that transplants are done only in major hospitals, typically university teaching hospitals, and patients not living in the city may have to relocate at least for a few months, often isolated from their families and at considerable expense. Post-transplant, patients need to follow a complex medication regimen consisting of immunosuppressants, cardiac, and often other medications. Also, considerable pressure is put on transplant patients to maintain an extremely healthy lifestyle: weight control and a healthy diet are crucial, as is a reasonable exercise program. Return to work is a viable prospect for some but certainly not all patients, and the transplantation often triggers deep existential questions: How is the donor family affected? Why do I deserve this heart? What is important for the rest of my life?

CONCLUDING COMMENTS

Given that 45% of all causes of death are cardiovascular in nature, the patient pool that may benefit from psychological support is vast. Furthermore, most CVD risk factors are interrelated and are in turn influenced by subjective well-being, thus creating ample opportunities for psychologists to contribute to cardiac health care; this may include the provision of services for prevention, early risk factor management, as well as rehabilitation and coping with chronic disease. Given the complexities of CVD and the very rich literature base on psychological factors in CVD, this chapter could only offer a sample of some of the major areas. Not covered here, for example (mostly due to lack of space), is the area of stroke, although it also has a high prevalence and it is emotionally distressing for patients and their families. Other areas only touched on, while highly relevant, are the contributions that psychology can make to facilitate smoking cessation, exercise uptake and maintenance, or the teaching of healthy eating habits. Each one of these can easily fill an entire book of its own. Furthermore, the reader might want to consider that behavioral science contributions to cardiac care are growing at a rapid pace and even the "experts" are struggling to keep up with the literature. It is fortunate for cardiac patients that cardiology itself is rapidly evolving but it represents yet another challenge for the psychologist interested in the latest developments in cardiac care.

Given that this book may be read by seasoned psychologists as well as those in training or considering respecialization, it may also be in order not only to discuss how psychology can contribute to cardiac care but to consider the role and the career path of the psychologist in cardiac care. Becoming a clinical health psychologist specializing in cardiac disease is not yet achievable via specialty training programs. Psychologists working in this area have typically acquired a Clinical Psychology degree with a subspecialization in Behavioral Medicine. Additional specialty knowledge and skill may have to be acquired on the job or, for a lucky few, can be obtained in post-doctoral training. Once psychologists find themselves in this kind of job, they usually become members of a multidisciplinary team (Kurz et al., 2001). While it is exciting to join a group of health care professionals with varying backgrounds and complementary skills, it also requires a strong self-definition, leadership skills, self-reliance, and confidence on the part of the psychologist because it usually means being the only psychologist on a team.

REFERENCES

American Heart Association (1973). *Coronary Risk Handbook*. (EM 629-PE 11-73-100M). Dallas, TX.

American Heart Association (2000). *Heart and Stroke Statistical Update*. Dallas, TX.

Appels, A., Siegrist, J. & DeVos, Y. (1997). "Chronic workload", "need for Control", and "vital exhaustion" in patients with myocardial infarction and controls: a comparative test of cardiovascular risk profiles. *Stress Medicine*, **13**, 117–121.

Appels, A., Bar, F., Lasker, J., Flamm, U. & Kop, M. (1997). The effect of a psychological intervention program on the risk of a new coronary event after angioplasty: a feasibility study. *Journal of Psychosomatic Research*, **43**, 209–217.

Appels, A., Bar, F.W., Bar, J., Bruggeman, C. & de Baets, M. (2000). Inflammation, depressive symptomatology, and coronary artery disease. *Psychosomatic Medicine*, **62**, 601–605.

Arthur, H.M., Daniels, D., McKelvie, R., Hirsh, J. & Rush, B. (2000). Effect of a preoperative intervention on preoperative and postoperative outcome in low-risk patients awaiting elective coronary artery bypass graft surgery. *Annals of Internal Medicine*, **133**, 253–262.

Blumenthal, J.A. & Emery, C.F. (1988). Rehabilitation of patients following myocardial infarction. *Journal of Consulting and Clinical Psychology*, **56**, 374–381.

Blumenthal, J.A., Jiang, W., Babyak, M.A., Krantz, D.S., Frid, D.J., Coleman, R.E., Waugh, R., Hanson, M., Appelbaum, M., O'Connor, C. & Morris, J.J. (1997). Stress management and exercise training in cardiac patients with myocardial ischemia. *Archives of Internal Medicine*, **157**, 2213–2223.

Califf, R.M., Krishnan, R.R. & O'Connor, C.M. (2001). Relationship of depression to increased risk for mortality and rehospitalization in patients with congestive heart failure. *Archives of Internal Medicine*, **161**, 1849–1856.

Con, A.H., Linden, W., Thompson, J.M. & Ignaszewski, A. (1999). The psychology of men and women recovering from coronary artery bypass surgery. *Journal of Cardiopulmonary Rehabilitation*, **19**, 152–161.

Cossette, S., Frasure-Smith, N. & Lesperance, F. (2001). Clinical implications of a reduction in psychological distress on cardiac prognosis in patients participating in a psychosocial intervention program. *Psychosomatic Medicine*, **63**, 257–266.

Davies, R.A., Rivard, M., Pflugfelder, P., Teo, K., Jlain, B., Champagne, F., Contandriopouos, A.P., Carrier, M., Latter, D., Chartrand, C., Daly, V., Gudas, V., Poirier, N., Sullivan, J. & Kostuk, W. (1996). *Heart transplantation in Canada and determinants of survival*. Paper presented at the Annual Meeting of the Canadian Cardiovascular Society, Montreal.

Denollet, J.K. (1999). Repressive coping predicts mortality in patients with coronary heart disease (CHD). Paper presented at the American Psychosomatic Society Conference, Vancouver.

Denollet, J., Sys, S.U. & Brutsaert, D.L. (1995). Personality and mortality after myocardial infarction. *Psychosomatic Medicine*, **57**, 582–591.

Dracup, K., Walden, J., Stevenson, L. & Brecht, M.L. (1992). Quality of life in patients with advanced heart failure. *Journal of Heart and Lung Transplantation*, **11**, 273–279.

Dusseldorp, E., Van Elderen, T., Maes, S., Meulman, J. & Kraail, V. (1999). A meta-analysis of psycho-educational programs for coronary heart disease patients. *Health Psychology*, **18**, 506–519.

ENRICHD Investigators (2000). Enhancing recovery in coronary heart disease patients: study design and methods. *American Heart Journal*, **139**, 1–9.

Fonarow, G.C., Stevenson, L.W., Walden, J.A., Livingston, N.A., Steimle, A.E., Hamilton, M.A., Moriguchi, J., Tillisch, J.H. & Woo, M.A. (1997). Impact of a comprehensive heart failure management program on hospital readmission and functional status of patients with advanced heart failure. *Journal of the American College of Cardiology*, **30**, 725–732.

Frasure-Smith, N. (1991). In-hospital symptoms of psychological stress as predictors of long term outcome after acute myocardial infarction in men. *American Journal Cardiology*, **67**, 121–127.

Frasure-Smith, N. & Prince, R. (1985). The Ischemic Heart Disease Life Stress Monitoring Program: impact on mortality. *Psychosomatic Medicine*, **47**, 431–445.

Frasure-Smith, N. & Prince, R. (1989). Long-term follow-up of the Ischemic Heart Disease Life Stress Monitoring Program. *Psychosomatic Medicine*, **51**, 485–513.

Frasure-Smith, N., Lesperance, F. & Talajic, M. (1995). Depression and 18-month prognosis after myocardial infarction. *Circulation*, **91**, 999–1005.

Frasure-Smith, N., Lesperance, F., Prince, R.H., Verrier, P., Garber, R.A., Juneau, M., Wolfson, C. & Bourassa, M.G. (1997). Randomised trial of home-based psychosocial nursing intervention for patients recovering from myocardial infarction. *Lancet*, **350**, 473–479.

Freedland, K.E., Carney, R.M., Hance, M.L. & Skala, J.A. (1996). Cognitive therapy for depression in patients with coronary artery disease (Abstract). *Psychosomatic Medicine*, **58**, 93.

Friedman, M., Thoreson, C., Gill, J., Powell, L., Ulmer, D., Thompson, L., Price, V., Rabin, D., Breall, W., Dixon, T., Levy, R. & Bourg, E. (1984). Alteration of type A behavior and reduction in cardiac recurrences in post-myocardial infarction patients. *American Heart Journal*, **108**, 237–248.

Gerin, W., Pickering, T.G., Glynn, L., Christenfeld, N., Schwartz, A., Carroll, D. & Davidson, K. (2000). A historical context for behavioral models of hypertension. *Journal of Psychosomatic Research*, **48**, 369–378.

Glaser, R., Rabin, B., Chesney, M., Cohen, S. & Natelson, B. (1999). Stress-induced immunomodulation. *JAMA*, **281**, 2268–2270.

Grady, K.L. (1993). Quality of life in patients with chronic heart failure. *Critical Care Nursing Clinics of North America*, 661–670.

Guyton, A.C. (1971). *Textbook of Medical Physiology*. Philadelphia: Saunders.

Habra, M.E., Linden, W., Anderson, J.C. & Weinberg, J. (in press). Type D personality is related to cardiovascular and neuroendocrine reactivity to acute stress. *Journal of Psychomatic Research*.

Helgeson, V. & Fritz, H. (1999). Cognitive adaptation as a predictor of new coronary events after percutaneous transluminal coronary angioplasty. *Psychosomatic Medicine*, **61**, 488–495.

Hogan, B.E., Linden, W. & Najarian, B. (2002). Social support interventions: do they work? *Clinical Psychology Review*, **22**, 381–440.

Irvine, M.J., Baker, B., Smith, J., Jandciu, S., Paquette, M., Cairns, J., Connolly, S., Roberts, R., Gent, M. & Dorian, P. (1999). Poor adherence to placebo or Amiodarone therapy predicts mortality: results from the CAMIAT study. *Psychosomatic Medicine*, **61**, 566–575.

Jacob, R.G., Chesney, M.A., Williams, D.M., Ding, Y. & Shapiro, A.P. (1991). Relaxation therapy for hypertension: design effects and treatment effects. *Annals of Behavioral Medicine*, **13**, 5–17.

Jones, D.A. & West, R.R. (1996). Psychological rehabilitation after myocardial infarction: multicentre randomized controlled trial. *British Medical Journal*, **313**, 1517–1521.

Jorgensen, R.S., Johnson, B.T., Kolodziej, M.E. & Schreer, G.E. (1996). Elevated blood pressure and personality: a meta-analytic review. *Psychological Bulletin*, **120**, 293–320.

JNC VI (1997). The sixth report of the joint national committee on prevention, detection, evaluation, and treatment of high blood pressure. *Archives of Internal Medicine*, **157**, 2413–2446.

Kamarck, T. & Jennings, J.R. (1991). Biobehavioral factors in sudden cardiac death. *Psychological Bulletin*, **109**, 42–75.

Kaplan, N.M. (1986). *Clinical Hypertension* (4th edn). Baltimore: Williams & Wilkins.

Ketterer, M.W., Mahr, G. & Goldberg, A.D. (2000). Psychological factors affecting a medical condition: Ischemic Coronary Heart Disease. *Journal of Psychosomatic Research*, **48**, 357–367.

Kop, W.J. (1999). Chronic and acute psychological risk factors for clinical manifestations of coronary artery disease. *Psychosomatic Medicine*, **61**, 476–487.

Kostis, J.B., Rosen, R.C., Cosgrove, N.M., Shindler, D.M. & Wilson, A.C. (1994). Nonpharmacologic therapy improves functional and emotional status in congestive heart failure. *Chest*, **106**, 995–1001.

Kostis, J.B., Rosen, R.C., Brondolo, E., Taska, L., Smith, D.E. & Wilson, A.C. (1992). Superiority of nonpharmacologic therapy compared to propranolol and placebo in men with mild hypertension: a randomized, prospective trial. *American Heart Journal*, **123**, 466–474.

Kubzansky, D.L. & Kawachi, I. (2000). Going to the heart of the matter: do negative emotions cause coronary heart disease? *Journal of Psychosomatic Research*, **48**, 323–338.

Kugler, J., Seelbach, H. & Krueskemper, G.M. (1994). Effects of rehabilitation exercise programmes on anxiety and depression in coronary patients. *British Journal of Clinical Psychology*, **33**, 401–410.

Kulik, J.A. & Mahler, H.I.M. (1989). Social support and recovery from surgery. *Health Psychology*, **8**, 221–238.

Kulik, J.A., Moore, P.J. & Mahler, H.I.M. (1993). Stress and affiliation: hospital room-mate effects on pre-operative anxiety and social interaction. *Health Psychology*, **12**, 118–124.

Kurz, R.W., Pirker, H., Doerrscheidt, W. & Uhlir, H. (2001). Einsparunspotential bei Antihypertensiva durch integriertes Hypertonikertraining. *Journal fuer Hypertonie*, **2**, 20–37.

Lau, J., Antman, E.M., Jimenez-Silva, J., Kupelnick, B., Mosteller, F. & Chalmers, T.C. (1992). Cumulative meta-analysis of therapeutic trials for myocardial infarction. *New England Journal of Medicine*, **327**, 248–254.

Lefkowitz, R.J. & Willerson, J.T. (2001). Prospects in cardiovascular research. *JAMA*, **285**, 581–587.

Linden, W. (1990). *Autogenic Training: A Clinical Guide*. New York: Guilford Press.

Linden, W. & Chambers, L.A. (1994). Clinical effectiveness of non-drug therapies for hypertension: a meta-analysis. *Annals of Behavioral Medicine*, **16**, 35–45.

Linden, W., Lenz, J.W. & Con, A.H. (2001). Individualized stress management for primary hypertension: a controlled trial. *Archives of Internal Medicine*, **161**, 1071–1080.

Linden, W., Rutledge, T. & Con, A. (1998). A case for the usefulness of laboratory social stressors. *Annals of Behavioral Medicine*, **20**, 310–316.

Linden, W., Stossel, C. & Maurice, J. (1996). Psychosocial interventions for patients with coronary artery disease: a meta-analysis. *Archives of Internal Medicine*, **156**, 745–752.

Liu, J.E., Roman, M.J., Pini, R., Schwartz, J.E., Pickering, T.G. & Devereux, R.B. (1999). Elevated ambulatory with normal clinic blood pressure ("white coat normotension") is associated with cardiac and arterial target organ damage. *Annals of Internal Medicine*, **131**, 564–572.

McGrady, A.V. & Higgins, J.T. Jr (1990). Effect of repeated measurements of blood pressure on blood pressure in essential hypertension: role of anxiety. *Journal of Behavioral Medicine*, **13**, 93–101.

McGrady, A. & Linden, W. (2003). Hypertension. In M.S. Schwartz (Ed.), *Biofeedback: A Practitioner's Handbook*. New York: Guilford Press.

McKelvie, R.S., Koon, K.T., McCartney, N., Humen, D., Montague, T. & Yusuf, S. (1995). Effects of exercise training in patients with congestive heart failure: a critical review. *Journal of the American College of Cardiology*, **25**, 789–796.

Mittag, O., Kolenda, K.D., Nordmann, K.J., Bernien, J. & Maurischat, C. (2001). Return to work after myocardial infarction/coronary artery bypass grafting: patients' and physicians' initial viewpoints and outcome 12 months later. *Social Science and Medicine*, **52**, 1441–1450.

Mittleman, M.A., Maclure, M., Sherwood, J.B., Mulry, R.P., Tofler, G.H., Jacobs, S.C., Friedman, R., Benson, H. & Muller, J.E. for the Determinants of Myocardial Infarction Onset Study Investigators (1995). Triggering of acute myocardial infarction onset by episodes of anger. *Circulation*, **92**, 1720–1725.

Murberg, T.A. & Bru, E. (2001). Coping and mortality among patients with congestive heart failure. *International Journal of Behavioral Medicine*, **8**, 66–79.

Nunes, E.V., Frank, K.A. & Kornfeld, D.S. (1987). Psychologic treatment for the type A behavior pattern and for coronary heart disease: a meta-analysis of the literature. *Psychosomatic Medicine*, **48**, 159–173.

Oldridge, N.B., Guyatt, G.H., Fischer, M.E. & Rimm, A.A. (1988). Cardiac rehabilitation after myocardial infarction: combined experience of randomized clinical trials. *JAMA*, **260**, 945–950.

Ornish, D., Brown, S.E., Scherwitz, L.S., Billings, J.H., Armstrong, W.T., Ports, T.A., McLanahan, S.M., Kirkeeide, R.L., Brand, R.J. & Gould, K.L. (1990). Can lifestyle change reverse coronary heart disease? *Lancet*, **336**, 129–133.

Ornish, D., Scherwitz, L.S., Doody, R.S., Kerten, D., McLanahan, S.M., Brown, S.E., DePuey, G., Sonnemaker, R., Haynes, C., Lester, J., McAlister, G.K., Hall, R.J., Burdine, J.A. & Gotto, A.M.

(1983). Effects of stress management training and dietary changes in treating ischaemic heart disease. *JAMA*, **249**, 54–60.

Ornish, D., Scherwitz, L.W., Billings, J.H., Gould, L., Merritt, T.A., Sparler, S., Armstrong, W.T., Ports, T.A., Kirkeeide, R.L., Hogeboorn, C. & Brand, R.J. (1998). Intensive lifestyle changes for reversal of coronary heart disease. *JAMA*, **280**, 2001–2007.

Profant, J. & Dimsdale, J.E. (2000). Psychosocial factors and heart failure. *International Journal of Behavioral Medicine*, **7**, 236–255.

Rozanski, A., Blumenthal, J.A. & Kaplan, J. (1999). Impact of psychological factors on the pathogenesis of cardiovascular disease and implications for therapy. *Circulation*, **99**, 2192–2217.

Rutledge, T., Reis, S.E., Olson, M., Owens, J., Kelsey, S.F., Pepine, C.J., Reichek, N., Rogers, W.J., Bairey Merz, C.N., Sopko, G., Cornell, C.E. & Matthews, K.A. (2001). Psychosocial variables are associated with atherosclerosis risk factors among women with chest pain: the WISE study. *Psychosomatic Medicine*, **63**, 282–288.

Sakakibara, M. & Hayano, J. (1996). Effect of slowed respiration on cardiac parasympathetic response to threat. *Psychosomatic Medicine*, **58**, 32–37.

Sakakibara, M., Takeuchi, S. & Hayano, J. (1994). Effect of relaxation training on cardiac sympathetic tone. *Psychophysiology*, **31**, 223–228.

Selenta, C., Hogan, B. & Linden, W. (2000). How often do office blood pressure measurements fail to identify true hypertension? *Archives of Family Medicine*, **9**, 533–540.

Shephard, R.J. & Franklin, B. (2001). Changes in the quality of life: a major goal of cardiac rehabilitation. *Journal of Cardiopulmonary Rehabilitation*, **21**, 189–200.

Sotile, W.M. (1996). *Psychosocial Interventions for Cardiopulmonary Patients*. Champaign, IL: Human Kinetics Press.

Spence, J.D., Barnett, P.A., Linden, W., Ramsden, V. & Taenzer, P. (1999). Recommendations on stress management. *Canadian Medical Association Journal*, **160**, S46–S50.

Van Dixhoorn, J. (1998). Cardiorespiratory effects of breathing and relaxation instruction in myocardial infarction patients. *Biological Psychology*, **49**, 123–135.

Van Dixhoorn, J., Duivenvoorden, H.J. & Pool, J. (1990a). Success and failure of exercise training after myocardial infarction: is the outcome predictable? *Journal of the American College of Cardiology*, **15**, 974–982.

Van Dixhoorn, J., Duivenvoorden, H.J., Pool, J. & Verhage, F. (1990b). Psychic effects of physical training and relaxation therapy after myocardial infarction. *Journal of Psychosomatic Research*, **34**, 327–337.

Van Dixhoorn, J., Duivenvoorden, H.J., Staal, H.A. & Pool, J. (1989). Physical training and relaxation therapy in rehabilitation assessed through a composite criterion for training outcome. *American Heart Journal*, **118**, 545–552.

Van Dixhoorn, J., Duivenvoorden, H.J., Staal, H.A., Pool, J. & Verhage, F. (1987). Cardiac events after myocardial infarction: possible effects of relaxation therapy. *European Heart Journal*, **8**, 1210–1214.

Wagdi, P., Vuilliomonet, A., Kaufmann, U., Richter, M. & Bertel, O. (1993). Ungenuegende Behandlungsdisziplin, Patienteninformation und Medikamentenverschreibung als Ursachen fuer die Notfallhospitalisation bei chronisch herzinsuffizienten Patienten. *Schweizer Medizinische Wochenschrift*, **123**, 108–112.

Ziegelstein, R.C., Fauerbach, J.A., Stevens, S.S., Romanelli, J., Richter, D.P. & Bush, D.E. (2000). Patients with depression are less likely to follow recommendations to reduce cardiac risk during myocardial recovery from a myocardial infarction. *Archives of Internal Medicine*, **160**, 1818–1823.

CHAPTER 7

Oncology and Psycho-oncology

Kristin M. Kilbourn
Northern Arizona University, USA
and
Patricia E. Durning
University of Florida, USA

INTRODUCTION

At its most basic level, cancer is a disorder of cellular growth and differentiation. Although the biological mechanisms by which normal cells initially transform have not been definitively determined, it has been demonstrated that as cancer develops, a transformed cell creates additional transformed cells that develop independence from normal cellular controls: cancer cells are not restricted to a specific location, a specific size, or a specific function. As cancerous cells invade a location, they grow and reproduce. Cancerous cells may be mechanically transported through the blood or lymphatic system to distant sites, where new tumors may then develop. Improvements in medical treatment for cancer have occurred as understanding of the processes by which malignant cells develop, reproduce, and spread has increased. Advances in surgery, chemotherapy, radiotherapy, and immunotherapy have all contributed to decreases in cancer mortality rates.

Despite improvements in cancer treatment, cancer is still the third leading cause of death internationally. Naturally, mortality may be reduced through reduction in cancer incidence. Prevention of cancer can be classified as either primary prevention or secondary prevention, with the former encompassing activities aimed at decreasing the occurrence of cancer and the latter encompassing activities aimed at improving detection of cancers in early stages, before cancerous cells have caused extensive local damage or have metastasized, or spread, to different locations.

Before effective treatments for cancer were developed, the disease was considered terminal. Accordingly, early psychological work with cancer patients focused on counseling and end-of-life issues. As prognoses for patients with cancer diagnoses improved, psychological work with cancer patients changed to include issues of coping with treatment and survivorship. Over the past several decades, research on the psychological and social factors

Handbook of Clinical Health Psychology. Edited by S. Llewelyn and P. Kennedy.
© 2003 John Wiley & Sons, Ltd.

associated with cancer have increased. The field variously identified as psycho-oncology, psychosocial oncology, or behavioral oncology includes not only research on primary and secondary prevention interventions, but also research on patients' adaptation to the illness. The 1176-page multi-authored textbook *Psycho-oncology* (Holland, 1998) provides an excellent example of the range and depth of the field.

This chapter summarizes results of psycho-oncology research in the areas of primary prevention, secondary prevention, adaptation to cancer, and interventions to improve quality of life and health outcome among cancer patients and cancer survivors.

PRIMARY PREVENTION

As noted above, primary prevention is aimed at decreasing the occurrence of cancer. A number of behavioral or lifestyle factors have demonstrated associations with the incidence of cancer of specific sites (see Table 7.1). Several of these behavioral factors are associated with development not only of cancer but also of several other disease processes; therefore, primary prevention interventions are often not focused solely on cancer prevention. Often, primary prevention interventions include behavioral strategies aimed at changing unhealthy behaviors and maintaining healthy behaviors. This may include interventions aimed at smoking cessation, decreasing alcohol consumption, improving diet and exercise habits, and decreasing sun exposure. A psychoeducational group format tends to be an effective and cost-efficient means of providing prevention and behavior modification information. The brief review below identifies several of the behavioral and lifestyle factors associated with cancer development.

Tobacco Use

Perhaps the strongest evidence for the association between behavior and cancer development is the consistently strong association between cigarette smoking and lung cancer. Tobacco use is also associated with the development of cancers of the head and neck, pancreas,

Table 7.1 Behavioral factors associated with cancer incidence

Behavioral factor	Cancer
Tobacco use	Lung; head and neck; esophagus; pancreas; urinary bladder; cervix
Diet and exercise	Colon; esophagus; stomach; oral cavity; prostate; breast; endometrium
Alcohol use	Liver (primary); mouth; esophagus; pharynx; larynx; (breast (possible association); colon/rectum (beer) only)
Sexual and reproductive behaviors	Cervix (infection with HPV); breast (nulliparity, advanced age at first birth, and use of birth control pills)
Sunlight exposure	Skin

Note: Level of empirical evidence for associations vary.

kidney, bladder, and cervix (WHO, 1995). The most successful cessation programs appear to combine education in cognitive-behavioral strategies for behavior change, social support, and psychopharmaceutical interventions, including nicotine replacement and antidepressant medications (Fiore, Jorenby & Baker, 1997).

Diet and Exercise

Dietary patterns may modify risk of cancer by both contributing to the development of cancer and protecting against cancer (Winters, 1998). High intake of dietary fat may be associated with the occurrence of colorectal, breast, prostate, and possibly gynecologic and pancreatic cancer. Very high intake of nitrates and salt (especially from salting, smoking, and pickling for food preservation) has been associated with incidence of stomach cancer. High intake of fruits and vegetables, conversely, may be associated with decreased occurrence of colorectal, breast, stomach, esophageal, pharyngeal, and oral cancer (WHO, 1995). Inadequate intake of dietary fiber has demonstrated association with incidence of colon, breast, and prostate cancer (Greenwald, 1993). Research examining the cancer-causing or cancer-preventing properties of macronutrients has produced promising results; however, further research is needed before the results can be considered conclusive (Osborne, Boyle & Lipkin, 1997; WHO, 1995). Independent of dietary fat, weight and lack of physical activity are associated with cancer development. Both weight at time of diagnosis and history of weight gain during adulthood may be linked to risk for colon and post-menopausal breast cancer; physical activity may decrease risk for these forms of cancer (Greenwald, 1993).

Substance Abuse

Associations between alcohol use and development of cancer of the head, neck, and liver have been clearly demonstrated (Lundberg & Passik, 1998). Alcohol's contributions to development of colorectal, stomach, breast, and pancreatic cancers have not been definitively identified. It has been proposed that alcohol and tobacco use have synergistic effects; because heavy alcohol and tobacco use often co-occur, it has been difficult to examine their effects independently. Moreover, poor diet and nutrition have been proposed as contributors to development of head and neck cancers: once again, poor diet and nutrition are often found among alcoholics, so examination of the independent effects of these behaviors is difficult (Lundberg & Passik, 1998).

Sexual Behavior

The primary risk factor for development of cervical cancer is infection with the human papilloma virus (HPV), which may be transmitted through sexual contact (Auchincloss & McCartney, 1998). Sexual behaviors associated with increased risk of HPV infection and cervical cancer include the following: young age at first intercourse, multiple sexual partners, and having a sexual partner who has had multiple partners (Auchincloss & McCartney, 1998). Human immunodeficiency virus (HIV), which may be transmitted through sexual contact, is associated with development of both Kaposi sarcoma and non-Hodgkins lymphoma. Primary prevention efforts for both HPV and HIV have promoted "safe" sexual practices (WHO, 1995).

Sunlight Exposure

Cancers of the skin (including basal and squamous cell cancers as well as the more dangerous malignant melanoma) may develop in cells that have been damaged by the ultraviolet radiation present in sunlight. Skin growths such as moles are also predictive of skin cancer risk; in fact, number of skin growths, or nevi, is the strongest risk factor for development of malignant melanoma. Because sun exposure at early ages may increase the number of nevi, sun exposure contributes to the relationship between nevi number and melanoma development (Harrison et al., 1994). Overall, the relationship between sun exposure and skin cancer development is more direct for non-melanoma than for melanoma skin cancers. However, for all forms of skin cancer, a causal relationship between sunlight exposure and skin cancer development has been demonstrated, although the association between sun exposure and risk may not be entirely linear (Ainsleigh, 1993; Armstrong, 1988).

Environmental Exposure

Exposure to carcinogens in the environment, particularly occupational environments, may also be associated with cancer risk. Similarly, exposure to certain viruses or parasites may increase relative risk of cancer development (WHO, 1995). Exposure to environmental carcinogens may be difficult to prevent on an individual level. However, educational programs may improve individuals' awareness of the risks, thereby enhancing their opportunities to limit their exposure. More importantly, reduction of carcinogens in the environment should reduce individuals' exposure and individual risk.

SECONDARY PREVENTION

Secondary prevention includes activities designed to identify cancers in early stages. Through screening of populations at risk for certain cancers, the probability of detecting cancer at early stages, when treatment is most effective, may be increased. Procedures recommended for cancer screening are listed in Table 7.2. As Bloom (1994) and others have pointed out, there are at least seven organizations that have promulgated screening guidelines; as would be expected, the concordance between these guidelines is not exact. Despite the lack of full agreement about specific recommendations, researchers have examined both the prevalence of screening behaviors and factors associated with screening.

Demographic characteristics that have been positively associated with increased use of screening in general include higher levels of education, higher socioeconomic class, and insurance status (Breen et al., 2001). Age has been negatively associated with screening, as it has been consistently found that screening behavior decreases with age (Rubenstein, 1994).

Psychological factors associated with screening compliance include knowledge, fear/worry, health beliefs, health locus of control, perceptions of benefits and barriers to

Table 7.2 Recommended screening procedures for early detection of cancer

Cancer site	Sex	Screening test
Breast	F	Breast self-exam Clinical breast exam Mammogram
Cervix	F	Pap test
Endometrium/ovaries	F	Clinical pelvic exam
Colorectal	F/M	Fecal occult blood test Flexible sigmoidoscopy Screening colonoscopy
Skin	F/M	Clinical skin exam Skin self-exam
Prostate	M	Prostate specific antigen blood test Digital rectal exam

screening, and attitude toward prevention in general. Although knowledge has been found in several studies to be positively associated with screening compliance, "knowledge" is not always measured as the same construct: it can include knowledge of screening tests, screening recommendations, cancer causes or warning signs (Bostick et al., 1993). Fear had been proposed as a model to explain non-compliance, with people who are fearful of receiving positive screening test results being less likely to have the tests. Results of a meta-analysis by McCaul et al. (1996), however, demonstrate that the opposite may be true: women who are more worried about being diagnosed with breast cancer are more likely to obtain screening for breast cancer. Health beliefs, health locus of control, perceptions of benefits and barriers to screening, and attitude toward prevention in general have all been demonstrated to be predictive of screening compliance (e.g., Kushnir et al., 1995; Lerman et al., 1990; Myers et al., 1990). Tests of models including these factors have included both predictions of behavior and compliance. The most consistent finding has been that physician recommendation affects screening behavior (Lerman et al., 1990). Therefore, a number of researchers have designed office-based interventions to increase either patient or physician screening behavior (e.g., Snall & Buck, 1996).

GENETIC SCREENING FOR CANCER

In addition to the behavioral contributions to cancer development enumerated above, genetic contributions to carcinogenesis also affect cancer risk. The genetic components of cancer were first recognized on the basis of familial patterns. For example, up to one-third of all individuals with breast cancer may have a family history positive for the disease (Gettig, Marks & Mulvihill, 1998). In the early 1990s, specific genes conferring risk for breast cancer susceptibility were identified, allowing for testing of breast cancer risk (Kash & Lerman, 1998). However, with only 5 to 10% of individuals with breast cancer testing positive for the marker genes, it is clear that not all individuals with positive family history have a genetic predisposition for the disease. The discrepancy between familial patterns and genetic patterns can be explained by non-genetic similarities within families: both environmental exposures and health-related behaviors are likely to be similar within families. Of course, it is possible that genetic markers for cancer risk currently unidentified also contribute to the familial patterns. To further complicate the issue, not all individuals who test positive for the genetic marker develop the disease. Nonetheless, knowledge of cancer risk may allow individuals who are at risk for cancer occurrence to modify their behavior or undergo procedures (e.g., prophylactic mastectomy) to decrease their cancer risk.

Because the relationships among genetic markers, disease occurrence, and disease progression may be complicated, specially trained genetic counselors may be employed to help individuals understand the genetic aspects of cancer. Individuals with high risk of cancer may be at high risk for psychological distress. Anxiety, sense of vulnerability, fear of disfigurement, fear of death, guilt, feelings of powerlessness, denial, and feelings of isolation may all be elevated in women who perceive themselves as at risk for breast cancer (Kash & Lerman, 1998). Provision of accurate information about genetic concepts and medical information may allow the genetic counselor to alleviate cancer-related distress, thereby allowing for more reasoned decision-making, which could include decision-making related to genetic testing.

If genetic susceptibility for cancer is verified through genetic testing, the person at risk may have to make difficult decisions about the means of preventing cancer. For a woman at genetic risk of breast cancer, for example, the prevention options could include prophylactic mastectomy or chemoprevention (i.e., prophylactic medications such as Tamoxifen). At the same time, secondary prevention or early detection of cancer (e.g., mammography and clinical breast exams to screen for breast cancer) may be recommended as viable alternatives to more aggressive preventive methods. Once a genetic susceptibility is identified within a family, moreover, family members must decide whether to undergo genetic testing themselves. Family relationships can become strained when some family members choose to learn their genetic risk while others do not (Kash & Lerman, 1998).

ADAPTATION TO CANCER

Even though improvements in detection and treatment of cancer have led to improvements in survival, cancer remains a potentially life-threatening disease; as such, it represents a potentially catastrophic stressor to those diagnosed with the disease. Although many people adapt well to a diagnosis of cancer, it is estimated that approximately one-third of all cancer patients experience some distress during the course of their illness (Zabora, 1998).

Estimates of the prevalence of psychological distress among patients with cancer have been somewhat varied, primarily as a result of inconsistencies in operational definitions. For example, in a meta-analytic review of studies relevant to this topic published between 1980 and 1994 (van't Spijker, Trijsburg & Duivenvoorden, 1997), prevalence rates of 0–46% for depression, 0.9–49% for anxiety, and 5–50% for psychological distress were identified. Even with this variability, patients with cancer diagnoses were found to score significantly higher than the general population, but significantly lower than psychiatric populations, on measures of depression. On the whole, however, the most consistently found prevalence rates for psychological distress among cancer patients have been in the range of 25–30% (Derogatis et al., 1983; Farber, Weinerman & Kuypers, 1984; Stefanek, Derogatis & Shaw, 1987; Zabora et al., 2001).

For anyone diagnosed with cancer, availability of appropriate resources may affect adaptation. Financial resources and access to appropriate medical care are primary concerns, particularly at the time of diagnosis. Personal and social resources also impact levels of distress and adjustment to cancer. Personal resources may include personality, knowledge, experiences, and coping skills. Social resources may include different forms of support from the people who interact with the patient.

One aspect of personality that has demonstrated an association with adaptation to cancer is optimism. In general, people with optimistic and pessimistic outlooks differ in their responses to stressful circumstances. Among cancer patients, optimism has been associated with lower levels of distress. For example, in a population of breast cancer patients, level of optimism prior to surgery was predictive of distress over the following year, even when controlling for initial distress level (Carver et al., 1993). Although optimism is generally considered a relatively stable personality trait, a recent study (Antoni et al., 2001) found that optimism increased as a result of a cognitive-behavioral stress management intervention. Confidence in dealing with a range of events may improve a person's confidence for dealing with traumatic events, such as diagnosis of cancer, by increasing optimism.

Knowledge and personal history may also have some impact on cancer-related distress. For example, a person who has limited knowledge of recent advances in cancer treatment or who has had a negative experience with cancer (e.g., death of a family member or friend) may believe that cancer is always a terminal illness. A more positive aspect of personal history is use of social support networks to cope with stressors. Social support has consistently been found to enhance adaptation to stressful situations, including significant illness. There is some evidence that social support may also serve as a buffer against disease progression (Smith et al., 1994). It appears that the patient's perception of support may be the most important element in this association. If a patient perceives that he or she has inadequate support, then the buffering effects of social support may be limited.

Although optimism and social support have been described as aspects of personality and of behavior, respectively, both have also been measured as indices of coping with cancer. In general, coping may encompass emotional, cognitive, and behavioral means of approaching (or avoiding) stressors in order to limit or reduce distress associated with the stressors. To assess the effectiveness of different coping styles or coping strategies, therefore, these are often measured along with distress. Because of wide variability in operational definitions of coping with cancer, generalizations must be made with caution. Results of a descriptive review of 58 studies assessing coping with cancer (van't Spijker et al., 1997) may provide a good indication of the commonly reported relationships among coping and distress. The authors identified two general clusters of coping responses commonly found among adults with cancer. The cluster of coping responses related to positive psychological adjustment included confrontation, fighting spirit, and optimism. The cluster of coping responses related to negative psychological adjustment included passive acceptance, avoidance, denial, feelings of loss of control, and fatalism (van't Spijker et al., 1997).

Although some mechanisms contributing to cancer-related distress levels (including optimism, availability of adequate social support, and positive coping styles) may be enhanced through interventions, other factors associated with distress levels (including demographic characteristics, diagnosis, and disease- and treatment-related variables) are not amenable to change. Knowledge of the associations between these factors and distress levels may help providers to identify patients at highest risk of distress. With respect to patient age, for example, studies have found significantly higher depression, anxiety, and general distress in younger patients than in older patients (Mor, Allen & Malin, 1994; van't Spijker et al., 1997). Therefore, providers should be alert to the possibility of distress among their younger patients. With respect to tumor site, patients with breast cancer may display lower levels of distress and patients with lung cancer may display higher levels of distress than patients with other forms of cancer (van't Spijker et al., 1997; Zabora et al., 2001). Specific treatment regimens may also be associated with increased risk of distress. For example, patients receiving radiation therapy for head and neck cancer report distress associated with difficulties with eating and swallowing and problems with verbal communication (De Boer et al., 1999).

Andersen (1992) proposed three categories of risk for psychological and behavioral morbidity based on illness- and treatment-related variables. The low risk group includes those with localized disease (i.e., Stage I or II) at diagnosis, single treatment modality, and favorable prognosis (e.g., 70–95% 5-year survival). The moderate risk group includes those with regional disease (i.e., Stage III at diagnosis or first recurrence for Stage I disease), combination treatment (e.g., surgery with adjuvant chemotherapy), and guarded prognosis (e.g., 40–60% 5-year survival). The high risk group includes those with distant spread of disease (i.e., Stage IV at diagnosis, first recurrence for regional disease, or all stages of rapidly progressive disease such as lung or pancreatic cancer), intensive treatment (i.e., possible surgery or radiation therapy for debulking or palliation, high likelihood of systemic chemotherapy, and possible invasive treatments for pain/symptom control), and dismal prognosis (e.g., 15–40% 1-year survival, 4–15% 5-year survival).

Positive Benefit Finding

While experience with cancer is typified as negative, recent research has found that most cancer patients ascribe some positive benefits to their cancer experience (Andrykowski, Brady & Hunt, 1993; Cordova et al., 2001). When confronted with their own mortality, individuals may re-evaluate goals and priorities and subsequently emerge with a greater appreciation of life, relationships, and spirituality (Tedeschi & Calhoun, 1995). Cognitive processing models also endorse benefit finding: developing new assumptions and coping skills in response to a life-altering experience may lead to a sense of personal growth (Parkes, 1971). Some evidence has shown that finding benefit in trauma may reduce later stress (McMillan, Smith & Fisher, 1997). Results of a recent cognitive-behavioral stress management intervention with breast cancer patients (Antoni et al., 2001) indicate that, overall, the participants saw their lives as positively changed as a result of their cancer diagnosis; the positive changes were unrelated to distress indices. Cordova and colleagues (2001) found that breast cancer patients had greater post-traumatic growth compared to healthy controls; again, the post-traumatic growth was independent of depression and well-being. These findings suggest that interventions should focus on both fostering positive experiences and reducing overall distress to be most effective.

Cancer-related Fatigue

Cancer-related fatigue (CRF) is one of the most common experiences among cancer patients and is often reported as the symptom that causes the most distress, the greatest level of interference in daily life activities, and the most negative impact on quality of life

(Cella, 1998; Portenoy & Miaskowski, 1998; Richardson, 1995; Vogelzang et al., 1997). It is estimated that 60–90% of cancer patients experience fatigue (Portenoy & Miaskowski, 1998; Vogelzang et al., 1997; Winningham et al., 1994). CRF is thought to be related to a number of factors, including underlying disease, direct effects of cancer-related treatments, side-effects associated with cancer treatments, poor nutritional status, sleep disturbances, decreased activity levels, various systemic disorders (e.g., anemia, infection, dehydration), and chronic pain (Piper, Lindsey & Dodd, 1991; Portenoy & Itri, 1999; Smets et al., 1993; Winningham et al., 1994). Cancer patients undergoing chemotherapy and radiotherapy are especially prone to fatigue, which tends to peak later in the treatment process and may persist for over a year following the end of adjuvant treatment (Greenberg, 1998; Irvine et al., 1994). Studies examining the impact of fatigue on quality of life in cancer patients have found that many patients report CRF to be more distressing and debilitating than pain (Vogelzang et al., 1997).

Although the relationship between distress and CRF is not well understood, CRF is consistently correlated with psychological disturbances such as depression and anxiety (Schwartz et al., 2000). This association may, in part, be related to the overlap of the symptoms of Major Depression (e.g., loss of energy, decreased motivation, anhedonia, and sleep difficulties) and CRF, making differential diagnosis somewhat difficult. Additionally, high levels of anxiety can lead to sleep difficulties, decreased pain tolerance and change in appetite. These somatic factors can compound or aggravate the symptoms of CRF.

Cancer-related Pain

Although the prevalence of pain among cancer patients varies by diagnosis, approximately 70% of cancer patients experience severe pain at some point during the course of their illness (Foley, 1985). Tumor-related variables (including tumor invasion of bone and tumor compression, invasion, or damage to nerves or other tissues) and treatment-related variables (including sequelae of surgery, chemotherapy, and radiotherapy) have been associated with up to 78% and 25%, respectively, of cancer patients' pain reports (Breitbart & Payne, 1998). Patients diagnosed with metastatic cancer may be at particular risk for pain if the metastases involve invasion of bone or invasion, compression, or damage of other tissue. Although the tumor- and treatment-related variables may explain the physiological etiology of cancer-related pain, the pain experience for each patient may also be influenced by cognitive, emotional, behavioral, and social factors. Positive associations between pain and psychological distress have been consistently identified (Derogatis et al., 1983). Patients who interpret pain as a marker of disease progression may experience the pain as more intense or more disruptive than patients who interpret the pain as a benign occurrence (Daut & Cleeland, 1982; Spiegel & Bloom, 1983).

THE CLINICAL HEALTH PSYCHOLOGIST'S ROLE IN ONCOLOGY SETTINGS

Although approximately two-thirds of adult cancer patients do not experience significant illness-related distress, all patients might benefit from psychological services. Given that such a wide variety of factors (e.g., illness-related factors, personal characteristics) may be associated with distress among cancer patients, there are numerous opportunities for clinical health psychologists to provide beneficial interventions. Patients who do not display significant distress might still report some degree of stress and/or display an inclination to work on positive growth. Those who do report significant distress can benefit from appropriate psychological services focused on decreasing distress.

Within a given oncology setting, the clinical health psychologist's role should be one that provides the best enhancement of patient care. For example, if no other psychosocial services are available to patients, then the psychologist may function primarily as a direct care provider for all distressed patients. If, on the other hand, some psychosocial services are available to patients through a service other than psychology (e.g., social work, pastoral counseling), then the psychologist may offer more targeted patient care. Clinical health psychologists may function as consultants, administrators, researchers, and educators (Tovian, 1991). To function most effectively in any of these roles, it is imperative for the psychologist to develop and maintain good working relationships with other health professionals. In addition to serving as consultants to health care providers, clinical health psychologists can assist in educating the medical staff on ways of identifying distress and maladaptive coping. Clinical health psychologists may also promote effective communication between patients and their providers, both by working with specific provider–patient pairs and by providing more general education about communication.

Of course, many of the issues listed above are relevant to psychologists working in any medical setting. Working in oncology settings may present additional issues specific to cancer patient populations. Most significantly, it is important to be aware of the expected side-effects of cancer treatment regimens in order to tailor services to patient populations. For example, both emotional and cognitive symptoms may result directly from certain chemotherapy agents; awareness of such relationships may allow for provision of most appropriate treatment. When working with cancer patients and their families, it is important to maintain a sense of flexibility. Patients may not be able to tolerate long therapy sessions or may need to cancel outpatient appointments due to sudden changes in their medical status. In addition, with frequent appointments, patients may have difficulty traveling to their medical appointments. The clinical health psychologist should be prepared for rapid changes in both appearance and health status associated with cancer treatment and/or disease progression (Tovian, 1991). A structured therapy approach requiring a set number of sessions may not be appropriate for patients for whom effects of disease and treatment may interfere with continuation in regular treatment.

CLINICAL ASSESSMENT OF CANCER PATIENTS

Although the most direct and thorough means of identifying distress levels and psychosocial needs of cancer patients is individual clinical assessment, it is impractical to conduct thorough interview-based assessments of all patients at high-volume oncology clinics, particularly given that only one-third of the patients would be expected to require psychosocial services (Zabora, 1998). A practical alternative to conducting interview assessments with all patients is to administer a self-report measure to all patients, then to provide more individualized services to those patients whose responses to the screening measure indicate that they might benefit from psychosocial services. In a recent review of distress screening protocols, Zabora (1998) identified five self-report instruments commonly used to screen for distress among cancer patient populations: the Brief Symptom Inventory (BSI; Derogatis, 1993), the Profile of Mood States (POMS; McNair, Lorr & Droppleman, 1971), the General Hospital Questionnaire (GHQ; Goldberg, 1978), the Hospital Anxiety and Depression Scale (HADS; Zigmond & Snaith, 1983), and the Medical Outcomes Study Short Form (SF-36; Ware et al., 1993). With the exception of the SF-36 (which, as a general quality of life measure, incorporates assessment of both psychological and physical symptoms) these instruments focus on psychological symptoms such as global distress, anxiety, and depression (Gotay & Stern, 1995).

An example of a screening instrument assessing both psychological and physiological symptoms of cancer patients is the Psycho-Oncology Screening Tool, or POST, which was developed by the Psycho-Oncology Program of the University of Florida Department of Clinical and Health Psychology. The instrument identifies the distress levels, fatigue and pain levels, and perceived needs of patients, incorporating elements of both distress and needs surveys. The one-page instrument (which can be completed in five minutes) is composed of four sections: distress and discomfort symptom level visual analogue scales, a depressive symptoms checklist, a social concerns checklist, and interest in psychosocial services questions. Among the initial 569 POST respondents, over one-third indicated interest in psychosocial services. Compared to the uninterested respondents, the interested respondents displayed significantly higher levels of anxiety, confusion, depression, anger, total distress, depressive symptoms, and social concerns (Durning et al., 2002). These results suggest that oncology patients with high levels of distress may tend to be amenable to receiving clinical services.

Once patients choose to pursue psychological services (either because they have been referred for services by health care providers, because their responses to a screening instrument prompted a referral, or because they independently sought services) more individualized and thorough assessments are warranted. As with any psychological assessment, the clinical interview may provide the most relevant and comprehensive clinical information. Table 7.3 provides an outline of interview topics relevant to cancer patient populations.

Table 7.3   Areas to assess when interviewing cancer patients

Medical status (stage, treatment, prognosis)
History and course of current and past medical conditions
Current medications
Cancer risk factors (behavioral, genetic, environmental)
Psychosocial history:
    Education/employment
    Current family situation
    Family of origin
    Alcohol and substance abuse use (past and present)
Knowledge and beliefs surrounding cancer diagnosis
Current stressors:
    Identify cancer and non-cancer related stressors
    Assess current coping strategies
Social support (family, friends, membership in religious and other organizations)
Psychological functioning/psychiatric history:
    Assess current mood (objective and subjective ratings)
    Past psychological history (therapy or counseling, psychiatric diagnosis and/or medications)
    Family history of psychiatric illness

Table 7.4 Common questionnaires used in oncology populations

Domain	Instrument	Reference
Overall distress	Profile of Mood States (POMS)	McNair et al. (1971)
	Brief Symptom Inventory (BSI)	Derogatis (1993)
	Symptom Checklist 90-R (SCL-90)	Derogatis (1983b)
	General Hospital Questionnaire (GHQ)	Goldberg (1978)
	Hospital Anxiety and Depression Scale (HADS)	Zigmond & Snaith (1983)
Adjustment to illness	Psychosocial Adjustment to Illness Scale (PAIS)	Derogatis (1983a)
Anxiety	State-Trait Anxiety Inventory (STAI)	Spielberger et al. (1983)
	Impact of Events Scale (IES)	Horowitz, Wilner & Alvarez (1979)
Depression	Beck Depression Inventory (BDI)	Beck et al. (1961)
	Center for Epidemiological Studies Depression (CES-D)	Radloff (1977)
Quality of life	Medical Outcomes Studies SF-36	Ware et al. (1993)
	Functional Assessment of Cancer Therapy (FACT)	Cella et al. (1993)
Fatigue	Multidimensional Fatigue Symptom Inventory (MFSI)	Stein et al. (1998)
	Functional Assessment of Cancer Therapy—Fatigue (FACT-F)	Cella (1997)
Pain	McGill Pain Questionnaire	Graham et al. (1980)
	Brief Pain Inventory (BPI)	Daut, Cleeland & Flanery (1983)
	Memorial Pain Assessment Card (MPAC)	Fishman et al. (1987)

Individualized assessments may also employ self-report inventories of particular domains. In addition to instruments assessing a global construct of distress, a number of instruments assessing specific aspects of functioning (e.g., depressive symptoms, fatigue) may be used to identify areas of concern for specific patients. Table 7.4 lists measures commonly used among cancer patients. Site-specific concerns (e.g., body image and arm edema for breast cancer patients) may be addressed through instruments designed specifically for those purposes. For example, the Functional Assessment of Cancer Therapy system (FACT; Cella et al., 1993) includes modules assessing concerns associated with particular cancer sites; modules are also available for assessing side-effects of treatment (such as fatigue and nausea) and additional issues such as spirituality.

INTERVENTIONS IN PSYCHO-ONCOLOGY

There are a variety of interventions used with cancer patients and cancer survivors. Psychosocial interventions can help to decrease distress and improve quality of life in those recently diagnosed with cancer or dealing with cancer progression or recurrence (Andersen, 1992; Fawzy et al., 1995; Goodwin et al., 2001; Meyer & Mark, 1995; Sheard & Maguire, 1999). Psychoeducation programs can also assist in increasing knowledge related to

Table 7.5 Interventions used to improve adjustment in cancer patients and their families

Individual therapy:
  Behavioral and Cognitive-behavioral Therapy
  Coping Skills Training
  Supportive Therapy
  Relaxation/Imagery

Group therapy (may consist of patients, families or caregivers):
  Stress-management/Coping Skills Training
  Psychoeducational
  Supportive-expressive

Family therapy
Couples therapy
Grief and bereavement counseling

treatment and/or decrease behaviors associated with increased risk of morbidity or mortality (Fawzy & Fawzy, 1998). A newly published review of the psychosocial intervention literature reports on both the psychosocial and biobehavioral outcomes of interventions for cancer patients (Andersen, 2002). Table 7.5 lists the types of interventions commonly used with cancer patient populations.

In planning implementation of interventions for cancer patients, it is important to consider several factors: (1) the target population (e.g., patients recently diagnosed, survivors of cancer, patients experiencing a recurrence or disease progression); (2) the primary goal of the intervention (e.g., decrease distress, decrease treatment side-effects, enhance health outcomes); and (3) the most appropriate modality (e.g., individual counseling, group therapy, community-wide interventions). Additionally, clinical health psychologists must be aware of available resources in order to provide high-quality programs in a cost-effective manner. For example, group interventions offer a means of providing high-quality services at less cost than traditional individual therapy. Community-wide interventions are especially cost-effective because a large number of people may be exposed to the intervention. The drawback of community interventions is that they are fairly general and cannot be tailored to meet the needs of all individuals. Practical concerns must also be addressed: if small numbers of patients are appropriate for a proposed group intervention, then enrolling participants and maintaining group membership may not be feasible. The following sections will present an overview of interventions used with cancer populations organized according to the factors listed above: target populations, intervention goals, and modalities. Of course, these are interactive factors in that each intervention should be for a specific population, have a specific goal, and employ a specific modality.

Interventions with Different Populations

Patients Newly Diagnosed with Cancer

The application of non-pharmacological, psychosocial interventions with cancer patients and their families has gained increased support and recognition over the past decade (Holland, 2001; Thomas & Weiss, 2000). Psychosocial interventions can provide a relatively quick and safe method of decreasing distress and improving quality of life in newly diagnosed cancer patients and their families. The goal of the intervention may vary as a function of the individual or the type of treatment. For example, the primary goal of many interventions is to decrease distress and assist with adjustment to current situations. Cancer patients commonly report feeling overwhelmed at the time of diagnosis; interventions can assist patients in gaining a sense of control over their situations. Interventions can also provide psychoeducation and may assist patients in making adaptive decisions related to treatment and long-term planning. They provide a safe place where cancer patients and their families can express their feelings without being judged or feeling as though they are burdening others with their problems or concerns. Additionally, interventions can help patients to manage some of the aversive side-effects of cancer treatment, including pain and cancer-related fatigue. Individual or group interventions can also assist patients in the development and refinement of various skills, such as managing stress, increasing social support, and improving coping skills. When newly diagnosed, some patients may need only limited assistance in learning how to apply existing skills to novel situations that may arise after a cancer diagnosis.

Cancer Survivors

Cancer survivorship presents its own set of stressors and challenges. Despite the fact that many oncology patients anticipate a decrease in distress and side-effects following the end of active treatment, many report increased post-treatment distress (Cella & Tross, 1986; Greaves-Otte et al., 1991). Cancer patients often spend the majority of their treatment focused on fighting their disease with little time to think about the long-term effects of cancer survivorship on their life. Some have described this as an existential challenge requiring confrontation with issues of mortality (Spiegel, 1994). This can be a time of productive inner growth for many individuals since it serves as a period when they may re-evaluate and re-prioritize goals and activities (Antoni et al., 2001; Cole & Pargament, 1999; Cordova et al., 2001).

Interventions aimed at cancer survivorship assist with the process of growth while helping patients to deal with their sense of powerlessness and loss of control over their futures. Many patients report heightened anxiety leading up to regular check-ups or follow-up tests (e.g., tumor markers, bone scans) that may uncover a recurrence of the cancer. Patients may also report hypervigilance to physical changes or minor aches and pains; this may be especially pronounced when medical monitoring becomes increasingly less frequent. Interventions focused on fostering growth, increasing social support, increasing pleasurable activities, and educating patients about stress-management and coping skills can be effective in decreasing distress and improving quality of life for those adapting to cancer survivorship (Cordova et al., 2001).

Patients with Cancer Recurrence or Progression

Cancer recurrence or progression presents a somewhat different challenge for the clinical health psychologist. Similar to those who are dealing with a new diagnosis of cancer, those diagnosed with a recurrence or progression may experience increased distress and difficulty adjusting to the new/changed diagnosis. Managing pain, decreasing or controlling adverse side-effects, and dealing with issues of loss are typically the focus of interventions with this population. Many patients may be interested in interventions that allow them to focus on spiritual and existential issues (Spiegel et al., 1989). Interventions may be conducted in individual, group or family therapy settings. Additionally, mind–body approaches to treatment (e.g., meditation, gentle yoga, prayer) may be especially helpful in this group in that such approaches provide patients with a sense of control and mastery, which is particularly important when medical control of the disease has decreased.

Interventions with Different Goals

Decreasing Distress and Improving Positive Psychosocial Adjustment

The diagnosis of cancer creates a great deal of disruption in the lives of cancer patients and their families. Additionally, problems that may have been present but manageable prior to the diagnosis of cancer may suddenly appear overwhelming. Therefore, stress-management interventions focusing on identifying and decreasing sources of stress and developing more effective coping techniques can be extremely beneficial to almost all newly diagnosed cancer patients. A number of studies have found that relaxation and stress-management interventions can impact distress and positive gains in cancer patients (Antoni et al., 2001; Fawzy et al., 1990a; Larsson & Starrin, 1992).

As discussed earlier, the incidence of severe and long-lasting distress in recently diagnosed cancer patients varies. Nevertheless, it is estimated that some patients will exhibit symptoms of moderate to severe depression. Pharmacotherapy, interpersonal therapy, and cognitive therapy all have been shown to be effective forms of treatment for depression (Barlow, 1996). Medication is recommended for patients who suffer from severe depression or those with longstanding moderate depression that has been resistant to psychotherapy (Lloyd-Williams, 2000). Among cancer patients referred for psychiatric evaluation, up to two-thirds may be appropriate candidates for antidepressant medication (Chaturvedi, Maguire & Hopwood, 1994). It is important that psychologists or other medical staff working with cancer patients pay close attention to levels of distress and work closely with psychiatrists (preferably who specialize in oncology) who can prescribe and monitor psychotropic medications. Early identification and management of depression among cancer patients is important so that patients may receive optimal treatment for both psychological and physical symptoms (Berney et al., 2000; Lloyd-Williams, 2000).

Controlling Treatment-related Responses and Behaviors

Interventions that instruct patients in self-help techniques to help to control treatment side-effects can have an enormous impact on quality of life as well as adherence to treatment (Redd, Montgomery & DuHamel, 2001). Psychological interventions targeting specific treatment-related responses or behaviors (see Table 7.6) have been proven effective in a number of studies (e.g., Andersen & Tewfik, 1985; Burish, Snyder & Jenkins, 1991; Burish et al., 1987; Decker, Cline & Gallagher, 1992; Vasterling et al., 1993). Because chemotherapy may induce various gastrointestinal symptoms, patients may develop anticipatory nausea; similarly, because radiotherapy procedures may induce fear reactions (including claustrophobia

Table 7.6 Interventions used to treat side-effects of medical treatment

Techniques and examples	Population	Targeted effect
Behavioral strategies:		
Contingency management	Children	Increase adherence
Systematic desensitization	Adults	Decrease anxiety/phobias
Modeling	Children	Decrease anxiety, increase adherence
Cognitive strategy:		
Cognitive restructuring	Adults	Decrease anxiety, increase adherence
Relaxation training:		
Hypnosis/imagery	Children/adults	Decrease pain, anxiety and fatigue
Relaxation training	Adolescents/adults	Decrease pain, anxiety and fatigue
Meditation	Adults	Decrease pain, anxiety and fatigue
Exercise interventions:		
Structured exercise programs	Adults	Decrease fatigue
Mind–body programs (e.g., yoga)	Adults	Decrease anxiety, fatigue, pain

related to the treatment machines), patients may develop anticipatory anxiety. If such symptoms increase in severity, a patient may become non-compliant with treatment. Therefore, the interventions focused on direct treatment-related effects may be effective in improving not only the presenting symptoms but also compliance with future treatment.

Controlling Physical Effects of Disease and Treatment

Very few studies have specifically examined the effectiveness of non-pharmaceutical interventions for the treatment of cancer-related fatigue (CRF). Suggested psychological interventions for CRF include education about fatigue and sleep hygiene (Fortin & Kirouac, 1976), stress-reduction/relaxation and psychotherapy (Cimprich, 1993), and exercise. However, there are no empirically tested guidelines that suggest the appropriate type or amount of exercise for cancer patients with CRF (Dimeo, Rumberger & Keul, 1998; Schwartz, 1998; Schwartz et al., 2001; Segal et al., 2001).

Pharmacological treatment of cancer pain may involve the use of non-opioid analgesics for mild to moderate pain and opioid analgesics for moderate to severe pain, with adjuvant analgesics (e.g., antidepressants, neuroleptics, psychostimulants, anticonvulsants, corticosteroids, and oral anesthetics) accompanying the opioid or non-opioid analgesics when indicated (Breitbart & Payne, 1998). Non-pharmacological interventions recommended for treating cancer-related pain and associated psychological symptoms include individual and group interventions composed of any of the following techniques: psychotherapy, cognitive-behavior therapy, relaxation exercises, imagery/distraction exercises, hypnosis, and/or biofeedback (Breitbart & Payne, 1998).

Changing Health-related Behaviors

As described above, primary prevention programs are aimed at modifying health-related behaviors (such as smoking, diet, or exercise) that are associated with increased vulnerability to the development of cancer. Similar lifestyle modification programs can be tailored to cancer patients. Programs may assist patients in developing new health behaviors that will decrease the probability of recurrence or the development of new cancers as well as limiting the development of other comorbid conditions, such as coronary heart disease, diabetes, or pulmonary disease (Demark-Wahnefried et al., 2000; Pinto, Eakin & Maruyama, 2000). Although there are few studies that include health behavior interventions for cancer patients, the results of dietary studies (Chlebowski et al., 1993; Kristal et al., 1997; Nordevang et al., 1992; Pierce et al., 1997) and exercise (Dimeo, Rumberger & Keul, 1998; Stoll, 1996) are promising. Unfortunately, research examining smoking cessation programs for cancer patients has shown relatively low long-term quit rates (Andersen, 2002).

Enhancing Health Outcome

Because psychological distress is associated with neuroendocrine and immune functioning, interventions have been designed to improve functioning of these systems. Cancer patients are vulnerable to profound changes in distress, fatigue, pain and general quality of life that may modulate neuroendocrine functions associated with disease progression (Andersen, Kiecolt-Glaser & Glaser, 1994; Andersen et al., 1998; Herbert & Cohen, 1993a, 1993b; Ironson, Antoni & Lutgendorf, 1995). The chronic challenge of dealing with cancer may play a role in neuroendocrine dysregulation that can lead to changes in immunity that may, in turn, contribute to disease progression (Turner-Cobb et al., 2000). Psychosocial interventions may impact stress-related variables and/or facilitate positive adaptations that may alter neuroendocrine and immune functions. It has been hypothesized that improvements in neuroendocrine and immune system functioning resulting from psychosocial interventions may lead to improved survival for the patients participating in the interventions. Although there are a few studies that have noted changes in immune or neuroendocrine measures related to psychological interventions (Cruess et al., 2000; Fawzy et al., 1990b; Gruber et al., 1993), evidence of a direct impact of psychosocial interventions on health outcomes is less compelling. To date, the handful of studies reporting on the impact of individual and group interventions on survival has lead to both positive (Fawzy et al., 1993; Kuchler et al., 1999; Ratcliffe, Dawson & Walker, 1995; Richardson et al., 1990; Spiegel et al., 1989) and negative findings (Cunningham et al., 1998; Edelman et al., 1999; Goodwin et al., 2001). Nevertheless, almost all of the studies examining the impact of a group intervention on patient survival have identified significant psychological and quality of life benefits (Spiegel, 2001).

Interventions of Different Modalities

Individual Interventions

Following a diagnosis of cancer, some patients may seek out individual psychotherapy or counseling aimed at decreasing distress and enhancing the recovery process. The screening of cancer patients may also identify those in need of additional psychological services. Individual therapy may range from cognitive-behavior therapy, focusing on the restructuring of negative thoughts and feelings, to emotional-expressive or supportive psychotherapy (see Table 7.5). Overall, the aim of individual therapy is to help the patient to adjust to changes associated with the diagnosis and to make plans for the future. Involvement in psychotherapy following a life-threatening event, such as the diagnosis and treatment of cancer, can be particularly productive because the patient may be ready to make changes in his or her life and to re-evaluate values and goals. Recent studies suggest that interventions with cancer patients can lead to decreases in distress and higher quality of life (Allen et al., 2000; Marchioro et al., 1996).

Group Interventions

Despite the fact that few studies have directly compared the efficacy of group versus individual treatment, available evidence indicates that both individual and group interventions are effective in reducing psychological and/or physical symptoms among oncology patients (Andersen, 2002; Fawzy, 1999; Sheard & Maguire, 1999). More recently, research in this area has focused on positive outcome measures that include positive feelings and positive growth (Andrykowski, Brady & Hunt, 1993; Antoni et al., 2001; Cordova et al., 2001).

One might presume that a structured group intervention may be more efficacious because it allows cancer patients to get emotional support and share information with those who have had similar experience. Group participants have the opportunity to practice new skills with other patients and witness how others handle the multiple stressors associated with cancer treatment and cancer survivorship. When planning group interventions, it is important to consider the membership of the group. The concerns and issues raised by group members may vary according to the site of the cancer. For example, breast cancer patients may raise issues related to sexuality, body image and relationship difficulties (Anllo, 2000; Carver et al., 1998). Head and neck cancer patients may be concerned about aspects of their appearance (such as weight loss or visible tattoos related to radiation) and problems associated with their treatment, such as loss of taste and smell, problems swallowing, and difficulties with verbal communication (De Boer et al., 1999; Moadel, Ostruff & Schantz, 1998). Those diagnosed with lung cancer often struggle with feelings of guilt and remorse because, for many of them, the cancer developed as a result of tobacco use (Faller, Schilling & Lang, 1995). Additionally, the severity of disease and stage of illness are important factors to consider. For example, the issues associated with a newly diagnosed cancer (primary tumor) are very different from those associated with disease progression or recurrence. For the group participants to optimally benefit, it is important to maintain some level of commonality among the members.

There is continued debate about the most effective type of group intervention. Some argue that the main purpose of a group intervention is to foster a feeling of cohesion and a safe environment where group members can talk about some of their feelings and experiences related to cancer (e.g., Spiegel's supportive-expressive group therapy). Others argue that psycho-educational groups provide more longlasting changes (Hegleson et al., 2000). While different types of interventions produce positive results, interventions that have demonstrated effectiveness contain the components of education, coping, emotional support, and psychotherapy. More thorough summaries of group interventions with cancer patients are available in several review articles (e.g., Fawzy, 1999; Fawzy et al., 1995; Spira, 1998).

Interventions with Families of Cancer Patients

Comprehensive reviews of research on the psychosocial functioning of the spouses, family members, and/or caregivers of adults with cancer (e.g., Lewis, 1986; Northouse, 1984; Sales,

1991) suggest that these significant others display levels of distress similar to those of the patients. While many display only slightly elevated distress, some display more significant psychological problems. Furthermore, the significant others' adjustment may be affected by the course of the disease, interactions with and needs of the patients, and levels of external support. Therefore, patients who are identified as in need of psychosocial services may also have spouses or family members who could benefit from services. Descriptive studies of interventions with significant others of cancer patients suggest that the interventions may produce positive results (Berger, 1984; Carter & Carter, 1994; Cohen, 1982; Cohen & Wellisch, 1978; Reele, 1994; Sabo, Brown & Smith, 1986; Walsh-Burke, 1992). Although controlled studies (e.g., Christensen, 1983; Goldberg & Wool, 1985; Heinrich & Schag, 1985; Toseland, Blanchard & McCallion, 1995) have yielded few significant results, the interventions appear to have been associated with improved functioning for some participants.

Family Therapy

When a family member is diagnosed with cancer, all members of the family are affected in some way. Cohen and Wellisch (1978) proposed that the cancer diagnosis can be viewed as an "accent" on the family's typical mode of functioning, which may result in either increased or decreased engagement among family members. When presenting for family therapy, the family may identify the cancer diagnosis as the primary problem, overlooking how all family members' reactions to the diagnosis may affect the functioning of the family (Cohen, 1982). The family therapist must assess the family's developmental level, unique style, and patterns of interaction in order to best assist the family in adjusting to changes precipitated by the cancer diagnosis. The therapist should also consider how the roles of each family member have changed since the diagnosis.

Couples Therapy

While focusing on the needs of loved ones diagnosed with cancer, spouses may overlook their own needs. In couples therapy, the needs of both the patient with cancer and his or her spouse should be directly addressed; this may require effort to shift focus from the patient to the spouse or to the relationship of the couple. In fact, the focus of the intervention may be learning to balance the needs of the patient and spouse so that both can provide support for each other. At the same time, consideration should be given to issues specific to the patient's diagnosis and treatment. For example, couples therapy following mastectomy for breast cancer may focus on issues of body image and sexuality that affect both the patient and her partner (Christensen, 1983).

SUMMARY AND CONCLUSIONS

Worldwide, it is estimated that 5 318 000 new cases of cancer will have been diagnosed and 3 522 000 people will have died from cancer in 2000 (Ferlay et al., 2001). Cancer is the third leading cause of death among adults internationally, with only cardiovascular disease and infectious/parasitic disease claiming more lives (WHO, 2001). Across geographic regions, incidence and mortality rates for specific cancers may vary based on environmental and lifestyle factors; however, the overall burden of cancer incidence and mortality is relatively evenly divided across developed and developing countries (Ferlay et al., 2001; Parkin, Pisani & Ferlay, 1999). Because the prevalence of cancer increases with age, the cancer incidence and mortality rates are expected to increase as the population continues to age. Given the number of people affected by cancer—and the likelihood that the number will continually increase—there is an ever-increasing need for clinical health psychologists to become involved in oncology.

As this review demonstrates, the field of psycho-oncology is extremely broad—and it continues to expand. Contributions to the field have come not only from clinical health psychology, but also from psychiatry, social work, nursing, epidemiology, and public health. Oncology offers a unique opportunity for psychologists to contribute to the care and well-being of a varied population that includes those at risk for the development of cancer as well as those with a diagnosis of cancer. Due to the importance of lifestyle factors in the development of cancer and psychological factors in early detection behavior, clinical health psychologists can assist in the design and implementation of behavior change strategies to improve both primary and secondary prevention. The fact that a high number of cancer patients report elevated distress and decreased quality of life indicates that there is ample opportunity for clinical health psychologists to provide an array of psychosocial interventions. Additionally, clinical health psychologists can serve a vital role in consultation and in education of medical staff involved in the care of cancer patients. Lastly, there are numerous opportunities for clinical health psychologists to become involved in research within the area of psycho-oncology. In a recent publication, Holland (2002) identified a number of areas for future research that included behavioral research focusing on lifestyle and health behaviors associated with cancer prevention for those at risk for cancer as well as cancer survivors; examination of behaviors and attitudes that impact screening and early detection of cancer; interventions to assist with symptom control during treatment; research examining the psychosocial issues of cancer survivors; continued investigation into the impact of psychosocial programs on biological variables as well as long-term survival; and the management of the psychosocial aspects of palliative and end of life care.

REFERENCES

Ainsleigh, H.G. (1993). Beneficial effects of sun exposure on cancer mortality. *Preventive Medicine*, **22**, 132–140.

Allen, S.M., Shah, A.C., Nezu, A.M., Nezu, C.M., Ciambrone, D., Hogan, J. & Mor, V. (2000). A problem-solving approach to stress reduction among younger women with breast cancer: a randomized controlled trial. *Cancer*, **94**, 3089–3100.

Andersen, B.L. (1992). Psychological interventions for cancer patients to enhance the quality of life. *Journal of Consulting and Clinical Psychology*, **60**, 552–568.

Andersen, B.L. (2002). Biobehavioral outcomes following psychological interventions for cancer patients. *Journal of Consulting and Clinical Psychology*, **70**, 590–610.

Andersen, B.L. & Tewfik, H.H. (1985). Psychological reactions to radiation therapy: reconsideration of the adaptive aspects of anxiety. *Journal of Personality and Social Psychology*, **48**, 1024–1032.

Andersen, B.L., Kiecolt-Glaser, J.K. & Glaser, R. (1994). A biobehavioral model of cancer stress and disease course. *American Psychologist*, **49**, 389–404.

Andersen, B.L., Farrar, W.B., Golden-Kreutz, D., Kutz, L.A., MacCallum, R., Courtney, M.E. et al. (1998). Stress and immune responses after surgical treatment for regional breast cancer. *Journal of the National Cancer Institute*, **90**, 30–36.

Andrykowski, M.A., Brady, M.J. & Hunt, J.W. (1993). Positive psychosocial adjustment in potential bone marrow transplant recipients: cancer as a psychosocial transition. *Psycho-oncology*, **2**, 261–276.

Anllo, L.M. (2000). Sexual life after breast cancer. *Journal of Sex and Marital Therapy*, **26**, 241–248.

Antoni, M.H., Lehman, J.M., Kilbourn, K.M., Boyers, A.E., Culver, J.L., Alferi, S.M. et al. (2001). Cognitive-behavioral stress management intervention decreases the prevalence of depression and enhances benefit finding among women under treatment for early-stage breast cancer. *Health Psychology*, **20**, 20–32.

Armstrong, B.K. (1988). Epidemiology of malignant melanoma: intermittent or total accumulated exposure to the sun? *Journal of Dermatologic Surgery and Oncology*, **14**, 835–849.

Auchincloss, S.S. & McCartney, C.F. (1998). Gynecologic cancer. In J.C. Holland (Ed.), *Psychooncology* (pp. 359–370). New York: Oxford University Press.

Barlow, D.H. (1996). Health care policy, psychotherapy research, and the future of psychotherapy. *American Psychologist*, **51**, 1050–1058.

Beck, A.T., Ward, C.H., Mendelson, M., Mock, J. & Erbaugh, J. (1961). An inventory for measuring depression. *Archives of General Psychiatry*, **4**, 561–571.

Berger, J. (1984). Crisis intervention: a drop-in support group for cancer patients and their families. *Social Work in Health Care*, **10**, 81–92.

Berney, A., Stiefel, F., Mazzocato, C. & Buclin, T. (2000). Psychopharmacology in supportive care of cancer: a review for the clinician. III. Antidepressants. *Supportive Care in Cancer*, **8**, 278–286.

Bloom, J.R. (1994). Early detection of cancer: psychologic and social dimensions. *Cancer*, **74**, 1464–1473.

Bostick, R.M., Sprafka, J.M., Virnig, B.A. & Potter, J.D. (1993). Knowledge, attitudes, and personal practices regarding prevention and early detection of cancer. *Preventive Medicine*, **22**, 65–85.

Breen, N., Wagener, D.K., Brown, M.L., Davis, W.W. & Ballard-Barbash, R. (2001). Progress in cancer screening over a decade: results of cancer screening from the 1987, 1992, and 1998 National Health Interview Surveys. *Journal of the National Cancer Institute*, **93**, 1704–1713.

Breitbart, W. & Payne, D.K. (1998). Pain. In J.C. Holland (Ed.), *Psychooncology* (pp. 450–467). New York: Oxford University Press.

Burish, T.G., Snyder, S.L. & Jenkins, R.A. (1991). Preparing patients for cancer chemotherapy: effect of coping preparation and relaxation interventions. *Journal of Consulting and Clinical Psychology*, **59**, 518–525.

Burish, T.G., Carey, M.P., Krozely, M.K. & Greco, F.A. (1987). Conditioned side effects induced by cancer chemotherapy: prevention through behavioral treatment. *Journal of Consulting and Clinical Psychology*, **55**, 42–48.

Carter, C.A. & Carter, R.E. (1994). Some observations on individual and marital therapy with breast cancer patients and their spouses. *Journal of Psychosocial Oncology*, **12**, 65–81.

Carver, C.S., Pozo, C., Harris, S.D., Noriega, V., Scheier, M.F., Robinson, D.S. et al. (1993). How coping mediates the effect of optimism on distress: a study of women with early-stage breast cancer. *Journal of Personality and Social Psychology*, **65**, 375–390.

Carver, C.S., Pozo-Kaderman, C., Price, A.A., Noriega, V., Harris, S.D., Derhagopian, R.P. et al. (1998). Concern about aspects of body image and adjustment to early stage breast cancer. *Psychosomatic Medicine*, **60**, 168–174.

Cella, D.F. (1997). The Functional Assessment of Cancer Therapy—Anemia (FACT-An) scale: a new tool for the assessment of outcomes in cancer anemia and fatigue. *Seminars in Hematology*, **34** (3, Suppl. 2), 13–19.

Cella, D. (1998). Factors influencing quality of life in cancer patients: anemia and fatigue. *Seminars in Oncology*, **25** (Suppl. 7), 43–46.

Cella, D.F. & Tross, S. (1986). Psychological adjustment to survival from Hodgkin's disease. *Journal of Consulting and Clinical Psychology*, **54**, 616–622.

Cella, D.F., Tulsky, D.S., Gray, G., Sarafian, B., Linn, E., Bonomi, A., Silberman, M., Yellen, S.B., Winicour, P., Brannon, J., Eckberg, K., Lioyd, S., Zpurl, S., Blendowski, C., Goodman, M., Barnicle, M., Stewart, I., McHale, M., Bonomi, P., Kaplan, E., Taylor, S., IV, Thomas, C.R., Jr & Harris, J. (1993). The Functional Assessment of Cancer Therapy Scale: development and validation of the general measure. *Journal of Clinical Oncology*, **11**, 570–579.

Chaturvedi, S., Maguire, P. & Hopwood, P. (1994). Antidepressant medications in cancer patients. *Psycho-oncology*, **3**, 57–60.

Chlebowski, R.T., Blackburn, G.L., Buzzard, M., Rose, D.P., Martino, S., Khandekar, J.D. et al. (1993). Adherence to a dietary fat intake reduction program in postmenopausal women receiving therapy for early breast cancer. *Journal of Clinical Oncology*, **11**, 2072–2080.

Christensen, D.N. (1983). Post-mastectomy couple counseling: an outcome study of a structured treatment protocol. *Journal of Sex and Marital Therapy*, **9**, 266–275.

Cimprich, B. (1993). Developing an intervention to restore attention in cancer patients. *Cancer Nursing*, **16**, 83–92.

Cohen, M.M. (1982). In the presence of your absence: the treatment of older families with a cancer patient. *Psychotherapy: Theory, Research and Practice*, **19**, 453–460.

Cohen, M.M. & Wellisch, D.K. (1978). Living in Limbo: psychosocial intervention in families with a cancer patient. *American Journal of Psychotherapy*, **32**, 561–571.

Cole, B. & Pargament, K. (1999). Re-creating your life: a spiritual/psychotherapeutic intervention for people diagnosed with cancer. *Psycho-oncology*, **8**, 395–407.

Cordova, M.J., Cunningham, L.L.C., Carlson, C.R. & Andrykowski, M.A. (2001). Posttraumatic growth following breast cancer: a controlled comparison study. *Health Psychology*, **20**, 176–185.

Cruess, D.G., Antoni, M.H., McGregor, B.A., Kilbourn, K.M., Boyers, A.E., Alferi, S.M. et al. (2000). Cognitive-behavioral stress management reduces serum cortisol by enhancing benefit finding among women being treated for early stage breast cancer. *Psychosomatic Medicine*, **62**, 304–308.

Cunningham, A.J., Edmonds, C.V., Jenkins, G.P., Pollack, H., Lockwood, G.A. & Warr, D. (1998). A randomized controlled trial of the effects of group psychological therapy on survival in women with metastatic breast cancer. *Psycho-oncology*, **7**, 508–517.

Daut, R.L. & Cleeland, C.S. (1982). The prevalence and severity of pain in cancer. *Cancer*, **50**, 1913–1918.

Daut, R.L., Cleeland, C.S. & Flanery, R.C. (1983). Development of the Wisconsin Brief Pain Questionnaire to assess pain in cancer and other diseases. *Pain*, **17**, 197–210.

De Boer, M.F., McCormick, L.K., Pruyn, J.F., Ryckman, R.M. & van den Borne, B.W. (1999). Physical and psychosocial correlates of head and neck cancer: a review of the literature. *Otolaryngol Head Neck Surgery*, **120**, 427–436.

Decker, T.W., Cline, E.J. & Gallagher, M. (1992). Relaxation therapy as an adjunct in radiation oncology. *Journal of Clinical Psychology*, **48**, 388–393.

Demark-Wahnefried, W., Peterson, B., McBride, C., Lipkus, I. & Clipp, E. (2000). Current health behaviors and readiness to pursue life-style changes among men and women diagnosed with early stage prostate and breast carcinomas. *Cancer*, **88**, 674–684.

Derogatis, L.R. (1983a). *Psychological Adjustment to Illness Scale: Administration, Scoring, and Procedures*. Baltimore: Clinical Psychometric Research.

Derogatis, L.R. (1983b). *The SCL-90 Administration, Scoring, and Procedures Manual, I*. Baltimore: Clinical Psychometric Research.

Derogatis, L.R. (1993). *The Brief Symptom Inventory: Administration, Scoring, and Procedures Manual*. Minneapolis, MN: National Computer Systems.

Derogatis, L.R., Morrow, G.R., Fetting, J.H., Penman, D., Piasetsky, S., Schmale, A.M. et al. (1983). The prevalence of psychiatric disorders among cancer patients. *Journal of the American Medical Association*, **249**, 751–757.

Dimeo, F., Rumberger, B.G. & Keul, J. (1998). Aerobic exercise as therapy for cancer fatigue. *Medicine and Science in Sports and Exercise*, **30**, 475–478.

Durning, P.E., Jump, R.L., Bishop, M.M. & Kilbourn, K.M. (2002, April). *Distress levels and interest in psychosocial services among radiotherapy patients*. Poster session presented at the annual meeting of the Society of Behavioral Medicine, Washington, DC.

Edelman, S., Lemon, J.A., Bell, D.R. & Kidman, A.D. (1999). Effect of group CBT on the survival time of patients with metastatic breast cancer. *Psycho-oncology*, **8**, 295–305.

Faller, H., Schilling, S. & Lang, H. (1995). Causal attribution and adaptation among lung cancer patients. *Journal of Psychosomatic Research*, **39**, 619–627.

Farber, J.M., Weinerman, B.H. & Kuypers, J.A. (1984). Psychosocial distress of oncology patients. *Journal of Psychosocial Oncology*, **2**, 109–118.

Fawzy, F.I. (1999). Psychosocial interventions for patients with cancer: what works and what doesn't. *European Journal of Cancer*, **35**, 1559–1564.

Fawzy, F.I. & Fawzy, N.W. (1998). Psychoeducational interventions. In J.C. Holland (Ed.), *Psychoon-cology* (pp. 676–693). New York: Oxford University Press.

Fawzy, F.I., Cousins, N., Fawzy, N., Kemeny, M.E., Elashoff, R. & Morton, D. (1990a). A structured psychiatric intervention for cancer patients: I. Changes over time in methods of coping and affective disturbance. *Archives of General Psychiatry*, **47**, 720–725.

Fawzy, F.I., Fawzy, N.W., Arndt, L.A. & Pasnau, R.O. (1995). Critical review of psychosocial inter-ventions in cancer care. *Archives of General Psychiatry*, **52**, 100–113.

Fawzy, F.I., Fawzy, N.W., Hyun, C.S., Elashoff, R., Guthrie, D., Fahey, J.L. et al. (1993). Malignant melanoma. Effects of an early structured psychiatric intervention, coping, and af-fective state on recurrence and survival 6 years later. *Archives of General Psychiatry*, **50**, 681–689.

Fawzy, F.I., Kemeny, M.E., Fawzy, N.W., Elashoff, R., Morton, D., Cousins, N. et al. (1990b). A structured psychiatric intervention for cancer patients. II. Changes over time in immunological measures. *Archives of General Psychiatry*, **47**, 729–735.

Ferlay, J., Bray, F., Pisani, P. & Parkin, D.M. (2001). *GLOBOCAN 2000: Cancer incidence, Mortality, and Prevalence Worldwide*. Version 1.0, IARC CancerBase No. 5. Lyon: IARC Press.

Fiore, M.C., Jorenby, D.E. & Baker, T.B. (1997). Smoking cessation: principles and practice based upon the AHCPR guideline, 1996. *Annals of Behavioral Medicine*, **19**, 213–219.

Fishman, B., Pasternak, S., Wallenstein, S.L., Houde, R.W., Holland, J.C. & Foley, K.M. (1987). The Memorial Pain Assessment Card: a valid instrument for the evaluation of cancer pain. *Cancer*, **60**, 1151–1158.

Foley, K.M. (1985). The treatment of cancer pain. *New England Journal of Medicine*, **63**, 845.

Fortin, F. & Kirouac, S. (1976). A randomized controlled trial of preoperative patient education. *International Journal of Nursing Studies*, **13**, 11–24.

Gettig, E., Marks, J.H. & Mulvihill, J.J. (1998). Genetic counseling for the oncology patient. In J.C. Holland (Ed.), *Psychooncology* (pp. 186–195). New York: Oxford University Press.

Goldberg, D. (1978). *Manual of the General Hospital Questionnaire*. Windsor, UK: NFER Publishing.

Goldberg, R.J. & Wool, M.S. (1985). Psychotherapy for the spouses of lung cancer patients: assessment of an intervention. *Psychotherapy and Psychosomatics*, **43**, 141–150.

Goodwin, P.J., Leszcz, M., Ennis, M., Koopmans, J., Vincent, L., Guther, H. et al. (2001). The effect of group psychosocial support on survival in metastatic breast cancer. *New England Journal of Medicine*, **345**, 1719–1726.

Gotay, C.C. & Stern, J.D. (1995). Assessment of psychological functioning in cancer patients. *Journal of Psychosocial Oncology*, **13**, 123–160.

Graham, C., Bond, S.S., Gerkovich, M.M. & Cook, M.R. (1980). Use of the McGill Pain Questionnaire in the assessment of cancer pain: replicability and consistency. *Pain*, **8**, 377–387.

Greaves-Otte, J.G.W., Greaves, J., Kruyt, P.M., van Leeuwen, O., van der Wouden, J.C. & van der Does, E. (1991). Problems at social reintegration of long-term cancer survivors. *European Journal of Cancer*, **27**, 178–181.

Greenberg, D.B. (1998). Radiotherapy. In J.C. Holland (Ed.), *Psychooncology* (pp. 269–276). New York: Oxford University Press.

Greenlee, R.T., Hill-Harmon, M.B., Murray, T. & Thun, M. (2001). Cancer statistics, 2001. *CA: Cancer Journal for Clinicians*, **51**, 15–36.

Greenwald, P. (1993). NCI cancer prevention and control. *Preventive Medicine*, **22**, 642–660.

Gruber, B.L., Hersh, S.P., Hall, N.R.S., Waletzky, L.R., Kunz, J.F., Carpenter, J.L. et al. (1993). Immunological responses of breast cancer patients to behavioral interventions. *Biofeedback and Self-Regulation*, **18**, 1–22.

Harrison, S.L., MacLennan, R., Speare, R. & Wronski, I. (1994). Sun exposure and melanocytic naevi in young Australian children. *Lancet*, **344**, 1529–1532.

Hegleson, V.S., Cohen, S., Schulz, R. & Yasko, J. (2000). Group support interventions for women with breast cancer: who benefits from what? *Health Psychology*, **19**, 107–114.

Heinrich, R.L. & Schag, C.C. (1985). Stress and activity management: group treatment for cancer patients and their spouses. *Journal of Consulting and Clinical Psychology*, **53**, 439–466.

Herbert, T. & Cohen, S. (1993a). Depression and immunity: a meta-analytic review. *Psychological Bulletin*, **113**, 472–486.

Herbert, T. & Cohen, S. (1993b). Stress and immunity in humans: a meta-analytic review. *Psychosomatic Medicine*, **41**, 209–218.

Holland, J.C. (Ed.) (1998). *Psychooncology*. New York: Oxford University Press.

Holland, J.C. (2001). Improving the human side of cancer care: psycho-oncology's contribution. *The Cancer Journal*, **7**, 458–471.

Holland, J.C. (2002). History of Psycho-oncology: overcoming attitudinal and conceptual barriers. *Psychosomatic Medicine*, **64**, 206–221.

Horowitz, M., Wilner, N. & Alvarez, W. (1979). Impact of event scale. *Psychosomatic Medicine*, **41**, 209–218.

Ironson, G., Antoni, M.H. & Lutgendorf, S. (1995). Can psychological interventions affect immunity and survival? Present findings and suggested targets with a focus on cancer and human immunodeficiency virus. *Mind/Body Medicine*, **1**, 85–110.

Irvine, D., Vincent, L., Graydon, J.E., Bubela, N. & Thompson, L. (1994). The prevalence and correlates of fatigue in patients receiving treatment with chemotherapy and radiotherapy: a comparison with the fatigue experienced by healthy individuals. *Cancer Nursing*, **17**, 367–378.

Kash, K.M. & Lerman, C. (1998). Psychological, social, and ethical issues in gene testing. In J.C. Holland (Ed.), *Psychooncology* (pp. 196–207). New York: Oxford University Press.

Kristal, A.R., Shattuck, A.L., Bowen, D.J., Sponzo, R.W. & Nixon, D.W. (1997). Feasibility of using volunteer research staff to deliver and evaluate a low-fat dietary intervention: the American Cancer Society Breast Cancer Dietary Intervention Project. *Cancer Epidemiology, Biomarkers and Prevention*, **6**, 459–467.

Kuchler, T., Henne-Bruns, D., Rappat, S., Graul, J., Holst, K., Williams, J.I. et al. (1999). Impact of psychotherapeutic support on gastrointestinal cancer patients undergoing surgery: survival results of a trial. *Hepato-gastroenterology*, **46**, 322–335.

Kushnir, T., Rabinowitz, S., Melamed, S., Weisberg, E. & Ribak, J. (1995). Health responsibility and workplace health promotion among women: early detection of cancer. *Health Care Women International*, **16**, 329–340.

Larsson, G. & Starrin, B. (1992). Relaxation training as an integral part of caring activities for cancer patients: effects on well-being. *Scandinavian Journal of Caring Sciences*, **6**, 179–186.

Lerman, C., Rimer, B., Trock, B., Balshem, A. & Engstrom, P.F. (1990). Factors associated with repeat adherence to breast cancer screening. *Preventive Medicine*, **19**, 279–290.

Lewis, F.M. (1986). The impact of cancer on the family: a critical analysis of the research literature. *Patient Education and Counseling*, **8**, 269–289.

Lloyd-Williams, W.M. (2000). Difficulties in diagnosing and treating depression in the terminally ill cancer patient. *Postgraduate Medical Journal*, **76**, 555–558.

Lundberg, J.C. & Passik, S.D. (1998). Alcohol and cancer. In J.C. Holland (Ed.), *Psychooncology* (pp. 45–48). New York: Oxford University Press.

Marchioro, G., Azzarello, G., Checchin, F., Perale, M., Segati, R., Sampognaro, E. et al. (1996). The impact of a psychological intervention on quality of life in non-metastatic breast cancer. *European Journal of Cancer*, **32A**, 1612–1615.

McCaul, K.D., Branstetter, A.D., Schroeder, D.M. & Glasgow, R.E. (1996). What is the relationship between breast cancer risk and mammography screening? A meta-analytic review. *Health Psychology*, **15**, 423–429.

McMillan, C., Smith, E.M. & Fisher, R.H. (1997). Perceived benefit and mental health after three types of disaster. *Journal of Consulting and Clinical Psychology*, **65**, 733–739.

McNair, D., Lorr, M. & Droppleman, L. (1971). *Manual for the Profile of Mood States*. San Diego: Educational and Industrial Testing Service.

Meyer, T.J. & Mark, M.M. (1995). Effects of psychosocial interventions with adult cancer patients: a meta-analysis of randomized experiments. *Health Psychology*, **14**, 101–108.

Moadel, A.B., Ostroff, J.S. & Schantz, S.P. (1998). Head and neck cancer. In J.C. Holland (Ed.), *Psychooncology* (pp. 314–323). New York: Oxford University Press.

Mor, V., Allen, S. & Malin, M. (1994). The psychosocial impact of cancer on older versus younger patients and their families. *Cancer*, **74** (7 Suppl.), 2118–2127.

Myers, R.E., Trock, B.J., Lerman, C., Wolf, T., Ross, E. & Engstrom, P.F. (1990). Adherence to colorectal cancer screening in an HMO population. *Preventive Medicine*, **19**, 502–514.

Nordevang, E., Callmer, E., Marmur, A. & Holm, L.E. (1992). Dietary intervention in breast cancer patients: effects on food choice. *European Journal of Clinical Nutition*, **46**, 387–396.

Northouse, L. (1984). The impact of cancer on the family: an overview. *Journal of Psychiatry in Medicine*, **14**, 215–243.

Osborne, M., Boyle, P. & Lipkin, M. (1997). Cancer Prevention. *Lancet*, **349** (Suppl. III), 27–30.

Parkes, C.M. (1971). Psychosocial transitions: a field for study. *Social Science and Medicine*, **5**, 101–115.

Parkin, D.M., Pisani, P. & Ferlay, J. (1999). Global cancer statistics. *CA: Cancer Journal for Clinicians*, **49**, 33–64.

Pierce, J.P., Faerber, S., Wright, F.A., Newman, V., Flatt, S.W. & Kealey, S. (1997). Feasibility of a randomized trial of a high-vegetable diet to prevent breast cancer recurrence. *Nutrition and Cancer*, **28**, 282–288.

Pinto, B.M., Eakin, E. & Maruyama, N.C. (2000). Health behavior change after a cancer diagnosis: what do we know and where do we go from here? *Annals of Behavioral Medicine*, **22**, 38–52.

Piper, B., Lindsey, A. & Dodd, M. (1991). Fatigue mechanisms in cancer patients: developing nursing theory. *Oncology Nursing Forum*, **14**, 17–23.

Portenoy, R. & Itri, L. (1999). Cancer-related fatigue: guidelines for evaluation and management. *The Oncologist*, **4**, 1–10.

Portenoy, R. & Miaskowski, C. (1998). Assessment and management of cancer-related fatigue. In A. Berger et al. (Eds), *Principles and Practice of Supportive Oncology* (pp. 109–1180). New York: Lippincott-Raven.

Radloff, L.S. (1977). The CES-D Scale: a self-report depression scale for research in the general population. *Applied Psychological Measurement*, **1**, 385–401.

Ratcliffe, M.A., Dawson, A.A. & Walker, L.G. (1995). Eysenck personality inventory L-scores in patients with Hodgkin's disease and non-Hodgkin's lymphoma. *Psycho-oncology*, **4**, 39–45.

Redd, W.H., Montgomery, G.H. & DuHamel, K.N. (2001). Behavioral intervention for cancer-treatment side-effects. *Journal of the National Cancer Institute*, **93**, 810–823.

Reele, B.L. (1994). Effect of counseling on quality of life for individuals with cancer and their families. *Cancer Nursing*, **17**, 101–112.

Richardson, A. (1995). Fatigue in cancer patients: a review of the literature. *European Journal of Cancer Care*, **4**, 20–32.

Richardson, J.L., Shelton, D.R., Krailo, M. & Levine, A.M. (1990). The effect of compliance with treatment on survival among patients with hematologic malignancies. *Journal of Clinical Oncology*, **8**, 356–364.

Rubenstein, L. (1994). Strategies to overcome barriers to early detection of cancer among older adults. *Cancer*, **74** (7 Suppl.), 2190–2193.

Sabo, D., Brown, J. & Smith, C. (1986). The male role and mastectomy: support groups and men's adjustment. *Journal of Psychosocial Oncology*, **4**, 19–31.

Sales, E. (1991). Psychosocial impact of the phase of cancer on the family: an updated review. *Journal of Psychosocial Oncology*, **9**, 1–18.

Schwartz, A.L. (1998). Patterns of exercise and fatigue in physically active cancer survivors. *Oncology Nursing Forum*, **25**, 485–491.

Schwartz, A.L., Mori, M., Gao, R., Nail, L.M. & King, M. (2001). Exercise reduces daily fatigue in women with breast cancer receiving chemotherapy. *Medicine and Science in Sports and Exercise*, **33**, 718–723.

Schwartz, A.L., Nail, L.M., Chen, S., Meek, P., Barsevick, A.M., King, M.E. et al. (2000). Fatigue patterns observed in patients receiving chemotherapy and radiotherapy. *Cancer Investigation*, **18**, 11–19.

Segal, R., Evans, W., Johnson, D., Smith, J., Colletta, S., Gayton, J. et al. (2001). Structured exercise improves physical functioning in women with stages I and II breast cancer: results of a randomized controlled trial. *Journal of Clinical Oncology*, **19**, 657–665.

Sheard, T. & Maguire, P. (1999). The effect of psychological interventions on anxiety and depression in cancer patients: results of two meta-analyses. *British Journal of Cancer*, **80**, 1770–1780.

Smets, E., Garssen, B., Schuster-Uitterhoeve, A. & de Haes, J. (1993). Fatigue in cancer patients. *British Journal of Cancer*, **68**, 220–224.

Smith, C.E., Fernengel, K., Holcroft, C. & Gerald, K. (1994). Metaanalysis of the associations between social support and health outcomes. *Annals of Behavioral Medicine*, **16**, 352–362.

Snall, J.L. & Buck, E.L. (1996). Increasing cancer screening: a meta-analysis. *Preventive Medicine*, **25**, 702–707.

Spiegel, D. (1994). Health caring. Psychosocial support for patients with cancer. *Cancer*, **74** (4 Suppl.), 1453–1457.

Spiegel, D. (2001). Mind matters—group therapy and survival in breast cancer. *New England Journal of Medicine*, **345**, 1767–1768.

Spiegel, D. & Bloom, J.R. (1983). Pain in metastatic breast cancer. *Cancer*, **52**, 341–345.

Spiegel, D., Bloom, J.R., Kraemer, H.C. & Gottheil, E. (1989). Effect of psychosocial treatment on survival of patients with metastatic breast cancer. *Lancet*, **2**, 888–891.

Spielberger, C., Gorsuch, R., Lushene, R., Vagg, P. & Jacobs, G. (1983). *Manual for the State-Trait Anxiety Inventory*. Palo Alto, CA: Consulting Psychologist Press.

Spira, J.L. (1998). Group therapies. In J.C. Holland (Ed.), *Psychooncology* (pp. 701–716). New York: Oxford University Press.

Stefanek, M.E., Derogatis, L.R. & Shaw, A. (1987). Psychosocial distress among oncology outpatients. *Psychosomatics*, **28**, 530–539.

Stein, K.D., Martin, S.C., Hann, D.M. & Jacobsen, P.B. (1998). A multidimensional measure of fatigue for use with cancer patients. *Cancer Practice*, **6**, 143–152.

Stoll, B.A. (1996). Diet and exercise regimens to improve breast carcinoma prognosis. *Cancer*, **78**, 2465–2470.

Tedeschi, R.G. & Calhoun, L.G. (1995). *Trauma and Transformation: Growing in the Aftermath of Suffering*. Thousand Oaks, CA: Sage.

Thomas, E.M. & Weiss, S.M. (2000). Nonpharmacological interventions with chronic cancer patients in adults. *Cancer Control*, **7**, 157–164.

Toseland, R.W., Blanchard, C.G. & McCallion, P. (1995). A problem solving intervention for caregivers of cancer patients. *Social Science and Medicine*, **40**, 517–528.

Tovian, S.M. (1991). Integration of clinical psychology into adult and pediatric oncology programs. In J.J. Sweet, R.H. Rozensky & S.M. Tovian (Eds), *Handbook of Clinical Psychology in Medical Settings* (pp. 331–352). New York: Plenum Press.

Turner-Cobb, J.M., Sephton, S.E., Koopman, C., Blake-Mortimer, J. & Spiegel, D. (2000). Social support and salivary cortisol in women with metastatic breast cancer. *Psychosomatic Medicine*, **62**, 337–345.

van't Spijker, A., Trijsburg, R.W. & Duivenvoorden, H.J. (1997). Psychological sequelae of cancer diagnosis: a meta-analytic review of 58 studies after 1980. *Psychosomatic Medicine*, **59**, 280–293.

Vasterling, J., Jenkins, R.A., Tope, D.M. & Burish, T.G. (1993). Cognitive distraction and relaxation training for the control of side effects due to cancer chemotherapy. *Journal of Behavioral Medicine*, **16**, 65–80.

Vogelzang, N., Breitbart, W., Cella, D., Curt, G.A., Groopman, J.E., Horning, S.J. et al. (1997). Patient, caregiver, and oncologist perceptions of fatigue: results of a tripartite assessment survey. *Seminars in Hematology*, **34** (Suppl. 2), 4–12.

Walsh-Burke, K. (1992). Family communication and coping with cancer: impact of the We Can Weekend. *Journal of Psychosocial Oncology*, **10**, 63–81.

Ware, J.E., Snow, K.K., Kosinski, M. & Gandek, B. (1993). *SF-36 Health Survey: Manual and Interpretation Guide*. Boston: The Health Institute, New England Medical Center.

Winningham, M., Nail, L., Burke, M., Brophy, L., Cimprich, B. & Jones, L.S. (1994). Fatigue and the cancer experience: the state of the knowledge. *Oncology Nursing Forum*, **16** (Suppl. 6), 27–34.

Winters, B.L. (1998). Diet and cancer. In J.C. Holland (Ed.), *Psychooncology* (pp. 49–57). New York: Oxford University Press.

WHO (1995). *National Cancer Control Programmes: Policies and Managerial Guidelines*. Geneva: World Health Organization.

WHO (2001). *World Health Report 2001: Mental Health: New Understanding, New Hope*. Geneva: World Health Organization.

Zabora, J.R. (1998). Screening procedures for psychosocial distress. In J.C. Holland (Ed.), *Psychooncology* (pp. 653–661). New York: Oxford University Press.

Zabora, J., Brintzenhofeszoc, K., Curbow, B., Hooker, C. & Piantadosi, S. (2001). The prevalence of psychological distress by cancer site. *Psycho-oncology*, **10**, 19–28.

Zigmond, A.S. & Snaith, R.P. (1983). The Hospital Anxiety and Depression Scale. *Acta Psychiatrica Scandinavica*, **67**, 361–370.

CHAPTER 8

Chronic Pain

Dennis C. Turk*
and
Elena S. Monarch
University of Washington, USA

INTRODUCTION

In most cases, acute pain is an adaptive response warning of potential bodily harm. When this signal reflects nociception—that is, an actual sensory event from peripheral sensory stimulation—it can be useful as a signal to prevent further injury to tissue. It is common to consider *pain* as synonymous with *nociception*. A clear distinction, however, must be made between these two separate but related phenomena. Nociception is limited to a sensory event and precedes the perception of pain. Although pain usually follows from nociception, non-sensory perceptual and interpretive processes such as cognition and emotion can modulate the perception and accompany the experience of pain. The International Association for the Study of Pain (Merskey & Bogduk, 1986) recognizes the distinction between nociception and pain by defining pain as "an unpleasant sensory *and* emotional experience associated with actual or *potential* tissue damage or *described* in terms of such damage" (emphasis added).

In the majority of cases physical factors instigate reports of pain. When pain is persistent, extending over many months and years, however, other factors, particularly psychosocial and behavioral ones, are capable of maintaining and exacerbating pain, influencing adjustment, and contributing to excessive disability. Research shows that these non-physiological factors, including fear, anger, beliefs, and contextual influences, can modulate the experience of pain (Turk & Okifuji, 2002).

Chronic pain poses a significant problem for the pain sufferer, the sufferer's significant others, the health care system, and society. Despite the prevalence of the problem, there is currently no adequate treatment that will completely eliminate pain for the majority of those afflicted. As we will illustrate in this chapter, chronic pain is a complex phenomenon with physical, psychosocial, and behavioral components. Failure to take into consideration each of these contributes to the failure of adequate treatment and excessive suffering. We will

---

* Please address all correspondence to Dr Dennis C. Turk.

Handbook of Clinical Health Psychology. Edited by S. Llewelyn and P. Kennedy.

begin by reviewing the most prominent models of chronic pain. Then we will discuss the important contributions of behavioral, cognitive, and affective factors to the experience of pain and briefly describe the components of psychological assessment. Next, we will outline a cognitive-behavioral approach to treatment of chronic pain patients, discuss how it has been incorporated within multidisciplinary rehabilitation programs, and summarize some of the outcomes of treatment. We will conclude with a discussion of some of the limitations of research highlighting some directions for future studies. Given this extensive agenda, we will obviously not be able to provide in-depth coverage of all the topics.

THEORETICAL PERSPECTIVES

Theoretical perspectives are important as they guide clinicians' assessment and treatment. Theoretical perspectives of pain can be grouped into two broad categories—unidimensional ones that focus on single causes of the symptoms, and multidimensional ones that focus on a range of factors.

Unidimensional Biomedical/Somatogenic Model

According to the biomedical or somatogenic view, the extent of pain reported should be proportional to the amount of detectable tissue damage. Health care providers often spend inordinate amounts of time and expense attempting to establish the specific link between tissue damage and pain reports. The expectation is that once *the* physical cause has been identified, appropriate treatment will follow. Biomedical treatment focuses on chemically or surgically eliminating the putative cause(s) of pain by removing the culprit or, failing that, by disrupting pain pathways.

There are, however, several perplexing findings related to chronic pain that do not fit within the biomedical model. One conundrum is that severe pain may be reported in the absence of any identified pathological processes. For example, in approximately 85% of cases, the cause of back pain is unknown (Deyo, 1986). Conversely, diagnostic imaging studies using computed tomography scans and magnetic resonance imaging have noted the presence of significant physical pathology in up to 35% of "asymptomatic" people (Jensen et al., 1994; Wiesel et al., 1984). Therefore, reports of significant pain are not always associated with identifiable pathology, and identifiable pathology is not always associated with reports of pain. Moreover, there is wide variation in response to identical treatments for patients with the same diagnosis.

Unidimensional Psychogenic Perspective

As is frequently the case in medicine, when physical explanations prove inadequate or "appropriate" treatments fail, psychological alternatives are invoked. This typically occurs when reported pain is deemed "disproportionate" (based on the opinion of someone else) to an objectively determined pathological process or if the report is recalcitrant to "appropriate" treatment.

Assessment based on the psychogenic perspective is directed toward identifying personality factors or psychopathological tendencies that initiate and maintain the reported pain.

Once identified, treatment is geared toward helping patients to gain "insight" into their maladaptive, predisposing psychological factors (Grzesiak, Ury & Dworkin, 1996). The assumption is that once patients become aware of the psychological causes of the symptoms they will be better able to deal with them and, as a result, the pain will be relieved. To date, there is no empirical evidence that insight is effective in alleviating chronic pain symptoms (Gamsa, 1994).

Unidimensional Motivational View

The motivational conceptualization is often posed as an alternative to the psychogenic perspective. From this view, a report of pain in the absence of or in excess of physical pathology is attributed to the patient's desire to obtain some benefit such as attention, time off from undesirable activities, or financial compensation. In contrast to the psychogenic perspective, a motivational view assumes that the patient's pain complaints are intentionally made in order to acquire desirable outcomes.

Assessment of patients from the motivational view focuses on identifying discrepancies between what patients say they are capable of doing and what they actually can do (Craig, Hill & McMurtry, 1998). A high degree of discrepancy between what the patient reports about his or her pain and physical functioning is taken as evidence that the patient is exaggerating or fabricating symptoms. Results of such assessments may be used to label patients as malingerers.

Treatment from the motivational perspective is simple: when there is a high degree of discrepancy between what patients claim and what they are observed to do—deny disability. The assumption is that denial of disability will lead to prompt resolution of the reported symptoms. Although this view is prevalent, especially among third-party payers, there is little evidence of dramatic variation of symptoms following denial of disability.

Unidimensional Operant Conditioning (Learning) Model

In 1976 Fordyce extended principles of operant conditioning to chronic pain. The main focus of operant conditioning is modification of the targeted behaviors that are maintained by their reinforcement contingencies. If the consequence of the given behavior is rewarding, the likelihood of its recurrence increases; if the consequence is aversive, the likelihood of its recurrence decreases.

The operant model focuses on "pain behaviors". These include verbal complaints (e.g., moaning), motor behaviors (e.g., limping), and help-seeking behaviors (e.g., requesting medications). These behaviors are hypothesized to serve a communicative function informing others that one is suffering. In acute pain, overt pain behaviors most likely result from reflexive avoidance of pain and serve as protective mechanisms to prevent further injury or the aggravation of existing symptoms. In chronic pain, however, there is only a modest correlation between intensity of pain and frequency of pain behaviors, suggesting that people do not exhibit pain behaviors simply because their pain is more intense (Fordyce et al., 1984). Other factors, acquired through operant (e.g., reinforcement schedules) and respondent processes (e.g., stimulus generalization), appear to influence the frequency of pain behaviors. Positive reinforcement, such as receiving sympathetic attention from others, and negative reinforcement, such as avoiding bothersome household chores, may underlie or at least contribute to the maintenance of pain behaviors (Romano et al., 1992; Turk, Kerns & Rosenberg, 1992). Operant processes are also involved in reduction of activity when physical performance and "well behaviors" are not adequately rewarded—more positive behaviors are extinguished and patients may become more disabled. The operant learning paradigm does not address the etiology of pain but focuses primarily on maintenance of pain behaviors and deficiency of well behaviors.

Operant treatment methods focus on changing reinforcement schedules of behaviors that may be related to pain. For example, pain behaviors can be minimized by withdrawal of attention and well behaviors can be increased by provision of attention.

Although operant factors may play an important role in the maintenance of disability, the unidimensional operant model has been criticized. Its exclusive focus on reinforcement does not integrate other factors such as sensory, emotional, and cognitive factors in the overall pain experience (Schmidt, 1985; Turk & Flor, 1987).

The biomedical, psychogenic, motivational, and operant views described are unidimensional in that the report of pain is ascribed to *either* physical *or* psychological factors. A growing body of evidence suggests that both physical *and* psychological components interact to create and influence the experience of pain.

Multidimensional Gate Control Model

The first attempt to develop an integrative model of chronic pain was the gate control theory (GCT) described by Melzack and Wall (1965). This model proposes the integration of peripheral stimuli with cortical variables, such as mood and cognitive processes, in the perception of pain. From the GC perspective, the experience of pain is an ongoing sequence of activities, largely reflexive at the outset, but modifiable even in the earliest stages by a variety of excitatory and inhibitory influences and by the integration of ascending and descending nervous system activity. Considerable potential for shaping the pain experience is implied because this theory invokes continuous interaction of multiple systems, specifically, sensory-discriminative, motivational-affective, and cognitive-evaluative.

Specifically, the GCT proposes that a *gate* is located in the dorsal horn of the spinal cord, the area responsible for receiving sensory input from the periphery. Within the dorsal horn, the substantia gelatinosa is thought to act as a spinal gating mechanism by modulating sensory input according to the balance of activity of large- and small-diameter fibers. According to Melzack and Wall (1965) the relative amount of excitatory activity in afferent, large-diameter (myelinated) and small-diameter (unmyelinated) fibers converging in the dorsal horns influences the spinal gating mechanism. Activity in large-diameter fibers tends to inhibit transmission of nociceptive signals and closes the gate while activity in small-diameter fibers tends to facilitate transmission (opens the gate) and prolong pain. In this way, it can inhibit or facilitate transmission of nerve impulses from the body to the brain. Melzack and Wall assert that the spinal gating mechanism is influenced not only by peripheral afferent activity but also by efferent neural impulses that descend *from* the brain. Within the brain, they suggest that the reticular formation functions as a central biasing mechanism. In this way, inhibition of the transmission of pain signals can occur at multiple synaptic levels of the somatosensory system.

The GCT's emphasis on the modulation of inputs in the dorsal horns and the dynamic role of the brain in pain processes and perception instigated the integration of psychological variables such as past experience, emotion, attention, and other cognitive activities into current pain research and therapy. Whereas prior to this formulation psychological processes were largely dismissed as reactions to pain, this new model suggested that treatments involving other factors from the brain were capable of modulating input. This theory promoted the idea that cutting nerves and pathways was insufficient and raised the importance of assessing and treating more than the anatomical and physiological parts of a person.

The physiological details of the GC model have been challenged, and it has been suggested that the model is incomplete. As additional knowledge has been gathered, specific points of posited mechanisms have required revision and reformulation. The theory does not include environmental and operant factors, and although it provides a conceptual basis for the role of psychological factors in pain, it does not address the nature of the interaction in any depth. Despite these shortcomings, the GCT has proven remarkably resilient and flexible in the face of accumulating scientific data and challenges. It continues to provide a powerful summary of the phenomena observed in the spinal cord and brain, and it has the capacity to explain many of the most mysterious and puzzling problems encountered in the clinic.

Multidimensional Biopsychosocial Model

The biopsychosocial model proposes that dynamic and reciprocal interactions among biological, psychological, and sociocultural variables shape the experience of pain (e.g., Turk, 1996; Turk & Flor, 1999). This model differs from the GCT in that it includes operant influences and gives greater attention to articulating the myriad of cognitive and affective influences. According to the biopsychosocial model, the pain experience begins when physiological changes produce peripheral nociceptive sensations within a conscious person with a prior learning history and within an idiosyncratic context. Peripheral fibers transmit these sensations but such sensations are not yet considered pain until subjected to higher order psychological and mental processing that involves appraisals. Unique appraisals and environmental circumstances influence people's responses and thereby explain the great variation in responses observed.

The biopsychosocial model incorporates cognitive-behavioral concepts in understanding chronic pain. Several assumptions characterize the cognitive-behavioral approach. One assumption is that both the environment and the person reciprocally determine behavior. People not only respond to their environment but elicit responses by their behavior. The person who becomes aware of a physical event (symptoms) and decides that the symptom requires attention from a health care provider initiates a set of circumstances different from a person with the same symptom who chooses to self-manage symptoms. Another assumption of the cognitive-behavioral perspective is that, in the same way as people are instrumental in the development and maintenance of maladaptive thoughts, feelings, and behaviors, they can, are, and should be considered active agents of change. Patients with chronic pain, despite their common beliefs to the contrary, are not helpless pawns of fate. They are instrumental in learning and carrying out more effective modes of responding.

Chronic pain sufferers often develop negative expectations about their own ability to exert any control over their pain. Maladaptive appraisals about their condition, situation, and their personal efficacy in controlling their pain or associated problems may lead to over-reaction to nociceptive stimulation, reduced effort, reduced perseverance in the face of difficulty, reduced activity, and increased psychological distress. Negative expectations may lead to feelings of frustration and demoralization. Pain sufferers frequently terminate efforts to develop new strategies to manage pain and reduce emotional distress, and instead turn to passive coping strategies such as inactivity, medication, or alcohol. They also absolve themselves of personal responsibility for managing their pain, and instead rely on family and health care providers. But research studies show that these potentially controllable factors (e.g., passive coping) contribute to the exacerbation, attenuation, and maintenance of pain, pain behaviors, affective distress, and dysfunctional adjustment to chronic pain (e.g., Council et al., 1988). The specific thoughts and feelings that patients experience prior to, during, or after an episode of pain can greatly influence the experience of pain.

From the biopsychosocial perspective, biomedical factors that may have initiated the original report of pain play a diminishing role in disability over time; secondary problems associated with deconditioning may exacerbate and maintain the problem. Inactivity leads to increased focus on and preoccupation with the body and pain, and these cognitive-attentional changes increase the likelihood of overemphasizing and misinterpreting symptoms, and perceiving oneself as being disabled.

CONTRIBUTION OF PSYCHOLOGICAL FACTORS

We will describe the various contributions of behavioral, cognitive, and affective factors in separate sections. It will become obvious, however, that they interact and are not independent.

Behavioral Influences on Pain

As noted, pain behaviors can be positively reinforced. They may also be maintained by escape from noxious stimulation through the use of drugs, rest, or avoidance of undesirable activities such as work. In addition, well behaviors (e.g., working) may not be positively reinforced by significant others, allowing pain behaviors to be more rewarding.

Health care professionals may reinforce pain and pain behavior by their responses. Physicians who prescribe medication when they observe pain behavior may, ironically, contribute to the occurrence of future pain behaviors. Patients learn that complaints elicit responses from physicians, and if these responses provide some relief of pain, then they may repeat these behaviors in order to obtain the desired outcome. This is the case when pain medication is prescribed on a "take as needed" (*prn*) basis. In this case the patients must indicate that pain has increased in order to take more medication. If the increased medication provides some reduction of pain, paying careful attention to indices of pain in the future is likely to continue. With the anticipated outcome of pain relief, patients are likely to pay attention to and consequently report higher levels of pain. The alternative for the physician is to prescribe routine time-contingent medication that is not dependent on reported level of pain.

Classical (respondent) conditioning also plays a central role in pain. For example, cancer patients who experience nausea and vomiting following chemotherapy feel nausea when confronted with neutral cues previously paired with chemotherapy, such as doctors, nurses, the hospital, and even patients' clothes (Carey & Burish, 1988). It is common to observe cancer patients long in remission who report nausea as soon as they see their doctors' faces, even years after completion of treatment. Once acquired, learned responses tend to persist over long periods.

Through classical conditioning, physical therapists and physicians may become potent cues for chronic pain patients to respond in certain ways. A patient, for example, who received a painful treatment from a physical therapist may become conditioned to experience a negative emotional response when in the presence of the therapist. The negative emotional reaction may lead to tensing of muscles and this in turn may exacerbate pain and strengthen the association between the presence of pain and otherwise neutral cues. Classically conditioned fear and anxiety may also elicit physiological reactivity and aggravate pain. Thus, psychological factors may directly affect nociceptive stimulation and need not be viewed as only reactions to pain. Over time, fear of pain may become associated with an expanding number of situations and behaviors, and many neutral or pleasurable activities may be avoided because they elicit or exacerbate pain.

Another way in which principles of learning influence pain is through *social learning*. There is evidence that some pain behaviors may be acquired by *observational* learning. For example, children learn how to interpret and respond to symptoms and physiological processes from their parents and social environment. But children can learn both appropriate and inappropriate responses to injury and disease and, as a result, be more or less likely to ignore or over-respond to symptoms (Richard, 1988).

Cognitive Influences on Pain

Studies have consistently demonstrated that patients' attitudes, beliefs, and expectancies about their plight, themselves, their coping resources, and the health care system influence their experience of pain, activity, disability, and response to treatment (e.g., Flor & Turk, 1988).

Beliefs about the meaning of pain and ability to function despite discomfort can make marked differences to patients' lives. For example, a cognitive representation that one has a very serious, debilitating condition, that disability is a necessary aspect of pain, that activity is dangerous, and that pain is an acceptable excuse for neglecting responsibilities will likely result in maladaptive responses. Similarly, if patients believe that pain signifies ongoing tissue damage or a progressive disease, this belief is likely to produce considerably more suffering and behavioral dysfunction than if it is viewed as being the result of a stable problem that is expected to improve or stay the same. Through a process of stimulus generalization, patients may avoid more and more activities, and soon become more physically deconditioned and disabled. A strong illness conviction, the firm belief that pain is caused by physical pathological processes and requires further medical intervention, compounded by the belief that physical activity may cause further damage, can all make adherence to a physical exercise program unlikely.

Spiegel and Bloom (1983) reported that ratings of pain severity by cancer patients could be predicted not only by their use of analgesics and affective state but also by their interpretations of pain. Patients who attributed their pain to a worsening of their disease experienced more pain despite levels of disease progression comparable to patients with more benign interpretations.

Once beliefs and expectancies about a disease are formed they become stable and are very difficult to modify. People tend to avoid experiences that could invalidate their beliefs and guide their behavior in accordance with these beliefs, even in situations where the belief is no longer valid. Chronic pain sufferers often mistakenly view hurt as synonymous with harm. Thus, if activities produce an increase in pain, they terminate the activity and avoid similar activities in the future. Consequently, they do not receive corrective feedback.

In chronically ill populations, people's beliefs about different aspects of pain and psychological factors appear to predict health care use better than the number or severity of physical symptoms (Flor & Turk, 1988; Sullivan et al., 1992). For example, pain-related beliefs have been found to be associated with psychological functioning (e.g., Jensen et al., 1999; Stroud et al., 2000), physical functioning (Stroud et al., 2000; Turner, Jensen & Romano, 2000), coping efforts (Anderson et al., 1995; Williams, Robinson & Geisser, 1994), pain behaviors (Buckelew et al., 1994; Jensen et al., 1999), and response to treatment (e.g., Jacob et al., 1993; Tota-Faucette et al., 1993).

Catastrophic thinking—experiencing extremely negative thoughts about one's plight and interpreting even minor problems as major catastrophes—appears to be a particularly potent way of influencing pain and disability. In a prospective study, Burton et al. (1995) found that catastrophizing was the most powerful predictor of back pain chronicity, almost seven times more important than the best of the clinical and historical variables. Flor, Behle and Birbaumer (1993) found that patients who improved following treatment showed a reduction in catastrophizing, whereas those who did not improve failed to reduce their levels of catastrophizing. Turk, Meichenbaum and Genest (1983) concluded, "What appears to distinguish low from high pain tolerant individuals is their cognitive processing, catastrophizing thoughts and feelings that precede, accompany, and follow aversive stimulation . . ." (p. 197).

A substantial number of patients with diverse chronic pain syndromes attribute the onset of their pain to some type of trauma such as a motor vehicle accident or a work-related injury. When patients believe that the cause of their symptoms is a traumatic injury, they tend to experience greater fear in association with their pain. Turk and Okifuji (1996) examined a sample of chronic patients and determined that 75% attributed the onset of their symptoms to a physical trauma. The authors found no significant differences in the physical pathology between the groups who reported a traumatic onset compared with those who reported an insidious onset. Yet patients who attributed their pain to a specific trauma reported significantly higher levels of emotional distress, more life interference, and higher levels of pain than patients who indicated that their pain had an insidious onset. This was the case even when they examined patients who were not seeking financial compensation for their pain. Turk et al. (1996) replicated the results with a sample of patients with fibromyalgia. Once again, the authors found no significant difference between those with a traumatic versus insidious onset of symptoms in physical pathology. Again, controlling for compensation status, Turk et al. (1996) found that the patients with traumatic onset of symptoms reported more pain, life interference, physical disability, and affective distress. The attribution of pain and related symptoms to a physical trauma and the resulting catastrophic thinking about pain and injury seem to add an additional burden and to exacerbate chronic pain patients' difficulties.

Self-efficacy—a personal conviction that one can successfully execute a course of action to produce a desired outcome in a given situation—is a major mediator of therapeutic change (Bandura, 1997). Given sufficient motivation to engage in a behavior, it is a person's self-efficacy beliefs that determine the choice of activities that he or she will initiate, the amount of effort that will be expended, and how long he or she will persist in the face of obstacles.

It is important to remember that coping behaviors are influenced by people's beliefs that the demands of a situation do not exceed their coping resources. For example, Council et al. (1988) asked patients to rate their self-efficacy as well as expectancy of pain related to performance during movement tasks. Patients' performance was highly related to their self-efficacy expectations, which in turn appeared to be determined by their expectancies regarding levels of pain that would be experienced.

Affective Influences on Pain

The interactive roles of sensory processes and affective states are supported by an overwhelming amount of evidence (Fernandez & Turk, 1992). The affective components of pain include many different emotions, but they are primarily negative. Depression, anxiety and anger have received the greatest amount of attention in chronic pain studies.

Research suggests that 40–50% of chronic pain patients suffer from depression (Romano & Turner, 1985). It is not surprising that chronic pain patients are depressed. It is interesting to ponder the other side of the coin. Given the nature of the symptoms and the problems created by chronic pain, why are not *all* depressed? Turk and colleagues (Rudy, Kerns & Turk, 1988; Turk, Okifuji & Scharff, 1995) examined this question and determined that two factors appear to mediate the pain–depression relationship: patients' appraisals of the effects of the pain on their lives, and appraisals of their ability to exert any control over their pain and lives. That is, those patients who believed that they could continue to function and that they could maintain some control despite their pain were less likely to become depressed.

Anxiety is also commonplace in chronic pain. Pain-related fear and concerns about harm-avoidance all appear to exacerbate symptoms (Vlaeyen et al., 1995a). Anxiety is an affective state that is greatly influenced by appraisal processes, to cite the stoic philosopher Epictetus, "There is nothing either bad or good but thinking makes it so." Thus, there is a reciprocal relationship between affective state and cognitive-interpretive processes. Thinking affects mood and mood influences appraisals and ultimately the experience of pain.

Threat of intense pain captures attention and it is difficult to disengage from it. Continual vigilance and monitoring of noxious stimulation and the belief that it signifies disease progression may render even low-intensity nociception less bearable. The experience of pain may initiate a set of extremely negative thoughts and arouse fears—fears of inciting more pain and injury, fear of their future impact (see Vlaeyen & Linton, 2000). Fear and anticipation of pain are cognitive-perceptual processes that are not driven exclusively by the actual sensory experience of pain and can exert a significant impact on the level of function and pain tolerance (Feuerstein & Beattie, 1995; Vlaeyen et al., 1999). People learn that avoidance of situations and activities in which they have experienced acute episodes of pain will reduce the likelihood of re-experiencing pain. Several investigators (e.g., Lenthem et al., 1983; Vlaeyen et al., 1995b) have suggested that fear of pain, driven by the anticipation of pain and not by the sensory experience of pain itself, produces strong negative reinforcement for the persistence of avoidance behavior and the alleged functional disability in chronic low back pain patients.

Avoidance behavior is reinforced in the short term, through the reduction of suffering associated with nociception (McCracken et al., 1993). Avoidance, however, can be a maladaptive response if it persists and leads to increased fear, limited activity, and other physical and psychological consequences that contribute to disability and persistence of pain. Studies have demonstrated that fear of movement and fear of (re)injury are better predictors of functional limitations than biomedical parameters (e.g., McCracken et al., 1993; Vlaeyen et al., 1995b). For example, Crombez, Vlaeyen and Heuts (1999) showed that pain-related fear was the best predictor of behavioral performance in trunk-extension, flexion, and weight-lifting tasks, even after partialing out the effects of pain intensity. Moreover, Vlaeyen et al. (1995b) found that fear of movement/(re)injury was the best predictor of self-reported disability among chronic back pain patients and that physiological sensory perception of pain and biomedical findings did not add any predictive value. Approximately two-thirds of chronic non-specific low back pain sufferers avoid back straining activities because of fear of (re)injury (Crombez et al., 1998). Interestingly, reduction in pain-related anxiety predicts improvement in functioning, affective distress, pain, and pain-related interference with activity (McCracken & Gross, 1998). Clearly, fear, pain-related anxiety, and concerns about harm-avoidance all play important roles in chronic pain and need to be assessed and addressed in treatment.

Frustrations related to persistence of symptoms, unknown etiology, and repeated treatment failures along with anger toward employers, insurers, the health care system, family, and themselves, all contribute to the general dysphoric mood of patients (Okifuji, Turk & Curran, 1999). Internalization of angry feelings is strongly related to measures of pain intensity, perceived interference, and frequency of pain behaviors (Kerns, Rosenberg & Jacob, 1994).

The precise mechanisms by which anger and frustration exacerbate pain are not known. One reasonable possibility is that anger exacerbates pain by increasing autonomic arousal. Anger may also block motivation for and acceptance of treatments oriented toward rehabilitation and disability management rather than cure. Yet rehabilitation and disability management are often the only treatments available for these patients.

It is important to be aware of the role of negative mood in chronic pain patients because it is likely to affect treatment motivation and adherence to treatment recommendations. For example, patients who are depressed and who feel helpless may have little initiative to adhere; patients who are anxious may fear engaging in what they perceive as physically demanding activities; and patients who are angry at the health care system are not likely to be motivated to respond to recommendations from yet another health care professional.

PSYCHOLOGICAL ASSESSMENT OF CHRONIC PAIN

As we have suggested, optimal treatment of chronic pain patients should begin with not only an examination of biomedical aspects of the pain condition but also comprehensive assessment of psychological factors related to the condition (Turk, Monarch & Williams, 2002).

From the biopsychosocial perspective, it is important to assess how patients perceive their pain conditions, for example, regarding the etiology of their pain, how pain affects quality of life, coping strategies and the efficacy of those strategies. In addition, patients' mood, the nature of their interpersonal relationships, and changes in their social, occupational, and physical activities may also be helpful in understanding the relationship between their chronic pain and current psychological functioning. Below we provide a list of components and sample questions that constitute a comprehensive psychology interview.

Because significant others may unwittingly contribute to pain and disability, a chronic pain evaluation must include an interview with a significant other. It is best to interview significant others individually, when they might feel more comfortable discussing details of the patient's situation. It is also worthwhile to observe patient and significant other interactions and to note any behaviors that might be related to the patient's disability. For example, are there indications that the significant other inadvertently reinforces pain behaviors?

People who feel that they have a number of successful methods for coping with pain may suffer less than those who feel helpless and hopeless. Thus assessments should focus on learning all factors that exacerbate and *ameliorate* the pain experience.

Components of a Chronic Pain Psychological Assessment

Experience of Pain and Related Symptoms

- Location and description of pain (e.g., "sharp", "burning")
- Onset and progression
- Perception of cause (e.g., trauma, virus, stress)
- What have they been told about their symptoms and condition? Do they believe that what they have been told is accurate?
- Exacerbating and relieving factors (e.g., exercise, relaxation, stress, massage). "What makes your pain worse?" "What makes your pain better?"
- Pattern of symptoms (e.g., symptoms worse certain times of day or following activity or stress)
- Sleep habits (e.g., difficulty falling to sleep or maintaining sleep, sleep hygiene)
- Thoughts, feelings, and behaviors that precede, accompany, and follow fluctuations in symptoms.

Treatments Received and Currently Receiving

- Medication (prescribed and over-the-counter)
- Pattern of medication use (*prn*, time-contingent)
- Physical modalities (e.g., physical therapy)
- Exercise (e.g., Do they participate in a regular exercise routine? Is there evidence of deactivation and avoidance of activity due to fear of pain or exacerbation of injury?)
- Complementary and alternative (e.g., chiropractic manipulation, relaxation training)
- Which treatments have they found the most helpful and why?
- Compliance/adherence with recommendations of health care providers
- Attitudes towards previous health care providers.

Compensation/Litigation

- Current disability status (e.g., receiving or seeking disability status, amount, percent of former job income, expected duration of support)
- Current or planned litigation (e.g., "Have you hired an attorney").

Responses by Patient and Significant Others

- Typical daily routine
- Changes in patient's activities and responsibilities (both positive and obligatory) due to symptoms ("What activities did you use to engage in prior to your symptoms?", "How has this changed since your symptoms began?")
- Changes in significant other's activities and responsibilities due to patient's symptoms
- Patient's behavior when pain intense or flares up ("What do you do when your pain is bothering you?", "Can others tell when your pain is bothering you?", "How do they know?")
- Significant other's response to behavioral expressions of pain ("What does your significant other do when he or she can tell your pain is bothering you?", "Are you satisfied with his or her responses?")
- What does the patient do when pain is not bothering him or her?
- Significant other's response when patient is active ("How does your significant other respond to your engaging in activities?")
- Impact of symptoms on interpersonal, family, marital, and sexual relations (e.g., changes in desire, frequency, or enjoyment)
- Activities that patient avoids because of symptoms ("Why do you avoid these activities?")
- Activities continued despite symptoms
- Pattern of activity and pacing of activity (activity diaries that ask patients to record their pattern of daily activities [time spent sitting, standing, walking, and reclining] for several days or weeks).

Coping

- How does the patient try to cope with his or her symptoms? (e.g., "What do you do when your pain worsens?") Does patient view self as having a role symptom management?
- Success/adequacy of coping efforts
- Current life stresses
- Pleasant activities ("What do you enjoy doing?").

Educational and Vocational History

- Education and work history
- Current work status (including home-making activities)
- Vocational and avocational plans.

Social History

- Relationships with family or origin
- History of pain or disability in family members
- History of substance abuse in family members
- History of current physical, emotional, or sexual abuse

- Marital history
- Quality of current marital and family relations.

Alcohol and Substance Use

- Current and history of alcohol use (quantity, frequency)
- History and current use of illicit psychoactive drugs
- History and current use of prescribed psychoactive drugs.

Psychological Dysfunction

- Current psychological symptoms/diagnosis (depression including suicidal ideation, anxiety disorders, somatization, post-traumatic stress disorder). Is the patient currently receiving treatment for these symptoms? (e.g., psychotherapy or psychiatric medications)
- History of psychiatric disorders/treatment including family counseling
- Family history of psychiatric disorders.

Concerns and Expectations

- Patient concerns/fears (e.g., Do you believe that you have serious physical problems that have not been identified? Or that your symptoms will become progressively worse? Do you worry that you will be told that the symptoms are all psychological?)
- Explanatory models (What have you been told is the cause of your symptoms?; What do you think is the cause of your pain now?)
- Expectations regarding the future and regarding treatment
- Attitude toward rehabilitation versus "cure"
- Treatment goals.

COGNITIVE-BEHAVIORAL APPROACH TO TREATMENT

The cognitive-behavioral (CB) perspective on pain management focuses on modifying sensory, affective, cognitive, and behavioral facets of the experience while providing patients with techniques to help them to gain a sense of control over the effects of pain on their lives. Cognitive techniques (e.g., self-monitoring to identify relationship among thoughts, mood, and behavior, or distraction using imagery) help to place cognitive, affective, behavioral, and sensory responses under patients' control. Studies demonstrate that patients are capable of more than they assumed, can reduce fear of activities, and increase their sense of personal competence.

Cognitive Restructuring

Most cognitive activities become automatic processes and we may not be conscious of the effects of our thoughts on mood, behavior, the environment, physiology, and pain. Cognitive restructuring is designed to help patients to identify and modify maladaptive thoughts. In order to accomplish this patients may be asked to monitor (1) the nature of a situation in which their pain is elevated, (2) their level of emotional and physiological arousal, and (3) thoughts they had and the impact of the thoughts on their emotions, behaviors and ultimately pain experience.

Once maladaptive thought patterns are identified, patients are asked to evaluate whether these thoughts might contribute to their suffering. They are then asked to examine the evidence in support of these thoughts. Finally, they are encouraged to generate evidence-based or adaptive thoughts (e.g., "Although I feel pain, my body is not being harmed"). These alternative thoughts emphasize adaptive ways of thinking to minimize emotional distress and behavioral dysfunction. Patients are instructed to practice identifying and modifying maladaptive thoughts outside of therapy sessions with home assignments using daily diaries.

Problem-solving

Problem-solving is an important concept for pain patients. If you ask patients about their problems they will likely say their only problem is pain; and once their pain is eliminated they will have no problems. Since it is improbable that all pain can be eliminated and unlikely that they appreciate problems created by pain (e.g., high levels of emotional arousal, poor communication with significant others, inability to do household chores), they often need assistance in shifting their view away from pain as the sole problem. Although it may not be possible to eliminate pain, there are things that patients can do to manage their difficulties.

Six steps of problem-solving (i.e., problem identification, goal selection, generation of alternatives, decision-making, implementation, and evaluation) can be introduced. Patients are informed that although there may not be perfect solutions, some solutions are more effective or adaptive than others. An important goal is to convey that the problems are manageable and that people can learn how to deal with these successfully and thereby foster their self-efficacy beliefs.

Coping Skills Training

Treatments that emphasize self-management aim at enhancing patients' adaptive coping; the goal is to help patients to resume a productive and enjoyable life *despite* pain. Coping strategies are thought to act by altering both the perception of intensity of pain and one's ability to manage or tolerate it. Self-management has the added benefit of contributing to a patient's self-efficacy.

Pain patients should be taught a variety of coping skills that they may select from, as appropriate. Behavioral coping strategies include rest, active relaxation, medication, reassuring oneself that the pain will diminish, seeking information, problem-solving, and distracting oneself from pain through physical or mental activities. Studies have shown that active coping strategies (i.e., efforts to function in spite of pain, such as distraction) are associated with adaptive functioning, and passive coping strategies (i.e., depending on others for help in pain control) are related to increased pain and depression. However, beyond this, there is no evidence supporting the greater effectiveness of any one active coping strategy compared to any other (Fernandez & Turk, 1989). It seems more likely that different strategies will be more effective than others for some individuals at some times but not necessarily for all people at all times.

Relaxation

Circumstances that are appraised as threatening are likely to heighten physiological reactions. Chronic increases in sympathetic nervous system activation, which leads to increased skeletal muscle tone, may set the stage for hyperactive muscle contraction and possibly for the persistence of a contraction following conscious muscle activation. It is common for someone in pain to needlessly "turn on" their sympathetic nervous system with their emotional distress or negative thoughts, which amplifies pain. In fact, simply seeing words describing migraine headaches on a screen produced increases in skin conductance response (hence sympathetic nervous system arousal) in patients suffering from recurrent migraine headaches (Jamner &Tursky, 1987).

Flor, Turk and Birbaumer (1985) demonstrated the direct effect of thoughts on muscle tension response. They found that when discussing their painful or stressful situations, back pain patients had significantly elevated muscle tension in their back, but not in their forehead or forearm. In contrast, neither a group of heterogeneous chronic (non-back) pain patients nor a healthy control group showed elevations in back muscle tension when discussing stress or pain.

Active relaxation is one way to manipulate autonomic nervous system activity. Generally, relaxation involves two steps. First, patients gain awareness of maladaptive physiological activity such that they are able to discriminate muscle tension and relaxation. Second, they learn how to purposefully modify autonomic activity. Relaxation skills can have a direct impact on pain perception by minimizing pain due to muscle spasm or tension. The skills can also reduce pain indirectly by (1) helping patients to minimize the impact of emotional distress, especially anxiety, on autonomic arousal, (2) diverting focus away from persistent pain and associated difficulties by serving as a distraction, and (3) providing patients with a sense of control over their bodies and, consequently, their pain.

Exposure to Feared Activities

As noted, one of the ways patients cope with fear of pain or injury is with avoidance. But in the long run this learned coping response can serve to maintain chronic pain conditions and result in greater disability. For example, following an accident in which a person hurts his back, he learns that certain movements make his pain worse. In response, he stops engaging in activities that exacerbate his pain and restricts his movements in an attempt to avoid pain and further injury. Consequently, he loses muscle strength, flexibility, and endurance. Here a vicious circle is created, for as the muscles become weaker, more and more activities begin to cause pain and are avoided. As the patient remains inactive and becomes more physically deconditioned, he becomes less likely to identify activities that build flexibility, endurance, and strength *without* risk of pain or injury. In addition, the distorted movements and postures that he assumes to protect himself from pain may cause further pain unrelated to his initial injury. For example, when he limps, he protects muscles on one side of his back, but the muscles on the other side of his back become overactive and can develop painful conditions of their own.

Avoidance of activity, although it is a seemingly rational way to manage a pain problem, can actually play a large role in *maintaining* chronic pain conditions and increasing disability. There is some preliminary evidence that exposure-based, counter-conditioning treatment focused on fear of movement is effective for patients with chronic back pain (Vlaeyen et al., 1995b).

Outcomes

A significant body of research supports the usefulness of psychological interventions with diverse pain states and syndromes such as low back pain (Bendix et al., 1997; Hildebrandt et al., 1997), headaches (Holroyd & Lipchik, 1999), fibromyalgia syndrome (e.g., Nielson, Harth & Bell, 1997; Turk et al., 1998a, 1998b), non-cardiac chest pain (Mayou et al., 1997), arthritis (e.g., Lorig, Mazonson & Holman, 1993), temporomandibular disorders (Mishra, Gatchel & Gardea, 2000), and whiplash-associated disorders (Vendrig, Van Akkerveeken & McWhorter, 2000).

Based on their meta-analysis of randomized-controlled trials comparing the effectiveness of CB therapy (CBT) to wait-list control and alternative-treatment control conditions, Morley, Eccleston and Williams (1999) concluded that CBT significantly improved pain experience, cognitive coping, appraisals and behavioral expressions of pain. Significant differences were not found, however, for dysphoric mood, negative appraisals, and social role functioning.

Currently, multidisciplinary pain rehabilitation programs (MPRPs) are the treatment of choice for patients with recalcitrant chronic pain. These comprehensive programs are more effective than no treatment, wait-list control, and monodisciplinary treatments (e.g., Flor, Fydrich & Turk, 1992; Guzman et al., 2001). They typically include medical management, physical therapy, occupational therapy, cognitive and behavioral components, and vocational counseling. The focus of these programs is to help patients to learn how to manage their pain and return to normal life activities with active coping skills, while reducing or eliminating their reliance on passive coping skills such as avoidance of activity or pain medication. Thus the emphasis is on functional restoration, not cure. Psychological concepts and techniques, particularly the cognitive and behavioral strategies described above, are incorporated into these programs.

FUTURE DIRECTIONS

There are some important limitations to the treatment outcomes studies outlined above. In order to demonstrate both the clinical and cost-effectiveness of these treatments, investigators will need to address these concerns.

For a treatment to be effective, at least two things have to occur: the treatment must be effective and patients have to adhere to treatment recommendations (Turk, Rudy & Sorkin, 1993). Treatment outcome studies of chronic pain rarely assess patients' adherence to recommendations. In addition to knowing whether patients adhere to treatment, it is important to know whether therapists administered treatment in the same manner (e.g., Jensen et al., 1997). *Treatment integrity* can be assessed by tape-recording samples of treatment sessions and having these tapes rated by independent observers. Treatment integrity can be improved by the use of standard treatment manuals, and having well-trained and supervised therapists.

Attrition from treatment is a major concern as large percentages of dropouts limits the validity and generalizability of results. Examination of treatment outcome studies reveals that up to 60% of patients dropped out of the studies with the attrition rates substantially higher in the waiting list and usual care groups (mean 24.6%) compared to the treated groups (mean 10.7%; Spence & Sharpe, 1993). Often those who drop out of treatment are eliminated from analyses and further interpretations of results. Because failure to include these patients may lead to inflated results, studies should use "intent-to-treat" analyses where patients who drop out are considered as treatment failures and are included in outcome analyses.

Future research in chronic pain needs to address the methodological issues described above. In addition to addressing methodological issues, however, research in chronic pain needs to be directed toward new pressing and interesting questions.

Predictors of Disability and Treatment Response

The vast majority of people who are injured recover and do not develop chronic disorders. Minimal attention has been given to those people who recover spontaneously or who make adequate and often exceptional accommodations to their conditions regardless of physical impairments and limitations. Much of what we know about chronic pain syndromes is based on patients who seek treatment. Since people are more likely to seek treatment when their symptoms are at their worst, research participants may not be a representative group. Parenthetically, we can note that treatment-seeking when symptoms are worse will likely result in almost any treatment appearing reasonably successful (regression to the mean). We must be cautious about generalizing from groups seeking treatment to all who might have the same diagnosis.

Similarly, a significant number of people who do develop chronic diseases associated with pain do *not* become physically and emotionally disabled. What protective factors are present in their lives? Although to date this question has not been fully answered, some efforts have been made to identify predictors of disability (e.g., Gatchel & Epker, 1999; Turk, 1997). These studies clearly show that degree of physical pathology has rather poor predictive power. Conversely, psychological factors are significant predictors of pain, distress, treatment-seeking, and disability (e.g., Boothby et al., 1999; Pfingsten et al., 1997). For example, Burton et al. (1995) reported that measures of physical pathology during acute back problems account for only 10% of the variance in disability one year following treatment-seeking, whereas psychosocial variables account for 59% of the variance in disability.

A number of prospective studies have identified high-risk psychosocial factors for the development of chronicity in acute unspecified low back pain (e.g., Crombez, Vlaeyen & Heuts, 1999) as well as acute sciatic pain (Hasenbring et al., 1994). These risk factors include: depression and daily stress (at work and in private life), maladaptive pain-coping patterns involving fear of pain and avoidance behavior, maladaptive operant behavior patterns and high levels of pain behaviors, and inability to search for and obtain social support. Other variables that appear to predict treatment outcome include whether patients are seeking disability compensation, have pending litigation, comorbid depression, and history of substance abuse. But identifying predictors is insufficient. The next steps are (1) to determine whether knowledge of predictors can guide treatment and (2) to develop strategies for improving outcome. To paraphrase the old behavioral adage, "Insight without changing behavior is a waste of time."

The average person treated at MPRPs averages over 85 months of pain (Flor, Fydrich & Turk, 1992). By this time, patients have become so disabled that rehabilitation becomes a Herculean task; the outcomes, although reasonably good, could improve if implemented at an earlier stage. Von Korff and colleagues (Moore et al., 2000; Von Korff et al., 1998) provide a detailed description of an early intervention program that was implemented in primary care. Prevention and earlier interventions hold promise for reduction in the extent of disability and should be a focus of future research.

Patient Differences and Treatment Matching

Although psychological treatments appear to be effective, not all patients benefit equally. Looking only at group effects may mask important issues related to the characteristics of patients who successfully respond to a treatment. Chronic pain syndromes are made up of heterogeneous groups of people, even if they have the same medical diagnosis (Turk, 1990). Patients with disease and syndromes as diverse as metastatic cancer, back pain, and headaches show similar adaptation patterns, whereas patients with the same diagnosis can show marked variability in their degrees of disability (Turk et al., 1998c).

A number of studies have identified subgroups of patients based on psychosocial and behavioral characteristics (e.g., Mikail, Henderson & Tasca, 1994; Turk & Rudy, 1988, 1990). Dahlstrom, Widmark and Carlsson (1997), Strategier et al. (1997), and Turk and colleagues (1998b) all found that when patients were classified into different subgroups based on their psychosocial and behavioral responses, they responded differentially to treatments. Recently Carmody (2001) reported differential dropout from treatment based on the same set of psychosocial and behavioral characteristics as subgroups identified by Turk and colleagues. Additional studies targeted toward matching interventions to specific patient characteristics are needed. The important question is not whether a treatment is effective but rather what treatment components delivered in what way and when produces the most successful outcomes for individual pain sufferers with what set of characteristics (Turk, 1990). Only a handful of studies have begun to demonstrate that matching treatments to patient characteristics is of benefit (e.g., Turk et al., 1998b). Developing treatments that are matched to patients' characteristics should lead not only to improved outcomes but also to greater cost-effectiveness.

Cost-effectiveness

Many third-party payers view pain rehabilitation programs as synonymous with expensive (Okifuji, Turk & Kalauokalani, 1999). With changes in health care, cost-effectiveness is assuming a role that is at least as important as clinical effectiveness. Specialized pain programs are expensive (Marketdata Enterprises, 1995). Little attempt has been made to isolate what features of MPRPs are necessary and sufficient to produce optimal outcomes. The trends for evidence-based health care require that we demonstrate the clinical and cost effectiveness of all components of treatments provided (Turk & Okifuji, 1998).

One of the ways that chronic pain patients and their health care providers can inadvertently exacerbate patient suffering is by viewing and treating chronic pain as an acute condition that will resolve following treatment. If we view chronic pain as a life-long disease, like other chronic diseases such as diabetes, we should expect treatment to be ongoing, requiring regular check-ups and continuing care. From the chronic disease perspective, treatment is not over after a few sessions or a three- to four-week rehabilitation program. We should expect and plan for the need to include long-term care such as booster sessions (Bendix et al., 1998; Lanes et al., 1995). Recognizing and appreciating the persistence and complexity of chronic pain is likely not only to facilitate care for these patients but also to do so in the most cost-effective manner.

CONCLUSION

Psychologists and psychological principles have played a major role in current understanding and treatment of people with persistent pain. Studies show that various psychological factors play important roles in the transition from acute to chronic pain, disability, adaptation, and response to treatments. In general, the results of outcome studies support the effectiveness of psychological treatment, especially CB interventions. The NIH Technology Assessment Panel (1996) and American Psychological Association's Division of Clinical Psychology's Task Force on the Promotion and Dissemination of Psychological Procedures have endorsed CBT as a *well-established* treatment approach for several pain problems (e.g., rheumatoid arthritis; Chambless et al., 1995). The importance of psychologists in the assessment and treatment of chronic pain has been accepted by a number of agencies and governmental bodies in the United States and Canada (e.g., United States Veterans Administration; United States Social Security Administration, Ontario Workplace Safety and Insurance Board). In fact, the Commission on the Accreditation of Rehabilitation Facilities in the United States *requires* involvement of psychologists in treatment for a program to be certified.

We have attempted to review some of the representative literature, described empirically based interventions, and point out a number of areas where research is likely to proceed over the next decade. We expect that psychological principles will continue to have an important place in understanding and treating chronic pain sufferers.

ACKNOWLEDGEMENTS

Preparation of this manuscript was supported in part by grants from the National Institute of Arthritis and Musculoskeletal and Skin Diseases (AR/AI44724; AR47298) and the National Institute of Child Health and Human Development (HD33989) awarded to the first author and AR44230 and AR46303 awarded to the second author.

REFERENCES

Anderson, K.O., Dowds, B.N., Pelletz, R.E., Edwarts, W.T. & Peeters-Asdourian, C. (1995). Development and initial validation of a scale to measure self-efficacy beliefs in patients with chronic pain. *Pain*, **63**, 77–84.

Bandura, A. (1997). *Self-efficacy: The Exercise of Control*. New York: W.H. Freeman.

Bendix, A.F., Bendix, T., Haestrup, C. & Busch, E. (1998). A prospective, randomized 5-year follow-up study of functional restoration in chronic low back pain patients. *European Spine Journal*, **7**, 111–119.

Bendix, A.F., Bendix, T., Lund, C., Kirkbak, S. & Ostenfeld, S. (1997). Comparison of three intensive programs for chronic low back pain patients: a prospective, randomized, observer-blinded study with one-year follow-up. *Scandinavian Journal of Rehabilitation Medicine*, **29**, 818–819.

Boothby, J.L., Thorn, B.E., Stroud, M.W. & Jensen, M.P. (1999). Coping with chronic pain. In R.J. Gatchel & D.C. Turk (Eds), *Psychosocial Factors in Pain: Critical Perspectives* (pp. 343–359). New York: Guilford Press.

Buckelew, S.P., Parker, J.C., Keefe, F.J., Deuser, W.E., Crews, T.M., Conway, R., Kay, D.R. & Hewett, J.E. (1994). Self-efficacy and pain behavior among subjects with fibromyalgia. *Pain*, **59**, 377–385.

Burton, A.K., Tillotson, K.M., Main, C.J. & Hollis, S. (1995). Psychosocial predictors of outcome in acute and subacute low back trouble. *Spine*, **20**, 722–728.

Carey, M. & Burish, T. (1988). Etiology and treatment of the psychological side effects associated with cancer chemotherapy: a critical review and discussion. *Psychological Bulletin*, **104**, 307–325.

Carmody, T.P. (2001). Psychosocial subgroups, coping, and chronic low-back pain. *Journal of Clinical Psychology in Medical Settings*, **8**, 137–148.

Chambless, D.L., Babich, K., Crits-Christoph, P. et al. (1995). Training and dissemination of empirically-validated psychological treatments: reports and recommendations. *Clinical Psychologist*, **48**, 3–23.

Council, J., Ahern, D., Follick, M. & Kline, C.L. (1988). Expectancies and functional impairment in chronic low back pain. *Pain*, **33**, 323–331.

Craig, K.D., Hill, M.L. & McMurtry, B. (1998). Detecting deception and malingering. In A.R. Block, E.F. Kremer & E. Fernandez (Eds), *Handbook of Pain Syndromes* (pp. 41–58). Mahwah, NJ: Lawrence Erlbaum.

Crombez, G., Vervaet, L., Lysens, R., Eelen, P. & Baeyerns, F. (1998). Avoidance and confrontation of painful, back straining movements in chronic back pain patients. *Behavior Modification*, **22**, 62–77.

Crombez, G., Vlaeyen, J.W. & Heuts, P.H. (1999). Pain-related fear is more disabling than pain itself: evidence on the role of pain-related fear in chronic back pain disability. *Pain*, **80**, 329–339.

Dahlstrom, L., Widmark, G. & Carlsson, S.G. (1997). Cognitive-behavioral profiles among different categories of orofacial pain patients: diagnostic and treatment implications. *European Journal of Oral Science*, **105**, 377–383.

Deyo, R.A. (1986). Early diagnostic evaluation of low back pain. *Journal of General Internal Medicine*, **1**, 328–338.

Fernandez, E. & Turk, D.C. (1989). The utility of cognitive coping strategies for altering pain perception: a meta-analysis. *Pain*, **38**, 123–135.

Fernandez, E. & Turk, D.C. (1992). Sensory and affective components of pain: separation and synthesis. *Psychological Bulletin*, **112**, 205–217.

Feuerstein, M. & Beattie, P. (1995). Biobehavioral factors affecting pain and disability in low back pain: mechanisms and assessment. *Physical Therapy*, **75**, 267–269.

Flor, H. & Turk, D.C. (1988). Chronic back pain and rheumatoid arthritis: predicting pain and disability from cognitive variables. *Journal of Behavioral Medicine*, **11**, 251–265.

Flor, H., Behle, D.J. & Birbaumer, N. (1993). Assessment of pain-related cognitions in chronic pain patients. *Behavior Research and Therapy*, **31**, 63–73.

Flor, H., Fydrich, T. & Turk, D.C. (1992). Efficacy of multidisciplinary pain treatment centers: a meta-analytic review. *Pain*, **49**, 221–230.

Flor, H., Turk, D.C. & Birbaumer, N. (1985). Assessment of stress-related psychophysiological reactions in chronic back pain patients. *Journal of Consulting and Clinical Psychology*, **53**, 354–364.

Fordyce, W. (1976). *Behavioral Methods in Chronic Pain and Illness*. St Louis: CV Mosby.

Fordyce, W.E., Lansky, D., Calsyn, D.A., Shelton, J.L., Stolov, W.C. & Rock, D.L. (1984). Pain measurement and pain behavior. *Pain*, **18**, 53–69.

Gamsa, A. (1994). The role of psychological factors in chronic pain: I. A half century of study. *Pain*, **57**, 5–15.

Gatchel, R.J. & Epker, J. (1999). Psychosocial predictors of chronic pain and response to treatment. In R.J. Gatchel & D.C. Turk (Eds), *Psychosocial Factors in Pain: Critical Perspectives* (pp. 412–434). New York: Guilford Press.

Grzesiak, R.C., Ury, G.M. & Dworkin, R.H. (1996). Psychodynamic psychotherapy with chronic pain patients. In R.J. Gatchel & D.C. Turk (Eds), *Psychological Approaches to Pain Management: A Practitioner's Handbook* (pp. 148–178). New York: Guilford Press.

Guzman, J., Esmail, R., Karjalainen, K., Malmivaara, A., Irvin, E. & Bombardier, C. (2001). Multi-disciplinary rehabilitation for chronic low back pain: systematic review. *British Medical Journal*, **322**, 1511–1516.

Hasenbring, M., Marienfeld, G., Kuhlendahl, D. & Soyka, D. (1994). Risk factors of chronicity in lumbar disc patients: a prospective investigation of biologic, psychologic, and social predictors of therapy outcome. *Spine*, **19**, 2759–2765.

Hildebrandt, J., Pfingsten, M., Saur, P. & Jansen, J. (1997). Prediction of success from a multidisciplinary program for chronic low back pain. *Spine*, **22**, 990–1001.

Holroyd, K. & Lipchik, G. (1999). Psychological management of recurrent headache disorders: progress and prospects. In R.J. Gatchel & D.C. Turk (Eds), *Psychosocial Factors in Pain: Critical Perspectives* (pp. 193–212). New York: Guilford Press.

Jacob, M.C., Kerns, R.D., Rosenberg, R. & Haythornthwaite, J. (1993). Chronic pain: intrusion and accommodation. *Behavior Research and Therapy*, **31**, 519–527.

Jamner, L. & Tursky, B. (1987). Discrimination between intensity and affective pain descriptors: a psychophysiological evaluation. *Pain*, **30**, 271–283.

Jensen, I., Dahlquist, C., Nygren, A., Royen, E. & Sternberg, M. (1997). Treatment for "helpless" women suffering from chronic spinal pain: a randomized controlled 18-month follow-up study. *Journal of Occupational Rehabilitation*, **7**, 225–238.

Jensen, M., Brant-Zawadski, M., Obuchowski, N., Modic, M.T. & Malkasian Ross, J.S. (1994). Magnetic resonance imaging of the lumbar spine in people without back pain. *New England Journal of Medicine*, **331**, 69–73.

Jensen, M.P., Romano, J.M., Turner, J.A., Good, A.B. & Wald, L.H. (1999). Patient beliefs predict patient functioning: further support for a cognitive-behavioral model of chronic pain. *Pain*, **81**, 94–104.

Kerns, R., Rosenberg, R. & Jacob, M. (1994). Anger expression and chronic pain. *Journal of Behavioral Medicine*, **17**, 57–67.

Lanes, T.C., Gauron, E.F., Spratt, K.F., Wernimont, T.J., Found, E.M. & Weinstein, J.N. (1995). Long-term follow-up of patients with chronic back pain treated in a multidisciplinary rehabilitation program. *Spine*, **20**, 801–806.

Lenthem, J., Slade, P.D., Troup, J.D.G. & Bentley, G. (1983). Outline of a fear-avoidance model of exaggerated pain perception—I. *Behavior Research and Therapy*, **21**, 401–408.

Lorig, K., Mazonson, P. & Holman, H. (1993). Evidence suggesting that health education for self-management in patients with chronic arthritis has sustained health benefits while reducing health care costs. *Arthritis and Rheumatism*, **36**, 439–446.

Marketdata Enterprises (1995). *Chronic Pain Management Programs: A Market Analysis*. Valley Stream, New York.

Mayou, R.A., Bryant, B.M., Sanders, D., Bass, C., Klimes, I. & Forfar, C. (1997). A controlled trial of cognitive behavioural therapy for non-cardiac chest pain. *Psychological Medicine*, **27**, 1021–1031.

McCracken, L.M. & Gross, R.T. (1998). The role of pain-related anxiety reduction in the outcome of multidisciplinary treatment for chronic low back pain: preliminary results. *Journal of Occupational Rehabilitation*, **8**, 179–189.

McCracken, L.M., Gross, R.T., Sorg, P.J. & Edmands, T.A. (1993). Prediction of pain in patients with chronic low back pain: effects of inaccurate prediction and pain-related anxiety. *Behavior Research and Therapy*, **31**, 647–652.

Melzack, R. & Wall, P. (1965). Pain mechanisms: a new theory. *Science*, **150**, 971–979.

Merskey, H. & Bogduk, N. (1986). International Association for the Study of Pain Classification of chronic pain. Descriptions of chronic pain syndromes and definitions of pain terms. *Pain*, **3**, S1–S226.

Mikail, S.F., Henderson, P.R. & Tasca, G.A. (1994). An interpersonally based model of chronic pain: an application of attachment theory. *Clinical Psychology Review*, **14**, 1–16.

Mishra, K.D., Gatchel, R.J. & Gardea, M.A. (2000). The relative efficacy of three cognitive-behavioral treatment approaches to temporomandibular disorders. *Journal of Behavioral Medicine*, **23**, 393–410.

Moore, J.E., von Korff, M., Cherkin, D., Saunders, K. & Lorig, K. (2000). A randomized trial of a cognitive-behavioral program for enhancing back pain self-care in a primary care setting. *Pain*, **88**, 145–153.

Morley, S., Eccleston, C. & Williams, A. (1999). Systematic review and meta-analysis of randomized controlled trials of cognitive behaviour therapy and behaviour therapy for chronic pain in adults, excluding headache. *Pain*, **80**, 1–13.

Nielson, W., Harth, M. & Bell, D. (1997). Out-patient cognitive-behavioral treatment of fibromyalgia: impact on pain response and health status. *Pain Research and Management*, **2**, 145–150.

NIH Technology Assessment Panel (1996). Integration of behavioral and relaxation approaches into the treatment of chronic pain and insomnia. *Journal of the American Medical Association*, **276**, 313–318.

Okifuji, A., Turk, D.C. & Curran, S.L. (1999). Anger in chronic pain: investigation of anger targets and intensity. *Journal of Psychosomatic Research*, **61**, 771–780.

Okifuji, A., Turk, D.C. & Kalauokalani, D. (1999). Clinical outcome and economic evaluation of multidisciplinary pain centers. In A.R. Block, E.F. Kremer & E. Fernandez (Eds), *Handbook of Pain Syndromes: Biopsychosocial Perspectives* (pp. 77–98). Mahwah, NJ: Lawrence Erlbaum.

Pfingsten, M., Hildebrandt, J., Leibing, E., Franz, C. & Saur, P. (1997). Effectiveness of a multimodal treatment program for chronic low-back pain. *Pain*, **73**, 77–85.

Richard, K. (1988). The occurrence of maladaptive health-related behaviors and teacher-related conduct problems in children of chronic low back pain patients. *Journal of Behavioral Medicine*, **11**, 107–116.

Romano, J.M. & Turner, J.A. (1985). Chronic pain and depression: does the evidence support a relationship? *Psychological Bulletin*, **97**, 18–34.

Romano, J.M., Turner, J.A., Friedman, L.S., Bulcroft, R.A., Jensen, M.P., Hops, H. & Wright, S.F. (1992). Sequential analysis of chronic pain behaviors and spouse responses. *Journal of Consulting and Clinical Psychology*, **60**, 777–789.

Rudy, T.E., Kerns, R.D. & Turk, D.C. (1998). Chronic pain and depression: toward a cognitive-behavioral mediation model. *Pain*, **35**, 129–140.

Rudy, T.E., Turk, D.C. & Brena, S.F. (1988). Differential utility of medical procedures in the assessment of chronic pain patients. *Pain*, **34**, 53–60.

Schmidt, A.J.M. (1985). Cognitive factors in the performance of chronic low back pain patients. *Journal of Psychosomatic Research*, **29**, 183–189.

Spence, S.H. & Sharpe, L. (1993). Problems of drop-out in the self-help treatment of chronic, occupational pain of the upper limbs. *Behavioral and Cognitive Psychotherapy*, **21**, 311–328.

Spiegel, D. & Bloom, J. (1983). Pain in metastatic breast cancer. *Cancer*, **52**, 341–345.

Strategier, L.D., Chwalisz, K., Altmaier, E.M., Russell, D.W. & Lehmann, T.H. (1997). Multidimensional assessment of chronic low back pain: predicting treatment outcomes. *Journal of Clinical Psychology in Medical Settings*, **4**, 91–110.

Stroud, M.W., Thorn, B.E., Jensen, M.P. & Boothby, J.L. (2000). The relation between pain beliefs, negative thoughts, and psychosocial functioning in chronic pain patients. *Pain*, **84**, 347–352.

Sullivan, M.J., Edgley, K., Mikail, S., Dehoux, E. & Fisher, R. (1992). Psychological correlates of health care utilization in chronic illness. *Canadian Journal of Rehabilitation*, **6**, 13–21.

Tota-Faucette, M.E., Gil, K.M., Williams, D.A., Keefe, F.J. & Goli, V. (1993). Predictors of response to pain management treatment. The role of family environment and changes in cognitive processes. *Clinical Journal of Pain*, **9**, 115–123.

Turk, D.C. (1990). Customizing treatment for chronic pain patients: who, what, and why. *Clinical Journal of Pain*, **6**, 255–270.

Turk, D.C. (1996). Biopsychosocial perspective on chronic pain. In R. Gatchel & D.C. Turk (Eds), *Psychological Approaches to Pain Management: A Practitioner's Handbook* (pp. 3–32). New York: Guilford Press.

Turk, D.C. (1997). Transition from acute to chronic pain: role of demographic and psychosocial factors. In T.S. Jensen, J.A. Turner & Z. Wiesenfeld-Hallin (Eds), *Proceedings of the 8th World Congress on Pain, Progress in Pain Research and Management* (pp. 185–213). Seattle: IASP Press.

Turk, D.C. & Flor, H. (1987). Pain behaviors: utility and limitations of the pain behavior construct. *Pain*, **31**, 277–295.

Turk, D.C. & Flor, H. (1999). Chronic pain: a biobehavioral perspective. In R. Gatchel & D.C. Turk (Eds), *Psychosocial Factors in Pain: Critical Perspectives* (pp. 18–34). New York: Guilford Press.

Turk, D.C. & Okifuji, A. (1996). Perception of traumatic onset, compensation status, and physical findings: impact on pain severity, emotional distress, and disability in chronic pain patients. *Journal of Behavioral Medicine*, **19**, 435–453.

Turk, D.C. & Okifuji, A. (1998). Treatment of chronic pain patients: clinical outcome, cost-effectiveness, and cost-benefits. *Critical Reviews in Physical Medicine and Rehabilitation*, **10**, 181–208.

Turk, D.C. & Okifuji, A. (2002). Psychological factors in chronic pain: evolution and revolution. *Journal of Consulting and Clinical Psychology*, **70**, 678–690.

Turk, D.C. & Rudy, T.E. (1988). Toward an empirically-derived taxonomy of chronic pain patients: integration of psychological assessment data. *Journal of Consulting and Clinical Psychology*, **56**, 233–238.

Turk, D.C. & Rudy, T.E. (1990). The robustness of an empirically derived taxonomy of chronic pain patients, *Pain*, **43**, 27–35.

Turk, D.C., Kerns, R.D. & Rosenberg, R. (1992). Effects of marital interaction on chronic pain and disability: examining the down-side of social support. *Rehabilitation Psychology*, **37**, 257–272.

Turk, D., Meichenbaum, D. & Genest, M. (1983). *Pain and Behavioral Medicine: A Cognitive-Behavioral Perspective*. New York: Guilford Press.

Turk, D.C., Monarch, E.S. & Williams, A.D. (2002). Psychological evaluation of patients diagnosed with fibromyalgia syndrome. Comprehensive approach. *Rheumatic Disease Clinics of North America.*, **28**, 219–233.

Turk, D.C., Okifuji, A. & Scharff, L. (1995). Chronic pain and depression: role of perceived impact and perceived control in different age cohorts. *Pain*, **61**, 93–101.

Turk, D.C., Rudy, T.E. & Sorkin, B.A. (1993). Neglected topics in chronic pain treatment outcome studies: determination of success. *Pain*, **53**, 3–16.

Turk, D.C., Okifuji, A., Sinclair, J.D. & Starz, T.W. (1998a). Interdisciplinary treatment for fibromyalgia syndrome: clinical and statistical significance. *Arthritis Care and Research*, **11**, 186–195.

Turk, D.C., Okifuji, A., Sinclair, J.D. & Starz, T.W. (1998b). Differential responses by psychosocial subgroups of fibromyalgia syndrome patients to an interdisciplinary treatment. *Arthritis Care and Research*, **11**, 397–404.

Turk, D.C., Okifuji, A., Starz, T.W. & Sinclair, J.D. (1996). Effects of type of symptom onset on psychological distress and disability in fibromyalgia syndrome patients. *Pain*, **48**, 423–430.

Turk, D.C., Sist, T.C., Okifuji, A., Miner, M.F., Florio, G., Harrison, P., Massey, J., Lema, M.L. & Zevon, M.A. (1998c). Adaptation to metastatic cancer pain, regional/local cancer pain and non-cancer pain: role of psychological and behavioral factors. *Pain*, **74**, 247–256.

Turner, J.A., Jensen, M.P. & Romano, J.M. (2000). Do beliefs, coping, and catastrophizing independently predict functioning in patients with chronic pain? *Pain*, **85**, 115–125.

Vendrig, A.A., Van Akkerveeken, P.F. & McWhorter, K.R. (2000). Results of multimodal treatment program for patients with chronic symptoms after whiplash injury of the neck. *Spine*, **25**, 238–244.

Vlaeyen, J.W.S. & Linton, S.J. (2000). Fear-avoidance and its consequences in chronic musculoskeletal pain: a state of the art. *Pain*, **85**, 317–332.

Vlaeyen, J.W.S., Kole-Snijders, A.M., Boeren, R.G.B. & van Eek, H. (1995a). Fear of movement/(re)injury in chronic low back pain and its relation to behavioral performance. *Pain*, **62**, 363–372.

Vlaeyen, J.W.S., Kole-Snijders, A., Rooteveel, A., Ruesink. R. & Heuts, P. (1995b). The role of fear of movement/(re)injury in pain disability. *Journal of Occupational Rehabilitation*, **5**, 235–252.

Vlaeyen, J.W.S., Seelen, H.A.M., Peters, M., de Jong, P., Aretz, E., Beisiegel, E. & Weber, W.E.J. (1999). Fear of movement/(re)injury and muscular reactivity in chronic low back pain patients: an experimental investigation. *Pain*, **82**, 297–304.

Von Korff, M., Moore, J.E., Lorig, K., Cherkin, D.C., Saunders, K., Gonzalez, V.M., Laurent, D., Rutter, C. & Comite, F. (1998). A randomized trial of a lay person-led self-management group intervention for back pain patients in primary care. *Spine*, **23**, 2608–2615.

Wiesel, S.W., Tsourmas, N., Feffer, H.L., Citrin, C.M. & Patronas, N. (1984). A study of computer-assisted tomography. I. The incidence of positive CAT scans in an asymptomatic group of patients. *Spine*, **9**, 549–551.

Williams, D.A., Robinson, M.E. & Geisser, M.E. (1994). Pain beliefs: assessment and utility. *Pain*, **59**, 71–78.

CHAPTER 9

Chronic Obstructive Pulmonary Disease: A Behavioural Medicine Approach

Margreet Scharloo*

and

Adrian A. Kaptein

Leiden University Medical Center, The Netherlands

INTRODUCTION

> *I have a terrible lack of energy. I get terribly,*
> *terribly tired and worn out very easily. You're*
> *always short of energy... Whether it's getting*
> *up in the morning, washing or dressing,*
> *anything, you get so damned tired and breathless.*
> (Williams, 1993, p. 65)

Chronic obstructive pulmonary disease (COPD) represents one of the most prevalent medical conditions in industrialised and developing countries (Murray & Lopez, 1997). Health care providers, patients, their partners and society will be faced with COPD and its associated medical, psychological and social costs to an ever-increasing degree. In their Global Burden of Disease study, Murray and Lopez (1997) predict that in 2020 COPD will be ranked as the third most prevalent chronic illness, following ischaemic heart disease (including cerebrovascular disease) and unipolar major depression, in terms of disease burden measured in disability-adjusted life years.

Despite a wealth of biomedical research on diagnostic and therapeutic measures, progress in this area is unimpressive (Kerstjens, Groen & van der Bij, 2001). The major reason for this state of affairs pertains to a relatively long duration of a period of therapeutic pessimism among pulmonary physicians about COPD. Only quite recently have research efforts been initiated on developing an animal model via which a more fundamental understanding of the

---

* Please address all correspondence to M. Scharloo.

Handbook of Clinical Health Psychology. Edited by S. Llewelyn and P. Kennedy.

pathogenesis of COPD might be achieved, resulting in, hopefully, more effective medical and pharmacological measures for patients with this respiratory disorder.

Psychologists also have shunned studying patients with COPD for a long time, for at least three reasons. In contrast to another highly prevalent respiratory disorder, asthma, no psychosomatic theories were developed on patients with chronic obstructive pulmonary disease. This led psychologists to ignore COPD patients in the first half of the twentieth century. Second, as smoking cigarettes is the major cause of COPD, quite a few psychologists joined others in the tendency to "blame the victim", and ignore the human suffering of COPD patients. Third, the typical COPD patient is quite well depicted by Schofield's (1964) acronym HOUND (Humble, Old, Unintelligent, Non-verbal, Dull)—most COPD patients prefer fighting their illness and its impressive consequences alone, rather than dis- cuss and address those consequences in therapeutic encounters with psychologists. COPD patients are a quite different group of patients than the YAVIS patients (Young, Attrac- tive, Verbal, Intelligent, Successful), preferred by psychotherapists; they tend to resist most forms of psychotherapeutic efforts (Goldstein, 1971).

Historically, the first study by psychologists on patients with COPD was done by Webb and Lawton (1961), using the Szondi test to examine psychosocial adjustment of COPD patients. Some 40 years later, psychologists are examining quality of life, cognitive- behavioural interventions and pulmonary rehabilitation programmes. A cautiously more optimistic view on the contribution of clinical health psychologists seems in order, as will be outlined in this chapter. Still, the number of empirical studies by clinical health psychol- ogists on COPD patients is only a fraction of the number of such studies on patients with cardiovascular disorders or cancer (Kaptein, 2002).

In this chapter we will describe and summarise the following topics as they relate to COPD:

- terminology
- epidemiology
- diagnostic issues
- quality of life
- therapeutic issues
- psychological interventions
- research agenda.

The reader who is interested in a more in-depth review of these areas is referred to Kaptein and Creer (2002), or to medical journals such as *American Journal of Respiratory and Critical Care Medicine*, *Chest*, *European Respiratory Journal*, and *Thorax*.

DISEASE CHARACTERISTICS

Definition of Chronic Obstructive Pulmonary Disease

The National Heart, Lung, and Blood Institute/World Health Organisation Global Initia- tive for Chronic Obstructive Lung Disease defines chronic obstructive pulmonary disease as: "a disease state characterised by airflow limitation that is not fully reversible. The air- flow limitation is usually both progressive and associated with an abnormal inflammatory response of the lungs to noxious particles or gases" (Pauwels et al., 2001, p. 1257). The critical feature that characterises COPD is that most of the lung impairment is fixed and cannot be reversed fully.

Disorder Description

The two major diseases of the lung that are grouped under COPD are chronic (obstructive) bronchitis and emphysema.

Pathologically, chronic bronchitis is characterised by the appearance of chronic cough with excess production of sputum lasting for more than three months of the year during two or more successive years. Chronic bronchitis is characterised by the lack of reversibility of pulmonary function in response to pharmacological agents. In the bronchi and bronchioles (small passageways in the lung) chronic inflammation leads to scar tissue that produces fixed airways obstruction.

Emphysema involves dilatation and destroying of the respiratory bronchioles. The lesions usually occur in the upper lung regions in milder disease, but may appear throughout the entire lung, destructing the pulmonary capillary bed in advanced cases. In emphysema, severe hyperinflation of the chest increases lung volumes, placing the respiratory muscles at a mechanical disadvantage, which reduces their force-generating capacity. Clinically, patients with emphysema exhibit varying degrees of dyspnoea on exertion. Dyspnoea may be defined as a sensation of difficulty in breathing.

Although chronic bronchitis and emphysema are both caused by cigarette smoking and frequently coexist, it is assumed that 85% of patients with COPD suffer primarily from chronic bronchitis and 15% from emphysema.

Aetiology

Cigarette smoking is responsible for almost 90% of the COPD cases. Usually it takes decades of tobacco smoking (one pack of cigarettes every day for more than 20 years) to develop COPD. The individual (genetic) susceptibility to the airway effects of smoking is very wide, such that approximately 10–15% of smokers will develop clinically significant COPD while approximately half will never develop any symptomatic physiological deficit (British Thoracic Society, 1997). Air pollution and some occupational exposures also represent risks for developing COPD. Gender, genetic features, presence of respiratory illness in childhood, long-standing asthma and family history (including socioeconomic status) should also be considered (Antó et al., 2001). There is also clear evidence about the role of alpha 1-antitrypsin deficiency causing emphysema, especially in patients who develop COPD at a young age (<45 years) (Sandford, Weir & Paré, 1997).

Diagnosis

The diagnosis of COPD is suspected in patients with a history of several decades of cigarette smoking who present with non-specific respiratory symptoms, such as wheezing, cough and sputum production. Although the presence of these symptoms is not a specific predictor for the subsequent development of COPD (Van den Boom et al., 1998), some studies show that chronic cough and mucus hypersecretion are associated with more hospital admissions and mortality (Vestbo, Prescott & Lange, 1996).

The diagnosis is established by spirometric testing which requires the patient to take a maximum inspiration, and then blow out all of the air into a spirometer as forcefully and as rapidly as possible. The volume of air exhaled within one second is referred to as forced expiratory volume in one second (FEV_1). It is expressed in litres and is considered to be the "gold standard" (Pauwels et al., 2001). Predicted forced expiratory volumes are expressed in terms of a normal range for age, sex and height. Airflow abnormality is usually demonstrated by a decreased FEV_1 and a decrease in the ratio of FEV_1 to forced vital capacity (FVC). FVC values represent the maximum volume of air that can be forcibly expelled after inhaling as deeply as possible. Reversibility of the airflow obstruction is tested by establishing spirometric values before and after an adequate dose of inhaled bronchodilator. Lung function (especially post-bronchodilator FEV_1) is a strong predictor of overall mortality in COPD (Anthonisen et al., 1986).

Course and Progression of Disease

People with COPD experience a gradual deterioration in functional status. Smokers may develop symptoms of COPD within years of starting smoking but the cough and sputum production are often ignored as normal for a smoker. The disease is usually not diagnosed until the smoker experiences symptoms (shortness of breath with mild exertion and fatigue) that interfere with activities of daily life. Patients often do not complain of exertional dyspnoea until their FEV_1 is between 40 and 59% of its predicted value (British Thoracic Society, 1997). Symptomatically, people with COPD experience progressive dyspnoea, and gradually reduce their physical activities to avoid experiencing dyspnoea. The sedentary lifestyle contributes to physical deconditioning, with generalised muscle weakness, a reduction in exercise tolerance, and poor survival rates (Maltais et al., 2000).

COPD is incurable. The lung function is constantly deteriorating and death rates increase. Smoking cessation results in an initial slight improvement and then a slower rate of lung function decline compared with continued smokers. Lung function decline then slows to the rate due to normal ageing alone (Anthonisen et al., 1994). However, FEV_1 values do not return to the normal level. Small losses of function can be tolerated without difficulty because there is about a 30% pulmonary function reserve in most people.

Patients with COPD usually experience progressively disabling dyspnoea with periods of relative clinical stability interrupted by recurrent exacerbations. Acute exacerbations are episodes of worsened dyspnoea, increased sputum production, and increased sputum purulence. They can be triggered by bacterial or viral infections, air pollution, and other serious conditions such as heart failure, non-pulmonary infections, and pulmonary embolism (Connors et al., 1996; Sherk & Grossman, 2000).

According to the National Heart, Lung, and Blood Institute/World Health Organisation Global Initiative for Chronic Obstructive Lung Disease (the GOLD study group) the risk of dying from an acute exacerbation is closely related to the presence of acidosis, comorbidities, and the need for ventilatory support (Pauwels et al., 2001). A report on outcomes following exacerbations in patients with COPD (the Study to Understand Prognoses and Preferences for Outcome and Risks of Treatment: SUPPORT) shows that approximately half of the patients required admission at the intensive care unit, with 11% of patients dying during hospital stay, 20% dying within 60 days, 33% within six months, 43% within one year, and 49% within two years after admission (Connors et al., 1996).

Data from the SUPPORT study on the last six months of life in patients with end-stage COPD who died within one year after study onset ($n = 416$) show that these patients spent 15–25% of their last six months in hospital. Moderate to severe physical symptoms that were present at least half of the time in the last six months included pain (25% of the sample), confusion (15%), and dyspnoea (70%). Depressed mood, anxiety scores and confusion gradually increased in patients who were hospitalised as patients came closer to death (Lynn et al., 2000).

A frequently occurring complication in patients with progressing COPD is weight loss (pulmonary cachexia). It is caused by elevated energy metabolism and inadequate dietary intake, and appears to be a determining factor of mortality, functional capacity, and quality of life. Prevalence rates of inadequate nutritional states in patients with COPD range from 20% in stable outpatients to 70% in hospitalised patients with acute respiratory failure (Ferreira et al., 2001; Wouters & Schols, 2000).

Disease Stages

The GOLD study group (Pauwels et al., 2001) recommends a simple classification of disease severity into four stages. The first stage (stage 0: at risk) is characterised by chronic cough and sputum production, but lung function (spirometry) is still normal. The second stage (stage I: mild COPD) is characterised by mild airflow limitation (post-bronchodilator $FEV_1 \geq 80\%$ predicted, $FEV_1/FVC < 70\%$). In the third stage (stage II: moderate COPD) patients have worsened airflow limitation (post-bronchodilator $FEV_1 \geq 30\%$ and $< 80\%$ predicted) and usually suffer the progression of symptoms, with shortness of breath on exertion. The fourth stage (stage III: severe COPD) is characterised by severe airflow limitation (post-bronchodilator $FEV_1 < 30\%$ predicted), or/and respiratory failure or clinical signs of right heart failure.

Comorbidity

In the National Heart, Lung, and Blood Institute Workshop Summary, Petty and Weinmann (1997) state that the relative risk for lung cancer incidence and mortality is nearly seven times higher in smokers with a low FEV_1 than in patients with normal airflow. Also, rapid decline in FEV_1 appears to be related to coronary heart disease mortality, whereas vital capacity values (FVC) are predictive of coronary heart incidence (Kannel, Hubert & Lew, 1983; Tockman et al., 1995).

A recent study on the prevalence of self-reported comorbidity in patients with COPD over the age of 40, comparing them with age-matched controls, shows that locomotive diseases, insomnia, sinusitis, migraine, depression, stomach or duodenal ulcers and cancer were significantly more common in patients with COPD. The majority of COPD patients (73%) reported one or more comorbid conditions (van Manen et al., 2001).

In a study by Mapel et al. (2000) diagnoses of chronic comorbid conditions in patients with COPD were compared to matched non-COPD controls (mean age: 67.5 years). Their study shows that patients with COPD had higher prevalence rates of ulcers or gastritis, coronary artery disease, other major cardiovascular diseases, non-metastatic cancers, non-stroke neurological diseases, and congestive heart failure.

Data from the SUPPORT study show that multiple comorbid conditions are common in patients with end-stage COPD (Lynn et al., 2000). In this group, 75% of the patients had two or three comorbidities, 39% had ≥ 3 comorbidities.

Mortality

Worldwide mortality from COPD ranked sixth in 1990. It is estimated that by the year 2020, COPD will become the third most common cause of death on a worldwide scale, exceeded only by heart attacks and stroke. It is the only leading cause of death due to illness in the 1990 top 10 that is expected to rise in prevalence (Murray & Lopez, 1997).

Statistics from the WHO on age-adjusted death rates (ages 35–74) for COPD in the year 1997 show that mortality rates in the USA were 46 per 100 000 population for males and 35 for females. The rates in the UK were 47 for males and 32 for females. The highest rates worldwide in women were observed in Scotland: 40 (53 for males) per 100 000, and in men in Hungary (1995 data): 75 per 100 000 (Hurd, 2000).

The prognosis of COPD is poor. Mortality 10 years after diagnosis is above 50% (Ferguson & Cherniack, 1994). Related to survival are post-bronchodilator FEV_1, hypoxaemia, age, gender, body weight and comorbidity. Also, in a study by Ashutosh, Haldipur and Boucher (1997) mortality could be predicted by overall psychological distress (higher MMPI scores) and a simple clinical score, irrespective of the degree of impairment in pulmonary function or oxygenation.

The main causes of death in patients with COPD are cardiovascular disease, COPD, lung cancer, and other tumours (Nishimura & Tsukino, 2000).

Prevalence

Prevalence data greatly underestimate the total number of patients with COPD because the disease is usually not diagnosed until it is already moderately advanced. The different classifications of COPD in different countries, the high costs of gathering epidemiological data, and the fact that COPD is more likely to be recorded as a secondary cause of death have made it hard to quantify COPD. Also, because the prevalence of COPD progressively increases with age, estimates greatly vary for samples with different age criteria.

Estimates derived from the National Health Interview Surveys from the National Center for Health Statistics in the USA suggest that chronic bronchitis and emphysema affected one in eight men and one in ten women >65 years in the USA in 1994 (Adams & Marano, 1995). It is estimated that in 1994 14.0 million US citizens suffered from chronic bronchitis and 2.2 million from emphysema. The number of patients with COPD in the USA has doubled in the past 25 years, with prevalence of COPD now rising faster in women than in men (Hurd, 2000). Studies of prevalence rates of COPD in European countries have indicated that

4–6% of the adult population has clinically relevant COPD (Gulsvik, 1999). A UK screening survey in a random sample of patients from north Lincolnshire, aged 60–75 years, showed the prevalence rate for COPD to be 9.9% (Dickinson et al., 1999).

Gender and Race Differences

Although men have had higher prevalence rates of COPD than women for decades, reflecting the historically higher smoking and occupational exposures in men, the increased smoking rates in females within the last several decades have been associated with steadily increasing rates of COPD in women. In 1994, the reported prevalence rate of chronic bronchitis and emphysema in the USA for females was respectively 63.1 and 6.0 per 1000, while the prevalence rate of chronic bronchitis and emphysema for males was respectively 44.5 and 9.7 per 1000 (Hurd, 2000). Also, some studies suggest that there are differences in the natural history of COPD in men and women. Women appear to be at higher risk of developing severe COPD than men (Silverman et al., 2000). They present with larger reductions in FEV_1 after adjustment for levels of tobacco smoke exposure. Also, it appears that women do not lose weight and maintain usual exercise ability until moderate or severe disease is present (Carter, Nicotra & Huber, 1994).

Black populations have generally lower prevalence levels of COPD than whites (both males and females) (Mannino et al., 2000). With regard to mortality, in the USA the age-adjusted death rate per 100 000 population was 25.5 in 1998 for white men, 20.9 for black men, 17.6 for white women, and 9.5 for black women. Compared with mortality rates in 1979 these rates have remained stable for white men (3% increase), have increased gradually in black men (22%), but have increased dramatically in white women (136%) and black women (157%) (American Lung Association, 2001).

Costs

The economic burden of COPD on individuals and on society is substantial. In the USA the National Heart, Lung, and Blood Institute estimated the annual total economic costs of COPD morbidity and mortality at $23.9 billion in 1993. This included $14.7 billion in direct health care costs (expenses due to admissions to hospitals, home visits, home care and drugs). In COPD, inpatient hospital care is the largest component of direct medical costs (Sullivan, Ramsay & Lee, 2000). More recent estimates are that the total economic costs for 2000 in the USA were $30.4 billion (National Institutes of Health and National Heart, Lung, and Blood Institute, 2000).

In the UK, the annual direct medical cost to the National Health Service has been estimated at £817.5 million in 1996, treating an estimated 6.5 million patients with COPD (Guest, 1999). In the Netherlands direct medical costs were estimated to be $US256 million in 1993. Annual costs were estimated to be $US813 per COPD patient, more than 2.5 times the annual costs per asthma patient. Assuming that starting and quitting rates for smoking as registered in 1993 would stay the same, costs for COPD in the Netherlands are predicted to increase by 61% to $US412.5 million (approximately €458 million at 2001 rates) by 2010 (Rutten-van Mölken et al., 1999a).

QUALITY OF LIFE

Assessment

Although traditional biomedical measures of COPD severity remain central to the clinical investigation of respiratory impairment and treatment of patients with COPD, quality of life (QoL) is increasingly being recognised as an important outcome parameter. Involvement of health psychologists in research and treatment in patients with COPD often originates from the recognition that ultimately the goal of medical management is to improve QoL. Assessment of QoL in COPD has become an important area of research (Maillé et al., 1996).

QoL measures ideally assess the patient's subjective experience of the effects of disease and treatment on satisfaction with life. However, as in other chronic diseases, little agreement has been attained on the definition or measurement of the construct (Carone & Jones, 2000). Also, the terms "quality of life", "functional performance", "health-related quality of life" and "health status" are used interchangeably in the respiratory medicine literature (Curtis, Martin & Martin, 1997). Broadly defined, QoL refers to the gap between what is desired and what is achievable in life. The more restrictive concept of health-related quality of life (HRQL) refers to the impact of disease on this gap (Carone & Jones, 2000).

Despite the diversity in definitions and preferred terms, in the last decade several disease-specific QoL measures for patients with COPD have been developed and the use of generic and disease-specific measures in COPD research has become well established (Maillé et al., 1996).

Generic Quality of Life Measures

The most widely used generic measures in COPD research are the Sickness Impact Profile (SIP) (Bergner et al., 1981), Medical Outcomes Study Short Form 36 (MOS SF-36) (Ware & Sherbourne, 1992), and the Nottingham Health Profile (NHP) (Hunt, McEwen & McKenna, 1986). For each instrument an example of a study employing the instrument in patients with COPD is given.

Using the SIP, Schrier et al. (1990) studied QoL in a variety of lung diseases. Patients rated their QoL (physical and psychosocial functioning) lower than did a healthy community sample, and patients with COPD were more impaired than patients with asthma.

The MOS SF-36 was used in a study by Stavem et al. (2000) to examine QoL across patients with COPD, angina pectoris, rheumatoid arthritis, and asthma. Patients with COPD were significantly more impaired on all QoL dimensions compared with a population reference. Also, in comparison to the other illnesses they had the lowest scores (indicating worse QoL) on five of the eight dimensions of the MOS SF-36 (physical functioning, general health, social functioning, physical role functioning, and emotional role functioning).

Jans, Schellevis and Van Eijk (1999) examined the psychometric properties of the NHP in asthma and COPD patients in general practice. Their results show that compared with scores in a healthy population, patients with COPD had higher scores (indicating worse

QoL) on the dimensions "physical mobility", "energy", "social isolation", and "emotional reactions", but not on the dimensions "pain" and "sleep".

Comparing the usefulness of these instruments for measuring change in COPD research, the SIP seems to be insensitive to changes in patients with mild/moderate disease severity and may have a greater sensitivity to deterioration in health than to improvement (Jones, 1999). The MOS SF-36 was found to be sensitive to changes after rehabilitation in severe patients (Boueri et al., 2001), after treatment with medication (Di Lorenzo et al., 1998), and after changes in dyspnoea (Mahler et al., 1995). The NHP was found to be sensitive to changes after rehabilitation in patients with moderate disease severity (Fuchs-Climent et al., 2001).

Disease-specific Instruments

Disease-specific instruments are commonly referred to as HRQL measures. The most widely used HRQL measures in COPD research are the St George's Respiratory Questionnaire (SGRQ) (Jones et al., 1992), the Chronic Respiratory (Disease) Questionnaire (CRQ) (Guyatt et al., 1987a), and the Breathing Problems Questionnaire (BPQ) (Hyland et al., 1994). The CRQ is also available in a recently developed self-administered version (Williams et al., 2001), and the BPQ is also available in a purpose-specific ten-item short version, designed for measuring outcome in pulmonary rehabilitation (Hyland et al., 1998). For each instrument an example of a study employing the instrument in patients with COPD is given.

The SGRQ was used in a study by Spencer et al. and the Inhaled Steroids in Obstructive Lung Disease (ISOLDE) Study Group (2001) examining health status decline in patients with COPD. Their results show that the baseline scores of patients with COPD were much higher (indicating worse QoL) on all the dimensions of the SGRQ ("symptoms", "activity", "impact" and "total score") than scores from a healthy reference population with the same age range.

Using the CRQ to assess the relation between QoL and depressive symptoms in patients with COPD, Yohannes et al. (1998a) found that patients with COPD had significantly lower CRQ total scores (reduced QoL) as compared to age-matched normal controls and a group of disabled controls (patients with Parkinson's disease, stroke, arthritis and amputation).

Yohannes et al. (1998b) assessed QoL in elderly COPD outpatients using both the BPQ and the CRQ. They found that patients with COPD had significantly higher scores on the BPQ and lower scores on the CRQ (indicating worse QoL) than age-matched controls.

Results from studies comparing the sensitivity and discriminative value of the three HRQL instruments are mixed. Singh et al. (2001) compared the sensitivity of the SGRQ, CRQ and BPQ SF-10 for evaluating outcome in pulmonary rehabilitation. Their study demonstrates much higher effect sizes for the CRQ as compared to the SGRQ and the BPQ. They conclude that the CRQ is the most sensitive to change, followed by the SGRQ and the BPQ. However, they state that the changes observed in the SGRQ may be more durable. Another study, comparing the sensitivity of the SGRQ and the CRQ to changes resulting from bronchodilator therapy, concludes that both instruments were equally sensitive and choices could be based on the size of the required sample (smaller for the CRQ) or availability of reference values (Rutten-van Mölken, Roos & van Noord, 1999). With regard to evaluating

HRQL cross-sectionally, in a study by Hajiro et al. (1998) the BPQ was found to be less discriminatory than the SGRQ or the CRQ. It appeared that the BPQ was highly skewed towards the very mild end of the scale. They suggest that the CRQ is more sensitive to psychological status. In contrast, in comparing the CRQ and the BPQ, Yohannes et al. (1998b) found that the BPQ was a better tool for differentiating elderly subjects with COPD from matched subjects with normal lung function.

The pros and cons of QoL instruments are discussed by Curtis, Martin and Martin (1997), Donner, Muir and the Rehabilitation and Chronic Care Scientific Group of the European Respiratory Society (1997), Hyland (2002), Jones (1999) and Maillé et al. (1996). In general, these authors suggest that generic instruments have lower levels of sensitivity to health status impairment and less power to detect changes than disease-specific instruments. However, if the primary goal is to compare disease status across different illnesses, the MOS SF-36 might be the best option for studying health status in patients with COPD. In discussing how to choose the best HRQL instrument, Hyland states that there is no "best" questionnaire. He suggests that "a good course of action is to compare the items in different scales against the kind of purpose for which the questionnaire is to be used" (Hyland, 2002, p. 243).

Other frequently assessed properties of COPD burden include measurement of functional status and activities of daily living (Functional Performance Inventory [Leidy, 1999], Pulmonary Functional Status Scale [Weaver & Narsavage, 1992], Nottingham Extended Activities of Daily Living Scale [Yohannes, Roomi & Connolly, 1998]), utility (Quality of Well Being Scale [Kaplan, Atkins & Timms, 1984]), dyspnoea rating scales (British Medical Research Council Dyspnoea Scale, Baseline Dyspnoea Index [ZuWallack, 2000]), exercise tolerance (timed walk test, treadmill or bicycle test [ZuWallack, 2000]) and psychological impact (Hospital Anxiety Depression Scale [Yohannes, Baldwin & Connolly, 2000]). Also, a screening tool for identifying psychosocial adjustment difficulties has been tested in patients with COPD (Psychosocial Adjustment to Illness Scale-Self Report [Stubbing, Haalboom & Barr, 1998]).

Impact of Illness

QoL measures assess the patients' subjective experience of the impact of illness in (preferably) several life domains. Most measurements include the dimensions of emotional functioning (mood changes), physical functioning (activities of daily living) and social functioning (employment, social or family relationships).

Patients with COPD typically experience a progressively worsening course of disease marked by a gradual increase in symptoms, which often results in emotional distress, reduced capacity for physical activities, loss of social roles, and deteriorations in cognitive functioning.

The primary activity-limiting symptom in patients with COPD is dyspnoea, which is often accompanied by chronic cough and wheezing. Other symptoms, such as fatigue, sleep difficulties and congestion, are also frequently reported (Guyatt et al., 1987b; Kinsman et al., 1983).

The emotional impact of the disease is reflected in the high prevalence of depression in patients with COPD (Yohannes, Baldwin & Connolly, 2000). According to Yohannes et al. (1998a) depression is frequently unrecognised in patients with COPD and may manifest as decreased energy levels, decreased libido, difficulty in performing activities, feelings of hopelessness, and social withdrawal. Anxiety and panic attacks are also common in patients with COPD (Smoller et al., 1996; Yohannes, Baldwin & Connolly, 2000).

The most commonly reported behavioural consequences of COPD are impairments in employment, recreational activities, household management and activities of daily living (McSweeny & Labuhn, 1996; Williams & Bury, 1989).

COPD can also have many effects on relationships and social contacts. Social isolation, loneliness, and sexual dysfunctioning are frequently reported (Keele-Card, Foxall & Barron, 1993; McSweeny & Labuhn, 1996; Sexton & Munrow, 1983). The pervasive influence of COPD on social and role functioning is demonstrated in studies comparing COPD with other chronic illnesses (Schlenk et al., 1998; Stavem et al., 2000).

Several studies have documented the impact on cognitive or neuropsychological functioning among chronic hypoxaemic patients. Deficits in attention, memory, complex visual motor processes, abstraction ability and verbal tasks have been reported (Incalzi et al., 1997; Stuss et al., 1997).

Recent qualitative studies in patients with COPD show that a sense of effectiveness ("being able") and connectedness ("being with") are important themes in patients' lives, and that QoL is seen as depending mainly on family relationships, sense of community and safety in the neighbourhood, mobility and independence in activities of daily living, and the absence of symptoms of comorbid conditions (Guthrie, Hill & Muers, 2001; Leidy & Haase, 1999).

Quantitative studies have shown that severity of disease in terms of its impact on QoL is poorly predicted by lung function tests. There is also some evidence that QoL scores in patients with COPD are predictive of use of acute services, (re-)admission to hospital, days in hospital, and nebuliser provision (Cox et al., 1993; Osman et al., 1997; Siu et al., 1993; Traver, 1988).

TREATMENT POSSIBILITIES

Treatments do not cure the patient, but may be able to benefit the patient's QoL. According to the GOLD study group (Pauwels et al., 2001) goals of effective management of COPD include preventing disease progression, relieving symptoms, improving exercise tolerance, improving health status, preventing and treating complications and exacerbations, and reducing mortality. A schematic overview of the treatment possibilities is given in Table 9.1.

Medical Management

Pharmacological Therapy

Unfortunately none of the pharmacological therapies has been shown to slow the progression of the disease or increase the survival rate. Although not all pharmacological treatments are evidence-based (Pauwels et al., 2001) and some are in fact not recommended or contra-indicated, medications prescribed for COPD patients include bronchodilators, corticosteroids, antibiotics, influenza vaccinations, mucolytics, cough suppressants, pain killers, sleeping pills, and tranquillisers.

Table 9.1 Overview of treatment possibilities in COPD

COPD treatment issues	Medical management	Psychosocial and behavioural management
Symptoms:		
Dyspnoea	Pharmacological treatment: • β-agonists • Anticholinergics • Methylxanthines • Corticosteroids—oral 　　　　　　　　—inhaled • Antibiotics • Influenza vaccination	Adherence issues: prevent overdoses, prevent going off medication abruptly, stimulate continued use, instructions to take exactly as directed, teaching inhaler techniques
	Oxygen therapy: • Home oxygen therapy • Ventilatory support—non-invasive 　　　　　　　　—invasive	Assist with acceptance of oxygen dependency, stimulate oxygen use during (outdoor) activities Failure to wean from ventilator Assist with breathing techniques
Mucus	Pharmacological treatment: • Mucolytics	
	Clearance through physical therapy: • Postural drainage • Chest percussion and vibration	Assist with forced expiration (coughing techniques) Fluid intake Exercise Positive expiratory pressure mask and flutter breathing (breathing techniques)
Cough	Suppressants	
Pain	Pain killers	
Sleep disorders	Hypnotic medication Nocturnal oxygen therapy	Sleep hygiene issues
Mood disorders:		
Depression	Anti-depressants	Stress reduction, relaxation
Anxiety	Anxiolytics	
Cor pulmonale	Diuretics Digitalis Oxygen therapy	
Undernutrition	Caloric supplementation Anabolic steroids Vitamin supplementation	Lifestyle changes (dietary: meals high in carbohydrate and fat)
Immobility/muscle wasting	Methylxanthines Oxygen	Lifestyle changes (exercise) Physiotherapy/exercise training
Smoking	Nicotine replacement Bupropion	Smoking cessation programmes
Cognitive deficits	Oxygen treatment	Evaluation and assessment of mental status
Emphysematous bullae	Surgery: • Lung volume reduction surgery • Lung transplantation	Recovery issues

Table 9.1 (*continued*)

COPD treatment issues	Medical management	Psychosocial and behavioural management
Somatising disorders		Cognitive modification
Prevention (environment) Passive smoking Air pollution Job-related	Education	Coping skills training
Family/relationship issues		Counselling
End-of-life issues	Life-sustaining treatment	Palliative care, end-of-life decisions

Bronchodilators (β_2-agonists, anticholinergics, methylxanthines) help to open narrowed airways, corticosteroids lessen inflammation of the airway walls, antibiotics fight infections, and influenza vaccination prevents pneumonia. In patients with mucous hypersecretion oral acetylcysteine is believed to have an antioxidant effect and may reduce exacerbations (Ferguson, 2000). Cough suppressants (e.g. codeine), pain killers (e.g. morphine), sleeping pills (e.g. barbiturates), psychoactive drugs (antidepressants and anxiolytic therapy) should be carefully selected and dosed in treating patients with COPD because generally they depress breathing.

Pharmacological treatment of cor pulmonale (right-heart failure due to lung problems) include diuretics that help to excrete excess fluid, and digitalis (nitric oxide) that strengthens the force of the heartbeat. Possibilities for treating undernutrition (although not widely used or studied) are caloric supplementation (oral supplements) and anabolic steroids. The effects of a high intake of vitamin C, vitamin E, β-carotene and fish oils continue to be evaluated and their routine use is not recommended. Respiratory muscle function can be improved by methylxanthines (theophylline). Theophylline benefits pulmonary vasodilation, which improves right ventricular function and exercise performance. Smoking cessation is considered the single most important therapeutic intervention in COPD. Nicotine replacement (transdermal patches, gums, nasal sprays, vapour inhalers) helps to reduce withdrawal symptoms improving smoking cessation rates with approximately 25% (at six months). Other pharmacological assistance (with approximately equal success rates) can be considered (e.g. the antidepressant bupropion) (Barnes, 2000; Ferguson, 2000).

Oxygen Therapy

In patients with severe stable COPD who suffer from hypoxaemia, optimal treatment may require the domiciliary administration of oxygen therapy during activities, or at night only, or patients can receive long-term oxygen therapy (LTOT) for more than 15 hours of the day (Criner, 2000; Petty, 1998; Tarpy & Celli, 1995).

In acute exacerbations of COPD treated in hospital, non-invasive positive pressure ventilation (NPPV) or invasive mechanical ventilatory support are applied (Lightower et al., 2003). NPPV involves the delivery of an inspiratory pressure boost via a close fitting nasal or oro-nasal mask and can also be used at home. Invasive ventilatory support involves endotracheal intubation. If patients fit the selection criteria (see GOLD guidelines, Pauwels et al., 2001), NPPV is the preferred mechanical ventilatory method since intubation is associated with more serious complications (pneumonia, laryngeal and tracheal trauma). Another hazard is the failure to wean to spontaneous ventilation (discontinuation from mechanical ventilation). In this stage the patient's own treatment wishes ("living will") should be the basis for decisions (Barnes, 2000; Cordova & Criner, 1997; Pauwels et al., 2001).

Secretion Clearance through Physical Therapy

Although implementation is not widely recommended, in some patients who produce a large amount of sputum postural bronchial drainage can enhance mucus transport and expectoration (Sutton et al., 1983). Manual or mechanical percussion and vibration do not seem to be as effective as forced expiration (huffing and coughing) in transporting mucus (Wollmer et al., 1985).

Lung Surgery

Lung volume reduction surgery (LVRS), in cases of diffuse emphysema, involves the resection of the most functionless areas of lung (20–30%) to improve ventilatory function (Young, Fry-Smith & Hyde, 1999).

Lung transplantation is only available for hypoxaemic patients with end-stage COPD ($FEV_1 < 25\%$ pred.) who are dependent on oxygen, have extreme limitation in activity, poor QoL, and are under 60 (for single) and under 50 (for bilateral transplantation). In addition they should be in a stable condition and not dependent on drugs, alcohol or nicotine. Due to the scarcity of donors waiting periods may be long (Trulock, 1998).

Pulmonary Rehabilitation

Definition and Principles

The American Thoracic Society (1999) proposes the following definition of pulmonary rehabilitation: "Pulmonary rehabilitation is a multidisciplinary programme of care for patients with chronic respiratory impairment that is individually tailored and designed to optimise physical and social performance and autonomy" (p. 1666).

The British Thoracic Society Standards of Care Subcommittee on Pulmonary Rehabilitation (2001) recently outlined five fundamental principles of rehabilitation:

1. *Rehabilitation follows (or continues alongside) optimal medical management.* Although pulmonary rehabilitation programmes may identify suboptimal medical management, it is assumed that lung function is optimised through medical treatment (pharmacological and oxygen therapy). Rehabilitation is appropriate for those patients who retain significantly disabled despite optimisation of medical therapy.

2. *Rehabilitation is aimed at reducing impairment, disability and handicap and at improving functional independence.* The central aim of pulmonary rehabilitation is to increase functioning. Rehabilitation should reduce limitations in activities and minimise social participation restrictions, aiming at the patients' domestic independence.

3. *Rehabilitation incorporates a multidimensional programme directed at individual needs of patients and their families.* Physical exercise training and disease education are considered mandatory key components of a multidimensional pulmonary rehabilitation programme. Additional components could include muscle strength training, psychological interventions, smoking cessation and nutritional therapy. Programmes should contain individual exercise prescriptions and may include other selected components of treatment depending on the needs of the patient.

4. *Rehabilitation is provided by a multiprofessional team.* Personnel involved in pulmonary rehabilitation programmes may include physicians, physiotherapists, nurses, dieticians, social workers, occupational therapists, pharmacists, lung function technicians, and patients who attended previous courses. Psychologists and exercise scientists may also contribute.

5. *Rehabilitation outcomes should be monitored with appropriate measures.* Outcome measures should reflect the goals of pulmonary rehabilitation. The gold standard for measuring impairment is exercise testing (peak oxygen uptake and dyspnoea during treadmill or cycle ergometer exercise tests). Impairment of lung function does not reverse with rehabilitation. Disability can be assessed by walking exercise tests (six-minute walk test, shuttle walking test), with dyspnoea or fatigue measured alongside. Handicap can be assessed with generic or disease-specific QoL tests or the Psychosocial Adjustment to Illness Scale-Self Report. Functioning can be assessed with pulmonary functional status scales, QoL questionnaires, and activities of daily living scales (see paragraph on QoL assessment).

Psychosocial and Behavioural Components in Pulmonary Rehabilitation

Although ATS and BTS guideline papers (American Thoracic Society, 1999; British Thoracic Society, 2001) include sections on the possible beneficial effects of incorporating psychosocial and behavioural interventions in pulmonary rehabilitation programmes, it is less clear what these interventions include and who should deliver them. According to the American College of Chest Physicians/American Association of Cardiovascular and Pulmonary Rehabilitation (ACCP/AACVPR, 1997) psychosocial intervention components include psychosocial intervention (stress-management, relaxation, patient education, support group addressing depression and anxiety, sexual relations, family and work relationships facilitating information and emotional support sharing), health behaviour intervention (smoking cessation, dietary change), adherence intervention (compliance with exercise and medical therapies), and education intervention (education classes on a wide variety of topics and active coaching). According to the BTS psychological and behavioural intervention is embedded in the structure of rehabilitation programmes through the delivery of education, small group discussions, and relaxation, with interventions targeting anxiety, depression, dyspnoea, self-efficacy and motivation (British Thoracic Society, 2001).

In their review of empirical papers on the effect of psychosocial support in pulmonary rehabilitation, Kaptein and Dekker (2000) identified ten studies with a randomised-controlled design. The types of psychosocial support used in these studies include relaxation aimed at more controlled and efficient breathing (applied in most studies), cognitive modification, coping skills training, stress-management, behaviour modification, cognitive-behaviour modification, panic control, supportive discussions and symptom control. In only one study the psychosocial intervention was explicitly provided by psychologists. Results from a survey on the provision of pulmonary rehabilitation services in the UK (Davidson & Morgan, 1998) reveal that psychologists participated in the programme in only 19 of the 91 hospitals that offered pulmonary rehabilitation and that a psychiatric input was reported in six hospitals. Although the role of psychologists in pulmonary rehabilitation may be more prominent in other countries, studies on this subject from other countries are lacking.

According to most guideline papers, the importance of psychosocial and behavioural interventions in improving outcome in pulmonary rehabilitation remains to be established. However, the review by Kaptein and Dekker (2000) shows that significant improvements are reported in QoL, dyspnoea, functional capacity and self-efficacy. Also, in their systematic overview of the rehabilitation literature Lacasse, Goldstein and Guyatt (1997) conclude that: "relaxation may relieve dyspnoea and anxiety acutely", and: "Cognitive and behaviour modification techniques as an adjunct to exercise training are effective in improving exercise tolerance and health-related quality of life" (p. 341).

Psychological Interventions

> as the fish that thrusts its jaw to water draw
> so I some air do seek to snare,
> and like the weanling goat upon the nipple I suck,
> but it is not milk so sweet I crave, but air, air so pure.
>   (Horowitz, 1996, p. 252)

Quite understandably, psychologists' first area of study is related to quantifying the psychological and social consequences of COPD for the patients. Webb and Lawton (1961) used the now outdated Szondi test to examine "basic personality traits characteristic of patients with primary obstructive pulmonary emphysema". Agle and Baum (1977) documented the psychological aspects of chronic obstructive pulmonary disease by psychiatric interview. Anxiety, depression, body preoccupation, alcoholism, paranoid states, sexual dysfunctions, and defence mechanisms were observed. In 1983 the first paper was published in which more adequate measures were applied in order to study the psychological responses of COPD patients to their condition. Kinsman et al. (1983) reported on levels of helplessness–hopelessness, fatigue, sleep disturbance, irritability, and anxiety in a sample of hospitalised patients with chronic bronchitis and emphysema.

A second area explored by clinical health psychologists (before the term "health psychologist" existed) concerns neuropsychological consequences of the disorder. A chronic insufficient level of oxygenation may translate into neuropsychological damage—studies on this topic, therefore, are done in patients with a severe grade of COPD. The study by Prigatano et al. (1983) is the first one on this topic. The authors report neuropsychological impairments (e.g. memory, tactual performance) in hypoxaemic COPD patients (see also Bender & Milgrom, 2002, for a recent review).

QoL represents the third major area of research by clinical health psychologists in COPD patients (see earlier in this chapter). A recent review of this area shows how the first paper on this subject was published in 1975 by Stewart, Hood and Block; currently, some 30 empirical papers per year are published in journals indexed in *Index Medicus* (Kaptein, 2002). This increase in publications on QoL in patients with COPD reflects how pulmonary physicians have become more interested in assessing the outcome of their medical management in broader terms than pulmonary function or functional capacity. For clinical health psychologists, QoL can quite often serve as a concept that facilitates discussion with respiratory physicians about initiating and performing studies in COPD patients. The overall term "quality of life" usually allows the addition in the design of concepts that are of particular interest to psychologists (e.g. self-efficacy, illness cognitions), but which may be met with the raising of an eyebrow in pulmonary physicians when discussed explicitly. This is not a cynical remark—it is merely a reflection of our experience with doing clinical health psychology research in the respiratory area. Emphasizing that "quality of life" is a major dependent variable in a study tends to reduce resistance in medical professionals about psychological research on patients with COPD.

The fourth major area in which behavioural scientists are involved is pulmonary rehabilitation for patients with COPD. This topic was discussed earlier in this chapter, so only some additional issues will be mentioned here briefly. Referral to pulmonary rehabilitation programmes sometimes equates an "elegant" way to "get the patient out of the waiting room". As described by Kinsman et al. (1983) and Van der Schoot and Kaptein (1990), patients who are referred to third-line medical management, i.e. inpatient or outpatient pulmonary rehabilitation programmes (first line being general practitioner care; second line, outpatient or short-stay hospital care), not only have serious medical problems. They usually also are characterised by severe psychological and social problems, which contributes to complicating the medical encounter. Referring a patient to a pulmonary rehabilitation programme may reflect difficulty experienced by the physician in the hospital or in primary care dealing with these problems in those patients.

Criteria for referring patients to pulmonary rehabilitation programmes do not encompass behavioural, psychological or social problems or indications explicitly. One of the tasks of the psychologist in the multidisciplinary team is to assess the precise reasons for referral. High drop-out rates may be reduced in this way. Those patients who do continue their rehabilitation sessions do benefit. A systematic review of studies with a randomised design examining behavioural interventions in pulmonary rehabilitation programmes tends to corroborate the view that psychological outcome measures (e.g. self-efficacy, shortness of breath, QoL, well-being) are positively affected (Kaptein & Dekker, 2000).

The fifth area of work by clinical health psychologists in COPD patients pertains to cognitive-behavioural interventions. As is true in the area of clinical health psychology overall, attempts to modify dysfunctional cognitive and behavioural responses of patients to their illness tend to produce quite positive outcomes. The study by Atkins et al. (1984) was the first study in the area of cognitive-behavioural interventions in COPD patients. The study still stands out as one of the best in this area, for methodological reasons in particular: patient selection, allocation of patients to the five experimental conditions, and assessment of independent and dependent variables must be qualified as "state-of-the-art". Patients in the cognitive-behavioural condition were taught to substitute unhelpful cognitions ("I can't walk very far without getting short of breath, so what's the use?") with more appropriate positive and goal-oriented self-statements ("This walking is uncomfortable, but I can handle it. Soon I will be able to walk farther") (p. 594). Compared to control conditions, patients in the cognitive-behavioural condition reported a higher exercise tolerance and a greater well-being. In an extension of their research, Ries et al. (1995) demonstrated how these effects could be replicated in an outpatient rehabilitation setting. Emery et al. (1998) report similar results in a more recent study (see Kaptein, 1997, for a review of this area).

Clinical health psychologists have come a long way over the past 40 years in studying patients with COPD. Descriptive studies are being replaced by intervention studies, with outcome measures in the psychological and social domains overtaking importance over pulmonary function measures. Given the high, and still increasing, prevalence of COPD, the associated psychological and social misery, and the evidence for the effectiveness of psychological interventions, COPD offers many opportunities for clinical health psychologists. Several areas are under-researched and deserve further study. The following topics are candidates for our research efforts:

- drop-out rates in pulmonary rehabilitation programmes
- sexuality
- effects of COPD on partners of patients
- contribution of patients themselves to cognitive-behavioural interventions
- integration of clinical health psychology into medical management of COPD
- strengthening the theoretical basis of clinical health psychology work in COPD.

A final remark. If no one smoked cigarettes, COPD would virtually cease to exist. COPD patients, almost by definition, have smoked cigarettes for at least 40 years. In our experience it is somewhat ludicrous to try to motivate those patients to stop smoking. Behavioural stop-smoking programmes are only moderately successful, pharmacological stop-smoking measures appear to share this fate. The efforts of health care providers, including clinical health psychologists, are currently limited to reducing the effects of smoking cigarettes in susceptible patients—a sober reminder of the limits of our work, and, for that matter, of the "condition humaine" (Arendt, 1958).

CONCLUSIONS AND FUTURE DIRECTIONS

As can be concluded from this chapter's section on disease characteristics, chronic obstructive pulmonary disease is a common, costly, potentially preventable disease that cannot be cured and that will remain one of the leading causes of morbidity and mortality in the industrialised and the developing countries. Although some gains have been made in recent decades, this is mainly due to refinements in medical treatments and not because medical therapeutic options have increased. For now, in order to alter the course and outcome of disease in patients with COPD, future research and treatment should focus on early detection (disease stages 0 and I), early warning and early interventions concentrating on smoking cessation (for an overview on smoking cessation see Nardini, 2000). Clinical or health psychologists could play an important role in the development and application of (more) effective smoking cessation or prevention programmes.

With respect to QoL it cannot be stressed enough that the goal of any treatment should be to increase QoL, with valid QoL measures being the primary outcome measure. Researchers and health care professionals involved in treating patients with COPD should be aware of the fact that exercise performance does not equal QoL. Quoting Lacasse, Guyatt and Goldstein (1998) on the subject: "Unfortunately, reports evaluating the efficacy of respiratory rehabilitation still focus too often on laboratory measures of exercise (. . .) However, measures of exercise capacity (either maximal or functional) correlate only weakly or moderately with quality-of-life instruments in chronic lung diseases" (pp. 2, 3).

Although the sections on psychosocial and behavioural interventions in medical guideline papers (especially those on rehabilitation) reveal that medical specialists assume that these kind of treatments could benefit their patients with COPD, their hunch is quite often not sub-stantiated by proper (randomised-controlled) studies. From the limited number of studies that qualify for inclusion in papers reviewing psychosocial and behavioural support it can be concluded that there is a great shortage of well-designed studies on the subject. Clinical or health psychologists could contribute a great deal to the management of COPD and apparently are needed to do so. Where evidence-based medicine is striving for A-levels (the highest level of scientific evidence of effectiveness of treatment) to support the recommen-dation of specific therapeutic interventions (for an overview of levels of recommendation see Lacasse & Goldstein, 1999), well-designed studies on psychosocial support in COPD would greatly increase the chances of behavioural scientists to become involved in the management of patients with COPD.

Future research using randomised-controlled designs, with psychosocial support added as an extra experimental condition to medical intervention/pulmonary rehabilitation, is needed to enable the evaluation of the additional value of psychosocial support for COPD patients. In addition, in these trials the content of psychosocial support should be precisely defined, should be theoretically based and trials should provide directions for the qualifications of health care providers responsible for the psychosocial support (Kaptein & Dekker, 2000).

The few well-designed psychosocial and behavioural intervention studies within the field of COPD and results from (intervention) studies addressing, for example, coping, self-efficacy, self-management and illness perceptions in patients with other chronic illnesses (Bourbeau et al., 2003; Clark & Hampson, 2001; Compas et al., 1998; Fawzy, Fawzy & Wheeler, 1996; Petrie et al. 2002; Scharloo et al., 1998, 1999, 2000a, 2000b), provide support that the participation of behavioural scientists in turn would increase QoL in patients with COPD.

Writing of this chapter was supported by research grants from the Dutch Asthma Foun-dation, project numbers 88.54, 90.37, and 98.15.

REFERENCES

Adams, P.F. & Marano, M.A. (1995). Current estimates from the National Health Interview Survey, 1994: National Center for Health Statistics. *Vital Health Statistics*, **10** (193), 1–128.

Agle, D.P. & Baum, G.L. (1997). Psychological aspects of chronic obstructive pulmonary disease. *Medical Clinics of North America*, **61**, 749–758.

American College of Chest Physicians/American Association of Cardiovascular and Pulmonary Rehabilitation Guidelines Panel (1997). Pulmonary Rehabilitation: joint ACCP/AACVPR evidence-based guidelines. *Chest*, **112**, 1363–1396.

American Lung Association (2001, March). Trends in chronic bronchitis and emphysema: morbidity and mortality. Retrieved, December 25, 2001, from http://www.lungusa.org/data/copd/copd1.pdf.

American Thoracic Society (1999). Pulmonary rehabilitation—1999. *American Journal of Respira-tory and Critical Care Medicine*, **159**, 1666–1682.

Anthonisen, N.R., Connett, J.E., Kiley, J.P., Altose, M.D., Bailey, W.C., Buist, A.S., Conway, W.A., Enright, P.L., Kanner, R.E., O'Hara, P., Owens, G.R., Scanlon, P.D., Tashkin, D.P., Wise, R.A. & The Lung Health Study Research Group (1994). Effects of smoking intervention and the use of an inhaled anticholinergic bronchodilator on the rate of decline of FEV_1. *Journal of the American Medical Association*, **272**, 1497–1505.

Anthonisen, N.R., Wright, E.C., Hodkin, J.E. & The IPPB Trial Group (1986). Prognosis in chronic obstructive pulmonary disease. *American Review of Respiratory Disease*, **133**, 14–20.

Antó, J.M., Vermeire, P., Vestbo, J. & Sunyer, J. (2001). Epidemiology of chronic obstructive pul-monary disease. *European Respiratory Journal*, **17**, 982–994.

Arendt, H. (1958). *The Human Condition*. Chicago: University of Chicago Press.

Ashutosh, K., Haldipur, C. & Boucher, M.L. (1997). Clinical and personality profiles and survival in patients with COPD. *Chest*, **111**, 95–98.

Atkins, C.J., Kaplan, R.M., Timms, R.M., Reinsch, S. & Lofback, K. (1984). Behavioral exercise programs in the management of chronic obstructive pulmonary disease. *Journal of Consulting and Clinical Psychology*, **52**, 591–603.

Barnes, P.J. (2000). Medical progress: chronic obstructive pulmonary disease. *New England Journal of Medicine*, **343**, 269–280.

Bender, B. & Milgrom, H. (2002). Neuropsychological and psychiatric side effects of medications used to treat asthma and allergic rhinitis. In A.A. Kaptein & T.L. Creer (Eds), *Respiratory Disorders and Behavioral Medicine* (pp. 175–196). London: Martin Dunitz Ltd.

Bergner, M., Bobbitt, R.A., Carter, W.B. & Gilson, B.S. (1981). The Sickness Impact Profile: development and final revision of a health status measure. *Medical Care*, **19**, 787–805.

Boueri, F.M.V., Bucher-Bartelson, B.L., Glenn, K.A. & Make, B.J. (2001). Quality of life measured with a generic instrument (Short Form-36) improves following pulmonary rehabilitation in patients with COPD. *Chest*, **119**, 77–84.

Bourbeau, J., Julien, M., Maltais, F., Rouleau, M., Beaupré, A., Bégin, R., Renzi, P., Nault, D., Borycki, E., Schwartzman, K., Singh, R. & Collet, J.P. for the Chronic Obstructive Pulmonary Disease axis of the Respiratory Networks, Fonds de la Recherche en Santé de Québec (2003). Reduction of hospital utilization in patients with chronic obstructive pulmonary disease. *Archives of Internal Medicine*, **63**, 586–591.

British Thoracic Society (1997). BTS guidelines for the management of chronic obstructive pulmonary disease. *Thorax*, **52** (Suppl. 5), 1–28.

British Thoracic Society Standards of Care Subcommittee on Pulmonary Rehabilitation (2001). Pulmonary rehabilitation. *Thorax*, **56**, 827–834.

Carone, M. & Jones, P.W. (2000). Health status "quality of life". *European Respiratory Monograph*, **13**, 22–35.

Carter, R., Nicotra, B. & Huber, G. (1994). Differing effects of airway obstruction on physical work capacity and ventilation in men and women with COPD. *Chest*, **106**, 1730–1739.

Clark, M. & Hampson, S.E. (2001). Implementing a psychological intervention to improve lifestyle self-management in patients with Type 2 diabetes. *Patient Education and Counseling*, **42**, 247–256.

Compas, B.E., Haaga, D.A.F., Keefe, F.J., Leitenberg, H. & Williams, D.A. (1998). Sampling of empirically supported psychological treatments from health psychology: smoking, chronic pain, cancer, and bulimia nervosa. *Journal of Consulting and Clinical Psychology*, **66**, 89–112.

Connors, A.F., Dawson, N.V., Thomas, C., Harrell, F.E., Desbiens, N., Fulkerson, W.J. et al. (1996). Outcomes following acute exacerbation of severe chronic obstructive lung disease. The SUPPORT investigators (Study to Understand Prognoses and Preferences for Outcomes and Risks of Treatments). *American Journal of Respiratory and Critical Care Medicine*, **154**, 959–967.

Cordova, F.C. & Criner, G.J. (1997). Management of advanced chronic obstructive pulmonary disease. *Comprehensive Therapy*, **23**, 413–424.

Cox, N.J., Hendricks, J.C., Binkhorst, R.A. & van Herwaarden, C.L. (1993). A pulmonary rehabilitation program for patients with asthma and mild chronic obstructive pulmonary disease (COPD). *Lung*, **171**, 235–244.

Criner, G.J. (2000). Effects of long-term oxygen therapy on mortality and morbidity. *Respiratory Care*, **45**, 105–118.

Curtis, R., Martin, D.P. & Martin, T.R. (1997). Patient-assessed health outcomes in chronic lung disease. *American Journal of Respiratory and Critical Care Medicine*, **156**, 1032–1039.

Davidson, A.C. & Morgan, M. (1998). A UK survey of the provision of pulmonary rehabilitation therapy. *Thorax*, **53** (Suppl. 4), 86.

Dickinson, J.A., Meaker, M., Searle, M. & Ratcliffe, G. (1999). Screening older patients for obstructive airways disease in a semi-rural practice. *Thorax*, **54**, 501–505.

Di Lorenzo, G., Morici, G., Drago, A., Pellitteri, M.E., Mansueto, P., Melluso, M., Norrito, F., Squassante, L., Fasolo, A. & the SLMT02 Italian Study Group (1998). Efficacy, tolerability, and effects on quality of life of inhaled salmeterol and oral theophylline in patients with mild-to-moderate chronic obstructive pulmonary disease. *Clinical Therapeutics*, **20**, 1130–1148.

Donner, C.F., Muir, J.F. & the Rehabilitation and Chronic Care Scientific Group of the European Respiratory Society (1997). Selection criteria and programmes for pulmonary rehabilitation in COPD patients. *European Respiratory Journal*, **10**, 744–757.

Emery, C.F., Schein, R.L., Hauck, E.R. & MacIntyre, N.R. (1998). Psychological and cognitive outcomes of a randomised trial of exercise among patients with chronic obstructive pulmonary disease. *Health Psychology*, **17**, 232–240.

Fawzy, F.I., Fawzy, N.W. & Wheeler, J.G. (1996). A post-hoc comparison of the efficiency of a psychoeducational intervention for melanoma patients delivered in group versus individual formats: an analysis of data from two studies. *Psycho-oncology*, **5**, 81–89.

Ferguson, G.T. (2000). Update on pharmacologic therapy for chronic obstructive pulmonary disease. *Clinics in Chest Medicine*, **21**, 723–738.

Ferguson, G.T. & Cherniack, R.M. (1994). Management of chronic obstructive pulmonary disease. *New England Journal of Medicine*, **328**, 1017–1022.

Ferreira, I.M., Brooks, D., Lacasse, Y. & Goldstein, R.S. (2001). Nutritional intervention in COPD: a systematic overview. *Chest*, **119**, 353–363.

Fuchs-Climent, D., Le Gallais, D., Varray, A., Desplan, J., Cadopi, M. & Préfaut, C.G. (2001). Factor analysis of quality of life, dyspnea, and physiologic variables in patients with chronic obstructive pulmonary disease before and after rehabilitation. *American Journal of Physical Medicine and Rehabilitation*, **80**, 113–120.

Goldstein, A.P. (1971). *Psychotherapeutic Attraction*. New York: Pergamon Press.

Guest, J.F. (1999). The annual cost of chronic obstructive pulmonary disease to the UK's National Health Service. *Disease Management and Health Outcomes*, **5**, 93–100.

Gulsvik, A. (1999). Mortality in and prevalence of chronic obstructive pulmonary disease in different parts of Europe. *Monaldi Archives for Chest Disease*, **54**, 160–162.

Guthrie, S.J., Hill, K.M. & Muers, M.F. (2001). Living with severe COPD. A qualitative exploration of the experience of patients in Leeds. *Respiratory Medicine*, **95**, 196–204.

Guyatt, G.H., Berman, L.B., Townsend, M., Pugsley, S.O. & Chambers, L.W. (1987a). A measure of quality of life for clinical trials in chronic lung disease. *Thorax*, **42**, 773–778.

Guyatt, G., Townsend, M., Berman, L. & Pugsley, S. (1987b). Quality of life in patients with chronic airflow limitation. *British Journal of Diseases of the Chest*, **81**, 45–54.

Hajiro, T., Nishimura, K., Tsukino, M., Ikeda, A., Koyama, H. & Izumi, T. (1998). Comparison of discriminative properties among disease-specific questionnaires for measuring health-related quality of life in patients with chronic obstructive pulmonary disease. *American Journal of Respiratory and Critical Care Medicine*, **157**, 785–790.

Horowitz, H.W. (1996). Night attack. *Lancet*, **348**, 252.

Hunt, S.M., McEwen, J. & McKenna, S.P. (1986). *Measuring Health Status*. London: Croom Helm.

Hurd, S. (2000). The impact of COPD on lung health worldwide. *Chest*, **117** (Suppl. 2), 1–4.

Hyland, M.E. (2002). Quality of life in respiratory disease. In A.A. Kaptein & T.L. Creer (Eds), *Respiratory Disorders and Behavioral Medicine* (pp. 233–253). London: Martin Dunitz Ltd.

Hyland, M.E., Bott, J., Singh, S. & Kenyon, C.A. (1994). Domains, constructs and the development of the breathing problems questionnaire. *Quality of Life Research*, **3**, 245–256.

Hyland, M.E., Singh, S.J., Sodergren, S.C. & Morgan, M.P.L. (1998). Development of a shortened version of the Breathing Problems Questionnaire suitable for use in a pulmonary rehabilitation clinic: a purpose-specific, disease-specific questionnaire. *Quality of Life Research*, **7**, 227–233.

Incalzi, R.A., Gemma, A., Marra, C., Capparella, O., Fuso, L. & Carbonin, P. (1997). Verbal memory impairment in COPD: its mechanisms and clinical relevance. *Chest*, **112**, 1506–1513.

Jans, M.P., Schellevis, F.G. & Van Eijk, J.Th.M. (1999). The Nottingham Health Profile: score distribution, internal consistency and validity in asthma and COPD patients. *Quality of Life Research*, **8**, 501–507.

Jones, P.W. (1999). Quality of life, health status, and functional impairment. In N.S. Cherniack, M.D. Altose & I. Homma (Eds), *Rehabilitation of the Patient with Respiratory Disease* (pp. 687–696). New York: McGraw-Hill.

Jones, P.W., Quirk, F.H., Baveystock, C.M. & Littlejohns, P.A. (1992). A self-complete measure for chronic airflow limitation: the St George's Respiratory Questionnaire. *American Review of Respiratory Disease*, **145**, 1321–1327.

Kannel, W.B., Hubert, H. & Lew, E.A. (1983). Vital capacity as a predictor of cardiovascular disease: the Framingham Study. *American Heart Journal*, **105**, 311–315.

Kaplan, R.M., Atkins, C.J. & Timms, R. (1984). Validity of a quality of well-being scale as an outcome measure in chronic obstructive pulmonary disease. *Journal of Chronic Diseases*, **37**, 85–95.

Kaptein, A.A. (1997). Behavioural interventions in COPD: a pause for breath. *European Respiratory Review*, **7**, 88–91.

Kaptein, A.A. (2002). Respiratory disorders and behavioral research. In A.A. Kaptein & T.L. Creer (Eds), *Respiratory Disorders and Behavioral Medicine* (pp. 1–17). London: Martin Dunitz Ltd.

Kaptein, A.A. & Creer, T.L. (Eds) (2002). *Respiratory Disorders and Behavioral Medicine*. London: Martin Dunitz Ltd.

Kaptein, A.A. & Dekker, F.W. (2000). Psychosocial support. *European Respiratory Monograph*, **13**, 58–69.

Keele-Card, G., Foxall, M.J. & Barron, C.R. (1993). Loneliness, depression, and social support of patients with COPD and their spouses. *Public Health Nursing*, **10**, 245–251.

Kerstjens, H.A.M., Groen, H.J. & van der Bij, W. (2001). Respiratory medicine. *British Medical Journal*, **323**, 1349–1353.

Kinsman, R.A., Fernandez, E., Schocket, M., Dirks, J.F. & Covino, N.A. (1983). Multidimensional analysis of the symptoms of chronic bronchitis and emphysema. *Journal of Behavioral Medicine*, **6**, 339–357.

Lacasse, Y. & Goldstein, R.S. (1999). Overviews of respiratory rehabilitation in chronic obstructive pulmonary disease. *Monaldi Archives for Chest Disease*, **54**, 163–167.

Lacasse, Y., Goldstein, R.S. & Guyatt, G.H. (1997). Respiratory rehabilitation in chronic obstructive pulmonary disease: summary of a systematic overview of the literature. *Reviews in Clinical Gerontology*, **7**, 327–347.

Lacasse, Y., Guyatt, G.H. & Goldstein, R.S. (1998). Is there really a controversy surrounding the effectiveness of respiratory rehabilitation in COPD? *Chest*, **114**, 1–4.

Leidy, N.K. (1999). Psychometric properties of the Functional Performance Inventory in patients with chronic obstructive pulmonary disease. *Nursing Research*, **48**, 20–28.

Leidy, N.K. & Haase, J.E. (1999). Functional status from the patient's perspective: the challenge of preserving personal integrity. *Research in Nursing and Health*, **22**, 67–77.

Lightower, J.V., Wedzicha, J.A., Elliott, M.W. & Ram, F.S.F. (2003). Non-invasive positive pressure ventilation to treat respiratory failure resulting from exacerbations of chronic obstructive pulmonary disease: Cochrane systematic review and meta-analysis. *British Medical Journal*, **326**, 185.

Lynn, J., Ely, E.W., Zhong, Z., Landrum-McNiff, K.L., Dawson, N.V., Connors, A., Desbiens, N.A., Claessens, M. & McCarthy, E.P. (2000). Living and dying with chronic obstructive pulmonary disease. *Journal of the American Geriatrics Society*, **48** (Suppl. 5), 91–100.

Mahler, D.A., Tomlinson, D., Olmstead, E.M. & Tosteson, G.T. (1995). Changes in dyspnea, health status and lung function in chronic airways disease. *American Journal of Respiratory and Critical Care Medicine*, **151**, 61–65.

Maillé, A.R., Kaptein, A.A., de Haes, J.C.J.M. & Everaerd, W.Th.A.M. (1996). Assessing quality of life in chronic non-specific lung disease: a review of empirical studies published between 1980 and 1994. *Quality of Life Research*, **5**, 287–301.

Maltais, F., LeBlanc, P., Jobin, J. & Casaburi, R. (2000). Peripheral muscle dysfunction in chronic obstructive pulmonary disease. *Clinics in Chest Medicine*, **21**, 665–677.

Mannino, D.M., Gagnon, R.C., Petty, T.L. & Lydick, E. (2000). Obstructive lung disease and low lung function in adults in the United States. *Archives of Internal Medicine*, **160**, 1683–1689.

Mapel, D.W., Hurley, J.S., Frost, F.J., Petersen, H.V., Picchi, M.A. & Coultas, D.B. (2000). Health care utilization in chronic obstructive pulmonary disease. *Archives of Internal Medicine*, **160**, 2653–2658.

McSweeny, A.J. & Labuhn, K.T. (1996). Quality of life in chronic obstructive pulmonary disease. In B. Spilker (Ed.), *Quality of Life and Pharmacoeconomics in Clinical Trials* (pp. 961–976). Philadelphia: Lippincott-Raven.

Murray, C.J.L. & Lopez, A.D. (1997). Alternative projections of mortality and disability by cause 1990–2020: global burden of disease study. *Lancet*, **349**, 1498–1504.

Nardini, S. (2000). Education and smoking cessation. *European Respiratory Monograph*, **13**, 41–57.

National Institutes of Health and National Heart, Lung, and Blood Institute (2000, May). *Morbidity and Mortality Chartbook 2000*. Retrieved December 25, 2001, from http://www.nhlbi.nih.gov/resources/docs/00chtbk.pdf.

Nishimura, K. & Tsukino, M. (2000). Clinical course and prognosis of patients with chronic obstructive pulmonary disease. *Current Opinion in Pulmonary Medicine*, **6**, 127–132.

Osman, L.M., Godden, D.J., Friend, J.A.R., Legge, J.S. & Douglas, J.G. (1997). Quality of life and hospital re-admission in patients with chronic obstructive pulmonary disease. *Thorax*, **52**, 67–71.

Pauwels, R.A., Buist, S.A., Calverley, P.M.A., Jenkins, C.R. & Hurd, S.S., on behalf of the GOLD Scientific Committee (2001). Global strategy for the diagnosis, management, and prevention of chronic obstructive pulmonary disease. *American Journal of Respiratory and Critical Care Medicine*, **163**, 1256–1276.

Petrie, K.J., Cameron, L.D., Ellis, C.J., Buick, D. & Weinman, J. (2002). Changing illness perceptions after myocardial infarction: an early intervention randomised controlled trial. *Psychosomatic Medicine*, **64**, 580–586.

Petty, T.L. (1998). Supportive therapy in COPD. *Chest*, **113** (Suppl. 4), 256–262.

Petty, T.L. & Weinmann, G.G. (1997). Building a national strategy for the prevention and management of and research in chronic obstructive pulmonary disease. *Journal of the American Medical Association*, **277**, 246–253.

Prigatano, G.P., Wright, E., Levin, D.C. & Hawryluk, G. (1983). Neuropsychological test performance in mild hypoxemic patients with chronic obstructive pulmonary disease. *Journal of Consulting and Clinical Psychology*, **51**, 108–116.

Ries, A.L., Kaplan, R.M., Limberg, T.M. & Prewitt, L.M. (1995). Effects of pulmonary rehabilitation on physiologic and psychosocial outcomes in patients with chronic obstructive pulmonary disease. *Annals of Internal Medicine*, **122**, 823–832.

Rutten-van Mölken, M., Roos, B. & van Noord, J.A. (1999b). An empirical comparison of the St George's Respiratory Questionnaire (SGRQ) and the Chronic Respiratory Disease Questionnaire (CRQ) in a clinical trial setting. *Thorax*, **54**, 995–1003.

Rutten-van Mölken, M., Postma, M.J., Joore, M.A., van Genugten, M.L.L., Leidl, R. & Jager, J.C. (1999a). Current and future medical costs of asthma and chronic obstructive pulmonary disease in the Netherlands. *Respiratory Medicine*, **93**, 779–787.

Sandford, A.J., Weir, T.D. & Paré, P.D. (1997). Genetic risk factors for chronic obstructive pulmonary disease. *European Respiratory Journal*, **10**, 1380–1391.

Scharloo, M., Kaptein, A.A., Weinman, J., Bergman, W., Vermeer, B.J. & Rooijmans, H.G.M. (2000a). Patients' illness perceptions and coping as predictors of functional status in psoriasis: a 1-year follow-up. *British Journal of Dermatology*, **142**, 899–907.

Scharloo, M., Kaptein, A.A., Weinman, J., Hazes, J.M., Breedveld, F.C. & Rooijmans, H.G.M. (1999). Predicting functional status in patients with rheumatoid arthritis. *Journal of Rheumatology*, **26**, 1686–1693.

Scharloo, M., Kaptein, A.A., Weinman, J., Hazes, J.M., Willems, L.N.A., Bergman, W. & Rooijmans, H.G.M. (1998). Illness perceptions, coping and functioning in patients with rheumatoid arthritis, chronic obstructive pulmonary disease and psoriasis. *Journal of Psychosomatic Research*, **44**, 573–585.

Scharloo, M., Kaptein, A.A., Weinman, J., Willems, L.N.A., Rooijmans, H.G.M. & Dijkman, J.H. (2000b). Physical and psychological correlates of functioning in patients with chronic obstructive pulmonary disease. *Journal of Asthma*, **37**, 17–29.

Schlenk, E.A., Erlen, J.A., Dunbar-Jacob, J., McDowell, J., Engberg, S., Sereika, S.M., Rohay, J.M. & Bernier, M.J. (1998). Health-related quality of life in chronic disorders: a comparison across studies using the MOS SF-36. *Quality of Life Research*, **7**, 57–65.

Schofield, W. (1964). *Psychotherapy. The Purchase of Friendship*. New Jersey: Prentice Hall.

Schrier, A.C., Dekker, F.W., Kaptein, A.A. & Dijkman, J.H. (1990). Quality of life in elderly patients with chronic nonspecific lung disease seen in family practice. *Chest*, **98**, 894–899.

Sexton, D. & Munrow, B.H. (1983). Impact of a husband's chronic illness (COPD) on the spouse life. *Research in Nursing and Health*, **8**, 83–90.

Sherk, P.A. & Grossman, R.F. (2000). The chronic obstructive pulmonary disease exacerbation. *Clinics in Chest Medicine*, **21**, 705–721.

Silverman, E.K., Weiss, S.T., Drazen, J.M., Chapman, H.A., Carey, V., Campbell, E.J., Denish, P., Silverman, R.A., Celedon, J.C., Reilly, J.J., Ginns, L.C. & Speizer, F.E. (2000). Gender-related differences in severe, early-onset chronic obstructive pulmonary disease. *American Journal of Respiratory and Critical Care Medicine*, **162**, 2152–2158.

Singh, S.J., Sodergren, S.C., Hyland, M.E., Williams, J. & Morgan, M.D.L. (2001). A comparison of three disease-specific and two generic health-status measures to evaluate the outcome of pulmonary rehabilitation in COPD. *Respiratory Medicine*, **95**, 71–77.

Siu, A.L., Reuben, D.B., Ouslander, J.G. & Osterweil, D. (1993). Using multidimensional health measures in older persons to identify risk of hospitalization and skilled nursing placement. *Quality of Life Research*, **2**, 253–261.

Smoller, J.W., Pollack, M.H., Otto, M.W., Rosenbaum, J.F. & Kradin, R.L. (1996). Panic anxiety, dyspnea, and respiratory disease: theoretical and clinical considerations. *American Journal of Respiratory and Critical Care Medicine*, **154**, 6–17.

Spencer, S., Calverley, P.M.A., Burge, P.S., Jones, P.W. on behalf of the ISOLDE Study Group (2001). Health status deterioration in patients with chronic obstructive pulmonary disease. *American Journal of Respiratory and Critical Care Medicine*, **163**, 122–128.

Stavem, K., Lossius, M.I., Kvien, T.K. & Guldvog, B. (2000). The health-related quality of life of patients with epilepsy compared with angina pectoris, rheumatoid arthritis, asthma and chronic obstructive pulmonary disease. *Quality of Life Research*, **9**, 865–871.

Stewart, B.N., Hood, C.I. & Block, A.J. (1975). Long-term results of continuous oxygen therapy at sea level. *Chest*, **68**, 486–492.

Stubbing, D.G., Haalboom, P. & Barr, P.J. (1998). Comparison of the Psychosocial Adjustment to Illness Scale-Self Report and clinical judgement in patients with chronic lung disease. *Journal of Cardiopulmonary Rehabilitation*, **18**, 32–36.

Stuss, D.T., Peterkin, I., Guzman, D.A., Guzman, C. & Troyer, A.K. (1997). Chronic obstructive pulmonary disease: effects of hypoxia on neurological and neuropsychological measures. *Journal of Clinical and Experimental Neuropsychology*, **19**, 515–524.

Sullivan, S.D., Ramsay, S.D. & Lee, T.A. (2000). The economic burden of COPD. *Chest*, **117** (Suppl. 2), 5–9.

Sutton, P.P., Parker, R.A., Webber, B.A., Newman, S.P., Garland, N., Lopez-Vidriero, M.T., Pavia, D. & Clarke, S.W. (1983). Assessment of the forced expiration technique, postural drainage and directed coughing in chest physiotherapy. *European Journal of Respiratory Diseases*, **64**, 62–68.

Tarpy, S.P. & Celli, B.R. (1995). Long-term oxygen therapy. *New England Journal of Medicine*, **333**, 710–714.

Tockman, M.S., Pearson, J.D., Fleg, J.L., Metter, E.J., Kao, S.Y., Rampal, K.G., Cruise, L.J. & Fozard, J.L. (1995). Rapid decline in FEV_1: a new risk factor for coronary heart disease mortality. *American Journal of Respiratory and Critical Care Medicine*, **151**, 390–398.

Traver, G.A. (1988). Measures of symptoms and life quality to predict emergent use of institutional health care resources in chronic obstructive airways disease. *Heart and Lung*, **17**, 689–697.

Trulock, E.P. (1998). Lung transplantation for COPD. *Chest*, **113** (Suppl. 4), 269–276.

Van den Boom, G., Rutten-van Mölken, M.H., Tirimanna, P.R.S., van Schayck, C.P., Folgering, H. & van Weel, C. (1998). Association between health-related quality of life and consultation for respiratory symptoms: results from the DIMCA programme. *European Respiratory Journal*, **11**, 67–72.

Van Manen, J.G., Bindels, P.J.E., IJzermans, C.J., van der Zee, J.S., Bottema, B.J.A.M. & Schadé, E. (2001). Prevalence of comorbidity in patients with a chronic airway obstruction and controls over the age of 40. *Journal of Clinical Epidemiology*, **54**, 287–293.

Van der Schoot, T.A.W. & Kaptein, A.A. (1990). Pulmonary rehabilitation in an asthma clinic. *Lung*, **168**, 495–501.

Vestbo, J., Prescott, E. & Lange, P. (1996). Association of chronic mucus hypersecretion with FEV_1 decline and chronic obstructive pulmonary disease morbidity. *American Journal of Respiratory and Critical Care Medicine*, **153**, 1530–1535.

Ware, J.E. & Sherbourne, C.D. (1992). The MOS short-form health survey (SF-36): 1, conceptual framework and item selection. *Medical Care*, **30**, 473–483.

Weaver, T.E. & Narsavage, G.L. (1992). Physiological and psychological variables related to functional status in chronic obstructive pulmonary disease. *Nursing Research*, **41**, 286–291.

Webb, M.W. & Lawton, A.H. (1961). Basic personality traits characteristics of patients with primary obstructive pulmonary emphysema. *Journal of the American Geriatrics Society*, **9**, 590–610.

Williams, J.E.A., Singh, S.J., Sewell, L., Guyatt, G.H. & Morgan, M.D.L. (2001). Development of a self-reported Chronic Respiratory Questionnaire (CRQ-SR). *Thorax*, **56**, 954–959.

Williams, S.J. (1993). *Chronic Respiratory Illness*. London: Routledge.

Williams, S.J. & Bury, M.R. (1989). Impairment, disability and handicap in chronic respiratory illness. *Social Science and Medicine*, **29**, 609–616.

Wollmer, P., Ursing, K., Midgren, B. & Eriksson, L. (1985). Inefficiency of chest percussion in the physical therapy of chronic bronchitis. *European Journal of Respiratory Diseases*, **66**, 233–239.

Wouters, E.F.M. & Schols, A.M.W.J. (2000). Nutritional support in chronic respiratory diseases. *European Respiratory Monograph*, **13**, 111–131.

Yohannes, A.M., Baldwin, R.C. & Connolly, M.J. (2000). Mood disorders in elderly patients with chronic obstructive pulmonary disease. *Reviews in Clinical Gerontology*, **10**, 193–202.

Yohannes, A.M., Roomi, J. & Connolly, M.J. (1998). Elderly people at home disabled by chronic obstructive pulmonary disease. *Age and Ageing*, **27**, 523–525.

Yohannes, A.M., Roomi, J., Baldwin, R.C. & Connolly, M.J. (1998a). Depression in elderly outpatients with disabling chronic obstructive pulmonary disease. *Age and Ageing*, **27**, 155–160.

Yohannes, A.M., Roomi, J., Waters, K. & Connolly, M.J. (1998b). Quality of life in elderly patients with COPD: measurement and predictive factors. *Respiratory Medicine*, **92**, 1231–1236.

Young, J., Fry-Smith, A. & Hyde, C. (1999). Lung volume reduction surgery (LVRS) for chronic obstructive pulmonary disease (COPD) with underlying severe emphysema. *Thorax*, **54**, 779–789.

ZuWallack, R.L. (2000). Outcome measures for pulmonary rehabilitation. *European Respiratory Monograph*, **13**, 177–200.

CHAPTER 10

Treatment of Obesity

Michael G. Perri*
University of Florida, USA
and
Joyce A. Corsica
Rush-Presbyterian-St Luke's Medical Center, Chicago, USA

INTRODUCTION

Obesity constitutes a major threat to health. Excess body weight contributes significantly to many chronic diseases, to diminished quality of life, and to decreased longevity. Despite the gravity of its consequences, success in the treatment of obesity has proven elusive. The identification of effective methods for long-term weight management continues to present a major challenge to health professionals and obese persons alike. In this chapter, we provide an overview of current treatments for obesity, including behavioral, pharmacological, and surgical methods. We begin with a context for understanding obesity as a major threat to public health. We review the increasing worldwide prevalence of obesity, and document the deleterious impact of excess weight on health and longevity. Next, we describe empirically tested treatments for obesity and evaluate methods designed to improve the maintenance of weight lost. We conclude the chapter with some specific recommendations for the clinical management of obesity.

Defining Obesity

Obesity refers to an excess accumulation of adipose tissue. However, direct and accurate measurement of total body fat is technically difficult and expensive (NHLBI, 1998). Thus, surrogate measures that rely on the weight-to-height ratio are commonly used. The Body Mass Index (BMI), calculated as weight in kilograms divided by the square of the height in meters (kg/m^2), has gained acceptance as the preferred surrogate method for classifying overweight and obesity in adults. For most individuals, BMI corresponds relatively closely to degree of adiposity (NHLBI, 1998).

---

* Please address all correspondence to Michael G. Perri.

Handbook of Clinical Health Psychology. Edited by S. Llewelyn and P. Kennedy.
© 2003 John Wiley & Sons, Ltd.

Table 10.1 World Health Organization classification system of overweight based on Body Mass Index

BMI	Category	Risk for comorbid conditions
<18.5	Underweight	Low[a]
18.5–24.9	Normal weight	Average
25.0–29.9	Pre-obese	Increased
30.0–34.9	Obese Class I	Moderate
35.0–39.9	Obese Class II	Severe
≥40.0	Obesity Class III	Very severe

[a] Risk for other clinical problems may be increased.

The World Health Organization (WHO, 1998) has developed a graded classification system for categorizing overweight and obesity in adults according to BMI. In the WHO system, overweight is defined as a BMI ≥ 25, and obesity is defined as a BMI ≥ 30. The WHO system employs six categories selected on the basis of the known risks of comorbid conditions associated with different BMI levels (see Table 10.1). For example, the risk of comorbid conditions is considered "average" in the normal weight category (BMI = 18.5–24.9) and "very severe" in the highest weight category, Class III obesity (BMI ≥ 40).

Prevalence

The past two decades have witnessed a striking increase in the rates of overweight and obesity throughout the industrialized world. In the USA, the prevalence of obesity has shown a marked increase over the past two decades, and the majority of adults (54%) are now overweight or obese (Flegal et al., 1998). European countries have observed increases of 10–40% in the prevalence of obesity (WHO, 1998). The most dramatic rise has been in the United Kingdom where the prevalence of obesity has more than doubled since 1980 (Department of Health, 2001). Figure 10.1 illustrates the changes in the prevalence of overweight and obesity in selected industrialized nations over the past two decades.

Seriousness of Obesity

Concern over the rising rates of obesity stems from clear evidence showing that excess weight has an adverse impact on health and longevity. Obesity-related conditions include hypertension, dyslipidemia, type 2 diabetes mellitus, coronary heart disease, stroke, osteoarthritis, respiratory disease, and certain types of cancer (NHLBI, 1998; WHO, 1998). The health risks associated with obesity also vary according to body fat distribution. Abdominal obesity (i.e., a waist circumference of >40 inches in men or >35 inches in women) confers increased risk for morbidity and mortality due to metabolic disorders and cardiovascular diseases (James, 1996; Melanson et al., 2001; NHLBI, 1998; Turcato et al., 2000).

The impact of obesity on life expectancy varies according to degree of overweight. Mortality ratios rise above average as BMI exceeds 25, and all-cause mortality rates increase by 50–100% when BMI surpasses 30 (Troiano et al., 1996). In the USA, more than 300 000

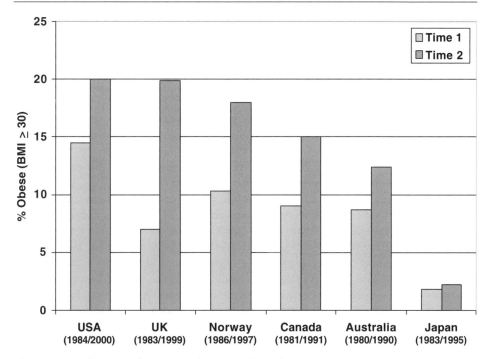

Figure 10.1   Changing obesity prevalence in selected countries

deaths per year are attributable to obesity-related causes (Allison et al., 1999), making obesity second only to smoking as the leading lifestyle contributor to mortality.

In addition to its adverse impact on health and longevity, obesity also diminishes quality of life (Wadden & Stunkard, 1993). Many obese persons experience social discrimination as a direct consequence of their obesity. For women, the psychological consequences may be particularly severe. The results of a large-scale, epidemiological study (Carpenter et al., 2000) recently showed that obesity was associated with major depressive disorder, suicidal ideation, and suicide attempts among women but not among men.

Causes of Obesity

Some individuals may be predisposed to obesity by genetic factors that control the regulation of body weight through energy intake, expenditure, and storage (Chagnon et al., 2000; Feitosa et al., 2000; Levin, 2000). Among the first genetic defects linked to obesity was the discovery of the ob gene and its protein product leptin (Zhang et al., 1994). Leptin, a hormone produced by fat cells, influences hypothalamic regulation of caloric consumption and energy expenditure. Laboratory mice that fail to produce leptin due to a genetic defect become obese as the result of excess energy intake and physical inactivity (Zhang et al., 1994). Moreover, the administration of recombinant leptin in such animals decreases food intake, increases physical activity, and reduces body weight (Campfield et al., 1995). In humans, however, only a very small percentage of obese individuals have leptin deficiencies (Montague et al., 1997), and trials of recombinant leptin as treatment for obesity have yielded relatively disappointing results (Heymsfield et al., 1999).

Several other single-gene defects have been discovered that contribute to obesity in animals (e.g., Levin, 2000). However, only one of these mutations (i.e., on the melanocortin-4 receptor) appears to be a contributor to human obesity, and it is been found to affect fewer than 4% of morbidly obese individuals (Farooqi et al., 2000; Vaisse et al., 2000). Moreover, because the human genome has not changed over the past 20 years, genetic factors alone cannot account for the recent rise in the prevalence of obesity. Rather, environmental changes that contribute to physical inactivity and the consumption of energy-dense diets constitute the fundamental causes of the current epidemic of obesity (Brownell, 1998; Poston & Foreyt, 1999).

In industrialized countries, people are exposed to an environment that promotes the overconsumption of energy-dense, nutrient-poor foods (Brownell, 1998; Kant, 2000). Tasty, low-cost, high-calorie items are readily available not only at fast-food restaurants, but also in supermarkets, food courts, vending machines, and even 24-hour service stations. Larger portion sizes, "supersizing", "value meals", and "2-for-1" deals, all provide additional opportunities and incentives for excess consumption. People are eating more meals outside the home and in doing so they are consuming larger portions of food. For example, in the early 1970s about 20% of the American household food dollar was spent on food outside the home but by 1995 that amount had doubled to 40% (Putnam & Allshouse, 1996). Eating away from home, particularly at fast-food restaurants, is associated with higher calorie and fat intake (French, Harnack & Jeffery, 2000), and "eating out" is a significant contributor to weight gain and the increasing prevalence of overweight (Binkley, Eales & Jekanowski, 2000; McCrory et al., 1999).

Sedentary lifestyle also appears to be a significant contributor to overweight and obesity. Few occupations now require vigorous levels of physical activity. Moreover, labor-saving devices such as cars, elevators, escalators, motorized walkways, and remote controls have had a significant cumulative impact in decreasing daily energy expenditure (Hill, Wyatt & Melanson, 2000; James, 1995). At the same time, levels of leisure time physical activity may have decreased as people spend more time in sedentary pursuits such as watching television and using computers rather than participating in physical pursuits that require greater amounts of energy expenditure. According to the US Centers for Disease Control (CDC, 2001), fewer than one in four adults engage in the recommended amounts of leisure time physical activity, and nearly 29% of the American population is totally sedentary.

Thus, the current epidemic of obesity may typify a "disease of civilization" resulting from the discordance between modern lifestyle and the lifestyles for which humans (and our genes) evolved over tens of thousands of years (Eaton & Konner, 1985). Decreases in physical activity and energy expenditure coupled with increases in exposure to an over-abundant supply of energy-dense foods have produced the dramatic worldwide rise in the prevalence of overweight and obesity.

TREATMENTS FOR OBESITY

Self-management of Body Weight

In the USA, surveys indicate that substantial numbers of adults are trying to lose weight. At any given point in time, about 44% of women and 29% of men report that they are dieting to lose weight (Serdula et al., 1999). The most common way that people attempt to regulate their body weight is through self-managed efforts to change their eating and activity patterns (Jeffery, Adlis & Forster, 1991). Self-management strategies include bibliotherapy, computer-assisted interventions, and self-help groups, and represent the most cost-effective methods of weight loss (Latner, 2001).

Some formerly overweight and obese individuals are very successful at weight management. In the USA, the National Weight Control Registry (NWCR) was founded in 1994 to study the strategies of successful maintainers of weight loss (Wing & Hill, 2001). More than 3000 individuals who have maintained a loss of 30 lb or more for at least one year are currently enrolled in the registry, and approximately 45% achieved their weight loss through self-management strategies (Wing & Hill, 2001). Successful maintainers commonly use three strategies for weight management. First, they regularly consume a low-calorie diet (i.e., <1400 kcal/day) that is low in fat (<25%) and high in carbohydrates (>55%). Second, they regularly engage in high levels of physical activity, about one hour per day of moderate activity such as brisk walking. Third, they regularly monitor their body weight: 44% weigh themselves daily and 31% weigh themselves at least once per week.

Obese individuals who seek professional assistance for weight loss tend to exhibit higher levels of distress and more pathological eating patterns compared to overweight persons in the general population (Fitzgibbon, Stolley & Kirschenbaum, 1993). At the current time, three major types of interventions are available to the obese person seeking professional assistance for weight management. These include behavioral or lifestyle treatment, pharmacological treatment, and bariatric surgery.

Behavioral Treatment

Behavior modification procedures have become the foundation of lifestyle interventions for weight loss (Wadden & Foster, 1992). Participants in behavioral treatment are taught to modify their eating and exercise habits so as to produce weight loss through a negative energy balance (i.e., the consumption of fewer calories than are expended). The key components typically used in behavioral interventions include: (a) goal-setting and daily self-monitoring of eating and physical activity; (b) nutritional training aimed at the consumption of a balanced low-calorie diet (i.e., typically 1000–1500 kcal/day)[1] sufficient to produce a weight loss of 0.5 kg per week; (c) increased physical activity through the development of a walking program and/or increased lifestyle activities; (d) arrangement of environmental cues and behavioral reinforcers to support changes in eating and exercise behaviors; (e) cognitive restructuring techniques to identify and change negative thoughts and feelings that interfere with weight-loss progress; and (f) training in problem-solving or relapse prevention procedures to enhance coping with setbacks and obstacles to progress.

Reviews of randomized trials (Jeffery et al., 2000; NHLBI, 1998; Perri & Fuller, 1995; Wadden, Sarwer & Berkowitz, 1999) show that behavioral treatment is safe and effective. Typically delivered in 15–26 weekly group sessions, such interventions produce mean losses of approximately 8.5 kg or approximately 9% reduction in body weight (Renjilian et al., 2001). Attrition rates over six months average less than 20%, and negative side-effects are rare. Improvements in blood pressure, glucose tolerance, and lipid profiles are commonly

---

[1] The use of very low calorie diets (i.e., <800 kcal/day) in behavioral treatment increases initial weight loss but does not produce greater long-term reductions than the use of low calorie diets (Wadden, Foster & Letizia, 1994).

observed, and participants often report decreases in depressive symptoms (NHLBI, 1998; Pi-Sunyer, 1999). Thus, behavioral treatment is recommended as the first line of professional intervention in a stepped-care approach to the management of overweight and obesity (NHLBI, 1998).

However, the long-term effectiveness of lifestyle interventions has remained an area of considerable concern. During the year following behavioral treatment, participants typically regain 30–40% of their lost weight (Jeffery et al., 2000; Wadden & Foster, 2000). Perri and Corsica (2002) recently summarized the results of behavioral treatment studies with follow-ups of two or more years and found a reliable pattern of gradual weight regain during the years following behavioral treatment. Nonetheless, the data show a mean weight loss of 1.8 kg from baseline to follow-up conducted on average 4.3 years after treatment.

When evaluating the long-term results of weight-loss interventions, several factors should be taken into account. Small net losses at long-term follow-up should be viewed in the context of what might have happened if the obese individual had never entered treatment. The natural course of weight change in untreated obese adults entails steady weight gain of about 0.5 kg per year (Shah, Hannan & Jeffery, 1991). Thus, long-term findings that show the maintenance of a small weight reduction may represent relatively favorable outcomes. In addition, the examination of group means can mask beneficial outcomes achieved by subgroups within study samples. For example, Kramer et al. (1989) found that 20% of their obese subjects succeeded in maintaining weight losses of 5 kg or more, 4–5 years after the completion of behavioral treatment. Similarly, a recent review of lifestyle interventions for weight loss indicated an overall median long-term success rate of 15% (Ayyad & Andersen, 2000).

Pharmacotherapy

Over the past five years, there have been major changes in the medications available for weight loss. The serotoninergic agents, fenfluramine and dexfenfluramine, were withdrawn from the US market in 1997 due to their association with valvular heart disease (Connolly et al., 1997). In 2000, the over-the-counter weight-loss products containing the noradrenergic ingredient, phenylpropanolamine, were removed from the market due to concerns about increased risk of stroke (FDA, Nov. 6, 2000). However, other noradrenergic agents, phentermine, mazindol, and diethylproporion, remain available on a prescription basis. In addition, since 1997, two new drugs, sibutramine (Meridia®; Knoll Pharmaceutical Company, 2000) and orlistat (Xenical®; Roche Pharmaceutical Company, 2000), have been approved for the treatment of obesity.

Noradrenergic agents are centrally acting drugs that suppress appetite by stimulating catecholamine neurotransmission. In a review of 23 studies, Bray and Gray (1988) found that over the course of three months the combination of a noradrenergic drug plus low-calorie diet produced a mean weight loss of 6.2 kg, compared with a 2.9 kg loss for placebo plus diet. Longer-term studies of noradrenergic drugs show that weight lost in treatment is almost completely regained when the drug is withdrawn. Because this type of agent is approved only for short-term use (i.e., two to three months), its usefulness in the long-term management of obesity is questionable.

Sibutramine is a combined noradrenaline and serotonin reuptake inhibitor. Sibutramine enhances satiety and may also produce a small increase in basal metabolic rate (Hansen et al., 1998). In controlled trials lasting 6–12 months, sibutramine (15 mg per day) produced mean weight loss of 6–7%, compared to 1–2% for placebo (Bray et al., 1999; Jones et al., 1995). Weight loss occurs in the first six months of use and tends to plateau thereafter. Sibutramine has also been used successfully as an adjunct treatment to enhance the effects of intensive dieting. For example, participants in one study who lost at least 6 kg through a four-week very low calorie diet increased their weight losses by almost 100% using sibutramine (losing an additional 5.2 kg), whereas subjects receiving placebo gained a small amount of weight during the same period (Apfelbaum et al., 1999).

Sibutramine produces a modest mean increase in blood pressure (about 2 mmHg systolic and diastolic at the 15 mg dose). However, some users (approximately 17%) experience an increase of >10 mmHg in blood pressure. Such an increase represents a serious concern given that a 2 mm rise in diastolic blood pressure increases the risk of coronary heart disease by 6% and increases the risk of stroke by 15% (Cook et al., 1995). As such, those on sibutramine must have their blood pressure monitored frequently, and patients with a history of heart disease, stroke, hypertension, or other risk factors for heart disease must not take sibutramine (Hensrud, 2000; Knoll Pharmaceutical, 2000). Because obesity is frequently associated with elevated blood pressure, this potential increase in blood pressure effectively eliminates this drug as a treatment option for many overweight patients.

Unlike most anti-obesity drugs, which act on the central nervous system, orlistat is a gastric and pancreatic lipase inhibitor, which acts by preventing the digestion or absorption of 30% of dietary fat. In a large-scale, randomized-controlled trial (Davidson et al., 1999), treatment with diet plus orlistat (120 mg, three times a day) for two years produced a 7.6% weight loss, whereas treatment with diet plus placebo resulted in a 4.2% loss. Maximum weight loss with orlistat typically occurs after 8–12 months of treatment, and 25–30% of the weight lost during the first year is regained during the following year, even with continued treatment (Davidson et al., 1999; Sjöstrom et al., 1998). Nonetheless, weight loss after two years of treatment with diet plus orlistat remains significantly greater than treatment with diet plus placebo (Davidson et al., 1999). Orlistat also reduces the regaining of lost weight (Hill et al., 1999).

The major side effects of orlistat include abdominal pain, flatus with discharge, fecal urgency, oily stools, increased defecation, and fecal incontinence. These side-effects are reported by 20–50% of users (Roche Pharmaceutical Company, 2000). The consumption of excessive quantities of fat increases the risk of these side-effects. Thus, in effect, orlistat may condition users to avoid high levels of dietary fat through the aversive consequences of consuming fats. Because of the unpleasant nature of these side-effects, many obese individuals refuse to consider orlistat as a treatment option.

While both sibutramine and orlistat enhance weight-loss success, these agents should not be used as the sole element of obesity management. Weight-loss medications are more effective when used as part of a comprehensive treatment regimen including lifestyle modification than when they are used alone (Wadden et al., 2001). In a randomized trial, the authors compared the use of sibutramine only, sibutramine plus a behavioral lifestyle program, and sibutramine plus behavioral lifestyle program plus a 1000 kcal/day portion-controlled diet to evaluate the effect of the addition of lifestyle training on weight loss in the context of pharmacological treatment of obesity. After treatment for one year, patients who used sibutramine combined with a behavioral lifestyle program lost twice as much weight as did those who took sibutramine only (10.8% vs 4.1%). Weight loss was increased to an even greater extent by combining sibutramine with lifestyle modification *and* a portion-controlled diet

(16.5% of initial weight—one of the largest mean weight losses reported in a randomized trial of weight-loss medication).

A current challenge with the new weight-loss medications is that their cost, at $120.00 per month, can be prohibitive for many obese patients. Despite empirical demonstrations of their safety and efficacy, weight-loss medications are rarely covered by insurance in the USA.

Bariatric Surgery

Class III obesity (BMI $\geq$ 40), also known as "morbid obesity", confers an extremely high risk for morbidity and decreased longevity. In the USA, morbid obesity affects about 3% of the population, approximately 12 million adults (Flegal et al., 1998). Because lifestyle and pharmacological interventions produce very limited benefits for these patients, bariatric surgery represents the treatment of choice for Class III obesity (Albrecht & Pories, 1999).

Gastroplasty and gastric bypass are the two major surgical procedures for weight loss. In vertical banded gastroplasty, the stomach is stapled to create a small vertical "pouch". This gastric pouch limits the amount of food that can be ingested in a single eating period to about 15 ml. A ring with a diameter of 9–10 mm is placed at the outlet of the pouch to slow the rate at which food passes through the remainder of the stomach and into the duodenum and jejunum (small intestine). Gastroplasty exerts a regulatory effect on eating behavior through aversive conditioning. Eating more than the small amount of solid food that the stomach pouch can accommodate typically results in vomiting, which provides a disincentive for overeating. Gastroplasty does not, however, provide a mechanism to limit the consumption of high-calorie liquids or soft foods. Consequently, as many as 30% of patients who have this surgery engage in the overconsumption of such foods (i.e., "soft calorie syndrome"), resulting in poor weight-loss outcome (Kral, 1989). An additional problem with gastroplasty is that over time the size of the pouch may expand, thereby limiting its long-term effectiveness.

The more effective Roux-en-Y gastric bypass procedure creates a small gastric pouch via stapling, and a limb of the jejunum is attached directly to the pouch. Ingested food bypasses 90% of the stomach, the duodenum, and a small portion of the proximal jejunum (Kral, 1995). The surgery facilitates weight loss in three ways. First, the pouch can only hold a small amount of food (15 ml), and overfilling the pouch results in regurgitation. Second, the emptying of partially digested food from the pouch into the small intestine results in malabsorption (i.e., a portion of calories consumed are not absorbed). Third, the consumption of sweets and foods containing refined sugar produces aversive consequences including nausea, lighted headedness, sweating, palpitations, and gastrointestinal distress. This constellation of symptoms, referred to as the "dumping syndrome", serves as a deterrent to the consumption of sweets.

Due to its superior weight-loss outcome, gastric bypass has replaced gastroplasty as the preferred type of bariatric surgery (Balsiger et al., 2000). Glenny and colleagues (Glenny et al., 1997) found that typical weight losses one year after gastric bypass ranged from 45 to 65 kg, whereas gastroplasty resulted in 30–35 kg weight loss. Similarly, the two-year follow-up of a large-scale trial of bariatric surgery in Sweden (Sjöstrom et al., 1999) found that patients who received gastric bypass had a 33% reduction in body weight compared to 23% for patients with gastroplasty. While long-term studies show some regaining of weight (about 5–7 kg over five years), gastric bypass patients commonly maintain 80–90% of their initial weight losses (Balsiger et al., 2000), making it by far the most successful treatment of obesity over the long term. Gastric bypass reduces or eliminates the major comorbid conditions experienced by severely obese patients, including hypertension, diabetes, dyslipidemia, asthma, and sleep apnea (Kral, 1995; Long et al., 1994; NIH, 1992). In addition, significant improvements in quality of life routinely accompany the large weight losses achieved by bariatric surgery patients (NIH, 1992). Along with its greater successes, however, come greater risks, including a mortality rate of approximately 0.5%, postoperative complications, micronutrient deficiencies, and late postoperative depression (NIH, 1992; Sjöstrom, Narbro & Sjöstrom, 1995).

MAINTENANCE STRATEGIES

With the exception of surgery, virtually all treatments for obesity show limited long-term effectiveness. A combination of physiological factors, such as reduced metabolic rate (Dulloo & Jacquet, 1998; Ravussin & Swinburn, 1993), and environmental factors, such as continuous exposure to an environment rich in tasty high-fat, high-calorie foods (Hill & Peters, 1998), prime the dieter to regain lost weight. This challenging combination of physiological and environmental barriers, in addition to psychological variables such as decreased motivation, makes long-term success a very difficult proposition. It is perhaps not surprising that most overweight individuals experience difficulties after completing weight-loss treatment. The most reinforcing aspect of treatment is weight loss, and weight loss generally slows or stops well before most patients reach their "desired" losses. As a result, many perceive a high behavioral "cost" associated with continued efforts at weight control precisely at the same time they are experiencing diminished "benefits" in terms of little or no additional weight loss. Weight regain often leads to attributions of personal ineffectiveness that can trigger negative emotions and a sense of hopelessness, resulting in an abandonment of the weight-control effort (Goodrick et al., 1992; Jeffery, French & Schmid, 1990).

Over the past 15 years, researchers have examined a wide array of strategies to improve long-term outcome in obesity treatment. These include: extended treatment, skills training, peer support, exercise/physical activity and multicomponent post-treatment programs. In Table 10.2, we summarize the apparent effectiveness of these strategies. In the following sections we describe those approaches that have been effective in improving long-term outcome.

Extended Treatment

Improving the long-term effectiveness of treatment involves finding ways to assist clients in sustaining key changes in the behaviors that regulate energy balance and weight loss. Perri and Corsica (2002) recently reviewed the results of 13 studies in which behavioral treatment was extended beyond six months, through the use of weekly or biweekly treatment sessions, for up to one year. Groups that received behavior therapy with extended contact succeeded in maintaining 96% of their initial losses, whereas groups without extended contact maintained about 67% of their initial weight reductions. Follow-up visits conducted nearly two years after treatment initiation showed that while the extended treatment group maintained 66%

Table 10.2   Strategies designed to improve long-term outcome

Strategy	Beneficial effect at 6–12 months	Beneficial effect at >13 months
Extended therapy		
Extended therapy (weekly/biweekly group sessions up to one year)	Yes	Yes
Therapist contact by phone/mail	Yes	Unknown
Telephone prompts by non-therapists	No	Unknown
Physical activity		
Supervised exercise	No	No
Use of personal trainers	No	No
Financial incentives	No	No
Home-based exercise	Yes	Unknown
Short-bout exercise + home exercise equipment	Yes	Unknown
Portion-controlled meals		
No-cost portion-controlled meals	Yes	Yes
Optional portion-controlled meals	Yes	No
Skills training		
RPT: initial treatment	No	Unlikely
RPT with post-treatment therapist contacts	Mixed	Unknown
Social support training		
Peer support training	No	Unlikely
Social support training for clients recruited with friends or relatives	Yes	Unknown
Multicomponent programs		
Therapist contact + increased exercise	Yes	Yes
Therapist contact + social support	Yes	Yes
Therapist contact + increased exercise + social support	Yes	Yes
Therapist contact + portion control foods	Yes	Yes
Therapist contact + pharmacotherapy	Yes	Unknown
Therapist contact + pharmacotherapy + portion-controlled meals	Yes	Unknown

Adapted and updated from Perri (2001).

of their initial reductions, those without extended contact maintained only 38% of their initial reductions. Collectively, these data strongly suggest extended treatment improves long-term outcome, a conclusion consistent with the findings of an independent review of long-term success in obesity treatment (Ayyad & Andersen, 2000).

Relapse Prevention Training

Relapse prevention training (RPT) involves teaching participants how to avoid or cope with slips and relapses (Marlatt & Gordon, 1985). Studies of the effectiveness of RPT on long-term weight management have revealed mixed results. While the inclusion of RPT during initial treatment has not been found to be effective, combining RPT with a post-treatment program of client–therapist contacts has improved the maintenance of weight loss in some studies (Baum, Clark & Sandler, 1991; Perri et al., 1984b). However, Perri et al. (2001) recently compared RPT and problem-solving therapy (PST) as year-long extended treatments for weight loss. PST showed better long-term outcome than the control group, but RPT did not. RPT in this study was administered as a standardized didactic program; it may be more effective when applied as an individualized therapy (Marlatt & George, 1998).

Telephone Contact

Post-treatment telephone contact may represent a more efficient mode of providing active follow-up care than in-person sessions. However, the use of telephone contact has yielded mixed results. Perri et al. (1984b) found that post-treatment contacts by telephone and mail significantly improved the maintenance of lost weight, but Wing et al. (1996) failed to find a beneficial effect from telephone prompts alone. However, these two studies differed in ways that may help to explain these divergent findings. In the Perri et al. (1984b) study, the clients' therapists made the phone calls and provided counseling about ways to cope with problems related to the maintenance of lost weight. In contrast, the contacts in the Wing et al. (1996) study were made by callers unknown to the clients who did not offer advice but simply prompted the clients to continue their self-management efforts. Telephone contact may be more effective when it includes an opportunity for counseling by the treatment provider with whom the client has a relationship.

Peer Support

Perri et al. (1987) examined the effects of a post-treatment peer support program compared to a post-treatment therapist support program and to a control condition that received no post-treatment contact. An 18-month follow-up assessment suggested a trend toward better maintenance of weight lost in both the peer-support and therapist contacts groups compared with the control condition. The effect of treating participants alone or with three friends or family members was recently tested by Wing and Jeffery (1999). The researchers used a partially randomized study design in assigning subjects (recruited alone versus with friends) to receive either standard behavior therapy or behavior therapy with social support training. The results of a relatively short follow-up (i.e., six months) indicated that the combination of joining with friends *and* receiving social support training significantly improved the maintenance of lost weight. These two studies (Perri et al., 1987; Wing & Jeffery, 1999) suggest a beneficial, albeit modest, effect for social support in long-term weight management.

Portion-controlled Meals

Can long-term weight control be improved through the use of portion-controlled meals? Jeffery and his colleagues (1993) provided obese patients with prepackaged, portion-controlled meals (ten per week at no cost) during initial treatment and the following year. Participants in the food provision groups showed significantly greater weight losses than those without food provision both during initial treatment and during the subsequent 12 months. However, the results of an additional 12-month follow-up, without food provision, revealed a significant regaining of weight (Jeffery & Wing, 1995). In a subsequent study, Wing et al. (1996) found that simply providing participants with the "opportunity" to purchase and use portion-controlled meals as a maintenance strategy was not effective, largely because the participants elected not to purchase the portion-controlled meals. Taken together, these studies show that the use of portion-controlled meals may be an effective maintenance strategy only when the meals are provided to participants at no cost. Consistent with these findings, Flechtner-Mors et al. (2000) found excellent long-term maintenance of lost weight for participants who were provided with extended treatment (i.e., monthly clinician contacts) and with no-cost portion-controlled meals and snacks (seven meals and seven snacks per week) over the course of a 48-month period.

Exercise/Physical Activity

Long-term weight loss is often associated with high levels of physical activity (e.g., Harris et al., 1994; McGuire et al., 1999; Sherwood, Jeffery & Wing, 1999; Wing & Hill, 2001). Nonetheless, an important question remains as to whether the addition of exercise/physical activity to dietary change can improve long-term weight loss. Wing (1999) reviewed six randomized-controlled trials that addressed this question. Only two of the studies showed significantly better maintenance of lost weight for the diet plus exercise condition versus diet alone; however, the direction of the findings in the four remaining studies suggested a favorable effect for the inclusion of exercise. The modest effects for the addition of exercise may have been due to several factors, including the short duration of the interventions, the relatively small amounts of exercise prescribed, and, most importantly, inconsistent adherence to the physical activity prescriptions. Given the obvious potential benefits of exercise in the management of obesity, a variety of strategies to improve exercise adherence have been examined including home-based exercise, the use of short bouts of exercise, the provision of home exercise equipment, monetary incentives for exercise, and follow-up programs focusing exclusively on exercise. We review each of these strategies next.

Several studies have demonstrated greater adherence to home-based exercise regimens compared with supervised group exercise (King et al., 1991; Perri et al., 1997). Moreover, Perri and colleagues (1997) found that participation in home-based exercise resulted in improvements in other domains including better attendance at treatment sessions, increased self-monitoring of food intake, and better long-term maintenance of lost weight. Similarly, Jeffery et al. (1998) also found that participants in a home-based exercise regimen showed superior maintenance of lost weight compared to those in supervised group-based exercise. Thus, the greater convenience and flexibility of home-based exercise may produce higher levels of exercise adherence, and continued participation in exercise may produce better adherence to other weight-control strategies and better maintenance of lost weight as well.

Adherence to home-based exercise routines may be enhanced by providing participants with exercise equipment and by allowing them to exercise in brief bouts. Jakicic et al. (1999) tested the effects of short-bout versus long-bout exercise (i.e., four 10-minute bouts per day versus one 40-minute bout per day) and the use of home exercise equipment (treadmills) on adherence, weight loss, and fitness. Benefits from exercise in short or long bouts were equivalent—an important finding for people who have difficulty finding time in their schedules for a longer bout of exercise. Further, participants who were provided with home exercise equipment maintained significantly higher levels of long-term exercise adherence and weight loss compared to subjects without exercise equipment.

Some exercise-related strategies have not proven to be helpful to weight management. For example, the use of personal exercise trainers and financial incentives for exercise completion[2] have improved attendance at supervised exercise sessions but have not increased weight loss (Jeffery et al., 1998). A focus on exercise alone as a maintenance strategy may not be sufficient to improve long-term weight control. For example, Leermakers et al. (1999) compared a maintenance program that focused exclusively on exercise adherence with a program that focused more generally on the maintenance of lost weight. A 12-month follow-up showed poorer maintenance of lost weight in the program that focused exclusively on exercise—a finding that highlights the necessity of focusing on dietary intake as well as energy expenditure for successful long-term weight management.

Multicomponent Post-treatment Programs

Several studies have demonstrated the effectiveness of post-treatment programs with multiple components. As noted previously, Flechtner-Mors et al. (2000) found excellent long-term maintenance of lost weight for participants who were provided with a multicomponent program consisting of extended treatment combined with no-cost, portion-controlled meals and snacks, and Wadden et al. (2001) demonstrated the effectiveness of combining lifestyle modification with pharmacotherapy and portion-controlled meals. Two studies (Perri et al., 1984a, 1986) have shown that multicomponent post-treatment programs consisting of peer group meetings combined with ongoing therapist contacts by mail and telephone improved the maintenance of lost weight compared to control conditions without follow-up care. Finally, Perri et al. (1988) examined the effects of adding increased exercise and a social influence program (or both) to a post-treatment therapist contact program consisting of 26 biweekly group sessions. Compared to a control condition that received behavioral therapy without post-treatment contact, all four post-treatment programs produced significantly greater weight losses at an 18-month follow-up evaluation. Collectively, the four maintenance groups succeeded in sustaining on average 83% of their initial weight losses, compared to 33% for the group without a post-treatment program. A common element in multicomponent programs is the addition of therapist contact following an initial period of weight-loss treatment. In most but not all studies (e.g., Perri et al., 2001), providing clients with follow-up care has resulted in improved maintenance of lost weight (Perri & Corsica, 2002). Such findings underscore the importance of programming a regimen of long-term care in the treatment of obese patients.

CLINICAL MANAGEMENT

We advocate four key elements in the clinical management of obesity. First, we argue for a greater recognition by clinicians and the general public of the nature of obesity as a serious health problem. Next, prior to undertaking treatment of obesity, we recommend a comprehensive assessment to determine risk of compromised health and quality of life

---

[2] Similarly, the use of financial incentives for weight loss in behavioral treatment has not increased the magnitude of weight reductions during initial treatment (Jeffery et al., 1993).

and to identify appropriate targets for intervention. Third, we advise matching treatments to patients based on the patient's weight status as well as other targets requiring change. Lastly, we argue for a "continuous care" approach which provides the overweight patient with long-term assistance in the management of obesity.

Recognizing the Nature of the Problem

Part of the difficulty in managing obesity stems from a failure to recognize not only its seriousness but also the contributors to its development and the options available for its treatment. In recent years, the detrimental impact of excess body weight has become increasingly apparent. For example, as a direct consequence of the dramatic rise in obesity among young people, type 2 diabetes mellitus, a disease most commonly seen in middle-aged obese adults, is now being observed in obese teenagers and young adults (Caprio & Tamborlane, 1999). Yet despite the ominous consequences of obesity, health care practitioners rarely provide overweight patients with advice about weight loss (Sciamanna et al., 2000). Moreover, when such advice is given, it is provided primarily to those who are already significantly obese, are middle-aged, and have comorbid conditions such as diabetes or hypertension (Sciamanna et al., 2000). Such findings suggest that health care providers may be missing significant opportunities to counsel overweight persons to lose weight or to maintain their weight and thereby avoid the development of comorbid conditions.

A greater awareness of the contribution of lifestyle factors to weight gain is also needed. Indeed, sedentary lifestyle and increased consumption of high fat foods constitute the major contributors to the increased prevalence of obesity. Accordingly, we must recognize those elements of our environment, at home, school, and work, that foster unhealthy patterns of eating and physical activity. Furthermore, we must acknowledge the necessity of environmental and lifestyle modifications to redress the problem.

Greater recognition must also be given to the range of empirically supported treatment options available for weight management. A common misconception, popular among many patients and health care providers, is that control of body weight represents a futile endeavor (Wilson, 1994). This perception stems largely from observations of relapse following treatment of obesity. It fails to take into account the fact that most obese people who experience relapses in weight management remain significantly lighter than their untreated overweight peers, who typically show a pattern of steady weight gain (Field et al., 2001; Shah et al., 1991). It also fails to take into account that among those treated for obesity, a substantial proportion (15–20%) demonstrate clear-cut, long-term success (Ayyad & Andersen, 2000; Kramer et al., 1989). In addition, substantial long-term weight losses accompanied by significant improvements in health are experienced by the overwhelming majority of morbidly obese patients who undergo bariatric surgery (MacDonald et al., 1997; Sjöstrom, Narbro & Sjöstrom, 1995).

Identifying Appropriate Targets for Change

An effective treatment plan for the obese person should begin with a comprehensive assessment of the effects of obesity on the individual's health and emotional well-being (Beliard, Kirschenbaum & Fitzgibbon, 1992; Kushner & Weinsier, 2000). In addition to a physical examination that specifically assesses risk for common comorbidities of obesity such as diabetes, dyslipidemia, and hypertension, the initial assessment should also include an evaluation of relevant behavioral and psychological factors, such as sedentary lifestyle, consumption of a poor-quality diet, binge eating, body image dissatisfaction, unrealistic weight-loss expectations, and symptoms of anxiety and depression. Each of these problems may represent an important target for change (Perri, Nezu & Viegener, 1992; Wadden & Foster, 1992), independent of a reduction in body weight.

Moreover, treatment goals should be framed in terms of behaviors that obese persons can control, such as the quantity and quality of food they consume and the amounts and types of physical activity they perform. Successful outcome in the care of the obese person should not be viewed solely in terms of weight loss. In some cases, the prevention of further weight gain may represent an appropriate goal of treatment. Beneficial changes in risk factors for disease and improvements in quality of life (Atkinson, 1993) often represent important indicators of success. Improvements in the quality of diet should be a component of care independent of whether weight reduction is an identified objective of care (Hill, Drougas & Peters, 1993). Reductions in amounts of dietary fats, particularly saturated fats, can improve health as well as assist in weight loss (Insull et al., 1990; NHLBI, 2001). Similarly, increased physical activity and a decrease in sedentary lifestyle can represent beneficial components of long-term care irrespective of the impact of exercise on weight loss (Lee, Blair & Jackson, 1999; Leermakers, Dunn & Blair, 2000). Finally, self-acceptance, independent of body weight, may also be a significant indicator of success in the psychological treatment of the obese person (Wilson, 1996).

Matching Treatments to Patients

We recommend that an initial treatment plan be devised and based on consideration of the range of appropriate treatment options that take into account both the patient's weight status and individualized targets for change identified by a comprehensive pretreatment assessment. Guidelines for a stepped-care approach for matching treatments to patients based on the severity of obesity and the presence of comorbid conditions have been described in several recent reports (NHLBI, 1998; WHO, 1998; see Table 10.3).

Table 10.3 A stepped-care approach to weight management

BMI	Presence of weight-related comorbidity	Recommended steps	Weight goal
<25	—	Self-management	Prevention of weight gain
25–29.9	No	1. Self-management 2. Lifestyle intervention	5–10% reduction
27–29.9	Yes	1. Lifestyle intervention 2. Lifestyle + pharmacotherapy	5–10% reduction 5–10% reduction
30–39.9	No	1. Lifestyle intervention 2. Lifestyle + pharmacotherapy	10% reduction 10% reduction
35–39.9	Yes	1. Lifestyle + pharmacotherapy 2. Bariatric surgery	10% reduction
≥40	—	Bariatric surgery	≥25% reduction

For people in the desirable weight range (i.e., BMI of 18.5–24.9), we recommend the prevention of weight gain and the maintenance, or if necessary the development, of healthy eating patterns and a physically active lifestyle. Indeed, high-fat diets and sedentary lifestyles represent increased risks for disease even in the absence of excess body weight (Blair & Brodney, 1999; Office of Disease Prevention and Health Promotion, 2000). For those in the overweight or obese Class I or II categories, lifestyle interventions represent the first line of treatment. In most cases, treatment goals typically will entail modification of eating and exercise behaviors so as to produce weight losses of 0.5–1.0 kg per week. Lifestyle or behavioral interventions can be expected to produce reductions of 5–10% in body weight (NHLBI, 1998). Losses of this magnitude are sufficient to produce clinically significant changes in risk for disease (Pi-Sunyer, 1999). The addition of pharmacotherapy to behavioral treatment may enhance the effectiveness of weight management efforts (Wadden et al., 2001). The combination of pharmacotherapy and behavioral treatment is generally reserved for those with a BMI in excess of 30 for whom lifestyle intervention alone has not produced adequate results. However, the presence of significant comorbidities may justify consideration of pharmacotherapy in patients with BMIs as low as 27. For patients with Class III obesity (i.e., BMI ≥ 40), bariatric surgery represents the treatment of choice. Here, also, the presence of significant comorbidities may justify consideration of surgery in patients with BMIs as low as 35.

Adopting a Lifelong Perspective

We believe that obesity should be viewed as a chronic condition requiring long-term, if not lifelong, care. The clinical challenge is not to persuade obese people that they need to be in treatment forever. Rather the challenge is to convince the overweight people that successful management of their weight will require constant vigilance and ongoing efforts at self-management of eating and exercise behaviors (Perri, Nezu & Viegener, 1992). Although weight management may become somewhat easier over time (McGuire et al., 1999), it is always likely to entail conscious efforts to maintain behavioral control of one's energy balance (Wing & Hill, 2001). In a compassionate manner, health providers must communicate to their obese patients not merely a recognition of the chronicity of the problem, but also an empathic understanding of the emotional aspects of what it means to be obese in a culture that values thinness.

Finally, clinicians need to assure obese patients of their ready availability to assist in the long-term management of weight and related issues. Indeed, the maintenance of weight loss is more likely to occur when clients are provided with interventions specifically designed to enhance long-term progress (e.g., Björvell & Rössner, 1992). Moreover, the most important maintenance strategy may consist of long-term clinical contact (Perri & Corsica, 2002). Such contact promotes vigilance to diet and exercise and provides opportunities for active problem-solving of obstacles to long-term success.

SUMMARY

Over the past two decades, the rates of overweight and obesity in the industrialized world have increased at an alarming pace. Obesity confers increased risk for morbidity and mortality and thereby constitutes a major public health problem. Although genetic factors may predispose some individuals to obesity, environmental factors comprise the major contributors to the current epidemic of overweight. Continuous exposure to an overabundance of high-calorie and high-fat foods coupled with decreased occupational and leisure time physical activity have resulted in the significant increases in body weights observed over the past two decades.

Weight loss can reverse many of the disadvantages associated with obesity, and progress has been made in the development of effective weight-loss treatments. Behavioral or lifestyle interventions that focus on moderate reductions in caloric intake, combined with increased energy expenditures through physical activity, produce weight reductions of sufficient magnitude to decrease the risk for many diseases. Moreover, new pharmacological agents can enhance the effectiveness of lifestyle interventions, and gastric bypass surgery now provides a viable treatment option for the very severely obese.

In spite of the considerable progress in producing clinically significant weight losses, all weight-loss interventions (with the possible exception of surgery) suffer from the problem of poor long-term maintenance of lost weight. However, providing obese patients with extended treatment and with long-term follow-up care has shown some benefit in this regard. The implementation of strategies to promote continued vigilance and adherence to changes in diet and physical activity may be required for long-term success in the management of obesity.

REFERENCES

Albrecht, R.J. & Pories, W.J. (1999). Surgical intervention for the severely obese. *Baillieres Best Practice Research and Clinical Endocrinology and Metabolism*, **13**, 149–172.

Allison, D.B. & Saunders, S.E. (2000). Obesity in North America. An overview. *Medical Clinics of North America*, **84**, 305–332.

Allison, D.B., Fontaine, K.R., Manson, J.E., Stevens, J. & Van Itallie, T.B. (1999). Annual deaths attributable to obesity in the United States. *Journal of the American Medical Association*, **282**, 1530–1538.

Apfelbaum, M., Vague, P., Ziegler, O., Hanotin, C., Thomas, F. & Leutenegger, E. (1999). Long term maintenance of weight loss after a very-low-calorie diet: a randomized blinded trial of the efficacy and tolerability of sibutramine. *American Journal of Medicine*, **106**, 179–184.

Atkinson, R.L. (1993). Proposed standards for judging the success of the treatment of obesity. *Annals of Internal Medicine*, **119**, 677–680.

Ayyad, C. & Andersen, T. (2000). Long-term efficacy of dietary treatment of obesity: a systematic review of studies published between 1931 and 1999. *Obesity Reviews*, **1**, 113–119.

Balsiger, B.M., Murr, M.M., Poggio, J.L. & Sarr, M.G. (2000). Bariatric surgery: surgery for weight control in patients with morbid obesity. *Medical Clinics of North America*, **84**, 477–489.

Baum, J.G., Clark, H.B. & Sandler, J. (1991). Preventing relapse in obesity through posttreatment maintenance systems: comparing the relative efficacy of two levels of therapist support. *Journal of Behavioral Medicine*, **14**, 287–302.

Beliard, D., Kirschenbaum, D.S. & Fitzgibbon, M.L. (1992). Evaluation of an intensive weight control program using a priori criteria to determine outcome. *International Journal of Obesity*, **16**, 505–517.

Binkley, J.K., Eales, J. & Jekanowski, M. (2000). The relation between dietary change and rising US obesity. *International Journal of Obesity*, **24**, 1032–1039.

Björvell, H. & Rössner, S. (1992). A ten year follow-up of weight change in severely obese subjects treated in a behavioural modification programme. *International Journal of Obesity*, **16**, 623–625.

Blair, S.N. & Brodney, S. (1999). Effects of physical inactivity and obesity on morbidity and mortality: current evidence and research issues. *Medicine and Science in Sports and Exercise*, **31** (Suppl. 11), S646–S662.

Bray, G.A. & Gray, D.S. (1988). Treatment of obesity: an overview. *Diabetes and Metabolism Review*, **4**, 653–679.

Bray, G.A., Blackburn, G.L., Ferguson, J.M., Greenway, F.L., Jain, A.K., Mendel, C.M., Mendels, J., Ryan, D.H., Schwartz, S.L., Scheinbaum, M.L. & Seaton, T.B. (1999). Sibutramine produces dose-related weight loss. *Obesity Research*, **7**, 189–198.

Brownell, K.D. (1998). Diet, exercise and behavioural intervention: the nonpharmacological approach. *European Journal of Clinical Investigation*, **28** (Suppl. 2), 19–21.

Campfield, L., Smith, F., Guisez, Y., Devos, R. & Burn, P. (1995). Recombinant mouse OB protein: evidence for peripheral signal linking adiposity and central neural networks. *Science*, **269**, 475–476.

Caprio, S. & Tamborlane, W.V. (1999). Metabolic impact of obesity in childhood. *Endocrinology and Metabolism Clinics of North America*, **28**, 731–747.

Carpenter, K.M., Hasin, D.S., Allison, D.B. & Faith, M.S. (2000). Relationship between obesity and DSM-IV major depressive disorder, suicide ideation, and suicide attempts: results from a general population study. *American Journal of Public Health*, **90**, 251–257.

Centers for Disease Control (2001). Physical Activity Trends: United States, 1990–1998. *Morbidity and Mortality Weekly Report*, **50**, 166–169.

Chagnon, Y.C., Perusse, L., Weisnagel, S.J., Rankinen, T. & Bouchard, C. (2000). The human obesity gene map: the 1999 update. *Obesity Research*, **8**, 89–117.

Connolly, H.M., Crary, J.L., McGoon, M.D., Hensrud, D.D., Edwards, B.S., Edwards, W.D. & Schaff, H.V. (1997). Valvular heart disease associated with fenfluramine-phentermine. *New England Journal of Medicine*, **337**, 581–588.

Cook, N.R., Cohen, J., Hebert, P.R., Taylor, J.O. & Hennekens, C.H. (1995). Implications of small reductions in diastolic blood pressure for primary prevention. *Archives of Internal Medicine*, **155**, 701–709.

Davidson, M.H., Hauptman, J., DiGirolamo, M., Foreyt, J.P., Halsted, C.H., Heber, D., Heimburger, D.C., Lucas, C.P., Robbins, D.C., Chung, J. & Heymsfield, S.B. (1999). Weight control and risk factor reduction in obese subjects treated for 2 years with orlistat: a randomized controlled trial. *Journal of the American Medical Association*, **281**, 235–242.

Department of Health (2001). *Health Survey for England: Trend Data for Adults 1993–1998*. Retrieved October 29, 2001, from Department of Health web site: http://www.doh.gov.uk

Dulloo, A.G. & Jacquet, J. (1998). Adaptive reduction in basal metabolic rate in response to food deprivation in humans: a role for feedback signals from fat stores. *American Journal of Clinical Nutrition*, **68**, 599–606.

Eaton, S.B. & Konner, M. (1985). Paleolithic nutrition: a consideration of its nature and current implications. *New England Journal of Medicine*, **312**, 283–289.

Farooqi, I.S., Yeo, G.S.H., Keogh, J.M., Aminian, S., Jebb, S.A., Butler, G., Cheetham, T. & O'Rahilly, S.O. (2000). Dominant and recessive inheritance of morbid obesity associated with melanocortin 4 receptor deficiency. *The Journal of Clinical Investigation*, **106**, 271–279.

Feitosa, M.F., Borecki, I., Hunt, S.C., Arnett, D.K., Rao, D.C. & Province, M. (2000). Inheritance of the waist to hip ratio in the National Heart, Lung, and Blood Institute Family Heart Study. *Obesity Research*, **8**, 294–301.

Field, A.E., Wing, R.R., Manson, J.E., Spiegelman, D.L. & Willett, W.C. (2001). Relationship of a large weight loss to long-term weight change among young and middle-aged US women. *International Journal of Obesity*, **25**, 1113–1121.

Fitzgibbon, M.L., Stolley, M.R. & Kirschenbaum, D.S. (1993). Obese people who seek treatment have different characteristics than those who do not seek treatment. *Health Psychology*, **12**, 342–345.

Flechtner-Mors, M., Ditschuneit, H.H., Johnson, T.D., Suchard, M.A. & Adler, G. (2000). Metabolic and weight loss effects of long-term dietary intervention in obese patients: four-year results. *Obesity Research*, **8**, 399–402.

Flegal, K.M., Carroll, M.D., Kuczmarski, R.J. & Johnson, C.L. (1998). Overweight and obesity in the United States: prevalence and trends, 1960–1994. *International Journal of Obesity*, **22**, 39–47.

Food and Drug Administration (2000, Nov. 6). *Public Health Advisory. Subject: Safety of Phenyl-propanolamine.*

French, S.A., Harnack, L. & Jeffery, R.W. (2000). Fast food restaurant use among women in the Pound of Prevention study: dietary, behavioral and demographic correlates. *International Journal of Obesity*, **24**, 1353–1359.

Glenny, A.M., O'Meara, S., Melville, A., Sheldon, T.A. & Wilson, C. (1997). The treatment and prevention of obesity: a systematic review of the literature. *International Journal of Obesity*, **21**, 715–737.

Goodrick, G.K., Raynaud, A.S., Pace, P.W. & Foreyt, J.P. (1992). Outcome attribution in a very low calorie diet program. *International Journal of Eating Disorders*, **12**, 117–120.

Hansen, D.L., Toubro, S., Stock, M.J., Macdonald, I.A. & Astrup, A. (1998). Thermogenic effects of sibutramine in humans. *American Journal of Clinical Nutrition*, **68**, 1180–1186.

Harris, J.K., French, S.A., Jeffery, R.W., McGovern, P.G. & Wing, R.R. (1994). Dietary and physical activity correlates of long-term weight loss. *Obesity Research*, **2**, 307–313.

Hensrud, D.D. (2000). Pharmacotherapy for obesity. *Medical Clinics of North America*, **84**, 463–476.

Heymsfield, S.B., Greenberg, A.S., Fujioka, K., Dixon, R.M., Kushner, R., Hunt, T., Lubina, J.A., Patane, J., Self, B., Hunt, P. & McCamish, M. (1999). Recombinant leptin for weight loss in obese and lean adults: a randomized, controlled, dose-escalation trial. *Journal of the American Medical Association*, **282**, 1568–1575.

Hill, J.O. & Peters, J.C. (1998). Environmental contributions to the obesity epidemic. *Science*, **280**, 1371–1374.

Hill, J.O., Drougas, H. & Peters, J.C. (1993). Obesity treatment: can diet composition play a role? *Annals of Internal Medicine*, **119**, 694–697.

Hill, J.O., Wyatt, H.R. & Melanson, E.L. (2000). Genetic and environmental contributions to obesity. *Medical Clinics of North America*, **84**, 333–346.

Hill, J.O., Hauptman, J., Anderson, J.W., Fujioka, K., O'Neil, P.M., Smith, D.K., Zavoral, J.H. & Aronne, L.J. (1999). Orlistat, a lipase inhibitor, for weight maintenance after conventional dieting: a 1-year study. *American Journal of Clinical Nutrition*, **69**, 1108–1116.

Insull, W., Henderson, M., Prentice, R., Thompson, D.J., Moskowitz, M. & Gorbach, S. (1990). Results of a feasibility study of a low-fat diet. *Archives of Internal Medicine*, **150**, 421–427.

Jakicic, J.M., Winters, C., Lang, W. & Wing, R.R. (1999). Effects of intermittent exercise and use of home exercise equipment on adherence, weight loss, and fitness in overweight women: a randomized trial. *Journal of the American Medical Association*, **282**, 1554–1560.

James, W.P.T. (1995). A public health approach to the problem of obesity. *International Journal of Obesity*, **19**, S37–S45.

James, W.P.T. (1996). The epidemiology of obesity. In D.J. Chadwick & G.C. Cardew (Eds), *The Origins and Consequences of Obesity* (pp. 1–16). Chichester: John Wiley & Sons.

Jeffery, R.W. & Wing, R.R. (1995). Long-term effects of interventions for weight loss using food provision and monetary incentives. *Journal of Consulting and Clinical Psychology*, **63**, 793–796.

Jeffery, R.W., Adlis, S.A. & Forster, J.L. (1991). Prevalence of dieting among working men and women: the healthy worker project. *Health Psychology*, **10**, 274–281.

Jeffery, R.W., French, S.A. & Schmid, T.L. (1990). Attributions for dietary failures: problems reported by participants in the Hypertension Prevention Trial. *Health Psychology*, **9**, 315–329.

Jeffery, R.W., Drewnowski, A., Epstein, L.H., Stunkard, A.J., Wilson, G.T., Wing, R.R. & Hill, D.R. (2000). Long-term maintenance of weight loss: current status. *Health Psychology*, **19** (Suppl. 1), 5–16.

Jeffery, R.W., Wing, R.R., Thorson, C. & Burton, L.R. (1998). Use of personal trainers and financial incentives to increase exercise in a behavioral weight-loss program. *Journal of Consulting and Clinical Psychology*, **66**, 777–783.

Jeffery, R.W., Wing, R.R., Thorson, C., Burton, L.R., Raether, C., Harvey, J. & Mullen, M. (1993). Strengthening behavioral interventions for weight loss: a randomized trial of food provision and monetary incentives. *Journal of Consulting and Clinical Psychology*, **61**, 1038–1045.

Jones, S.P., Smith, I.G., Kelly, F. & Gray, J.A. (1995). Long term weight loss with sibutramine. *International Journal of Obesity*, **19** (Suppl. 2), 41.

Kant, A.K. (2000). Consumption of energy-dense, nutrient-poor foods by adult Americans: nutritional and health implications. The Third National Health and Nutrition Examination Survey, 1988–1994. *American Journal of Clinical Nutrition*, **72**, 929–936.

King, A.C., Haskell, W.L., Taylor, C.B., Kraemer, H.C. & DeBusk, R.F. (1991). Group- vs. home-based exercise training in healthy older men and women. A community-based clinical trial. *Journal of the American Medical Association*, **266**, 1535–1542.

Knoll Pharmaceutical Co. (2000). Meridia (sibutramine hydrochloride monohydrate). Prescribing information. *Physician's Desk Reference* (pp. 1509–1513). Montvale, NJ: Drug Information Services Group.

Kral, J.G. (1989). Surgical treatment of obesity. *Medical Clinics of North America*, **73**, 251–269.

Kral, J.G. (1995). Surgical interventions for obesity. In K.D. Brownell & C.G. Fairburn (Eds), *Eating Disorders and Obesity: A Comprehensive Handbook* (pp. 510–515). New York: Guilford Press.

Kramer, F.M., Jeffery, R.W., Forster, J.L. & Snell, M.K. (1989). Long-term follow-up of behavioral treatment for obesity: patterns of weight regain among men and women. *International Journal of Obesity*, **13**, 123–136.

Kushner, R.F. & Weinsier, R.L. (2000). Evaluation of the obese patient. Practical considerations. *Medical Clinics of North America*, **84**, 387–399.

Latner, J.D. (2001). Self-help in the long-term treatment of obesity. *Obesity Reviews*, **2**, 87–97.

Lee, C.D., Blair, S.N. & Jackson, A.S. (1999). Cardiorespiratory fitness, body composition, and all-cause and cardiovascular disease mortality in men. *American Journal of Clinical Nutrition*, **69**, 373–380.

Leermakers, E.A., Dunn, A.L. & Blair, S.N. (2000). Exercise management of obesity. *Medical Clinics of North America*, **84**, 419–440.

Leermakers, E.A., Perri, M.G., Shigaki, C.L. & Fuller, P.R. (1999). Effects of exercise-focused versus weight-focused maintenance programs on the management of obesity. *Addictive Behaviors*, **24**, 219–227.

Levin, B.E. (2000). The obesity epidemic: metabolic imprinting on genetically susceptible neural circuits. *Obesity Research*, **8**, 342–347.

Long, S.D., O'Brien, K., MacDonald, K.G. Jr, Leggett-Frazier, N., Swanson, M.S., Pories W.J. & Caro, J. (1994). Weight loss in severely obese subjects prevents the progression of impaired glucose tolerance to type-II diabetes. A longitudinal intervention study. *Diabetes Care*, **17**, 372–375.

MacDonald, K.G. Jr, Long, S.D., Swanson, M.S., Brown, B.M., Morris, P., Dohm, G.L. & Pories, W.J. (1997). The gastric bypass operation reduces the progression and mortality of non-insulin-dependent diabetes mellitus. *Journal of Gastrointestinal Surgery*, **1**, 213–220.

Marlatt, G.A. & George, W.H. (1998). Relapse prevention and the maintenance of optimal health. In S.A. Shumaker, E.B. Schron, J.K. Ockene & W.L. McBee (Eds), *The Handbook of Health Behavior Change* (2nd edn, pp. 33–58). New York: Springer.

Marlatt, G.A. & Gordon, J.R. (1985). *Relapse Prevention: Maintenance Strategies in the Treatment of Addictive Behaviors*. New York: Guilford Press.

McCrory, M.A., Fuss, P.J., Hays, N.P., Vinken, A.G., Greenberg, A.S. & Roberts, S.B. (1999). Overeating in America: association between restaurant food consumption and body fatness in healthy adult men and women ages 19 to 80. *Obesity Research*, **7**, 564–571.

McGuire, M., Wing, R., Klem, M., Lang, W. & Hill, J. (1999). What predicts weight regain in a group of successful weight losers? *Journal of Consulting and Clinical Psychology*, **67**, 177–185.

Melanson, K.J., McInnis, K.J., Rippe, J.M., Blackburn, G. & Wilson, P.F. (2001). Obesity and cardiovascular disease risk: research update. *Cardiology Review*, **9**, 202–207.

Montague, C.T., Farooqi, I.S., Whitehead, J.P., Soos, M.A., Rau, H., Wareham, N.J., Sewter, C.P., Digby, J.E., Mohammed, S.N., Hurst, J.A., Cheetham, C.H., Earley, A.R., Barnett, A.H., Prins, J.B. & O'Rahilly, S. (1997). Congenital leptin deficiency is associated with severe early-onset obesity in humans. *Nature*, **387**, 903–908.

National Heart, Lung, and Blood Institute (1998). Obesity education initiative expert panel on the identification, evaluation, and treatment of overweight and obesity in adults. *Obesity Research*, **6** (Suppl. 2).

National Institutes of Health (1992). Gastrointestinal surgery for severe obesity. Proceedings of a National Institutes of Health Consensus Development Conference. *American Journal of Clinical Nutrition*, **55**, S487–S619.

Office of Disease Prevention and Health Promotion. (2000). Healthy People 2010. Retrieved October 22, 2001, from Office of Disease Prevention and Health Promotion web site: http://odphp.osophs.dhhd.gov

Perri, M.G. (2001). Improving maintenance in behavioural treatment. In K.D. Brownell & C.G. Fairburn (Eds), *Eating Disorders and Obesity: A Comprehensive Handbook* (2nd edn, pp. 593–598). New York: Guilford Press.

Perri, M.G. & Corsica, J.A. (2002). Improving the maintenance of weight lost in behavioral treatment of obesity. In T.A. Wadden & A.J. Stunkard (Eds), *Handbook of Obesity Treatment* (pp. 367–389). New York: Guilford Press.

Perri, M.G. & Fuller, P.R. (1995). Success and failure in the treatment of obesity: where do we go from here? *Medicine, Exercise, Nutrition and Health*, **4**, 255–272.

Perri, M.G., Nezu, A.M. & Viegener, B.J (1992). *Improving the Long-Term Management of Obesity: Theory, Research, and Clinical Guidelines*. New York: John Wiley & Sons.

Perri, M.G., McAdoo, W.G., McAllister, D.A., Lauer, J.B., Jordan, R.C., Yancey, D.Z. & Nezu, A.M. (1987). Effects of peer support and therapist contact on long-term weight loss. *Journal of Consulting and Clinical Psychology*, **55**, 615–617.

Perri, M.G., McAdoo, W.G., McAllister, D.A., Lauer, J.B. & Yancey, D.Z. (1986). Enhancing the efficacy of behavior therapy for obesity: effects of aerobic exercise and a multicomponent maintenance program. *Journal of Consulting and Clinical Psychology*, **54**, 670–675.

Perri, M.G., McAdoo, W.G., Spevak, P.A. & Newlin, D.B. (1984a). Effect of a multi-component maintenance program on long-term weight loss. *Journal of Consulting and Clinical Psychology*, **52**, 480–481.

Perri, M.G., McAllister, D.A., Gange, J.J., Jordan, R.C., McAdoo, W.G. & Nezu, A.M. (1988). Effects of four maintenance programs on the long-term management of obesity. *Journal of Consulting and Clinical Psychology*, **56**, 529–534.

Perri, M.G., Martin, A.D., Leermakers, E.A., Sears, S.F. & Notelovitz, M. (1997). Effects of group-versus home-based exercise in the treatment of obesity. *Journal of Consulting and Clinical Psychology*, **65**, 278–285.

Perri, M.G., Nezu, A.M., McKelvey, W.F., Shermer, R.L., Renjilian, D.A. & Viegener, B.J. (2001). Relapse prevention training and problem-solving therapy in the long-term management of obesity. *Journal of Consulting and Clinical Psychology*, **69**, 722–726.

Perri, M.G., Shapiro, R.M., Ludwig, W.W., Twentyman, C.T. & McAdoo, W.G. (1984b). Maintenance strategies for the treatment of obesity: an evaluation of relapse prevention training and posttreatment contact by mail and telephone. *Journal of Consulting and Clinical Psychology*, **52**, 404–413.

Pi-Sunyer, F.X. (1999). Co-morbidities of overweight and obesity: current evidence and research issues. *Medicine and Science in Sports and Exercise*, **31** (Suppl. 11), S602–S608.

Poston, W.S. & Foreyt, J.P. (1999). Obesity is an environmental issue. *Atherosclerosis*, **146**, 201–209.

Putnam, J.J. & Allshouse, J.E. (1996). *Food Consumption, Prices, and Expenditures, 1970–1994*. Washington, DC: US Department of Agriculture.

Ravussin, E. & Swinburn, B.A. (1993). Metabolic predictors of obesity: cross-sectional versus longitudinal data. *International Journal of Obesity*, **17** (Suppl. 3), S28–S31.

Renjilian, D.A., Perri, M.G., Nezu, A.M., McKelvey, W.F., Shermer, R.L. & Anton, S.D. (2001). Individual versus group therapy for obesity: effects of matching participants to their treatment preference. *Journal of Consulting and Clinical Psychology*, **69**, 717–721.

Roche Pharmaceutical Company (2000). Xenical (orlistat). Prescribing information. *Physician's Desk Reference* (pp. 2693–2696). Montvale, NJ: Drug Information Services Group.

Sciamanna, C.N., Tate, D.F., Lang, W. & Wing, R.R. (2000). Who reports receiving advice to lose weight? Results from a multistate survey. *Archives of Internal Medicine*, **160**, 2334–2339.

Serdula, M.K., Mokdad, A.H., Williamson, D.F., Galuska, D.A., Medlein, J.M. & Heath, G.W. (1999). Prevalence of attempting weight loss and strategies for controlling weight. *Journal of the American Medical Association*, **282**, 1353–1358.

Shah, M., Hannan, P.J. & Jeffery, R.W. (1991). Secular trends in body mass index in the adult population of three communities from the upper mid-western part of the USA: the Minnesota Heart Health Program. *International Journal of Obesity*, **15**, 499–503.

Sherwood, N.E., Jeffery, R.W. & Wing, R.R. (1999). Binge status as a predictor of weight loss treatment outcome. *International Journal of Obesity*, **23**, 485–493.

Sjöstrom, L., Narbro, K. & Sjöstrom, D. (1995). Costs and benefits when treating obesity. *International Journal of Obesity*, **19** (Suppl. 6), S9–S12.

Sjöstrom, C.D., Lissner, L., Wedel, H. & Sjöstrom, L. (1999). Reduction in incidence of diabetes, hypertension and lipid disturbances after intentional weight loss induced by bariatric surgery: the SOS Intervention Study. *Obesity Research*, **7**, 477–484.

Sjöstrom, L., Rissanen, A., Andersen, T., Boldrin, M., Golay, A., Koppeschaar, H.P. & Krempf, M. (1998). Randomised placebo-controlled trial of orlistat for weight loss and prevention of weight regain in obese patients. European Multicentre Orlistat Study Group. *Lancet*, **352**, 167–172.

Troiano, R.P., Frongillo, E.A., Sobal, J. & Levitsky, D.A. (1996). The relationship between body weight and mortality: a quantitative analysis of combined information from existing studies. *International Journal of Obesity*, **20**, 63–75.

Turcato, E., Bosello, O., Francesco, V.D., Harris, T.B., Zoico, E., Bissoli, L., Fracassi, E. & Zamboni, M. (2000). Waist circumference and abdominal sagittal diameter as surrogates of body fat distribution in the elderly: their relation with cardiovascular risk factors. *International Journal of Obesity*, **24**, 1005–1010.

Vaisse, C., Clement, K., Durand, E., Hercberg, S., Guy-Grand, B. & Froguel, P. (2000). Melanocortin-4 receptor mutations are a frequent and heterogeneous cause of morbid obesity. *The Journal of Clinical Investigation*, **106**, 253–262.

Wadden, T.A. & Foster, G.D. (1992). Behavioral assessment and treatment of markedly obese patients. In T.A. Wadden & T.B. Van Itallie (Eds), *Treatment of the Seriously Obese Patient* (pp. 290–330). New York: Guilford Press.

Wadden, T.A. & Foster, G.D. (2000). Behavioral treatment of obesity. *Medical Clinics of North America*, **84**, 441–461.

Wadden, T.A. & Stunkard, A.J. (1993). Psychosocial consequences of obesity and dieting. In A.J. Stunkard & T.A. Wadden (Eds), *Obesity: Theory and Therapy* (pp. 163–167). New York: Raven Press.

Wadden, T.A., Foster, G.D. & Letizia, K.A. (1994). One-year behavioral treatment of obesity: comparison of moderate and severe caloric restriction and the effects of weight maintenance therapy. *Journal of Consulting and Clinical Psychology*, **62**, 165–171.

Wadden, T.A., Sarwer, D.B. & Berkowitz, R.I. (1999). Behavioral treatment of the overweight patient. *Best Practice and Research Clinical Endocrinology and Metabolism*, **13**, 93–107.

Wadden, T.A., Berkowitz, R.I., Sarwer, D.B., Prus-Wisniewski, R. & Steinberg, C.M. (2001). Benefits of lifestyle modification in the pharmacologic treatment of obesity: a randomized trial. *Archives of Internal Medicine*, **161**, 218–227.

WHO (1998). *Obesity: Preventing and Managing the Global Epidemic*. Report of a WHO Consultation on Obesity. Geneva: World Health Organization.

Wilson, G.T. (1994). Behavioral treatment of obesity: thirty years and counting. *Advances in Behaviour Research and Therapy*, **16**, 31–75.

Wilson, G.T. (1996). Acceptance and change in the treatment of eating disorders and obesity. *Behavior Therapy*, **27**, 417–439.

Wing, R.R. (1999). Physical activity in the treatment of the adulthood overweight and obesity: current evidence and research issues. *Medicine and Science in Sports and Exercise*, **31**, S547–S552.

Wing, R.R. & Hill, J.O. (2001). Successful weight loss maintenance. *Annual Review of Nutrition*, **21**, 323–341.

Wing, R.R. & Jeffery, R.W. (1999). Benefits of recruiting participants with friends and increasing social support for weight loss and maintenance. *Journal of Consulting and Clinical Psychology*, **67**, 132–138.

Wing, R.R., Jeffery, R.W., Hellerstedt, W.L. & Burton, L.R. (1996). Effect of frequent phone contacts and optional food provision on maintenance of weight loss. *Annals of Behavioral Medicine*, **18**, 172–176.

Zhang, Y., Proenca, R., Maffei, M., Barone, M., Leopold, L. & Friedman, J.M. (1994). Positional cloning of the mouse obese gene and its human homologue. *Nature*, **372**, 425–432.

CHAPTER 11

Diabetes Mellitus

Suzanne Bennett Johnson
Florida State University College of Medicine, USA

and

Dawn Newman Carlson
University of Florida Health Sciences Center, USA

INTRODUCTION

Diabetes mellitus comprises a heterogeneous group of disorders characterized by high blood glucose levels (hyperglycemia). The World Health Organization (WHO, 1999) has defined four major types of diabetes: Type 1 diabetes, Type 2 diabetes, Gestational Diabetes, and diabetes secondary to other conditions. Type 1 and Type 2 diabetes are the focus of this chapter. Type 1 diabetes is associated with low or absent levels of endogenous insulin; daily insulin injections are necessary for survival. Type 2 diabetes is the more common form of the disease and is associated with insulin insufficiency or insulin resistance; the patient does not require insulin injections for survival but injections may be used to manage hyperglycemia. Disease onset for Type 1 diabetes usually occurs in childhood or adolescence. Disease onset for Type 2 diabetes usually occurs in persons >40 years of age (Harris, 1995).

Since Type 1 and Type 2 diabetes differ in etiology, onset-age, and treatment, this chapter discusses Type 1 and Type 2 diabetes separately. However, the chapter's discussion of Type 1 and Type 2 diabetes is organized using a similar format: Classification, Incidence, and Prevalence; Etiology, Morbidity and Mortality; Treatment; Challenges and Adaptation; and Prevention. We end the chapter with a summary of clinical health psychology's role in diabetes management and highlight opportunities for greater contributions in both patient care and research.

TYPE 1 DIABETES

Classification, Incidence, and Prevalence

Onset of Type 1 diabetes is characterized by classic signs and symptoms: urinary frequency, thirst, rapid weight loss, fatigue, and ketonuria. Blood glucose levels are very elevated

Handbook of Clinical Health Psychology. Edited by S. Llewelyn and P. Kennedy.
© 2003 John Wiley & Sons, Ltd.

(>200 mg/dl or 11.1 mmol/l). The patient has little or no circulating endogenous insulin and without injected insulin will die (Harris, 1995). Disease onset may occur at any age but typically occurs in youth, with the highest incidence rates during the adolescent years. Although Type 1 diabetes is diagnosed far less frequently than Type 2 diabetes, it remains one of the most common chronic diseases of childhood. In the USA, for example, over 120 000 children and 180 000 adults were living with Type 1 diabetes in 1990. Approximately 30 000 new cases are diagnosed each year; 13 000 of these cases are children. It is important to recognize the large international differences in the incidence of Type 1 diabetes, ranging from 0.7 cases per 100 000 in Shanghai, China, to 35.3 cases per 100 000 in Finland; this international variation is one of the largest seen in any noncommunicable disease. As might be expected, there are large racial differences with incidence greatest among whites (LaPorte, Matsushima & Chang, 1995).

Etiology, Morbidity and Mortality

Type 1 diabetes results from an autoimmune-mediated destruction of the pancreas. However, the rate of destruction can be slow or rapid, the latter occurring most often in children (WHO, 1999). Genes that confer susceptibility to Type 1 diabetes are located in the HLA region of chromosome 6. However, genetic susceptibility does not tell the whole story, since the concordance for Type 1 diabetes in monozygotic twins is only ~36%. Consequently, environmental factors must play a role although their nature and mechanism of action remains unknown (Dorman et al., 1995).

In the USA, Type 1 diabetes is associated with reduced life expectancy of approximately 15 years. More than 15% of young people diagnosed with this disease will die by the age of 40 years. However, there is considerable across-country variation, with Finland reporting lower age-adjusted death rates for patients with this disease than the USA and Japan reporting higher (Portuese & Orchard, 1995). Type 1 diabetes is associated with a host of serious complications. In the early years after diagnosis, acute coma is the leading cause of death. After 15 years, the long-term complications of diabetes become evident: renal failure, retinopathy, neuropathy, and cardiovascular disease (Harris, 1995). Maintaining blood glucose levels in the near normal range prevents or delays the onset of these complications (DCCT Research Group, 1993, 1994).

Treatment

Type 1 diabetes requires exogenous insulin replacement by injection two or more times per day, or by an insulin pump. Insulin administration must be timed in relationship to meals, with frequent small meals and snacks recommended. Foods that induce hyperglycemia (those high in concentrated sweets) are generally to be avoided. The goal of treatment is to maintain blood glucose levels in the near normal range (80–120 mg/dl or 4.4–6.6 mmol/l). A variety of insulins are available that vary in onset and duration of action; insulin types are often combined to improve glycemic control. However, since exogenous insulin replacement only approximates normal pancreatic function, blood glucose excursions do occur outside of the normal range. When available insulin is too high relative to available glucose, the result is hypoglycemia (blood glucose levels <60 mg/dl or 3.3 mmol/l). Hypoglycemia is often the consequence of variations in dietary intake or exercise. Hyperglycemia (blood glucose levels >160 mg/dl or 8.9 mmol/l) occurs when available insulin is too low relative to available glucose and is often the result of excessive food intake, insufficient insulin administration or illness. Because blood glucose levels can fluctuate throughout the day, patients are instructed to monitor their blood glucose levels multiple times a day and to take corrective action. Hypoglycemia requires immediate treatment with a fast-acting carbohydrate; left untreated, it can result in coma, seizures and death.

Persistent hyperglycemia is sometimes associated with ketonuria. Consequently, patients are instructed to test for urine ketones when blood glucose levels are >240 mg/dl (>13.3 mmol/l); left untreated, ketoacidosis can result in coma, seizures and death. Blood glucose testing is normally done using sophisticated computerized meters that hold in memory the time and result of the test. The patient obtains a drop of blood using a finger stick that is placed on a reagent strip and "read" by the meter. The patient's blood glucose testing records also provide important information to the physician and guide insulin dose adjustment. The physician will also monitor the patient's blood glucose control using the glycosylated hemoglobin assay (HbA_{1c}). This assay provides an estimate of the patient's average blood glucose levels in the preceding two to four months. People without diabetes have HbA_{1c} values in the 4–6% range. People with diabetes are considered in excellent control if their HbA_{1c} values are 6–7% (Skyler, 1998).

Challenges and Adaptation

Type 1 diabetes is obviously a complex disease to manage with multiple daily insulin injections, blood glucose tests, and dietary constraints. Exercise is encouraged because it improves insulin action. However, food intake and exercise must be coordinated in order to avoid hypoglycemia, which requires immediate action to avoid coma and death. Prolonged hyperglycemia is equally serious since it promotes the long-term complications of diabetes (retinopathy, neuropathy, kidney disease, cardiovascular disease). For this reason, patients are often encouraged to undertake intensive therapy, increasing the frequency of insulin administration and blood glucose testing and making daily insulin adjustments using blood glucose test results. While intensive therapy may reduce the risk of long-term complications, it is associated with increased hypoglycemia (DCCT Research Group, 1993, 1994). Clearly, Type 1 diabetes represents a challenge to patients in terms of diabetes regimen adherence, management of hypoglycemia, and general psychological adaptation.

Regimen Adherence

Given the complex array of behaviors involved in the management of this disease, it is no surprise that poor regimen adherence is a common problem. Insulin administration in Type 1 patients is associated with high compliance rates (>90%) but the timing of its administration is poor. Diet and exercise prescriptions are even more problematic. Patients acknowledge following their dietary prescriptions only 60–70% of the time. Although the American Diabetes Association (ADA, 2002) recommends restricting fats to <30% of daily calories, studies consistently report fat consumption rates >40%. Only 30% of Type 1 patients report adhering to their exercise prescriptions. A substantial number of patients fail to test their blood glucose regularly or conduct fewer tests than prescribed, with noncompliance rates varying from 36 to 82% (see Johnson, 1992, for a review).

A variety of factors seem to underlie patients' difficulties in adhering to the treatment regimen. Sometimes noncompliance is inadvertent; through patient–provider miscommunication, or knowledge or skill deficits, the patient believes he or she is compliant with the treatment regimen but is actually behaving in ways that are contrary to provider recommendations. Inadvertent noncompliance is actually very common. For example, Page et al. (1981) compared recommendations given by health care providers in a childhood diabetes clinic with patients' and parents' recall of those recommendations. Providers gave an average of seven recommendations per patient. Patients (and parents of younger children) recalled an average of two recommendations. However, 40% of the recommendations patients and parents recalled were not made by the provider! Obviously, we cannot expect patients to be adherent with their treatment regimen if they fail to accurately grasp their providers' recommendations.

Because Type 1 diabetes is usually diagnosed in childhood, developmental issues contribute to difficulties with treatment adherence. Younger children often do not have the necessary cognitive abilities and fine motor skills to draw up and administer insulin accurately or to make appropriate treatment decisions in the face of hypo- or hyperglycemia (Johnson, 1995; Perwien et al., 2000). Adolescents have a better understanding of their disease, but are far less adherent than younger children. Parental supervision declines during the adolescent years, adolescents become less rule-oriented about their care, and are more likely to experiment and respond to peer group social pressures (Johnson, 1995; Johnson & Meltzer, 2002).

A number of studies have demonstrated that regimen adherence can be improved in Type 1 populations using behavioral strategies including self-monitoring, corrective feedback, reinforcement, modeling, behavioral contracting, and conflict resolution. Most interventions involve both the patient and parent in the program and are often conducted in a group format (see Lemanek, Kamps & Chung, 2001; Plante, Lobato & Engel, 2001; and Rapoff, 1999, for reviews).

Management of Hypoglycemia

Hypoglycemia can be a frightening experience for the patient and family. Left untreated, the patient may become disoriented and sometimes combative. Unconsciousness and seizures may occur. There is some evidence that serious hypoglycemia can have long-term neuropsychological effects (Northam et al., 1999). Many patients become extremely fearful of hypoglycemia and may remain hyperglycemic as a consequence (Cox et al., 1987; Green, Wysocki & Reineck, 1990). Issues surrounding hypoglycemia management have become increasingly salient in the current environment where many providers are encouraging patients to engage in intensive therapy to reduce the long-term complications of diabetes; intensive therapy is associated with increased hypoglycemia (DCCT Research Group, 1993, 1994).

Most diabetes education programs teach patients a standard set of symptoms that are presumed to be associated with hypoglycemia and a different set of standard symptoms that are presumed to be associated with hyperglycemia. However, the available literature suggests that patients vary in their ability to accurately estimate their own blood glucose levels

(Cox et al., 1985a, 1985b; Eastman et al., 1983; Freund et al., 1986; Nurick & Johnson, 1991; Ruggiero et al., 1991). Further, numerous studies have demonstrated that there are no standard symptoms that are predictive of hypoglycemia (or hyperglycemia) for all, or even most, patients with Type 1 diabetes. Instead, most patients have unique symptoms that are predictive of hypo- or hyperglycemia for the individual patient, although most patients are unaware of their unique predictive symptoms (Freund et al., 1986; Nurick & Johnson, 1991). Carefully designed intervention programs developed by Cox and his colleagues have demonstrated that teaching patients about their own unique predictive symptoms can improve blood glucose estimation accuracy, leading to improved early detection of impending hypoglycemia (Cox et al., 2001; Nurick & Johnson, 1991).

Psychological Adjustment

A Type 1 diabetes diagnosis is associated with increased distress and depression in both children and parents; however, this negative affect tends to dissipate over time (Kovacs et al., 1990a, 1990b; Northam et al., 1996). After an initial period of distress, most patients adjust remarkably well (Jacobson et al., 1997; Rubin & Peyrot, 1992).

While children and adolescents with diabetes often perform within the normal range on general measures of psychological adjustment, some studies have documented an increased risk for eating disorders, particularly bulimia (Neumark-Sztainer et al., 1996). It is generally accepted that eating disorder behaviors, such as binge-eating or food restriction, will disrupt a patient's glycemic control (Meltzer et al., 2001). Further, the necessity of closely monitoring food intake for individuals with Type 1 diabetes may potentiate disordered eating characteristics. More controversial is whether the Type 1 patient population suffers from an increased prevalence of eating disorders per se (Bryden et al., 1999; Meltzer et al., 2001; Peveler et al., 1992; Pollock, Kovacs & Charron-Prochownik, 1995; Striegel-Moore, Nicholson & Tamborlane, 1992).

Type 1 diabetes places numerous demands upon a family, as parents attempt to manage the child's illness while providing a home environment supportive of normal growth and development. Mothers may be particularly affected as they most often serve as the child's primary caretaker (Hauenstein et al., 1989; Kovacs et al., 1985; Wysocki et al., 1989). Good diabetes management occurs in families that are organized but flexible, with low family conflict and frequent diabetes-specific supportive behaviors (Anderson et al., 1999; Johnson & Perwien, 2001). Sibling relationships could be affected, although this has been the subject of little empirical research. Data from a population survey (Cadman, Boyle & Offord, 1988) and a multisite collaborative study (Sahler et al., 1994) suggest that there is an increased prevalence of behavioral and emotional problems in siblings of chronically ill youngsters compared to siblings of well children; nevertheless, the majority of chronically ill youngsters' siblings are well adjusted. Little research of this type has focused specifically on the siblings of youngsters with Type 1 diabetes. However, research that examines sibling adjustment, rather than sibling roles within the family, may miss subtle illness-related differences in parental disciplinary practices, family chore assignment, relative time parents spend with each child, etc. Further, sibling gender and birth order relative to the ill child may be important determinants of sibling adjustment (Silver & Frohlinger-Graham, 2000).

Prevention

Since Type 1 diabetes results from an autoimmune destruction of the pancreatic beta cells, it is now possible to identify people at risk for diabetes before disease onset. A blood test can detect the presence of islet cell antibodies (ICA), a potent risk factor for Type 1 diabetes. ICA+ first-degree relatives of Type 1 patients have a risk of developing diabetes 50–500 times the risk of individuals without ICA (Dorman et al., 1995). Several large-scale prevention trials have been initiated with ICA+ persons. In the USA, the Diabetes Prevention Trial for Type 1 Diabetes (DPT-1) is testing the use of subcutaneous insulin or oral insulin as possible interventions to prevent or delay the onset of the disease. The European Nicotinamide Diabetes Intervention Trial (ENDIT) study is testing whether nicotinamide will reduce the rate of progression to Type 1 diabetes in ICA+ individuals (Schatz & Bingley, 2001). Since specific genes that confer susceptibility to Type 1 diabetes have been identified, genetic screening studies are underway with newborns in the USA and Europe (Kupila et al., 2001).

Prevention studies of this type raise a number of psychosocial concerns. Individuals are informed of their at-risk status when no known methods to prevent the disease are available. Risk notification itself is an extremely complex issue and there is increasing evidence that patients and parents fail to understand risk information accurately (Johnson, 2001). Since Type 1 diabetes is usually diagnosed in childhood, screening children to identify those at risk for the disease further complicates the situation. A number of studies have suggested that risk notification can lead to high levels of anxiety in both the at-risk individual and in family members although this anxiety tends to dissipate over time (Johnson & Tercyak, 1995; Johnson et al., 1990; Roth, 2001; Weber & Roth, 1997). How an individual copes with the news appears to influence anxiety post-notification, with avoidance, wishful thinking and self-blame associated with greater maintenance of anxiety over time (Johnson & Carmichael, 2000).

The American Diabetes Association (ADA, 2002) currently recommends that interventions for the prevention of Type 1 diabetes should be attempted only in the context of defined clinical studies with Institutional Review Board oversight. Further, screening of any population is discouraged outside the context of defined research studies. Better integration of psychosocial research into screening and prevention trials would help to address the ethical concerns raised by such trials and improve their scientific quality (Johnson, 2001; Roth, 2001; Weber & Roth, 1997).

TYPE 2 DIABETES

Classification, Incidence and Prevalence

Fasting blood glucose levels >126 mg/dl (7 mmol/l) or levels >200 mg/dl (11.1 mmol/l) two hours after an oral glucose tolerance test indicate the presence of Type 2 diabetes (WHO, 1999). Only half of patients with Type 2 diabetes present with classic signs and symptoms (frequent urination, thirst, fatigue, weight loss). Many are diagnosed during routine medical examinations, through diabetes-screening programs, or while being treated for another medical condition (Harris, 1995). Type 2 diabetes is reaching epidemic proportions throughout the world. It comprises approximately 90–95% of all diagnosed cases of diabetes in the USA and its incidence has been rising substantially in recent years. Currently, 6% of the US population has Type 2 diabetes. Although Type 2 diabetes is typically diagnosed after age 45, with increasing incidence with increasing age, there are growing numbers of children with the disease (CDCP, 1998, 1999). Differences in prevalence of Type 2 diabetes worldwide are dramatic. It is virtually nonexistent among the Mapuche Indians in Chile while 50% of the Pima Indians in the USA have the disease (Rewers & Hamman, 1995). The disorder is far more common among US blacks, Hispanics, Japanese Americans and native Americans than non-Hispanic whites (Kenny, Aubert & Geiss, 1995).

Etiology, Morbidity and Mortality

Type 2 diabetes is the result of insufficient insulin production or insulin resistance. The etiology of Type 2 diabetes appears to be heterogeneous, including a complex interplay of genetics, environment, lifestyle risk factors (obesity and low physical activity) and insulin abnormalities. The disease is associated with initial insulin resistance and hyperinsulinemia with secondary beta cell failure. Although concordance rates among monozygotic twins are high (~60%), insulin resistance and beta cell failure have multiple genetic and nongenetic causes (Rewers & Hamman, 1995). Obesity is present in approximately 80% of patients with Type 2 diabetes and is believed to play a significant role in the increasing incidence of the disease (Zimmerman, 1998). Patients go through a period of impaired glucose tolerance before developing full-blown Type 2 diabetes. For many patients, the onset of Type 2 diabetes occurs approximately ten years before clinical diagnosis. In fact, approximately half of Americans with Type 2 diabetes are undiagnosed (Harris, 1995). A host of complications are associated with Type 2 diabetes: retinopathy, nephropathy, neuropathy, peripheral vascular disease, and cardiovascular disease. Reduction in life expectancy is five to ten years for those with disease onset in middle age, with little or no reduction in those diagnosed at age >70 years. Most patients with diabetes die of cardiovascular disease (Geiss, Herman & Smith, 1995). In the USA, Type 2 diabetes is the seventh leading cause of death by disease (CDCP, 1999).

Treatment

The goal of treatment is to reduce blood glucose levels to the near normal range. Data from the United Kingdom Prospective Diabetes Study Group (1998) provided strong evidence that maintaining near normal blood glucose levels will minimize or prevent the development of long-term complications. HbA_{1c} levels should be reduced to less than 7%. This is accomplished through patient education, lifestyle modification (i.e., nutrition and physical activity), self-monitoring of blood glucose, regularly scheduled doctor's visits, and, when necessary, the use of pharmacological agents (i.e., oral medication and insulin) (ADA, 2002).

The National Standards for Diabetes Self-Management Education is a valuable framework for offering this essential treatment component (ADA, 2002). The educational program includes information about the diabetes disease process and treatment options, the importance of incorporating appropriate nutrition and physical activity into daily life, use of medications (if applicable), monitoring blood glucose and using the results to improve glycemic control, and preventing, detecting, and treating both acute and chronic complications of the disease. Interventions of this type have been shown to improve HbA_{1c} levels in Type 2 adults an average of 1.9% (Task Force on Community Preventive Strategies, 2001).

Not all patients can effectively manage their diabetes with education alone. More extensive behavioral interventions aimed at improving nutrition and increasing exercise may be necessary (Wing, 1993). However, if the desired level of glycemic control is not attained via diabetes self-management education or more extensive behavioral interventions, pharmacologic agents are added to the treatment plan. Oral medications Acarbose, Metformin, and Troglitazone all enhance the effectiveness of available insulin. Repaglinide and the Sulfonylureas increase the secretion of insulin (Zimmerman, 1998). Due to the fact that a single oral agent is unlikely to maintain glycemic control for more than a few years, combination therapy is quite common (Riddle, 1999). Combining oral medications is often more effective than stopping one agent and substituting another. In the majority of patients with Type 2 diabetes, the failure of combining two oral agents in an effort to restore glucose control requires the introduction of insulin injections either alone or in addition to oral agents (Riddle, 1999). Although insulin injections are not usually a first-line treatment for Type 2 diabetes, nearly 50% of patients with Type 2 diabetes eventually need insulin to control their hyperglycemia (Buse et al., 1998).

Unlike the adult population, a large number of Type 2 pediatric patients are initially misdiagnosed with Type 1 diabetes and are treated with insulin at the time of diagnosis. In most cases, once a diagnosis of Type 2 diabetes is made, the patient is weaned off insulin (Pinhas-Hamiel & Zeitler, 1997). It is important to note that there is an extensive body of literature on the effects of oral pharmacologic agents, alone and in combination, in the adult population. However, the benefits of oral agents among the pediatric population have not been extensively studied.

Challenges and Adaptation

Managing Type 2 diabetes presents a considerable challenge. The disease is usually diagnosed in late adulthood, after nutrition and exercise habits have been established for many years, making lifestyle change exceedingly difficult. The large number of patients with the disease means that most are seen by a primary care provider, not a diabetes specialist; the latest in disease management may be the exception rather than the rule.

Provider Behavior

Although guidelines for diabetes management are available (e.g., ADA, 2002), few patients with Type 2 diabetes receive appropriate care. In the USA, for example, only 40% of Type 2 patients receive any formal education about their diabetes and only 24% have their HbA_{1c} measured more than once per year. While close monitoring of complications associated with diabetes is considered essential, only 56% of these patients have an annual eye examination (Task Force on Community Preventive Strategies, 2001). Primary care providers rate diabetes as "harder to treat" than hypertension, angina, hyperlipidemia, arthritis, and heart failure. US primary care providers fail to adhere to standards of diabetes care for a variety of reasons: provider frustrations with the disease itself; complexity of the treatment regimen (i.e., medications, glucose monitoring, diet and exercise education, screening for and prevention of complications); treatment components that are outside of the provider's control (i.e., patient lifestyle change); insufficient provider training to promote behavioral change; provider training in the acute rather than chronic disease model; discrepancy between provider and patient perceptions of diabetes control; and a perceived lack of support from society and the health care system to control diabetes (Larme & Pugh, 1998).

There is strong evidence that health care system interventions designed to assure an organized, proactive, multicomponent approach to diabetes care can have significant positive effects on patient outcomes. Further, case management is recommended for patients at risk for poor outcomes. Case management involves assigning authority to one professional (usually not the direct health care provider) who oversees and coordinates all components of the patient's care. On average, health care system interventions improve patient HbA_{1c} levels 0.4 to 0.5% (Task Force on Community Preventive Strategies, 2001). Such interventions may be more easily put in place in countries with universal health care systems and the economic capacity to address the multicomponent nature of this disease.

Regimen Adherence

Given the extent of provider noncompliance with recommended medical care, it is no surprise that patients often fail to engage in ideal disease management. Patients report following their exercise prescriptions only half of the time and only 42% test their blood glucose levels more than once a day (Johnson, 1992; Task Force on Community Preventive Strategies, 2001). Many patients fail to understand what is expected of them. Early studies by Hulka and colleagues documented the extent of provider–patient miscommunication; only 66% of the physician instructions were accurately understood by the patients and many patients were misinformed as to the function of their medication and the timing of its administration (Hulka et al., 1975, 1976).

While behavioral change intervention programs can yield significant improvements in metabolic control among overweight individuals with Type 2 diabetes (Cox & Gonder-Fredrick, 1992; Wing, 1993), the patient's nonadherence to the prescribed treatment regimen often precludes success (Smith & Wing, 1991). Potential barriers to success include the patient's resistance to change, negative attitudes toward exercising, poor awareness of health risks, previous unsuccessful experiences with weight control, lack of social support, as well as negative perceptions about the time required and the financial costs (Gumbiner, 1999; NHLBI Obesity Education Expert Panel, 1998). Even patients who are initially successful often fail to maintain their gains over time (Wing et al., 2001).

Although weight-loss programs aimed at children with Type 2 diabetes have received little or no research attention, programs developed for overweight children without diabetes have shown maintenance of treatment effects five and ten years postintervention (Epstein et al., 1990, 1994; Jelalian & Saelens, 1999; Knip & Nuutinen, 1993). As Epstein et al. (1998) have pointed out, there are a number of reasons why pediatric obesity may be more amenable to treatment than adult obesity. Children do not have as well-established dietary and eating practices as adults; thus, it may be easier to mobilize families to address a child's obesity than an adult's. Children are also growing in height, permitting weight maintenance to translate into lower weight relative to height.

Recent research has suggested that patient motivation may need to be more effectively targeted. A pilot study conducted by Smith et al. (1997) explored the use of motivational interviewing (Miller & Rollnick, 1991) in a behavioral obesity intervention program for patients with Type 2 diabetes. The results suggested that the addition of motivational interviewing to a standard behavioral weight-control program may significantly enhance adherence to the treatment regimen as well as assist patients to achieve improved glucose control.

Psychological Adjustment

Recent research has focused on the comorbidity of mental illness and Type 2 diabetes. There is convincing evidence that depression is more common in Type 2 patients, occurring at least twice the prevalence rates found in nondiabetic adults (Anderson et al., 2001; Lustman & Gavard, 1995). Wing et al. (1990) found that depression symptoms were greater in obese patients with Type 2 diabetes than in their similarly obese spouses without the disease. Medical disorders of all types are associated with increased prevalence of depression. It is unclear whether the increased prevalence of depression in Type 2 diabetes is greater than that found in other somatic illnesses. Although it is widely believed that depression is secondary to the complications and demands of the disease, the research literature has failed to document such an association (Lustman & Gavard, 1995).

On the other hand, depression appears to be strongly linked to reporting of diabetes symptoms. Symptoms of poor diabetes control (e.g., thirst, frequent urination, fatigue), gastrointestinal motor difficulties (e.g., abdominal pain, diarrhea, constipation), and erectile dysfunction are significantly correlated with depression. These findings suggest that psychological as well as physiological factors may contribute to symptom reporting (Lustman & Gavard, 1995).

Depression also appears to be linked to glycemic control, although the effect size is small (0.13–0.21) (Lustman et al., 2000a). There are a few studies suggesting that pharmacological treatment of depression may provide symptom relief and possible improvement in glycemic control. However, conventional antidepressants have side-effects (weight gain, sexual dysfunction, anticholinergic effects) that may limit their use with Type 2 patients. Cognitive-behavioral treatments for depression may prove particularly helpful with this population. However, controlled trials are needed (Lustman & Gavard, 1995; Lustman et al., 2000b).

Although depression has been the primary focus of psychological adjustment studies in Type 2 patients, there has been a recent interest in eating disorders. The prevalence of eating disorders of all types does not appear to differ in Type 2 compared to Type 1 patient populations. However, binge-eating is far more common in Type 2 patients and appears to predate disease onset, suggesting that it is one of the causes of obesity (Herpertz et al., 1998; Kenardy et al., 1994).

Prevention

Type 2 diabetes is increasing at an alarming rate and appears to be associated with the increasing prevalence of obesity and a sedentary lifestyle. For the first time, Type 2 diabetes is being diagnosed in children rather than being limited to overweight older adults. Both weight and physical activity appear to contribute independently to the development of the disease. Because behavioral factors play such a strong role in the etiology of Type 2 diabetes, it is considered a preventable disorder. For this reason the National Institutes of Health in the USA launched a multicenter trial to determine whether lifestyle or pharmacological (metformin) intervention could prevent Type 2 diabetes in adults with impaired glucose tolerance (Diabetes Prevention Program Research Group, 1999). The results of the trial were impressive. Compared to placebo, the lifestyle intervention reduced the incidence of Type 2 diabetes by 58% and metformin reduced the incidence by 31%. The lifestyle intervention was significantly more effective than metformin (Diabetes Prevention Program Research Group, 2002). These results are consistent with prior studies conducted in countries other than the USA that have documented the effectiveness of diet and exercise in the prevention of Type 2 diabetes (Eriksson & Lindgarde, 1991; Pan et al., 1997).

CLINICAL HEALTH PSYCHOLOGY'S CONTRIBUTIONS TO DIABETES MANAGEMENT

Clinical health psychology has made major contributions to the management of both Type 1 and Type 2 diabetes. These are disorders where behavior plays a major role in daily disease management. Consequently, psychologists have brought their expertise to the patient–provider encounter, the assessment of disease management skills and adherence behaviors, and have developed interventions to improve medical regimen adherence and the management of severe hypoglycemia. As psychologists, they have also been sensitive to the psychological cost of diabetes on the patient and family, exploring psychological factors in the etiology and management of this disease.

Clinical health psychologists play an important role on the medical treatment team. They serve as communicators and facilitators, helping patients to understand provider recommendations and helping providers to develop realistic patient expectations. Their assessment skills permit them to identify skill deficits, poor or inadequate diabetes management behaviors and barriers to ideal care. Their treatment skills assist the patient with setting realistic goals, developing problem-solving skills, and identifying family and social support to assist patients in reaching those goals. Their mental health training enables them to be sensitive to signs of comorbid psychological disorders, such as depression or eating disorders that may further interfere with the patient's diabetes management and quality of life. Clinical health psychologists understand that patients live in systems—family, school, work, community, and health care systems—that can either promote or interfere with their diabetes care. Articulating this systems perspective and devising treatment plans accordingly are some of the most important ways that clinical health psychologists can contribute to the diabetes management team.

OPPORTUNITIES FOR IMPROVED PATIENT CARE AND FUTURE RESEARCH

The full potential of clinical health psychology to diabetes management has not yet been realized. For example, although studies suggest that adherence behaviors and management of hypoglycemia can be improved in Type 1 populations using behavioral interventions, this approach has not been widely integrated into usual practice. In most clinical settings, patient–provider miscommunication is rampant; psychologists need to become part of interdisciplinary treatment and research teams, offering their expertise to assure clearer communication and provider adherence to a high standard of medical care. In Type 2 populations, issues of maintenance of lifestyle change present a major challenge. Patients often are able to make initial changes in diet and exercise but have great difficulty maintaining their treatment gains over time. The particular concerns of minority populations, for whom Type 2 diabetes is so common, need to be addressed. Children are now being diagnosed with Type 2 diabetes, demanding carefully designed intervention programs that will effectively meet their needs. Issues of comorbid mental health conditions, particularly depression and eating disorders, demand our attention. The particular needs of family members, spouses and children, parents and siblings, cannot be forgotten as this is the social context within which the patient lives.

Efforts to prevent the disease bring new challenges and new opportunities. ICA and genetic screening for Type 1 diabetes raises numerous psychosocial issues, including how diabetes risk is communicated, the psychological impact of risk assessment when no viable intervention is available to prevent the disease, and issues surrounding recruitment and retention of at-risk children into prevention trials. The data suggest that Type 2 diabetes can be prevented but the challenge presented by ever-increasing rates of obesity and sedentary behavior is sobering. Psychologists must expand their efforts beyond the clinical encounter, to the community, schools, family, and workplace.

Clinical health psychologists are well-suited to both clinical practice and research. Participation in multidisciplinary treatment teams will inform their research and their research will inform the kind of care patients receive.

ACKNOWLEDGEMENT

This chapter was supported in part by HL69736 from the National Institutes of Health.

REFERENCES

American Diabetes Association (2002). Clinical practice recommendations. *Diabetes Care*, **25** (Suppl. 1). Available: http://care.diabetesjournals.org/content/vol25/suppl_1/

Anderson, B., Brackett, J., Ho, J. & Laffel, L. (1999). An office-based intervention to maintain parent–adolescent teamwork in diabetes management. Impact on parent involvement, family conflict, and subsequent glycemic control. *Diabetes Care*, **22**, 713–721.

Anderson, R., Freedland, K., Clouse, R. & Lustman, P. (2001). The prevalence of comorbid depression in adults with diabetes: a meta-analysis. *Diabetes Care*, **24**, 1069–1078.

Bryden, K., Neil, A., Mayou, M., Peveler, R., Fairburn, C. & Dunger, D. (1999). Eating habits, body weight, and insulin misuse. A longitudinal study of teenagers and young adults with type 1 diabetes. *Diabetes Care*, **22**, 1956–1960.

Buse, J.B., Faja, B.W., Gumbiner, B., Whitcomb, R.W., Mathias, N.P. & Nelson, D.M. (1998). Troglitazone use in insulin-treated type 2 diabetic patients. *Diabetes Care*, **21**, 1455–1461.

Cadman, D., Boyle, M. & Offord, D. (1988). The Ontario Child Health Study: social adjustment and mental health of siblings of children with chronic health problems. *Journal of Developmental and Behavioral Pediatrics*, **13**, 11–16.

CDCP (1998). *National Diabetes Fact Sheet*. Atlanta, GA: Centers for Disease Control and Prevention. Available: http://www.cdc.gov/diabetes/pubs/facts98.htm

CDCP (1999). *1999 Diabetes Surveillance Report*. Atlanta, GA: Centers for Disease Control and Prevention. Available: http://www.cdc.gov/diabetes/statistics/index.htm

Cox, D.J. & Gonder-Fredrick, L. (1992). Major developments in behavioral diabetes research. *Journal of Clinical Psychology*, **60**, 628–638.

Cox, D.J., Clarke, W.L., Gonder-Frederick, L.A., Pohl, S.L., Hoover, C., Snyder, A., Zimbelman, L., Carter, W., Bobbitt, S. & Pennebaker, J.W. (1985a). Accuracy of perceiving blood glucose in IDDM. *Diabetes Care*, **8** (6), 529–536.

Cox, D., Gonder-Frederick, L., Pohl, S., Carter, W., Clarke, W., Johnson, S.B., Rosenbloom, A., Bradley, C. & Moses, J. (1985b). Symptoms and blood glucose levels in diabetics. *Journal of the American Medical Association*, **253**, 1558.

Cox, D., Gonder-Frederick, L., Polonsky, W., Schlundt, D., Kovatchev, B. & Clarke, W. (2001). Blood glucose awareness training (BGAT-2): Long-term benefits. *Diabetes Care*, **24**, 637–642.

Cox, D., Irvine, A., Gonder-Frederick, L., Nowacek, G. & Butterfield, J. (1987). Fear of hypoglycemia: quantification, validation, and utilization. *Diabetes Care*, **10**, 617–621.

Diabetes Prevention Program Research Group (1999). Design and methods for a clinical trial in the prevention of type 2 diabetes. *Diabetes Care*, **22**, 623–634.

Diabetes Prevention Program Research Group (2002). Reduction in the incidence of Type 2 diabetes with lifestyle intervention or metformin. *New England Journal of Medicine*, **346**, 393–403.

DCCT Research Group (1993). The effect of intensive treatment of diabetes on the development and progression of long-term complications in insulin-dependent diabetes mellitus. *New England Journal of Medicine*, **329**, 977–986.

DCCT Research Group (1994). Effect of intensive diabetes treatment on the development and progression of long-term complications in adolescents with insulin-dependent diabetes mellitus: diabetes Control and Complications Trial. *Journal of Pediatrics*, **125**, 177–188.

Dorman, J., McCarthy, B., O'Leary, L. & Koehler, A. (1995). Risk factors for insulin-dependent diabetes. National Diabetes Data Group. *Diabetes in America* (2nd edn). Bethesda, MD: National Institutes of Health, NIH Publication No. 95-1468. Available: http://www.niddk.nih.gov/health/diabetes/dia/

Eastman, B., Johnson, S.B., Silverskin, J., Spillar, R. & McCallum, M. (1983). Understanding of hypo- and hyperglycemia by youngsters with diabetes and their parents. *Journal of Paediatric Psychology*, **8**, 229–243.

Epstein, L., Myers, M., Raynor, H. & Saelens, B. (1998). Treatment of pediatric obesity. *Pediatrics*, **101**, 554–570.

Epstein, L., Valoski, A., Wing, R. & McCurley, J. (1990). Ten-year follow-up of behavioral family-based treatment for obese children. *Journal of the American Medical Association*, **264**, 2519–2523.

Epstein, L., Valoski, A., Wing, R. & McCurley, J. (1994). Ten-year outcomes of behavioral family-based treatment for childhood obesity. *Health Psychology*, **13**, 373–383.

Eriksson, K. & Lindgarde, F. (1991). Prevention of type 2 (non-insulin-dependent) diabetes mellitus by diet and physical exercise. *Diabetologia*, **34**, 891–898.

Freund, A., Johnson, S.B., Rosenbloom, A.L., Alexander, B. & Hansen, C.A. (1986). Subjective symptoms, blood glucose estimation, and blood glucose concentrations in adolescents with diabetes. *Diabetes Care*, **9**, 236–243.

Geiss, L., Herman, W. & Smith, P. (1995). National Diabetes Data Group. *Diabetes in America* (2nd edn). Bethesda, MD: National Institutes of Health, NIH Publication No. 95-1468. Available: http://www.niddk.nih.gov/health/diabetes/dia/

Green, L., Wysocki, T. & Reineck, B. (1990). Fear of hypoglycemia in children and adolescents with diabetes. *Journal of Pediatric Psychology*, **15**, 633–641.

Gumbiner, B. (1999). The treatment of obesity in type 2 diabetes mellitus. *Primary Care*, **26**, 869–883.

Hauenstein, E., Marvin, R., Snyder, A. & Clarke, W. (1989). Stress in parents of children with diabetes mellitus. *Diabetes Care*, **12**, 18–19.

Harris, M. (1995). Classification, diagnostic criteria, and screening for diabetes. National Diabetes Data Group. *Diabetes in America* (2nd edn). Bethesda, MD: National Institutes of Health, NIH Publication No. 95-1468. Available: http://www.niddk.nih.gov/health/diabetes/dia/

Herpertz, S., Albus, C., Wagener, R., Kocnar, M., Wagner, R., Henning, A., Best, F., Foerster, H., Schleppinghoff, B., Thomas, W., Kohle, K., Mann, K. & Senf, W. (1998). Comorbidity of diabetes and eating disorders. Does diabetes control reflect disturbed eating behavior? *Diabetes Care*, **21**, 1110–1116.

Hulka, B.S., Cassel, J.C., Kupper, L.L. & Burdette, J.A. (1976). Communication, compliance and concordance between physicians and patients with prescribed medications. *American Journal of Public Health*, **66**, 847–853.

Hulka, B.S., Kupper, L.L., Cassel, J.C. & Mayo, F. (1975). Doctor–patient communication and outcomes among diabetic patients. *Journal of Community Health*, **1**, 15–27.

Jacobson, A., Hauser, S., Willett, J., Wolfsdorf, J., Dvorak, R., Herman, H. & de Groot, M. (1997). Psychological adjustment to IDDM: 10-year follow-up of an onset cohort of child and adolescent patients. *Diabetes Care*, **20**, 811–818.

Jelalian, E. & Saelens, B.E. (1999). Empirically supported treatments in pediatric psychology: pediatric obesity. *Journal of Pediatric Psychology*, **24**, 223–248.

Johnson, S.B. (1992). Methodological issues in diabetes research: measuring adherence. *Diabetes Care*, **15**, 1658–1667.

Johnson, S.B. (1995). Managing insulin dependent diabetes mellitus: a developmental perspective. In J. Wallander & L. Siegel (Eds), *Advances in Pediatric Psychology II: Perspectives in Adolescent Health* (pp. 265–288). New York: Guilford Publications.

Johnson, S.B. (2001). Screening programs to identify children at risk for diabetes mellitus: psychological impact on children and parents. *Journal of Pediatric Endocrinology and Metabolism*, **14** (Suppl. 1), 653–659.

Johnson, S.B. & Carmichael, S. (2000). At-risk for diabetes: coping with the news. *Journal of Clinical Psychology in Medical Settings*, **7**, 69–78.

Johnson, S.B. & Meltzer, L. (2002). Disentangling the effects of current age, onset age, and disease duration: parent and child attitudes toward diabetes as an exemplar. *Journal of Pediatric Psychology*, **27**, 77–86.

Johnson, S.B. & Perwien, A. (2001). Insulin-dependent diabetes mellitus. In H. Koot & J. Wallander (Eds), *Quality of Life in Children and Adolescents: Concepts, Methods, and Findings*. Brighton, UK: Brunner-Routledge.

Johnson, S.B. & Tercyak, K. Jr (1995). Psychological impact of islet cell antibody screening for IDDM on children, adults, and their family members. *Diabetes Care*, **18**, 1370–1372.

Johnson, S.B., Riley, W., Hansen, C. & Nurick, M. (1990). The psychological impact of islet cell antibody (ICA) screening: preliminary results. *Diabetes Care*, **13**, 93–97.

Kenardy, J., Mensch, M., Bowen, K. & Pearson, S. (1994). A comparison of eating behaviors in newly diagnosed NIDDM patients and case-matched control subjects. *Diabetes Care*, **17**, 1197–1199.

Kenny, S., Aubert, R. & Geiss, L. (1995). Prevalence and incidence of non-insulin-dependent diabetes. National Diabetes Data Group. *Diabetes in America* (2nd edn). Bethesda, MD: National Institutes of Health, NIH Publication No. 95-1468. Available: http://www.niddk.nih.gov/health/diabetes/dia/

Knip, M. & Nuutinen, O. (1993). Long-term effects of weight reduction on serum lipids and plasma insulin in obese children. *American Journal of Clinical Nutrition*, **54**, 490–493.

Kovacs, M., Finkelstein, R., Feinberg, R., Crouse-Novak, M., Paulauskas, S. & Pollack, M. (1985). Initial psychological responses of parents to the diagnosis of insulin-dependent diabetes mellitus in their children. *Diabetes Care*, **8**, 568–575.

Kovacs, M., Iyengar, S., Goldston, D., Obrosky, D., Stewart, J. & Marsh, J. (1990a). Psychological functioning among mothers of children with insulin-dependent diabetes mellitus: a longitudinal study. *Journal of Consulting and Clinical Psychology*, **58**, 189–195.

Kovacs, M., Iyengar, S., Goldston, D., Stewart, J., Obrosky, D. & Marsh, J. (1990b). Psychological functioning of children with insulin-dependent diabetes mellitus: a longitudinal study. *Journal of Pediatric Psychology*, **15**, 619–632.

Kupila, A., Muona, P., Simell, T., Arvilommi, P., Savolainen, H., Hamalainen, A., Korhonen, S., Kimpimaki, T., Sjoroos, M., Honen, J., Knip, M. & Simell, O. (2001). Feasibility of genetic and immunological prediction of Type 1 diabetes in a population-based birth cohort. *Diabetologia*, **44**, 290–297.

Larme, A.C., & Pugh, J.A. (1998). Attitudes of primary care providers toward diabetes: barriers to guideline implementation. *Diabetes Care*, **21**, 1391–1396.

LaPorte, R., Matsushima, M. & Chang, Y. (1995). Prevalence and incidence of insulin-dependent diabetes. National Diabetes Data Group. *Diabetes in America* (2nd edn).

Bethesda, MD: National Institutes of Health, NIH Publication No. 95-1468. Available: http://www.niddk.nih.gov/health/diabetes/dia/

Lemanek, K., Kamps, J. & Chung, N. (2001). Empirically supported treatments in pediatric psychology: regimen adherence. *Journal of Pediatric Psychology*, **26**, 253–275.

Lustman, P. & Gavard, J. (1995). Psychosocial aspects of diabetes in adult populations. National Diabetes Data Group. *Diabetes in America* (2nd edn). Bethesda, MD: National Institutes of Health, NIH Publication No. 95-1468. Available: http://www.niddk.nih.gov/health/diabetes/dia/

Lustman, P., Anderson, R., Freedland, K., de Groot, M., Carney, R. & Clouse, R. (2000a). Depression and poor glycemic control: a meta-analytic review of the literature. *Diabetes Care*, **23**, 934–942.

Lustman, P., Freedland, K., Griffith, L. & Clouse, R. (2000b). Fluoxetine for depression in diabetes: a randomized double-blind placebo-controlled trial. *Diabetes Care*, **23**, 618–623.

Meltzer, L., Johnson, S.B., Prine, J., Banks, R., Desrosiers, P. & Silverstein, J. (2001). Disordered eating, body mass, and glycemic control in adolescents with type 1 diabetes. *Diabetes Care*, **24**, 628–682.

Miller, W.R. & Rollnick, S. (1991). *Motivational Interviewing: Preparing People to Change Addictive Behavior*. New York: Guilford Press.

Neumark-Sztainer, D., Story, M., Toporoff, E., Cassuto, N., Resnick, M. & Blum, R. (1996). Psychosocial predictors of binge eating and purging behaviors among adolescents with diabetes mellitus. *Journal of Adolescent Health*, **19**, 289–296.

NHLBI Obesity Education Expert Panel (1998). *Clinical Guidelines on the Identification, Evaluation, and Treatment of Overweight and Obesity in Adults: The Evidence Report*. Bethesda, MD. National Institutes of Health, NIH Publication No. 98-4083. Available: http://www.nhlbi.nih.gov/guidelines/obesity/ob_gdlns.pdf

Northam, E., Anderson, P., Adler, R., Werther, G. & Warne, G. (1996). Psychosocial and family functioning in children with insulin-dependent diabetes at diagnosis and one year later. *Journal of Pediatric Psychology*, **21**, 699–717.

Northam, E., Anderson, P., Werther, G., Warne, G. & Andrewes, D. (1999). Predictors of change in neuropsychological profiles in children with Type 1 diabetes 2 years after disease onset. *Diabetes Care*, **22**, 1438–1443.

Nurick, M.A. & Johnson, S.B. (1991). Enhancing blood glucose awareness in adolescents and young adults with IDDM. *Diabetes Care*, **14**, 1–7.

Page, P., Verstraete, D., Robb, J. & Etzwiler, D. (1981). Patient recall of self-care recommendations in diabetes. *Diabetes Care*, **4**, 96–98.

Pan, X., Li, G., Hu, Y., Wang, J., Yang, W., An, Z., Hu, Z., Lin, J., Xiao, J., Cao, H., Liu, P., Jiang, X., Jiang, Y., Wang, J., Zheng, H., Zhang, H., Bennett, P. & Howard, B. (1997). Effects of diet and exercise in preventing NIDDM in people with impaired glucose tolerance: the Da Qing IGT and Diabetes Study. *Diabetes Care*, **20**, 537–544.

Perwien, A., Johnson, S.B., Dymtrow, D. & Silverstein, J. (2000). Blood glucose monitoring skills in children with type 1 diabetes. *Clinical Pediatrics*, **39**, 351–357.

Peveler, R., Fairburn, C., Boller, I. & Dunger, D. (1992). Eating disorders in adolescents with IDDM: a controlled study. *Diabetes Care*, **15**, 1356–1360.

Pinhas-Hamiel, O. & Zeitler, P. (1997). A weighty problem: diagnosis and treatment of type 2 diabetes in adolescents. *Diabetes Spectrum*, **10**, 292–298.

Plante, W., Lobato, D. & Engel, R. (2001). Review of group interventions for pediatric chronic conditions. *Journal of Pediatric Psychology*, **26**, 435–453.

Pollock, M., Kovacs, M. & Charron-Prochownik, D. (1995). Eating disorders and maladaptive dietary/insulin management among youths with childhood-onset insulin-dependent diabetes mellitus. *Journal of the American Academy of Child and Adolescent Psychiatry*, **34**, 291–296.

Portuese, E. & Orchard, T. (1995). Mortality in insulin-dependent diabetes. National Diabetes Data Group. *Diabetes in America* (2nd edn). Bethesda, MD: National Institutes of Health, NIH Publication No. 95-1468. Available: http://www.niddk.nih.gov/health/diabetes/dia/

Rapoff, M. (1999). *Adherence to Pediatric Medical Regimens*. New York, Boston, Dordrecht, London, Moscow: Kluwer Academic/ Plenum Publishers.

Rewers, M. & Hamman, R. (1995). Risk factors for non-insulin-dependent diabetes. National Diabetes Data Group. *Diabetes in America* (2nd edn). Bethesda, MD: National Institutes of Health, NIH Publication No. 95-1468. Available: http://www.niddk.nih.gov/health/diabetes/dia/

Riddle, M.C. (1999). Oral pharmacologic management of type 2 diabetes. *American Family Physician*, **60**, 2613–2620.

Roth, R. (2001). Psychological and ethical aspects of prevention trials. *Journal of Pediatric Endocrinology and Metabolism*, **14** (Suppl. 1), 669–674.

Rubin, R. & Peyrot, M. (1992). Psychosocial problems and interventions in diabetes. A review of the literature. *Diabetes Care*, **15**, 1640–1657.

Ruggiero, L., Kairys, S., Fritz, G. & Wood, M. (1991). Accuracy of blood glucose estimates in adolescents with diabetes mellitus. *Journal of Adolescent Health*, **12**, 101–106.

Sahler, O., Roghmann, K., Carpenter, P., Mulhern, R., Dolgin, M., Sargent, J., Barbarin, O., Copeland, D. & Zeltzer, L. (1994). Sibling adaptation to childhood cancer collaborative study: prevalence of sibling distress and definition of adaptation levels. *Journal of Developmental and Behavioral Pediatrics*, **15**, 353–366.

Schatz, D. & Bingley, P. (2001). Update on major trials for the prevention of type 1 diabetes mellitus: the American Diabetes Prevention Trial (DPT-1) and the European Nicotinamide Diabetes Intervention Trial (ENDIT). *Journal of Pediatric Endocrinology and Metabolism*, **13** (Suppl. 1), 619–622.

Silver, E. & Frohlinger-Graham, M. (2000). Brief report: psychological symptoms in healthy female siblings of adolescents with and without chronic conditions. *Journal of Pediatric Psychology*, **25**, 279–284.

Skyler, J. (1998). *Medical Management of Type 1 Diabetes* (3rd edn). Alexandria, VA: American Diabetes Association.

Smith, D.E. & Wing, R.R. (1991). Diminished weight loss and behavioral compliance during repeated diets. *Health Psychology*, **10**, 378–383.

Smith, D., Heckemeyer, C., Kratt, P. & Mason, D. (1997). Motivational interviewing to improve adherence to a behavioral weight-control program for older obese women with NIDDM: a pilot study. *Diabetes Care*, **20**, 52–54.

Striegel-Moore, R.H., Nicholson, T.J. & Tamborlane, W.V. (1992). Prevalence of eating disorder symptoms in preadolescent and adolescent girls with IDDM. *Diabetes Care*, **15**, 1361–1367.

Task Force on Community Preventive Strategies (2001). Strategies for reducing morbidity and mortality from diabetes through health-care system interventions and diabetes self-management education in community settings. *Morbidity and Mortality Weekly Report*, **50**, No. RR-16, 1–15. Available: http://www.cdc.gov/mmwr/preview/mmwrhtml/rr5016a1.htm

United Kingdom Prospective Diabetes Study Group (1998). Effect intensive blood control with metformin and complications in overweight patients with type 2 diabetes. *Lancet*, **352**, 854–865.

Weber, B. & Roth, R. (1997). Psychological aspects in diabetes prevention trials. *Annals of Medicine*, **29**, 461–467.

Wing, R. (1993). Behavioral treatment of obesity: its application to type II diabetes. *Diabetes Care*, **16**, 193–199.

Wing, R., Goldstein, M., Acton, K., Birch, L., Jakicic, J., Sallis, J., Jr, Smith-West, D., Jeffery, R. & Surwit, R. (2001). Behavioral science research in diabetes: lifestyle changes related to obesity, eating behavior, and physical activity. *Diabetes Care*, **24**, 117–123.

Wing, R.R., Marcus, M.D., Blair, E., Epstein, L.H. & Burton, L.R. (1990). Depressive symptomatology in obese adults with type 2 diabetes. *Diabetes Care*, **13**, 170–172.

WHO (1999). *Definition, Diagnosis and Classification of Diabetes Mellitus and its Complications*. Geneva: Department of Noncommunicable Disease Surveillance, World Health Organization. Available: http://www.staff.ncl.ac.uk/philip.home/who_dmc.htm#Heading

Wysocki, T., Huxtable, K., Linscheid, T. & Wayne, W. (1989). Adjustment to diabetes mellitus in preschoolers and their mothers. *Diabetes Care*, **12**, 524–529.

Zimmerman, B. (1998). *Medical Management of Type 2 Diabetes* (4th edn). Alexandria, VA: American Diabetes Association.

CHAPTER 12

Working with Cognitively Impaired Clients

Jeri Morris
Northwestern University Medical School, Chicago, USA

INTRODUCTION

In many settings, both inpatient and outpatient, we encounter clients who have deficits to their cognitive functioning. Clients may come into the world with congenital deficits that affect their ability to learn, work, or socialize. Others may acquire problems through illness or injury. Even when we are not with an individual primarily to treat his cognitive deficits, we often must take those problems into account when treating that person. For example, a client who comes for treatment of alcohol dependency needs to be able to remember what was said in treatment to benefit appropriately from the experience. An individual who seeks psychotherapy for depression that has kept him from working following a mild stroke may have slowed mentation that is a consequence of the physical effects of the stroke and needs to function more quickly to return to his job. While we may see clients for more traditional psychological problems, we may be more helpful if we can provide treatment for cognitive deficits as well as behavioral problems. To accomplish this, there is a need for a thoughtful approach to treatment.

ADDRESSING COGNITIVE PROBLEMS: HOW DO WE BRING ABOUT CHANGE?

It is critical for any clinician working with neurologically impaired individuals to take time to consider the mechanisms of therapeutic change in order to develop a reasonable philosophy of treatment from which to make treatment decisions. While that concept may seem obvious once articulated, too often treatment is initiated without appropriate consideration of what specific factors bring about a change in function.

This is true not only for those providing cognitive treatment to brain-impaired individuals but also for more traditional psychotherapeutic and behavioral treatments. Treatment options are often inadequately considered by the clinician, without sufficient thought to a philosophy of treatment, resulting in inefficient or even irrelevant care. It is quite common

Handbook of Clinical Health Psychology. Edited by S. Llewelyn and P. Kennedy.
© 2003 John Wiley & Sons, Ltd.

for a clinician to identify symptoms, search his or her repertoire for treatment, and apply that treatment without thoughtful consideration of the underpinnings of change and how they can be incorporated into methods of treatment. In "traditional" psychotherapy, for example, the focus of treatment may be to help clients to gain insight into the causes or determinants of their symptoms. If this occurs without thought to how those clients will make alternative choices in their behavior, there may be little change or improvement in symptomatology despite insight. A client's relief in having found understanding can be short-lived in the face of continued depression, anxiety, rage, or other negative symptoms. On the other hand, behavioral treatments that are instituted without insight into aspects of an individual's life that reinforce those symptoms also are unlikely to bring about enduring change. Fortunately, in the area of psychotherapy, there has been considerable research over the past several decades that has encouraged more thoughtful and, as a result, more effective treatment.

This problem of failure to develop a philosophy of treatment is particularly acute in the treatment of brain-injured clients. Even in many formal, well-established, and well-regarded treatment programs that specialize in the treatment of brain-impaired individuals, treatment is often based on exercises and activities that have some superficial relationship to the client's problem(s) while little depth of thought is given to consideration of the mechanisms of change. In response to the question, "What do you do to bring about change in your clients?" many clinicians in such programs answer, "We use a multidisciplinary approach." Without a coherent philosophy of treatment, it is difficult to make basic treatment decisions such as which tools to use, and to decide what the order of treatment might be, that is, which problem should be worked on next.

What follows is a philosophy of treatment that addresses the mechanisms of change in brain-impaired individuals, not simply by superficial consideration of symptoms and tools for eliminating those symptoms, but one that is based upon research over the past 50 years that has, in particular, provided a great deal of information about how the brain functions (Lezak, 1995; Mills, Cassidy & Katz, 1997). It is also based upon research revealing changes in functioning that correspond to damage to the brain through illness or injury.

THE COMMONALITY TO CHANGES IN FUNCTIONING AFTER NEUROLOGIC ILLNESS/INJURY

After damage to the brain has occurred, the most pervasive effect, regardless of the specific impairments, is the fact that cognitive functions that once were automatic no longer occur automatically. In order to perform those cognitive functions, the individual must now do on a conscious and intentional basis what once occurred without the need for conscious intent.

Clients typically have little understanding of their metacognition prior to the acquisition of brain impairment (Berwick et al., 1995). Because much of our cognitive functioning is automatic, they had little reason to consider metacognitive processes in everyday life. As a result, after experiencing a brain injury or the onset of a neurologic illness, many have little sense that they have a problem in functioning, even when that problem is quite apparent to others and, in fact, is interfering in their life. Some, for example, may be accustomed to having a good memory and excellent problem-solving skills and may assume that they continue to have those abilities. It is impossible to consider a problem that one is not aware of. Others may know they have some cognitive problem but have little idea of specifically what that problem is. They are not likely to solve a problem they cannot understand.

Those who have no idea that they have a problem tend to be the individuals standing by the door asking to leave the treatment program, or calling their families to come to take them home, or complaining that staff are keeping them against their will, or refusing to go to outpatient treatment because they believe it is boring or irrelevant. Hostility between the client and the therapist can develop quickly when the individual believes that the therapist has identified non-existent problems, and resistance to treatment can then be intense and an insurmountable obstacle to improvement. These individuals reject direct treatments or compensations that are offered to them.

Those clients who know they have some cognitive problem but misidentify, mislabel, and misdefine that problem cannot develop a specific understanding of the existence and specific nature of a cognitive problem (Ben-Yishay & Prigatano, 1990). Because of this, even when willing or even enthusiastic about receiving treatment and suggestions, these individuals cannot know when to employ what they are given. As a consequence, treatment is not optimally effective.

The Matter of Awareness

It follows, then, that if cognitive functions that once were automatic now must be done on a voluntary, intentional basis, the client must reach a conscious awareness of the specific areas of his cognitive functioning that have been affected by his illness or injury (Lam et al., 1998; Piasetsky, 1982; Rebman & Hannon, 1995; Weinberg et al., 1977, 1979, 1982).

The fact is that most individuals in treatment programs—even those specifically designed to treat cognitive deficits—have no understanding of the actual goals of their own treatment. They may be given a list of deficits (e.g., short-term memory problems; visuospatial deficits) for which they have no understanding and to which they cannot connect to everyday functioning. As a consequence, treatment often seems irrelevant. Ask clients in a full-day cognitive treatment program what they did during the day and they typically will reply, "I went to Speech Therapy", or "I went to Occupational Therapy". Asked further to explain what they did in those treatments, they will say, "I worked in workbooks", or "I cooked brownies". To the clients, these activities bear no relation to their lives and are dismissed as unimportant. Even if the client realizes that his therapies should be important to him, unless that individual has an awareness of his impairments, there is no way that the activities can be meaningful and, as a consequence, the therapy cannot generalize beyond the treatment setting.

Interestingly, once clients have genuine awareness of their deficits, they often can think of solutions to overcome or deal with those deficits. In addition, any compensations that are provided by the treatment team can then actually be used by the client, not just during the treatment session itself, but also in the individual's life outside the facility. Further, treatment is more effective and efficient when the clients are genuine participants because they understand how the activities/tools/exercises are applicable to their lives. Awareness of metacognitive deficits promotes the client's motivation for treatment. This motivation can range from tolerance for treatment to active enthusiasm, whereas without such awareness, few could reasonably be expected to have any use for treatment.

The Importance of Appropriate Conceptualization of Metacognition

If the clients must be aware of their very specific metacognitive deficits in order to be an active participant in treatment, it follows that those deficits must be presented in a way that accurately describes them (Berwick et al., 1995).

First, giving clients vague or meaningless terms to describe their problems cannot be helpful because that does not promote genuine understanding. For example, imagine that a therapist administers tests to a client, the client does poorly on a test said to measure visual memory, and the therapist then provides the feedback that the client has a "visual memory deficit". Little is communicated because the label for the problem is too general. There are many reasons why an individual may show impairment for memory of visual information. That individual may have difficulty with visual scanning, or may not be able to discern which visual details are relevant, or may have problems imagining objects in a different orientation from the one presented, or may have difficulty keeping track of multiple stimuli, or may not be able to see the gestalt in an image and, as a consequence, miss the "big picture". Or the client actually may be unable to consolidate new visual information into long-term storage.

Second, treatment would be quite different, depending on which problem the client actually had (Berwick et al., 1995). The treatment for visual scanning is not the same as the treatment for keeping track of multiple stimuli, though a deficit to either might well bring about poor results on a test of "visual memory". Therefore, if you do not give specific information about the problem in a way that can be understood, no particular treatment is implied. No client can think of solutions to a problem he does not understand, so lack of understanding results in a loss of the client's capacity to be a part of the solution. And it may result in a rejection, as meaningless and valueless, of what the clinician has to offer.

It is clear, then, that if a therapist is to be of effective use to a client, the therapist must have an adequate understanding of the client's problems, and this requires appropriate assessment. Therefore, assessment must be thorough and must address the underlying metacognitive issues.

Recognizing the Difference between Remediation and Compensation

In selecting which metacognitive problems might be addressed, it is important to consider expectations. Techniques for treatment will be quite different if a deficit can be remediated than if an impairment can only be compensated for. Remediation is the attempt to facilitate improvement to a particular ability. It is never possible to know the degree to which actual improvement can be made, but working on remediating or improving an area of weakness is always preferable to teaching a compensation. Unfortunately, impairments to many cognitive functions can only be compensated for and might never actually be improved upon. Giving compensatory methods is nearly always less satisfactory than remediating a problem, but there are many times when it is the only means available to us. In the treatment examples for "mental speed" and "short term memory" given below, the former is something that can often be remediated to some extent, while the latter typically requires compensatory strategies. Though remediation is preferable, providing compensatory strategies can also make a meaningful improvement to an individual's life if he understands when and how they might be used.

Developing a Therapeutic Alliance

While awareness is fundamental to conducting treatment that will generalize, communicating the client's problems in a way that can be accepted by the individual can be extremely difficult. No one wants to know they have cognitive impairments, or feel intellectually weaker than they once were. In fact, becoming aware of cognitive deficits often results in a narcissistic injury to the individual's sense of self. This is frequently extremely painful if not devastating and can undermine the patient's sense of self-worth, ability to see his remaining positive attributes, and capacity to enjoy and have a meaningful life (Ruff & Neiman, 1990). Yet awareness is fundamental to effective treatment.

The challenge is to communicate information that will lead to awareness of deficits in a way that increases the likelihood that the patient will accept rather than reject treatment. This is not easy to accomplish. To communicate such a powerfully negative message without a consequent rejection of the therapist and treatment, the therapist must be seen to be coming from a position of benevolence—an ally trying to help. Too frequently, we find therapists insisting to the client that the client has cognitive deficits. The therapist may become anxious when the client denies the reality of those deficits and may find himself imploring the client to cooperate, pointing out that there is only limited time to take advantage of the treatment. As the client rejects the message, the therapist insists even more, and an adversarial relationship develops, each feeling as though he were on opposite sides of a battle that has serious consequences. To avoid the development of an adversarial relationship or to put an end to one that has started and, instead, to develop an alliance, the therapist must "climb over" onto the side of the client. There are a variety of techniques that foster such an alliance.

First, the therapist must make certain that the client feels the therapist is approaching him as an actual person, separate from other clients. It is very difficult for a relationship of mutual trust to develop if the client feels that the therapist is approaching the client as a "brain injured" or "ill" individual rather than as an individual. Beginning by acknowledging past achievements and accomplishments while taking a history often can be helpful. Looking for places within the history-taking in which one can make a personal comment can help to get across the point that the history-taking is not merely a formality and that the therapist is genuinely interested in knowing the client as a person.

Seeking out times within the initial session(s) in which the therapist can interject an empathic comment also can be helpful in building an alliance. For example, for the client who may be complaining about treatment, it may be useful to comment, "I don't blame you a bit for feeling that way. No one really wants to have to come here. But I'll try to do the best I can, and hopefully you'll find it was worthwhile." At times, the therapist can initiate such an interaction by making a comment such as, "This must be really difficult for you. It must be tough to go through this." Acknowledging the difficulty of treatment can be helpful, as well.

It is important to remember that an aspect of gaining enough of an alliance to deliver bad news to a client is to establish credibility as a professional. A therapist may have the most extensive curriculum vitae and professional reputation, but this may well mean nothing to the client. It is our responsibility to establish our credibility with each client if we want to be taken seriously and seen as an ally. We need to recognize that this often takes time. Ironically, we may need to delay aspects of treatment while we are gaining the respect and acceptance of the client.

In the meantime, while establishing our relationship with the individual, we can be assessing that person and providing opportunities for him to make errors that can be capitalized on. After a person has made several errors, we then may be able to make an observation that characterizes those errors (e.g. "I notice you keep bumping into things on the left"). After there is sufficient trust within the therapeutic relationship, we then can label those errors (e.g., "We call that 'left-side neglect'") without provoking an argument or jeopardizing our opportunity to have the client understand and cooperate in treatment.

SPECIFIC TREATMENTS

Improving Mental Speed: A Problem Amenable to Remediation

Many disorders of brain functioning affect speed of mentation (Lezak, 1995; Sohlberg & Mateer, 2001). These disorders include AIDS-related dementia, head trauma, and cerebral vascular disease, to name but a few. The individual can be confused in conversation, particularly when speaking with more than one other person, because he cannot keep up with what is said and has lost track of the topic. The client may be very poor in novel situations or those that require problem-solving because he cannot think quickly enough to deal with what is occurring around him. He may not remember what has been said to him because information was presented more quickly than he could take it in. Slow motor speed often accompanies slow mentation. This can affect speed of gross motor movements, very fine motor movements such as those needed for writing, and even the speed to which the facial muscles react to what the client is thinking. Further, speed of speech is often affected along with mental speed. This is associated with slow thought processes and impaired capacity to use oral musculature quickly enough to form words.

These speed-related problems affect the individual's capacity to function, and they also contribute to the appearance of disability, a separate problem. One can be normal but appear disabled, and this will have an impact on relationships, particularly with those with which the individual is less familiar. A client who looked quite impaired as a consequence of his spinal injury wore a hat that said, "It talks." He did this in an attempt at irony and to underscore the fact that simply because he appeared to be disabled did not mean that his intellect was impaired. It was an acknowledgement of the fact that individuals often mistake one disability for another and make negative judgments about the disabled person. Reducing the appearance of disability (in this instance, speed of speech) can help a person to reduce negative impressions that others may incorrectly form.

Therefore, because speed of functioning occurs in conjunction with many disorders, affects so many aspects of functioning, and frequently can actually be remediated, at least to some degree, it is worthwhile to attempt to focus on ways that might improve it. Improvement is sometimes quite dramatic, but even where change is less impressive, results are often meaningful to the client.

The tool (or activity) one uses to increase speed is not the treatment itself. In fact, many tools or activities can be used interchangeably to achieve results, as long as the treatment is emphasized consistently. The client must come to understand that his functioning is slow and that the purpose for the treatment is to increase speed.

An activity might be to write one's name and address ten times, while someone keeps track of the time. The time can then be compared to the trials the preceding days, and progress can be charted and understood. Virtually any timed activity that can improve with practice can be used. Sorting colored objects, mirror writing, reading words aloud, copying shapes, walking around a track, all could be used to keep track of speed.

It is critical that any activity or tool used be one wherein the client's behavior is observable and measurable (Fluharty & Priddy, 1993; Schmitter-Edgecombe et al., 1995; Sohlberg & Mateer, 2001). This is the only way that the therapist can know if the client is actually improving. This is relevant because it is important to have evidence and acknowledge that the treatment is helping, and it allows one to know when the client's improvement has stopped or slowed significantly. Knowing that treatment has helped is a great motivator for further treatment and also can give a client increased self-confidence. Knowing that progress has stopped or slowed dramatically can introduce reality into the situation. Consider the case of an individual sent for treatment following a head injury. The first session began with the client taking a glass of water, putting it to his lips, and setting it back down. This took more than one minute for him to accomplish. He then stated, excruciatingly slowly, that his goal was to return to work as an air traffic controller. Clearly, this was an unrealistic goal, but it was equally clear that the client did not realize this and had no awareness of how slow he was. We began to work on speed, and kept a chart of his improvement. After initial improvement, there followed a period in which there was little change. Because we kept track of the time, and the client understood his goal and the relationship to his life, he eventually commented, "At this rate, it will take me 120 years to get back to my job." Sad as this was, it meant he understood and could accept the reality of his situation and was willing to consider alternative goals for himself in order to have a more satisfying life.

Other clients have improved their speed to the point that they can function normally. To do a job, one must be accurate, *within time*. Accuracy alone is not enough. Once individuals understand that they are functioning slowly, they can put effort into speeding their own functioning and taking an active part in the remediation procession. To do this, as a part of the record, it is important for the therapist to write (or have the clients write) what occurred during the session. This needs to be phrased in a manner that includes a reiteration of the clients' problems and the methods used for treating those problems (not simply the tool or activity). Therefore, a client must keep a personal record after each therapy session (Fluharty & Priddy, 1993; Solberg & Mateer, 2001).

For example, the therapist or client might write, "Tuesday, January 3, 20–, we worked on increasing my speed by writing my name and address as fast as I could ten times, and we kept track of how long it took." This method of keeping track:

- reinforces the orientation by giving the day and date
- reiterates the client's problem so that awareness of the problem is increased
- emphasizes the relevance of the treatment
- emphasizes the goal of the treatment
- allows for consideration of progress and of reality issues.

Improving Memory Functioning: A Problem Amenable to Compensation

Memory functioning is another aspect of cognitive functioning that is seen across many illnesses and can interfere dramatically to reduce effective functioning in everyday life situations. However, the underlying processes involved in memory deficits are often not understood, and, as a consequence, are not dealt with effectively when, in fact, effective compensations may be available (Baddeley, Wilson & Watts, 1989; Lam et al., 1998; Schmitter-Edgecombe et al., 1995; Squire & Schachter, 2002). It should be noted that memory is not a muscle that can be exercised. Simply reading something, looking away, and then trying to explain what one read will not increase memory capacity. Only compensations can be effective.

The most common misconception about memory deficits centers around the concept of "short-term memory" (Butterfield, Wambold & Belmont, 1973; Cermak, 2001; Lam et al., 1998; Squire & Schachter, 2002). Therapists as well as text books operationally define "short-term memory" in a wide variety of ways, yet how one defines terms is important, because unless terms are defined appropriately, reflecting how the brain actually works, it is very difficult to think of how they might be compensated for effectively. For example, one of the most common deficits that masquerades as a "short-term memory problem" should be thought of in terms of storage and retrieval. Many kinds of neurologic problems (such as head trauma, some effects of alcoholism, many strokes, and even congenital learning disabilities) involve deficits to storage of new declarative memory with relative preservation of retrieval processes. Understanding this is crucial to compensating for the problem.

Declarative memory includes semantic memory, or memory for words and their meanings, and episodic memory, or memory for events and occurrences that have a temporal or spatial component (Glisky & Delaney, 1996; Squire & Schachter, 2002; Wilson, 1987). Storage of new semantic and episodic memory is often impaired following the neurologic disorders mentioned above, as well as others that might affect the functioning of the hippocampus. Any impairment to hippocampal functioning is likely to bring with it a consequent impairment to storage of semantic and episodic material. Examples of semantic memory include learning new words and the meaning of new words. In adult clients, since the neurologic disorders affect storage of new material but leave relative preservation of previously learned information, semantic memory storage deficits are often not obvious and not a significant impediment to functioning. By adulthood, we have learned most of the words we need to use, and, for most individuals, there is not usually a great pressure to learn new ones. Episodic memory impairments are more obvious and typically more of an impediment. These include memory for events (e.g., what one did last weekend), for what has occurred (including what someone has said or what the individual has said to someone else), for the experience of having learned something (e.g., not the rules of how to operate a copy machine as much as the recollection of the experience of having learned or been taught in whatever setting and by whom).

The importance of understanding that the problem is one of storage of declarative memory rather than "short-term memory" is in the compensation process. The consequences of head injury can be used to illustrate the issue most vividly. When an individual is first injured, he may experience a loss of consciousness followed by a period of post-traumatic amnesia (Cicerone et al., 1996; Glisky & Delaney, 1996). During that amnestic period, the patient may appear normal to those around him and be able to converse and answer questions about himself, but later cannot recall what was experienced during the amnestic period. The patient can speak and answer questions about himself because memory retrieval is not disturbed, but he does not recall the amnestic period because no new memories were being stored. This is a severe disturbance of memory storage with relative preservation of memory retrieval that occurs because the hippocampus is commonly injured following head injury, causing the memory storage deficit, while other parts of the brain, where previously learned material is maintained, are relatively intact (Wilson, 1987). In head injury, this occurs so often because of the location of the hippocampus in relation to the bony prominence of the skull against which the brain typically impacts physically. After the period of post-traumatic amnesia begins to resolve, we see the same problem but with less severity. The individual begins to store new memories and is said to be oriented to his circumstances. He then begins to remember at least some events from one day to the next, as his memory storage processes improve. However, to the extent that the memory problem persists, it remains in the same pattern, with reasonably preserved retrieval processes and impairment to the quantity of new information that is stored. When these individuals are examined periodically after their injuries, we find that they can store less than the average individual. However, what does get stored can be retrieved later, just as can information learned prior to the injury. It is not a retrieval problem, it is a storage problem. Because such individuals are easily overwhelmed and take in less than the usual amount of information, less is retained. But what is retained can be recalled later. Clearly, then, the problem becomes one of thinking of ways to increase the chances that new information will be stored.

It should be obvious why it is important to correctly define the deficit. If one mis-labels this type of problem as a "short-term memory" deficit, it is difficult to think of what to do about the problem (Zencus, Wesolowski & Burke, 1990). But if we define the problem in terms of the way the brain actually functions, it becomes apparent that strategies that increase the likelihood that new declarative memories will be stored can be of value to the client, as he will be able to retrieve that stored information later, since retrieval is not a problem.

There are a number of ways we can increase the likelihood that new declarative memories will be stored.

1. When attempting to learn, the client should read or listen to only a small amount of information and then learn that well with repeated practice before going on to learn more.
2. The individual will probably require more than the usual amount of overlearning to store new material. Overlearning is continued practice past the point of initial mastery. Thus clients need to practice even after they believe they have taken in information so that the likelihood that it will be stored is increased.
3. The individual should take frequent breaks when studying and repeated practice should be distributed over time rather than massed (as in "cramming"). While intuitively, those who retain little would seem to benefit from more practice at any given time, in reality, continued practice will be counter-productive for the individual with this problem because he will simply become overwhelmed. In those circumstances, the client will remember less rather than more.
4. Because immediate recall can be so much better than recall after a half-hour, it would be easy for the client (and those working with the client) to err and expect the individual to retain information that actually is never stored. Before going on to learn additional material, clients should review what they have previously studied to be certain they have retained it. There is no point in going on if the individual has not yet mastered the material.
5. For learning long passages (for example, for a student who wishes to return to school or an employee who must learn new information associated with work), reducing material

to outline form and then learning the outline piece by piece can be effective. Again, short sessions and overlearning are important. Learning piece one, then one and two, then one, two and three, and so on is a method that can be used to allow an individual with a significant memory storage problem to eventually learn a considerable amount of information. This method also helps a person to assess whether enough time has been spent studying or if additional time and effort are required.

Again, keeping a personal record after each session with the client will help to orient the individual, underscore the problem, and emphasize the relevance and goals of treatment (Laatsch, 1983).

For example, the therapist or client might write, "Wednesday, January 4, 20–, we worked on increasing the amount of new information I can store by practicing my method of learning small amounts with lots of repetition, and I took frequent breaks. We kept a record of what I was able to remember after each ten-minute interval." This method:

- reinforces the orientation by giving the day and date
- reiterates the client's problem so that awareness of the problem is increased
- emphasizes the relevance of the treatment
- emphasizes the goal of the treatment
- allows for consideration of progress and of reality issues.

Because memory can only be compensated for, the effects of treatment are not as satisfying as they would be if the problem could be remediated (Laatsch, 1983). Nevertheless, if clients become aware of the nature of their memory problem, they can use compensations (and even think of their own) because they will make sense (Langer & Padrone, 1992). Helping the client to understand and be aware of memory storage deficits also can give the therapist greater credibility with that person, because the explanation is likely to seem "right" and make sense, and will have the consequent benefits of increasing the client/therapist alliance and the client's motivation for treatment.

With a thoughtful approach to treatment, we can enhance treatment of behavioral problems in those who have cognitive deficits. A program that includes cognitive treatments designed to generalize to situations outside treatment setting can have the additional benefit of giving encouragement and optimism. In the context of the therapeutic alliance, awareness can be built that allows greater client participation in treatment and increased likelihood that compensations will be used in other situations.

REFERENCES

Baddeley, A.D., Wilson, B.A. & Watts, F. (1989). *Handbook of Memory Disorders*. New York: John Wiley & Sons.

Ben-Yishay, Y. & Prigatano, G.P. (1990). Cognitive remediation. In M. Rosenthal, M.R. Bond, E.R. Griffith & J.D. Miller (Eds), *Rehabilitation of the Adult and Child with Traumatic Brain Injury* (2nd edn). Philadelphia: F.A. Davis.

Berwick, K.D., Raymond, J.J, Malia, K.B. & Bennett, T.L. (1995). Metacognition as the ultimate executive: techniques and tasks to facilitate executive functions. *NeuroRehabilitation*, **5**, 367–375.

Butterfield, E.C., Wambold, C. & Belmont, J.M. (1973). On the theory and practice of improving short term memory. *American Journal of Mental Deficiency*, **77**, 644–669.

Cermak, L.S. (2001). *Handbook of Neuropsychology* (2nd edn): *Memory and its Disorders.* New York: Elsevier Science.

Cicerone, K.D., Smith, L.C., Ellmo, W., Mangel, H.E., Nelson, P., Chase, R.F. & Kalmar, K. (1996). Neuropsychological rehabilitation of mild traumatic brain injury. *Brain Injury*, **10**, 277–286.

Fluharty, G. & Priddy, D. (1993). Methods of increasing client acceptance of a memory book. *Brain Injury*, **7**, 85–88.

Glisky, E.L. & Delaney, S. (1996). Implicit memory and new semantic learning in posttraumatic amnesia. *Journal of Head Trauma Rehabilitation*, **11**, 31–42.

Laatsch, L. (1983). Development of a memory training program. *Cognitive Rehabilitation*, **1**, 15–18.

Lam, C., McMahon, B., Priddy, D. & Geherd-Schultz, A. (1998). Deficit awareness and treatment performance among traumatic head injury adults. *Brain Injury*, **2**, 235–242.

Langer, K.G. & Padrone, F.J. (1992). Psychotherapeutic treatment of awareness in acute rehabilitation of traumatic brain injury. *Neuropsychological Rehabilitation*, **2**, 235–242.

Lezak, M.S. (1995). *Neuropsychological Assessment* (3rd edn). New York: Oxford University Press.

Mills, V.M., Cassidy, J.W. & Katz, D.I. (1997). *Neurologic Rehabilitation: A Guide to Diagnosis, Prognosis, and Treatment Planning.* Malden, MA: Blackwell Science.

Piasetsky, E.B. (1982). The relevance of brain-behavior relationships. In L.E. Trexler (Ed.), *Cognitive Rehabilitation.* New York: Plenum Press.

Rebman, M.J. & Hannon, R. (1995). Treatment of unawareness deficits in adults with brain injury: three case studies. *Rehabilitation Psychology*, **40**, 279–280.

Ruff, R.M. & Neiman, H. (1990). Cognitive rehabilitation versus day treatment in head-injured adults: is there an impact on emotional and psychosocial adjustment? *Brain Injury*, **4**, 339–347.

Schmitter-Edgecombe, M., Fahy, J., Whelan, J. & Long, C. (1995). Memory remediation after severe closed head injury: notebook training versus supportive therapy. *Journal of Consulting and Clinical Psychology*, **63**, 484–489.

Sohlberg, M.D. & Mateer, C.A. (2001). *Cognitive Rehabilitation.* New York: Guilford Press.

Squire, L.R. & Schachter, D.L. (2002). *Neuropsychology of Memory* (3rd edn). New York: Guilford Press.

Weinberg, J., Diller, L., Gordon, W.A., Gerstman, L.J., Lieberman, A., Lakin, P., Hodges, G. & Ezrachi, O. (1977). Visual scanning training effect on reading-related tasks in acquired right-brain damage. *Archives of Physical Medicine and Rehabilitation*, **58**, 479–496.

Weinberg, J., Diller, L., Gordon, W.A., Gerstman, L.J., Lieberman, A., Lakin, P., Hodges, G. & Ezrachi, O. (1979). Training sensory awareness and spatial organization in people with right brain damage. *Archives of Physical Medicine and Rehabilitation*, **60**, 491–496.

Weinberg, J., Piasetsky, E., Diller, L. & Gordon, W. (1982). Treating perceptual organization deficits in nonneglecting RBD stroke patients. *Journal of Clinical Neuropsychology*, **4**, 59–75.

Wilson, B.A. (1987). *Rehabilitation of Memory.* New York: Guilford Press.

Zencus, A., Wesolowski, M.D. & Burke, W.H. (1990). A comparison of four memory strategies with traumatically brain-injured clients. *Brain Injury*, **4**, 33–38.

CHAPTER 13

Psychological Aspects of Acquired Hearing Impairment and Tinnitus

Laurence McKenna
Royal National Throat, Nose and Ear Hospital, London, UK
David Mark Baguley
Addenbrooke's Hospital, Cambridge, UK
and
Gerhard Andersson
Uppsala University, Sweden

INTRODUCTION

The fundamental importance of the sense of hearing, and its contribution to communication, safety and the enjoyment of music, have been remarked upon throughout history. The handicap and disability associated with acquired hearing loss and tinnitus (ringing or buzzing in the ear) has been similarly evident. The British statesman and man of letters Philip Dormer Stanhope (4th Earl of Chesterfield, 1694–1773) stated: ". . . I swear that I do not know how to be deaf: I cannot get used to it, and I am as humiliated and distressed by it today as I was during the first week. No philosophy in the world can palliate deafness" (Barrell, 1980). Such experiences are still apparent in clinical practice with hearing-impaired and tinnitus patients today, and indicate the need for effective, timely and patient-centred rehabilitation. With this in mind, this chapter aims to explore the psychological issues around the experiences of acquired hearing loss and tinnitus and to describe the therapeutic approaches commonly employed. The amount of psychological research done in this area has not matched that seen in other areas of health care such as pain management, primarily because the numbers of psychologists involved in audiology is still relatively few. Nonetheless, psychologists have made important contributions to our understanding of the nature and management of distressing audiological symptoms. Our objective is that the reader should have an increased understanding of the challenges facing individuals with an acquired hearing and/or tinnitus, and perceive the rationale for psychological formulations and interventions in these

Handbook of Clinical Health Psychology. Edited by S. Llewelyn and P. Kennedy.
© 2003 John Wiley & Sons, Ltd.

conditions. We will discuss hearing loss first and then tinnitus. In each case we will provide an outline to the audiological background before discussing the psychological issues
surrounding the symptoms.

AUDIOLOGICAL ASPECTS OF ACQUIRED DEAFNESS

Hearing loss has traditionally been characterised by the site of the lesion causing that loss.
In such a framework a lesion of the conductive auditory pathway (the outer ear, ear drum
and middle ear) causes a conductive hearing loss, with an associated reduction in hearing
sensitivity but no reduction in discrimination abilities if a sound is sufficiently intense as to
be audible. A cochlear hearing loss is by definition associated with cochlear dysfunction,
usually involving the delicate micro-mechanical structures of the cochlea, and specifically
the hair cells. These structures are involved in the transduction of sound from vibration in air.
The cochlear fluid and the neural impulses are not merely passive receptors, but rather have
active processes that are involved in fine frequency, time and intensity discrimination. Thus a
cochlear hearing loss may involve not only a reduction in hearing sensitivity, but also reduced
abilities in auditory discrimination. A lesion arising from or impinging upon the auditory
nerve, such as the rare tumour named vestibular schwannoma, may also cause a hearing
loss that would again be associated with both reduced sensitivity and discrimination, though
such symptoms would very rarely occur in isolation from other manifestations of disease.
Finally, a category of central auditory processing disorder (CAPD) has been identified in
which cochlear function may be normal, but the individual may have auditory perceptual
problems particularly in background noise. The categories of cochlear, retrocochlear, and
central auditory dysfunction have often been subsumed into an inclusive category of sensori-
neural hearing loss (SNHL).

The majority of adults who experience an acquired hearing loss do so because of cochlear
dysfunction. The most common aetiology is that of presbyacusis, or age-related hearing loss.
Pathophysiological models of presbyacusis are complex and varied, but there is a consensus
that cochlear hair cell dysfunction is a major factor, with the consequent difficulties in
discrimination as described above. Davis (1997) reports data that indicate an overall adult
(aged 18–80) population prevalence of 13.9% of SNHL equal or worse than 25 dB (thus the
level of a whisper) in the individual's better ear. This prevalence rises sharply with age such
that 42% of the age range 61–80 years were in this position. This criteria of SNHL represents
the point at which an individual might benefit from a hearing aid. Unfortunately, the shortfall
in provision is such that it has been estimated that there are 6.3 million adults in England and
Wales, for example, who would benefit but who have not tried a hearing aid (Davis, 1997).

While much more rare than presbyacusis, the experience of those adults with unilateral
SNHL is worthy of note. Even in the presence of one normally hearing ear, a hearing
impairment in the other may cause considerable hearing handicap, with difficulties in sound
localisation and in hearing in noise. The causes of unilateral deafness are varied. Noise
exposure can be more marked in one ear than in the other, and this may be evident in
a patient examined after extended rifle shooting. If a unilateral hearing loss is associated
with symptoms of imbalance, a specialist clinical opinion should be sought, in particular to
consider the diagnosis of treatable otological pathology.

Acquired profound deafness is rare, but the consequences may be devastating. While
some individuals appear to undergo progressive cochlear failure in adulthood that may be
ascribed to auto-immune problems or genetic causes, in others this situation occurs suddenly

following meningitis. Such a sudden bilateral profound hearing loss has immediate consequences for the individual and his or her family, and must be addressed in an urgent and comprehensive manner, involving psychological and audiological interventions at an early stage.

THE AUDIOLOGICAL TREATMENT OF ACQUIRED HEARING IMPAIRMENT

As stated above, the aetiology of conductive hearing impairment is almost always a structural lesion of the conductive auditory pathway, examples being wax in the ear canal, a perforation of the tympanic membrane, fluid in the middle ear (glue ear) or dislocation of the ossicular chain. Many of these structural lesions are amenable to surgical or medical treatment by an otologist, and in such cases the surgery is undertaken with the joint aim of removing disease and restoring hearing. In SNHL, however, where the most common cause of the hearing impairment is cochlear dysfunction, effective surgical intervention is not possible, with the exception of cochlear implantation which is discussed below. Herein lies the overarching irony of audiological management of hearing loss: those patients with conductive hearing impairment, who would do well with hearing aids as they have well-preserved auditory discrimination abilities, do not receive them as a rule, as they progress to medical and surgical treatment of their condition. Those patients with SNHL, however, with reduced discrimination have no medical or surgical option, and thus can only undergo treatment with hearing aids: but that reduced auditory discrimination ability means that even optimal hearing aid prescription will not result in normal hearing abilities. Modern sophisticated hearing aids, in particular digital speech-processing devices, have however allowed the audiologist to more closely match the needs of the patient with the aid prescription, and in particular have facilitated the amplification level of speech to a programmed desired sensation level while reducing background noise. There is emergent evidence that the issue of such sophisticated hearing aids can result in improved patient satisfaction over traditional analogue hearing aids.

Another area where technological advance has resulted in patient benefit is the application of cochlear implants to individuals with severe and profound hearing loss. Initial experiments in the 1960s, with simple single-channel cochlear implants, enabled deafened patients to perceive rhythms and intonations of speech. Today cochlear implants are complex multichannel devices that allow some patients to have excellent abilities to discriminate speech without lip-reading (and thus are able to use the telephone). A danger exists with such advances in technology, however—that therapy becomes technology and device centred rather than patient centred. The case for a psychological approach to the problems faced by people with hearing impairment is often as compelling as that for a technological one. A technological approach to the management of hearing impairment is often rejected, or at least poorly complied with by patients (Baumfield & Dillon, 2001; Brooks, 1985). At best both strategies should be considered in tandem.

PSYCHOLOGICAL PROFILE OF PEOPLE WITH ACQUIRED HEARING LOSS

A popular image of people with hearing impairment is that they suffer from psychological disturbances such as depression or paranoia (Jones & White, 1990); however this idea has been only partly investigated in the empirical literature (Andersson, 1995). It has also been observed that people who use hearing aids are regarded less favourably by others than people without a hearing aid (Danhauer et al., 1985). There are certainly good reasons to suppose that hearing loss might influence the onset of psychological disturbance, and the link between hearing loss and psychological status has been investigated in a number of ways. One approach has been to examine the prevalence of psychological problems among a population of hearing-impaired people. For example, McKenna, Hallam and Hinchcliffe (1991) reported that 27% of people attending a neuro-otology clinic with a main complaint of hearing loss were suffering from significant psychological disturbance. This is considerably higher than the prevalence of psychological disturbance among the general population but is lower than the prevalence rates reported to be associated with other audiological symptoms such as tinnitus or vertigo (Asmundson, Larsen & Stein, 1998; McKenna, Hallam & Hinchcliffe, 1991; Meric et al., 1998). A different approach to the question has been to examine the extent of hearing loss among populations of known psychiatric patients, but it has proved difficult to draw conclusions from the results of this approach. There is the potential for a hearing loss to lead to mis-classification in psychiatric cases and it is important for this to be taken into account in the diagnostic process (Kreeger et al., 1995). When other health problems have been taken into consideration, the correlations between hearing loss and anxiety and depression are weaker. The experience of multiple symptoms leads to a greater likelihood of a person suffering from significant psychological distress. The high comorbidity between hearing loss and tinnitus is particularly relevant in this respect.

What is clear is that the relationship between hearing loss and psychological well-being is a complex one. This point is highlighted by the fact that many people, particularly older people, do not complain about their hearing loss. It has been noted that some people deny that they have a hearing problem even when confronted by audiometric evidence of a hearing loss (Gilhome Herbst & Humphrey, 1980). The complexity of the relationship between hearing loss and psychological status is further highlighted by the fact that audiological measures of hearing loss do not predict the extent of psychological disturbance (Gilhome Herbst & Humphrey, 1980; Kerr & Cowie, 1997; Mahapatra, 1974; Thomas & Gilhome Herbst, 1980). One study (Thomas & Gilhome Herbst, 1980), however, suggested that while for most of the population assessed there was no clear relationship between degree of hearing loss and psychological disturbance, there was a higher degree of disturbance among a subgroup of people with particularly severe hearing loss, poor speech discrimination and who received little benefit from hearing aids. The uncertain relationship between hearing loss and psychological well-being may, in part, be because of an overly simple approach to assessing psychological status. Many studies (e.g. Ingalls, 1946; Knapp, 1948; Mahapatra, 1974; Singerman, Reidner & Folstein, 1980; Thomas & Gilhome Herbst, 1980) have used an approach that classifies people as either psychiatrically disturbed or not. This runs the risk of neglecting those people who experience emotional distress but who fall short of a classification as dysfunctional. Not everyone experiencing an adjustment reaction to hearing loss will react in ways that would allow them to be classified as psychiatrically dysfunctional.

A different approach to the study of hearing loss was taken by Kerr and Cowie (1997). They examined the subjective experiences of people with acquired hearing loss and described the effects of hearing loss in terms of six factors derived from a factor analysis of questionnaire responses. Only one of the factors obtained referred to the communication problems that one might expect to be associated with hearing loss. One factor was concerned with social restrictions such as employment difficulties and strained family relationships.

Another referred to poor interactions on the part of others, i.e. deafened people perceive others as using strategies that undermine the hearing-impaired person. The other factors emphasized psychosocial dimensions of the experience. One of these factors was concerned with the distress associated with interactions and a sense of social isolation. Another highlighted a sense of loss and bereavement and a sense that hearing people do not understand what it is like to be deafened. The last factor was concerned with positive experiences associated with hearing loss such as social support and greater inner philosophical resources. In common with other studies, Kerr and Cowie (1997) found that audiological factors did not allow one to say how much impact a hearing loss would have on a person's life. The finding that hearing loss might be associated with some positive consequences may seem surprising. There are, however, other sources of evidence that the effects of hearing loss are not always those that one might intuitively think of. For example, it is worth noting that not all cochlear implant users report a positive psychological outcome, even when the implant provides obvious acoustic benefit. Sometimes the "restoration of hearing" provided by an implant does not lead to the changes in life that the person hoped for. In behavioural terms the act of wearing the implant is not reinforced. Just as with hearing aids, a proportion of implant recipients do not use their devices (McKenna, 1986).

The complexity of the relationship between hearing loss and psychological status is due to the fact that hearing loss does not occur in a vacuum but rather within the "rich tapestry of life". Two people with the same level of hearing loss may have quite different life experiences. The World Health Organization (WHO, 1980) classification of impairment, disability, and handicap has been appealed to when seeking to explain the imprecise relationship between hearing loss and psychological disturbance. Stephens and Hetu (1991) provided definitions of impairment, disability, and handicap within this context. They defined impairment as the defective function that may be measured using psycho-acoustical techniques, and suggested that it is independent of psychosocial factors. They defined disability as the auditory problem experienced by the individual and handicap as the non-auditory problems that result from hearing impairment and disability. Handicap is determined by the social and cultural context and because it refers to the disadvantage that the individual experiences, there is not a direct relationship between impairment, disability, and handicap.

The WHO (1980) model has been challenged, notably by Johnson (1996), who found that it could not account for her observations of people suffering from physical disorders. Johnson (1996) argued that levels of disability are influenced by a combination of an intention to behave in a certain way and perceived control over being able to do so, and cited the Theory of Planned Behaviour (Azjen, 1988) in this context. This theory suggests that a person's intention to perform a task is determined by a combination of a change in attitudes to the behaviour, the subjective norm for the behaviour, and the person's perception of control over the behaviour. Johnson (1996) contended that physical impairment influences mental representations that, in turn, determine behavioural intentions and disabled behaviour. In summary, the suggestion is that disability, like handicap, refers to *behaviour* that is subject to manipulation in the same way as any other behaviour. The Theory of Planned Behaviour has not been formally applied with an audiology setting but these ideas do have some resonance in the clinical observations made within that setting. In an audiology context the behaviour in question might be speaking with others. A change in attitude associated with this might be "I feel embarrassed when I mishear people and I dislike embarrassment". The subjective norm might be "my spouse wishes to do the talking for me and I am happy to go along with this" and an example of perceived control over the behaviour could be "I am not confident that I can hear what people say". The ideas of Skinner (1957) add to this view of hearing. During his later years, Skinner extended his theories into the field of ageing and hearing loss (Skinner & Vaughan, 1983). Hearing can be viewed as an operant, i.e. a behaviour that is under the influence of contingencies of reinforcement. Skinner advocated an assertive approach while acknowledging that when it is impossible to hear: "You do your best to stop trying to hear things when you are having trouble. You are probably not enjoying what is said in a television program if you are straining to hear it" (Skinner & Vaughan, 1983, p. 44).

The point that social factors influence the level of disability was recognised by Stephens and Hetu (1991). While it is widely recognised that social barriers act as determinants of disability (Finkelstein, 1980, 1990), (e.g. a wheelchair user is disabled because there are steps rather than a ramp), Johnson's (1996) argument extends this idea by also highlighting cognitive determinants of disability. The roles of social and psychological factors in audiological disability are discussed by Arnold (1998). While the notion that hearing-impaired people face social barriers is now considered self-evident (e.g. a hearing-impaired person is disabled by background noise), from a clinical point of view it is also apparent that they encounter psychological obstacles through factors such as anxiety or reduced motivation. The evidence suggests that the effects of acquired hearing loss go beyond communication problems and there are strands of support for the idea that psychological factors influence hearing disability directly. One piece of research from the field of cochlear implants (McKenna & Denman, 1993) adds to this picture. An assessment was carried out of a group of implant users' retrospective perceptions of changes in their psychological status. The assessment indicated that almost all of the group believed that their lives were close to ideal prior to the onset of hearing loss, and that this was radically changed by hearing loss. It seems implausible that so many in any group would have had near perfect lives before losing their hearing. It seems unlikely that this perception is the consequence of only social factors. It is more likely that this represents a cognitive shift. The effect is to increase the perception of the loss experienced and this in turn is likely to be a determinant of the subsequent disability behaviour.

A new classification of impairments, disability and handicap has been proposed by the WHO (2000). This refers to: losses or abnormalities of bodily function and structure (previously referred to as impairments), limitations of activities (previously disabilities) and restriction in participation (previously handicaps), and contextual factors. The proposed new classification is set within the context of the social model of disability. It suggests that disablement occurs within and by means of social, environmental and personal contextual factors. This new classification is broad enough to incorporate the ideas put forward within the psychological model (Johnson, 1996); however, Johnson's (1996) suggestions more clearly delineate the role of psychological factors. The application of the new WHO definition in audiology was recently reviewed by Stephens and Kerr (2000).

PSYCHOLOGICAL TREATMENT PERSPECTIVES REGARDING HEARING LOSS

From a psychological point of view, much of the emphasis within a clinical setting has been on providing a psychotherapeutic response to the emotional consequences of hearing loss. In the first instance an emphasis is often placed on working through a grief process; however, the scarcity of services means that most people in this position do not see a psychologist. In a well-provided service they will receive practical support and counselling from a hearing therapist but most people will not have their psychological needs identified or met in this respect. In reality it is only when a patient suffers more enduring psychological distress that a referral to a psychologist is made. In such cases the problems persist usually because the patient holds overly negative beliefs about the implications of the loss with the result that the adjustment process is interrupted. Usually a cognitive therapy (Beck, 1976) approach is taken in such situations. Moorey (1996) discussed the use of cognitive therapy in adverse life circumstances. Hearing loss, like many other physical symptoms, can be associated with beliefs that, although negative, are not necessarily irrational. For example, a belief such as "I can no longer hear well" is accurate. Similarly, negative beliefs about the consequences of hearing loss such as "people think that if you are deaf (popular misuse of terms) you are stupid" may be at least partially accurate. As Moorey (1996) pointed out, however, patients can over-generalise the implications of illness; this is as true for people with hearing loss as it is for people with life-threatening problems. Apparently accurate beliefs that hearing impairment makes some things more difficult or that some people hold prejudiced attitudes about hearing impairment can form the basis for ideas such as "I cannot do anything I like any more" or "no one will accept me".

A behavioural perspective to the management of people with hearing loss has also been suggested. McKenna (1987) described a behavioural approach to audiological rehabilitation based on goal-planning principles. Within an auditory rehabilitation setting it is important to identify the patient's listening or communication strategies and to determine the factors that influence these behaviours. It is recommended that clear behavioural language is used to describe the patient's needs. For example, rather than having a vague objective for a patient, such as "better communication", specific goals may be stated such as "he needs to tell people how to talk to him". Similarly, the things that each person involved in the rehabilitation programme will do are clearly specified. For example, the patient and his wife will spend 20 minutes each day talking, in a quiet environment, while the patient wears his hearing aid. Goals are broken down into achievable steps. An emphasis is placed on abilities rather than disabilities and positive language is used, e.g. "the patient needs to practise relaxation techniques" rather than "he cannot relax". Goal-planning is a means of stating what should be achieved but does not dictate the method of intervention.

A cognitive-behavioural approach to the management of hearing loss in elderly people has been described in a series of studies by Andersson and colleagues (Andersson, Green & Melin, 1997; Andersson et al., 1994, 1995a, 1995b). These have focused on the use of hearing tactics, i.e. the methods used by hearing-impaired people to solve the everyday hearing problems. Examples of good hearing tactics are ensuring that the hearing-impaired person is face to face with the speaker, that light is shining on the speaker's face, and that he or she speaks slowly and clearly and does not shout. Individualised treatment goals are set and behavioural tasks and communication strategies are devised to help to achieve these. Strategies used include the rehearsal of tactics, and teaching relaxation and coping skills. Andersson and coworkers found that patients treated in this way were better able to cope with their hearing loss. They concluded that disability resulting from hearing impairment could be regarded as a behavioural problem and that this behaviour can be the central focus of rehabilitation. They suggested that cognitive, and especially motivational, factors are of central importance in the way hearing disability is viewed. Their work supports the application of Johnson's (1996) ideas about disability in this context. Recently the work on hearing tactics was reconsidered in the light of coping research. In a review, Andersson and Willebrand (in press) suggested that some of the effects of hearing tactics may have more to do with changes in appraisal than the actual practice of hearing tactics. Moreover, they concluded that coping research has yet to be fully applied in research on hearing loss, as the concept of coping has been used as equivalent to communication strategies, or distress in relation to communication failure. This should be contrasted with the more complex concept of coping endorsed by health psychologists (Lazarus, 1993).

AUDIOLOGICAL ASPECTS OF TINNITUS

Tinnitus has been remarked upon from the beginnings of medicine, and indeed receives six mentions in the writings of Hippocrates. The word tinnitus, which derives from the Latin *tinnire* (to ring), is first recorded in use in 1693 in Blanchard's *Physician's Dictionary*, as follows:

"Tinnitus Aurium, a certain buzzing or tingling in the Ears proceeding from obstruction, or something that irritates the Ear, whereby the Air that is shut up is continually moved the beating of the Arteries, and the Drume of the Ear is lightly verberated, whences arises a Buzzing and a Noife" (p. 201).

In an attempt at a more modern and scientific definition, McFadden (1982) considered that: "Tinnitus is the conscious expression of a sound that originates in an involuntary manner in the head of its owner, or may appear to him to do so." This definition has been widely adopted (e.g. Coles, 1987; Davis & Rafaie, 2000; Stephens, 2000). This definition includes such somatosounds as pulsatile tinnitus caused by blood flow, or awareness of breathing sounds. It is possible to classify somatosounds differently from tinnitus without a mechanical cause; however the management of these sounds is likely to be similar to pure tinnitus.

There have been many attempts to determine the prevalence of tinnitus, but the most robust and comprehensive has been undertaken by the MRC Institute of Hearing Research and reported by Davis and Rafaie (2000). In this study, questions about tinnitus were incorporated in a longitudinal study of hearing ($n = 48\,313$), and 10.1% of adults were found to have experienced prolonged (>5 minutes) spontaneous tinnitus, and in 5% of the adult population this was reported to be moderately or severely annoying. In 0.5% tinnitus was said to have a severe effect upon their ability to lead a normal life.

It may be assumed by the reader that these experiences are intimately associated with cochlear dysfunction, but there is evidence that this may not be the case. Heller and Bergman (1953) undertook an interesting experiment, and their study is often cited. Eighty adults (age range 18–60) with "apparently normal hearing" and in whom no tinnitus experience was reported were asked to sit in a "sound proof chamber" for approximately five minutes, and to write a note of any sounds heard. The results were that: "Audible tinnitus was experienced by 94% of the apparently normal hearing adults." The inference made was that: "Tinnitus, which is sub-audible, may be a physiological phenomenon in an intact auditory apparatus"; thus the presence of perceived tinnitus in an individual does not mean that they are necessarily suffering from ear disease. This conclusion is probably correct although it has been difficult to replicate this finding. For example, in a replication, Levine (2001) found that 55% of normal hearing subjects reported tinnitus. This is, of course, also a remarkably high figure, but not as dramatic as in the study by Heller and Bergman. In addition, Davis and Rafaie (2000) found that while in the large epidemiological study described above there were indications that increased age, and particularly high-frequency hearing thresholds, were predictors of tinnitus experience, many individuals reported troublesome tinnitus who did not have hearing loss.

Observations such as these have led to a move away from models of tinnitus that focus on the cochlea to an understanding that places greater emphasis on central processes. The neurophysiological model of tinnitus (Jastreboff, 1990; Jastreboff & Hazell, 1993) suggests that tinnitus may originate from a pathological lesion in the auditory pathway, or may arise by abnormal perception of normal background activity in the auditory system. Normally, neural filtering networks in the brainstem suppress such signals. It is suggested that tinnitus distress comes about because a neutral tinnitus signal becomes associated with an unpleasant event or other emotionally arousing circumstance and so comes to evoke the same emotional reaction as that event. This process is said to involve classical conditioning and the distress is the result of a conditioned physiological reflex arc. The normal filtering fails, allowing the tinnitus signal to be perceived at a cortical level and limbic system and autonomic nervous processes are activated. It is suggested that these processes increase the sensitivity of the auditory system to that tinnitus signal, producing a positive feedback loop. Although this model is referred to as "neurophysiological" it is not free from the philosophical and theoretical underpinnings of psychology and it will be discussed further below.

MEDICAL AND AUDIOLOGICAL TREATMENT APPROACHES TO TINNITUS

A number of medical and surgical approaches have been taken to the management of tinnitus, but have very largely proven ineffective (Dobie, 1999). Where tinnitus is found to be a symptom of ear disease, surgery may be undertaken for that condition, but will rarely result in improvement in tinnitus. Hopes for a pharmacological treatment for tinnitus were raised by the discovery that the intravenous infusion of lignocaine reduced tinnitus intensity in two-thirds of subjects (Martin & Colman, 1980). The failure, however, of other sodium-channel blocking agents and lignocaine-analogues means that these hopes remain unfulfilled to date (Dobie, 1999). In practice, the most commonly used medicines are antidepressants and sleeping pills for the management of the distress associated with tinnitus.

The traditional audiological approach to the management of tinnitus has been to use external noise to obscure or otherwise alleviate it (Vernon & Meikle, 2000). This is usually achieved through the use of a tinnitus masker, a device resembling a hearing aid that emits a noise, often a broad spectrum noise, into the patient's ear. Tinnitus masking produced some symptomatic relief while the masking was in place but rarely had any more enduring benefits. Today, masking is not recommended as it is thought to be counterproductive in the long term and instead an emphasis is placed on using sound at a level just below that of the tinnitus to reduce the impact of the tinnitus. It has been suggested that such *sound enrichment* serves to disrupt neuronal networks that process tinnitus information (Jastreboff & Hazel, 1993). Sound enrichment is often achieved by the use of a noise generator (i.e. a masker used at an intensity below that of the tinnitus) but for some people it is achieved simply through the use of low-level background noise. Efforts are usually also made to reassure the patient that tinnitus is benign. The evidence in support of this approach is still emerging, but to date there is no compelling evidence for the efficacy of sound therapy alone (Kröner-Herwig et al., 2000).

PSYCHOLOGICAL ASPECTS OF TINNITUS

Tinnitus is associated with a variety of negative consequences (e.g. Fowler, 1948; Hallam, 1989; Hallam, Jakes & Hinchcliffe, 1988; Hallam, Rachman & Hinchcliffe, 1984; Tyler & Baker, 1983) such as sleep disturbance, emotional disturbance, concentration problems, as well as auditory perceptual disorders such as interference with hearing or sensitivity to noise. Evidence is now emerging that children's experiences of tinnitus parallel that of adults but expressed in age-appropriate terms; sleep disturbance seems to be the main issue in children (Kentish, Crocker & McKenna, 2000). The link between tinnitus and emotional distress has been investigated in several studies (Collet et al., 1990; Halford & Anderson, 1991; Harrop-Griffiths et al., 1987; Kirsch, Blanchard & Parnes, 1989; McKenna, Hallam & Hinchcliffe, 1991; Simpson et al., 1988; Stephens & Hallam, 1985; Wood et al., 1983). For example, McKenna, Hallam and Hinchcliffe (1991) reported that 45% of those attending hospital with tinnitus as a main complaint showed signs of significant psychological disturbance. Simpson et al. (1988) found that 63% of tinnitus sufferers could be classified as psychiatrically disturbed and 46% had mood disorder as assessed by the Structured Interview for the DSM-III-R (SCID). Some studies have suggested a link between problematic tinnitus and depression (Hinchcliffe & King, 1992; Wilson et al., 1991) while others have highlighted the importance of anxiety, particularly trait anxiety (McKenna & Hallam, 1999; McKenna, Hallam & Shurlock, 1995). Erlandsson (1990) theorised that there are two psychological reactions to tinnitus; one characterised by anxiety and one by depression but these thoughts have not yet been validated empirically. The authors' clinical experience suggests that tinnitus distress is associated with autonomic arousal either in the form of anxiety or agitated depression. There is a popular idea, held by many patients and professionals, that tinnitus acts as a trigger for suicide. There is no good evidence to support this idea. Only a few studies have been conducted on this subject (Johnson & Walker, 1996; Lewis, Stephens & Huws, 1992; Lewis, Stephens & McKenna, 1994) and these have been post mortem in nature. The conclusion that these permit is that those tinnitus patients who committed suicide were at high risk of suicide anyway but that tinnitus probably acts as an additional stressor, particularly in the first two years after onset.

It should be noted, however, that most studies on the emotional consequences of tinnitus have been conducted on highly selective samples of patients with severe tinnitus distress (e.g. Briner et al., 1990) and the conclusions drawn may not apply to all tinnitus patients, let alone all people with tinnitus. It is important to note that there are large individual differences in the extent to which people experience these problems. Indeed, the epidemiology of tinnitus indicates that a minority of people who experience tinnitus are distressed by it (Davis & Rafaie, 2000). Even among those who do complain about tinnitus there is variation in the extent to which other problems are present. For example, McKenna (2000) suggests that no more than about 50% of patients seen in a tinnitus clinic suffer from sleep problems. As with hearing impairment, psycho-acoustic measures (e.g. matching of tinnitus loudness) have not been found to be good predictors of tinnitus discomfort (Dobie, 1999). A simple biological model of tinnitus is therefore inadequate and any model must take account of psychological factors.

The most significant contribution from psychologists within this field was Hallam, Rachman and Hinchcliffe's (1984) model of tinnitus. The authors suggested that the natural history of tinnitus is characterised by the process of habituation and that distress associated with tinnitus represents a failure of habituation. They suggested that habituation to tinnitus follows the same rules as habituation to any other constant stimulus. Habituation is slowed by factors such as a high level of tonic arousal and by the tinnitus acquiring an emotive significance. These authors cited epidemiological data in support of their argument. They noted the lack of relationship between tinnitus complaint and perceived loudness, and pointed to a study by Tyler and Baker (1983) that reported a diminishing range, and intensity, of problems associated with tinnitus the longer that tinnitus had been present. As further evidence they pointed to the observations that people complaining of tinnitus tend to be more persistently aware of it than people who do not complain, and with time, people change from presenting with tinnitus as a main complaint among audiological symptoms to reporting it among the other symptoms. As further support for their model the authors also cited anecdotal clinical evidence that tinnitus patients do acquire tolerance and that this tolerance is reduced by stress. This original model has, however, been challenged (Carlsson & Erlandsson, 1991). Dishabituation may be another way of describing the process of developing tinnitus-related distress (Baltissen & Boucsein, 1986), however there is relatively little evidence to support these other approaches, and Hallam, Rachman and Hinchcliffe's (1984) model remains the main inspiration for clinical work.

The phantom nature of tinnitus as a symptom presents clinicians and researchers with a challenge when it comes to measurement or assessment. A number of self-report scales for the assessment of tinnitus-related distress have been developed, such as the Tinnitus Questionnaire (Hallam, 1996), the Tinnitus Handicap Inventory (Newman, Jacobson & Spitzer, 1996; Newman, Sandridge & Jacobson, 1998) and the Tinnitus Reaction Questionnaire (Wilson et al., 1991). Most of these scales have good psychometric properties. The Tinnitus Questionnaire has British normative data; it has also been adapted for use in Germany and Sweden (Andersson, 1996; Hiller & Goebel, 1992). The usefulness of these scales within both clinical and research contexts has been recognised and recommended (Baguley, Humphriss & Hodgson, 2000; McCombe et al., 2001). Daily measures of tinnitus distress and loudness on Visual Analogue Scales have been used in clinical and research settings (Lindberg et al., 1989). Other self-report measures, such as the Beck Depression Inventory (Beck, Steer & Brown, 1996), the Beck Anxiety Inventory (Beck & Steer, 1990) and the General Health Questionnaire (Goldberg, 1978), are commonly used in both clinical and research settings. A structured interview has been developed in Uppsala, Sweden, with which all patients referred to the psychologist for tinnitus treatment are assessed. The interview is structured along cognitive-behavioural principles and information is sought about antecedent variables (affecting changes in tinnitus) and consequences (Andersson, Lyttkens & Larsen, 1999). The information gathered then guides the psychological treatment offered.

There has been a focus on central factors in tinnitus perception in recent years and this has led to studies on measures such as evoked potentials (Attias et al., 1993; Colding-Jorgensen et al., 1992), auditory brain-stem responses (Rosenhall & Axelsson, 1995) and PET scanning (Andersson et al., 2000b) in tinnitus patients. It has also led to a small series of studies on a hitherto neglected aspect of tinnitus complaint, viz. concentration problems (McKenna, 1997; McKenna & Hallam, 1999; McKenna, Hallam & Shurlock, 1995). The results of these studies suggest that tinnitus patients do experience some inefficiency in cognitive processing that cannot be accounted for in terms of emotional disturbance. The exact nature of the difficulties experienced is still unclear but a likely possibility is that tinnitus interferes with the performance of mundane tasks more than with high-priority tasks. This work has led to the suggestion that tinnitus can be regarded as a "changing-state" stimulus (e.g. it comes and goes because of masking environmental sound or it is a variable stimulus in itself) (Andersson, Khakpoor & Lyttkens, 2002). This reasoning is influenced by the finding that an auditory stimulus that changes in pitch has the capacity to negatively effect cognitive processing to an equal degree as irrelevant speech (Jones & Macken, 1993). This view of tinnitus provides a possible explanation for patients' complaints of concentration problems, and for why many people do not manage to habituate to tinnitus.

PSYCHOLOGICAL TREATMENT APPROACHES TO TINNITUS

Hallam, Rachman and Hinchcliffe's (1984) model provides the main inspiration for the psychological treatment of tinnitus patients. It suggests that psychological treatment should focus on reducing patients' arousal and changing the emotional significance of the tinnitus, i.e. a cognitive-behaviour therapy (CBT) approach to tinnitus management. This approach to tinnitus management has also been suggested by others (Scott et al., 1985). Other psychological treatments have also been suggested for the management of tinnitus but most, like CBT, are aimed at decreasing the psychological distress associated with tinnitus, rather than lessen the sound itself.

Perhaps the most challenging aspect of Hallam, Rachman and Hinchcliffe's (1984) model is its emphasis on the central role of beliefs in the distress experienced by tinnitus patients. Many patients do not find this an intuitively appealing idea and, as in other clinical health psychology settings, a certain amount of convincing or "socialising" of patients to this model is often needed. As with hearing loss, and many other physical symptoms, tinnitus can be accompanied by negative beliefs that are not necessarily irrational. Beliefs such as "I have tinnitus", "It will never go away", or "I will never hear silence again" are reasonably accurate. Their apparent accuracy can lead people into a therapeutic blind alley. The supposed implications of these beliefs, such as "I will never have peace and quiet again and I will have a nervous breakdown" or "I will never be able to enjoy life again", provide a better focus for therapy. It is common practice to combine the challenging of the latter type of beliefs with education about the natural course of tinnitus. One of the most common experiences of new tinnitus patients is being told by a doctor: "This is tinnitus and you must learn to live with it." The patient has usually consulted the doctor in a state of understandable apprehension about the onset of the new symptom and often interprets the doctor's words as suggesting that he or she must learn to live with feeling as bad as they do at that moment. A failure to identify and distinguish irrational beliefs from accurate ones can lead an adjustment reaction to turn to anxiety. An account of CBT management of tinnitus has been prepared by Henry and Wilson (2001).

The effects of psychological treatment have been reviewed, and most recently in a meta-analysis (Andersson & Lyttkens, 1999). Overall, the effects are well established and while the strongest effects have been found immediately following treatment, there is evidence that positive treatment effects are maintained at follow-up. The effects, however, are mostly seen with regard to tinnitus annoyance and to a lesser extent on the perceived loudness of tinnitus. One of the most recent outcome studies is that reported by Henry and Wilson (1999). They reported that 74% of their tinnitus patients benefited from CBT; the success criteria was a reduction in score of at least 50% on their tinnitus complaint questionnaire and with the final score representing no more than mild distress. In another recent study, self-help treatment via the Internet was evaluated. Results showed that tinnitus-related distress, depression, and diary ratings of annoyance caused by tinnitus decreased significantly. Effects on reduced tinnitus annoyance were found in a one-year follow-up (Andersson et al., 2002).

THE PSYCHOLOGICAL AND NEUROPHYSIOLOGICAL MODELS COMPARED AND CONTRASTED

There are striking parallels between Hallam, Rachman and Hinchcliffe's (1984) model and the more recent neurophysiological model of tinnitus suggested by Jastreboff (1990). Although different language is used, both view habituation as a key process and both highlight the importance of the emotional significance of the tinnitus and of autonomic nervous system arousal; it might be argued that the neurophysiological model owes much to its psychological predecessor. There is, however, an important difference in emphasis between the two models. While the neurophysiological model acknowledges the role of cognitions in tinnitus suffering, it suggests that subconscious classical conditioning is the key process in understanding the production of tinnitus distress. The difference between this and a modern CBT approach is highlighted in the respective treatment implications. The treatment that derives from the neurophysiological model is known as Tinnitus Retraining Therapy (TRT) and involves a combination of counselling and sound enrichment. It is suggested that sound enrichment serves to disrupt neuronal networks that process tinnitus information. The counselling is directive in nature and involves educating the patients about the neurophysiological model and reassuring them of the benign nature of tinnitus. There has been a debate about the relative merits of TRT and CBT. Early papers on the neurophysiological model, which used the terms "directive counselling" and "cognitive therapy" interchangeably, suggested that the intention of the directive counselling process is to change patients' beliefs about their tinnitus (Jastreboff, 1990; Jastreboff & Hazell, 1993). Psychologists (Wilson et al., 1998) have, however, suggested that directive counselling does not equate with cognitive therapy as it does not meet the rigorous standards and protocols of that therapy. Jastreboff (1999a) also sought to highlight differences between TRT and cognitive therapy but the distinctions suggested are far from clear. The proponents of the neurophysiological model (Jastreboff, 1999a, 1999b) asserted that lasting benefit cannot be achieved through the use of a cognitive approach and that passive extinction of the subconscious conditioned response is required. The evidence, to date, does not support this contention. A number of methodological difficulties with TRT studies have been highlighted by Wilson et al. (1998) and it is not yet clear that the benefits of TRT extend beyond those that might be offered by directive counselling alone. Thus there is no case for suggesting that TRT is superior to a CBT approach and the latter remains an essential therapeutic approach.

CONCLUSIONS

A biopsychosocial model is required for an adequate understanding of tinnitus and hearing loss. Whether or not hearing loss or tinnitus are problematic is dependent as much, if not more, on psychological factors as on physical ones. People's responses to tinnitus and to hearing loss are not always easily predictable. They depend on cognitive, behavioural and social influences as well as the changes in acoustic ability. An approach to auditory rehabilitation that focuses only on an attempt to alter acoustic input runs the risk of ignoring fundamental aspects of the experience and therefore faces the prospect of only limited success. This was recognised almost 20 years ago when Goldstein and Stephens (1981) recommended that aural rehabilitation should address psychological factors. Since then our understanding of the issues involved has improved and the argument for the involvement of clinical health psychologists in this field becomes all the more persuasive. The future direction for psychology within the field of hearing loss may be in manipulating the determinants of disability as much as in moderating the handicap. Psychological treatment of tinnitus is now well established in major centres. There is, however, a need for these treatments to be refined so that they become efficacious across a wider spectrum of tinnitus complaint. For example, the efficacy of psychological treatments on tinnitus-related insomnia is limited, and not well studied (McKenna, 2000). To date, the treatment strategies have not specifically addressed sleep disturbance and it seems likely that psychological treatments that specifically tackle insomnia may lead to greater success. Given the limited success that psychological treatments have had on auditory perceptual aspects of tinnitus complaint, it may be that this is another area in which a refinement of treatment approaches would lead to greater success. The greater understanding of tinnitus complaint that psychologists have developed in recent years, including the difficulties in concentration associated with tinnitus, may lead to a more sophisticated and more useful cognitive model of tinnitus.

In summary, ongoing research in this area deals with many different aspects closely related to clinical health psychology. For example, intensive research efforts are devoted to developing suitable self-report inventories, often informed by psychological research on personality and psychometrics. Next, cognitive processing issues in tinnitus are being investigated in the form of experimental and clinical work. While this has been investigated more deeply in the area of hearing impairment (for example, lip-reading), some research on cognitive bias in tinnitus patients has begun to emerge (Andersson, Ingerholt & Jansson, in press). Finally, treatment research is conducted on hearing loss and tinnitus. This is often, but not always, done within a cognitive-behavioural framework.

There are, however, many things left to study. For example, there is only one study on the role of the family members and adult attachment when coping with tinnitus (Granqvist et al., 2001). Several other concepts from psychology could be applied in the study of hearing loss and tinnitus. This includes the role of "lay theories" (e.g. Furnham & Thomson, 1996) for how hearing-impaired persons are perceived by people without hearing loss. Aural rehabilitation has long struggled with compliance issues (for example, use of hearing aids), and the relevance of the stages-of-change model for behaviour change could be studied (Prochaska, DiClemente & Norcross, 1992). As mentioned, studies on cognitive processing in tinnitus patients are being conducted (e.g. Andersson et al., 2000a), but the field of tinnitus research lags far behind the knowledge on cognitive processing bias in the field of chronic pain (Pincus & Morley, 2001). In conclusion, there is a great potential for clinical health psychology to make a lasting contribution to audiology. By necessity, this is a multidisciplinary task and it is hoped that future generations of clinical health psychologists take on this challenge.

REFERENCES

Andersson, G. (1995). *Hearing as behaviour. Psychological aspects of acquired hearing impairment in the elderly.* Doctoral dissertation. Uppsala: Acta Universitas Upsaliensis.

Andersson, G. (1996). The role of optimism in patients with tinnitus and in patients with hearing impairment. *Psychology and Health*, **11**, 697–707.

Andersson, G. & Lyttkens, L. (1999). A meta-analytic review of psychological treatments for tinnitus. *British Journal of Audiology*, **33**, 201–210.

Andersson, G. & Willebrand, M. (in press). What is coping? A critical review of the construct and its application in audiology. *International Journal of Audiology*.

Andersson, G., Green, M. & Melin, L. (1997). Behavioural hearing tactics: a controlled trial of a short treatment programme. *Behavior Research and Therapy*, **35**, 523–530.

Andersson, G., Ingerholt, C. & Jansson, M. (in press). Autobiographical memory in patients with tinnitus. *Psychology and Health*.

Andersson, G., Khakpoor, A. & Lyttkens, L. (2002). Masking of tinnitus and mental activity. *Clinical Otolaryngology*, **27**, 270–274.

Andersson, G., Lyttkens, L. & Larsen, H.C. (1999). Distinguishing levels of tinnitus distress. *Clinical Otolaryngology*, **24**, 404–410.

Andersson, G., Eriksson, J., Lundh, L.-G. & Lyttkens, L. (2000a). Tinnitus and cognitive interference: a Stroop paradigm study. *Journal of Speech, Hearing, and Language Research*, **43**, 1168–1173.

Andersson, G., Lyttkens, L., Hirvela, C., Furmark, T., Tillfors, M. & Fredrikson, M. (2000b). Regional cerebral blood flow during tinnitus: a PET case study with lidocaine and auditory stimulation. *Acta Otolaryngology*, **120** (8), 967–972.

Andersson, G., Melin, L., Scott, B. & Lindberg, P. (1994). Behavioural counselling for subjects with acquired hearing loss. A new approach to hearing tactics. *Scandanavian Audiology*, **23**, 249–256.

Andersson, G., Melin, L., Scott, B. & Lindberg, P. (1995a). A two-year follow-up examination of a behavioural treatment approach to hearing tactics. *British Journal of Audiology*, **29**, 347–354.

Andersson, G., Melin, L., Scott, B. & Lindberg, P. (1995b). An evaluation of a behavioural treatment approach to hearing impairment. *Behavior Research and Therapy*, **33**, 283–292.

Andersson, G., Strömgren, T., Ström, T. & Lyttkens, L. (2002). Randomised controlled trial of Internet based cognitive behavior therapy for distress associated with tinnitus. *Psychosomatic Medicine*, **64**, 810–816.

Arnold, P. (1998). Is there still a consensus on impairment, disability and handicap in audiology? *British Journal of Audiology*, **32**, 265–271.

Asmundson, G.J.G., Larsen, D.K. & Stein, M.B. (1998). Panic disorder and vestibular disturbance: an overview of empirical findings and clinical implications. *Journal of Psychosomatic Research*, **44**, 107–120.

Attias, J., Urbach, D., Gold, S. & Sheemesh, Z. (1993). Auditory event related potentials in chronic tinnitus patients with noise induced hearing loss. *Hearing Research*, **71**, 106–113.

Azjen, I. (1988). *Attitudes, Personality and Behaviour*. Milton Keynes: Open University Press.

Baguley, D., Humphriss, R.L. & Hodgson, C.A. (2000). Convergent validity of the tinnitus handicap inventory and the tinnitus questionnaire. *Journal of Laryngology Otology*, **114** (11), 840–843.

Baltissen, R. & Boucsein, W. (1986). Effects of a warning signal on reactions to aversive white noise stimulation: does warning "short-circuit" habituation? *Psychophysiology*, **23**, 224–231.

Barrell, R.A. (Ed.) (1980). *The French Correspondence of the 4th Earl of Chesterfield* (vol. I, p. 108; trans. James Gray). Ottawa: Borealis Press.

Baumfield, A. & Dillon, H. (2001). Factors affecting the use and perceived benefit of ITE and BTE hearing aids. *British Journal of Audiology*, **35** (4), 247–258.

Beck, A. (1976). *Cognitive Therapy and the Emotional Disorders*. Madison, CT: International Universities Press.

Beck, A. & Steer, R. (1990). *Manual of the Beck Anxiety Inventory*. The Psychology Corporation. San Antonio: Harcourt Brace & Company.

Beck, A., Steer, R. & Brown, G. (1996). *Manual of the Beck Depression Inventory* (2nd edn). The Psychology Corporation. San Antonio: Harcourt Brace & Company.

Blanchard (1693). *Physician's Dictionary* (2nd edn). London.

Briner, W., Risey, J., Guth, P. & Noris, C. (1990). Use of the million clinical multiaxial inventory in evaluating patients with severe tinnitus. *American Journal of Otolaryngology*, **11**, 334–337.

Brooks, D.N. (1985). Factors relating to the under-use of postaural hearing aids. *British Journal of Audiology*, **19** (3), 211–217.

Carlsson, S. & Erlandsson, S. (1991). Habituation and tinnitus: an experimental study. *Journal of Psychosomatic Research*, **35**, 509–514.

Colding-Jorgensen, E., Lauritzen, M., Johnsen, N., Mikelsen, K. & Saermark, K. (1992). On the evidence of auditory evoked magnetic fields as objective measures of tinnitus. *Electroencephology and Clinical Neurophysiology*, **83**, 322–327.

Coles, R.R.A. (1987). Tinnitus and its management. In D. Stephens (Ed.), *Adult Audiology, Volume 2, Scott Brown's Otolaryngology* (5th edn). London: Butterworths.

Collet, L., Moussu, M., Disant, F., Ahami, T. & Morgon, A. (1990). Minnesota Multiphasic personality inventory in tinnitus disorders. *Audiology*, **29**, 101–106.

Danhauer, J., Johnson, C.E., Kasten, R. & Brimacombe, J. (1985). The hearing aid effect. Summary, conclusions and recommendations. *Hearing Journal*, **38**, 12–14.

Davis, A.C. (1997). Epidemiology. In D. Stephens (Ed.), *Adult Audiology, Volume 4, Scott Brown's Otolaryngology* (5th edn). London: Butterworths.

Davis, A.C. & Rafaie, E.A. (2000). Epidemiology of tinnitus. In R.S. Tyler (Ed.), *Tinnitus Handbook*. San Diego: Singular.

Dobie, R.A. (1999). A review of randomized controlled trials in tinnitus. *Laryngoscope*, **109**, 1202–1211.

Erlandsson, S. (1990). *Tinnitus: Tolerance or threat? Psychological and psychophysiological perspectives*. Doctoral Thesis. Department of Psychology, University of Goteborg.

Finkelstein, V. (1980). *Attitudes and Disabled People*. New York: World Rehabilitation Fund,.

Finkelstein, V. (1990). "We" are not disabled, "you" are. In S. Gregory & G. Hartley (Eds), *Constructing Deafness* (pp. 265–271). London: Pinter/Milton Keynes: OUP.

Fowler, E. (1948). The emotional factor in tinnitus aurium. *Laryngoscope*, **58**, 145–154.

Furnham, A. & Thomson, L. (1996). Lay theories of heroin addiction. *Social Science and Medicine*, **43**, 29–40.

Gilhome Herbst, K. & Humphrey, C. (1980). Hearing impairment and mental state in the elderly living at home. *British Medical Journal*, **281**, 903–905.

Goldberg, D. (1978). *Manual of the General Health Questionnaire*. Slough, UK: National Foundation for Educational Research.

Goldstein, D.P. & Stephens, S.D.G. (1981). Audiological rehabilitation: management model I. *Audiology*, **20**, 432–452.

Granqvist, P., Lantto, S., Ortiz, L. & Andersson, G. (2001). Adult attachment, perceived family support, and problems experienced by tinnitus patients. *Psychology and Health*, **16**, 357–366.

Halford, J. & Anderson, S. (1991). Anxiety and depression in tinnitus sufferers. *Journal of Psychosomatic Research*, **35**, 383–390.

Hallam, R.S. (1989). *Living with Tinnitus: Dealing with the Ringing in Your Ears*. Wellingborough, UK: Thorsons.

Hallam, R.S. (1996). *Manual of the Tinnitus Questionnaire*. The Psychology Corporation. London: Harcourt Brace & Company.

Hallam, R.S., Jakes, S. & Hinchcliffe, R. (1988). Cognitive variables in tinnitus annoyance. *British Journal of Clinical Psychology*, **27**, 213–222.

Hallam, R.S., Rachman, S. & Hinchcliffe, R. (1984). Psychological aspects of tinnitus. In S. Rachman (Ed.), *Contributions to Medical Psychology*, Vol. 3. Oxford: Pergamon Press.

Harrop-Griffiths, J., Katon, W., Dobie, R., Sakai, C. & Russo, J. (1987). Chronic tinnitus: association with psychiatric diagnoses. *Journal of Psychosomatic Research*, **31**, 613–621.

Heller, M.F. & Bergman, M. (1953). Tinnitus in normally hearing persons. *Annals of Otology*, **62**, 73–83.

Henry, J. & Wilson, P. (1999). Cognitive behavioural therapy for tinnitus related distress: an experimental evaluation of initial treatment and relapse prevention. In J. Hazell (Ed.), *Proceedings of the Sixth International Tinnitus Seminar*. Cambridge, UK.

Henry, J.L. & Wilson, P.H. (2001). *Psychological Management of Chronic Tinnitus: A Cognitive-Behavioral Approach*. Boston: Allyn & Bacon.

Hiller, W. & Goebel, G. (1992). A psychometric study of complaints in chronic tinnitus. *Journal of Psychosomatic Research*, **36**, 337–348.

Hinchcliffe, R. & King, P. (1992). Medicolegal aspects of tinnitus. 1: Medicolegal position and current state of knowledge. *Journal of Audiological Medicine*, **1**, 38–58.

Ingalls, G. (1946). Some psychiatric observations on patients with hearing deficit. *Occupational Therapy and Rehabilitation*, **25**, 62–66.

Jastreboff, M. (1999a). Controversies between cognitive therapies and TRT counselling. In J. Hazell (Ed.), *Proceedings of the Sixth International Tinnitus Seminar*. Cambridge, UK: The Tinnitus and Hyperacusis Centre.

Jastreboff, P. (1990). Phantom auditory perception (tinnitus): mechanisms of generation and perception. *Neuroscience Research*, **8**, 221–254.

Jastreboff, P. (1999b). The neurophysiological model of tinnitus and hyperacusis. In J. Hazell (Ed.), *Proceedings of the Sixth International Tinnitus Seminar*. Cambridge, UK: The Tinnitus and Hyperacusis Centre.

Jastreboff, P. & Hazell, J. (1993). A neurophysiological approach to tinnitus: clinical implications. *British Journal of Audiology*, **27**, 7–17.

Johnson, M. (1996). Models of disability. *The Psychologist*, May, 205–210.

Johnson, M. & Walker, M. (1996). Suicide in the elderly: recognising the signs. *General Hospital Psychiatry*, **18**, 257–260.

Jones, D. & Macken, W. (1993). Irrelevant tones produce an irrelevant speech effect. *Journal of Experimental Psychology, Learning, Memory, and Cognition*, **19**, 369–381.

Jones, E. & White, A.J. (1990). Mental health and acquired hearing impairment. A review. *British Journal of Audiology*, **24**, 3–9.

Kentish, R., Crocker, S. & McKenna, L. (2000). Children's experiences of tinnitus: a preliminary survey of children presenting to a psychology department. *British Journal of Audiology*, **34**, 335–340.

Kerr, P. & Cowie, R. (1997). Acquired deafness: a multidimensional experience. *British Journal of Audiology*, **31**, 177–188.

Kirsch, C., Blanchard, E. & Parnes, S. (1989). Psychological characteristics of individuals high and low in their ability to cope with tinnitus. *Psychosomatic Medicine*, **51**, 209–217.

Klockhoff, I. & Lindblom, U. (1967). Menière's disease and hydrochlorothiazide (Dichlotride®)—a critical analysis of symptoms and therapeutic effects. *Acta Otolaryngology (Stockholm)*, **63**, 347–365.

Knapp, P. (1948). Emotional aspects of hearing loss. *Psychosomatic Medicine*, **10**, 203–222.

Kreeger, J.L., Raulin, M.L., Grace, J. & Priest, B.L. (1995). Effect of hearing enhancement on mental status ratings in geriatric psychiatric patients. *American Journal of Psychiatry*, **152**, 629–631.

Kröner-Herwig, B., Biesinger, E., Goebel, G., Greimel, K.V. & Hiller, W. (2000). Retraining therapy for chronic tinnitus. *Scandinavian Audiology*, **29**, 67–78.

Lazarus, R.S. (1993). Coping theory and research: past, present, and future. *Psychosomatic Medicine*, **55**, 234–247.

Levine, R.A. (2001). Diagnostic issues in tinnitus: a neuro-otological perspective. *Seminars in Hearing*, **22**, 23–36.

Lewis, J., Stephens, S.D.G. & Huws, D. (1992). Suicide in tinnitus sufferers. *Journal of Audiological Medicine*, **1**, 30–37.

Lewis, J., Stephens, S.D.G. & McKenna, L. (1994). Tinnitus and suicide. *Clinical Otolaryngology*, **19**, 50–54.

Lindberg, P., Scott, B., Melin, L. & Lyttkens, L. (1989). The psychological treatment of tinnitus: an experimental evaluation. *Behaviour Research and Therapy*, **27**, 593–603.

McCombe, A., Baguley, D., Coles, R., McKenna, L., McKinney, C. & Windle-Taylor, P. (2001). Guidelines for the grading of tinnitus severity: the results of a working group commissioned by the British Association of Otolaryngologists, Head and Neck Surgeons, 1999. *Clinical Otolaryngology*, **26**, 388–393.

McFadden, D. (1982). *Tinnitus: Facts, Theories and Treatments*. Report of Working Group89, Committee on Hearing Bioacoustics and Biomechanics. National Research Council National Academy Press, Washington, DC.

McKenna, L. (1986). The psychological assessment of cochlear implant patients. *British Journal of Audiology*, **20**, 29–34.

McKenna, L. (1987). Goal planning in audiological rehabilitation. *British Journal of Audiology*, **21**, 5–11.

McKenna, L. (1997). *Audiological disorders: Psychological state and cognitive functioning*. Unpublished doctoral thesis, The City University, London, UK.

McKenna, L. (2000). Insomnia and tinnitus. In R. Tyler (Ed.), *Tinnitus Handbook*. San Diego: Singular.

McKenna, L. & Denman, C. (1993). Repertory grid technique in the assessment of cochlear implant patients. *Journal of Audiological Medicine*, **2**, 75–84.

McKenna, L. & Hallam, R. (1999). Concentration problems in tinnitus patients: a neuropsychological study. In J. Hazell (Ed.), *Proceedings of the Sixth International Tinnitus Seminar*. Cambridge, UK: The Tinnitus and Hyperacusis Centre.

McKenna, L., Hallam, R.S. & Hinchcliffe, R. (1991). The prevalence of psychological disturbance in neuro-otology outpatients. *Clinical Otolaryngology*, **16**, 452–456.

McKenna, L., Hallam, R. & Shurlock, L. (1995). Cognitive functioning in tinnitus patients. In G. Reich (Ed.), *Proceedings of the Fifth International Tinnitus Seminar*. Portland, USA.

Mahapatra, S. (1974). Deafness and mental health: psychiatric and psychosomatic illness in the deaf. *Acta Psychiatrica Scandinavica*, **50**, 596–611.

Martin, F.W. & Colman, B.H. (1980). Tinnitus: a double blind cross over controlled trial to evaluate the use of lignocaine. *Clinical Otolaryngology*, **5**, 3–11.

Meric, C., Gartner, M., Collet, L. & Chéry-Croze, S. (1998). Psychopathological profile of tinnitus sufferers: evidence concerning the relationship between tinnitus features and impact on life. *Audiology and Neuro-otology*, **3**, 240–252.

Moorey, S. (1996). When bad things happen to rational people: cognitive therapy in adverse life circumstances. In P. Salkovskis (Ed.), *Frontiers of Cognitive Therapy*. New York: Guilford Press.

Newman, C., Jacobson, G. & Spitzer, J. (1996). Development of the Tinnitus Handicap Inventory. *Archives of Otolaryngology, Hear and Neck Surgery*, **122**, 143–148.

Newman, C., Sandridge, S. & Jacobson, G. (1998). Psychometric adequacy of the Tinnitus Handicap Inventory (THI) for evaluating treatment outcome. *Journal of the American Academy of Audiology*, **9**, 153–160.

Pincus, T. & Morley, S. (2001). Cognitive-processing bias in chronic pain: a review and integration. *Psychological Bulletin*, **127**, 599–617.

Prochaska, J.O., DiClemente, C.C. & Norcross, J.C. (1992). In search of how people change. Applications to addictive behaviors. *American Psychologist*, **47**, 1102–1114.

Rosenhall, U. & Axelsson, A. (1995). Auditory brainstem response latencies in patients with tinnitus. *Scandinavian Audiology*, **24**, 97–100.

Scott, B., Lindberg, P., Melin, L. & Lyttkens, L. (1985). Psychological treatment of tinnitus. An experimental group study. *Scandinavian Audiology*, **14**, 223–230.

Singerman, B., Reidner, E. & Folstein, M. (1980). Emotional disturbance in hearing clinic patients. *British Journal of Psychiatry*, **137**, 58–62.

Simpson, R., Nedzelski, J., Barber, H. & Thomas, M. (1988). Psychiatric diagnoses in patients with psychogenic dizziness or severe tinnitus. *Journal of Otolaryngology*, **17**, 325–330.

Skinner, B.F. (1957). *Verbal Behavior*. New York: Appleton-Century-Crofts, Inc.

Skinner, B.F. & Vaughan, M.E. (1983). *Enjoy Old Age. A Program for Self-management*. London: Hutchinson.

Stephens, S.D.G. (2000). A history of tinnitus. In R.S. Tyler (Ed.), *Tinnitus Handbook*. San Diego: Singular.

Stephens, S.D.G. & Hallam, R. (1985). The Crown Crisp experiential index in patients complaining of tinnitus. *British Journal of Audiology*, **19**, 151–158.

Stephens, S.D.G. & Hetu, R. (1991). Impairment, disability and handicap in audiology: towards a consensus. *Audiology*, **30**, 185–200.

Stephens, S.D.G. & Kerr, P. (2000). Auditory displacements: an update. *Audiology*, **39**, 322–332.

Thomas, A. & Gilhome Herbst, K. (1980). Social and psychological implications of acquired deafness for adults of employment age. *British Journal of Audiology*, **14**, 76–85.

Tyler, R. & Baker, L. (1983). Difficulties experienced by tinnitus sufferers. *Journal of Speech and Hearing Disorders*, **48**, 150–154.

Vernon, J.A. & Meikle, M.B. (2000). Tinnitus masking. In R.S. Tyler (Ed.), *Tinnitus Handbook*. San Diego: Singular. Thomson Learning.

Wilson, P.H., Henry, J.L., Andersson, G., Hallam, R.S. & Lindberg, P. (1998). A critical analysis of directive counselling as a component of tinnitus retraining therapy. *British Journal of Audiology*, **32**, 273–286.

Wilson, P.H., Henry, J.L., Bowen, M. & Haralambous, G. (1991). Tinnitus reaction questionnaire: psychometric properties of a measure of distress associated with tinnitus. *Journal of Speech and Hearing Research*, **34**, 197–201.

Wood, K., Webb, W., Orchik, D. & Shea, J. (1983). Intractable tinnitus: psychiatric aspects of treat-
    ment. *Psychosomatics*, **24**, 559–565.
WHO (1980). *International Classification of Impairments, Disabilities, and Handicaps*. Geneva:
    World Health Organisation.
WHO (2000). *International Classification of Functioning, Disability and Health*. Prefinal draft. Full
    version. Geneva: World Health Organisation.

CHAPTER 14

Spinal Cord Injury

Jane Duff
Stoke Mandeville Hospital NHS Trust, Aylesbury, UK
and
Paul Kennedy
University of Oxford, UK

INTRODUCTION

The spinal cord is a long cylindrical structure containing neurons that convey sensory and motor information to and from the brain. The cord is protected by a vertebral column that extends from the brain to the lower back area. The column is composed of 24 individual vertebrae of the cervical, thoracic and lumbar regions, and fused vertebrae that make up the sacral and coccygeal areas. The spinal cord passes through the centre of each vertebra, and injury can occur through a tear, severing, stretching or compression of the cord, and may also include a fracture or dislocation/displacement of the vertebrae. As the cord carries motor and sensory impulses for all areas of the body, injury to the cord and vertebrae can therefore impair motor, bladder, bowel and sexual function below the level of injury.

The degree to which a person's function is impaired depends on the degree of damage to the cord and location (level) of injury. A complete injury of the cord results in complete loss of sensation and voluntary movement below the level of injury, whereas an incomplete injury involves a degree of sensory or motor sparing. There are two forms of measuring completeness, which are largely similar: Frankel Grade (Frankel et al., 1969), and the American Spinal Injuries Association scales (ASIA, 1996). Frankel or ASIA grade A refers to total motor and sensory loss, and both systems rate the degree of loss through to a grade of "no functional deficit" (grade E). Injury in the cervical region of the spinal cord may result in tetraplegia, impairment of neurological function in all four limbs. Injury at this level may also include impairment in function of the diaphragm and there may be a requirement for permanent or intermittent ventilation if the injury is above the level of the fourth cervical vertebra. Injury to the thoracic area and below may result in paraplegia, impairment of function in the lower limbs alone.

Unlike many physical injuries, spinal cord injury (SCI) is a complex, multisystem impairment. Because of this, the treatment and rehabilitation approaches to this injury are not organised around specific body systems, traditional within medical practice, but around the

Handbook of Clinical Health Psychology. Edited by S. Llewelyn and P. Kennedy.
© 2003 John Wiley & Sons, Ltd.

concept of whole system rehabilitation, which requires skills and knowledge from a number of specialities and different professional groups (Thomas, 1995). Rehabilitation and treatment for people who sustain SCI has been developed since the 1940s. Prior to this, 80% of people who sustained a SCI died within the first few weeks of the condition (Guttmann, 1976). The concept of SCI rehabilitation and systematic management of the consequences of injury in terms of skin, bladder and bowel care was pioneered by Sir Ludwig Guttmann in the UK, and developed concurrently in other areas of Europe and in the USA. It was this systematic approach to managing the consequences of injury that increased the survival rates to the extent that life expectancy is now rarely compromised except for the highest levels of injury (DeVivo & Stover, 1995). However, following injury individuals need to develop a regimen of life-long management of skin, bladder and bowel function in order to avoid complications and threat to life. Whiteneck et al. (1992) conducted retrospective research on the mortality and morbidity of 834 individuals who had been injured more than 20 years. They found failure of the genitourinary system (the development of conditions such as renal failure) to be the leading cause of death, followed by cardiovascular problems and then respiratory difficulties. The leading cause of morbidity was found to be pressure sores, followed by bladder infections.

The incidence of SCI in the UK and other European countries is approximately 10–15 per million each year, and approximately 30–40 per million of the population in the USA (Go, DeVivo & Richards, 1995). There is no absolute calculation of the number of persons living with SCI, but in the USA this is thought to be somewhere between 183 000 and 230 000 (Go, DeVivo & Richards, 1995) and approximately 40 000 in the UK. SCI can be sustained through both traumatic and non-traumatic circumstances. In the UK and other European countries, the most common cause of injury is road traffic accidents (approximately 40–50% of injuries), while falls account for approximately 25% of injuries, with sporting injuries, most commonly diving, accounting for 15–20% (Go, DeVivo and Richards, 1995; Grundy & Swain, 1996; Kennedy, 1995). The aetiology of SCI changes across countries and cultures, for example in the USA approximately 16% of injuries occur through acts of violence (predominantly gunshot) (Go, DeVivo & Richards, 1995). Hoque, Grangeon and Reed (1999) conducted an epidemiological study in Bangladesh between 1994 and 1995. They found three main causes of injury: falls from a height, such as a tree, were the most common (43%), 20% of injuries were associated with falling while carrying a heavy load on the head (a common practice in Bangladesh), and 18% of injuries were sustained through a road traffic accident (RTA). Non-traumatic aetiology can include SCI developing during surgery as a consequence of disrupted blood flow to the spinal cord, or following tumour. However, these account for a minority of injuries.

In terms of age, SCI occurs most frequently in those aged 16–30 years (Go, DeVivo & Richards, 1995). However, SCI can occur throughout the life span. At present approximately 24% of all SCIs in the USA are to those over 50 years of age, and 12% are to those aged over 65 years (Whiteneck, 2000). However, there is evidence of an increasing trend of injuries among older adults, in both the USA and Australia, where often a high-level incomplete injury is sustained following a fall (O'Connor, 2000; Whiteneck, 2000). SCI occurs substantially more frequently in males than in females. The Model Systems database in the USA, which records demographic statistics, indicates the male : female proportion to be about 4 : 1, but comments that this proportion is in keeping with the mortality rate due to unintentional injuries in the general population (about three times higher for males than for females aged 15–24 years, and four times higher for the 25–44 age group), because young males are more likely to engage in high-risk activities (Go, DeVivo & Richards, 1995). The Model Systems database also suggests that slightly more people sustain tetraplegia (52.9%) than paraplegia (46.2%), 0.9% experiencing complete neurological recovery at the time of discharge. The most commonly occurring level of injury at discharge is the fifth cervical vertebra (Go, DeVivo & Richards, 1995). Someone of this level of injury is likely to require assistance to dress, transfer from a wheelchair to a bed or car and may require help propelling across carpeted and non-level surfaces (Consortium for Spinal Cord Medicine, 1999).

Although an infrequent occurrence in epidemiological terms, SCI is often substantial in terms of the degree of physiological damage and impairment, and presents a significant challenge to an individual and his or her family's psychological resources. Research has suggested a higher incidence of depression (Frank et al., 1985; Kennedy et al., 2000) and suicide (DeVivo et al., 1991) following SCI in comparison to incidence within the general population. Evidence is only starting to be collated about the exact long-term psychosocial consequences of SCI, but Craig et al. (1990) comment that the incidence of suicide, self-neglect, divorce and drug abuse are an indication that management of the psychological impact of SCI is crucial in relation to long-term adjustment and quality of life.

Understanding the psychological impact of SCI has been considered necessary and important since the early days of systematic rehabilitation (Berger & Garrett, 1952). Historically, adjustment has been viewed as a sequential stage process. Guttmann (1976) proposed the two basic stages: shock and realisation, with patients experiencing anxiety, depression or pain in the latter. Subsequently, Stewart (1977) commented that patients experience a period of denial followed by depression prior to undergoing a "restitution" phase. The number of stages has varied between authors. However, Tucker (1980), in an article summarising much of the stage literature, produced a five-stage model which included phases of severe depression, anger, confusion, withdrawal, followed by acceptance. Tucker considered that patients who experience initial depression are more likely to experience better long-term adjustment, but commented that patients were most commonly "stuck" in the depression or anger stages following injury. In essence such models view adjustment as a linear process, and one in which an individual can fail to proceed adequately. Also implicit is the assumption that depression is an expected part of a "grieving" process and that failure to express depressive symptoms is maladaptive. Siller (1969) suggested that all patients experience depression and are required to do so for adjustment to occur. Indeed failure to experience depression within this model is considered denial. Although depression is considered a stage in most if not all the theories developed, there is a failure to adequately define what is meant by this (Howell et al., 1981).

The development and content of the stage models were largely informed by clinical impression and the bereavement, psychodynamic and personality literature of the time. While useful in terms of describing a number of emotions that may be commonly experienced, empirical research has challenged the three fundamental assumptions of the theories, namely: linearity; the assumption that depression is an inevitable post-injury reaction; and that the primary predictor of response is acquiescence to loss rather than individual characteristics. Frank et al. (1987), in a systematic review of the literature, suggested that individuals vary in their coping style and personal resources prior to injury and that these factors more than any other moderate an individual's psychological response to SCI. Perhaps most significantly they argue that, far from being a necessary process, symptoms of depression may be part of a maladaptive reaction. Frank and Elliott (1987) sought to compare the stage models with a life stress model (Folkman & Lazarus, 1986) by investigating whether passage of time (as suggested by the stage theories) alleviates distress. They found that passage of time did not moderate psychological well-being and suggested that the Folkman and Lazarus's model replace the stage theories as a way of understanding adjustment. Buckelew et al. (1991) further challenged the stage approach by demonstrating the role and importance of individual characteristics upon the adjustment process rather than time since injury per se. Research such as that above led to the demise of stage models as a way of understanding adjustment following SCI, and to the development and research into alternative models formulated on individual response and an understanding about coping process.

Coping models are as much concerned with recognising the types of strategy and approach that facilitate coping, as they are about identifying when coping efforts lead to distress and dysfunction, and as such are a major departure from the tenets of the stage theories. Within coping models, issues such as self-efficacy, previous coping style, locus of control and social support, as well as societal and environmental aspects, are all recognised as influencing an adjustment process. Folkman and Lazarus (1980) conceptualised coping with stress as an individual appraising a condition in terms of a threat or challenge which, in turn, determines the coping effort required. They developed a transactional model of stress which recognised the dynamic nature of the coping process and have defined coping as "the cognitive and behavioural efforts to master, reduce or tolerate the internal and/or external demands that are created by a stressful transaction" (Folkman, 1984). The model considers response to stress to consist of three processes: primary appraisal (in which threat is perceived), secondary appraisal (in which the threat is considered with respect to the resources available to meet the demand, which may be biological, social or psychological) and coping (the execution of a response).

The initial formulation was that coping could be divided into cognitive or behavioural strategies but this was later reformulated to consider the purpose of coping in terms of whether it is problem or emotion focused. A problem-focused strategy is one in which active attempts are made to modify or eliminate the source of stress. Emotion-focused strategies are concerned with the emotional consequences of a stressor and act to manage the stress and maintain equilibrium. Within the model, emotion-focused strategies are particularly important when problems are not amenable to change, making problem-focused strategies less productive or redundant. The model does not therefore identify positive and negative approaches to coping, but rather sees coping as a process. This model has been expanded to include more cognitive components in terms of appraisal of threat and reappraisal, with a recognition that the threat appraisal process is constantly changing during a stressful encounter as a result of changes in the person–environment relationship (Folkman et al., 1991).

Sustaining SCI poses a number of challenges to an individual. Within an adjustment model, the appraisal and meaning attached to such a significant injury influences the emotional impact, and, as a consequence, the adjustment process. The potential threats or challenges are numerous, but may include coping with mobility changes and losses which impact on work or leisure interests, managing threats to self-esteem and sense of self which can result from changed body image or may be the consequences of lifestyle changes necessitated by SCI. By its nature, SCI not only affects the individual, but also impacts upon someone's social network. This can be significantly disrupted immediately following injury when an individual is likely to spend between three and eight months in hospital participating in rehabilitation. The following two sections discuss the emotional and psychological impact of SCI and provide research evidence about the incidence of adverse emotional reactions as well as the factors that facilitate adjustment. The subsequent sections consider a range of interventions, both individual, group and systemic with this client group, including the application of an adjustment model. This chapter concludes with a discussion about issues related to longer-term adjustment and ageing with SCI.

ADJUSTMENT AND EMOTIONAL IMPACT

Depression and Anxiety

Frank et al. (1987) effectively challenged the assumption that depression was an inevitable consequence of SCI. Depression was almost encouraged in rehabilitation settings as a therapeutic prerequisite for optimal adjustment. In contrast, the absence of depression was considered to be unhealthy and suggestive of denial. Elliott and Frank (1996) reviewed the literature and concluded that studies reliant on DSM-III criteria using relatively small samples of recently injured individuals and stringent interview systems have found the rate of major depressive episodes among persons with SCI ranges from 22.7 to over 30%.

Hancock et al. (1993) compared 41 persons with SCI for depression and anxiety with 41 able-bodied controls matched for age, sex and education, and found that approximately one-quarter of the SCI group were anxious compared to less than 5% of the control group, and approximately 25% of the SCI group were depressed compared to around 3% of the control group. However, Elliott and Frank (1996) lamented that no studies had been published on the treatment of depression (this will be presented later) and criticised existing SCI literature for the lack of longitudinal research investigating depression and anxiety. Bracken and Shepard (1980) examined anxiety and depression in SCI over the first four years following injury, but they found only moderate changes over time that were generally in a positive direction. However, the use of one-item questions to measure effective reactions does not provide an empirically sound basis for comparison.

Kennedy and Rogers (2000a) examined the prevalence of anxiety and depression longitudinally in a cohort of 104 patients with SCI. They used a prospective longitudinal multiple wave panel design with measures taken on 14 observational periods. They utilised the Beck Depression Inventory and the State Anxiety Inventory to measure depression and anxiety. The mean scores of anxiety and depression obtained illustrated a specific pattern of mood during the first two years post-injury. In the acute phase of hospital care between the initial week of contact and week 18, there was a modest decrease in scores of anxiety and depression. At week 18 a gradual increase commenced and rose to a peak at week 48, at which time the mean scores were above the clinical cut-off for both the Beck Depression Inventory and the State Anxiety Inventory. However, following discharge, scores decreased notably to within a similar though slightly lower range, as identified in the acute phase of care. Roughly a third of the participants scored above the clinical cut-off for depression and a quarter for anxiety.

Self-report measures such as the Beck Depression Inventory and the State Anxiety Inventory represent a cluster of behaviours that may not directly reflect the diagnosis of depression and anxiety. Symptoms of depression include: low mood and hopelessness;

impaired concentration and attention; increased propensity for negative thinking; increased suicidal ideation; and behavioural symptoms such as impaired sleep, appetite and engagement in self-care activity. Clearly these problems may present increased challenges for those engaged in active rehabilitation and increase vulnerability to secondary conditions such as urinary tract infections (UTIs) and pressure sores. Social barriers such as poor social support and unemployment and physical barriers such as architectural inaccessibility and high levels of fatigue may confound further depressive symptomatology.

Fuhrer et al. (1993) studied such symptomatology in a community-based sample of 140 people with SCI. Using the Center for Epidemiology Studies Depression Scale (CES-D) they concluded that the level of depressive symptomatology for persons with SCI living in the community was higher than for persons in the general population. They also found that the mean score for women was higher than that for men. Furthermore, Krause, Kemp and Coker (2000) found that 48% of a sample of 1391 persons with a traumatic SCI reported clinically significant symptoms of depression. They used the Older Adult Health and Mood Questionnaire and a 22-item measure of depressive symptoms designed following DSM-III-R. They also found that minority participants, particularly women, were at a substantially higher risk for depressive symptoms.

Mood and Coping Strategies

Kennedy et al. (2000) used a longitudinal method to examine the predictive nature of coping strategies on emotional adjustment. Individuals were assessed for coping strategies utilised, functional independence, depression, anxiety and social support. This study produced three major findings. Firstly, psychological outcomes and coping strategies across time were found to be stable. Secondly, high correlations were found between depression, anxiety and a variety of coping strategies coined as maladaptive by previous researchers (Kennedy et al., 1995), including behavioural disengagement, drug and alcohol use ideation and denial. The third finding related to the results of the regression models that were used to predict outcome over a two-year period. These analyses found that coping strategies such as behavioural disengagement, acceptance (negative coefficient), alcohol and drug use ideation accounted for a significant proportion of the variance in depression and anxiety across all assessment periods. Coping strategies at six weeks were also found to predict 67% of the variance in depression at one year.

Reidy, Caplan and Shawaryn (1991) found that depression had a strong positive correlation with escape and avoidance coping strategies. Galvin and Godfrey (2001) concluded that a wide array of literature now exists which supports a stress and coping model of rehabilitation in relation to the management of the consequences of SCI. The stress and coping model and its contribution to the treatment of depression will be described later in this chapter.

PSYCHOLOGICAL ASPECTS

The suicide rate in individuals with SCI is between two and six times greater than that for able-bodied persons (Charlifue & Gerhart, 1991). Suicide is a leading cause of death in individuals with SCI younger than 55 years of age, and 75% of the suicides occur within four to five years post-injury. Although it is acknowledged that depression is linked with increased suicidal ideation, Beck et al. (1985) found that it is actually the degree of hopelessness experienced that is predictive of eventual attempts, rather than depression per se. In a recent study of hopelessness in SCI, Beedie and Kennedy (2002) found that satisfaction with social support was highly predictive of the degree of hopelessness experienced. Support appeared to have an increasing impact on psychological well-being as the individual began to progress through the first few months of their rehabilitation programme.

Heinemann (1995) suggests that certain specific characteristics appear to place people at risk for suicide. These characteristics include pre- and post-injury despondency, a sense of shame, apathy, hopelessness, family disruption before injury, alcohol abuse, active involvement in SCI aetiology and antisocial behaviour. It is also important to acknowledge that death due to septicaemia secondary to infection, or a pressure sore that the patient has left untreated, may be suicide by self-neglect (Hartkopp et al., 1998). As mentioned, direct involvement in the SCI itself may increase an individual's vulnerability.

Kennedy et al. (1999) retrospectively reviewed outcomes when SCI was the result of a suicide attempt. Schizophrenia and depression accounted for almost 60% of the psychiatric illness identified. However, most individuals who sustained SCI secondary to a suicide attempt did not reattempt suicide, but a small proportion did (7.3%). Again, it is imperative to provide appropriate psychiatric and psychological assessment and treatment for those admitted as a result of self-harm.

Substance Abuse

Heinemann (1995) highlights how alcohol and other drug abuse contribute to the onset of SCI by increasing risk-taking among intoxicated individuals, limits rehabilitation gains by impairing learning, and hampers rehabilitation outcomes by contributing to increased morbidity and mortality. O'Donnell et al. (1981–82) reported a 68% rate of self-reported alcohol use at onset of SCI with 68% resuming drinking during hospitalisation. Johnson (1985) reported that vocational rehabilitation and independent living centre clients with SCI exhibited a rate of moderate or heavy drinking that was nearly twice the rate reported in the general population (46% in SCI, 25% general population). Heinemann (1995) concluded that substance use and abuse among SCI persons occurs frequently and may complicate the rehabilitation process as well as limiting long-term outcomes and the capacity for independent living.

Post-traumatic Stress Disorder

Post-traumatic stress disorder (PTSD) may also complicate effective psychological adjustment to SCI. Radnitz et al. (1995) found that 11% of their sample of veterans met the diagnosis for current PTSD, and 29% met the criteria for lifetime PTSD. Despite this research being conducted with veterans, their injury demographics were very similar to that of the general SCI population. Kennedy and Evans (2001) found that high levels of distress were evident in 14% of the sample, and Duff (1997) found a similar level of PTSD following SCI. In a large multicentre study between the United Kingdom and Switzerland,

Lude et al. (2002) found that the incidence of PTSD symptoms was similar to that of previous studies, and lower than levels found following trauma caused by other factors such as road traffic accidents and rape. There was no significant difference between the levels of PTSD in the two countries, and the rates found were comparable to those seen in the Swiss able-bodied population. Lude et al. (2002) also highlighted the role of coping, finding denial, focusing on and venting of emotions, and mental disengagement to be predictive factors in post-traumatic distress.

In relation to children who sustain SCI, 33% of those in Boyer, Tollen and Kafkalas's (1998) study exhibited symptoms that met one diagnostic criteria for PTSD with an additional 19% meeting two of the diagnostic criteria.

Danner and Radnitz (2000) examined the effects of protective factors, including current family structure, level of education and perceived social support on post-traumatic disorder symptomatology in veterans with SCI. They found that the most consistent predictor of PTSD symptomatology was perceived social support from friends. Furthermore, Radnitz, Schlein and Hsu (2000) found that those who had served in a war zone had more difficulty in recovering from PTSD following SCI than non-war veterans.

Acquired Cognitive Impairment

Between 40 and 60% of acute traumatic SCI patients demonstrated cognitive dysfunction resulting from various cerebral damage, including concurrent premorbid closed head injury, chronic alcohol or substance abuse and other causes, according to Roth et al. (1989). In this controlled study, SCI patients were found to have poor attention span, reduced concentration ability, impaired memory function and altered problem-solving ability. Clearly these deficits interfere with the rehabilitation process. It is recommended that some form of routine rudimentary assessment of cognitive ability should be performed post-SCI with more in-depth formal neuropsychological evaluations considered for those who showed evidence of significant impairment. Richards, Kewman and Pierce (2000) emphasised that it is important not to overestimate or underestimate the significance of cognitive deficits in this population. Mild concomitant traumatic brain injury may have few long-term implications, but more moderate and severe concomitant brain injuries may present cognitive and behavioural difficulties that will persist over time. Such injuries may have significant implications for personal and social functioning.

Chronic Pain

Chronic pain is a possible significant complication of SCI with prevalence estimates ranging from 25 to 45% (Kennedy et al., 1997). Various taxonomies of SCI pain have been proposed. Brittell and Mariano (1991) divided SCI pain into the following three main categories: mechanical pain, ridicular pain, and central spinal cord dysaesthesia. Siddall and Loeser (2001) confirmed chronic pain as a major impediment to effective rehabilitation and current treatments employed included a variety of pharmacological, surgical, physical and psychological approaches. Evidence for many of the treatments in use is still limited and there are no well-controlled outcome studies of psychosocial interventions for SCI pain. Therefore the clinician is left with the techniques that are proven efficacious for other chronic pain populations, with appropriate modifications for people with SCI (Richards, Kewman & Pierce, 2000).

Sexual Issues

Sexual dysfunction following SCI is a major issue. Sipski and Alexander (1992) in their review highlight that between 70 and 93% of males with complete upper motor neurone lesions retained reflex erections, but none sustained psychogenic erections. Ejaculation and orgasm are also unlikely in this group. Changes in the sexual physiology of women include impaired vaginal responsiveness and inability to experience orgasm. Jackson et al. (1995) suggest that participation in sexual intercourse diminishes somewhat post-injury for women and that self-reported orgasm decreases markedly.

Sipski and Alexander (1993) examined sexual activities, response and satisfaction in a sample of 25 SCI women. Sexual intercourse was the favourite activity pre-injury, whereas kissing, hugging and touching were the most favoured post-injury. White et al. (1993) reported on a representative sample of 40 women selected from a community-based sampling frame that 65% reported having had a physical relationship in the past 12 months, although their sex life ranked tenth in importance and tenth in satisfaction with respect to 11 other areas of life.

Alexander, Sipski and Findley (1993) examined sexual activities, desire and satisfaction in males pre- and post-SCI. Thirty-eight SCI males participated in the study. They found that sexual satisfaction decreased post-injury and was positively correlated with both the patients' and their partners' interest in penile–vaginal intercourse. Twenty-seven per cent reported sexual adjustment difficulties and 74% reported relationship difficulties. White et al. (1993) examined sexual activities and concerns in a community sample of 79 men post-SCI. Of the sample, 67% reported having had a physical relationship, although not necessarily including intercourse, in the past 12 months.

Areas of sexual activity about which respondents were most concerned included not satisfying the partner, getting and giving a sexual disease, urinary accidents and not getting enough personal satisfaction. Kreuter, Sullivan and Siösteen (1996) found that the most important correlates of sexual fulfilment in a sample of 167 persons with SCI were the use of a varied repertoire of sexual behaviours and their perception that the partner enjoys and is satisfied with the sexual aspects of the relationship. These and other studies highlight the importance of addressing the issue of sexuality and sexual counselling post-SCI.

PSYCHOLOGICAL INTERVENTION

Coping with SCI involves engaging in activities that maintain psychological integrity. The previous sections highlighted potential psychological sequelae and the impact of SCI, and the research identified a number of strategies that facilitate coping and adjustment. This section discusses intervention approaches in the light of the above evidence and highlights a clinical care pathway. A model of adjustment is presented and the role of a clinical health psychologist in direct work with both individuals and groups is discussed.

While the introductory section of this chapter demonstrated the lack of evidence supporting the stage approach to conceptualising adjustment to SCI, there is evidence that a number
of the emotional responses commented on within the theories may occur. During the acute
phase following injury, an individual will be experiencing shock and perhaps acute stress,
and will be seeking to understand what has occurred physically and make psychological
sense of the situation. Part of understanding about an injury involves either implicitly or explicitly thinking about its implications: on your immediate and future view of yourself and
your roles as an individual within a family or social network. Emotions commonly experienced may be low mood when thinking about losses sustained, anxiety about the future and
questions about how to manage with changed mobility or work prospects, or perhaps anger
about the circumstances or cause of injury. These are all natural emotions and are part of
a normal process following trauma. At this stage the intervention requirement is to convey
a sense of safety and that the initial trauma is over, to normalise the individual's emotions
and help the person to make sense of the experience (Janoff-Bulman, 1999). Supporting
someone in gaining an understanding of the diagnosis and prognosis, extent of injury and
consequences, and discussing fears are all part of this process.

There are a number of pre-injury factors which influence adjustment. An individual's
previous history of emotional distress, self-schema and self-worth, preferred coping style
and social, environmental and biological resources affect an individual's assessment (or appraisal) of his or her capacity to cope. Self and world schema play an important role in influencing how a person perceives the threat posed by SCI. A further factor which is relevant and
influences appraisal is an individual's fundamental assumptions about the world, including
concepts such as a belief in benevolence and meaning, and just world ideas (Janoff-Bulman,
1999). Such assumptions influence how an individual makes sense of the occurrence of life
events, a common question at this stage is "why me?", or perhaps a sense of injustice, which
may require schema-focused intervention to help the person to reconstruct his or her assump-
tive world (Janoff-Bulman, 1999). Higgins and Leibowitz (1999) suggest that adjustment
involves reality negotiation, in which the therapist is required to offer the individual plausible
attributions. They suggest that the individual makes causal attributions when initially injured
in an attempt to maintain his connectedness to the social environment and preserve a sense of
control and self-concept, but in time these are replaced or altered as the individual develops
a connectedness to his new situation. A further factor that influences someone's appraisal
and perception about whether SCI is "manageable" are the beliefs the individual holds
about disability. People often have little or no experience of SCI or disability prior to injury,
and society and the media often promote negative images about disability which inform an
individual's general belief system. Olver (2001) found that able-bodied people consistently
predicted quality, value and meaning of life following SCI to be significantly lower than people with tetraplegia's ratings of these factors (see "Spinal cord injury across the life span",
below).

The introductory section presented the principles of the Cognitive Model of Stress and
Coping (Folkman & Lazarus, 1980; Folkman et al., 1991). Figure 14.1 presents a model
developed by the authors which highlights the central elements involved in adjustment to
SCI. Conceptually this model has been developed from and complements the Cognitive
Model of Stress and Coping but emphasises particular aspects of adjustment and coping
relevant to SCI. The model postulates that the appraisal process is influenced by the factors
discussed in the above section.

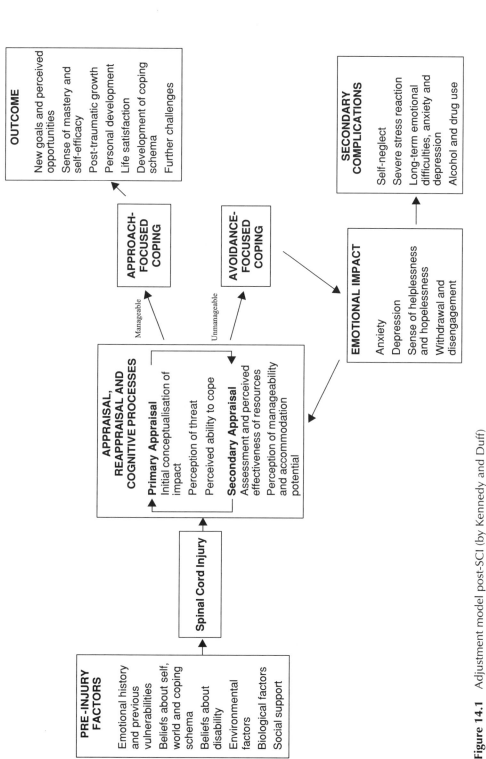

Figure 14.1 Adjustment model post-SCI (by Kennedy and Duff)

The primary appraisal process involves an initial conceptualisation of the impact. Folkman and Lazarus (1980) consider primary appraisal to be an assessment of a stressor's capacity to do harm; a judgement about whether it is a threat, challenge or benign. Sub-evaluations are then made about novelty, certainty and predictability. SCI is frequently a new situation about which an individual has no prior knowledge or experience, therefore uncertainty and fear of the unknown is a common feeling. Within SCI, developing a belief that this is a situation that can be managed, and perceiving that you can control or influence the situation, is an appraisal which facilitates coping and adjustment. Individuals appraise their SCI to be unmanageable when they perceive themselves to be in a situation that is beyond their control and for which they have no resources to cope. The appraisal process influences the coping approach and strategies used.

The earlier section highlighted the types of coping strategies found to be helpful when adjusting to SCI. Folkman and Lazarus (1980) make the distinction between problem and emotion-focused coping. Clinically many coping approaches involve both processes, so the distinction made within the model presented here is between those coping strategies that are approach focused (such as thinking about one's injury, acceptance, planning and problem-solving) and avoidance strategies (such as alcohol and drug use, behavioural or mental disengagement and denial). The selection of approach- or avoidance-focused strategies are influenced by the primary and secondary appraisal process. Within SCI this process is affected by the individual's belief and perception about whether this is a manageable or unmanageable situation. Avoidance-focused strategies lead to difficulties managing the emotional impact of SCI and may result in anxiety and depression, or other emotional difficulties. If this reaction is unmanaged and the appraisal process is unchanged, a number of secondary complications can arise, such as a long-term stress reaction, severe depression and mood disturbance, and in relation to SCI there can also be health implications in terms of pressure management neglect. Krause and Crewe (1987) in a series of studies examining adjustment over time found that poor personal adjustment to injury was linked to preventable deaths through complications such as pressure sores and other health-related factors. However, when primary and secondary appraisal processes facilitate a belief that this is a situation the individual can manage, the use of approach-coping strategies leads to a number of positive occurrences such as the individual having a sense of mastery and self-efficacy, development of coping schema and a sense of life satisfaction as highlighted in the model.

There are a number of points of intervention that can facilitate adjustment. Adjustment counselling focuses on the management of current distress, perhaps including specific cognitive and behavioural strategies to manage symptoms of anxiety and depression, but also includes discussion of fears, doubts and losses as well as irrational beliefs about the consequences of SCI. Fundamentally, adjustment counselling involves enabling the person to sustain an integrated view of self while constructing a new reality that is both hopeful and credible. Tirch and Radnitz (2000) suggest that there are six categories of cognitive distortion that are particularly relevant following SCI. These include (1) an overly negative view of self and others; (2) appraisals about self-worth following injury; (3) expectations about rejection from others and inadequacy; (4) expectations about consistent failure; (5) development of excessive personal entitlement; and (6) an over-developed sense of vulnerability.

Sustaining an injury does not necessarily threaten a person's self-theory or schema, but, as highlighted earlier, can often threaten his or her sense of being in control. When someone sustains an SCI, that person moves from a position of independence and control to one in which he or she becomes highly dependent on others to preserve life. Therefore key issues as someone proceeds through rehabilitation is the re-establishment of control and a sense of mastery so that internal attributions regarding competency are re-established. The process of adaptation and adjustment to SCI involves moving from making sense and negotiating a relationship with initial trauma to negotiating the ongoing demands of living and re-establishment of control (Higgins & Leibowitz, 1999). Facilitating this process clinically may involve behavioural strategies of problem-solving and rehearsal, specific cognitive work regarding the appraisals made about individual stressors, or the development of new or more adaptive coping strategies. Intervention may also include specific work on challenging negative beliefs about SCI and aspects of self-schema that are dissonant following injury.

Reviewing the literature, cognitive-behavioural approaches are the most commonly used therapeutic orientation within SCI and many other physical health conditions. However, psychodynamic interventions, although not as widely published, are also used. Backman (1989) cites examples of work within peptic ulcer disease, cardiac disease, cancer, and pre-operative preparation and reviews a variety of psychotherapeutic approaches within physical health. Backman considers that an assault of the ego, the central core of self, can occur in which all previous sense of reality is shattered and states that the "why me?" question is common, and that "the sense of being punished, justly or injustly, is strong" (p. 7).

Psychodynamic approaches within chronic conditions focus predominantly on the personal meaning attributed to the situation and the threat to self that the situation brings. In the review of this area, Backman states "people go through various stages in their attempt to adjust to a serious illness" (p. 8) and cites a clinical example of work involving the stages of denial, despair, negotiation and acceptance. Backman highlights many of the emotional processes discussed earlier, but comments on two that are particularly relevant for psychodynamic work: ego-control and ego-mastery failure. "Ego-control failure" occurs when a person is forced into a passive or powerless role, which can in turn lead to extreme anxiety or depression. The opposite of this, but just as potentially damaging, is "ego-mastery failure", when in order to gain control of the situation an individual may go to the library and read numerous medical journals in an attempt to achieve mastery. Backman comments that this latter process can lead to greater stress and difficulties when the desire for taking action and regaining control is thwarted.

The Journal of Rational-Emotive and Cognitive-Behaviour Therapy has dedicated two special issues (1990 and 1997) to discussing Rational Emotive Behaviour Therapy (REBT) within physical health and disability. Balter (1997) comments that REBT "helps the client reconceptualise minor and major hassles associated with living with a disability and not to overvalue the messages given them by family, friends and 'well-meaning others'" (p. 191). Clinical work using REBT with patients faced with illness or disability has been cited for a number of years (Ellis, 1978), with Albert Ellis discussing the use of REBT as a way of approaching the increasing disability he was experiencing from diabetes (Ellis, 1997). One of its strengths is the emphasis it has that a person has value and worth beyond the role the individual plays within life. Calabro (1997) discusses a range of behavioural and rational emotive interventions which can be used to resolve the emotional discomforts experienced within each category of Maslow's hierarchy of human needs (Maslow, 1943), which Calabro terms "psychological priorities". For example, Calabro comments that within many physical health conditions, including SCI, once hunger and thirst are satisfied, the primary goal is to avoid pain, the experience of which is inevitably involved in physical rehabilitation, and also provides examples of managing other needs such as security and predictability, affiliative, self-worth, and vital absorption priorities. Wallace and Maddox (as cited in Calabro, 1997) give an example of how to use the approach to treat the embarrassment associated with the functional difficulties caused by physical disability. Balter (1997) comments that self-acceptance is the key process that REBT aims to facilitate, and that this process can often be best achieved through group work with others with a similar disability, because validation from others reinforces positive self-concepts.

Lazarus and Folkman's (1984) Cognitive Model of Stress and Coping has also been developed into a group intervention programme, called Coping Effectiveness Training (CET; Chesney & Folkman, 1994; Folkman et al., 1991). CET aims to teach appraisal skills and how to select and apply coping strategies that are appropriate to the appraisal and situation. The programme teaches a range of standard cognitive-behavioural interventions, such as activity scheduling and challenging negative thoughts, as well as relaxation and problem-solving skills. King and Kennedy (1999) applied and developed the programme for people with SCI within an inpatient hospital rehabilitation centre. Using a matched control trial, they found that intervention group participants ($n = 19$) showed significantly greater reduction in levels of depression and anxiety than the controls post-intervention and at six-week follow-up. Kennedy et al. (2003a) extended the above research to 45 participants and replicated the findings for anxiety and depression. In addition, the intervention group completed measures of self-perception. Significant decreases were found in the discrepancy between participants' "ideal" self and "as I am", and between "as I would be without the injury" and "as I am" following the intervention and at follow-up. However, neither study found significant differences between the groups in relation to the coping strategies used. The studies also sought participant feedback about the group. Aspects highlighted as particularly beneficial were the sharing of views and experiences of group members and the discussion of "real life" scenarios.

Hanson et al. (1993) investigated coping strategies and adjustment following SCI over a five-year period, and suggested that interventions that best assist post-rehabilitation adjustment were those specifically aimed at enhancing cognitive-restructuring and information-seeking strategies, and applying these to the reduction of wish-fulfilling strategies (which were associated with poorer adjustment). The incorporation of "real life" scenarios and accompanying discussion which includes cognitive restructuring and problem-solving/coping also facilitates the coping adaptation process.

Craig et al. (1998) have also applied a group intervention to people with SCI. The intervention was cognitive behavioural in orientation and addressed management of anxiety and depression, self-esteem, assertion, sexuality and family relations. No significant main effects of a reduction of anxiety or depression were found between the intervention and control groups across time. However, further analysis revealed that the control group demonstrated higher levels of depression in the one- to two-year follow-up than the intervention group. This intervention aimed at relieving symptoms of anxiety and depression, rather than specific teaching of appraisal skills. Although the results of the latter group are more limited, the evidence suggests that brief focused group interventions can help ameliorate the impact of SCI and facilitate adjustment. We would suggest that group adjustment work can be particularly beneficial because of the peer interaction that is implicit within the process, with participants learning from other attendees' accounts of how to manage situations.

REHABILITATION AND GOAL-PLANNING

Much of the focus of rehabilitation is on challenging behaviour. Trieschmann and Willems (1980) conceptualised rehabilitation in behavioural terms and Norris-Baker et al. (1981) concluded that behavioural engagement in rehabilitation was the best predictor of both medical and behavioural status post-discharge. Kennedy, Fisher and Pearson (1988), in an observational study of a spinal rehabilitation centre, found that patients spent a considerable proportion of their time in solitary and disengaged behaviours. Goal-planning provides a systematic framework for incorporating behavioural change principles into the rehabilitation process. The common features of goal-directed action include those which are generated within the individual, have a significant association with the management of need and recognise the interplay between physiological, cognitive and environmental factors. Rehabilitation is a process of active change by which a person who has SCI can acquire the knowledge and skills for optimal physical, psychological and social functioning.

Treatment theory (Keith & Lipsey, 1993) identified the need for assessment measures that explicitly account for the processes that occur in the transformation from input to output, define problems for the specific populations, specify the critical inputs and identify the important steps to produce the desired affects, mode of delivery and expected outcome. There are many variants in goal-planning, but they generally share the following elements. The first concerns patient involvement, a practice that is client-centred rather than therapist-centred and recognises the need to engage the SCI person throughout the rehabilitation as an active participant. Secondly, there is a need to identify the individual's strengths and for the therapist and rehabilitation team members to build on such strengths. These strengths not only compensate for loss of function, but enable maximum control and independence. By emphasising needs, rather than disabilities, goal-planning identifies difficult areas and explores ways in which they can be realistically tackled. Goals need to be set by the person with SCI in collaboration with the team members. The team will then review the targets and small steps that are required to achieve a goal. When setting goals it is important to specify who will be carrying out the activity, what the behaviour is that is required and under what conditions and how often it should take place. This system provides an ongoing assessment of adherence and engagement in rehabilitation and enables a more systematic and continued delivery of positive social reinforcement.

When people are initially engaged in the rehabilitation process, they are often overwhelmed by their needs and a goal-planning programme can help to provide a scaffold to enable progress and advancement in rehabilitation. The needs addressed may include: activities of daily living; bladder and bowel management; skin management; mobility and wheelchair and equipment needs; discharge planning and community issues; and psychological and personal needs. People with SCI need to draw upon skills, knowledge and support of all of the multidisciplinary team which may include medical doctors, nurses, physiotherapists, occupational therapists as well as clinical psychologists, speech therapists, social workers and care managers. Many goal-planning programmes utilise a keyworker as part of the process to help empower and involve the person with SCI. The keyworker generally coordinates, advocates and supports the individual within the rehabilitation process. This approach to rehabilitation planning not only provides a safety net for the person, but highlights gaps in services and unmet needs. It also supports the rehabilitation team in minimising role ambiguity and role conflict which can undermine team effort, essentially demonstrating needs and achievements over disabilities and losses (Kennedy, 1998). In a comparative study of goal achievement during rehabilitation for older and younger spinal cord injured adults, Kennedy et al. (2003b) reported that older adults' rehabilitation gains were comparable to those of younger adults. Both groups demonstrated significant improvements in all areas of need; however there were specific areas of need (i.e. maintaining skin integrity) where older adults do not achieve similar levels of independence. These results highlight important considerations for the rehabilitation of older adults and emphasise the need for adaptive, individually tailored rehabilitation programmes. Special attention needs to be paid to the problems presented by spinal cord injured population subgroups.

Kirschner et al. (2001), in a study of the issues that rehabilitation clinicians found most troubling in clinical practice, found that the second most common problem (17%) involved conflicts between patients, physicians, team members and families around goal-setting, thereby highlighting the importance of programme clarity in rehabilitation. Pot et al. (1999) utilised a similar needs assessment system which highlighted patient needs related to symptoms, and was found to be a useful tool to signal aspects of rehabilitation that required improvement, thereby enhancing quality management. MacLeod and MacLeod (1996) evaluated client and staff satisfaction with a goal-planning programme in a SCI centre and found that both patients and staff were positive about the perceived benefits, despite staff acknowledging an increase in their workload.

SPINAL CORD INJURY ACROSS THE LIFE SPAN

The previous sections and model highlighted the processes which facilitate adjustment following SCI and the prevalence of emotional reactions among those who have sustained injury. This section discusses issues related to longer-term adjustment and quality of life, as well as considering lifespan issues such as ageing with a SCI and the provision of services following acute injury.

Studies concerning quality of life following SCI have commonly been considered as part of research examining adjustment over time, with a large body of evidence stemming from studies of those who have aged with SCI. It is beyond the scope of this chapter to discuss the merits of the construct quality of life, its definition and relationship with aspects such as life satisfaction, meaning and value of life and their respective measures, so for the purpose of this review these aspects shall be considered synonymous.

Possibly the two most significant studies in this area are those conducted by Krause and Crewe in Atlanta, USA, and Whiteneck and colleagues at the Craig Hospital, Colorado, USA. Both groups have conducted large-scale research into the long-term impact of SCI in relation to quality of life and ageing.

In a series of longitudinal studies, Crewe and Krause (1991) found that adjustment to SCI was largely stable over time, with an increase in perceptions of quality of life the greater the time since injury. Krause (1998) examined the data collected at four time intervals over a 20-year period with participants injured for an average of 28.7 years. Subjective well-being was found to increase over time, with length of time injured correlating positively with adjustment. Participants reported feeling more engaged in their lives, with an improvement in career opportunities and finances, and noted a decrease in negative emotions during the course of the study. There was also found to be a reduction in hospitalisation and days in hospital over time within the sample. Whiteneck et al. (1992) examined ageing and adjustment among those who were 20 or more years post-injury. Three-quarters of the participants in the sample rated current quality of life as good or excellent (on a five-point scale), with evidence of increased life satisfaction over time. These studies are discussed further in relation to ageing with SCI.

In assessing quality of life following SCI, comparisons have also been made with non-disabled peer groups. Post et al. (1998) and Olver (2001) used matched able-bodied control groups and found quality of life between those with and without injury to be comparable. Post et al. (1998) also examined the factors within and contributing to quality of life and found that those with SCI were less satisfied than their peers with respect to their sexual life and self-care, a finding replicated by Olver (2001). Eisenberg and Saltz (1991) compared war veterans with SCI with veterans without an injury and found that those with an injury reported a higher quality of life. Cushman and Hassett (1992), in a study examining the impact of SCI 10 and 15 years post-injury, found that two-thirds of participants considered their life to be comparable to or better than that of their peers. The third who rated their life satisfaction as "somewhat" or "much worse" than their peers had lower rates of employment. Clayton and Chubon (1994) interviewed 100 people who had been injured between two and 37 years. They replicated many of the above findings, but also identified the importance of income and educational status within perceptions of quality of life. Studies have also assessed long-term outcome in those who sustained SCI as a child. Vogel et al. (1998) found that the level of life satisfaction in those injured as children was also similar to non-injured peers. High educational achievement and social interaction were found for this sample, but a low level of employment. Kannisto et al. (1998) compared adults who sustained a paediatric injury with those who had been injured as adults and found the former group to have greater physical performance and quality of life.

It is perhaps difficult for non-disabled people to comprehend how an individual's quality of life following SCI can be defined in the above terms. Albrecht and Devlieger (1999) consider this to be a "disability paradox" which stems from a common misunderstanding about quality of life. They suggest that the assumptions made within non-disabled groups are that quality of life refers to being in good health, experiencing subjective well-being and life satisfaction, with the implicit assumption that people with disability are not in good health and do not possess a high level of life satisfaction. The corollary of this assumption within society is that someone with a disability is limited in function and role performance, stigmatised and under-privileged. However, the research cited demonstrates that an individual's perceptions of personal health, well-being and life satisfaction are often discordant with objective health status and disability. Olver (2001) examined this paradox by matching an able-bodied group with SCI individuals in relation to psychological status, gender, socio-economic background and employment. Able-bodied controls were asked to rate the quality, value and meaning of life of someone with complete tetraplegia on the basis of a clinical vignette. The able-bodied group expected these aspects to be about 20%, whereas the matched tetraplegic sample assessed their own quality, value and meaning of life to be about 70%. Furthermore no significant differences were found between the spinal cord injured and able-bodied groups' ratings of current value placed on life and meaning of life.

However, it is recognised that a significant minority of those with a SCI have long-term difficulties with adjustment and mood. Research has therefore considered the factors which affect quality of life and long-term adjustment following SCI and has identified a number of elements. A consistent finding is the lack of correlation between life satisfaction or quality of life and extent of spinal cord paralysis. Whiteneck (1989) investigated the quality of life in people with SCI who were permanently ventilated and found that 92% of those interviewed were glad to be alive, with only 10% rating their quality of life as poor. However, factors that have been found to influence perceived quality of life are social integration, mobility, perceived control, and self-assessed health status (Fuhrer et al., 1992), coping effectiveness (Nieves, Charter & Aspinall, 1991), and mood and social support (Siösteen et al., 1990), indicating the impact of adjustment processes and community integration following SCI. Lundqvist et al. (1991), in a longitudinal study of 98 new SCI patients over a four-year period, found that mobility, social activities and contacts increased throughout the study, but most substantially within the first two years post-injury, highlighting the importance of managing the consequences of injury from an early stage. No significant differences were found between this group and the able-bodied control group with respect to psychosocial function, mood and perception of quality of life. Although it was a much smaller study, Stensman (1994) assessed the consecutive quality of life and coping approaches of 17 participants from six months to five years post-injury. This research provides some evidence of the relationship between coping and quality of life and the detrimental impact that chronic pain and unemployment can have upon these processes. The study also began to identify factors which impacted on quality of life, with relationships with family and friends making positive contributions and pain, problems with bowel management and functional loss detracting from quality of life.

Weizenkamp et al. (2000) compared the quality of life ratings of 195 men between 23 and 49 years post-injury with large-scale community ratings of components of quality of life (Flanagan, 1978). They found differences in the ratings of the spinal cord popula-tion compared to the general population. Spinal cord injured men rated relationships with relatives, learning, creative expression, reading and other quiet leisure activities as more important, and material comfort, having and raising children, work and participating in governmental and local affairs as less important than their counterparts. The study found that the aspects rated as important were related to things the spinal cord injured men had achieved, and proposed that as a process of adjustment, priority shifting may occur so that people make judgements about quality of life in terms of what they believe is possible for them to achieve rather than what they actually achieve.

As indicated earlier, adjustment to SCI is a process, and one that takes place in the context of each individual's culture and society. Kennedy and Rogers (2000b) examined quality of life ratings at one month and six months post-discharge. They found across the two time points that the importance attached to specific needs was consistently greater than the degree to which the needs were met. They identified a number of specific needs of people with SCI that are not being met in the community: helping others, participation in activities relating to local government, learning and expressing oneself. Viemerö and Krause (1998) examined the quality of life among a group of people with physical disabilities (including SCI) from cities in Finland and Sweden. This study had a mixture of people defined as coping well/well adjusted and those defined as being poorly adjusted. They found that satisfaction with life was highly dependent on occupational status, meaningful activities, social integration and having psychological resources to cope with stressful situations, and that satisfaction in general and satisfaction with social relationships explained most of the variance in measures of psychological resources. They comment that disability per se does not decrease the disabled individual's quality of life, but that factors such as psychological resources, ability to cope with everyday life, engagement in occupation or meaningful activities as well as social integration impact on quality of life, and need to be fostered and developed in intervention programmes to facilitate adjustment.

Albrecht and Devlieger (1999) consider that the development of a "can do" approach to life following disability is important in the explanation of the adjustment process and the "disability paradox". They suggest that this develops from a sense of having control over bodies, minds and spirits, being able to perform expected roles, maturity gained from their individual experience, a reorientation about what is important in life and satisfaction received from providing emotional support to others, which leads to a balanced view of themselves as whole people. They also suggest that one of the factors within quality of life becomes a judgement about how well the person is doing with the disability and a feeling of satisfaction when comparing oneself to others' capabilities. However, Albrecht and Devlieger (1999) also identify aspects which contribute towards a poor or fair quality of life: the impact of pain and fatigue upon an individual's ability to plan, perform roles and live a full life, a sense of loss of control and unpredictability, and a discrepancy between now and what someone would like to do and can do, or between now and what they used to do.

Many of the above longitudinal studies have assessed quality of life while examining the impact of ageing with SCI. Approximately 40% of the 179 000 spinal cord injured survivors in the USA are aged over 45 years, with one in four having lived 20 years or more with the injury (Gerhart et al., 1993). When examining factors impacting upon ageing with injury, researchers have tried to distinguish between ageing, and ageing with injury, and also age at injury, and posed the question whether the ageing process intensifies with injury.

Menter and Hudson (1995) reviewed the impact of physiologic ageing with injury by examining the Model Systems database of SCI maintained in the USA. They found that level of injury and degree of completeness can affect the ageing process. For example, people with paraplegia, rather than those with complete tetraplegia, often experience premature ageing or "wearing out" of neurologically intact arms because of the demands of using these limbs to transfer from a bed to a wheelchair. They suggest that there is an incremental increase in the number of potential ageing effects, such as increased urinary tract infections, scoliosis (curvature of the spine), pressure sores and spasticity, with each five-year period post-injury. However, they comment that both frequency of hospitalisation and mean number of days spent in hospital decreases as the time from the initial injury increases.

Gerhart et al. (1993) examined ageing and functional decline among 279 spinal cord injured individuals derived from two UK spinal units. Seventy-eight per cent of participants reported needing no greater amount of physical assistance than earlier in their injuries, with 22% considering that they now needed more assistance. Those who needed more help were significantly older, and those with cervical injuries who reported needing more help were significantly younger than counterparts with lower level injuries (cervical injuries requiring help were on average 49 years old compared with 54 years for the paraplegic participants). In terms of perceptions of quality of life, the ratings of those requiring extra help declined as a function of the extra support required.

Whiteneck et al. (1992), in a major study in this area, examined ageing and adjustment in those over 20 years post-injury. They found that the largest reported decline in quality of life was among those aged over 50 years who had been injured for 30 years or more, and a pattern of increasing satisfaction with time since injury until this point with a decline following it. They comment that there is a clear interplay between the normal ageing process and SCI in terms of increased medical complications and morbidity, but that this relationship is a complicated one. There is evidence that the longer people live with injury, the greater the move away from an SCI-related death such as renal failure, with causes of death becoming more like those observed within the general population. In an attempt to explore these aspects more fully, Krause (2000) examined the relationship between secondary complications and age at onset during the first 20 years of injury among 347 participants. A number of conditions were examined; for example, those aged 40 at onset were six times more likely to have heart problems than those aged 18 or under at onset. The odds for experiencing a "bowel obstruction" increased with increasing age at injury, whereas developing kidney stones had greatest decrease in prevalence with increasing age. Krause suggests that the first ten years post-injury are critical for the development of several of the secondary conditions, whereas conditions that do not occur in the first ten years may then be unlikely to occur at all. Also, some conditions are unrelated to ageing, such as pressure ulcers, but ageing may impact on the recurrence of such problems.

From the systematic reviews of the ageing process following SCI and the evidence regarding the occurrence of secondary complications, the above studies provide recommendations about the need for service provision following SCI. Gerhart et al. (1993) comment that interventions to develop strength, prevention of weight gain and postural deformities can delay or minimise the need for additional help as people age and highlight the importance of ongoing assessment and review. Most SCI rehabilitation centres provide a lifelong service following injury for these reasons, and recognise the importance of preventative health care and need for ongoing maintenance of health behaviour following injury. There is a general consensus regarding the importance of such a provision, but relatively few published studies on the impact of this. Dunn, Love and Ravesloot (2000), in one of the few outcome studies, found there was a decrease in subjective health ratings and independence, and increase in levels of depression with increasing age in a group of 136 people who did not receive follow-up compared with those who received lifelong support following injury. Similar types of secondary conditions were found to occur between the groups, but severity and frequency were less in the people who received lifelong support.

SUMMARY

SCI is a multisystem, complex injury that can have a significant impact on an individual's coping. Research indicates that most people who sustain SCI do cope and adjust well to these demands, and obtain a comparable quality of life with peers and pre-injury levels. However, a significant minority experience long-term adjustment difficulties. This chapter has highlighted the need for a sophisticated, multilevel approach for psychological services for people with SCI and provided evidence to challenge previous assumptions that depression is an inevitable post-injury reaction. An adjustment model incorporating appraisal and coping theories as well as recognition of the cognitive components influencing these processes was presented to aid in the formulation of these complex needs, and individual, group and systemic intervention approaches for working with this client group were also considered. The evidence base for SCI rehabilitation processes and psychological management has developed substantially over the past decade. Clinical challenges within this area include developing coping and adjustment models further, particularly in relation to appraisal processes and understanding about family adjustment processes.

REFERENCES

Albrecht, G.L. & Devlieger, P.J. (1999). The disability paradox: high quality of life against all odds. *Social Science and Medicine*, **48**, 977–988.

Alexander, C.J., Sipski, M.L. & Findley, T.W. (1993). Sexual activities, desire, and satisfaction in males pre- and post-spinal cord injury. *Archives of Sexual Behavior*, **22** (3), 217–228.

ASIA (1996). American Spinal Injuries Association Scales. *Outcomes Following Traumatic Spinal Cord Injury: Clinical Practice Guidelines for Health-Care Professionals*. USA: Consortium for Spinal Cord Medicine, Paralyzed Veterans of America.

Backman, M.E. (1989). *The Psychology of the Physically Ill Patient—A Clinician's Guide*. New York: Plenum Press.

Balter, R. (1997). Introduction to the Special Issue. *Journal of Rational-Emotive and Cognitive-Behavior Therapy*, **15** (3), 191–192.

Beck, A.T., Steer, R.A., Kovacs, M. & Garrison, B. (1985). Hopelessness and eventual suicide: a 10-year prospective study of patients hospitalized with suicidal ideation. *American Journal of Psychiatry*, **142** (5), 559–563.

Beedie, A. & Kennedy, P. (2002). Quality of social support predicts hopelessness and depression post spinal cord injury. *Journal of Clinical Psychology in Medical Settings*, **9** (3), 227–234.

Berger, S. & Garrett, J. (1952). Psychological problems of the paraplegic patient. *Journal of Rehabilitation*, **18** (5), 15–17.

Boyer, B.A., Tollen, L.G. & Kafkalas, C.M. (1998). A pilot study of post traumatic stress disorder in children and adolescents with spinal cord injury. *SCI Psychosocial Processes*, **11**, 75–81.

Bracken, M. & Shepard, M. (1980). Coping and adaptation to acute spinal cord injury: a theoretical analysis. *Paraplegia*, **18**, 74–85.

Brittell, W.W. & Mariano, A.J. (1991). Chronic pain in spinal cord injury. In N.E. Walsh (Ed.), *Physical Medicine and Rehabilitation: Rehabilitation of Chronic Pain* (pp. 71–82). Philadelphia: Hanley & Belfus.

Buckelew, S.P., Frank, R.G., Elliot, T.R., Chaney, J. & Hewett, J. (1991). Adjustment to spinal cord injury: stage theory re-visted. *Paraplegia*, **29**, 125–130.

Calabro, L.E. (1997). "First Things First": Maslow's hierarchy as a framework for REBT in promoting disability adjustment during rehabilitation. *Journal of Rational-Emotive and Cognitive-Behavior Therapy*, **15** (3), 193–213.

Charlifue, S.W. & Gerhart, K.A. (1991). Behavioural and demographic predictors of suicide after traumatic spinal cord injury. *Paraplegia*, **72**, 488–492.

Chesney, M.A. & Folkman, S. (1994). Psychological impact of HIV disease and implications for intervention. *Psychiatric Clinics of North America*, **17**, 163–182.

Clayton, K.S. & Chubon, R.A. (1994). Factors associated with the quality of life of long-term spinal cord injured persons. *Archives of Physical Medicine and Rehabilitation*, **75**, 633–638.

Consortium for Spinal Cord Medicine (1999). *Outcomes following Traumatic Spinal Cord Injury: Clinical Practice Guidelines for Health-Care Professionals*. USA: Paralyzed Veterans of America.

Craig, A.R., Hancock, K., Chang, E. & Dickson, H.G. (1998). Immunising against depression and anxiety after spinal cord injury. *Archives of Physical Medicine and Rehabilitation*, **79** (4), 375–377.

Craig, A.R., Hancock, K.M., Dickson, H.G., Martin, J. & Chang, E. (1990). Psychological consequences of spinal injury: a review of the literature. *Australian and New Zealand Journal of Psychiatry*, **24**, 418–425.

Crewe, N.M. & Krause, J.S. (1991). An eleven year follow-up of adjustment to spinal cord injury. *Rehabilitation Psychology*, **35**, 205–210.

Cushman, L.A. & Hassett, J. (1992). Spinal cord injury: 10 and 15 years after. *Paraplegia*, **30**, 690–696.

Danner, G. & Radnitz, C.L. (2000). Protective factors and posttraumatic stress disorder in veterans with spinal cord injury. *International Journal of Rehabilitation and Health*, **5** (3), 195–203.

DeVivo, M.J. & Stover, S.L. (1995). Long-term survival and causes of death. In S.L. Stover, J.A. DeLisa & G.G. Whiteneck (Eds), *Spinal Cord Injury: Clinical Outcomes from the Model Systems*. Maryland: Aspen.

DeVivo, M.J., Black, K.J., Richards, J.S. & Stover, S.L. (1991). Suicide following spinal cord injury. *Paraplegia*, **29**, 620–627.

Duff, J.S. (1997). *The psychological sequelae of trauma following spinal cord injury*. Unpublished doctoral thesis. University of Southampton.

Dunn, M., Love, L. & Ravesloot, C. (2000). Subjective health in spinal cord injury after outpatient healthcare follow-up. *Spinal Cord*, **38**, 84–91.

Eisenberg, M.C. & Saltz, C.C. (1991). Quality of life among spinal cord injured patients: long term rehabilitation outcomes. *Paraplegia*, **29**, 514–520.

Elliot, T.R. & Frank, R.G. (1996). Depression following spinal cord injury. *Archives of Physical Medicine and Rehabilitation*, **77**, 816–823.

Ellis, A. (1978). *Brief Psychotherapy in Medical and Health Practice*. New York: Springer Publishing Co.

Ellis, A. (1997). Using rational-emotive-behavior therapy techniques to cope with disability. *Professional Psychology: Research and Practice*, **1**, 17–22.

Flanagan, J.C. (1978). A research approach to improving quality of life. *American Psychologist*, **2**, 138–147.

Folkman, S. (1984). Personal control and stress and coping processes: a theoretical analysis. *Journal of Personality and Social Psychology*, **46**, 839–852.

Folkman, S. & Lazarus, R.S. (1980). An analysis of coping in a middle-aged community sample. *Journal of Health and Social Behaviour*, **21**, 219–239.

Folkman, S. & Lazarus, R.S. (1986). Stress processes and depressive symptomatology. *Journal of Abnormal Psychology*, **95**, 107–113.

Folkman, S., Chesney, M., McKusick, L., Ironson, G., Johnson, D.S. & Coates, T.J. (1991). Translating Coping Theory into an Intervention. In J. Eckenrode (Ed.), *The Social Context of Coping*. New York: Plenum Press.

Frank, R.G. & Elliott, T.R. (1987). Life stress and psychologic adjustment following spinal cord injury. *Archives of Physical Medicine and Rehabilitation*, **68**, 344–347.

Frank, R.G., Elliott, T.R., Corcoran J.R. & Wonderlich, S.A. (1987). Depression after spinal cord injury: is it necessary? *Clinical Psychology Review*, **7**, 611–630.

Frank, R.G., Kashani, J.H., Wonderlich, S.A., Lising, A. & Viscot, L.R. (1985). Depression and adrenal function in spinal cord injury. *American Journal of Psychiatry*, **142**, 252–253.

Frankel, H.L., Hancock, D.O., Hyslop, G., Melzak, J., Michaelis, L.S., Ungar, G.H., Vernon, J.D. & Walsh, J.J. (1969). The value of postural reduction in the initial management of closed injuries of the spine with paraplegia and tetraplegia. *Paraplegia*, **7** (3), 179–192.

Fuhrer, M.J., Rintala, D.H., Hart, K.A., Clearman, R. & Young, M.E. (1992). Relationship of life satisfaction to impairment, disability, and handicap among persons with spinal cord injuries. *Archives of Physical Medicine and Rehabilitation*, **73**, 552–557.

Fuhrer, M.J., Rintala, D.H., Hart, K.A., Clearman, R. & Young, M.E. (1993). Depressive symptomatology in persons with spinal cord injury who reside in the community. *Archives of Physical Medicine and Rehabilitation*, **74** (3), 255–60.

Galvin, L.R. & Godfrey, H.P. (2001). The impact of coping on emotional adjustment to spinal cord injury (SCI): review of the literature and application of a stress appraisal and coping formulation. *Spinal Cord*, **39** (12), 615–627.

Gerhart, K.A., Bergstrom, E., Charlifue, S.W., Menter, R.R. & Whiteneck, G.G. (1993). Long-term SCI: functional changes over time. *Archives of Physical Medicine and Rehabilitation*, **74**, 1030–1034.

Go, B.K., DeVivo, M.J. & Richards, J.S. (1995). The epidemiology of spinal cord injury. In S.L. Stover, J.A. DeLisa & G.G. Whiteneck (Eds), *Spinal Cord Injury: Clinical Outcomes from the Model Systems*. Maryland: Aspen.

Grundy, D. & Swain, A. (1996). *ABC of Spinal Cord Injury* (3rd edn). London: BMJ.

Guttmann, L. (1976). *Spinal Cord Injuries: Comprehensive Management and Research* (2nd edn). Oxford: Blackwell Scientific.

Hancock, K.M., Craig, A.R., Dickson, H.G., Chang, E. & Martin, J. (1993). Anxiety and depression over the first year of spinal cord injury: a longitudinal study. *Paraplegia*, **31**, 349–357.

Hanson, S., Buckelew, S.P., Hewett, J. & O'Neal, G. (1993). The relationship between coping and adjustment after SCI: a five-year follow-up study. *Rehabilitation Psychology*, **38** (1), 41–52.

Hartkopp, A., Bronnum-Hansen H., Seidenschnur, A.M. & Biering-Sorensen, F. (1998). Suicide in a spinal cord injured population: its relation to functional status. *Archives of Physical Medicine and Rehabilitation*, **79** (11), 1356–1361.

Heinemann, A.W. (1995). Spinal cord injury. In A.J. Goreczny (Ed.), *Handbook of Health and Rehabilitation Psychology* (pp. 341–360). New York: Plenum Press.

Higgins, R.L. & Leibowitz, R.Q. (1999). Reality negotiation and coping. In C.R. Snyder (Ed.), *Coping: The Psychology of What Works*. New York: Oxford University Press.

Hoque, M.F., Grangeon, C. & Reed, K. (1999). Spinal cord lesions in Bangladesh: an epidemilogical study 1994–1995. *Spinal Cord*, **37**, 858–861.

Howell, T., Fullerton, D.T., Harvey R.F. & Klein, M. (1981). Depression in spinal cord injured patients. *Paraplegia*, **19**, 284–288.

Jackson, A.J., Wadley, V.G., Richards, J.S. & DeVivo, M.J. (1995). Sexual behaviour and function among spinal cord injured women. *Journal of Spinal Cord Medicine*, **18**, 141.

Janoff-Bulman, R. (1999). Rebuilding shattered assumptions after traumatic life events. In C.R Snyder (Ed.), *Coping: The Psychology of What Works*. New York: Oxford University Press.

Johnson, D.C. (1985). *Alcohol Use by Persons with Disabilities*. Unpublished report. Wisconsin Department of Health and Social Services.

Kannisto, M., Merikanto, J., Alaranta, H., Hokkanen, H. & Sintonen, H. (1998). Comparison of health-related quality of life in three subgroups of spinal cord injury patients. *Spinal Cord*, **36**, 193–199.

Keith, R.A. & Lipsey, M.W. (1993). The role of theory in rehabilitation assessment, treatment, and outcomes. In R.L. Glueckauf, L.B. Sechrest, G.R. Bond & E.C. McDonel (Eds), *Improving Assessment in Rehabilitation and Health* (pp. 33–60). California: Sage.

Kennedy, P. (1995). *Psychological aspects of spinal cord injury: behavioural approaches, emotion and impact in coping strategies* (Volume 2). Unpublished doctoral thesis, University of Ulster.

Kennedy, P. (1998). Spinal cord injuries. In A.S. Bellack & M. Hersen (Eds), *Comprehensive Clinical Psychology* (pp. 445–462). New York: Pergamon.

Kennedy, P. & Evans, M. (2001). Evaluation of post traumatic distress in the first 6 months following SCI. *Spinal Cord*, **39**, 381–386.

Kennedy, P. & Rogers, B.A. (2000a). Anxiety and depression after spinal cord injury: a longitudinal analysis. *Archives of Physical Medicine and Rehabilitation*, **81**, 932–937.

Kennedy, P. & Rogers, B. (2000b). Reported quality of life of people with spinal cord injuries: a longitudinal analysis of the first 6 months post discharge. *Spinal Cord*, **38**, 498–503.

Kennedy, P., Fisher, K. & Pearson, E. (1988). Ecological evaluation of a rehabilitative environment for spinal cord injured people: behavioural mapping and feedback. *British Journal of Clinical Psychology*. **27** (3), 239–246.

Kennedy, P., Duff, J., Evans, M. & and Beedie, A. (2003a). Coping Effectiveness Training reduces depression and anxiety following traumatic spinal cord injuries. *British Journal of Clinical Psychology*, **42**, 41–52.

Kennedy, P., Evans, M., Berry, C. & Mullin, J. (2003b). Comparative analysis of goal achievement during rehabilitation for older and younger adults with spinal cord injury. *Spinal Cord*, **41**, 44–52.

Kennedy, P., Frankel, H., Gardner, B. & Nuseibeh, I. (1997). Factors associated with chronic pain following traumatic spinal cord injuries. *Spinal Cord*, **35**, 814–817.

Kennedy, P., Lowe, R., Grey, N. & Short, E. (1995) Traumatic spinal cord injury and psychological impact: a cross-sectional analysis of coping strategies. *British Journal of Clinical Psychology*, **34**, 627–639.

Kennedy, P., Marsh, N., Lowe, R., Grey, N., Short, E. & Rogers, B. (2000). A longitudinal analysis of psychological impact and coping strategies following spinal cord injury. *British Journal of Health Psychology*, **5**, 157–172.

Kennedy, P., Rogers, B., Speer, S. & Frankel, H. (1999). Spinal cord injuries and attempted suicide: a retrospective review. *Spinal Cord*, **37** (12), 847–852.

King, C. & Kennedy, P. (1999). Coping effectiveness training for people with spinal cord injury: preliminary results of a controlled trial. *British Journal of Clinical Psychology*, **38**, 5–14.

Kirschner, K.L., Stocking, C., Wagner, L.B., Foye, S.J. & Siegler, M. (2001). Ethical issues identified by rehabilitation clinicians. *Archives of Physical Medicine and Rehabilitation*, **82**, S2–S8.

Krause, J.S. (1998). Changes in adjustment after spinal cord injury: a 20-year longitudinal study. *Rehabilitation Psychology*, **43** (1), 41–55.

Krause, J.S. (2000). Aging after spinal cord injury: an exploratory study. *Spinal Cord*, **38**, 77–83.

Krause, J.S. & Crewe, N.M. (1987). Prediction of long-term survival of persons with spinal cord injury: an 11-year prospective study. *Rehabilitation Psychology*, **32**, 205–213.

Krause, J.S., Kemp, B. & Coker, J. (2000). Depression after spinal cord injury: relation to gender, ethnicity, aging, and socioeconomic indicators. *Archives of Physical Medicine and Rehabilitation*, **81** (8), 1099.

Kreuter, M., Sullivan, M. & Siösteen, A. (1996). Sexual adjustment and quality of relationship in spinal paraplegia: a controlled study. *Archives of Physical Medicine and Rehabilitation*, **77** (6), 541–548.

Lazarus, R.S. & Folkman, S. (1984). *Stress, Appraisal and Coping*. New York: Springer.

Lude, P., Kennedy, P., Evans, M., Lude, Y. & Beedie, A. (2002). Post traumatic distress symptoms following spinal cord injury: a comparative review of British and Swiss samples. Manuscript submitted for publication.

Lundqvist, M.D., Siösteen, R.P.T., Blomstrand, C., Lind, B. & Sullivan, M. (1991). Clinical, functional and emotional status. *Spine*, **16** (1), 78–83.

MacLeod, G.M. & MacLeod, L. (1996). Evaluation of client and staff satisfaction with a Goal Planning project implemented with people with spinal cord injuries. *Spinal Cord*, **34**, 525–530.

Maslow, A.H. (1943). A theory of human motivation. *Psychology Review*, **50**, 370–396.

Menter, R.R. & Hudson, L.M. (1995). Effects of age at injury and the aging process. In S.L. Stover, J.A. DeLisa & G.G. Whiteneck (Eds), *Spinal Cord Injury: Clinical Outcomes from the Model Systems*. Maryland: Aspen.

Nieves, C.C., Charter, R.A. & Aspinall, M.J. (1991). Relationship between effective coping and perceived quality of life in spinal cord injured patients. *Rehabilitation Nursing*, **16**, 129–132.

Norris-Baker, C., Stephens, M.A., Rintala, D.H. & Willems, E.P. (1981). Patient behavior as a predictor of outcomes in spinal cord injury. *Archives of Physical Medicine and Rehabilitation*, **62** (12), 602–608.

O'Connor, P. (2000, November). *Australian data on elderly acute SCI patients*. Paper presented at the meeting of the International Medical Society of Paraplegia (IMSOP), Sydney, Australia.

O'Donnell, J.J., Cooper, J.E., Gessner, J.E., Shehan, I. & Ashley, J. (1981–82). Alcohol, drugs and spinal cord injury. *Alcohol Health Research World*, **6** (2), 27–29.

Olver, L.R. (2001). *Predicting the quality, value and meaning of life with tetraplegia following traumatic spinal cord injury*. Unpublished doctoral thesis, University of Plymouth, England.

Post, W.M., Van Dijk, A.J., Van Asbeck, F.W.A. & Schrijvers, A.J.P. (1998). Life satisfaction of persons with spinal cord injury compared to a population group. *Scandinavian Journal of Rehabilitation Medicine*, **30**, 23–30.

Pot, J.W., Van Harten, W.H., Seydel, E.R. & Snoek, G. (1999). Development of a needs assessment system in rehabilitation. *International Journal of Rehabilitation Research*, **22** (3), 155–159.

Radnitz, C.L., Schlein, I.S. & Hsu, L. (2000). The effect of prior trauma on the development of PTSD following spinal cord injury. *Journal of Anxiety Disorders*, **14** (3), 313–324.

Radnitz, C.L., Schlcin, I.S., Walczak, S., Broderick, C.P., Binks, M., Tirch, D., Willard, J., Perez-Strumulo, L., Festa, J., Lillian, L.B., Bockian, N., Cytryn, A. & Green, L. (1995). The prevalence of post traumatic stress disorder in veterans with spinal cord injury. *SCI Psychosocial Processes*, **8**, 145–149.

Reidy, K., Caplan, B. & Shawaryn, M. (1991). *Coping strategies following spinal cord injury: accommodation to trauma and disability*. Paper presented at the 68th Annual Meeting of the American Congress of Rehabilitation Medicine, Washington.

Richards, J.S., Kewman, D.G. & Pierce, C.A. (2000). Spinal cord injury. In R.G. Frank & T.R. Elliot (Eds), *Handbook of Rehabilitation Psychology*. Washington, DC: American Psychological Association.

Roth, E., Davidoff, G., Thomas, P., Doljanac, R., Dijkers, M., Berent, S., Morris, J. & Yarkony, G. (1989). A controlled study of neuropsychological deficits in acute spinal cord injury patients. *Paraplegia*, **27** (6), 480–489.

Siddall, P.J. & Loeser, J.D. (2001). Pain following spinal cord injury. *Spinal Cord*, **39** (2), 63–73.

Siller, J. (1969). Psychological situation of the disabled with spinal cord injuries. *Rehabilitation Literature*, **30**, 290–296.

Siösteen, A., Lunqvist, C., Blomstrand, C., Sullivan, L. & Sullivan, M. (1990). The quality of life of three functional spinal cord injury subgroups in a Swedish community. *Paraplegia*, **28**, 476–488.

Sipski, M. & Alexander, C.J. (1992). Sexual function and dysfunction after spinal cord injury. *Physical Medicine and Rehabilitation Clinics of North America*, **3**, 811–828.

Sipski, M.L. & Alexander, C.J. (1993). Sexual activities, response and satisfaction in women pre- and post-spinal cord injury. *Archives of Physical Medicine & Rehabilitation*, **74** (10), 1025–1029.

Stensman, R. (1994). Adjustment to traumatic spinal cord injury. A longitudinal self-reported measure. *Paraplegia*, **32**, 416–422.

Stewart, T.D. (1977). Coping behaviour and the moratorium following spinal cord injury. *Paraplegia*, **15**, 338–342.

Thomas, J.P. (1995). The model spinal cord injury concept: development and implementation. In S.L. Stover, J.A. DeLisa & G.G. Whiteneck (Eds), *Spinal Cord Injury: Clinical Outcomes from the Model Systems*. Maryland: Aspen.

Tirch, D.D. & Radnitz, C.L. (2000). Spinal cord injury. In C.L. Radnitz (Ed.), *Cognitive Behaviour Therapy for Persons with Disabilities*. New Jersey: Jason Aronson Inc.

Trieschmann, R.B. & Willems, E.P. (1980). Behavioral programs for the physically disabled. In D. Glenwick & L. Jason (Eds), *Behavioural Community Psychology: Progress and Prospects* (pp. 45–57). New York: Praeger.

Tucker, S.J. (1980). The psychology of spinal cord injury: patient–staff interaction. *Rehabilitation Literature*, **41**, 114–121.

Viemerö, V. & Krause, C. (1998). Quality of life in individuals with physical disabilities. *Psychotherapy and Psychosomatics*, **67** (6), 317–322.

Vogel, L.C., Klaas, S.J., Lubiky, J.P. & Anderson, C.J. (1998). Long-term outcomes and life satisfaction of adults who had pediatric spinal cord injuries. *Archives of Physical Medicine and Rehabilitation*, **79**, 1496–1503.

Weizenkamp, D.A., Gerhart, K.A., Charlifue, S.W., Whiteneck, G.G., Glass, C.A. & Kennedy, P. (2000). Ranking the criteria for assessing quality of life after disability: evidence for priority shifting among long-term spinal cord injury survivors. *British Journal of Health Psychology*, **5**, 57–69.

White, M.J., Rintala, D.H., Hart, K.A. & Fuhrer, M.J. (1993). Sexual activities, concerns and interests of women with spinal cord injury living in the community. *American Journal of Physical Medicine and Rehabilitation*, **72** (6), 372–378.

Whiteneck, G. (1989). Long-term outlook for persons with quadraplegia. In G. Whiteneck, C. Alder & R.E. Carter (Eds), *The Management of High Quadraplegia* (pp. 353–391). New York: Demos Publications.

Whiteneck, G. (2000, November). *Demographics—the extent of the problem*. Paper presented at the meeting of the International Medical Society of Paraplegia (IMSOP), Sydney, Australia.

Whiteneck, G.G., Charlifue, S.W., Frankel, H.L., Fraser, B.M., Gardner, B.P., Gerhart, M., Krishnan, K., Menter, R.R., Nuseibeh, I., Short, D. & Silver, J. (1992). Mortality, morbidity and psychosocial outcomes of persons spinal cord injured more than twenty years ago. *Paraplegia*, **30**, 617–630.

CHAPTER 15

Clinical Practice Issues in Solid Organ Transplantation

Michelle R. Widows
and
James R. Rodrigue*
University of Florida Health Sciences Center, USA

INTRODUCTION

Organ transplantation offers many patients the opportunity for life extension and better quality of life. Patients who most certainly would have died from their disease or its complications 10 or 20 years ago are now enjoying longer and healthier lives due to transplantation. Profound advances in transplant surgery and pharmacology have been made in the last two decades and these advances have extended the reach of transplantation to more and more patients. Clinical health psychologists are increasingly asked to serve as integrated members of transplant teams or as consultants to transplant centers. They may be asked to evaluate psychological strengths and liabilities of patients being considered for transplantation, to design and deliver interventions to reduce behavioral health liabilities (e.g., smoking cessation, improve adherence, weight loss), to provide psychotherapy following transplantation to enhance the likelihood of positive health outcomes, or to conduct behavioral health research. In addition, clinical health psychologists may be called upon to educate physicians, medical/surgical residents, nurse coordinators, and other allied health professionals about behavioral health issues and their application to the transplant process. The purpose of this chapter, therefore, is to provide a summary of the predominant clinical issues that may confront the clinical health psychologist practicing in the field of solid organ transplantation. We provide a brief overview of the medical indications for transplantation and associated patient survival rates. Next, the key components of the pre-transplant psychological assessment are reviewed. Finally, we highlight the range of interventions that might be expected with patients awaiting or receiving transplantation.

---

* Please address all correspondence to James R. Rodrigue.

Handbook of Clinical Health Psychology. Edited by S. Llewelyn and P. Kennedy.
© 2003 John Wiley & Sons, Ltd.

SOLID ORGAN TRANSPLANTATION: INCIDENCE, INDICATIONS, AND OUTCOMES

The number of solid organ transplants performed annually in the United States and Europe has increased by about 30% in the last decade. Surgical advances have contributed to an expanding range of patients who might benefit from transplant surgery, thus increasing the number of patients evaluated and wait-listed for this intervention. Unfortunately, a severe shortage of suitable organ donors has led to substantially more patients waiting longer periods of time and, consequently, more deaths on transplant waiting lists. It can be conservatively estimated that over 175 000 patients worldwide are currently in need of or wait-listed for solid organ transplantation and that more than 25 000 patients will die within the next year before receiving this potentially life-saving intervention.

Transplantation of the kidney, pancreas, liver, heart, and lung are now routinely performed worldwide. The medical conditions that lead to transplantation and associated survival rates vary by transplant type and transplant center. Nevertheless, the information compiled by the United Network for Organ Sharing (UNOS, 2000) in the United States is generally considered representative of the indications and outcomes reported at centers worldwide. Table 15.1 lists the most common indications for each of the solid organ transplants and associated patient survival rates.

Kidney transplantation is appropriate for patients with chronic and end-stage renal disease (ESRD). The most common conditions leading to transplantation include diabetes, chronic glomerulonephritis, polycystic kidney disease, nephrosclerosis (hypertension), systemic lupus erythematosus (SLE), and interstitial nephritis. Kidney transplantation offers substantial improvement in quality of life and longer life duration, and it is generally more effective than long-term dialysis treatment (Schnuelle, Lorenz & Trede, 1998). Patient survival rates following kidney transplantation are generally high. The most critical factor related to patient survival is the donor source, with patients who receive a living donor kidney (especially from an antigen-matched sibling) having superior survival rates than those who receive a cadaveric kidney.

Pancreas transplantation, historically performed as part of a simultaneous pancreas–kidney transplant, is used for patients with type I (or insulin-dependent) diabetes mellitus and chronic or ESRD. In a much smaller percentage of patients, a pancreas is transplanted in those who already have a functional kidney transplant or in those for whom a subsequent kidney transplant may be avoided. The primary goal of pancreas transplantation, apart from relief from dialysis, is to prevent, slow the progression of, or reverse secondary organ complications that are commonly associated with diabetes. Patient survival rates have steadily improved in the last ten years, and are now comparable to those of cadaveric kidney transplantation alone (Kaufman, 2000).

Once used as a last resort for patients with end-stage liver disease who were on life support, liver transplantation is now an appropriate intervention for patients in earlier stages of chronic liver disease. Liver failure secondary to infectious (hepatitis B and C), toxic (acetaminophen, alcohol), inherited (biliary atresia, inborn errors of metabolism), and immunological (autoimmune hepatitis, primary biliary cirrhosis) causes are now considered indications for transplant consideration. Patient survival rates have improved substantially in recent years and complete rehabilitation can be expected for approximately two-thirds of recipients (Adams et al., 1995). Live donor liver transplantation has recently expanded in the United States and Europe, but has been the primary form of liver transplantation in

Table 15.1 Primary medical conditions leading to solid organ transplantation and 1-, 3-, and 5-year patient survival rates[a]

Indications for transplant	Survival rates[b]		
	1 year	3 years	5 years
*Kidney transplantation (CD[c])	95%	89%	82%
(LD[d])	98%	95%	91%
Type I diabetes mellitus			
Hypertension			
Glomerulonephritis			
*Congenital anomalies			
Kidney–pancreas transplantation	94%	88%	83%
Type I diabetes mellitus			
Liver transplantation	88%	79%	74%
Alcoholic cirrhosis			
Hepatitis B, C			
Primary biliary cirrhosis			
Sclerosing cholangitis			
Autoimmune chronic active hepatitis			
Hepatocellular carcinoma			
Fulminant hepatic failure			
Budd–Chiari syndrome			
Heart transplantation	86%	77%	70%
Ischemic cardiomyopathy			
Idiopathic cardiomyopathy			
Lung transplantation	77%	58%	44%
Emphysema/chronic obstructive pulmonary disease (COPD)			
Cystic fibrosis			
Idiopathic pulmonary fibrosis			
Primary pulmonary hypertension			
Alpha-1 antitrypsin deficiency			

[a] The medical conditions listed here are those that are most common. This list is not intended to be exhaustive.
[b] *Source:* UNOS (2000)
[c] CD = cadaveric donation
[d] LD = living donation

Eastern countries (e.g., Japan) due largely to societal norms limiting cadaveric donation (Hashikura et al., 2001). Nevertheless, long-term patient survival data for adult recipients of live donor liver transplantation are as yet unavailable across multiple transplant centers.

Heart transplantation is appropriate therapy for ischemic idiopathic cardiomyopathies. Generally, patients with heart disease refractory to medical management and an estimated survival of less than two years without transplantation are considered for heart transplantation. Regarding outcomes, over 90% of patients achieve a New York Heart Association class I or II status and long-term survival (i.e., ten years) hovers around 50–60%. Median survival after transplantation is approximately nine years, but increases to 12 years when deaths in the first post-transplant year are removed from analysis (Hosenpud et al., 1999).

Lung transplantation has emerged in the last decade as a viable treatment for various end-stage pulmonary diseases, including emphysema, cystic fibrosis, and pulmonary hypertension. Functional outcomes, including exercise tolerance and pulmonary function tests, generally reflect significant improvement, particularly for patients undergoing bilateral lung transplantation. There may be a slight survival advantage for those receiving bilateral vs single lung transplantation as well, although single lung transplantation remains the most common procedure due largely to the organ donor shortage. While lung volume reduction surgery has garnered support as a viable alternative treatment for patients with chronic obstructive pulmonary disease (Cooper et al., 1995), transplantation remains the treatment of choice for those who meet listing criteria.

PSYCHOLOGICAL ASSESSMENT OF TRANSPLANT CANDIDATES

Rationale

Given the shortage of viable cadaveric donor organs, the fair selection of patients who would benefit optimally from transplantation is of utmost concern. Assessment of potential organ transplant candidates typically occurs within a multidisciplinary context, within which the clinical health psychologist's role is to provide an assessment of the behavioral health strengths and limitations of each patient, particularly as they relate to the potential for positive health outcomes. This might include: an evaluation of informed consent and educability; the patient's ability to form a collaborative relationship with the transplant team and to adhere to medical regimens and recommendations; identification of coping resources, psychopathology, and substance use problems in order to plan for services aimed at intervention or relapse prevention; identification of the psychosocial needs of the family in order to plan for appropriate services; and baseline measurement of cognitive functioning (Levenson & Olbrisch, 2000). It is important to note that the clinical health psychologist is not typically expected to provide a decision as to whether or not a patient should be accepted for transplantation but rather to advise the transplant team about any issues that may impact or interfere with the patient's ability to benefit optimally from transplantation.

Domains of Assessment

The clinical health psychologist's assessment is typically guided by biopsychosocial and systems models of health and illness (Engel, 1980; McDaniel, Hepworth & Doherty, 1992). In addition to the traditional areas of assessment included in a general psychological diagnostic interview, the pre-transplant psychological evaluation must also encompass those domains specific to transplant adaptation and outcome. The psychosocial domains specific to transplantation and subject to evaluation by clinical health psychologists are listed in Table 15.2 and may include: informed consent; motivation for and barriers to transplant; quality of life; cognitive functioning; adherence; behavioral health practices; substance use; psychopathology; coping; and social support. Assessment of the caregiver's psychological functioning and ability to care for the patient are also important domains of the

Table 15.2 Primary domains of the pre-transplant psychological assessment

Informed consent
Motivation for and barrier to transplantation
Quality of life
Cognitive functioning
Adherence
Behavioral health practices
Substance use
Psychopathology
Coping resources
Social support availability and stability

clinical health psychologist's evaluation. A description of the unique aspects of each of these transplant-specific domains follows.

Informed Consent

Given the emotional context of being diagnosed with a life-threatening medical condition that may necessitate major surgery, physical rehabilitation, and the lifelong need for immunosuppressant medication, it is important for the clinical health psychologist to directly assess the individual's informed consent for transplant. Ethically, the ability to give informed consent comprises three key elements: adequate information, adequate decision-making capacity, and freedom from coercion (President's Commission for the Study of Ethical Problems in Medicine and Biomedical and Behavioral Research, 1982). To this end, there should be an assessment of obvious cognitive limitations that may impact decision-making capacity (e.g., mental retardation, active psychosis) and the thought processes associated with the decision to undergo transplantation should be carefully examined. For example, a patient with an active psychiatric disturbance (e.g., schizophrenia) may express desire for transplantation, but his or her cognitive disorganization may have implications for judgment and decision-making capacity that could negatively impact health outcomes. This patient may not fully appreciate their potential for adherence problems and subsequent poor outcome. In terms of adequate information, the clinical health psychologist may assess the patient's knowledge of their medical condition and prognosis, the transplant process itself (e.g., length of surgery and recovery period, caregiving needs, need for immunosuppressant medications, rejection, and infection precautions), and associated risks and benefits. As an example of the importance of the adequate provision of information, a patient may make an emotionally driven initial decision to pursue transplantation but may then later change his or her mind as more information is gathered regarding the full range of risks and benefits in terms of quality of life issues.

Motivation for and Barriers to Transplantation

Motivation to pursue transplantation follows from informed consent. A patient may overtly express informed consent to the transplant team in order to optimize his or her chances to be wait-listed but may continue to experience some ambivalence about the procedure. This ambivalence may present as direct questioning about whether the benefits of transplantation outweigh its potential negative impact on quality of life or as spiritual concerns about possessing someone else's organ. Cultural and religious belief structures also play a role in one's motivation for transplant. While most religious denominations support organ donation and transplantation, certain sects may erect barriers to transplantation by virtue of their concomitant belief systems. For example, a transplant candidate who was self-identified as a Jehovah's Witness informed a clinical health psychologist that his religion would not serve as a barrier to acceptance of a cadaveric organ but would preclude the use of blood transfusions during the transplant surgery. Implicit in the psychologist's assessment of motivation and belief structure barriers to transplantation is the goal of allocating scarce organs to those individuals most likely to obtain positive outcomes following transplant. A transplant candidate who refuses blood products during transplant surgery has the potential for greater mortality should intraoperative complications arise. Potential for negative outcome is less obvious, but no less important, in the individual who was never highly motivated for transplant and who subsequently experiences significant morbidity and ultimate mortality secondary to poor adherence to the post-transplant medication regimen.

Quality of Life

Quality of life is an important clinical marker for evaluating both the patient's illness progression prior to transplant and the relative success of transplantation. By the time a patient has reached the point of evaluation for transplantation, he or she has usually experienced a number of functional limitations and impairments in quality of life. By conducting an assessment of the patient's quality of life, the clinical health psychologist provides the transplant team with information about the patient's functional limitations and establishes a baseline assessment to which subsequent quality of life measurements can be compared. Furthermore, pre-transplant assessment can identify those quality of life domains that may be targets for intervention should they persist following transplantation. The patient's inability to continue working and subsequent reliance on disability benefits, stress associated with taking time off from work if still currently employed, inability to complete activities of daily living, significant fatigue, decreased ability to engage in activities previously enjoyed and changes in role functioning, mood, and cognition are examples of quality of life domains to be examined in the context of this assessment.

Cognitive Functioning

Many medical conditions requiring transplantation can produce changes in cognitive functioning. For instance, encephalopathy, uremia, hypoxia, and hypercarbia are not uncommon in transplant patients (Wijdicks, 1999). The screening and assessment of cognitive functioning, therefore, may provide valuable information about disease progression and other factors that may affect health outcomes following transplantation. In addition to obtaining verbal reports of cognitive status changes from both patients and their caregivers, the clinical health psychologist may also employ behavioral observation and/or screening measures with high sensitivity (e.g., Neurobehavioral Cognitive Status Exam [Kiernan et al., 1987], Trail

Making Tests [Reitan & Wolfson, 1993], Grooved Pegboard [Matthews & Klove, 1964], Rey-Osterrieth Complex Figure Test [Meyers & Meyers, 1995]). Identification of cognitive functioning decrements that are inconsistent with the expected disease course may suggest the need for further neuropsychological and/or neurological testing. Such findings could also have important implications for the development and implementation of appropriate cognitive rehabilitation services.

Adherence

A patient's potential ability to adhere to medical regimens and recommendations is a central issue in the transplant evaluation process. Adherence history speaks to the transplant candidate's ability to form a collaborative relationship with the team, complete required rehabilitation programs prior to and following transplantation, and be compliant with lifelong immunosuppressant medication regimens following transplantation. The potential importance of an individual's adherence cannot be understated, as poor post-transplant adherence to immunosuppressant medications can lead directly to rejection episodes, graft loss, and patient death (see Dew et al., 2001, and Laederach-Hofmann & Bunzel, 2000, for reviews). Typically, the clinical health psychologist uses a variety of approaches to assess adherence behaviors, including direct questioning, corroborative reports, review of medical records, and consultation with physicians and other health providers. Areas of direct patient inquiry about adherence to medication regimens may include: the patient's attitudes toward medication use; knowledge of current medications and their functions, dosages, and instructions for use; and history of previous adherence to medication regimens (e.g., frequency of missed dosages, completion of antibiotic prescriptions to prevent antibody development). Medical appointment adherence should also be assessed through direct patient inquiry, review of medical records, and consultation with health care providers given that it is tied to medication adherence (Laederach-Hofmann & Bunzel, 2000). A history of poor medical appointment adherence or limited contact with health care providers may result in missed or delayed appointments such as post-transplant blood draws, which could reveal episodes of rejection or drug toxicity. Given their immunocompromised status, it is imperative for the transplant recipient to notify their physician of early symptoms of infection such as fever or cough, as delays in seeking medical care could lead to advanced infection, such as pneumonia, that becomes resistant to treatment and ultimately results in death. Medical appointment adherence is also significant in terms of the transplant patient's increased risk of cancer given their immunocompromised status; avoidance of routine screening could ultimately lead to lack of diagnosis and subsequent death. Finally, history of adherence to physician recommendations such as weight loss, dietary recommendations (e.g., salt, sugar, or protein restrictions), sunscreen use, and discontinuation of substance use following initial diagnosis are important to consider when assessing a transplant candidate's overall adherence.

Because transplant candidates are likely to present themselves in a favorable manner in order to "pass" the evaluation process and be accepted for transplant, relying exclusively on patient self-report is discouraged. Obtaining collateral information, such as through a separate interview with the patient's spouse or caregiver and telephone contact with the patient's primary care physician, is highly recommended. Throughout this assessment process, careful attention should be given to the specific barriers to adherence that may be experienced by the patient and how these barriers might be minimized or eliminated throughout the transplant process.

Other Behavioral Health Issues

While adherence is the behavioral health practice with the most obvious impact on transplant outcome and patient survival, other behavioral health issues are important to address in the psychological evaluation. For instance, obesity has been shown to be related to higher transplant waiting list mortality and to post-transplant morbidity and mortality in some solid organ transplant patients (Grady et al., 1999; Kanasky et al., 2002; Sawyer, Pelletier & Pruett, 1999). Clinical health psychologists are appropriately trained to assess the psychological and sociocultural factors that may be associated with obesity and to design interventions to facilitate weight loss.

A transplant candidate's hygiene practices may affect post-transplant recovery via their association with other adherence behaviors or may have a direct impact on post-transplant outcome given that transplant patients are at high risk for infection. For instance, patients who come into contact with animal waste, such as feline feces, are at increased risk of infection due to their immunocompromised status as are those individuals who engage in poor dental care. Individuals who engage in promiscuous sexual practices may be at elevated risk for sexually transmitted diseases, such as hepatitis and human immunodeficiency virus.

Substance Use

The significance of substance use in an individual's candidacy for transplant varies both across and within transplant centers. Substance use may be considered a contraindication to transplantation or an issue requiring intervention before transplant listing by some transplant programs, but not others (Levenson & Olbrisch, 2000). Nevertheless, the clinical health psychologist may be called upon to evaluate issues associated with tobacco, alcohol, illicit drug, and prescribed narcotics use.

Estimates of current tobacco use or history of tobacco abuse range from 12 to 42% among kidney transplant patients to 68–94% among heart transplant patients (Durning & Perri, 2001). Pre-transplant tobacco use is associated with both intraoperative and postoperative complications and has been found to be associated with renal allograft failure and death (Cosio et al., 1999). Additionally, tobacco use places greater stress on transplanted organs responsible for filtering toxins and increases the risk of cancer and cardiovascular disease. As such, solid organ transplant programs may identify tobacco use as a contraindication or barrier to transplant. The clinical health psychologist may be in the best position to comprehensively assess tobacco use and risk for relapse to smoking, and to make appropriate recommendations for intervention. Specific areas of inquiry may include: length of time spent smoking; average and highest levels of use; types of products used; last use of tobacco or nicotine products and reason for quitting at that time; number of prior quit attempts; longest period of smoking cessation; whether or not previous periods of smoking cessation occurred exclusively in the context of restricted environments (e.g., during hospitalization or inpatient substance use treatment); use of smoking cessation aids or techniques; current struggles to remain nicotine and tobacco free; and willingness to engage in smoking cessation and to adopt a nicotine and tobacco free lifestyle if the transplant candidate has not already done so. Based on this information, the clinical health psychologist may then determine the patient's risk for relapse and make recommendations for intervention.

Alcohol use is another important area of assessment for the clinical health psychologist because its use has potential implications for post-transplant recovery and survival. It has been estimated that 29% of liver transplants performed are secondary to alcohol-related liver diseases (Everhart & Beresford, 1997). Furthermore, 15–54% of liver transplant candidates and 4–42% of liver transplant recipients have been found to have a history of alcohol abuse or dependence as well as alcohol-related liver disease (Durning & Perri, 2001). Some controversy has existed as to whether individuals who actively contributed to their disease (e.g., alcohol-related liver disease) should compete equally for transplantation, given the shortage of organs and the number of less "blameworthy" individuals who die while awaiting a new liver. However, there is some empirical evidence that liver transplant recipients with a history of alcohol abuse or dependence do not have higher rates of post-transplant relapse and that *carefully selected* transplant patients do not necessarily have poorer outcome than transplant recipients without such a history (Tringali et al., 1996). As such, rather than excluding from transplantation those patients with alcohol-related disease or a history of problematic alcohol consumption, many transplant programs have established guidelines for accepting such patients for evaluation and transplantation. For instance, many liver transplant programs in the United States require random alcohol screens, specified periods of abstinence (e.g., 6 or 12 months) from alcohol before placement on the waiting list, and/or participation in a relapse prevention program (Everhart & Beresford, 1997; Gastfriend et al., 1989). However, these practices are not without controversy (Weinrieb et al., 2000) and research suggests that length of abstinence is not strongly associated with risk of relapse (Beresford & Lucey, 1994).

A thorough evaluation by the clinical health psychologist should include: the patient's pattern of alcohol consumption over time; patterns of heaviest alcohol consumption; preferred alcoholic beverage; number of prior attempts at abstinence; involvement in treatment programs or efforts to aid in abstinence; number and length of periods of abstinence and whether or not abstinences have occurred exclusively in the context of restricted environments; last alcohol consumption and stated reason for abstinence; history of negative consequences associated with past alcohol consumption; tolerance; withdrawal symptoms; current difficulties maintaining abstinence; and willingness to engage in and adopt an alcohol-free lifestyle. Based on this information, and other assessment instruments (e.g., Inventory of Drinking Situations [Annis, Graham & Davis, 1987]), the clinical health psychologist may then provide the transplant team with an assessment of the patient's risk of relapse and appropriate treatment recommendations.

Estimates of illicit substance abuse range from 5 to 60% across solid organ transplant populations (Durning & Perri, 2001). While not an absolute contraindication for transplantation for many programs (Levenson & Olbrisch, 2000), a history of illicit drug use and the associated risk for relapse should be carefully assessed during the pre-transplant evaluation. This group of patients has a potentially higher risk of infection and nonadherence to prescribed medical regimens due to the disorganized lifestyle associated with active drug use (Gastfriend et al., 1989). The clinical health psychologist, therefore, should obtain a thorough history of the patient's illicit and intravenous drug use, in line with the type of evaluation previously described for assessing tobacco and alcohol history, risk of relapse, and intervention needs.

Use of narcotic pain medications warrant similar evaluation. Although attitudes toward narcotic pain medication use are likely to vary by transplant program, the clinical health psychologist's evaluation may identify those patients who are at elevated risk for problematic use of or dependence on narcotic pain medication post-transplant. While narcotic pain medication use may not necessarily directly impact morbidity and mortality following transplant, it may impact the management of the transplant recipient. Relevant areas of inquiry include: the patient's previous pattern of narcotic pain medication use; types of narcotic pain medications taken; the maximum amount of narcotic pain medication taken within a 24-hour period; taking narcotic pain medication in ways other than as prescribed (e.g., taking it more frequently than prescribed and running out before a prescription is eligible for refill); borrowing other people's narcotic pain medication; obtaining narcotic pain medications from street sources; obtaining prescriptions from several different physicians or emergency room staff; euphoric effects; mixing narcotic pain medication with other substances; increased tolerance; withdrawal symptoms; and history of other opioid abuse. For those patients at risk for opioid abuse or addiction post-transplant, the transplant physician may consider tapering narcotic pain medications prior to transplant, using appropriate trials of non-narcotic pain medications, and careful post-transplant monitoring of narcotic pain medication use. The clinical health psychologist may also help the patient acquire nonpharmacological, or psychological, pain management techniques.

Psychopathology

While psychopathology is not necessarily a contraindication to transplantation per se, the information that the clinical health psychologist can provide to the transplant team regarding current and prior psychological disturbance has implications for transplant recipient selection, patient management, and service needs planning. Psychological disturbance among transplant candidates is fairly common, with incidence rates for depression, anxiety, and personality disturbances estimated to be higher than in the general population (Chacko et al., 1996). Such distress has been shown to be associated with poorer post-transplant health outcomes in some studies (Deshields et al., 1996; Dew, 1994; Shapiro et al., 1995), but not in others (Skotzko et al., 1999; Woodman et al., 1999). Despite the equivocal nature of these findings, the patient's psychological status has implications for decision-making capacity and ability to provide informed consent, as well as for the delivery of appropriate psychological services.

The potential for psychological disturbance during the post-transplant period is heightened by the use of corticosteroids, immunosuppressants, antifungals, antibiotics, and antivirals (Robinson & Levenson, 2001). Prednisone, a corticosteroid used commonly in the post-transplant period, is associated with mood swings, irritability, depression, and mania; these symptoms may be exacerbated among those with previous psychiatric disturbance. Additionally, delirium secondary to immunosuppressant medications may be more common among individuals with a history of psychiatric disturbance. The potential for the occurrence of these psychological symptoms raises practical concerns about patient management during transplant hospitalization as well as concerns about adherence. For example, adherence to medication regimens may be limited by the chaos surrounding a patient's immunosuppressant-induced mania or, alternatively, by the passive suicidal ideation experienced by a depressed transplant recipient. The psychological evaluation, therefore, has the potential to provide valuable aid in treatment planning and in optimizing recovery for such individuals.

Coping

The coping resources available to patients are another important component of the assessment process. In general, active and approach-based coping strategies have been consistently found by researchers to be associated with better psychological adjustment in chronically ill patients. It is important to recognize, however, that coping represents a fluid process characterized by many different strategies, with both adaptive and maladaptive qualities depending on the stage of illness and/or treatment. For example, denial and avoidance may be adaptive at mild levels in those situations where a patient has little control, but may be more dysfunctional when they interfere with a patient's decision-making and adherence behaviors.

Coping strategies that are maladaptive may be an important target of psychological intervention. For instance, patients wait-listed for heart transplantation in the United States may be hospitalized for several months before transplant. Psychological adjustment may be facilitated by the patient's successful coping with the numerous stressors that accompany extended hospitalizations, including isolation from family and friends, adapting to the patient role, anxiety and guilt surrounding the wait for a donor organ and financial concerns (Olbrisch et al., 2002; Porter et al., 1994). The clinical health psychologist can play an important role in developing and implementing a systematic intervention program designed to build effective coping skills in patients awaiting transplantation.

Social Support

Most transplant centers require that patients have at least one identified caregiver who can provide instrumental assistance throughout the transplant process. Indeed, researchers have found that the greater availability and/or higher quality of the support system at various stages in the transplant process are associated with better psychological adjustment and lower psychological distress (Christensen et al., 1989; Dew et al., 1994; Frazier, Davis-Ali & Dahl, 1995), good adherence behaviors (Dew et al., 1996; Shapiro et al., 1995), and longer survival (Rodrigue, Pearman & Moreb, 1999). It is recommended that the clinical health psychologist conduct a separate clinical interview with the primary caregiver. This interview typically follows a course similar to that outlined for the transplant patient (see Table 15.2), but also includes assessment of the marital and/or family system and provides an opportunity to further inquire about concerns that may have developed during the patient interview (e.g., patterns of substance use). Moreover, the assessment should address factors that may functionally limit an individual's ability to serve in a caregiver capacity, such as chronic medical conditions, available work release time or vacation/sick time, employer supportiveness, financial stress associated with taking time off from work, and availability of childcare. In addition to the potential for functional limitations, spouses and other family members may experience some reservations or ambivalence about taking on the responsibility of serving in the caregiver capacity, leading to concerns about the stability of the relationship and support network. Upon identification of areas of potential concern, the transplant psychologist may make recommendations to the transplant team aimed at optimizing the caregiver's ability to serve in such a capacity (e.g., psychological intervention) or identifying alternative caregivers in the family system.

Limitations of Assessment

Socially desirable responses and impression management are distinct possibilities during the transplant evaluation (Carnrike, McCracken & Aikens, 1996). Indeed, the transplant evaluation process assumes a high degree of disclosure about behaviors that may impact suitability as a transplant recipient. Beyond impression management behaviors, some patients may purposefully conceal or misrepresent behaviors that they believe will be perceived negatively, such as recent or ongoing substance use. Thus, the clinical health psychologist's evaluation and subsequent recommendations are limited by the veracity of the reports obtained. As was discussed previously, collateral information, such as record review, separate clinical interview with the patient's spouse, and consultation with relevant health providers, may aid in deflating the impact of social desirability, concealment, and misrepresentation.

COMMON MEASUREMENT STRATEGIES AND TOOLS

The semi-structured clinical interview is perhaps the most widely used means of obtaining a large amount of information in the most time-efficient manner (Levenson & Olbrisch, 2000). Clinical interviews allow for great flexibility, particularly in a time-limited context in which a seasoned clinician may quickly discern that a particular psychosocial domain may be irrelevant for a specific patient and does not warrant further extensive questioning. This greater flexibility, however, also raises the potential that some factors relevant to determining a patient's suitability for transplant may be overlooked. More structured clinical interviews increase the reliability of evaluations, although this may in turn have some limitations on the degree of flexibility available to the clinician.

The Structured Interview for Renal Transplantation (SIRT; Mori, Gallagher & Milne, 2000) is a semi-structured clinical interview designed specifically for use with kidney transplant candidates that allows for reliable assessment of transplant-specific domains within the context of a psychiatric interview. The SIRT is a comprehensive yet fairly flexible protocol through its use of multiple-choice, Likert-ratings, checklist, and open-ended items. It provides cues for seven domains of assessment relevant to determining an individual's appropriateness for renal transplant: (1) background/demographic information; (2) understanding of illness (i.e., diagnosis, current medical and dialysis regimen, and transplant procedure), in order to ascertain informed consent as well as an individual's compliance with medical regimens; (3) education/socioeconomic status, to identify learning barriers that may impact a candidate's educability about the transplant procedure or post-transplant regimens; (4) brief family history, to assess available support; (5) coping/personality style, in order to further assess social support as well as identifying coping deficits and strengths; (6) psychiatric history, including substance use and family history; and (7) mental status exam. The SIRT also has an additional section in which results of psychological testing, laboratory findings, and medications can be recorded. In addition to providing cues for assessment of the aforementioned domains in the clinical interview, the SIRT provides for medical chart review corroboration of patient reports of behavioral health issues. In summary, the SIRT appears to be a comprehensive tool to assist the clinical health psychologist in completing a thorough evaluation of the kidney transplant candidate and may be particularly useful in training situations where evaluators do not have transplant-specific experience. Additionally, the SIRT has the potential to be easily modifiable to reflect the specific issues of differing organ transplant populations.

Even with increased structure in the clinical interview, the interpretation and weighting of the information obtained through clinical interview may vary across professionals, yielding implications for the fair selection of transplant recipients. As such, supplemental rating scales have been developed in order to promote reliability and equanimity in patient selection for transplantation. These scales may aid in the reliable identification of candidate strengths and weaknesses in the relevant domains of interest.

The Psychosocial Assessment of Candidates for Transplant (PACT; Olbrisch, Levenson & Hamer, 1989) is a clinical rating scale that is intended to supplement the clinical interview. The PACT consists of an initial rating of the patient's suitability for transplant based on the clinician's impression from the clinical interview. Using a five-point scale, the clinician then rates the transplant candidate on eight psychosocial domains relevant to a patient's suitability for transplant: (1) family or support system stability; (2) family or support system availability; (3) psychopathology and stable personality factors; (4) risk for psychopathology; (5) healthy lifestyle and ability to sustain change in lifestyle; (6) drug and alcohol use; (7) compliance with medications and medical advice; and (8) relevant knowledge and receptiveness to education. Based on these ratings, the clinician then makes a final rating of the patient's suitability for transplant using a five-point scale (0 = poor, surgery contraindicated; 4 = excellent candidate). Adequate discriminant and convergent validity, as well as interrater reliability, have been reported for the PACT (Olbrisch, Levenson & Hamer, 1989; Olbrisch et al., 1992).

The Transplant Evaluation Rating Scale (TERS; Twillman et al., 1993) is a transplant candidate classification scale adapted from the Psychosocial Levels Systems (PLS; Futterman et al., 1991), a system developed for rating overall adjustment during bone marrow transplantation. Used in conjunction with a clinical interview, the TERS yields three levels of ratings (level 1 = mild/minimal; level 3 = severe) on ten separate biopsychosocial domains that are weighted to make up a final summary rating of the candidate's appropriateness for transplant. The ten biopsychosocial domains rated on the TERS, in order of relative weighting in the final rating, are: (1) DSM-IV (APA, 1994) Axis I psychiatric history; (2) DSM-IV (APA, 1994) Axis II psychiatric history; (3) substance use/abuse; (4) compliance; (5) health behaviors; (6) quality of family/social support; (7) prior history of coping; (8) coping with disease and treatment; (9) quality of affect; and (10) mental status (past and present). The TERS has demonstrated only moderate interrater reliability (kappa range = 0.40 to 0.56), although retrospective ratings were found to be significantly correlated with levels of compliance, substance use, health behaviors, and quality of life one to three years post-transplant (Twillman et al., 1993).

In comparing the relative advantages of the TERS and the PACT, the five-point rating scale of the PACT may allow for greater flexibility in rating candidates on each psychosocial domain than the three-level rating scale of the TERS. The formal weighting system would appear to be an advantage of the TERS in terms of reliability and validity, although this has not been statistically demonstrated. One could argue that the clinician's individual judgment of the relative weight of each domain in the final PACT rating contributes to the validity of determining a patient's suitability for transplant given that different domains may be more relevant to different patients.

Although formal psychometric assessment of psychological functioning is not an integral component of the pre-transplant evaluation at all transplant centers, clinical health psychologists have begun to develop transplant-specific norms for certain psychological instruments (Deshields et al., 1996; Putzke et al., 1997; Rodrigue et al., 2001b; Sears et al., 1999; Streisand et al., 1999). Such norms allow for appropriate within group comparisons, in line with the goal of appropriate and ethical use of psychological tests. Based on this work, transplant population norms are now available for measures of cognitive functioning (e.g., Mini-Mental State Exam [Folstein, Folstein & McHugh, 1975], Trail Making Tests A and B [Reitan & Wolfson, 1993], WAIS-R scales [Wechsler, 1981]), affective and symptom distress (e.g., Beck Anxiety Inventory [Beck & Steer, 1990], Beck Depression Inventory [Beck, 1987], State-Trait Anger Expression Inventory [Speilberger, 1984], State-Trait Anxiety Inventory [Speilberger, 1983], and Symptom Checklist-90-R [Derogatis, 1983]), adjustment to illness (e.g., Psychosocial Adjustment to Illness Scale-Revised [Derogatis & Lopez, 1983]), coping (e.g., Medical Coping Modes Questionnaire [Feifel, Strack & Nagy, 1987]), and quality of life (e.g., Medical Outcomes Study SF-36 Health Survey [Ware, 1993]).

PSYCHOLOGICAL INTERVENTIONS WITH TRANSPLANT PATIENTS AND THEIR FAMILIES

Given that poor behavioral health practices and psychological distress may occur during both the pre-transplant waiting period and post-transplant recovery period, the clinical health psychologist has the opportunity to provide clinical services aimed at optimizing psychological adjustment and transplant outcome. Unfortunately, published empirical investigations examining the effectiveness of such psychological interventions with transplant patients are limited. Rather, the literature consists primarily of descriptive reports of interventions that may be relevant to the psychological treatment of transplant patients.

Behavioral Contracting

A behavioral contingency contract is a written and signed agreement between the transplant patient and the transplant team that identifies the behavior to be changed, the method used to change such behavior, and the outcome or consequence if behavior change does not occur (Cupples & Steslow, 2001). Behavioral contracting may be useful in modifying a number of behavioral health practices that may place a patient at risk for poor outcome following transplant. Use of a behavioral contract promotes standardization of behaviors required for transplant, conveys clear expectations to the transplant candidate, defines the behavior rather than the patient as the problem, enables patients to take responsibility for their behavior, allows for monitoring of the behavior, and facilitates a collaborative relationship (Cupples & Steslow, 2001; Nelson et al., 1995). For example, some transplant programs require that patients at high risk for relapse (e.g., alcohol, tobacco, etc.) meet certain conditions as a contingency for transplant listing. These conditions can be set forth in a behavioral contract and failure to adhere to the agreed upon behaviors would result in the consequence set forth in the contract, such as being removed from active status on the waiting list until the conditions of the contract are met. Table 15.3 provides an example of such a policy or contract in use with the University of Florida liver transplant program. Behavioral contingency contracting is perhaps most widely used by transplant teams for

Table 15.3 The University of Florida Liver Transplant Program Policy on Substance Abuse

The Shands hospital at the University of Florida Liver Transplant Program requires that all patients with a history of substance dependence or abuse agree to the following conditions prior to being accepted for liver transplantation. Please indicate your agreement to each condition by initialing the box to the right and by signing at the end.

1. I understand that at least six months of out-of-hospital abstinence is required ☐
   before transplant listing. Abstinence is defined as "no use in any circumstances"
   and pertains to alcohol and other drugs of dependence or abuse. Continued
   lifetime abstinence may enhance the likelihood of positive health outcomes.
   Therefore, I understand that the transplant program expects continued lifetime
   abstinence and I agree to adopt this as an expectation for myself as well.

2. I agree to participate in a psychological evaluation and behavioral health ☐
   assessment by the transplant psychologist. I understand that my primary
   caregiver is expected to participate in this evaluation as well.

3. I understand that if I am listed for transplantation, I will be required to see the ☐
   transplant psychologist every 90 days while on the transplant list. I understand
   that my primary caregiver is expected to be present for these appointments as
   well.

4. I understand that participation in a relapse prevention program is required for ☐
   those with an abstinence period less than 18 months. In most instances,
   participation in the Shands at the University of Florida Liver Transplant
   Program's relapse prevention program will be required. Exceptions to this latter
   requirement will be made by the Transplant Program only in rare circumstances
   and after appropriate review of treatment program records to ensure
   compliance with the Transplant Program's relapse prevention program criteria.

5. If participating in a relapse prevention program, I agree to provide the ☐
   transplant program with monthly written reports (usually in the form of a letter
   by the treating professional) of my progress in treatment. This is a requirement
   of continued transplant listing until I have been successfully discharged from
   treatment.

6. I understand that any use of any prescription narcotics or sedatives must be ☐
   pre-approved by the transplant physician.

7. I agree to undergo random urine and/or blood screens for substance use as ☐
   requested by the transplant program. Refusal to undergo such testing will be
   treated the same as a positive screen.

8. Substance use during the evaluation process or while listed for transplantation ☐
   will be examined promptly by the transplant team. Any non-approved substance
   use will result in being moved immediately from active to inactive listing status.
   I further understand that, at such time, I will be required to participate in
   another evaluation by the transplant psychologist. Following this evaluation,
   the transplant program may require me to participate in another substance
   abuse treatment program or remove me from the transplant list permanently.

9. I agree to inform my primary caregiver *and* either the transplant coordinator, ☐
   transplant physician, transplant social worker, or transplant psychologist of any
   doubts that I may have about my continued abstinence. Such an open dialogue
   with the team will allow us to work together to ensure continued abstinence
   before relapse occurs.

10. I agree to inform the transplant coordinator, transplant physician, transplant ☐
    social worker, or transplant psychologist about any significant changes in my
    life circumstances (e.g., relationship with primary caregiver, financial
    difficulties, depression, etc.).

(Continues overleaf)

Table 15.3   *(Continued)*

I have read this policy and the transplant psychologist has reviewed it with me. I have had the opportunity to ask questions and these questions have been answered to my satisfaction. I agree to follow what is in this policy. I have been given a copy of this policy for future reference.
Patient Signature_____ Date_____

I have participated in the review of this policy and agree to help the patient follow it. I have been given a copy of this policy for future reference.
Primary Caregiver_____ Date_____

I have explained the above policy to the patient and primary caregiver and have answered their questions.
Transplant Psychologist_____ Date_____

substance use, but it has applicability to other health behaviors such as diet and weight loss, exercise and physical rehabilitation, adherence to medication and medical regimens, safe sexual practices, and hygiene practices.

Substance Use Treatment

Formal substance use treatment or relapse prevention services may be set forth by the transplant team as a specific requirement for transplant listing. Biopsychosocial approaches may include pharmacological treatment, residential and outpatient treatment programs, behavioral treatment, and psychotherapy (Durning & Perri, 2001). Such requirements for treatment may be individualized and may be available from the clinical health psychologist or other treatment providers.

While some individuals are able to quit smoking "cold turkey" or with the aid of nicotine replacement or pharmacotherapy, some patients may require further assistance in adopting a smoke-free lifestyle. Patients may benefit from educational materials provided by community organizations (e.g., American Cancer Society, American Lung Association) or through involvement with agency-sponsored support groups. Individualized smoking cessation programs that deal more extensively with the behavioral and psychological aspects of smoking may be necessary for some patients who have difficulty with smoking cessation. Components of such programs focus on identifying situations and "triggers" associated with smoking, identifying smoking reinforcers, developing more adaptive alternative coping strategies, and developing a relapse prevention plan. Additionally, motivational interviewing techniques appear to be useful in assisting the patient with resolution of ambivalence toward smoking cessation (Miller & Rollnick, 1991).

With regard to alcohol consumption, estimates of "any drinking" after liver transplant range from 0 to 95% while estimates of "problem drinking" after liver transplant range from 0 to 40% (Durning & Perri, 2001), highlighting the potential for intervention with subsamples of patients. A number of treatment approaches may be useful for patients who exhibit problematic alcohol or illicit drug use or who may be at high risk for relapse. Active alcohol/drug abuse or dependence may require inpatient or outpatient treatment in a designated substance abuse treatment program or center. For some patients, regular participation in Alcoholics Anonymous or Narcotics Anonymous (NA) with a sponsor may be sufficient in terms of treatment and relapse prevention, although some individuals do not achieve benefit from this approach due to philosophical conflicts with the tenets of these organizations.

Individualized and structured relapse prevention programs are an alternative that may be helpful in maintaining abstinence (Wagner, Haller & Olbrisch, 1996). Relapse prevention programs aim to help individuals develop a relapse-resistant lifestyle through use of analysis of substance use patterns, identification of high relapse risk situations, development of more adaptive coping strategies, and identification of a relapse prevention plan. Transplant patients referred for relapse prevention may differ from the typical substance abuser who presents for treatment in that transplant patients may have never perceived their substance use as problematic and thus may have limited motivation for behavioral change. Again, motivational interviewing techniques may therefore be helpful in facilitating a transplant patient's readiness to change alcohol and drug behaviors (Miller & Rollnick, 1991).

Psychotherapy

Supportive and cognitive-behavioral individual psychotherapy may be indicated for transplant candidates and recipients due to the potential for psychological distress and adjustment difficulties during the pre-transplant waiting period and post-transplant recovery. The transplant patient is faced with a number of stressors during these periods and may benefit from a supportive therapeutic relationship within which to discuss their concerns. During the pre-transplant period, patients may experience depression and anxiety and struggle with denial, death and dying issues, fears and concerns about the procedure, guilt associated with benefiting from the death of the donor, financial stress, and family stress (Olbrisch et al., 2002). Following transplantation, affective distress, fear of graft rejection, reintegration into the family system, body image changes, existential concerns, and unrealistic expectations for recovery may be prominent themes in individual psychotherapy. Couples or marital therapy may also be useful in addressing caregiving stressors, communication difficulties, and role changes in the relationship.

A variety of psychotherapeutic interventions have been suggested as potentially beneficial in the treatment of the depression, anxiety, and adjustment difficulties experienced by transplant patients (Olbrisch et al., 2002). Cognitive-behavior therapy might focus on unrealistic expectations, irrational thought patterns, and behavioral exercises aimed at increasing patient activity level. Anxiety reduction techniques such as systematic desensitization, relaxation training, guided imagery, and hypnosis have potential utility throughout the transplant process. Such techniques may also be beneficial as adjuncts to pharmacological management of pain, as some patients present with significant post-surgical pain. Skill building techniques, such as stress management, anger management, and coping skills training, may facilitate patient adjustment and may be particularly relevant for certain transplant patients, especially those who may be hospitalized for several months before transplantation. Additionally, specific trauma-focused interventions may be effective with transplant patients experiencing post-traumatic stress symptoms secondary to transplant (DuHamel et al., 2000; Stukas et al., 1999). To our knowledge, there have been no systematic investigations of the use and effectiveness of such interventions with solid organ transplant patients, although their utility has been demonstrated in cancer populations (Trijsburg, van Knippenberg & Rijpma, 1992). For instance, Gaston-Johansson and colleagues (2000) found that use of a comprehensive coping strategy program (CCSP) consisting of preparatory information, cognitive restructuring, relaxation, and guided imagery was associated with decreased nausea, fatigue, and anxiety among 52 breast cancer patients treated with autologous bone marrow transplantation. Additionally, relaxation and imagery, cognitive-behavioral coping skills training (Syrjala et al., 1995), and hypnosis (Syrjala, Cummings & Donaldson, 1992) have been found to reduce pain during cancer treatment. An interesting study found that massage therapy for autologous bone marrow transplantation was associated with im-mediate reductions in distress, fatigue, nausea, and anxiety, although the authors were unable to evaluate how long these effects were maintained (Ahles et al., 1999). A meta-analytic review of empirical studies of psychological interventions with cancer patients prior to 1992 demonstrates the effectiveness of a number of various intervention strategies. Specifically, behavioral interventions were found to be effective in the treatment of anxiety and pain, structured counseling (i.e., educational and behavioral components) was found to decrease depression and distress, and tailored counseling (i.e., counseling and support) had effects on distress, self-concept, health locus of control, fatigue, and sexual problems (Trijsburg, van Knippenberg & Rijpma, 1992).

Support Groups

Support groups are widely available to transplant patients and offer the opportunity for patients to gather emotional support and information from others who have shared simi-lar experiences. Again, while no known empirical data are available with regard to their effectiveness, several reports provide information regarding the nature of the support groups typically conducted with transplant populations (Abbey & Farrow, 1998; Stewart et al., 1995). The structure of the transplant support group may vary across settings, ranging from groups run by transplant patients or paraprofessionals for their supportive benefit to more structured groups with psychoeducational and psychotherapeutic components. The more structured support groups typically focus on family and role relationships, health beliefs and maintenance, financial stressors, coping and stress tolerance, self-perception, and substance use, but may also provide a forum for the exploration of existential issues and psychological distress (Stewart et al., 1995). Some transplant programs have developed quite extensive and comprehensive group treatment programs for their pre- and post-transplant patients, con-sisting of linear combinations of interpersonal and supportive-expressive therapy groups, supportive and psychoeducational discussion groups, and education seminars (Abbey & Farrow, 1998). In addition to expanding the support system base, such groups may effec-tively integrate family members into the transplant process.

LONG-TERM FOLLOW-UP AND RECOVERY ISSUES

The literature examining long-term follow-up of transplant recipients is very limited. Most studies reporting on the long-term functioning of transplant recipients have focused exclu-sively on measuring quality of life. In general, solid organ transplantation appears to lead to significant improvements in quality of life (see Dew et al., 2000, for a comprehensive re-view). However, it is also clear from these studies that some patients continue to experience difficulties long after transplant surgery, including fatigue, work-related difficulties, and affective distress. Additional long-term recovery issues may include: body image concerns (e.g., secondary to surgical scars and corticosteroid-induced weight gain, skin changes, and hair growth); financial concerns; family system disruption; unrealistic expectations for recovery; depression and anxiety related to graft rejection, infection, and retransplantation;

and death and dying. The availability of long-term psychological follow-up and intervention for transplant recipients should be a priority for transplant programs, and should include periodic monitoring and assessment of psychological functioning and other behavioral health issues that may warrant intervention.

While the literature has focused largely on identifying the psychological costs of transplantation (i.e., prevalence of depression, anxiety, stress, etc.), it should be emphasized that positive psychological outcomes are also possible. For instance, the concept of "post-traumatic growth" (Tedeschi, Park & Calhoun, 1998) following life-threatening medical illness may hold particular relevance for transplant patients. Changes in self-perception, relationships with others, and one's philosophy of life may characterize such growth. Positive changes in self-perception may include identification as a survivor (vs victim) and greater self-reliance. Positive changes in a patient's relationships with others may include greater self-disclosure and emotional expressiveness, more compassion for and sensitivity toward others, and sustained efforts at improving relationships. Patients who are faced with a traumatic event may rely on their social network to discuss their experiences and may become more sensitive to the suffering and experiences of others. A changed philosophy of life may be evident through reprioritization, greater appreciation of life, finding a sense of meaning, and spiritual growth. While no empirical investigations have been published regarding the presence of post-traumatic growth among solid organ transplant recipients, our clinical experience suggests that many of our patients do experience these positive changes, even in the presence of psychological distress and poor quality of life.

LIVING ORGAN DONATION

This chapter would not be complete without some discussion of the clinical health psychologist's role in living organ donation. It is generally recognized that the number of individuals on transplant waiting lists has grown substantially in recent years and has far outpaced the number of available organ donors. This widening gap has meant an increase in the number of deaths while waiting for organ transplantation. While many efforts have been made to better understand the factors that affect organ donation decisions, transplant programs and patients are confronted with rapidly expanding waiting lists, more deaths on waiting lists, only slight increases in cadaveric organ donation, and new organ distribution policies. Living organ donation represents a critical step toward increasing the number of transplants that are done, reducing waiting times, and saving the lives of those in need of transplantation (Tarantino, 2000). In addition to freeing the number of cadaveric kidneys for other recipients, living donation affords several advantages. For instance, it allows for the scheduling of transplantation at a time of optimal donor and recipient health, the avoidance of dialysis for some kidney transplant patients, the pre-empting of a rapidly deteriorating quality of life, the use of potentially better quality organs than those from cadavers, lower rates of acute rejection, and higher graft and patient survival rates. Moreover, graft and patient survival rates are higher for living donor transplants.

In years past, living organ donation was restricted to individuals with a genetic or a strong emotional connection to the recipient. In more recent years, however, there has been an increase in the number of "Good Samaritan donors" (Olbrisch et al., 2001), those with an indirect or a distant relationship to the recipient, and "donors-at-large" (or stranger donors), those who are not aware of a particular patient in need and who simply want to donate an organ to the waiting list. Good Samaritan donors and donors-at-large raise important ethical

Table 15.4 Primary domains of the living donor interview

Donor motives
Decision-making process
Prior attitudes and beliefs about organ donation
Ambivalence about donation
Cognitive functioning and ability to provide informed consent
Knowledge of the surgical procedure and associated risks
Expectations about recovery as well as recipient morbidity and mortality
Subtle and/or overt forms of coercion from recipient or family members
Nature and stability of donor–recipient relationship
Attitudes of significant others toward donation decision
Coping resources
Past and/or current psychological problems and associated interventions
Substance use history (tobacco, alcohol, drugs, pain medications)
Spirituality and/or religious barriers
Current life stress
Availability and stability of both emotional and instrumental support
History of pain tolerance and pain management strategies

---

and clinical issues, and there is a clear consensus that clinical health psychologists should play a prominent role in evaluating these prospective candidates for living donor surgery.

Clinical health psychologists are increasingly called upon to conduct evaluations of potential living organ donors and to assess outcomes following donation (Olbrisch et al., 2001; Rodrigue, Bonk & Jackson, 2001a). As highlighted in Table 15.4, initial clinical interviews typically focus on many issues pertinent to the donation decision, understanding of the risks and benefits, and psychological stability. Socially desirable responding is common in the context of donor evaluations, so careful attention must be given to the possibility that prospective donors may deceive the evaluator about unethical arrangements or may conceal highly relevant information (e.g., substance abuse).

Until recent, the primary outcomes of interest for living donors were mortality and morbidity. Mortality figures for living donation are quite favorable for kidney and liver donation (Broelsch et al., 2000; Najarian et al., 1992). Post-operative and long-term morbidity may include pain and discomfort, pulmonary embolus, the need for splenectomy, development of proteinuria, hypertension, or progressive renal or liver failure, and the need for transplantation, to name only a few. Today, there is a burgeoning interest in health-related outcomes that extend beyond mortality and morbidity. These include health-related quality of life, psychological risks and benefits, changes in donor–recipient relationships, and health service utilization. Several studies across different transplant centers have reported good of quality of life in the months and years following living donation, with some even reporting significantly better quality of life than the general population. Positive psychological outcomes (e.g., higher self-esteem and self-image, increased happiness, feelings of being a better person, improved relationship with the recipient) have also been reported, although some negative ramifications have included concerns about physical health, appearance, and sexuality, as well as feelings of depression (see Switzer, Dew & Twillman, 2000, for a comprehensive review).

The degree to which the living donation experience affects the relationship between the donor and the recipient has been of substantial clinical interest. However, there has not been any systematic study of how, if at all, the donor–recipient relationship changes over time following living donation. In our own experience, many donors and recipients report positive changes in the relationship (i.e., feeling closer to each other) and some of these perceptions have been reported in retrospective investigations (Simmons et al., 1987). Negative changes in the donor–recipient relationship have also been observed when, for instance, the recipient engages in health-compromising behaviors (e.g., noncompliance, substance use) or when the donor demands too much praise for his or her sacrifice. Of course, it is also possible that the donor–recipient relationship does not change at all. Changes in the donor–recipient relationship that do occur may be moderated by other factors, including the functioning of the graft, the recipient's health behaviors and quality of life, and the donor's psychological status and quality of life. One additional factor that may be related to such relationship changes is the type of donor–recipient relationship. For instance, there may be important implications for relationship outcomes based on whether the donor and recipient are genetically related (e.g., parent, sibling), emotionally related (e.g., spouse), or emotionally unrelated (e.g., friend, coworker). The precise nature and extent to which such donor–recipient types impact relationships in the short- and long-term are unknown and clearly warrant investigation.

In summary, living organ donation holds the potential to extend the lives of many individuals who are currently awaiting organ transplantation. With a relatively flat rate of cadaveric donation, the increase in living organ donation has become a major focus in efforts to close the gap between actual donation rates and the number of patients on transplant waiting lists. Clinical health psychologists can play a prominent role in the evaluation and treatment of candidates for living organ donation, as well as in the evaluation of outcomes following donation.

SUMMARY

Solid organ transplantation holds great promise for many patients with end-stage organ failure. Its broad reach is now limited primarily by a severe organ shortage. Within the context of transplantation, clinical health psychologists are increasingly asked to play a key role in the evaluation and treatment of transplant patients and their families. We strongly encourage the development and implementation of routine psychological services as components of all transplant programs. Such services should include: (1) initial evaluation services to identify patients' behavioral health strengths and liabilities, psychological resources, and social support availability and stability; (2) the implementation of psychological or behavioral health interventions to enhance the likelihood of positive health outcomes both before and after transplantation; and (3) the routine assessment of patients in the months and years after transplantation to identify in a timely manner those in need of follow-up psychological services. It is our belief that the integration of these services into all transplant programs is essential if the full benefit of solid organ transplantation is to be realized.

ACKNOWLEDGMENT

The preparation of this chapter was supported in part by Grant No. R01 DK55706 02 from the National Institute of Diabetes and Digestive and Kidney Diseases awarded to James R. Rodrigue.

REFERENCES

Abbey, S. & Farrow, S. (1998). Group therapy and organ transplantation. *International Journal of Group Psychotherapy*, **48**, 163–185.

Adams, P.C., Ghent, C.N., Grant, D.R. & Wall, W.J. (1995). Employment after liver transplantation. *Hepatology*, **21**, 140–144.

Ahles, T.A., Tope, D.M., Pinkson, B., Walch, S., Hann, D., Whedon, M., Dain, B., Weiss, J.E., Mills, L. & Silberfarb, P.M. (1999). Massage therapy for patients undergoing autologous bone marrow transplantation. *Journal of Pain and Symptom Management*, **18**, 157–163.

Annis, H.M., Graham, J.M. & Davis, C.S. (1987). *Inventory of Drinking Situations: User's Guide.* Toronto: Addiction Research Foundation.

APA (1994). *Diagnostic and Statistical Manual of Mental Disorders* (4th edn). Washington, DC: American Psychiatric Association.

Beck, A.T. (1987). *Beck Depression Inventory.* San Antonio, TX: The Psychological Corporation.

Beck, A. & Steer, R.A. (1990). *Beck Anxiety Inventory.* San Antonio, TX: The Psychological Corporation.

Beresford, T. & Lucey, M.R. (1994). Alcoholics and liver transplantation: facts, biases, and the future. *Addiction*, **89**, 1043–1048.

Broelsch, C.E., Malago, M., Testa, G. & Gamazo, C.V. (2000). Living donor liver transplantation in adults: outcome in Europe. *Liver Transplantation*, **6**, S64–S65.

Carnrike, C.L.M., McCracken, L. & Aikens, J.E. (1996). Social desirability, perceived stress, and PACT ratings in lung transplant candidates: a preliminary investigation. *Journal of Clinical Psychology in Medical Settings*, **3**, 57–67.

Chacko, R.C., Harper, R.G., Kunik, M. & Young, J. (1996). Relationship of psychiatric morbidity and psychosocial factors in organ transplant candidates. *Psychosomatics*, **37**, 100–107.

Christensen, A.L., Turner, C.W., Slaughter, J.R. & Holman, J.M. (1989). Perceived family support as a moderator of psychological well-being in end-stage renal disease. *Journal of Behavioral Medicine*, **12**, 249–265.

Cooper, J.D., Trulock, E.P., Triantafillou, A.M., Patterson, G.A., Pohl, M.S., Deloney, P.A., Sundaresan, R.S. & Roper, C.L. (1995). Bilateral pneumonectomy (volume reduction) for chronic obstructive pulmonary disease. *Journal of Thoracic and Cardiovascular Surgery*, **109**, 106–119.

Cosio, F.G., Falkenhain, M.F., Pesavento, T.E., Yim, S., Alamir, A., Henry, M.L. & Ferguson, R.M. (1999). Patient survival after renal transplantation: II. The impact of smoking. *Clinical Transplantation*, **13**, 336–341.

Cupples, S.A. & Steslow, B. (2001). Use of behavioral contingency contracting with heart transplant candidates. *Progress in Transplantation*, **11**, 137–144.

Derogatis, L.R. (1983). *SCL-90: Administration, Scoring, and Procedures Manual for the Revised Version.* Baltimore, MD: Clinical Psychometric Research.

Derogatis, L.R. & Lopez, M.C. (1983). *Psychosocial Adjustment to Illness Scale.* Baltimore, MD: Clinical Psychometric Research.

Deshields, T.L., McDonnough, M.E., Mannen, K. & Miller, L.W. (1996). Psychological and cognitive status before and after heart transplantation. *General Hospital Psychiatry*, **18**, S62–S69.

Dew, M.A. (1994). Behavioral factors in heart transplantation: quality of life and medical compliance. *Journal of Applied Biobehavioral Research*, **2**, 28–54.

Dew, M.A., Dunbar-Jacob, J., Switzer, G.E., DiMartini, A.F., Stilley, C. & Kormos, R.L. (2001). Adherence to the medical regimen in transplantation. In J.R. Rodrigue (Ed.), *Biopsychosocial Perspectives on Transplantation* (pp. 93–124) New York: Kluwer Academic/Plenum Publishers.

Dew, M.A., Goycoolea, J.M., Switzer, G.E. & Allen, A.S. (2000). Quality of life in organ transplantation: effects on adult recipients and their families. In P.T. Trzepacz & A.F. DiMartini (Eds), *The Transplant Patient: Biological, Psychiatric, and Ethical Issues in Organ Transplantation* (pp. 67–145). Cambridge: Cambridge University Press.

Dew, M.A., Roth, L.H., Thompson, M.E., Kormos, R.L. & Griffith, B.P. (1996). Medical compliance and its predictors in the first year after heart transplantation. *Journal of Heart and Lung Transplantation*, **15**, 631–645.

Dew, M.A., Simmons, R.G., Roth, L.H., Schulberg, H.C., Thompson, M.E., Armitage, J.M. & Griffith, B.P. (1994). Psychosocial predictors of vulnerability to distress in the year following heart transplantation. *Psychological Medicine*, **24**, 929–945.

DuHamel, K.N., Ostroff, J.S., Bovbjerg, D.H., Pfeffer, M., Morasco, B.J., Papadoupoulos, E. & Redd, W.H. (2000). Trauma-focused intervention after bone marrow transplantation: a case study. *Behavior Therapy*, **31**, 175–186.

Durning, P.E. & Perri, M.G. (2001). Substance abuse and transplantation. In J.R. Rodrigue (Ed.), *Biopsychosocial Perspectives on Transplantation* (pp. 125–149). New York: Kluwer Academic/Plenum Publishers.

Engel, G.L. (1980). The clinical application of the biopsychosocial model. *American Journal of Psychiatry*, **137**, 535–544.

Everhart, J.E. & Beresford, T.P. (1997). Liver transplantation for alcoholic liver disease: a survey of transplantation programs in the United States. *Liver Transplantation and Surgery*, **3**, 220–226.

Feifel, H., Strack, S. & Nagy, V.T. (1987). Coping strategies and associated features of medically ill patients. *Psychosomatic Medicine*, **49**, 616–625.

Folstein, M.F., Folstein, S.E. & McHugh, P.R. (1975). Mini-Mental State. A practical guideline for grading the cognitive state of patients for the clinician. *Journal of Psychiatric Research*, **12** (3), 189–198.

Frazier, P.A., Davis-Ali, S.H. & Dahl, K.E. (1995). Stressors, social support, and adjustment in kidney transplant patients and their spouses. *Social Work in Health Care*, **21**, 93–108.

Futterman, A.D., Wellisch, D.K., Bond, G. & Carr, C.R. (1991). The Psychosocial Levels System: a new rating scale to identify and assess emotional difficulties during bone marrow transplantation. *Psychosomatics*, **32**, 177–186.

Gastfriend, D.R., Surman, O.S., Gaffey, G.K. & Dienstag, J.L. (1989). Substance abuse and compliance in organ transplantation. *Substance Abuse*, **10**, 149–153.

Gaston-Johansson, F., Fall-Dickson, J.M., Nanda, J., Ohly, K. Krum, S. & Kennedy, M. (2000). The effectiveness of the comprehensive coping strategy program on clinical outcomes in breast cancer autologous bone marrow transplantation. *Cancer Nursing*, **23**, 277–285.

Grady, K.L., White-Williams, C., Naftel, D., Costanzo, M.R., Pitts, D., Rayburn, B., VanBakel, A., Jaski, B., Bourge, R., Kirklin, J. & the Cardiac Transplant Research Database (CTRD) Group. (1999). Are preoperative obesity and cachexia risk factors for post heart transplant morbidity and mortality? A multi-institutional study of preoperative weight-height indices. *Clinical Heart Transplantation*, **18**, 750–763.

Hashikura, Y., Kawasaki, S., Terada, M., Ikegami, T., Nakazawa, Y., Urata, K., Chisuwa, H., Mita, A., Ohno, Y. & Miyagawa, S. (2001). Long-term results of living-related donor liver transplantation: a single-center analysis of 110 transplants. *Transplantation*, **72**, 95–99.

Hosenpud, J.D., Bennett, L.E., Keck, B.M., Fiol, B., Boucek, M.M. & Novick, R.J. (1999). The registry of the international society for heart and lung transplantation: sixteenth official report—1999. *Journal of Heart and Lung Transplantation*, **18**, 611–626.

Kanasky, W.F., Anton, S.D., Rodrigue, J.R., Perri, M.G., Szwed, T. & Baz, M.A. (2002). Impact of body weight on long-term survival after lung transplantation. *Chest*, **121**, 401–406.

Kaufman, D.B. (2000). Kidney transplantation. In F.P. Stuart, M.M. Abecassis & D.B. Kaufman (Eds), *Organ Transplantation* (pp. 105–144). Georgetown, TX: Landes Bioscience.

Kiernan, R.J., Mueller, J., Langston, J.W. & Van Dyke, C. (1987). The Neurobehavioral Cognitive Status Examination. *Annals of Internal Medicine*, **107**, 481–485.

Laederach-Hofmann, K. & Bunzel, B. (2000). Noncompliance in organ transplant recipients: a literature review. *General Hospital Psychiatry*, **22**, 412–424.

Levenson, J.L. & Olbrisch, M.E. (2000). Psychosocial screening and selection of candidates for organ transplantation. In P.T. Trzepacz & A. DiMartini (Eds), *Psychiatric Issues in Organ Transplantation* (pp. 21–41). Oxford: Oxford University Press.

Matthews, C.G. & Klove, H. (1964). *Instruction Manual for the Adult Neuropsychology Test Battery*. Madison, WI: University of Wisconsin Medical School.

McDaniel, S.H., Hepworth, J. & Doherty, W.J. (1992). *Medical Family Therapy: A Biopsychosocial Approach to Families with Health Problems*. New York: Basic Books.

Meyers, J. & Meyers, K. (1995). *The Meyers Scoring System for the Rey Complex Figure and the Recognition Trial: Professional Manual*. Odessa, FL: Psychological Assessment Resources.

Miller, W.R. & Rollnick, S. (1991). *Motivational Interviewing*. New York: Guilford Press.

Mori, D.L., Gallagher, P. & Milne, J. (2000). The Structured Interview for Renal Transplantation—SIRT. *Psychosomatics*, **41**, 393–406.

Najarian, J.S., Chavers, B.M., McHugh, L.E. & Matas, A.J. (1992). 20 years or more of follow-up of living kidney donors. *Lancet*, **340**, 807–810.

Nelson, M.K., Presberg, B.A., Olbrisch, M.E. & Levenson, J.L. (1995). Behavioral contingency contracting to reduce substance abuse and other high-risk health behaviors in organ transplant patients. *Journal of Transplant Coordination*, **5**, 35–40.

Olbrisch, M.E., Levenson, J.L. & Hamer, R. (1989). The PACT: a rating scale for the study of clinical decision making in psychosocial screening of organ transplant candidates. *Clinical Transplantation*, **3**, 164–169.

Olbrisch, M.E., Benedict, S.M., Ashe, K. & Levenson, J.L. (2002). Psychological assessment and care of organ transplant patients: a review. *Journal of Consulting and Clinical Psychology*, **70**, 771–783.

Olbrisch, M.E., Benedict, S.M., Haller, D.L. & Levenson, J.L. (2001). Psychosocial assessment of living organ donors: clinical and ethical considerations. *Progress in Transplantation*, **11**, 40–49.

Olbrisch, M.E., Levenson, J.L., Sherwin, E.D. & Best, A.M. (1992, May). *Concurrent validation of the PACT in 40 cardiac transplant candidates*. Paper presented at the Second Working Conference on Psychiatric, Psychosocial and Ethical Aspects of Organ Transplantation, Pittsburgh, PA.

Porter, R.R., Krout, L., Parks, V., Gibbs, S., Luers, E.S., Nolan, M.T., Cupples, S.A., Lepley, D., Givan, D.A., Ohler, L. & Nunes, N. (1994). Perceived stress and coping strategies among candidates for heart transplantation during the organ waiting period. *Journal of Heart and Lung Transplantation*, **13**, 102–107.

President's Commission for the Study of Ethical Problems in Medicine and Biomedical and Behavioral Research (1982). *Making Health Care Decisions*. Washington, DC: US Government Printing Office.

Putzke, J.D., Williams, M.A., Millsaps, C.L., Azrin, R.L., LaMarche, J.A., Bourge, R.C., Kirklin, J.K., McGiffin, D.C. & Boll, T.J. (1997). Heart transplant candidates: a neuropsychological descriptive database. *Journal of Clinical Psychology in Medical Settings*, **4**, 343–355.

Reitan, R.M. & Wolfson, D. (1993). *The Halstead–Reitan Neuropsychological Test Battery: Theory and Clinical Interpretation*. Tucson, AZ: Neuropsychology Press.

Robinson, M.J. & Levenson, J.L. (2001). Psychopharmacology in transplantation. In J.R. Rodrigue (Ed.), *Biopsychosocial Perspectives on Transplantation* (pp. 151–172). New York: Kluwer Academic/Plenum Publishers.

Rodrigue, J.R., Bonk, V. & Jackson, S. (2001a). Psychological considerations of living organ donation. In J.R. Rodrigue (Ed.), *Biopsychosocial Perspectives on Transplantation* (pp. 59–70). New York: Kluwer Academic/Plenum Publishers.

Rodrigue, J.R., Pearman, T.P. & Moreb, J. (1999). Morbidity and mortality following bone marrow transplantation: predictive utility of pre-BMT affective functioning, compliance, and social support stability. *International Journal of Behavioral Medicine*, **6**, 241–254.

Rodrigue, J.R., Kanasky, W.F., Marhefka, S.L., Perri, M.G. & Baz, M. (2001b). A psychometric normative database for pre-lung transplantation evaluations. *Journal of Clinical Psychology in Medical Settings*, **8**, 229–236.

Sawyer, R.G., Pelletier, S.J. & Pruett, T.L. (1999). Increased early morbidity and mortality with acceptable long-term function in severely obese patients undergoing liver transplantation. *Clinical Transplantation*, **13**, 126–130.

Schnuelle, P., Lorenz, D. & Trede, M. (1998). Impact of renal cadaveric transplantation on survival in end-stage renal failure: evidence for reduced mortality risk compared with hemodialysis during long-term follow-up. *Journal of the American Society of Nephrology*, **9**, 2135–2141.

Sears, S.F., Rodrigue, J.R., Sirois, B.C., Urizar, G.G. & Perri, M.G. (1999). Extending psychometric norms for pre-cardiac transplantation evaluations: the Florida cohort, 1990–1996. *Journal of Clinical Psychology in Medical Settings*, **6**, 303–316.

Shapiro, P.A., Williams, D.L., Foray, A.T., Gelman, I.S., Wukich, N. & Sciacca, R. (1995). Psychosocial evaluation and prediction of compliance problems and morbidity after heart transplantation. *Transplantation*, **60**, 1462–1466.

Simmons, R.G., Klein Marine, S. & Simmons, R.L. (1987). *Gift of Life: The Effect of Organ Transplantation on Individual, Family, and Societal Dynamics*. New York: Transaction Books.

Skotzko, C.E., Rudis, R., Kobashigawa, J. & Laks, H. (1999). Psychiatric disorders and outcome following cardiac transplantation. *Journal of Heart and Lung Transplantation*, **18**, 952–956.

Speilberger, C.D. (1983). *Manual for the State-Trait Anxiety Inventory*. Palo Alto, CA: Consulting Psychologists Press.

Speilberger, C.D. (1984). *The State-Trait Anger Expression Inventory: Research Edition*. Odessa, FL: Psychological Assessment Resources.

Stewart, A.M., Kelly, B., Robinson, J.D. & Callender, C.O. (1995). The Howard University Hospital transplant and dialysis support group: twenty years and going strong. *International Journal of Group Psychotherapy*, **45**, 471–488.

Streisand, R.M., Rodrigue, J.R., Sears, S.F., Perri, M.G., Davis, G.L. & Banko, C.G. (1999). A psychometric normative database for pre-liver transplantation evaluations: the Florida cohort 1991–1996. *Psychosomatics*, **40**, 479–485.

Stukas, A.A., Dew, M.A., Switzer, G.E., DiMartini, A., Kormos, R.L. & Griffith, B.P. (1999). PTSD in heart transplant recipients and their primary family caregivers. *Psychosomatics*, **40**, 212–221.

Switzer, G.E., Dew, M.A. & Twillman, R.K. (2000). Psychosocial issues in living organ donation. In P. Trzepacz & A. DiMartini (Eds), *The Transplant Patient: Biological, Psychiatric and Ethical Issues in Organ Transplantation* (pp. 42–66). Cambridge: Cambridge University Press.

Syrjala, K.L., Cummings, C. & Donaldson, G.W. (1992). Hypnosis or cognitive-behavioral training for the reduction of pain and nausea during cancer treatment: a controlled clinical trial. *Pain*, **48**, 137–146.

Syrjala, K.L., Donaldson, G.W., Davis, M.W., Kippes, M.E. & Carr, J.E. (1995). Relaxation and imagery and cognitive-behavioral training to reduce pain during cancer treatment. *Pain*, **63**, 189–198.

Tarantino, A. (2000). Why should we implement living donation in renal transplantation? *Clinical Nephrology*, **53**, 55–63.

Tedeschi, R.G., Park, C.L. & Calhoun, L.G. (1998). Posttraumatic growth: conceptual issues. In R.G. Tedeschi, C.L. Park & L.G. Calhoun (Eds), *Posttraumatic Growth: Positive Changes in the Aftermath of Crisis*. Mahwah, NJ: Lawrence Erlbaum Associates.

Trijsburg, R.W., van Knippenberg, F.C.E. & Rijpma, S.E. (1992). Effects of psychological treatment on cancer patients: a critical review. *Psychosomatic Medicine*, **54**, 489–517.

Tringali, R.A., Trzepacz, P.T., DiMartini, A. & Dew, M.A. (1996). Assessment and follow-up of alcohol-dependent liver transplant patients: a clinical cohort. *General Hospital Psychiatry*, **18**, S70–S77.

Twillman, R.K., Manetto, C., Wellisch, D.K. & Wolcott, D.L. (1993). The Transplant Evaluation Rating Scale: a revision of the psychosocial levels system for evaluating organ transplant candidates. *Psychosomatics*, **34**, 144–153.

UNOS (2000). *Annual Report of the US Scientific Registry for Transplantation Recipients and the Organ Procurement and Transplant Network*. Richmond, VA: United Network for Organ Sharing, Division of Transplantation.

Wagner, C.C., Haller, D.L. & Olbrisch, M.E. (1996). Relapse prevention treatment for liver transplant patients. *Journal of Clinical Psychology in Medical Settings*, **3**, 387–398.

Ware, J.E. (1993). *SF-36 Health Survey: Manual and Interpretation Guide*. Boston: Nimrod Press.

Wechsler, D. (1981). *Wechsler Adult Intelligence Scale—Revised Manual*. New York: The Psychological Corporation.

Weinrieb, R.M., Van Horn, D.H.A., McLellan, A.T. & Lucey, M.R. (2000). Interpreting the significance of drinking by alcohol-dependent liver transplant patients: fostering candor is the key to recovery. *Liver Transplantation*, **6**, 769–776.

Wijdicks, E.F.M. (Ed.) (1999). *Neurologic Complications in Organ Transplant Recipients*. Boston: Butterworth-Heinemann.

Woodman, C.L., Geist, L.J., Vance, S., Laxson, C., Jones, K. & Kline, J.N. (1999). Psychiatric disorders and survival after lung transplantation. *Psychosomatics*, **40**, 293–297.

CHAPTER 16

Chronic Fatigue Syndrome

Michael Sharpe
University of Edinburgh, UK

WHAT IS CHRONIC FATIGUE SYNDROME?

Fatigue

We all know what the feeling of fatigue is like but it is difficult to define it in words. It is essentially a generalized subjective state that must be differentiated from local weakness, decrements in performance and from physiological mechanisms (Berrios, 1990). Fatigue has been described as a feeling of aversion towards activity and perceived inability to perform (Bartley & Chute, 1947). It has a number of synonyms such as tiredness, weariness, and exhaustion. However statistical analysis of fatigue questionnaire responses suggests that these synonyms refer to essentially the same concept; the only clear distinction being between physical and mental fatigue (Chalder et al., 1993).

The feeling of fatigue becomes a symptom when the sufferer regards it as a problem (Dohrenwend & Crandell, 1970). Twenty per cent of the general population report fatigue to be a problem for them (Chen, 1986). However, relatively few of those people regard themselves as ill, and consequently only a small minority seek a medical opinion. Even so, the complaint of problematic fatigue is one of the commonest clinical presentations in primary care (Morrison, 1980).

When it is persistent and associated with impairment of functioning, fatigue can also be considered an illness (Mayou & Sharpe, 1995). The feeling of fatigue can be a manifestation of a large range of diseases. However, an illness characterized by persistent disabling fatigue and frequently accompanied by other symptoms, including poor concentration, irritability and muscle pain, but not explained by disease, has been recognized at least since the latter half of the last century and probably much longer (Straus, 1991).

Fatigue and Hypothesized Diseases

In the latter half of the last century the illness characterized as chronic disabling fatigue was called neurasthenia. The clinical descriptions of neurasthenia recorded at that time have a remarkable similarity to the modern descriptions of chronic fatigue syndrome (CFS)

Handbook of Clinical Health Psychology. Edited by S. Llewelyn and P. Kennedy.
© 2003 John Wiley & Sons, Ltd.

(Wessely, 1990). A predominant theory of neurasthenia was of a problem in the supply of energy to the central nervous system. Overwork and the stress of "modern" society were seen as causes, and treatment was by rest and electrical stimulation to regenerate energy (Macmillan, 1976). This model of neurasthenia fell out of favour when the developing science of neuropathology failed to find any observable abnormality in the nervous system. Sigmund Freud believed in a physical mechanism for neurasthenia (Freud, 1895), but Janet subsequently developed a psychogenic understanding (Costa e Silva & De Girolamo, 1990) and the symptoms previously described by this diagnosis were increasingly reattributed to the new psychiatric diagnoses. Hence fatigue on the slightest exertion became a symptom of anxiety and most of the other symptoms previously attributed to neurasthenia were attributed to depression (Greenberg, 1990).

The idea of fatigue as illness, distinct from depression and anxiety, did not disappear, however. Neurasthenia has persisted as a residual psychiatric diagnostic category in the International Classification of Diseases (WHO, 1992), no doubt reflecting its continuing usage in certain countries, especially the Far East. Furthermore, patients have continued to present to physicians with fatigue and received diagnoses such as "chronic nervous exhaustion" (Macy & Allen, 1934), chronic glandular fever or chronic Epstein–Barr virus infection (Straus, 1991).

Myalgic Encephalomyelitis

The term myalgic encephalomyelitis (ME) was originally used to describe an epidemic of symptoms among the staff of the Royal Free Hospital in 1955 (Anonymous, 1956). The proposed explanation for this epidemic centred on infection, and specifically a possible viral link with poliomyelitis. Although this hypothesis remained unconfirmed, it was not until 1970 that an alternative theory was published. In that year the psychiatrists MacEvedy and Beard reviewed the evidence and suggested that the symptoms were not due to viral infection but to "mass hysteria" (McEverdy & Beard, 1970). Although the truth of the Royal Free epidemic will now probably never be known, the term myalgic encephalomyelitis (ME) has survived. Some doctors and patient organizations still use it (for example, the ME Association and ME Action Campaign).

By and large ME is now used principally as an alternative name for the syndrome described as CFS. However, it carries an implication of pathology. Indeed some hold the view that ME represents a more severe or "core" CFS syndrome that is "medical" rather than "psychiatric"(Dowsett et al., 1990). Indeed, it is currently, although controversially, also listed as a neurological disease in the International Classification of Diseases (David & Wessely, 1993).

In the United States, where the explanation of chronic fatigue has been more immunological, the term chronic fatigue and immune dysfunction syndrome (CFIDS), which also implies disease pathology, has been similarly used.

Chronic Fatigue Syndrome

One by one the hypothetical disease diagnoses for chronic fatigue illness have failed to be substantiated, and have been abandoned (Wooley, 1976). By the late 1980s research had effectively disproved that Epstein–Barr virus (EBV) was the cause in the majority of cases of chronic fatigue (Jones & Straus, 1987). A problem existed until a working group of physicians met at the Centers for Disease Control (CDC) in Atlanta, USA, in 1997 and defined a new illness which they termed chronic fatigue syndrome (CFS) (Holmes, 1991). This new illness was operationally defined in terms of symptoms rather than hypothesized disease. The definition required that the patient complained of chronic fatigue that had been present for six months and had led to at least a 50% decrease in pre-illness activity. It also required that the patient had six or eight additional symptoms. Patients with alternative medical or psychiatric explanations for their illness were excluded according to an extensive list. This was a tremendous step forward for researchers; there was now an operational definition for the problem. Unfortunately, it soon became clear that it had major shortcomings, both theoretical and practical.

Because of the manifest shortcomings of these original criteria, a group of British researchers organized a consensus conference in Oxford, the aim of which was to achieve a UK consensus on new improved diagnostic criteria for research into CFS. These so-called Oxford criteria (Sharpe et al., 1991) are shown in Figure 16.1. As can be seen the problem of defining the feeling of fatigue was circumvented by allowing it to remain a broad concept and the problem of defining a threshold for severity was circumvented by setting criteria for duration and associated disability.

Revised American CDC criteria were then published in 1994 (Fukuda et al., 1994). The new CDC criteria, also referred to as the International Criteria, borrowed heavily from the Oxford criteria and are shown in Figure 16.2.

However, both these definitions have limitations: first, it must be remembered that committees designed them and hence they embody arbitrary judgements—for example, why

---

Inclusion criteria

- A syndrome characterized by fatigue as a principal symptom
- A syndrome of definite onset that is not lifelong
- The fatigue is severe, disabling and affects both physical and mental functioning
- The symptoms of fatigue should have been present for a minimum of six months during which it was present for more than half of the time
- Other symptoms may be present, particularly myalgia, mood and sleep disturbances, although these are not required to make the diagnosis.

Exclusion criteria

- Patients with established medical conditions known to produce chronic fatigue (for example, severe anaemia). Such a patient should be excluded where the medical condition is diagnosed at presentation or subsequently. All patients should have a history and physical examination performed by a competent physician.
- Patients with a current diagnosis of schizophrenia, manic-depressive illness, substance abuse, eating disorder, or proven organic brain disease. Other psychiatric disorders including depressive illness, anxiety disorders and hyperventilation syndrome are not necessarily reasons for exclusion.

Figure 16.1   The 1991 Oxford diagnostic criteria for CFS (Sharpe et al., 1991)

Inclusion criteria

Clinically evaluated, medically unexplained fatigue of at least six months duration that is:

- Of new onset (not lifelong)
- Not result of ongoing exertion
- Not substantially alleviated by rest
- A substantial reduction in previous level of activities.

The occurrence of four or more of the following symptoms:

- Subjective memory impairment
- Sore throat
- Tender lymph nodes
- Muscle pain
- Joint pain
- Headache
- Unrefreshing sleep
- Post-exertional malaise lasting more than 24 hours.

Exclusion criteria

- Active, unresolved or suspected disease
- Psychotic, melancholic or bipolar depression (but not major depression)
- Psychotic disorders
- Dementia
- Anorexia or bulimia nervosa
- Alcohol or other substance misuse
- Severe obesity.

Figure 16.2 International (1994 CDC) case definition of CFS (Fukuda et al., 1994)

require six months duration and not five? Second, the patient group that it defines is likely to be heterogeneous. Third, CFS as defined overlaps with other symptom-defined conditions (for example, fibromyalgia). Finally, the name itself remains controversial with patients' organizations, who claim that it trivializes their suffering. Overall, however, until such time as a better definition is proposed, a descriptive name and a descriptive operational definition has provided an invaluable basis for research.

THEORETICAL PERSPECTIVES

The cause of CFS remains unknown. Over the last 20 years, there have been many competing theories proposed from medical, psychiatric and psychological perspectives. Central to much of the controversy about CFS has been whether it is best regarded as a "medical" or as a "psychiatric or psychological" condition (Sharpe, 1998).

Medical Perspectives

This term is use for approaches that focus exclusively on biological and particularly pathological processes.

Infection

Patients often report that their illness began with a "viral infection". Perhaps surprisingly viral infection in general does not seem to cause CFS (Wessely et al., 1995). There is, however, some evidence that people who get certain infections (Epstein–Barr virus and Q fever agent) are more likely to go on to get CFS (Ayres et al., 1998; White et al., 1995). However, if infection has a role it seems to be more as a trigger than as a persisting cause.

Immune Functioning

Immune disturbance has been suggested as the persisting cause. A wide range of immune abnormalities has been reported (Lloyd, Wakefield & Hickie, 1993; Vollmer-Conna et al., 1998). However, the importance of these findings remains uncertain. The changes found are relatively small and inconsistent in nature. Furthermore, their specificity is in doubt as they can occur in patients with depressive disorder (Herbert & Cohen, 1993).

Muscle Pathology and Physical Fitness

The observation that muscle pain and subjective muscle weakness were common complaints of patients with CFS led to the investigation of muscle structure and function. However, the findings do not seem to indicate that these problems are due to a fault in the muscles themselves (Edwards, Newham & Peters, 1991) although controversy continues about this matter (Lane et al., 1998; McCully & Natelson, 1999). Also of interest is the role of a generally reduced physical fitness in CFS. This has been frequently found (Fulcher & White, 2000) but, alone, clearly does not adequately explain all the clinical phenomena of CFS.

Central Nervous System

The common symptoms of CFS, namely fatigue, sleep disturbance and poor concentration, suggest a problem with the central nervous system (CNS). One way to address this is by neuropsychological testing. Studies suggest that people with CFS find it more difficult to do complex mental tasks. However, similar abnormalities are also found in depression and the specificity of this finding remains uncertain (Wearden & Appleby, 1997). New methods of looking at the structure of the brain with CT and MRI scans have been used to study CFS/ME. Despite some reports to the contrary there remains no good evidence that the structure of the brain is abnormal (Cope & David, 1996).

If there are no problems in the structure of the brain we might ask if the problem is in how it is working, that is, in its functioning. Studies using SPECT, MRI and PET have examined functioning and have reported a slightly lower blood flow (hypo-perfusion) in certain areas of the brain (though different researchers have found this in different areas). These findings suggest changes in the demand for blood by certain areas of the brain because they are more, or less, active than in comparison patients (Fischler et al., 1996). However, the findings are not consistent and remain difficult to distinguish from those observed in depressed patients (Machale et al., 2000).

Another way to find out about brain functioning is by using neuroendocrine function tests. These have been found to be abnormal in some patients with CFS (Sharpe et al., 1996a). There is also evidence that the changes found may differ from those usually seen in people who are depressed (Cleare et al., 1995).

Functioning of the Hypothalamo–pituitary–adrenal Axis (HPA Axis)

It has been suggested that it is the brain's control of stress hormones that is defective in CFS. This idea, based on Selye's seminal work on stress (Selye, 1936), was reported in chronic fatigue in 1981 (Poteliakhoff, 1981). More recent evidence comes from the finding that patients with CFS have lower urinary cortisol excretion than healthy controls (Demitrack et al., 1991) and, indeed, than patients with melancholic depression (Demitrack, 1994). The abnormalities found so far are small, however, and are only definable in group comparisons. Similar changes may be reproduced in healthy persons by disrupting the sleep–wake cycle (Leese et al., 1996). Furthermore, the benefits of giving cortisol as a medicine to people with CFS/ME remain unclear (Cleare et al., 1999; McKenzie et al., 1998).

Circadian Rhythms and Sleep Problems

Patients with CFS commonly report disturbed sleep, mostly broken, unrefreshing and altered times of sleep (Sharpe et al., 1992), and studies of sleep using a polysomnogram have confirmed patients' reports of broken sleep (Morriss et al., 1993). However, a further study that excluded patients with confounding depression or anxiety diagnoses revealed only minor abnormalities which were thought inadequate to explain the patients' symptoms (Sharpley et al., 1997). The role of sleep disturbance remains unclear.

Changes in Blood Pressure—Postural Hypotension

More recently it has been found that a proportion of patients with CFS show an unusually large drop in their blood pressure when moving from lying to a standing position, leading to the theory that CFS is due to neurally mediated hypotension (Rowe et al., 1995). This hypothesis has been investigated using tilt table tests. Blood pressure and symptoms are monitored while the tilt table is moved from horizontal to vertical. There is a suggestion from these experiments that dizziness and fatigue are made worse in some patients when they stand up (and their blood pressure goes down). However, it is still unclear just how common this problem really is in people with CFS (LaManca et al., 1999) and whether it is a cause of the illness, or simply an effect of anxiety (Cohen et al., 2000) or inactivity (Kottke, 1966).

The Effects of Inactivity

Prolonged inactivity, even in fit persons, has been long known to cause fatigue and make it harder to be active (Zorbas & Matveyev, 1986). It has also been shown to have profound effects on the body and mind, such as changes in blood pressure regulation leading to postural hypotension, changes in the body's ability to tolerate activity, changed temperature regulation and actual physical changes in the functioning and the bulk of muscles (Sandler & Vernikos, 1986). Some people with CFS become persistently inactive and for them it appears likely that inactivity contributes to their symptoms (Sharpe & Wessely, 1998).

Psychiatric and Psychological Approaches

These have focused on factors known to be associated with conditions conventionally deemed psychiatric, such as depression.

Stress and Life Events

Stress (as used in this context) is the name given to physical, psychological and social pressures on a person that make them feel "stressed" or under strain (Butler, 1993). Patients with CFS/ME commonly report suffering a period of stress prior to the onset of the illness. There is some evidence that stress may be a causal factor in that an increase in life events before the onset of illness has been noted (Theorell et al., 1999). While most clinicians think stress is an important factor in many cases of CFS, the scientific evidence to support this is limited.

"Somatization" and CFS

Somatization, or somatoform disorders as described in DSM-IV, refers to the process in which the patient has somatic symptoms that are not explained by a medical condition and where psychological factors are assumed to be operating (APA, 1994). Somatization is a psychoanalytic word implying that mental factors have been made physical (Steckel, 1943). It is a theoretical construct and its measurement is problematic. In its clinical use the somatoform concept is little more than a description of somatic symptoms that are not readily explained by disease, with the questionable assumption that they are therefore psychological in origin (Bass & Tyrer, 2000). A more rigorous operationalization of somatization required that the patient has positive evidence of emotional disorder, and that it is the somatic symptoms of these disorders that account for the symptoms (Bridges & Goldberg, 1985).

Depression, Anxiety and CFS

If depression and anxiety are to account for the phenomena of CFS they must: (a) have similar symptoms; and (b) be detectable in patients with CFS. The symptoms are similar. Fatigue is a prominent symptom of both depressive and anxiety syndromes, as are the other key symptoms of CFS, namely poor concentration and muscle pain (WHO, 1992). Depression and anxiety have been reported to be diagnosable in most hospital-referred patients with CFS (Lane, Manu & Matthews, 1991), and many studies have addressed this issue. Those that also contained a comparison group are summarized in Table 16.1.

There is some evidence for the "somatization" view of CFS, but there are also some difficulties. First, depression and anxiety cannot be diagnosed in all patients with CFS (Wessely, 1991). Second, the attribution of the symptoms of CFS to emotional disorder depends on one's starting assumption about CFS. If CFS is assumed to be a medical disease, as many patients and some clinicians do, then this hypothesis may be considered inappropriate (Johnson, DeLuca & Natelson, 1996a).

In practice, the differentiation between CFS and emotional disorder is influenced by the attributional preference of those making the judgement. For example, a doctor who believes that we know more about anxiety and depression and regards these as more useful diagnoses is likely to diagnose emotional disorder. Conversely, patients (or doctors) who believe in a distinct medical condition called CFS (or ME) will attribute symptoms to this rather than to a psychiatric problem (Deale & Wessely, 2000). This issue highlights how beliefs are inextricably tangled up with the very concept of CFS.

A Cognitive-behavioural Perspective on CFS

A more integrated approach that combines the positive findings obtained from both the medical and psychiatric research and emphasizes the role of the patients' beliefs and coping behaviour has been proposed. It is often referred to as a cognitive-behavioural model although its components are not restricted to cognitions and behaviours. An important component of the cognitive-behavioural approach to CFS is the idea that the illness is perpetuated by an interaction of factors, including the patient's ideas. This perspective is, in fact, not new. In 1909, Waterman, a neurologist, described his understanding of and treatment approach for chronic fatigue, emphasizing the role of beliefs about the illness, the effect of focusing on fatigue and the avoidance of activity.

Characteristics of the Model

The main characteristics of the cognitive-behavioural model (see Figure 16.3) are:

- A focus on illness-perpetuating factors
- An assumption of the importance of beliefs and behaviours in illness perpetuation
- An assumption that the illness perpetuating factors interact
- An assumption of reversibility.

Table 16.1 Psychiatric disorder reported in studies of CFS patients recruited from hospital settings that included a comparison group

Reference	N	Sample	Interview	Findings Cases	Findings Controls
Deale & Wessely (2000)	24	CFS clinic, UK	DIS	67% lifetime MDD	(Healthy) 29% lifetime MDD
Wessely & Powell (1989)	47	Neurological Hospital, UK	SADS	72% psychiatric diagnosis; 47% MDD; 15% SD	(Neurological controls) 36%
Hickie et al. (1990)	48	CFS clinic, Australia	SCID	46% MDD; 2% SD; MDD pre-illness 13%	(Depressive patients) MDD pre-illness 62%
Gold et al. (1990)	26	Viral clinic, USA	DIS	42% current MDD; 73% lifetime MDD	(Healthy) No current MDD; 22% lifetime MDD
Wood et al. (1991)	34	CFS clinic, UK	PSE	41% psychiatric disorder	(Muscular disease) 15% psychiatric disorder
Katon et al. (1991)	98	CFS clinic, USA	DIS	45% psychiatric disorder; 15% MDD; 17% GAD; 46% SD	(Rheumatoid arthritis) 6% psychiatric disorder
Pepper et al. (1993)	45	Neurology clinic, USA	SCID	23% psychiatric disorder; (lifetime 51%) most MDD	(Multiple sclerosis) 8% (lifetime 32%)
Farmer et al. (1995)	100	CFS clinic, UK	SCAN (PSE)	34% somatoform; 34% depression; 23% anxiety	(Healthy) 0% somatoform; 8% depression, 18% anxiety
Johnson, DeLuca & Natelson (1996b)	48	CFS clinic, USA	DIS	45% psychiatric disorder; 31% MDD	(Multiple sclerosis) 11% MDD
Fischler et al. (1997)	53	CFS clinic, Belgium	SCID	77% current psychiatric disorder: 30% MDD; 57% GAD	(Medical controls) 50% psychiatric: 10% MDD; 14% GAD

MDD = Major Depressive Disorder; GAD = Generalized Anxiety Disorder; SD = Schizoaffective Disorder

• Cognitions	Negative views about prognosis Belief in a fixed physical cause Concern that symptoms may indicate harm Belief that rest is better than activity
• Behaviour	Avoidance of activities that lead to exacerbation of symptoms Failure to address psychological problems
• Mood	Depressed and anxious mood
• Physiology	Physiological results of inactivity Physiological concomitants of anxiety and depression (Other physiological factors)
• Social factors	Social reinforcement of the above beliefs and behaviours

Figure 16.3   Components of the cognitive-behavioural model of CFS

A Focus on Illness Perpetuating Factors

Patients with CFS will, by definition, have been ill for at least six months. As with any chronic illness the factors that initiated it may well not be those that perpetuate it. For example, although the illness may be precipitated by a viral infection, the patient's symptoms and disability are likely to be perpetuated by other factors such as the effects of inactivity. This situation has been well illustrated by Lishman (1988) in his description of the post-concussional syndrome. In the early days after head injury organic factors directly related to brain trauma are likely to be most important. As time passes, however, many secondary factors come into play. Hence, psychological factors such as depression and anxiety and social factors such as loss of occupation may not only result from the injury but may, as time passes, go on to account for an increasing proportion of the symptoms and disability. It is proposed, therefore, that effective treatment must be aimed at these "illness perpetuating" factors, rather than at the original cause of symptoms.

An Assumption of the Importance of Beliefs and Behaviours in Illness Perpetuation

The cognitive-behavioural approach takes a broad view of the patient's illness. The biological perspective is expanded to include the patient's beliefs and thoughts about the illness, their predominant mood, the coping behaviour they adopt, reversible aspects of their physiological state and their social situation. It should be noted that this approach does not seek to replace a biological explanation with a psychological one but rather to achieve a wider biopsychosocial perspective (Engel, 1977).

An Assumption that the Illness Perpetuating Factors Interact

The hypothesized interactions are (see Figure 16.4):

1. Fatigue is, at least in part, a consequence of the same factors that give rise to the symptoms of depression. Perceived disability and helplessness to overcome the condition in turn exacerbates depression.

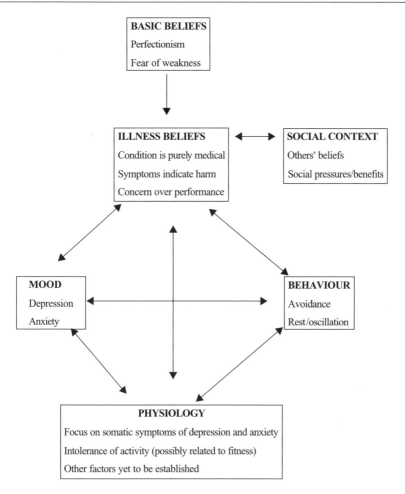

Figure 16.4 A hypothetical cognitive-behavioural model of perpetuating factors in CFS

2. The belief that fatigue and other symptoms are indications of disease leads to avoidance of activity (either persistent or intermittent) associated with them and hence to disability. Perceived disability in turn leads to the belief that one has disease.
3. Social factors act by reinforcing these fears and beliefs. Unhelpful information that portrays the illness as ME, and as an irreversible neurological disease which is worsened by activity reinforces the above beliefs. Similarly, disbelief by others may also serve to entrench such illness beliefs as a reaction to a perceived denial of their suffering and disability.
4. Inactivity leads to physiological changes that in turn exacerbate the symptoms arising from activity.

An Assumption of Reversibility

In contrast to medical models of CFS that assume it is the expression of a "disease process" and can therefore only be treated by a specific medical intervention that targets the disease

(Behan & Behan, 1988), the cognitive-behavioural approach assumes that many of the factors perpetuating the patient's illness (e.g. emotional disorder, beliefs and behaviours, and physiological processes) are readily reversible. As such, CFS could be seen as a functional disorder in the nineteenth-century sense.

Advantages of the Cognitive-behavioural Perspective

The perspective outlined above offers several potential advantages over a narrow biological model. First, the factors important in perpetuating the illness are, for the most part, apparent from appropriate clinical assessment and do not require complex investigation. Second, the formulation can be individualized to cope with the manifest heterogeneity among patients with CFS. Third, it integrates multiple factors from biological, psychological, and social realms into a single model. Finally, it offers an optimistic approach to an otherwise untreatable illness. Ultimately, however, the utility of this perspective depends on whether it leads to effective treatment.

Cognitive-behavioural Therapy for CFS

A cognitive-behavioural therapy (CBT) for CFS based on the above model has been constructed.

Aims

The aim of CBT in relation to this model of CFS would be to release patients from the vicious circles that perpetuate their illness and to return them to normal functioning. It is hypothesized that the principal obstacle to return to normal functioning is unhelpful beliefs about the illness symptoms.

Targets

The first target of therapy is the disease attribution. If patients see their illness as having an uncontrollable external cause, they will be rendered helpless to overcome the illness and will not believe that they can recover by means of changes in their beliefs and behaviour. The main way this belief is addressed is by showing patients that they can, in fact, improve their functioning and that the biological basis of CFS is therefore at least partially reversible.

The second target is to reduce the degree to which symptoms induced by activity are interpreted in a catastrophic way. Symptoms that are seen as dangerous are also likely to be a focus of attention and lead to a perceived increase in their magnitude. The main way symptoms are decatastrophized is to demonstrate that activity may be increased without persistent exacerbation of symptoms if it is done on a gradual basis.

The third target of therapy is to reduce the obstacles to recovery located in the external world. These obstacles may be the beliefs and behaviours of other people including partners, parents, and patient groups. Other practical obstacles to functional recovery include difficulty with finance and employment that are often perceived as insoluble.

Effects

It is assumed that the emotional and physiological aspects of the illness will tend to improve, as the patients feel less helpless about their situation and less fearful of their symptoms, and increase their participation in normal activities.

In summary, the aim is to help patients to change their understanding of their illness from an uncontrollable externally caused medical condition with frightening symptoms, to a controllable reversible physiological disorder with symptoms that may be annoying but not dangerous. The main way this is achieved is by the behavioural experiment of demonstrating that people can regain control over their lives with increases in activity without suffering an ever-increasing increase in symptoms.

EVIDENCE FOR THE COGNITIVE-BEHAVIOURAL PERSPECTIVE

The evidence in support of the cognitive-behavioural perspective will be considered, first, as evidence for the model and, second, as evidence for the efficacy of cognitive-behavioural therapy.

Evidence for the Model

There has now been a substantial amount of research investigating the cognitive-behavioural approach to CFS. Most of this research takes the form of descriptive studies in which the individual components of a cognitive-behavioural model are assessed. These findings support the hypothesis that most patients with CFS believe that their illness is predominantly physical. Studies also show that catastrophic beliefs about symptoms (mainly that doing more will make the symptoms worse/cause harm) and a strong belief in the illness (illness identity) are associated with disability. Coping by avoiding activity or disengaging from activity is very common and associated with disability.

In summary, beliefs and behaviours emphasized by the cognitive-behavioural model in particular are manifest by many patients with CFS (see Tables 16.2, 16.3 and 16.4).

This work has a number of methodological limitations, however, a major one being the nature of the sample studied as these are often highly selected. A second limitation is the variety and inadequacy of the measures used. Perhaps the most important limitation is the difficulty in demonstrating not only that the components of the cognitive-behavioural model are present, but also that they actually interact in a way that is hypothesized.

Perhaps the most convincing way to demonstrate the causal role of illness beliefs and behaviours in CFS would be to see if one could give someone the illness. This would be akin to testing the pathogenicity of a virus by infecting a laboratory rat. Clearly, however, this is neither an ethical nor a possible way to proceed. In the absence of this level of testing the hypothesis, the next best alternative is to see whether specifically manipulating beliefs and behaviours is associated with improvement.

Table 16.2 Reports of attributions for illness and symptoms in patients with CFS

Reference	N	Source	Measure	Findings
Matthews, Manu & Lane (1989)	100	Medical clinic	Patient report	75/100 (75%) physical attributions
Wessely & Powell (1989)	47	Neurology clinic	Five-item scale	39/47 (83%) believed in a physical cause
Sharpe et al. (1992)	144	Medical clinic	Three-point scales	Most believed virus a cause (although many also endorsed stress); belief in virus infection associated with disability
Wood et al. (1991)	34	Medical clinic	Questions about aetiology	19/34 (56%) regarded the illness as predominantly physical; 15/34 (44%) used the label ME
Schweitzer et al. (1994)	40	Fatigue clinic	Illness behaviour questionnaire	CFS patients had a high degree of conviction that they had a physical illness
Trigwell et al. (1995)	98	Medical clinic	Illness behaviour questionnaire	CFS patients had high disease conviction and hypochondriasis and low psychological versus somatic concern (NB: similar to patients with MS)
Moss-Morris & Petrie (1996)	233	Support group	Illness perception questionnaire	Most attributed CFS to medical causes although stress also acknowledged
Vercoulen et al. (1996)	264	CFS clinic	Likert scale	86% reported a physical explanation for the fatigue
Clements et al. (1997)	66	Medical clinic	Qualitative interviews	45% attributed illness exclusively to physical disease
Neerinckx et al. (2000)	192	Medical clinic	Questionnaire	Only 5% made psychological attribution (most mixed attribution); extreme physical attributions more common in patient group members
Butler, Chalder & Wessely (2001)	50	CFS clinic	Symptom interpretation questionnaire	CFS patients made predominantly somatic attributions for their illness (more than fracture clinic patients); their partners also do

Table 16.3 Reports of illness beliefs other than simple attributions in patients with CFS

Reference	N	Sample	Measure	Findings
Petrie, Moss-Morris & Weinman (1995)	282	Support group	Catastrophic thinking on questionnaire	87/282 (31%) expressed beliefs regarded as catastrophic in regard to symptoms (these had more fatigue and disability)
Moss-Morris & Petrie (1996)	233	Support group	Illness perception questionnaire	Strongest correlations with disability were illness identity and serious consequences
Clements et al. (1997)	66	Medical clinic	Qualitative interviews	Limited control over symptoms—mainly by avoidance
Heijmans (1998)	98	Patient group	Illness perception questionnaire	Greater "illness identity" associated with worse illness
Edwards et al. (2001)	173	CFS clinic	Illness perception questionnaire	High illness identity and anticipated negative consequences predicted fatigue in a regression model

Table 16.4 Reports of coping behaviour in patients with CFS

Reference	N	Sample	Measure	Findings
Blakely et al. (1991)	38	CFS clinic	Ways of coping scale	More avoidance in CFS than in health controls
Sharpe et al. (1992)	144	Medical clinic	Four-point scales	Half reported avoiding exercise; avoidance related to disability
Ray et al. (1993)	208	Medical clinic	Illness management questionnaire	Accommodating to illness related to disability
Lewis, Cooper & Bennett (1994)	47	Medical clinic	Ways of coping scale	CFS patients used more escape-avoidance after onset of illness than IBS and healthy controls
Antoni et al. (1994)	65	CFS clinic	COPE	Disengagement and denial predominant and associated with disability
Vercoulen et al. (1994)	298	CFS clinic	Four questions	96% reported avoidance or physical activity
Cope et al. (1996)	64	Primary care	Ways of coping scale	More than half avoided activity for fear of exacerbating fatigue
Clements et al. (1997)	66	Medical clinic	Qualitative analysis of interviews	Most reduced activity (either avoid or rest in anticipation of activity)
Ray, Jefferies & Weir (1995/1997)	137	Medical clinic	COPE scale and locus of control	Perceived controllability and behavioural disengagement associated with worse outcome
Afari et al. (2000)	62	Twins discordant for CFS	Ways of coping scale	Twin with CFS used more avoidance

Evidence for the Efficacy of Cognitive-behavioural Therapy

There have now been five randomized trials of a cognitive-behavioural type of intervention for CFS. All of these, apart from the first one, which used a brief therapy given by non-specialist therapists, have shown a substantial treatment effect. Furthermore, there is evidence that this treatment effect is not merely the product of non-specific attention, as it does not occur with treatment conditions such as simple relaxation (see Table 16.5).

There have also been trials of simple behavioural treatment in the forms of graded increases and activity. These show advantages but unless patients are highly selected and the graded activity given in a context of a great deal of explanation (in which case it could be said to be approximating cognitive-behavioural therapy) there is a poor acceptance and adherence rate (see Table 16.6).

A recent major systematic review of all published treatment trials in patients with CFS concluded that only cognitive-behavioural therapy and graded activity had evidence of efficacy (Whiting et al., 2001).

There are limitations with these trials, however. They are relatively small and use different outcome measures, making it difficult to amalgamate the findings in meta-analyses and many, but not all, have selected the patients included so that they may not be representative of the wider population of people with CFS.

Another major limitation in interpreting these trials as the test of the cognitive-behavioural model is that the cognitive-behavioural interventions are complex. That is the treatment given has a range of components including not only the targeting of the patients' beliefs and coping behaviour, but also general advice about activity, rest, and problem-solving. In order to explore the possible mechanism of behavioural and cognitive-behavioural treatments in patients with CFS, some of the studies have examined change in intermediate process variables and sought to correlate change in these with clinical improvement. In general, these show that the increase in activity does not appear to operate by an increase in physical fitness. They also suggest that the mechanism of change produced by cognitive therapy is not by altering attributions, as patients who improve may continue to believe that they have a physical illness called ME that has a viral causation. However, there is some evidence that specific beliefs that activity should be avoided and is harmful are key, and that changes in these may be correlated with more active coping and reduced tendency to avoid activity (see Table 16.7).

One of the most interesting trials is by Powell et al. (2001) which evaluated the effect of giving patients a greater knowledge of the known physiological disturbances associated with CFS, rather than emphasizing the role of psychological factors. Patients were encouraged to improve their sleep and activity on the basis that this would improve the "functional" disturbance in physiology. They appeared to do as well as those who had more elaborate CBT. This trial raises interesting issues for the application of so-called psychological therapies to patients with predominantly somatic complaints.

FUTURE RESEARCH AND POLICY

Having reviewed the theoretical perspectives on CFS and the evidence for them, it is interesting to identify some potential future directions for both research and policy.

Table 16.5 Randomized trials of CBT for patients with CFS

Reference	Treatment	Comparison	No.	Result	Follow-up	Comments
Lloyd et al. (1993)	Rehabilitative but brief (6 individual sessions)	Medical care	41 + 49	No difference	3 months	Complex design including immunotherapy may have compromised CBT
Sharpe et al. (1996b)	Rehabilitative with strong cognitive emphasis (16 sessions)	Medical care	30 + 30	Greater reduction in disability, fatigue and depression	8 months	Difference between groups increased during follow-up; first positive result in RCT
Deale et al. (1997)	Rehabilitative with behavioural emphasis (13 individual sessions)	Relaxation therapy (13 sessions)	30 + 30	Greater reduction in disability, fatigue and depression	6 months	Shows that effect of CBT not "non-specific"; improvement with CBT increased overtime
Prins et al. (2001)	Rehabilitative (16 individual sessions)	Group sessions and no treatment	93 + 94 + 91	Greater reduction in disability and fatigue	6 months	Many refusals and dropouts. Improvement with CBT increased over time
Powell et al. (2001)	Educational and graded activity (CBT) (2–7 sessions)	3 intensities of therapy and usual care	34 + 37 + 39 + 38	Greater reduction in disability and fatigue	8 months	Brief somatically oriented therapy effective; self-rated outcome only

Table 16.6 Randomized trials of graded exercise therapy (GET) for patients with CFS

Reference	Design	Treatment	Comparison	No.	Result	Follow-up	Comments
Fulcher & White (1997)	Randomized-controlled trial with cross-over	Graded aerobic exercise	Flexibility exercise	33 + 33	Greater improvement in global self-rating, physical function, fatigue, and physical fitness	One year	Selected sample: 3 dropouts each group; gain maintained in those followed up
Wearden et al. (1998)	Randomized-controlled trial (4 arms)	Graded aerobic exercise (with or without antidepressant drug therapy)	Follow-up only (with or without antidepressant drug therapy)	67 + 69	Greater improvement in physical fitness only	None	High dropout rate in exercise therapy—improvement in fatigue in completers only

Table 16.7 Process measures where reported in randomized treatment trials

Reference	Treatment	Process measures and outcome	Comment
Deale et al. (1997); Deale, Chalder & Wessely (1998)	CBT	Physical illness attributions did not change; beliefs that "symptoms indicate harm" and "activity should be avoided" changed more in CBT group and were associated with improvement	These findings are very similar to those found in the Oxford trial
Wearden et al. (1998)	GET	Positive but low correlation between improvement and increase in fitness	Activity may help by reducing fear of activity induced symptoms rather than by a direct effect on physical fitness
Fulcher & White (1997)	GET	No correlation between improvement and increase in fitness	Activity may help by reducing fear of activity induced symptom rather than by a direct effect on physical fitness
Powell et al. (2001)	CBT	In CBT group the belief in viral causation did not change; there was an increased belief in physical deconditioning as a cause of symptoms and a reduced avoidance of exercise	Changes mirror model of therapy; again, suggest fear of symptoms is important

Case Definition

The case definition needs improving, first by defining more homogeneous groups of patients—but homogeneous in terms of what? On the basis of the findings discussed above there may be a case for defining patients with CFS in terms of beliefs and behaviours as well as symptoms, as is currently the case for anorexia nervosa.

The second issue is whether patients with CFS are usefully considered separately from patients with other unexplained symptom conditions. The most commonly diagnosed of these are fibromyalgia (widespread pain unexplained by unidentifiable pathological process) and irritable bowel syndrome (bowel symptoms unexplained by identifiable pathological process). From the specialist perspective, these are separate conditions. However, there is now mounting evidence that not only are patients with one of these conditions more likely to have the others, but that these conditions overlap in terms of their constituent symptoms and association (Wessely, Nimnuan & Sharpe, 1999). There is therefore now a growing consensus that CFS should not be regarded as entirely separate from these other functional disorders. Hence, rather than define functional conditions separately according to symptoms, we might wish to regard them as a general functional disorder that is subdivided on the terms of dimensions of belief, behaviour, mood and identifiable physiological processes (Mayou, Bass & Sharpe, 1995).

Measures

We need a core set of simple measures to use for CFS. As in the case of pain (Downie et al., 1978), simple measures of fatigue are likely to be as useful as more complex ones, although this needs to be empirically established. Similarly, simple measures of disability such as the physical function scale of SF-36 (Stewart, Hays & Ware, 1988) and the Karnofsky performance scale (Karnofsky et al., 1948) are more likely to achieve general use than complex measures such as a sickness impact profile (SIP) (Bergner et al., 1981). Greater use could be made of more behavioural measures such as a timed walking test (Butland et al., 1982), and activity measurement using actigraphs (Vercoulen et al., 1997).

Evaluations of Treatment

We have reached a most interesting point in the development of treatment for CFS. The initial enthusiasm for a variety of specific pharmacological agents such as antiviral therapy has waned, and there is steady accumulating evidence for the role of non-pharmacological behavioural treatments such as CBT and graded exercise therapy (GET). Perhaps more than any other somatic condition there is now a general acceptance that these are currently the treatments of choice.

It seems clear that we need a large pragmatic multicentre trial, which dismantles the complex intervention called CBT. To some extent, examining the role of graded exercise has already done this. However, the interesting question is whether very brief education interventions such as that evaluated by Powell and colleagues (Powell et al., 2001) can be effective as more elaborate therapy. Ideally, we would do a trial large enough to be able to give more information on what kind of patient responds best to what kind of treatment.

There is also a need for earlier intervention for at-risk groups. Although designed only for research purposes, the six-month duration of illness required for a diagnosis of CFS has tended to inhibit early intervention in clinical practice. There is much to learn from the simple information and advice interventions such as that pioneered as early intervention for back pain (Linton & Andersson, 2000).

Integrated Approaches

There is now quite a large literature of essentially descriptive case control studies, which have examined a variety of potential biological and psychological aetiological factors. They result in an emerging consensus view that CFS is best regarded from a biopsychosocial perspective (Yeomans & Conway 1991). We are at last starting to get more robust findings about the biology of CFS, particularly in terms of brain and hypothalamo–pituitary axis function (Lloyd, Hickie & Peterson, 1999). We are also starting to get a clearer picture of the importance of beliefs and behaviours as potential perpetuating factors. However, although most clinicians would point to the role of interpersonal and social factors in the perpetuation of CFS, we still know little about how these might operate. One aspect of this that has received little attention, but clinically appears to be very important, is the iatrogenic harm that doctors can do, for example, by giving unhelpful explanations of the illness and by over-prescribing symptom-relieving medications (Kouyanou, Pither & Wessely, 1997).

Other Aspects of CFS to be Addressed by a Comprehensive Model

A biopsychosocial approach, as hypothesized by the comprehensive cognitive-behavioural model, would also have to address in more detail the role of other psychological factors such as personality as well as social and biological factors. There has been relatively little research on coping prior to the onset of illness, or on personality problems. The exploration of social factors has also been limited to date. Preliminary research has suggested that factors such as medical retirement (Deale et al., 2001) and excessive caring by spouses (Schmaling, 2000) is associated with worse illness.

A cognitive-behavioural model must also address possible biological factors. Physical fitness could be further explored although its importance in CFS remains unclear (Bazelmans et al., 2001). Other biological factors have been proposed more recently, but have not been universally found (Komaroff & Buchwald, 1998). Certainly, the evidence concerning beliefs, behaviour and emotional disorder presented here does not rule out the possibility that there are pathological processes associated with at least some cases of CFS.

We may conclude that the cognitive-behavioural model applies to some degree to at least a proportion of the patients in this sample with CFS. It seems likely that CFS will turn out to be heterogeneous and the cognitive-behavioural model will have greater applicability to some patients with CFS than to others. However, we need to address additional factors, including personality, physiology, and social processes.

POLICY

The main policy implication of these findings is that we now have a treatment that will be of substantial benefit to a large proportion of patients suffering from CFS.

However, this therapy is not widely available. The reasons for this are both complex and interesting. The following factors appear to be relevant: first, there is the lack of appropriately interested and skilled cognitive therapists; second, there is major difficulty in funding and delivering psychological treatments for "medical" conditions; third, there is the reluctance of patient organizations to support the development of this sort of therapy.

Given the accumulation of evidence supporting the role of rehabilitative approaches (CBT and GET) for CFS (Whiting et al., 2001), patient organizations have begun to cautiously accept their role. However, this is often with the caveat that treatments may be suitable for the subset of patients who have "more psychiatric" types of CFS with poor coping ability and depression, but not for the core ME patients who, in their view, do not have a psychological component to their illness.

There are various ways to interpret this disagreement between professionals and patients. The first possibility is that patients' views are simply incorrect and that their views reflect a psychological process of interpretive bias as described by exponents of somatization, whereby symptoms that have their basis in emotional disorder are misattributed (Bridges & Goldberg, 1985) to a medical disease process in order to avoid stigma and blame, but with unhelpful consequences for the patients' treatment and prognosis.

The second possibility is that the patients are right and the professionals wrong. Those favouring this scenario would anticipate that research will eventually identify a pathological disease process and that CFS will come to be unambiguously classified as a medical condition.

The third, and perhaps most interesting, possibility is that both professionals and patients are wrong. That is, the whole debate about the aetiology of CFS simply highlights the shortcomings of the traditional and dichotomous "medical" or "psychiatric" classification of illness (Sharpe & Carson, 2001). Our understanding of such "unexplained" or "functional" illness is developing and it is become increasingly apparent that while neither CFS nor other functional syndromes are characterised by the presence of observable pathology, this does not necessarily mean that they are "purely psychological". Rather they are better regarded as having biological, psychological and social aspects (Wessely, Nimnuan & Sharpe, 1999).

Indeed, it could be argued that the current "state of the art" understanding of CFS and related conditions would probably be that these illnesses are best understood as psychophysiological states associated with identifiable abnormalities in cerebral functioning and neuroendocrine status, but not conventionally defined "tissue pathology", and are influenced by the social context.

If one takes this position one may then reasonably ask if the patients are right or wrong in regarding their illness as predominantly physical? Perhaps it is just the wrong question. If we are to make cognitive-behavioural approaches more available to patients with somatic complaints we need to be mindful of these issues when designing psychological treatments and services to provide them (Sharpe & Carson, 2001). In particular, there are a number of changes we will have to make. First, we will have to develop therapies that are acceptable to patients and congruent with their own illness beliefs. Second, we will have to train therapists who feel comfortable treating patients with predominantly physical symptoms, and, finally, we will have to develop psychological treatment services that are much more integrated with medical clinics and physical rehabilitation services. This is a major challenge for clinical health psychology.

REFERENCES

Afari, N., Schmaling, K.B., Herrell, R., Hartman, S., Goldberg, J. & Buchwald, D.S. (2000). Coping strategies in twins with chronic fatigue and chronic fatigue syndrome. *Journal of Psychosomatic Research*, **48** (6), 547–554.

APA (1994). *Diagnostic and Statistical Manual of Mental Disorders* (4th edn). Washington, DC: American Psychiatric Association.

Anonymous (1956). A new clinical entity? *Lancet*, **1**, 789–790.

Antoni, M.H., Brickman, A., Lutgendorf, S.K., Klimas, N.G., Imia Fins, A., Ironson, G., Quillian, R., Miguez, M.J., van Riel, F. & Morgan, R. (1994). Psychosocial correlates of illness burden in chronic fatigue syndrome. *Clinical Infectious Diseases*, **18** (Suppl. 1), S73–S78.

Ayres, J.G., Flint, N., Smith, E.G., Tunnicliffe, W.S., Fletcher, T.J., Hammond, K., Ward, D. & Marmion, B.P. (1998). Post-infection fatigue syndrome following Q fever. *Quarterly Journal of Medicine*, **91** (2), 105–123.

Bartley, S.H. & Chute, E. (1947). *Fatigue and Impairment in Man*. New York: McGraw-Hill.

Bass, C. & Tyrer, P. (2000). The somatoform conundrum: a question of nosological valves. *General Hospital Psychiatry*, **22** (1), 49–51.

Bazelmans, E., Bleijenberg, G., Van der Meer, J.W. & Folgering, H. (2001). Is physical deconditioning a perpetuating factor in chronic fatigue syndrome? A controlled study on maximal exercise performance and relations with fatigue, impairment and physical activity. *Psychological Medicine*, **31** (1), 107–114.

Behan, P.O. & Behan, M.H. (1988). Postviral fatigue syndrome. *CRC Critical Reviews in Neurobiology*, **4**, 157–179.

Bergner, M., Bobbitt, R.A., Carter, W.B. & Gilson, B.S. (1981). The Sickness Impact Profile: development and final revision of a health status measure. *Medical Care*, **19**, 787–805.

Berrios, G.E. (1990). Feelings of fatigue and psychopathology: a conceptual history. *Comprehensive Psychiatry*, **31**, 140–151.

Blakely, A.A., Howard, R.C., Sosich, R.M., Murdoch, J.C., Menkes, D.B. & Spears, G.F. (1991). Psychiatric symptoms, personality and ways of coping in chronic fatigue syndrome. *Psychological Medicine*, **21**, 347–362.

Bridges, K.W. & Goldberg, D.P. (1985). Somatic presentation of DSM-III psychiatric disorders in primary care. *Journal of Psychosomatic Research*, **29**, 563–569.

Butland, R.J.A., Pang, J., Gross, E.R., Woodcock, A.A. & Geddes, D.M. (1982). Two-, six-, and 12-minute walking test in respiratory disease. *British Medical Journal*, **284**, 1607–1608.

Butler, G. (1993). Definitions of stress. *Occasional Papers of the Royal College of General Practitioners*, No. 61, 1–5.

Butler, J.A., Chalder, T. & Wessely, S. (2001). Causal attributions for somatic sensations in patients with chronic fatigue syndrome and their partners. *Psychological Medicine*, **31** (1), 97–105.

Chalder, T., Berelowitz, G., Pawlikowska, T., Watts, L., Wessely, S., Wright, D.J. & Wallace, E.P. (1993). Development of a fatigue scale. *Journal of Psychosomatic Research*, **37**, 147–153.

Chen, M.K. (1986). The epidemiology of self-perceived fatigue among adults. *Preventative Medicine*, **15**, 74–81.

Cleare, A.J., Bearn, J., Allain, T., McGregor, A., Wessely, S., Murray, R.M. & O'Keane, V.O. (1995). Contrasting neuroendocrine responses in depression and chronic fatigue syndrome. *Journal of Affective Disorders*, **35**, 283–289.

Cleare, A.J., Heap, E., Malhi, G.S., Wessely, S., O'Keane, V. & Miell, J. (1999). Low-dose hydrocortisone in chronic fatigue syndrome: a randomised crossover trial. *Lancet*, **353** (9151), 455–458.

Clements, A., Sharpe, M., Borrill, J. & Hawton, K.E. (1997). Chronic fatigue syndrome: a qualitative investigation of patients' beliefs about the illness. *Journal of Psychosomatic Research*, **42**, 615–624.

Cohen, T.J., Thayapran, N., Ibrahim, B., Quan, C., Quan, W. & von Zur, M.F. (2000). An association between anxiety and neurocardiogenic syncope during head-up tilt table testing. *Pacing and Clinical Electrophysiology*, **23** (5), 837–841.

Cope, H. & David, A.S. (1996). Neuroimaging in chronic fatigue syndrome. *Journal of Neurology, Neurosurgery and Psychiatry*, **60**, 471–473.

Cope, H., Mann, A., Pelosi, A. & David, A. (1996). Psychosocial risk factors for chronic fatigue and chronic fatigue syndrome following presumed viral illness: a case-control study. *Psychological Medicine*, **26**, 1197–1209.

Costa e Silva, J.A. & De Girolamo, G. (1990). Neurasthenia: history of a concept. In N. Sartorious et al. (Eds), *Psychological Disorders in General Medical Settings* (pp. 69–81). Toronto: Hogrefe & Huber.

David, A.S. & Wessely, S. (1993). Chronic fatigue, ME, and ICD-10. *Lancet*, **342**, 1247–1248.

Deale, A. & Wessely, S. (2000). Diagnosis of psychiatric disorder in clinical evaluation of chronic fatigue syndrome. *Journal of the Royal Society of Medicine*, **93** (6), 310–312.

Deale, A., Chalder, T. & Wessely, S. (1998). Illness beliefs and treatment outcome in chronic fatigue syndrome. *Journal of Psychosomatic Research*, **45** (1; Spec. No.), 77–83.

Deale, A., Chalder, T., Marks, I. & Wessely, S. (1997). Cognitive behavior therapy for chronic fatigue syndrome: a randomized controlled trial. *American Journal of Psychiatry*, **154** (3), 408–414.

Deale, A., Husain, K., Chalder, T. & Wessely, S. (2001). Long-term outcome of cognitive behavior therapy versus relaxation therapy for chronic fatigue syndrome: a 5-year follow-up study. *American Journal of Psychiatry*, **158** (12), 2038–2042.

Demitrack, M.A. (1994). Chronic fatigue syndrome: a disease of the hypothalamic–pituitary–adrenal axis? *Annals of Medicine*, **26**, 1–5.

Demitrack, M.A., Dale, J.K., Straus, S.E., Laue, L., Listwak, S.J., Kreusi, M.J., Chrousos, G.P. & Gold, P.W. (1991). Evidence for impaired activation of the hypothalamic–pituitary–adrenal axis in patients with Chronic Fatigue Syndrome. *Journal of Clinical Endocrinology and Metabolism*, **73**, 1224–1234.

Dohrenwend, B.P. & Crandell, D.L. (1970). Psychiatric symptom in community, clinic, and mental hospital groups. *American Journal of Psychiatry*, **126**, 1611–1621.

Downie, W.W., Leathan, P.A., Rhind, V.M., Wright, V., Branco, J. & Anderson, J.A. (1978). Studies with pain rating scales. *Annals of Rheumatic Diseases*, **37**, 378–381.

Dowsett, E.G., Ramsay, A.M., McCartney, R.A. & Bell, E.J. (1990). Myalgic encephalomyelitis—a persistent enteroviral infection? *Postgraduate Medical Journal*, **66**, 526–530.

Edwards, R.H.T., Newham, D.J. & Peters, T.J. (1991). Muscle biochemistry and pathophysiology in postviral fatigue syndrome. *British Medical Bulletin*, **47**, 826–837.

Edwards, R., Suresh, R., Lynch, S., Clarkson, P. & Stanley, P. (2001). Illness perceptions and mood in chronic fatigue syndrome. *Journal of Psychosomatic Research*, **50** (2), 65–68.

Engel, G.L. (1977). The need for a new medical model: a challenge for biomedicine. *Science*, **196**, 129–196.

Farmer, A., Jones, I., Hillier, J., Llewellyn, M., Borysiewicz, L.K. & Smith, A.P. (1995). Neurasthenia revisited. *British Journal of Psychiatry*, **167**, 496–502.

Fischler, B., Cluydts, R., De Gucht, Y., Kaufman, L. & De Meirleir, K. (1997). Generalized anxiety disorder in chronic fatigue syndrome. *Acta Psychiatrica Scandinavica*, **95** (5), 405–413.

Fischler, B., D'Haenen, H., Cluydts, R., Michiels, V., Demets, K., Bossuyt, A., Kaufman, L. & De Meirleir, K. (1996). Comparison of 99m Tc HMPAO SPECT scan between chronic fatigue syndrome, major depression and healthy controls: an exploratory study of clinical correlates of regional cerebral blood flow. *Neuropsychobiology*, **34** (4), 175–183.

Freud, S. (1895). *Heredity and the Aetiology of the Neuroses* (standard edn). London: Hogarth Press.

Fukuda, K., Straus, S.E., Hickie, I.B., Sharpe, M., Dobbins, J.G. & Komaroff, A.L. (1994). Chronic Fatigue Syndrome: a comprehensive approach to its definition and management. *Annals of Internal Medicine*, **121** (12), 953–959.

Fulcher, K.Y. & White, P.D. (1997). Randomised controlled trial of graded exercise in patients with the chronic fatigue syndrome. *British Medical Journal*, **314** (7095), 1647–1652.

Fulcher, K.Y. & White, P.D. (2000). Strength and physiological response to exercise in patients with chronic fatigue syndrome. *Journal of Neurology, Neurosurgery and Psychiatry*, **69** (3), 302–307.

Gold, D., Bowden, R., Sixbey, J., Riggs, R., Katon, W.J., Ashley, R.L., Obrigewitch, R. & Corey, W. (1990). Chronic fatigue. A prospective clinical and virologic study. *Journal of the American Medical Association*, **264**, 48–53.

Greenberg, D. (1990). Neurasthenia in the 1980s: chronic mononucleosis, chronic fatigue syndrome, and anxiety and depressive disorders. *Psychosomatics*, **31**, 129–137.

Heijmans, M.J. (1998). Coping and adaptive outcome in chronic fatigue syndrome: importance of illness cognitions. *Journal of Psychosomatic Research*, **45** (1; Spec. No.), 39–51.

Herbert, T.B. & Cohen, S. (1993). Depression and immunity: a meta-analytic review. *Psychological Bulletin*, **113**, 472–486.

Hickie, I.B., Lloyd, A.R., Wakefield, D. & Parker, G. (1990). The psychiatric status of patients with chronic fatigue syndrome. *British Journal of Psychiatry*, **156**, 534–540.

Holmes, G.P. (1991). Defining the chronic fatigue syndrome. *Reviews of Infectious Diseases*, **13** (Suppl. 1), S53–S55.

Johnson, S.K., DeLuca, J. & Natelson, B.H. (1996a). Assessing somatization disorder in the chronic fatigue syndrome. *Psychosomatic Medicine*, **58**, 50–57.

Johnson, S.K., DeLuca, J. & Natelson, B.H. (1996b). Depression in fatiguing illness: comparing patients with chronic fatigue syndrome, multiple sclerosis and depression. *Journal of Affective Disorders*, **39** (1), 21–30.

Jones, J.F. & Straus, S.E. (1987). Chronic Epstein–Barr virus infection. *Annual Reviews of Medicine*, **38**, 195–209.

Karnofsky, D.A., Abelmann, W.H., Craver, L.F. & Burchenal, J.H. (1948). The use of the nitrogen mustards in the palliative treatment of carcinoma. *Cancer*, **1**, 634–656.

Katon, W.J., Buchwald, D.S., Simon, G.E., Russo, J.E. & Mease, P. (1991). Psychiatric illness in patients with chronic fatigue and rheumatoid arthritis. *Journal of General Internal Medicine*, **6**, 277–285.

Komaroff, A.L. & Buchwald, D.S. (1998). Chronic fatigue syndrome: an update. *Annual Review of Medicine*, **49**, 1–13.

Kottke, F.J. (1966). The effect of limitation of activity upon the human body. *Journal of the American Medical Association*, **196**, 825–830.

Kouyanou, K., Pither, C.E. & Wessely, S. (1997). Iatrogenic factors and chronic pain. *Psychosomatic Medicine*, **59** (6), 597–604.

LaManca, J.J., Peckerman, A., Walker, J., Kesil, W., Cook, S., Taylor, A. & Natelson (1999). Cardiovascular response during head-up tilt in chronic fatigue syndrome. *Clinical Physiology*, **19** (2), 111–120.

Lane, R.J., Barrett, M.C., Woodrow, D., Moss, J., Fletcher, R. & Archard, L.C. (1998). Muscle fibre characteristics and lactate responses to exercise in chronic fatigue syndrome. *Journal of Neurology, Neurosurgery and Psychiatry*, **64** (3), 362–367.

Lane, T.J., Manu, P. & Matthews, D.A. (1991). Depression and somatization in the chronic fatigue syndrome. *American Journal of Medicine*, **91**, 335–344.

Leese, G., Chattington, P., Fraser, W., Vora, J., Edwards, R.H.T. & Williams, G. (1996). Short-term night-shift working mimics the pituitary-adrenocortical dysfunction in chronic fatigue syndrome. *Journal of Clinical Endocrinology and Metabolism*, **81**, 1867–1870.

Lewis, S., Cooper, C.L. & Bennett, D. (1994). Psychosocial factors and chronic fatigue syndrome. *Psychological Medicine*, **24**, 661–671.

Linton, S.J. & Andersson, T. (2000). Can chronic disability be prevented? A randomized trial of a cognitive-behavior intervention and two forms of information for patients with spinal pain. *Spine*, **25** (21), 2825–2831.

Lishman, W.A. (1988). Physiogenesis and psychogenesis in the postconcussional syndrome. *British Journal of Psychiatry*, **153**, 460–469.

Lloyd, A.R., Hickie, I. & Peterson, P.K. (1999). Chronic fatigue syndrome: current concepts of pathogenesis and treatment. *Current Clinical Topics in Infectious Diseases*, **19**, 135–159.

Lloyd, A.R., Hickie, I.B., Brockman, A., Hickie, C., Wilson, A., Dwyer, J. & Wakefield, D. (1993). Immunologic and psychologic therapy for patients with chronic fatigue syndrome: a double-blind, placebo-controlled trial. *American Journal of Medicine*, **94**, 197–203.

Lloyd, A.R., Wakefield, D. & Hickie, I.B. (1993). Immunity and the pathophysiology of chronic fatigue syndrome. *Ciba Foundation Symposium*, **173**, 176–187.

Machale, S.M., Lawrie, S.M., Cavanagh, J.T., Glabus, M.F., Murray, C.L., Goodwin, G.M. & Ebmeier, K.P. (2000). Cerebral perfusion in chronic fatigue syndrome and depression. *British Journal of Psychiatry*, **176**, 550–556.

Macmillan, M.B. (1976). Beard's concept of neurasthenia and Freud's concept of the actual neuroses. *Journal of the History of Behavioral Science*, **12**, 376–390.

Macy, J.W. & Allen, E.V. (1934). A justification of the diagnosis of chronic nervous exhaustion. *Annals of Internal Medicine*, **7**, 861–867.

Matthews, D.A., Manu, P. & Lane, T.J. (1989). Diagnostic beliefs among patients with chronic fatigue. *Clinical Research*, **37**, 820A.

Mayou, R.A. & Sharpe, M. (1995). Diagnosis, illness and disease. *Quarterly Journal of Medicine*, **88**, 827–831.

Mayou, R.A., Bass, C. & Sharpe, M. (1995). *Treatment of Functional Somatic Symptoms*. Oxford: Oxford University Press.

McCully, K.K. & Natelson, B.H. (1999). Impaired oxygen delivery to muscle in chronic fatigue syndrome. *Clinical Science*, **97** (5), 603–608.

McEverdy, C. & Beard, A. (1970). Royal Free Epidemic of 1955: a reconsideration. *British Medical Journal*, **1**, 7–11.

McKenzie, R., O'Fallon, A., Dale, J., Demitrack, M., Sharma, G., Deloria, M., Garcia-Borreguero, D., Blackwelder, W. & Straus, S.E. (1998). Low-dose hydrocortisone for treatment of chronic fatigue syndrome: a randomized controlled trial. *Journal of the American Medical Association*, **280** (12), 1061–1066.

Morrison, J.D. (1980). Fatigue as a presenting complaint in family practice. *Journal of Family Practice*, **10**, 795–801.

Morriss, R.K., Sharpe, M., Sharpley, A., Cowen, P.J., Hawton, K.E. & Morris, J.A. (1993). Abnormalities of sleep in patients with chronic fatigue syndrome. *British Medical Journal*, **306**, 1161–1164.

Moss-Morris, R. & Petrie, K.J. (1996). Functioning in chronic fatigue syndrome: do illness perceptions play a regulatory role? *British Journal of Health Psychology*, **1**, 15–25.

Neerinckx, E., Van Houdenhove, B., Lysens, R., Vertommen, H. & Onghena, P. (2000). Attributions in chronic fatigue syndrome and fibromyalgia syndrome in tertiary care. *Journal of Rheumatology*, **27** (4), 1051–1055.

Pepper, C.M., Krupp, L.B., Friedberg, F., Doscher, C. & Coyle, P.K. (1993). A comparison of neuropsychiatric characteristics in chronic fatigue syndrome, multiple sclerosis, and major depression. *Journal of Neuropsychiatry and Clinical Neurosciences*, **5**, 200–205.

Petrie, K.J., Moss-Morris, R. & Weinman, J. (1995). The impact of catastrophic beliefs on functioning in chronic fatigue syndrome. *Journal of Psychosomatic Research*, **39** (1), 31–38.

Poteliakhoff, A. (1981). Adrenocortical activity and some clinical findings in acute and chronic fatigue. *Journal of Psychosomatic Research*, **25**, 91–95.

Powell, P., Bentall, R.P., Nye, F.J. & Edwards, R.H. (2001). Randomised controlled trial of patient education to encourage graded exercise in chronic fatigue syndrome. *British Medical Journal*, **322** (7283), 387–390.

Prins, J.B., Bleijenberg, G., Bazelmans, E., Elving, L.D., de Boo, T.M., Severens, J.L., Van der Wilt, G.J., Spinhoven, P. & Van der Meer, J.W. (2001). Cognitive behaviour therapy for chronic fatigue syndrome: a multicentre randomised controlled trial. *Lancet*, **357** (9259), 841–847.

Ray, C., Jefferies, S. & Weir, W.R. (1995). Coping with chronic fatigue syndrome: illness responses and their relationship with fatigue, functional impairment and emotional status. *Psychological Medicine*, **25** (5), 937–945.

Ray, C., Jefferies, S. & Weir, W.R. (1997). Coping and other predictors of outcome in chronic fatigue syndrome: a 1-year follow-up. *Journal of Psychosomatic Research*, **43** (4), 405–415.

Ray, C., Weir, W., Stewart, D., Miller, P.M. & Hyde, G. (1993). Ways of coping with chronic fatigue syndrome: developement of an illness management questionnaire. *Social Science in Medicine*, **37**, 385–391.

Rowe, P.C., Bou Holaigah, I., Kan, J.S. & Calkins, H. (1995). Is neurally mediated hypotension an unrecognised cause of chronic fatigue? *Lancet*, **345**, 623–624.

Sandler, H. & Vernikos, J. (1986). *Inactivity: Physiological Effects*. London: Academic Press.

Schmaling, K.B.P. (2000). Significant other responses are associated with fatigue and functional status among patients with chronic fatigue syndrome. *Psychosomatic Medicine*, **62** (3), 444–450.

Schweitzer, R., Robertson, D.L., Kelly, B. & Whiting, J. (1994). Illness behaviour of patients with chronic fatigue syndrome. *Journal of Psychosomatic Research*, **38**, 41–49.

Selye, H. (1936). A syndrome produced by diverse nocuous agents. *Nature*, **138**, 32.

Sharpe, M. (1998). Doctors' diagnoses and patients' perceptions: lessons from chronic fatigue syndrome. *General Hospital Psychiatry*, **20**, 335–338.

Sharpe, M. & Carson, A.J. (2001). "Unexplained" somatic symptoms, functional syndromes, and somatization: do we need a paradigm shift? *Annals of Internal Medicine*, **134** (9; Suppl. (Part 2)), 926–930.

Sharpe, M. & Wessely, S. (1998). Putting the rest cure to rest—again. *British Medical Journal*, **316**, 796.

Sharpe, M., Archard, L.C., Banatvala, J.E., Borysiewicz, L.K., Clare, A.W., David, A.S., Edwards, R.H.T., Hawton, K.E., Lambert, H.P., Lane, R.J.M., McDonald, E.M., Mowbray, J., Pearson, D.J., Peto, T.E.A., Preedy, V.R., Smith, A.P., Smith, D.G., Taylor, D.J., Tyrrell, D., Wessely, S. & White, P.D. (1991). A report—chronic fatigue syndrome: guidelines for research. *Journal of the Royal Society of Medicine*, **84**, 118–121.

Sharpe, M., Clements, A., Hawton, K.E., Young, A.H., Sargent, P. & Cowen, P.J. (1996a). Increased prolactin response to buspirone in chronic fatigue syndrome. *Journal of Affective Disorders*, **41**, 71–76.

Sharpe, M., Hawton, K.E., Seagroatt, V. & Pasvol, G. (1992). Patients who present with fatigue: a follow-up of referrals to an infectious diseases clinic. *British Medical Journal*, **305**, 147–152.

Sharpe, M., Hawton, K.E., Simkin, S., Surawy, C., Hackmann, A., Klimes, I., Peto, T., Warrell, D. & Seagroatt, V. (1996b). Cognitive behaviour therapy for the chronic fatigue syndrome: a randomized controlled trial. *British Medical Journal*, **312**, 22–26.

Sharpley, A.L., Clements, A., Hawton, K.E. & Sharpe, M. (1997). Do patients with "pure" chronic fatigue syndrome (Neurasthenia) have abnormal sleep? *Psychosomatic Medicine*, **59**, 592–596.

Steckel, W. (1943). *The Interpretation of Dreams*. New York: Liveright.

Stewart, A.L., Hays, R.D. & Ware, J.E. (1988). The MOS Short-Form General Health Survey: reliability and validity in a patient population. *Medical Care*, **26**, 724–735.

Straus, S.E. (1991). History of chronic fatigue syndrome. *Reviews of Infectious Diseases*, **13** (Suppl. 1), S2–S7.

Theorell, T., Blomkvist, V., Lindh, G. & Evengard, B. (1999). Critical life events, infections, and symptoms during the year preceding chronic fatigue syndrome (CFS): an examination of CFS patients and subjects with a nonspecific life crisis. *Psychosomatic Medicine*, **61** (3), 304–310.

Trigwell, P., Hatcher, S., Johnson, M., Stanley, P. & House, A. (1995). "Abnormal" illness behaviour in chronic fatigue syndrome and multiple sclerosis. *British Medical Journal*, **311** (6996), 15–18.

Vercoulen, J.H., Bazelmans, E., Swanink, C.M., Fennis, J.F., Galama, J.M., Jongen, P.J., Hommes, O., Van der Meer, J.W. & Bleijenberg, G. (1997). Physical activity in chronic fatigue syndrome: assessment and its role in fatigue. *Journal of Psychiatric Research*, **31** (6), 661–673.

Vercoulen, J.H., Swanink, C.M., Fennis, J.F., Galama, J.M., Van der Meer, J.W. & Bleijenberg, G. (1994). Dimensional assessment of chronic fatigue syndrome. *Journal of Psychosomatic Research*, **38**, 383–392.

Vercoulen, J.H., Swanink, C.M., Fennis, J.F., Galama, J.M., Van der Meer, J.W. & Bleijenberg, G. (1996). Prognosis in chronic fatigue syndrome (CFS): a prospective study on the natural course. *Journal of Neurology, Neurosurgery and Psychiatry*, **60**, 489–494.

Vollmer-Conna, U., Lloyd, A., Hickie, I. & Wakefield, D. (1998). Chronic fatigue syndrome: an immunological perspective. *Australian and New Zealand Journal of Psychiatry*, **32** (4), 523–527.

Waterman, G.A. (1909). The treatment of fatigue states. *Journal of Abnormal Psychology*, **4**, 128–139.

Wearden, A.J. & Appleby, L. (1997). Cognitive performance and complaints of cognitive impairment in chronic fatigue syndrome (CFS). *Psychological Medicine*, **27** (1), 81–90.

Wearden, A.J., Morriss, R.K., Mullis, R., Strickland, P.L., Pearson, O., Appleby, L., Campbell, I.T. & Morris, J.A. (1998). Randomised, double-blind, placebo-controlled treatment trial of fluoxetine and graded exercise for chronic fatigue syndrome. *British Journal of Psychiatry*, **172**, 485–490.

Wessely, S. (1990). Old wine in new bottles: neurasthenia and "ME". *Psychological Medicine*, **20**, 35–53.

Wessely, S. (1991). Chronic fatigue syndrome. *Journal of Neurology, Neurosurgery and Psychiatry*, **54**, 669–671.

Wessely, S. & Powell, R. (1989). Fatigue syndromes: a comparison of chronic "postviral" fatigue with neuromuscular and affective disorder. *Journal of Neurology, Neurosurgery and Psychiatry*, **52**, 940–948.

Wessely, S., Nimnuan, C. & Sharpe, M. (1999). Functional somatic syndromes: one or many? *Lancet*, **354** (9182), 936–939.

Wessely, S., Chalder, T., Hirsch, S.R., Pawlikowska, T., Wallace, P. & Wright, D.J. (1995). Postinfectious fatigue: prospective cohort study in primary care. *Lancet*, **345**, 1333–1338.

White, P.D., Thomas, J.M., Amess, J., Grover, S.A., Kangro, H.O. & Clare, A.W. (1995). The existence of a fatigue syndrome after glandular fever. *Psychological Medicine*, **25**, 907–916.

Whiting, P., Bagnall, A., Sowden, A., Cornell, J.E., Mulrow, C. & Ramirez, G. (2001). Interventions for the treatment and management of chronic fatigue syndrome: a systematic review. *Journal of the American Medical Association*, **286**, 1360–1368.

Wood, G.C., Bentall, R.P., Gopfert, M. & Edwards, R.H.T. (1991). A comparative psychiatric assessment of patients with chronic fatigue syndrome and muscle disease. *Psychological Medicine*, **21**, 619–628.

Wooley, C.F. (1976). Where are the diseases of yesteryear? DaCosta's syndrome, soldiers heart, the effort syndrome, neurocirculatory asthenia—and the mitral valve prolapse syndrome. *Circulation*, **53**, 749–751.

WHO (1992). *The ICD-10 Classification of Mental and Behavioural Disorders* (10th edn). Geneva: World Health Organization.

Yeomans, J.D. & Conway, S.P. (1991). Biopsychosocial aspects of chronic fatigue syndrome (myalgic encephalomyelitis). *Journal of Infection*, **23**, 263–269.

Zorbas, Y.G. & Matveyev, I.O. (1986). Man's desirability in performing physical exercises under hypokinesia. *International Journal of Rehabilitation Research*, **9**, 170–174.

CHAPTER 17

Gynaecology

Pauline Slade
University of Sheffield, UK

INTRODUCTION

The gynaecological system forms the basis of women's reproductive capacity and can be crucial in the fulfillment of important life goals such as the development of satisfying sexual relationships and becoming a mother. It has the potential to influence the taking on of particular roles as well as impacting upon a woman's quality of life. The gynaecological system encompasses the ovaries, fallopian tubes, uterus and vaginal area and is influenced by both centrally derived (hypothalamic and pituitary) and peripheral hormones. However, psychological factors are also of relevance. The aims of this chapter are, firstly, to consider the relationships between gynaecological symptoms in general and psychological distress and, secondly, to select three major areas of difficulty for women: symptoms related to the menstrual cycle, the menopause, and chronic pelvic pain, and to consider in detail these main areas for consultation in terms of relevant psychological factors and clinical implications.

RELATIONSHIPS BETWEEN GYNAECOLOGICAL SYMPTOMS AND PSYCHOLOGICAL DISTRESS

The idea that women consulting with difficulties relating to their reproductive systems and hence suffering from gynaecological symptoms may show high levels of psychological or psychiatric difficulties has received considerable attention over the last 20 years. Essentially the current consensus is that, at first outpatient appointment, 25–35% of women show significant psychological or psychiatric distress (Slade, Anderton & Faragher, 1988; Sundstrom et al., 2001). Types of distress have focused on depressive and anxiety symptoms with different studies showing slightly different patterns. Of interest is the fact that an equivalent study in Nigeria produced very similar figures (Abiodun, Adetoro & Ogunbode, 1992).

More specialist clinics such as those set up for the menopause (Hay, Bancroft & Johnstone, 1994) showed caseness levels of depressive symptoms in approximately 50% of new attenders. Stewart et al. (1992), in a Canadian menopausal clinic sample, found particularly high levels of distress on the Brief Symptom Inventory in both perimenopausal (during the

---

phase of menstrual irregularity prior to total cessation of menstruation) and menopausal attender samples. Obviously in these settings there is greater potential for confounding of reason for consulting with level of distress. However, there is no doubt that these levels of "probable caseness" are well above those reported in community samples of women based upon the National Survey of Psychiatric Morbidity of Great Britain (Jenkins et al., 1997) or many consulting populations in other medical specialties.

The relative importance of causes or consequence is less clear. In the only longitudinal study of psychological distress and gynaecological symptoms in an outpatient population, which followed women up for a year after first referral, Slade and Anderton (1992) suggested that, in general, psychological symptoms diminished in response to gynaecological improvement. Failure of gynaecological symptoms to remit was followed by an increase in depressive symptoms. These patterns would suggest the importance of psychological distress, at least in part as a response to the experience of gynaecological difficulties.

This does not, of course, deal with the issue of when and why individuals seek help. Social cognition models emphasise the importance of the sense that people make of their symptoms. There is relatively little specific work about the factors triggering help seeking in gynaecological conditions. In the context of the menopause, Montero, Ruiz and Hernandez (1993) suggest that when consulters for menopausal symptoms were compared with a matched community sample, the former showed higher psychiatric morbidity, higher social dissatisfaction, lower levels of social support and a higher frequency of severe life events. Where the significance of symptoms is ambiguous, as is often the case in gynaecological problems, it seems likely that those with greater psychological distress, either in response to or coincidental with gynaecological problems, and those with lower levels of support and higher frequencies of other stressors, may be more likely to consult. Some of this distress is likely to remit with gynaecological improvement but it is likely that psychological distress may itself interact with this process.

The need for routine consideration of psychological distress in gynaecological outpatient settings has been clearly made. Indeed, some suggestions have been proposed for suitable screening instruments including the General Health Questionnaire (GHQ) (Goldberg & Williams, 1988). However, this is purposeless if identification is not followed by the potential for appropriate care. Studies in the United States (Spitzer et al., 2000) and Australia (Phillips, Dennerstein & Farrish, 1996) have considered whether psychological difficulties have been identified and whether intervention has been offered. There is unanimity that difficulties are common, identification is rare, and offer of intervention rarer. In many ways this situation may mirror the hidden morbidity noted in general practice settings where many patients with high levels of psychological distress go undetected and deprived of opportunities for effective intervention.

The structure of this chapter is to consider our understandings of psychological aspects of some of the more common gynaecological complaints: premenstrual symptoms, menopausal complaints and chronic pelvic pain. An assumption is made that the reader is familiar with the basic concept of the biopsychosocial model as a way of understanding experiences.

THE MENSTRUAL CYCLE AND PREMENSTRUAL SYMPTOMS

Women in Western societies are likely to experience reasonably regular menstrual cycles from around the age of 12 years as a typical age of menarche to an average of 50 years with the menopause being defined as the last menstrual period. It must be noted that this typical duration of 38 years may be punctuated by intervals without menstruation when a woman is pregnant or breast-feeding. In England and Wales overall pregnancy rates are reducing and at six to ten weeks postpartum the Department of Health Infant Feeding Survey (2000) suggests that only around two-thirds of mothers are breast-feeding. In previous eras and different societies, menarche, being strongly influenced by nutrition, would have occurred later, many more children would have been born, breast-feeding more commonly engaged in and for longer duration. It can be seen that experience of regular menstrual cycles for long phases of life is a relatively recent development and a function of lifestyle of Westernised women. In addition, with increasing longevity, women now expect to live one-third of their lives postmenopause. The salience of both the menstrual cycle and the menopause is therefore likely to be significantly increased in societies in which these changes have occurred. Two other major changes have been the artificial regulation of the menstrual cycle through use of oral contraceptives and prolongation of cyclical bleeding although not fertility with some forms of hormone replacement therapy (HRT).

One of the major areas of difficulty related to menstruation which leads to consultation concerns premenstrual symptoms. The typical components are both psychological, characterised by irritability, anxiety and low mood, often coupled with an intolerance of social contact, together with physical symptoms of water retention and weight gain. A common third feature involves headache and general aches and pains. Cyclicity is characterised by symptoms occurring in the week leading up to menstruation with a reduction following the first day of bleeding.

It is generally agreed that retrospective assessment of cyclical symptoms is unreliable and that many women who view themselves as suffering from these changes fail to show them when daily ratings are used (Hardie, 1997). Two commonly used assessment scales are the Calendar of Premenstrual Experience (COPE) (Mortola et al., 1990) and the Daily Symptom Scale derived from the Moos Menstrual Distress Questionnaire (Blake et al., 1998). Sufferers are expected to show a 30% increase between the premenstrual and postmenstrual weeks with a minimum level of premenstrual symptoms also specified. A recent review of assessment methods is provided by Haywood, Slade and King (2002).

A second method of definition is via the DSM-IV criteria for Premenstrual Dysphoric Disorder (PMDD) (APA, 1994) which requires luteal phase (second half of cycle) experience of core mood symptoms which must not be present in the follicular phase. These must be confirmed by daily ratings in two prospective cycles with symptoms causing marked interference with lifestyle. There must also be an absence of other diagnoses. In contrast, under the DSM-IV rubric for premenstrual syndrome only one of a whole range of symptoms is required.

It is estimated that between 3 and 8% of women experiencing menstrual cycles may experience significant premenstrual symptoms. However, estimates of prevalence are fraught with difficulty. While reliance on the women's own retrospective assessments has been shown to be unreliable, a requirement for two months of daily data involves its own hidden selection bias. Only a proportion of women are prepared to complete longitudinal measures and samples may be biased towards the better organised and less distressed groups. In terms of predictive factor there are suggestions that clinic attenders tend to be older (in their 30s) and parous (with children). There are also suggestions that more severe cyclical symptoms may occur in more stressful life circumstances (Woods, Dery & Most, 1982). In terms of cross-cultural studies there are certainly indications of different patterns, with pain symptoms predominating in Nigerian women, Japanese samples showing the lowest overall cyclical symptom prevalence and Western developed countries, particularly the USA, showing highest levels of negative emotional symptoms (Janiger, Reffenburgh & Kersch, 1972). More recently a study of diverse ethnic communities in Australian society (Hasin, Dennerstein & Gotts, 1988) suggested associations between complaints of emotional cyclical symptoms and duration of stay in Australia, which the authors suggest as a society may socialise women into a culture of premenstrual suffering.

Explanatory models for premenstrual symptoms can be divided roughly into three perspectives: biomedical, radical feminist and biopsychosocial. The biomedical model takes the view that symptoms are due to an underlying disruption of physiological functioning, either peripheral or central, which, if rectified, will provide a cure. This has formed the basis for the vast majority of research work in this area. At the other end of the spectrum the radical feminist model suggests that normal behaviours and concerns are labelled as unwomanly, because of their cultural unacceptability in a patriarchal society. As such they are pathologised as illness requiring treatment (Rome, 1986). The biopsychosocial model incorporates physiological changes and then considers how attitudes and expectations affect detection, appraisal and attributions. The latter influence the meaning made of the symptoms and coping strategies employed which then directly influence the experienced distress (Reading, 1993).

While one might expect the biopsychosocial model to have developed considerable credence, the reality is that treatment when offered is rarely within this model. There are numerous studies of hormonal, serotonergic and other drug-based intervention with only a handful of psychological studies and virtually no combinations. The area is hampered by the lack of integration of work. This bias in intervention work is particularly significant in that in a study of preferences among women consulting for premenstrual syndrome (PMS) there was a clear demand for *both* hormonal and psychological input (Hunter, Swann & Ussher, 1995).

INTERVENTIONS FOR PMS

Interventions for PMS have been many and varied. Within the biomedical model many different hormonal approaches have been used. The typical pattern of publication with a new substance has moved from individual case studies and single blind trials with encouraging results to disappointing double blind trials where both active agent and placebo have been efficacious for around 40% of each sample. This has certainly been the case for progesterone, a treatment which has received much attention in the media. Beliefs about the utility of progesterone have been extremely strong to the degree that interruption in treatment has been used as an effective defence in murder trials. Interestingly the hormonal intervention now under most rigorous investigation is the use of oestrogen patches.

In terms of non-hormonal biological approaches, fluoxetine (a serotonin reuptake inhibitor), more commonly known as prozac, has shown substantive results with two-thirds of women showing benefit. A deficit in the sensitivity of the serotonergic system is postulated. These studies are reviewed by Steiner (1997) who concluded that this approach is showing more encouraging results than all prior hormonal or psychoactive drugs. However, one-third of women will not respond and, as already stated, many women are unhappy with an approach via medication particularly in terms of mood-enhancing drugs. There is also the issue of the longevity of the effect and the impact of stopping medication. In studies of depressive symptoms unrelated to the menstrual cycle, equivalent initial outcomes have been shown with antidepressant medication, but with longer follow-up the latter has been more efficacious, probably because it equips the individual with skills to manage mood fluctuations. In the case of menstrual cycle symptoms, there are therefore many reasons why an approach focusing upon self-management strategies is likely to be helpful and well received. Abraham, Llewellyn Jones and Perz (1994) suggest that PMS symptoms are an important predictor of many menopausal symptoms and hence, untreated, the duration of distress may be extensive. Other approaches such as self-help, which are often advocated, have received little systematic attention. A dietary intervention through exclusion of caffeine and sucrose was investigated in one small study and benefits were suggested (Daiss & Krietsch, 1997).

The literature in terms of psychological interventions is surprisingly limited. All the approaches are underpinned by the biopsychosocial model with the woman herself being viewed as an active agent in her own change and with aims of coping rather than cure.

Slade (1989) published a series of case studies of women with established cyclical emotional changes with promising results. This involved eight sessions of psychological work focusing on understanding ongoing stressors and triggers for problematic responses, together with a combination of problem-solving, relaxation and cognitive work focusing on attributions for symptoms.

Morse et al. (1991) compared coping skills group approaches with relaxation and hormonal treatment (progesterone). Although all groups led to symptomatic reductions, only in the coping skills sample was improvement sustained at three months. A second group approach, utilising coping skills, was reported by Kirkby (1994) who included awareness through movement as an attention control group. The former group showed a greater reduction in self-reported premenstrual symptoms and irrational thinking. Goodale, Domar and Benson (1990) also considered relaxation as a group intervention. When compared to a control sample, the intervention group showed a significantly greater reduction in symptoms. From a cross-cultural perspective, Sridevi and Krishna-Rao (1996) have reported on the benefits of the practice of yoga with menstrual cycle symptoms.

This area has been significantly advanced by Blake (1995) and Blake et al. (1998) in two papers which respectively detail and evaluate a cognitive therapy approach to PMS. The 12-session intervention is significantly more effective than the wait list control. The details of the underlying mechanisms proposed by Blake concern responses to minor symptoms, characterised by thoughts of loss of control, leading to increased anxiety and depressed mood. One of two pathways is hypothesised to be activated, either through guilt and increased effort, leading to a sense of failure, or through resentment about demands and lack of support triggering an irritable outburst which, in turn, leads to feelings of guilt. Both pathways are hypothesised to lead to further endorsing the perception of loss of control. Essentially symptoms are viewed as a trigger for certain problematic cognitive schema. It is the nature of these which is hypothesised to determine response to symptoms and therefore distress.

Finally Slade, Escott and King (1998) developed a case formulation approach. This has tentatively identified certain commonalities in the cognitive patterns of women complaining of PMS. These are identified as a need for perfectionism and a difficulty in tolerating lowered performance, a difficulty in asking for help and looking after her own needs, coupled with an overdeveloped sense of responsibility for the well-being of others. These patterns were often coupled with or indeed possibly dependent on a perception of having been critically parented. These ideas are currently being further evaluated.

The questions that these studies raise are numerous and include: How do psychological interventions compare to fluoxetine? Are 12 sessions necessary and what level of expertise is needed to deliver this approach? What are the vital components in therapy? We need to know much more about typical problematic cognitions and related behavioural patterns. While the evidence is intriguing, it is still rather limited.

In terms of service delivery, as well as considering the provision of more psychologically based individual care, the fact that literature suggests that most cognitive approaches adapt well and without loss of efficacy to a group format (Morrison, 2001) offers a possible development. A recent survey of family doctors and practice nurses (Slade & Mathers, 2001) indicated that they received frequent consultations for premenstrual problems. A large proportion of staff found these difficult or extremely difficult to manage and would particularly welcome group approaches to intervention carried out in the primary care setting. Interventions in primary care with involvement of practice nurses as well as specialist input may also be a potential initiative. In the context of the current body of evidence, however, the following clinical guidelines are suggested.

Current Clinical Implications

Developing engagement and appropriate initial assessment is crucial in this area. Explaining the relevance of psychological approaches and checking the woman's own views on this is vital. Educating referrers is also crucial in this so that women feel they are gaining access to a valuable resource rather than having their symptoms discounted in some way. It is often helpful to talk about this in terms of finding different ways to manage some of the feelings and symptoms, so that they create less distress and disruption to life.

A second step involves asking the woman to complete two months of daily forms rating physical and emotional symptoms and noting the occurrence of menstruation—for example, Calendar of Premenstrual Experience (COPE; Mortola et al., 1990; or Daily Modified MDQ; Blake et al., 1998). Daily records need to be on individual sheets rather than a cumulative chart in which a previous day's data is displayed. It is important that these daily ratings are as independent as possible so the instructions should ask the woman to place the completed form at the bottom of the pile and not look at it again. This is introduced as a collaborative enterprise to explore, together, the most problematic symptoms and when they occur. As a part of this process it is helpful to agree to produce a graph in order to feed back patterns in symptoms.

The graph needs to show days and symptom levels with menstruation clearly marked. Sometimes the data is obviously cyclical, but sometimes not. In the latter circumstances the process of viewing the data she has provided often frees a woman to consider alternative mechanisms for distress and facilitates other work.

Where information appears cyclical it is useful to discuss the concept of a psychological overlay, i.e. that some women have an underlying pattern of increased symptoms premenstrually, but that it is often what we make of these (our cognitions about the changes) that determines our overall level of distress. While our psychological work will not remove the underlying cyclical patterns it can be very effective in reducing the overlying distress.

One could then work in a cognitive-behavioural framework based upon an individualised formulation, taking into account the commonly reported problematic schema already identified.

THE MENOPAUSE

On average, the menopause (defined as the last menstrual period) occurs at the age of 50 years. While the term menopause is commonly used, the term climacterium is a word often used in research and has been endorsed by the World Health Organisation. This encapsulates the notion of a process of hormonal change extending over 10–15 years with the actual menopause (occurring at the time of the last menstrual period) as a final stage. During this time, women move away from a cyclical pattern characterised by peaks of gonadotrophins (follicle-stimulating hormone and luteinising hormone) from the pituitary gland which stimulate production of oestrogens. Premenopausally these exert negative feedback to reduce gonadotrophins thereby creating the menstrual cycle. After menopause this feedback system no longer operates and a steady state of high gonadotrophins and low oestrogens is maintained. This process is associated with declining fertility.

The menopause has been said to be associated with a multitude of different symptoms across the physical and psychological spectrum. Key issues here are vasomotor symptoms (hot flushes and night sweats), sexual problems, psychological difficulties such as depressive symptoms and panic attacks, and cognitive concerns regarding memory in particular. In addition to reports of symptoms, there are increased risks of health problems such as heart disease and osteoporosis where the menopause is clearly implicated, as protection previously conveyed by oestrogens is lost. There seems little doubt that the experience of hot flushes and night sweats relates to the reduction in oestrogen. This responds well to HRT. Similarly, sexual problems, in particular dyspareunia (pain on intercourse), are often related to vaginal dryness, and the thinning of vaginal walls appears to be related to reductions in oestrogens. However, the evidence concerning the relationship of the menopause to other symptoms is somewhat more equivocal.

A key issue is whether psychological symptoms occur in women more commonly around the menopause. There are two main sources of information: large-scale cross-sectional studies and rather smaller longitudinal projects. Cross-sectional studies rarely show any increase in emotional symptoms around the menopause, e.g. Holte's (1991) study of 1800 Norwegian women or the study by McKinlay, McKinlay and Brambrilla (1987) of 8000 Canadian women. Similarly, if one studies the data from the General National Household Survey carried out in the UK in 1995, the figures fail to demonstrate increased emotional distress in the tranche of time when the majority of the cohort would experience their menopause. More recently, a large-scale study of Dutch women concluded that only vasomotor symptoms could rightly be called menopausal and there was no evidence for a significant rise in emotional distress around this time (Vanwesenbeeck, Vennis & van de Wiel, 2001).

This does not exclude the possibility that some women may be particularly affected around this stage of life or by their hormonal changes. Cooke and Green (1981) completed some innovative work which has yet to be improved upon in this area. They studied a sample of Scottish women and divided in terms of their approximate climacteric status, based upon age premenopausal <25–34 years, early 35–44, late 45–54 and postmenopausal 55–64 years. Emotional symptoms peaked in the early climacteric group, i.e. 35–44 years, and this pattern was mirrored by certain patterns in their lives, namely "death exits". These were bereavements of close family members. This raises another issue which concerns the social context at different stages of life. Interestingly in their studies vasomotor symptoms (hot flushes) peaked in the late climacteric which incorporates the actual mean age of menopause.

EXPLANATORY THEORIES FOR MENOPAUSAL SYMPTOMS

While the evidence for routine emotional change related to the menopause per se is somewhat equivocal, explanatory psychological theories for menopausal symptoms still abound. For example, relating any psychological changes to the loss of reproductive capacity or the so-called "empty nest syndrome" when children leave home, to psychological changes. The former explanation is given little support by Avis and McKinlay (1991) who found that the most common emotional response to menopause was one of relief. It will be interesting to see whether the recent increases in typical age of child-bearing and consequent infertility, together with economic patterns that have led to changes in patterns of family dispersal, impact on perceptions of emotional changes around the menopause as social and biological events become more disconnected in time.

Attitudes towards the menopause have been identified as factors in relation to emotional symptoms around the menopause. Hunter (1992), in a longitudinal study of depressive symptoms in the premenopause, found that pre-existing negative attitudes towards the menopause were one of the strongest predictors of symptoms. In concert with a history of depression and not being employed, these accounted for approximately half of the variance in emotional symptoms. This contrasted with 2% for actual menopausal status. Similarly, Avis and McKinlay (1991), in the Massachusetts Women's Health Study, a longitudinal study of 2500 women, found that negative attitudes were the best predictors of subsequent symptoms. They concluded that: "*The so called menopause syndrome may be related more to personal characteristics than menopause per se.*" Abraham, Llewelyn and Jones Perz's (1994) longitudinal study also suggested that expectations for the menopause to be a relief or nuisance were generally verified at ten-year follow-up. In addition they found that women actually experienced less depressive symptoms and fewer hot flushes when assessed post-menopausally than they had predicted premenopausally. This substantiates other findings of menopausal and post-menopausal women evaluating the menopause more positively than premenopausal women, suggesting that expectation is generally worse than reality.

If attitudinal factors are significant, how may these be influenced? An intriguing study by Shoebridge and Steed (1999) assessed the content of women's magazines in Australia in terms of articles relating to the menopause over a ten-year period. Their thematic analysis indicated that these could be encapsulated under the terms "illness, medical intervention and fear". The authors suggest that the media portrayal of the menopause is essentially pathologising.

Another dimension to this debate involves the role of culture. One potential implication concerns the way the menopause is construed within different societies, and the impact of ageing on status. In Westernised societies these are essentially considered as negative changes and hence the experience of the menopause as a sign of ageing may be experienced in this way. Interestingly, a recent study of menopausal symptoms in South East Asian countries suggested that these were experienced to a much milder degree than in more Westernised societies (Boulet ct al., 1994). A study of Chinese women living in Taiwan (Chen, Voda & Mansfield, 1998) indicated that menopause was viewed in a positive and holistic way, with descriptions ranging from "no longer young, getting old" to "wisdom and maturation", "a symbol of achievement" and "a time to start enjoying life". Unfortunately, alongside this study there was no assessment of symptoms. However, the meaning of ageing and the menopause within a society is likely to have the potential to influence experience, and warrants much greater exploration.

FLUSHING

While information about routine linkage between the menopause and emotional symptoms is equivocal, the data on hot flushes and night sweats is persuasive. Many women report daily hot flushes with one-third experiencing these on more than ten occasions in a day. They generally last one to five minutes and are described as sensations of heat, sweating and flushing spreading up through the body and over the face. Objective and subjective measurements of hot flushes show good concordance and the suggestion is that these occur in response to small changes in the body's core temperature (Freedman, 2001). Interestingly there is an association between the experience of hot flushes and disturbed sleep. The psychological impact of hot flushes is extremely variable, with many women being unconcerned. Others respond with high anxiety and distress but the frequency and/or duration of flushing holds little predictive power for emotional response. It appears that the personal and social meanings attributed to the flushing (e.g. this is a sign of my degenerating body; no one will want to employ someone at this time of their life; everyone can see I'm menopausal) are important factors.

An interesting study by Reynolds (1997) suggests that perceived control over flushing is associated with lower frequency of flushing. However, whether coping strategies are employed or deemed successful or unsuccessful is less important than another factor. The key issue appeared to be an individual's attitudes to the strategies she uses and the meaning she makes of their use. For example, two women may both adopt strategies of wearing cotton fabrics to keep cool with equivalent impact or lack of impact; one may view this with equanimity while another may view this as her biology restricting her freedom with consequent resentment. Again, the role of beliefs about the meaning of both the symptoms and steps taken to manage them appear to be crucial mediators of distress rather than the frequency or severity of symptoms, or even the efficacy of coping.

Considering hot flushes in particular, interesting psychological interventions based on cognitive-behavioural principles have been piloted with promising results (Hunter & Liao, 1996). In this study triggers and cognitions were identified, lending greater predictability and potential for challenge. In addition to modification of cognitions, stress reduction techniques were employed. While both hormone replacement and cognitive-behavioural therapy samples showed reductions in frequency of flushing, only the latter approach was effective in reducing anxiety and perceived level of problem from the women's perspective.

COGNITIVE DIFFICULTIES

One final area of controversy relating to the menopause concerns the prevalence of cognitive difficulties, in particular, memory problems. Such difficulties are undoubtedly reported by some women attending menopause clinics, and there is evidence that after surgical menopause, treatment with oestrogens improves verbal memory functioning (Phillips & Sherwin, 1992). However, as Hurrell and Slade (2001) conclude, there is little substantive evidence linking the natural menopause, where less dramatic hormonal decline occurs, with reduction in memory functioning. Indeed a study of perception of memory problems in female community samples failed to find any effect of age or menopausal status (Ford, 2002). There was a trend for women on HRT to report higher perceived difficulties. It could be that those with perceived difficulties were already receiving intervention, but unless there was initially a greater decrement this was clearly ineffective. It is notable that studies of women using HRT (Kuh, Wadsworth & Hardy, 1997) have suggested that they are more distressed than non-users, across a variety of parameters. The question therefore arises as to whether the prescription of HRT is being utilised by medical practitioners as a mid-life panacea.

PREVENTION OF MENOPAUSAL SYMPTOMS

Another consideration is whether there is scope for prevention of menopausal symptoms through the provision of information and shaping of attitudes. Liao and Hunter (1998) have completed innovative work in this area through the running of premenopausal groups with such aims. While their impact must be considered modest at best, the extensive evidence available about the salience of attitudes means that such approaches merit further consideration.

Current Clinical Implications

For assessment of symptoms, the Women's Health Questionnaire (Hunter, 2000) provides consideration of all the relevant symptom domains. In addition, evaluation is required of the role of attitudes to ageing, the meaning of the loss of reproductive capacity and consideration of losses or missed opportunities in this regard in the form of infertility, miscarriages or terminations. Assessment of recent events, particularly bereavements and response to these together with the availability of support, particularly from the partner, are key issues in working with women in the menopause.

Interventions relating to challenging assumptions, considering issues of loss and helping to plan a path forward in a new phase of life, are useful approaches depending on the particular presenting problems and contextual issues. The use of cognitive-behavioural interventions to reduce distress associated with hot flushes is clearly an option. Finally, the development and further testing of preventative interventions is also highly desirable.

CHRONIC PELVIC PAIN

One of the most common reasons for referral to a gynaecologist is the experience of pelvic pain. A range of physical problems may be implicated and the normal process of care involves an investigatory operation, a laparoscopy (a procedure involving the insertion of an optical device through a cut in the abdominal wall) through which the internal state of the pelvic organs can be examined. However, studies suggest that the rate of abnormal findings ranges from 8 to 88%, with endometriosis (migration of tissue from the lining of the womb) and pelvic adhesions some of the more common findings. In other cases the pain may be attributed to pelvic congestion, cervical stenosis or other systems of the body such as abnormalities of bowel functioning. Women are often discharged from gynaecology clinics having been provided with "reassurance" after a "negative" laparoscopy (i.e. an investigation of the gynaecological structures where no abnormality is found) and no further care is provided.

For many the pelvic pain becomes chronic (defined as lasting for more than six months) and a repeated ineffective cycle of care may be instigated with some women having as many as 14 laparoscopies. McGowan, Pitts and Carter (1999), who surveyed family doctors' perspectives, suggested that "where there is no clear abnormality women are caught in a futile cycle of referral and investigation". What is very clear is that for many women treatment becomes idiosyncratic and ineffective. In a study of family doctors' perspective on providing care for psychological aspects of gynaecological conditions, dealing with chronic pelvic pain (CPP) was rated as the most problematic (Slade & Mathers, 2001).

As a result of the apparent dichotomy between "functional and organic" causation, a great deal of time was spent by researchers attempting to identify predictive psychological factors to account for what was construed as "psychogenic" pain. One particular pathophysiological mechanism suggested was pelvic congestion. This condition, in which a woman may develop chronically dilated pelvic veins, has been hypothesised to occur in response to stress. One group of workers has suggested increased rates of child abuse in women with CPP showing pelvic congestion (Fry et al., 1997). This remains a possible avenue for consideration; however, definitive venographic studies remain to be completed.

The majority of more recent studies have failed to find psychological differences in terms of personality profiles or mood states between women with CPP with and without pathology (for a review, see Savidge & Slade, 1997). However, there are certainly differences between these groups and non-pain comparison groups in that levels of depressive symptoms are elevated in the former. Hence current thinking suggests that psychological distress is a response to, rather than a cause of, the pain. It must also be noted that identifying pathological causation is an imprecise process, which is limited by current knowledge and techniques. Secondly, the presence of abnormality does not necessarily mean that this is the actual cause. Many women around the age of 40, a typical time for consultation about pelvic pain, show signs of endometriosis which, in a CPP patient, would be designated as identifiable pathology but report no pain or are certainly not consulting for CPP.

Interestingly, a study by Richter et al. (1998) suggests that the presence or absence of pathology has no discernible impact in terms of outcomes in long-term follow-up. Similar conclusions are drawn by Elcombe, Gath and Day (1999) who randomly allocated 71 women to wait two or ten weeks for laparoscopy. Pain ratings reduced following laparoscopy. However, the main predictors of this reduction were not pain chronicity or level of pathology but changes in beliefs about the pain and the woman's own evaluation of the seriousness of her condition. The importance of appraisal factors is clearly emphasised.

The potential role of sexual abuse in women with CPP has only recently been appreciated. Walker et al. (1988), for example, have suggested elevated rates of childhood or adult sexual trauma (58%) in CPP patients. In a group of 106 women with chronic pelvic pain without pathology (CPPWOP), Reiter et al. (1991) suggested a rate of 48% compared to 6% in a pain-free gynaecological outpatient control group. However, findings are not totally consistent, with Rapkin et al. (1990) finding no significant differences in prevalence between CPP groups, other chronic pain groups and a no-pain group. The former did, however, show high rates of physical abuse in childhood. Interestingly, a very recent study by Raphael, Widom and Lange (2001) has taken a prospective view identifying a large number of childhood victims and following them up as adults to assess their rate of medically explained and unexplained pain complaints. The odds of reporting medically unexplained pain symptoms were not elevated in those who were childhood victims of abuse. However, if one considered retrospective assessments of abuse, then having one or more unexplained pain symptoms was associated with recollections of victimisation. There may therefore be an issue of mood-congruent memory in that experiencing pain may facilitate the recall of memories encoded in a similar state.

Toomy et al. (1993) suggest that women with CPP who had experienced abuse reported less perceived life control and a more punishing response to the pain and higher levels of global distress compared to women with CPP and no history of abuse. They concluded that a combination of abuse and CPP is likely to lead to a particularly high somatic preoccupation. Other linkages suggested are that greater exposure to illness and death in CPPWOP leads to increased attention to health and illness, and provide a schema in which the likelihood of perceiving sensory input from the pelvis is high. An additional strand of work by Heim et al. (1998) has suggested that childhood sexual abuse changes the responsivity of the hypothalamic pituitary adrenal axis and increases susceptibility to CPP. Early experiences are therefore potentially of relevance in CPP but relationships are likely to be complex and involve a variety of physiological and psychological mechanisms including appraisal and response to pain.

A high prevalence of adult sexual dysfunction has been suggested to occur in women with CPP. Several studies have related this to the rates of sexual abuse. However, CPP is associated with depressive symptoms and hence a reduction in libido. In addition, the pain experienced is in the area of reproductive organs and therefore it may not be surprising that difficulties are common.

WOMEN'S OWN EXPERIENCES OF CPP

There is no doubt that CPP is associated with considerable ongoing distress. From a clinical perspective we need to understand the experiences of women with CPP and how services may be of best help to them. Understanding women's own perspectives are crucial in this process. Qualitative studies which have explored the women's experience are rare but highly informative in this context. Savidge et al. (1998) report on a series of interviews with women with CPP, 12–18 months after a laparoscopy, where no abnormality was detected. Almost all the women held specific beliefs about the causes of their pain, which often focused on the assumption of some physical damage from a reproductive event such as labour, miscarriage, termination or sterilisation. A second category of explanation related the experience of life stressors such as a bereavement or serious illness of a family member. These ideas were rarely explored by clinicians. Prior to the laparoscopy, the most important aspects of quality of care concerned the nature of the relationship with the family doctor. The most positively evaluated aspects were characterised by listening, taking time to explain and showing concern and sympathy.

Following referral, women's expectations of the consultation with the gynaecologist were typically high, focusing on gaining a solution to their pain. Only a quarter found these expectations realised and these women felt reassured by the information that there was nothing wrong. However, a majority of women were very dissatisfied about how information was relayed following the laparoscopy. Typically they received information from a nurse or doctor, not previously met, some while still recovering from the anaesthetic. There were obvious difficulties in processing information and having the opportunity to ask appropriate questions. Only a quarter received any medical follow-up. Explanations provided were either that there was no identifiable cause or it might be a bowel problem. While, as already stated, a quarter felt reassured, many expressed confusion/upset or anger and a feeling of not being taken seriously.

In terms of the ongoing impact, two-thirds were still experiencing pain 12 to 18 months later and most reported an ongoing negative emotional impact together with adverse effects on several aspects of their lives, including sexual activities, their leisure and work. The summary of identified themes encapsulating their experience emphasised the need to ensure that others understood how much they hurt and did not dismiss their pain. The emotional impact was often intensified by a sense of not being believed, and fuelled by the sense of uncertainty generated by the lack of information. The final points concerned a sense of being helpless, isolated, coping alone and not knowing where to turn.

There are obvious implications relating to the process of care in the initial gynaecological consultation in terms of the importance of professionals taking time to listen, validating the experience of pain and exploring women's own beliefs about causation. After the operation there needs to be adequate time to recover from the anaesthetic before being given feedback together with time for clarification of and questioning of explanations. Essentially the main difficulty is that a chronic problem is being treated within an acute medical model.

In many localities there is little provision for help in managing and coping with pain rather than attempting to cure it. This is clearly crucial given the information already provided about how beliefs impinge on pain experience. It may also be helpful to provide educational materials indicating the fact that CPP is common, and that it is often the case that clear explanations are unavailable, together with some possible explanations about mechanisms underpinning the experience of pain. Options for educational follow-up together with the potential for pain management programmes are clear. Other options that have been explored concern group therapy (Albert, 1999) and individualised work. Clearly there are opportunities to look at how histories of sexual abuse may be influencing current experience, but as yet there are no published intervention studies.

Current Clinical Implications

It is crucial that in the initial discussions about the woman's pain that psychological and physical strands are considered together. This avoids the all too common scenario of a woman being referred to psychologists after multiple investigations have enhanced her belief in severity and pathology, leading to feelings of being "fobbed" off with distress unvalidated and disbelieved. This can be avoided by working closely with gynaecologists in initial stages of assessment.

Processes of care need to be organised to recognise the potential chronicity of the condition. It is important that the aim is management of difficulties, i.e. to reduce distress and increase quality of life rather than cure. Pain management programmes and mechanisms to reduce isolation and distress need to be developed to deal with the specific needs of CPP patients.

The clinician needs to be alert to the issues of sexual difficulties and physical and sexual abuse.

SUMMARY

This chapter has selected just a few of the difficulties that may lead women to be referred to a gynaecology service. In all these areas psychological factors are likely to be of considerable relevance and there is some knowledge available about potentially helpful psychological input. For the areas particularly considered, several common themes can be extracted. Firstly, there is the importance of the personal meanings of experienced symptoms and how these appraisals dramatically influence suffering and distress. Secondly, there is the inadequacy of current psychological care, both within gynaecological and within primary care settings where much gynaecological care occurs. There is considerable potential for more integrated services with gynaecologists and for working with practice nurses and GPs on these issues. Finally, if attitudes play such a crucial role, then further attention needs to be given to the potential for preventative education.

REFERENCES

Abiodun, O.A., Adetoro, O.O. & Ogunbode, O.O. (1992). Psychiatric morbidity in a gynaecology clinic in Nigeria. *Journal of Psychosomatic Research*, **36**, 485–490.

Abraham, S., Llewellyn Jones, D. & Perz, J. (1994). Changes in Australian women's perceptions of menopause and menopausal symptoms before and after the climacterium. *Maturitas*, **20**, 121–128.

Albert, H. (1999). Psychosomatic group treatment helps women with chronic pelvic pain. *Journal of Psychosomatic Obstetrics and Gynaecology*, **20**, 216–225.

APA (1994). *Diagnostic and Statistical Manual*. Washington, DC: American Psychiatric Association.

Avis, N.E. & McKinlay, S.M. (1991). A longitudinal analysis of women's attitudes toward the menopause: results from the Massachusetts Women's Health Study. *Maturitas*, **13**, 65–79.

Blake, F. (1995). Cognitive therapy for premenstrual syndrome. *Cognitive and Behavioural Practice*, **2**, 167–185.

Blake, F., Salkovskis, P., Gath, D., Day, A. & Garrod, A. (1998). Cognitive therapy for premenstrual syndrome: a controlled trial. *Journal of Psychosomatic Research*, **45**, 307–318.

Boulet, M.J., Oddens, B.J., Lehert, P. & Verner, H. (1994). Climacteric and menopause in 7 South East Asian countries. *Maturitas*, **19**, 157–176.

Chen, Y.L.D., Voda, A.M. & Mansfield, P.K. (1998). Chinese midlife women's perceptions and attitudes about the menopause. *Journal of the North American Menopause Society*, **5**, 28–34.

Cooke, D.J. & Green, J.G. (1981). Types of life events in relation to symptoms at the climacterium. *Journal of Psychosomatic Research*, **25**, 5–11.

Daiss, S. & Krietsch, K. (1997). Use of dietary interventions in PMS. *Journal of Psychological Practice*, **3**, 174–185.

Department of Health Infant Survey (2000). www.statistics.gov

Elcombe, S., Gath, D. & Day, A (1999). The psychological effects of laparoscopy on women with chronic pelvic pain. *Psychological Medicine*, **27**, 1041–1050.

Ford, N. (2002). *Perceptions of memory functioning: the impact of age and menopausal status*. DClinPsy thesis, University of Sheffield.

Freedman, R.R. (2001). Ambulatory monitoring of menopausal hot flushes. In *Progress in Ambulatory Assessment* (chap. 28, pp. 493–503). Gottingen, Germany: Hagrefe & Huber.

Fry, R.P.W., Beard, R.W., Crisp, A.H. & McGuigan, S. (1997). Sociopsychological factors in women with chronic pelvic pain with and without pelvic venous congestion. *Journal of Psychosomatic Research*, **42**, 71–83.

Goldberg, D.P. & Williams, P. (1988). *A User's Guide to the General Health Questionnaire*. Windsor: NFER.

Goodale, I.L., Domar, A.D. & Benson, H. (1990). Allieviation of premenstrual syndrome symptoms with the relaxation response. *Obstetrics and Gynaecology*, **74**, 649–665.

Hardie, E.A. (1997). Prevalence and predictors of cyclic and non cyclic affective change. *Psychology of Women Quarterly*, **21**, 299–314.

Hasin, M., Dennerstein, L. & Gotts, L.G. (1988). Menstrual cycle complaints: a crosscultural study. *Journal of Psychosomatic Obstetrics and Gynaecology*, **9**, 35–42.

Hay, A.G., Bancroft, J. & Johnstone, E.C. (1994). Affective symptoms in women attending a menopause clinic. *British Journal of Psychiatry*, **164**, 513–516.

Haywood, A., Slade, P. & King, H. (2002). Assessing the assessment measures for menstrual cycle symptoms: a guide for researchers and clinicians. *Journal of Psychosomatic Research*, **52**, 223–237.

Heim, C., Ehlert, U., Hanker, J.P. & Hellhammer, D.H. (1998). Abuse related post traumatic stress disorder and alterations to the hypothalamic–pituitary–adrenal axis in women with chronic pelvic pain. *Psychosomatic Medicine*, **60**, 309–318.

Holte, A. (1991). Prevalence of climacteric complaints in a representative sample of middle aged women in Oslo, Norway. *Journal of Psychosomatic Obstetrics and Gynaecology*, **12**, 303–317.

Hunter, M. (1992). The South East England longitudinal study of climacteric and postmenopausal women. *Maturitas*, **14**, 117–126.

Hunter, M. (2000). The development, standardisation and application of a measure of mid aged women emotional and physical health. *Quality of Life Research*, **9**, 733–738.

Hunter, M. & Liao, K.L. (1996). Evaluation of a four session cognitive behavioural intervention for menopausal hot flushes. *British Journal of Health Psychology*, **1**, 113–125.

Hunter, M., Swann, C. & Ussher, J.M. (1995). Seeking help for premenstrual syndrome. Women's self reports and treatment preferences. *Sexual and Marital Therapy*, **10**, 253–262.

Hurrell, E. & Slade, P. (2001). Memory and the perimenopausal woman: clinical implications of recent research findings. *Journal of the Menopause Society*, **7**, 61–67.

Infant Feeding Patterns (2000). Department of Health Report (www.statistics.gov.uk)

Janiger, O., Reffenburgh, R. & Kersch, R. (1972). Cross cultural study of premenstrual symptoms. *Psychosomatics*, **13**, 226–235.

Jenkins, R., Lewis, G., Bebbington, P., Brugha, T., Farrell, M., Gill, B. & Meltzer, H. (1997). The National Psychiatric Morbidity Surveys of Great Britain—initial findings from the Household Survey. *Psychological Medicine*, **27**, 775–789.

Kirkby, R.J. (1994). Changes in premenstrual symptoms and irrational thinking following cognitive behavioural coping skills training. *Journal of Consulting and Clinical Psychology*, **62**, 1026–1032.

Kuh, D.L., Wadsworth, M. & Hardy, R. (1997). Women's health in mid life, the influence of the menopause, social factors and health earlier in life. *British Journal of Obstetrics and Gynaecology*, **104**, 923–933.

Liao, K.L.M. & Hunter, M. (1998). Preparation for menopause, a prospective evaluation of a health education intervention for mid aged women. *Maturitas*, **29**, 215–224.

McGowan, L., Pitts, M. & Carter, D.C. (1999). Chronic pelvic pain: the general practitioner's perspective. *Psychology Health and Medicine*, **4**, 303–317.

McKinlay, J.B., McKinlay, S.M. & Brambrilla, D. (1987). The relative contributions of endocrine changes and social circumstances to depression in mid aged women. *Journal of Health and Social Behaviour*, **28**, 345–363.

Montero, I., Ruiz, I. & Hernandez, I. (1993). Social functioning as a significant factor in women's help-seeking behaviour during the climacteric period. *Social Psychiatry and Psychiatric Epidemiology*, **28**, 178–183.

Morrison, N. (2001). Group cognitive therapy: treatment of choice or suboptimal option. *Behavioural and Cognitive Therapy*, **29**, 311–321.

Morse, C.A., Dennerstein, L., Farrell, E. & Varnavides, K. (1991). A comparison of hormone therapy, coping skills training, and relaxation for the relief of premenstrual syndrome. *Journal of Behavioural Medicine*, **14**, 469–489.

Mortola, J.T., Girton, L., Beck, L. & Yen, S.S.C. (1990). Diagnosis of premenstrual syndrome by a simple prospective and reliable instrument: the calendar of premenstrual experience. *Obstetrics and Gynaecology*, **76**, 302–307.

Phillips, N., Dennerstein, L. & Farish, S. (1996). Psychiatric morbidity in obstetric and gynaecology patients. Testing the need for an expanded psychiatric service in obstetric and gynaecology services. *Australian and New Zealand Journal of Psychiatry*, **30**, 74–81.

Phillips, S.M. & Sherwin, B.B. (1992). Effects of estrogen on memory function in surgically menopausal women. *Psychoneuroendocrinology*, **17**, 484–495.

Raphael, K.G., Widom, C.S. & Lange, G. (2001). Childhood victimization and pain in adulthood: a prospective investigation. *Pain*, **92**, 283–293.

Rapkin, A.J., Kames, L.D., Darke, L.L., Stampler, F.M. & Naliboff, B.D. (1990). History of physical and sexual abuse in women with chronic pelvic pain. *Obstetrics and Gynaecology*, **76**, 92–96.

Reading, A.E. (1993). Cognitive model of premenstrual syndrome. *Clinics in Obstetrics and Gynaecology*, **35**, 693–700.

Reiter, R.C., Shakerin, L.R., Gambone, D.O. & Milburn, A.K. (1991). Correlation between sexual abuse and somatization in women with somatic and non somatic chronic pelvic pain. *American Journal of Obstetrics and Gynaecology*, **165**, 104–109.

Reynolds, F.A. (1997). Perceived control over menopausal hot flushes, exploring the correlates of a standardised measure. *Maturitas*, **27**, 215–221.

Richter, H.E., Holley, R.L., Chandraiah, S. & Varner, R.E. (1998). Laparoscopic and psychologic evaluation of women with chronic pelvic pain. *International Journal of Psychiatry in Medicine*, **28**, 243–253.

Rome, E. (1986). Premenstrual syndrome (PMS) examined through a feminist lens. *Health Care for Women International*, **7**, 145.

Savidge, C. & Slade, P. (1997). Psychological aspects of chronic pelvic pain. *Journal of Psychosomatic Research*, **42**, 433–444.

Savidge, C., Slade, P., Stewart, P. & Li, T.C. (1998). Women's perspectives on their experiences of chronic pelvic pain and medical care. *Journal of Health Psychology*, **3**, 103–116.

Shoebridge, A. & Steed, L. (1999). Discourse about menopause in selected print media. *Australian and New Zealand Journal of Public Health*, **23**, 475–481.

Slade, P. (1989). Psychological therapy for premenstrual symptoms. *Behavioural Psychotherapy*, **17**, 135–150.

Slade, P. & Anderton, K.J. (1992). Gynaecological symptoms and psychological distress: a longitudinal study of their relationship. *Journal of Psychosomatic Obstetrics and Gynaecology*, **13**, 51–64.

Slade, P. & Mathers, N. (2001). *"An Unmet Need": GP and Practice Nurse Perspectives on the Provision of Care for Psychological Issues Related to Women's Reproductive Health*. Report from the Institute of General Practice and Psychological Health, Sheffield.

Slade, P., Anderton, K.J. & Faragher, E.B. (1988). Psychological aspects of gynaecological outpatients. *Journal of Psychosomatic Obstetrics and Gynaecology*, **8**, 77–94.

Slade, P., Escott, D. & King, H. (1998). *An Evaluation of the Need for Psychological Services to the Women's Health Clinic*. Report to Community Health Sheffield Trust.

Spitzer, R.L., Williams, J.B.W., Kroenke, K., Hornyak, R. & McMurray, J. (2000). Validity and utility of the PRIME-MD Patient Health Questionnaire in assessment of 3000 obstetric–gynaecologic patients: the PRIME-MD Patient Health Questionnaire Obstetric Gynaecology study. *American Journal of Obstetrics and Gynaecology*, **183**, 759–769.

Sridevi, K. & Krishna-Rao, P.V. (1996). Yoga practice and menstrual distress. *Journal of the Indian Academy of Applied Psychology*, **22**, 47–54.

Steiner, M. (1997). Premenstrual syndromes. *Annual Review of Medicine*, **48**, 447–455.

Stewart, D.E., Boydell, K.M., Derzko, C. & Marshall, V. (1992). Psychological distress during menopausal years in women attending a menopause clinic. *International Journal of Psychiatry in Medicine*, **22**, 213–220.

Sundstrom, I.M.E., Bixo, M., Bjorn, I. & Astrom, M. (2001). Prevalence of psychiatric symptoms in gynaecological outpatients. *American Journal of Obstetrics and Gynaecology*, **184**, 8–13.

Toomy, T.C., Hernandez, J.T., Gitterlman, D.F. & Hulka, J.F. (1993). Relationship of sexual and physical abuse to pain and psychological assessment variables in chronic pelvic pain patients. *Pain*, **53**, 105–109.

Vanwesenbeeck, I., Vennis, P. & van de Wiel, H. (2001). Menopausal symptoms: associations with menopausal status and psychosocial factors. *Journal of Psychosomatic Obstetrics and Gynaecology*, **22**, 149–158.

Walker, E., Katon, W., Harrop-Griffiths, J., Holm, L., Russo, L.J. & Hickok, L.R. (1988). Relationship of chronic pelvic pain to psychiatric diagnoses and childhood sexual abuse. *American Journal of Psychiatry*, **145**, 75–80.

Woods, N.F., Dery, G.K. & Most, A. (1982). Stressful life events and premenstrual symptoms. *Journal of Human Stress*, **8**, 12–31.

CHAPTER 18

Accident and Trauma

Gary Latchford
University of Leeds, UK

INTRODUCTION

Most people would consider the care of people after accidents as one of the core functions of an acute hospital. This aspect of modern health care is a common feature of our cultural experience, whether through our own personal experience or through the media, where it is frequently represented in dramas and documentaries. An assumption that we share is that people who are seriously injured need specialist care, and may have particular physical and psychological needs—the term "trauma" has both a physical and a psychological meaning. Most people have less understanding of the range of injuries that people may suffer, or of the changes in care—and of outcome—which have taken place over the last 20 years. This chapter focuses on the psychological care of those suffering traumatic injuries, some of whom are so badly injured that there is a significant possibility of mortality, and long-term disability of some kind is almost certain. For such patients, survival and rehabilitation perhaps represents the greatest challenge to a health service.

ORTHOPAEDIC SURGERY AND PSYCHOLOGY

Orthopaedic surgery—surgery to the bones in the body—may be grouped into two types, elective and traumatic. Elective orthopaedic surgery refers to non-emergency surgery, usually to correct the effects of a congenital or deteriorating condition. In many areas, psychological factors are now receiving increased attention, such as the positive benefits of providing psychiatric consultation for patients undergoing procedures such as hip replacement (Strain et al., 1991). Traumatic orthopaedic surgery refers to surgery undertaken following a traumatic injury, with the aim of saving the life of the patient and reducing the physical disability that may result from the injury. This chapter will focus on this group of patients, whose experiences are characterised by sudden and unexpected injury and hospital admission, with all the psychological consequences that this entails.

Handbook of Clinical Health Psychology. Edited by S. Llewelyn and P. Kennedy.
© 2003 John Wiley & Sons, Ltd.

WHY FOCUS ON TRAUMA PATIENTS?

Many patients will pass through the emergency facilities of acute hospitals for a variety of reasons, including onset of acute medical symptoms such as chest pain, attempted suicide, and accidental injury. Of the latter, most patients are discharged home without being admitted and are rarely referred for psychological help, though many may have unmet psychological needs (Mayou, Bryant & Duthie, 1993). The present chapter, however, is concerned with those who suffer physical injuries severe enough for them to be admitted, when their psychological needs may become obvious and interventions requested.

The scale and cost of orthopaedic trauma is much greater than most people imagine. US data indicates that trauma accounts for a greater financial loss to society in terms of lost working days than heart disease and cancer combined (Glancy et al., 1992). Injury is the leading cause of death and disability in young men under the age of 45 (Holbrook et al., 1998). The study of survivors of orthopaedic injury, with the aim of achieving a greater understanding of their needs, has become increasingly important over the last 20 years as new systems of care have led to increased rates of survival (Ornato et al., 1985).

DEFINING PHYSICAL TRAUMA

Internationally, the most widely used measuring instruments for physical injury are the Abbreviated Injury Scale (AIS; AAAM, 1985) and the Injury Severity Score (ISS; Baker et al., 1974). The former categorises each injury on two axes: body area and severity, scored from 0 (no injury) to 5 (practically unsurvivable injury). The ISS is then calculated by summing the squares of the three highest AIS values for the three most severely injured body areas. A score of 16 or higher is taken as an indication of polytrauma—a term indicating the presence of severe multiple injuries.

Causes of trauma vary from site to site, but the most common single cause is road traffic accidents (RTA[1]) involving motor vehicles or motorcycles. Other possible causes include industrial accidents, falls, and physical assaults (including gunshot wounds). Severe physical trauma is more common in younger people and in males, though there is an interaction with mechanism of injury (e.g. more young men are injured in motorcycle accidents than women).

MEDICAL CARE OF TRAUMA PATIENTS

The initial aim of medical care is to promote survival, followed by a concern to limit long-term disability—for example, by pursuing alternatives to limb amputation. This depends on a smooth transition between emergency services and surgical care, initial damage limitation, and coordinated intensive care provision. Recent years have seen a move towards early surgical intervention to stabilise long bone fractures but delayed reconstructive work (MacKenzie et al., 1993). Successful outcome both in the short term and long term depends upon coordinated care, and the input of many different health professionals.

---

[1] This abbreviation will be used instead of MVA (Motor Vehicle Accident) throughout this chapter.

There are several differences in the approach to management of traumatic injury across different nations. Germany and the United States have pioneered an approach that involves the development of Level 1 Regional Trauma Centres, receiving patients with severe injuries 24 hours a day, and with all key specialties in the treatment of trauma care on the same site. Specialties with particular relevance are accident and emergency physicians, orthopaedic and spinal surgery, neurosurgery, thoracic surgery, general surgery, vascular surgery, maxillofacial surgery, plastic surgery, and paediatric surgery. The Level 1 centre is supported by a network of district acute hospitals with less comprehensive emergency facilities.

The situation in the UK is different, with only six acute hospitals providing the full range of surgical services (Templeton, 2000). Also, trauma care varies within many nations. Across the USA, for example, nearly one half of the states have no organised systems of trauma care, with rural coverage being a particular problem (Bass, Gainer & Carlini, 1999). A comprehensive trauma system is necessarily a public health strategy, and this has caused problems in the USA where the requirement of trauma centres to refer on less severely injured patients has led to financial problems in many centres, most famously in Los Angeles in 1992 (Mullins, 1999). There have been recent calls in the USA for the magnitude of the problems caused by trauma to be recognised in the funding available for research and service provision (Institute of Medicine, 1999).

Nevertheless, the US model has been a major influence on the organisation of trauma services in other nations. In the UK there are current proposals to develop Level 1 centres along similar lines, with each centre serving a population of around three million people and supported by acute general hospitals (Templeton, 2000).

Finally, many countries have introduced the Advanced Trauma Life Support training programme, developed in the USA, which is increasingly being seen internationally as the gold standard for clinical protocols and specialist training in the care of the seriously injured patient.

The Experience of Patients

An example of the experience of a patient following severe injury is given below. This patient's experiences of the trauma and subsequent medical intervention may be characterised as a series of stages, beginning with the accident and ending with discharge from the orthopaedic consultant:

1. The traumatic incident
2. Initial admission and surgery
3. Resident in Intensive Care
4. Resident on Orthopaedic Ward
5. Discharge home, with regular outpatient attendance for physiotherapy and readmissions for follow-up surgery
6. Discharge from consultant orthopaedic surgeon, long-term adjustment.

In cases of serious injury the time period from the accident to discharge by the surgeon or other specialist is usually several years, with latter years often complicated by factors such as physical disability and compensation claims.

Case Example: Barry

Barry is a 24-year-old man injured while riding a motorcycle when he was in collision with a motorist overtaking a tractor in a rural lane. He was conscious after the accident and in considerable pain. He suffered multiple fractures of one hip, both legs and one arm, and underwent extensive surgery on his admission to hospital. As his condition remained critical, he subsequently spent one week on an intensive care unit before being transferred to an orthopaedic ward. He underwent further surgery while on the ward. He was also seen by the acute pain team, a physiotherapist, and—because he had lost a large amount of weight—a dietician.

He was discharged home after ten weeks on the ward. He worked as a machinist in a local factory but was unable to return to his previous employment. He lived alone in a small house that was not suitable due to his mobility problems, and moved back to live with his parents for six months.

He returned to the hospital twice a week for physiotherapy for eight months, and also underwent two further operations.

He was discharged by the orthopaedic surgeon three and a half years after the accident. At that time he still had not returned to full employment, and still reported significant mobility problems and pain.

OUTCOME AFTER MAJOR TRAUMA

Physical Outcome

Survival and functional outcome after serious injury is extremely variable, with factors such as extent and site of injury, injury mechanism, sociodemographic status, social support and psychological sequelae cited as potentially important in different reports, although there is little consistency across the literature (Holbrook et al., 1998).

In general, although functional outcome reduces as amount of injury increases, most surviving the initial stages of the trauma will experience significant recovery in the first half year after the injury, and further slight recuperation subsequently, although a significant minority will remain severely disabled (Van der Sluis, ten Duis & Geertzen, 1995). The majority of patients who have suffered multiple injuries report a decreased quality of life, citing a negative impact on areas such as general health, employment and social activities (Thiagarajan et al., 1994). Although the majority of those employed previously do return to work (MacKenzie et al., 1988) this is not necessarily to the same job, and many report being forced to change their leisure activities. Factors influencing outcome include social support and educational background (Van der Sluis et al., 1998).

There is no simple correlation between impairment (the extent of physical injury) and disability (limitations in daily living). In a six-month follow-up of 302 patients with lower extremity fracture, MacKenzie et al. (1993) found little correlation between severity of injury and subsequent disability, as reflected in return to work, home management or recreation. They suggest that other factors may play an important role in influencing outcome, including economic and social resources, and general affective personality traits. Similarly, Glancy et al. (1992), in a six-month follow-up of 441 trauma patients, found that although injury severity and age did predict return to previous functioning, this was also influenced by a number of social and psychological variables, including educational level and pre-injury hostility.

Finally, Michaels et al. (2000) have reported a 12-month follow-up study of 247 trauma patients, in which work status, general health and overall satisfaction with recovery was dependent on their mental health. They call for greater awareness of the importance of psychological problems in trauma patients.

Psychological Outcome

In terms of psychological outcome, it is known that victims of orthopaedic trauma are extremely vulnerable to psychiatric disorders in the months and years following the trauma (Malt, 1988), especially post-traumatic stress disorder (PTSD). Blanchard et al. (1995) showed that the risk of developing PTSD following an accident was directly related to the severity of the injuries sustained and the perception of the risk to life, though they also cited cases that did not fit this pattern. Similarly, other researchers (e.g. Frommberger et al., 1999) have shown that extent of injury following accidents interacts with personality factors and predicts psychological health at six months.

A series of studies has investigated outcome following traffic accidents in which patients were hospitalised. In 1997, Mayou, Tyndel and Bryant reported the results of a five-year follow up in which 10% were reported to be suffering from full PTSD, 60% reported travel anxiety and 55% reported an adverse effect on quality of life. Jeavons (2000) has examined possible predictors of PTSD following RTAs and found that emotional coping was associated with poorer outcome. She also looked at severity of injury and found that it was associated with psychological outcome, but at 12-month follow-up and not earlier. Interestingly, Joy et al. (2000) suggest that distress in the acute stage after injury is related to pre-trauma functioning. Depression is also common. In a study of 1048 seriously injured trauma patients, 60% were found to be depressed at discharge, and 31% at six-month follow-up (Holbrook et al., 1998). Depression was found to be associated with functional outcome, as was post-traumatic stress symptoms.

Apart from the distress such psychological symptoms cause patients, research previously described indicates that they are also implicated in influencing physical outcome, particularly return to previous levels of functioning. Although the mechanism is not yet known, psychological state may influence adherence to treatment, as well as self-directed rehabilitation.

Overview of Research Evidence

As medical techniques have improved, increasing numbers of patients are surviving serious physical injury. The current literature suggests that many will suffer long-term physical disability, that psychological problems are also a likely outcome, and that physical and psychological factors may interact. Many studies do not provide clear information on the extent of the physical trauma, however, and measures of psychological functioning are sometimes crude. There is widespread agreement among researchers that outcome in orthopaedic trauma must move on from a focus on survival statistics, and incorporate quality of life indices which includes psychological health (Naughton & Shumaker, 1997). This consensus was recently summarised in a report on the future of services in the UK:

> There are no large cohort studies of the disabilities of the increased numbers of surviving
> patients nor knowledge of this burden of human suffering and cost. Both are likely to
> be considerable and require urgent investigation. (RCSE/BOA, 2000, p. 16)

Additional Factors Affecting Outcome

Several other factors may further complicate the medical and psychological needs of these
patients. In some cases a limb may need to be amputated, patients may sustain spinal injuries
leading to paralysis, or burns injuries that require specialist medical intervention. Also, head
injury is a relatively common complication of severe physical injury, and again requires
specialist intervention.

In addition, variables relating to the traumatic incident, the personality of the patient and
the involvement of others may have a big impact on recovery. These will be discussed below.

PSYCHOLOGICAL INTERVENTIONS WITH TRAUMA PATIENTS

What follows is a guide to the likely needs of patients during different stages of their
treatment and recovery, and psychological interventions appropriate for each stage. Patients
who survive serious physical trauma are subjected to a number of different stressors in the
weeks, months and years following the injury. These may be grouped into three main
factors:

1. The psychological impact of the traumatic event.
2. The psychological impact of sudden hospitalisation.
3. The psychosocial impact of the resulting physical impairment.

Although there are many individual variations in the reactions of patients to these three
factors, this is a useful framework and the relative impact of these factors at different stages
of recovery will be used as a guide in this section.

Stage 1: The Trauma

As described above, there are many possible causes of traumatic injury. Psychological
help is not available at the scene, but aspects of the traumatic event may have important
consequences for later adaptation. Table 18.1 lists some important variables, some examples
of pertinent issues, and possible consequences. It is important to keep these issues in mind
during later assessment.

Stage 2: Admission to Hospital

For the severely injured, the patient undergoes medical assessment on arrival and usually
undergoes surgery very soon after. Many will have brief and sometimes confused memories

Table 18.1 The trauma: important factors in later adaptation

Variable	Example	Possible consequences
Responsibility	• Was patient responsible for injury to others? • Was patient responsible for own injuries? • Was someone else responsible for the trauma? Are they known?	• Guilt; denial of importance of accident • Anger at self, but may increase perception of control • Anger. If person not known, anger may be debilitating
Immediate consequences	• Was the patient conscious following the trauma? • Was there a long duration before help arrived? • Was the patient trapped? • Did patient play any part in self-rescue?	• Flashbacks to scene of accident • Anxiety • Claustrophobia; increased risk of PTSD • May increase perception of control and self-worth
Involvement of others	• Were children involved? • Were there any fatalities?	• Increased risk of PTSD • Bereavement; sadness

from this period, and these may feature in later adaptation—for example, they may have vivid and distressing memories of their family arriving at the hospital. For some, the seriousness of their condition may have become apparent to them at this time, and they may have become aware of the possibility of dying.

Stage 3: Admission to Intensive Care

Following initial surgery, seriously injured patients are usually admitted to an intensive care unit where their physical signs can be closely monitored. At this time there is often still a significant risk of mortality, and patients are usually sedated. Opportunities to work psychologically with patients in intensive care are limited by their level of consciousness.

One important factor here is the occurrence of "intensive care syndrome". Although not well understood, this refers to a condition in which the patient experiences disorientation and memory problems. Several factors are thought to contribute, including sensory deprivation, isolation, high doses of medication, and helplessness exacerbated by an inability to communicate because of intubation. Patients may become delirious, withdrawn or occasionally euphoric (Gammon, 1999). The experience may present as a problem to the patient some time after, and can lead to nightmares and intrusive images from this period to recur. Sometimes the patients may be reluctant to disclose hallucinations for fear of not being believed.

Stage 4: Transfer to Ward

Initially, transfer from intensive care to a hospital ward may be unsettling for patient and family. Levels of nursing are lower, and the patient may be in a room with others. Adjusting to a period of residence on a hospital ward is often a difficult psychological task. Trauma patients are at a disadvantage in three important respects:

1. Their entry to hospital has been sudden and they have had no time in which to prepare, either psychologically or practically, for a period of prolonged admission.
2. They have suffered severe physical injuries that may make them totally dependent on the staff of the ward.
3. The experience of the trauma may already have rendered them extremely vulnerable psychologically.

At this stage patients will often have their first opportunity to begin the process of comprehending what has happened to them, and to anticipate the likely consequences. The immediate concern of patients is usually their physical injuries, current pain, and the short-term plan for medical treatment. This may be confounded by psychological factors such as emotional lability (tearfulness) and nightmares, and difficulties adjusting to the ward.

The Effect of Hospitalisation

Patients on a hospital ward find themselves in an alien environment controlled by others, separated from their loved ones and everyday normal life (Salmon, 2000). Life on the ward for trauma patients is characterised by an extreme loss of control magnified by the physical restrictions imposed by their injuries. They are usually unable to wash or go to the toilet unaided. They have little or no choice over timing and content of meals, and often have no choice over whom they talk to. They often feel that they have little personal dignity or privacy. Unlike most other inpatients they experience extreme dependence on the staff for the basic elements of survival. This loss of control is particularly important for this group, as they have often experienced feelings of powerlessness in connection with the original trauma. This may be particularly hard for those with no prior experience of any period of hospitalisation, those who have previously been very independent, those who have previously worked in a caring role (e.g. health professionals), and those (especially older adults) who are distressed by their lack of privacy.

In addition, patients may be very fearful of medical treatments (including surgery) and of the prospects for the future. They may be extremely worried about something going wrong, and may check their body for signs of problems. They may become anxious, and misinterpret bodily signs. They may consistently request reassurance that things are going well. Information is not always easily available and staff may not have clear answers about the extent of physical recovery possible and not wish to speculate. As a result, however, patients may misinterpret information passed on by different professionals. Often, patients may feel afraid and express a strong desire to get home, and frustration at the time it will take.

Physically, patients may be in some discomfort. Pain is very common, and the vast majority will be prescribed analgesics of varying strength. Sleep is often a problem because of pain, physical discomfort, or anxiety that often increases when the patient is alone at night. Also, many report suffering from muscle spasms as they drift to sleep, which can be very unsettling.

As concern with physical injury becomes less immediate over time, patients may begin to worry about the wider impact of the trauma. They may be concerned for the effect on their home-life and on family and friends. They may be worried about the financial implications (and in some countries the cost of treatment), or the prospect of not returning to work. For many, especially manual workers (who are more at risk of injury), return to the same form of employment is not likely.

During this period, the most useful psychological intervention is one of providing psychological support: listening to fears, communicating understanding and helping to normalise reactions. The experience of a ward has been likened to deciphering the social conventions and rules of a foreign country (Salmon, 2000). Patients have a powerful expectation of passivity (Peerbhoy et al., 1998) and are concerned with "fitting-in". One of the roles of those offering psychological support may therefore be seen as acting as an interpreter:

> When the psychologist reached Mrs G's bed, she was clearly quite distressed. She explained that she had been worried since having her surgery the day before. That morning the surgeon had passed by the end of her bed. She had looked up to talk to him but he had not said anything to her. She explained that she thought that the reason was that he had very bad news for her and was avoiding her. This was not, in fact, the case, and the psychologist and Mrs G discussed alternative explanations, such as the surgeon being in a rush, and the different social conventions often seen on the ward.

Patients who become distressed may have problems engaging in rehabilitation and there may be implications for the pace of recovery. Anxiety management is often a useful strategy at this time, and should combine relaxation training with cognitive techniques to challenge erroneous thinking, such as catastrophising bodily signs. Physical injuries usually make imaginal rather than progressive muscle relaxation more useful, and relaxation tapes on audiocassette can often be left with the patient. Imagining a different location, perhaps from memory, can also offer a safe refuge from the ward. Relaxation may help alleviate anxiety, give the patient a greater sense of control, and may also help with sleep.

Sometimes there may be friction between patient and ward staff, and consultancy work may be necessary to identify problems and work on a solution. Ideally, psychological support should be provided by all of the staff on the ward. In practice, however, pressure of time and lack of training can make this difficult, and psychological support often has a low priority. Nicholls (1995) has argued that changing the prevailing culture on wards so that patients' individual needs are addressed (and in the process the needs of the staff) should be a major priority. The concept of "patient-centredness" (Mead & Bower, 2000) describes an approach to patient care based on a biopsychosocial model, with an emphasis on a therapeutic alliance between patient and health professional and sharing power and responsibility. Fostering this development is an important role for psychologists.

Psychological Symptoms

As shown above, patients with serious injury are at great risk of developing PTSD. The symptoms listed in the criteria for PTSD outlined in the fourth *Diagnostic and Statistical Manual of Mental Disorders* (APA, 1994) are grouped along three axes: re-experiencing phenomena, such as intrusive recollections; avoidance or emotional numbing; and increased arousal, indicated by symptoms such as sleep disturbance and an exaggerated startle reflex.

More relevant in the month immediately following the trauma is acute stress disorder (ASD), which is characterised by similar symptoms to PTSD (though it separates avoidance from dissociative symptoms such as emotional numbing), but which lasts a minimum of two days and maximum of four weeks. It is predictive of later development of PTSD.

There is a long history of attempts to pre-empt the development of PTSD, initially in combat survivors and later in civilian populations. Mitchell (1983) and Dyregrov (1989) independently developed a technique for debriefing survivors of trauma in small groups. The process involves encouraging participants to talk through their memories, thoughts and feelings about the event in order to help them to process their experiences. Following initial enthusiasm, however, the method was criticised for the lack of a clear evidence base. In 1998 a systematic review of debriefing was published (Wesseley, Rose & Bisson, 1998) which showed that it might actually increase symptoms at follow-up. Mitchell has, in turn, criticised the methodologies of the papers included in the review: the index trauma and facilitator varied greatly, and all utilised individual debriefing, unlike the group debriefing as described in Mitchell's original model (Everly & Mitchell, 2000).

Reviewing the evidence, it seems plausible that encouraging patients to describe their traumatic experiences soon after the trauma may in some cases undermine their preferred coping behaviour and therefore risk causing secondary traumatisation. Also, there is a lack of clear evidence for the effectiveness of debriefing in a one-to-one situation, reinforced by a recent finding that debriefing is ineffective when used with uninjured RTA victims (Mayou, Ehlers & Hobbs, 2000). It is therefore not recommended for use with patients on the ward.

What interventions may be useful? Perhaps the most interesting issue about PTSD in this group is that many people do not develop it. It is, however, misleading to assume that those without full-blown PTSD or ASD have no problems. In fact, many patients on the ward will experience individual symptoms—or clusters of symptoms—which though not constituting PTSD are nonetheless severely disabling and may pose a serious problem for rehabilitation. It is more useful clinically to consider individual post-traumatic stress reactions rather than focus only on those diagnosed with a disorder.

In such cases the most effective intervention at this stage is likely to be psycho-educational, and involves explaining to patients the likely origin of their symptoms, offering reassurance that such reactions are natural, and suggesting coping strategies such as relaxation. Patients commonly worry about these symptoms, generating further stress, and normalising the experience can have a dramatic therapeutic effect. It is advisable to have information materials that can be given to the patient. This may also help patients to identify persistent problems in the future before they become established. Sometimes a patient may wish to talk through the trauma as part of the process of adaptation, and this may be helpful if the patient is allowed control over the process. Some common psychological symptoms are listed below:

- *Emotionalism* (e.g. tearfulness)*:* Repeated episodes of tearfulness, triggered by a number of previously innocuous cues such as sad songs, or seeing friends and family. This is a common reaction to a traumatic health event. Patients are usually able to appreciate that their emotions are much closer to the surface and that this is a natural reaction. Some, particularly young men, may find this embarrassing and out of character. (*"I was watching some silly programme on the television and I started crying."*)

- *Hyperarousal:* Patients may appear anxious and "jumpy". Often, an exaggerated startle reflex is apparent. (*"I looked around, and I suddenly saw a window cleaner outside the window. It made me jump so much I actually jumped out of the bed, though my arm was still all wired up."*) Patients usually understand that their anxiety has something to do with a response to the fear that they have felt, and normalising it as an extended fear response (for example, using the metaphor of a car alarm continuing to sound) can be helpful.

- *Rumination:* Thoughts about the accident and the "what ifs" surrounding it are common. Patients may go over the sequence of events in their mind many times, but do appreciate that there is no solution to be found. (*"I keep thinking, what if I had decided to stay at home that day, or had gone the other way to work."*) Cognitions about the accident such as perceived threat to life are more strongly related to subsequent PTSD than severity (Jeavons, Greenwood & Horne, 2000).

- *Nightmares:* These may be about the accident, or appear at first to have little connection to it: they may feature an important aspect of it—such as feeling trapped or being aware that something is about to happen and unable to stop it—but feature people or events that were not connected to the real event. They are often felt to be very disturbing. Again, normalising the experience (for example, as attempts by the unconscious to process what has happened) may be helpful. They often resolve naturally over time. (*"In the dream my leg was being crushed in the accident, but the people who were around me were people from years ago, who didn't work with me any more."*)

- *Shock and disbelief:* Some patients may initially appear to have problems in grasping what has happened to them. (*"It feels as though it has happened to someone else."*) This should be distinguished from a more prolonged emotional numbness described below.

- *Emotional numbing:* Patient may appear withdrawn with a diminished range of affect, speak in a monotone, and feel distant or cut off from others. It has been argued that emotional numbing is a product of chronic hyperarousal (Flack et al., 2000). An alternative hypothesis is that it reflects an unconscious psychological defence against the full impact of the event, and may therefore be more common in individuals where the emotional impact of the trauma may be greater—e.g. where they have been responsible for the death of others or have lost a loved one. In such cases the patient may minimise what has happened or avoid thinking about it. Offering an explanation may be helpful for the patient and family, but it is important that any intervention to enable processing of the traumatic material is postponed until the chronic nature of the problems has become apparent and the patient is ready.

- *Guilt:* In some cases the patient may feel intense guilt, either about causing or contributing to the accident, or for surviving it when others have not. (*"I keep worrying about the other driver, whether they are alright."*) In some cases in which the patient has caused accidental injury to others, there are serious long-term psychological problems including suicide risk.

- *Anger:* This is not often expressed to a great extent in the weeks following a trauma, but may become more pronounced when the patient is confronted by the multiple conse-quences of the trauma. In the short term the anger may be directed at medical staff; in the longer term it may be directed at whoever is perceived to be responsible, or associated with the experience (such as solicitors involved in a compensation claim).

- *Dissociation:* Dissociation, or a psychological distancing of the self from the trauma, is potentially reflected in many different symptoms. In more extreme cases it may be characterised by chronic emotional numbness. A much less serious but extremely common symptom is the perception that time was extended during the trauma itself. (*"It felt as if the accident was happening in slow motion."*)

Assessing and intervening for distress during the inpatient period may be extremely important. Richmond and Kauder (2000), in their study of 109 seriously injured patients, found that distress increased from 32% of individuals during hospitalisation to 49% three months after discharge, and that distress during hospitalisation was the best predictor of later distress.

Reaction of Others

Traumatic events do not happen in isolation. They may complicate existing problems, such as relationship difficulties or separation. Friends and relatives may be an important source of social support, or may themselves be traumatised by the event. They may be angry with the patient if they feel he or she has contributed to the accident. The patient may attempt to protect loved ones from the full implications of the trauma, or be too embarrassed or afraid to confide difficult feelings. A common reaction of others (including medical staff) is to tell the patient that he or she is lucky to have survived. Though some find this thought reassuring, most do not find this helpful, since they do not feel particularly lucky. The notion that the only reason for survival is luck can also be a very unsettling concept, reinforcing a sense of powerlessness.

Stage 5: Discharge

In general, patients are desperate to be discharged home. It should be noted, however, that for many, returning home is not possible if they live alone and need further care or if their home is not suitable (e.g. if it has narrow stairs). A minority will never be able to return to their previous accommodation.

Returning home can also act as a catalyst for emotion, and it is often helpful to prepare patients for this. Three factors are particularly important. First, patients tend to feel much more secure in their own home and will feel easier about releasing emotions there. This is particularly important if the patient has had no time alone with a loved one. Second, patients are prevented from participating in most self-care activities in hospital, and on returning home to a familiar environment can often be shocked at the extent to which their injuries intrude in day-to-day living. Third, in hospital there are medical staff to answer worries at all times, and patients may initially become anxious at home.

Stage 6: Long-term Adaptation

Many patients will face very real problems in adapting to their injuries. The months following discharge are usually a time of great uncertainty. For those with severe orthopaedic injuries, it may be two years before the extent of recovery of function is known. There is also an increased risk of arthritic conditions in future years. Some will require further surgery, and the prospect of returning to hospital may generate much anticipatory anxiety.

Depending on the extent of the injuries, many different aspects of life will be disrupted, some permanently: for example, sports and hobbies that require physical fitness (e.g. squash, running); house maintenance and improvements (e.g. house painting); shopping (e.g. carrying heavy bags); and sexual activity. Return to work depends on injuries and type of work. Even where a job is non-manual, it may prove difficult, for example, if the patient is required to sit down most of the day and this generates pain. The impact of any of these changes depends on the meaning of the activity to the patient, and his or her ability to find alternatives. Some people may be particularly vulnerable to the effect of serious injury; for example, a man who has always worked long hours in manual jobs, and prided himself in being the main wage-earner in the household and in maintaining the house, may find his self-esteem threatened by enforced changes. It is important that patients receive employment and benefits advice, and are informed about support groups.

The majority of injured patients will return to some form of employment, but this is usually after months or years of gradual recovery and rehabilitation, which is often felt to be extremely frustrating. Some may be self-conscious about their appearance (e.g. if they have an amputated limb), and may become socially isolated. In addition, the trauma may place increasing strains on close relationships. Finally, increased alcohol or drug use is an important risk, particularly in those who are in pain, and who find it difficult to adjust to not working.

Particular issues of concern during this time include the following:

- *Travel anxiety:* Many patients injured in RTAs become anxious (or phobic) about travelling (Mayou, Tyndel & Bryant, 1997). This includes those injured when travelling as a passenger (in some cases the reaction is worse, magnified by the loss of control felt in the accident). Patients may find it hard to understand, and be embarrassed to talk about it. It may be expressed as an avoidance of travelling, or excessive anxiety (e.g. using "safety behaviours" such as over-using the rear-view mirror, or shouting warnings to the driver). The best intervention is a combination of the psycho-educational (normalising the symptoms) and cognitive-behavioural, in which relaxation is used with systematic desensitisation through a graded hierarchy of feared stimuli, together with cognitive restructuring of dysfunctional beliefs about RTAs.
- *Irritability:* Some patients may report becoming much more short tempered, particularly with family and friends, though this may take many months to become apparent. ("*I used to be so patient with my grandchildren, but I just lose my temper all the time now.*") Potential causes include pain and poor sleep, low mood, frustration at lack of progress and anxiety. It may be a sign that other post-traumatic stress symptoms are present.
- *Post-traumatic stress reactions:* A significant minority of patients will develop PTSD (Mayou, Tyndel & Bryant, 1997). This may be expressed, for example, as chronic and debilitating nightmares about the accident. Pain may be a particular trigger for intrusive images. An intervention is advised; for example, using an exposure-based intervention known to be effective (Foa, Keane & Friedman, 2000).
- *Changes in mood:* The experience of a trauma and its aftermath has a powerful effect on emotions. Depression present before the trauma may not be present after, but the development of depression after traffic accidents is common in those who also develop PTSD (Blanchard et al., 1995), and mood may be adversely affected by the changes in lifestyle caused by injury. Many patients report a lack of confidence, and some withdraw from social activity.

- *Changes in outlook:* The literature on post-traumatic stress conceptualises the condition as a combination of hyper-arousal and the attempt to deal with emotionally difficult material, characterised by alternating episodes of intrusion and avoidance. These are the outward, observable signs of changes at a much deeper level, in terms of the core beliefs and assumptions that the individual holds about the world. The patients who are the focus of the present chapter will almost invariably have survived a situation in which they may easily have died, and coming to terms with this fact is not easy. If the patient has always considered the world to be a just and predictable place, and held a view that he or she was fairly invulnerable (or if the patient has not given much thought to these issues at all), then constructing a new world view is a major undertaking. This is not always a negative process, and there are now many references to a positive change in outlook following trauma (Joseph, Williams & Yule, 1993). Patients may re-evaluate previously held priorities and begin valuing friends and family much more, for example. They may experience strong spiritual beliefs, sometimes for the first time. They may see themselves as emerging from this period of their life as a "better person".

Adaptation can be affected by a number of factors. One important complicating factor is the involvement of other agencies, particularly insurance companies dealing with a compensation claim, which may take many years to resolve. There is no strong evidence that this litigation influences symptom presentation (Blanchard et al., 1996), but patients often find it stressful and impersonal, and experience very little control over the process: (*"I get a letter or a report from the insurance company every week, and every time I open one, it brings the accident back to me."*)

In working with patients at this stage in recovery, it is useful to keep these factors in mind. A summary of the main factors, together with some example questions to consider, is given in Table 18.2.

Following a serious injury, most patients are desperately keen for a return to a "normal life". For many, however, a simple return to a previous lifestyle is not possible, and patients need a period of time in which they can alter aspects of their previous lifestyle to meet their current restrictions (e.g. learning to use an automatic transmission in their car) or accept the end of some activities and interests and develop new ones (e.g. giving up coaching the youth football team but taking over management). This is a process without a clear end, but some events may serve a purpose for the individual by marking a transition, whether it is being discharged by the orthopaedic surgeon, a return to full-time employment, or the end of a compensation claim: (*"I needed a sense of closure, and when the compensation claim was finally settled I made a big bonfire out of all the documentation I'd built up over the years."*)

ISSUES IN WORKING WITH TRAUMA PATIENTS

Assessment

For the most part, assessments of psychological state such as the revised Beck Depression Inventory (Beck, Steer & Brown, 1996) are also valid with this client group. Some caution in interpretation needs to be taken, however, where symptoms may have a physical cause, such as sleep disturbance due to pain. The Hospital Anxiety and Depression Scale (HADS; Zigmond & Snaith, 1983) was designed for a hospital outpatient population with

Table 18.2 Factors relevant to longer-term work

Factor	Examples
Life situation at time of trauma	Has the trauma left other issues current at that time unresolved? (e.g. the future of a relationship)
Previous coping style	Has the patient coped with traumatic events before? How well?
Social support	Are there close confiding relationships? Are there others who can offer practical help? What effect has the trauma had on others?
Personal resources	Does the patient have educational qualifications and some flexibility in employment?
Social resources	Does the patient have financial worries?
Psychological resources	Does the patient have a vulnerable self-identity (e.g. is it bound up in employment which is now under threat)?
Expectation of recovery	Does the patient have realistic expectations of recovery?
Certainty of recovery	Is there uncertainty about the physical outcome (e.g. might an amputation still be needed)?
Prolonged trauma	Is the patient suffering from a condition that involves repeated traumatic experiences (e.g. burns injuries)?
Current psychological state	Check for: sleep problems, intrusions, nightmares, concentration problems, travel anxiety, irritability, guilt, emotional numbness, bereavement, depression. Is PTSD intervention needed?
Legal complications	Is there an ongoing compensation claim? How does the patient feel about this?

this problem in mind, and is worth considering. It is also useful to administer an assessment of post-traumatic stress such as the Impact of Events Scale (IES; Horowitz, Wilner & Alvarez, 1979), which is very widely used, or the newer revised version which includes hyper-arousal items (Weiss & Marmar, 1995). For general assessment of quality of life the SF-36 (Ware & Sherbourne, 1992) is a short and well-researched instrument.

One decision is whether to administer paper and pencil tests during the inpatient stay. If it is practicable (e.g. the patient is able to write) it is often appropriate to ask the patient to complete selected assessments on the ward.

The Importance of Culture

There are clearly individual differences in the extent to which some people are influenced by their culture. People from all cultures are vulnerable to post-traumatic stress reactions, but culture may influence the perception and interpretation of events, and the expression of symptoms. For example, people from oriental cultures tend to somatise emotional problems (de Silva, 1999). A potentially important factor is the influence of culture on an individual's worldview. Some Asian religions include the concept of Karma, in which negative events are seen as part of a natural process, and in which a person's actions are thought to influence later events. For some patients, this may feed ruminations on why the event has happened to them.

The Therapeutic Relationship

An acute medical ward is not an ideal setting for therapy. It is often difficult to locate a private room in which to see the patient, and many patients are not physically able to leave the bed. Drawing curtains affords some privacy, but may give a false sense of security as other people can still hear conversations. Interruptions by medical staff can be frequent. In addition, patients are particularly vulnerable; they are often in their pyjamas, feeling ill, in pain, or low in mood. Sessions may need to be short if the patient is unwell.

Patients see many different health professionals, often for brief consultations, and are usually unclear about what different people do. Care should always be taken to obtain consent from the patient to be seen. It is good practice to arrange follow-up appointments with the patient, and leave an appointment card with a contact number. Other professions tend not to do this, but it may give the patient a greater feeling of control. Similarly, it is often useful to consult with ward staff, and an entry should be made in hospital notes, which requires that confidentiality be respected while also communicating useful information for patient care.

There are some advantages in making contact with a patient so early since early intervention may prevent later problems. In cases where long-term work is needed, working with a patient in the early stages after a trauma may enable a particularly strong relationship to be established—the psychologist is in some respects a participant in the patient's experiences, and may be trusted more than someone consulted some time after the event.

Impact on the Psychologist

One issue easily neglected but extremely important is self-care. This is, of course, an issue for all health care professionals. In most areas, however, the professional is aware of potential areas of vulnerability with particular clients—we normally know whether abusive events have occurred in our own childhoods, for example. The boundary between the experiences of clients and health care professionals is much more blurred in clinical health psychology. Ill health will at some time in our lives affect all of us, either directly or indirectly through our loved ones. This uncertainty is even greater when working with victims of accidents, in which involvement in the accident is often the only thing separating psychologist and client. This can be particularly unsettling if the client shares some similarity with the psychologist, such as age and family background.

In addition, a psychologist working with this client group will inevitably be exposed to sights that may at first be disturbing. For example, metalwork is commonly used by orthopaedic surgeons to hold bones together. Finally, accidents can have a dramatic effect on people's lives and, as in other areas of clinical health psychology, hearing details about such events can sometimes be extremely sad.

CONCLUSIONS

This chapter has attempted to present an overview of current research into this group of patients, and offer guidance on psychological care. Changes in medical treatment has meant that more and more patients with severe injuries are surviving, and we have yet to develop a clear picture of the implications for their quality of life, or their needs at different stages of the recovery process. There is therefore little established evidence-based practice for the psychologist working in this field, but psychological knowledge from many different areas may usefully be applied.

The chapter has described a series of stages through which patients pass, starting with the accident itself, and moving on to hospitalisation, discharge, and long-term adaptation. At each stage important issues for assessment and treatment have been described. Suggestions for appropriate interventions at each stage have also been made, ranging from offering psychological support, normalising of emotional reactions, anxiety management, and treatment of PTSD. Working with this patient group offers a number of challenges, as these patients have to come to terms with an event that has often touched every part of their lives and led to truly profound changes (Van der Sluis, ten Duis & Geertzen, 1995), and the provision of early intervention may make a real difference to their future quality of life.

REFERENCES

AAAM (1985). *The Abbreviated Injury Scale (Revised)*. Des Plaines, IL: American Association of Automotive Medicine.

APA (1994). *Diagnostic and Statistical Manual of Mental Disorders IV*. Washington, DC: American Psychiatric Association.

Baker, S., O'Neill, B., Haddon, W. & Long, W. (1974). The injury severity score: a method for describing patients with multiple injuries and evaluating emergency care. *The Journal of Trauma*, **14**, 187.

Bass, R., Gainer, P. & Carlini, A. (1999). Update on trauma system development in the United States. *Journal of Trauma-Injury Infection and Critical Care*, **47** (3 Suppl.), S15–S21.

Beck, A., Steer, R. & Brown, G. (1996). *Beck Depression Inventory—Second Edition Manual*. San Antonio: The Psychological Corporation.

Blanchard, E., Hickling, E., Mitnick, N., Taylor, A., Loos, W. & Buckley, T. (1995). The impact of severity of physical injury and perception of life threat in the development of post-traumatic stress disorder in motor vehicle accident victims. *Behaviour Research and Therapy*, **33**, 529–534.

Blanchard, E., Hickling, E., Taylor, A., Loos, W., Forneris, C. & Jaccard, J. (1996). Who develops PTSD from motor vehicle accidents? *Behaviour Research and Therapy*, **34**, 1–10.

De Silva, P. (1999). Cultural aspects of posttraumatic stress disorder. In W. Yule (Ed.), *Post-traumatic Stress Disorder: Concepts and Therapy*. Chichester: John Wiley & Sons.

Dyregrov, A. (1989). Caring for helpers in disaster situations: psychological debriefing. *Disaster Management*, **2**, 25–30.

Everly, G.S. & Mitchell, J.T. (2000). The debriefing "controversy" and crisis intervention: a review of lexical and substantive issues. *International Journal of Emergency Mental Health*, **2**, 211–225.

Flack, W., Litz, B., Hsieh, F., Kaloupek, D. & Keane, T. (2000). Predictors of emotional numbing, revisited: a replication and extension. *Journal of Traumatic Stress*, **13**, 611–618.

Foa, E., Keane, T. & Friedman, M. (2000). Guidelines for treatment of PTSD. *Journal of Traumatic Stress*, **13**, 539–588.

Frommberger, V., Stieglitz, R., Straub, S., Nyberg, E., Schlickewei, W., Kuner, E. & Berger, M. (1999). The concept of "sense of coherence" and the development of post traumatic stress disorder in traffic accident victims. *Journal of Psychosomatic Research*, **46**, 1343–1348.

Gammon, J. (1999). The psychological consequences of source isolation: a review of the literature. *Journal of Clinical Nursing*, **8**, 13–21.

Glancy, K., Glancy, C., Lucke, J., Mahurin, K., Rhodes, M. & Tinkoff, G. (1992). A study of recovery in trauma patients. *Journal of Trauma*, **33**, 602–609.

Holbrook, T., Anderson, J., Sieber, W., Browner, D. & Hoyt, D. (1998). *Journal of Trauma: Injury, Infection and Critical Care*, **45**, 315–323.

Horowitz, M., Wilner, N. & Alvarez, W. (1979). Impact of events scale: a measure of subjective stress. *Psychosomatic Medicine*, **41**, 209–218.

Institute of Medicine (1999). *Reducing the Burden of Injury: Advancing Prevention and Treatment*. Washington, DC: National Academy Press.

Jeavons, S. (2000). Predicting who suffers psychological trauma in the first year after a road accident. *Behaviour Research and Therapy*, **38**, 499–508.

Jeavons, S., Greenwood, K. & Horne, D. (2000). Accident cognitions and subsequent psychological trauma. *Journal of Traumatic Stress*, **13**, 359–365.

Joseph, S., Williams, R. & Yule, W. (1993). Changes in outlook following disaster: the preliminary development of a measure to assess positive and negative responses. *Journal of Traumatic Stress*, **6**, 271–279.

Joy, D., Probert, R., Bisson, J. & Shepherd, J. (2000). Post traumatic stress reactions after injury. *Journal of Trauma: Injury Infection and Critical Care*, **48**, 490–494.

MacKenzie, E., Cushing, B., Jurkovich, G., Morris, J., Burgess, A., deLateur, B., McAndrew, M. & Swiontkowski, M. (1993). Physical impairment and functional outcomes six months after lower extremity fractures. *Journal of Trauma*, **34**, 528–539.

MacKenzie, E., Siegel, J., Shapiro, S., Moody, M. & Smith, R. (1988). Functional recovery and medical costs of trauma: an analysis by type and severity of injury. *Journal of Trauma*, **28**, 281–297.

Malt, U. (1988). The long term psychiatric consequences of accidental injury: a longitudinal study of 107 adults. *British Journal of Psychiatry*, **153**, 810–818.

Mayou, R., Bryant, B. & Duthie, R. (1993). Psychiatric consequences of road traffic accidents. *British Medical Journal*, **307**, 647–651.

Mayou, R., Ehlers, A. & Hobbs, M. (2000). Psychological debriefing for road traffic accident victims: three-year follow-up of a randomised controlled trial. *British Journal of Psychiatry*, **176**, 589–593.

Mayou, R., Tyndel, S. & Bryant, B. (1997). Long-term outcome of motor vehicle accident injury. *Psychosomatic Medicine*, **59**, 578–584.

Mead, N. & Bower, P. (2000). Patient-centeredness: a conceptual framework and review of the empirical literature. *Social Science and Medicine*, **51**, 1087–1110.

Michaels, A., Michaels, C., Smith, J., Moon, C., Peterson, C. & Long, W. (2000). Outcome after injury: general health, work status and satisfaction. 12 months after trauma. *Journal of Trauma: Injury, Infection and Critical Care*, **48**, 841–850.

Mitchell, J. (1983). When disaster strikes. *Journal of Emergency Medical Services*, **8**, 36–39.

Mullins, R. (1999). A historical perspective of trauma system development in the United States. *Journal of Trauma: Injury, Infection and Critical Care*, **47** (3, Suppl.), S8–S14.

Naughton, M. & Shumaker, S. (1997). Assessment of health-related quality of life in orthopaedic outcomes' studies. *Arthroscopy*, **13**, 107–113.

Nicholls, K. (1995). Institutional versus client-centred care in general hospitals. In A. Broome & S. Llewelyn (Eds), *Health Psychology: Processes and Applications* (2nd edn). London: Chapman & Hall.

Ornato, J.P., Craren, E.J., Nelson, N.M. & Kimball, K.F. (1985). Impact of improved emergency medical services and emergency trauma care on the reduction in mortality from trauma. *Journal of Trauma*, **25**, 575–577.

Peerbhoy, D., Hall, G., Parker, C., Shenkin, A. & Salmon, P. (1998). Patients' reactions to attempts to increase passive or active coping with surgery. *Social Science and Medicine*, **47**, 595–601.

Richmond, T. & Kauder, D. (2000). Predictors of psychological distress following serious injury. *Journal of Traumatic Stress*, **13**, 681–692.

RCSE/BOA (2000). *Better Care for the Severely Injured*. Working Party Report of the Royal College of Surgeons of England & British Orthopaedic Association.

Salmon, P. (2000). *Psychology of Medicine and Surgery*. Chichester: John Wiley & Sons.

Strain, J., Lyons, J., Hammer, J. & Fahs, M. (1991). Cost offset from a psychiatric consultation-liaison intervention with elderly hip fracture patients. *American Journal of Psychiatry*, **148**, 1044–1049.

Templeton, J. (2000). The organisation of trauma services in the UK. *Annals of the Royal College of Surgeons of England*, **82**, 49–50.

Thiagarajan, J., Taylor, P., Hogbin, E. & Ridley, S. (1994). Quality of life after multiple trauma requiring intensive care. *Anaesthesia*, **49**, 211–218.

Van der Sluis, C., ten Duis, H. & Geertzen, J. (1995). Multiple injuries: an overview of the outcome. *Journal of Trauma: Injury, Infection and Critical Care*, **38**, 681–686.

Van der Sluis, C., Eisma, W., Groothoff, J. & ten Duis, H. (1998). Long-term physical, psychological and social consequences of severe injuries. *Injury*, **29**, 281–285.

Ware, J. & Sherbourne, C. (1992). The MOS 36-item short form health survey (SF-36). I. Conceptual framework and item selection. *Medical Care*, **30**, 473–483.

Weiss, D. & Marmar, C. (1995). The Impact of Events Scale—Revised. In J. Wilson & T. Keane (Eds), *Assessing Psychological Trauma and PTSD: A Practitioner's Handbook*. New York: Guilford Press.

Wesseley, S., Rose, S. & Bisson, J. (1998). *A Systematic Review of Brief Psychological Interventions ("Debriefing") for the Treatment of Immediate Trauma Related Symptoms and the Prevention of Post Traumatic Stress Disorder*. Oxford, UK: The Cochrane Library.

Zigmond, A. & Snaith, R. (1983). The hospital anxiety and depression scale. *Acta Psychiatrica Scandinavica*, **67**, 361–370.

CHAPTER 19

Reproductive Health

Beth Alder

Napier University, Edinburgh, UK

INTRODUCTION

This chapter will discuss the biopsychosocial model and some of the concepts of health psychology as applied to reproductive health. Patterns of reproduction over the life span are described, and a number of central findings will be presented. These are that: the experience of infertility has psychological consequences and may have psychological causes, although these are uncertain; that miscarriage and therapeutic abortion may both have psychological impacts; that prenatal screening has developed rapidly in recent years and may be associated with anxiety; that antenatal preparation has attempted to reduce anxiety in childbirth and enhance later postnatal adjustment; that breast-feeding is a behaviour that has a direct effect on the health of the child; and, lastly, that research in reproductive health behaviour is difficult and there are many methodological pitfalls and some ethical issues to be considered.

THE BIOPSYCHOSOCIAL MODEL

The biopsychosocial model suggests that biological, psychological and social aspects of a person's life affect health and illness (Schwartz, 1982). *Biological factors* include genetic inheritance; gender differences are mostly determined by chromosome differences between males and females; individuals differ in their vulnerability to disease (e.g. cystic fibrosis) and in their physical make-up (e.g. congenital heart problems); and their physical functioning may be determined by early experience (e.g. a childhood illness or accident) or later behaviour (e.g. smoking or substance abuse). All these interact with each other, and health is a dynamic process. *Psychological factors* include cognition, emotion and motivation, which are familiar concepts to psychologists. In the context of health, a cognition might be the experience and interpretation of pain, emotion might be the fear of hospitals, and motivation might account for differences in health behaviour. Psychological factors influencing health behaviour are, in fact, far more complex than these suggest and social

Handbook of Clinical Health Psychology. Edited by S. Llewelyn and P. Kennedy.
© 2003 John Wiley & Sons, Ltd.

cognition models have been developed to understand health behaviour (Conner & Norman, 1996). *Social factors* include a society that values health and a community that affects our physical health (e.g. environmental pollution), our health behaviour and our use of health care. Health behaviours may be learned mainly in the family, and social relationships within the family affect health and illness behaviour.

The biopsychosocial model can be well illustrated by the changes to parents during the first postnatal year (Holden, 1991; Kumar & Brockington, 1988; Oates, 1989). Females give birth and breast-feed (bio), beliefs and attitudes influence parenting (psycho) and the social context will have a major influence on the postnatal experience (social). Clinical health psychology has made use of the research traditions of psychology and is strongly evidence based. In this chapter the author has tried to report research studies that are well designed and relatively free from bias. Where there are methodological problems these have been described. There is a vast amount of research published in heath psychology journals, clinical psychology journals and specialised subject areas. This selection is intended to convey the application of clinical health psychology to reproductive issues, rather than attempting to be comprehensive.

REPRODUCTIVE BEHAVIOUR

Epidemiology

The average age of women having their first child has increased in recent years from 27.5 years in 1990 to 29.1 in 2000 (Shaw, 2001). Fertility among women in their thirties and early forties has risen while that of women in their twenties has fallen.

In 1999 there were an estimated 42 000 conceptions in under-18-year-olds with only over half going on to deliver. Conception rates in teenagers could be due to lack of knowledge about contraception, difficulties of access to contraception, unavailability of contraception at the time of sexual intercourse, barriers to the use of contraception, or even the desire to become pregnant.

We can assume that most teenagers know that unprotected intercourse carries a risk of becoming pregnant, but they may underestimate the extent of that risk. There is no single reason why teenagers become pregnant and it is not simply a lack of information or access to contraception (Woodward, 1995). Johnson et al. (1994) found that of those who had had intercourse before age 16, almost half the women and over half the men reported not using contraception the first time that they had intercourse. This may not be because they lack knowledge of contraception. Churchill et al. (2000) found in a case control study that 71% of women under 20 who had conceived had discussed contraception during the year before conception.

Pregnancies could also result from positive attitudes towards pregnancy and child-bearing even though the pregnancy may later be reported as being unplanned at the time of sexual intercourse. Sutherland (1997) suggests that young women may choose to become pregnant because it demonstrates their independence, they may feel that it shows devotion to their boyfriend; they may desire something of their own to love, they have no employment prospects or they are worried about later infertility. These feelings need to be interpreted in the context of the young person's cultural context, and for some young people a pregnancy in late teens is a positive event.

Reproductive Choice

Some couples choose to remain childless and increasing numbers of couples delay the birth of their first child. The proportion of women who never have children appears to be increasing. It is expected that over a third of women born in 1967 will be childless at the age of 30 (Matheson & Babb, 2002). Some societies may assume that, for women, bearing children is a natural expression of femininity and that, for men, having children is a duty. At the same time there is a global concern about the burgeoning worldwide population (Morse, 2000). Women in industrial countries have effective means of fertility control and can choose the timing of their pregnancies, and the number. In some countries there are state policies to regulate fertility and limit family size. In others there is concern about the proportionate increase in the ageing population with fewer young people to care for them. In both types of societies, sociopolitical pressures may centre on the role of women.

Women who want children may include women who have unplanned, but not unwanted, pregnancies and those who would like to become pregnant but are subfertile. In their study of nearly 400 couples Miller and Pasta (1995) found that child-timing intentions followed by child-bearing intentions were the most important factors in predicting attempts to conceive. Women are expected to conform to society's expectations of the right time to have children and the right number. Woollett (1996) describes how women are expected to be free to choose how many children they have as long as it is not "no children", not "only one child" and not "too many". They are not expected to have children when they are "too young" or "too old".

INFERTILITY

Psychological Factors

Most couples probably make a conscious decision to stop using contraception in order to have children, and most women will become pregnant if they have unprotected intercourse for a year. About 15–19% of couples are involuntarily infertile. Infertility in couples who have never had children is called primary infertility, and in those who have already had children, secondary infertility. In a quarter of couples with infertility problems it will be unexplained, although this depends on the length of time of investigation and the extent to which the couple are prepared to undergo prolonged and invasive investigations.

Recent suggestions that the sperm count may be falling in men have given rise to anxiety about future conception rates (Irvine et al., 1996), and sexual problems may reduce the chances of conception. Sexual problems in men, such as impotence and retrograde ejaculation (when the semen is not fully expelled), will reduce fertility. Sexual activity may not include vaginal intercourse and not all sexual behaviour could result in pregnancy (Read, 1999). Excessive use of alcohol, drug abuse or medical disorders such as diabetes will also impair fertility.

Psychiatric illnesses such as anorexia nervosa are associated with infertility. A higher prevalence of eating disorders was found in two surveys of women attending infertility clinics compared with normal populations (Stewart et al., 1990; Thommen, Vallach & Kienke, 1995). About half of women suffering from bulimia nervosa will have amenorrhoea or oligomenorrhoea. McCluskey, Lacey and Pearce (1992) found that a third of women with polycystic ovary syndrome had reported bulimic eating behaviour, and Morgan (1999) suggests that these women should be routinely screened for abnormal eating behaviour. Women with eating disorders who wish to have children may ask for infertility treatment rather than treatment of their eating disorder and it is suggested that many women do not inform their gynaecologist or obstetrician about their past or present eating problems (Franko & Spurrell, 2000; Franko & Walton, 1993). Norré, Vandereycken and Gordts (2001) suggest that women with eating disorders should get psychological help before becoming pregnant. In their clinic in Belgium they found that women did not easily accept referral to a psychologist as the next step in their treatment progress, although this was the practice in Sydney (Abraham, 1999). Many couples denied that they had a psychological problem or that it could be related to their infertility.

Psychological Causes and Consequences

If there are no apparent physical causes of infertility it remains unexplained, and couples, and possibly therapists, may be tempted to seek psychological causes. These must be distinguished from psychological consequences. Research studies have found little evidence for psychogenic effects on infertility. Studies that attempt to compare characteristics of patients with apparent organic infertility with those with unexplained infertility are difficult because the extent of unexplained infertility may reflect the sophistication of the infertility investigations.

Edelmann and Connolly (1996) reviewed studies between 1972 and 1983 and concluded that there were no differences in personality characteristics. O'Moore and Harrison (1991) found that stress-related factors distinguished couples with unexplained infertility and couples who were normally fertile. They found significantly higher scores of anxiety, measured by the STAI, in infertile women compared with controls. They suggest that stress may raise anxiety levels that influence hormone levels. Demyttaenaere et al. (1988) found that initial trait anxiety levels were related to the number of treatment cycles necessary for conception by donor insemination. Counselling may reduce the anxiety and guilt associated with failure to conceive but, even without treatment, a proportion will conceive. Connolly, Edelmann and Cooke (1987) found that the emotional well-being of couples was affected by prolonged periods of clinical investigation and these were greater if the cause of the infertility lay with the man. In a study of 20 women undergoing attempts to conceive by in vitro fertilisation in an early programme, we found that they were generally positive about the very stressful and invasive procedures (Alder & Templeton, 1985). Even though they were unsuccessful in conceiving, they thought that it was their only chance and some felt that they could then begin to accept their childlessness *because* they had made an effort. Both medical staff and lay people may assume that women may be more upset than men if they cannot bear children, but this may be culturally and psychologically determined.

Lampman and Dowling-Guyer (1995) gave six scenarios describing couples with different family situations to over 200 undergraduate students. They rated the scenarios on characteristics of the couples and their relationships. The results showed negative ratings towards voluntary childlessness but they were less negative towards involuntary childlessness. The general public may, however, be sympathetic to those with infertility problems. Alder et al. (1986) surveyed nearly 2000 women attending a family planning clinic and found that the majority were in favour of research into in vitro fertilisation and embryo transfer.

Berg and Wilson (1995) looked at the pattern of distress in 104 couples with primary infertility attending for infertility investigations. Forty per cent of men and 49% of women met caseness criteria on the SCL-90-R scale (Derogatis, 1977). In a third of couples, neither was distressed, in 18% the male only, in 22% the female only and in 27% both partners were distressed. Edelmann and Connolly (1996) assessed sex-role type (Bem, 1974) on psychological functioning in a sample of 130 couples presenting with primary infertility but before diagnosis. Masculine men were the least anxious but there were no relationships between anxiety and sex-role type in women. Depressive symptoms may be associated with infertility but infertility may also be associated with the use of antidepressant drug therapy (Lapane et al., 1995).

Recognition of the problem and the feeling that something is being done may be very reassuring. Couples who have difficulty in conceiving probably discuss their reasons for having children and think through their reproductive choices in a way that most couples do not. Issues about lack of fertility may arise in a non-medical context, e.g. in consultation for marital problems. Burns (1995) reviewed the extent of sexual problems among infertile couples. Non-consummation may be under-reported.

Pfeffer and Woollett (1988) describe the emotional reaction to infertility and the pressures of medical investigations. For those who want children but are unable to have them, grief can be very intense and their pattern of grief may resemble that described for bereavement (Kubler Ross, 1969). Their initial reaction to the diagnosis may be shock and disbelief. Pfeffer and Woollett, who had themselves experienced infertility investigations, suggest that the couple should be told the results of the tests together and given time to absorb and return to ask questions later. Denial may result in rejection of the clinic's findings and a renewed search for medical advice.

The diagnostic procedures involved in fertility investigations are very invasive in the psychological sense. Taking basal temperature, planning the frequency and timing of sexual intercourse and post-coital semen samples may affect sexual relationships (Bell & Alder, 1994). Couples may feel very guilty about their feelings and may resent other women who are pregnant or who have as many children as they want. Their feelings of anger may be directed at themselves, perhaps for a previous termination, venereal disease or premarital promiscuity. The angry feelings may also be directed at the infertile partner so disrupting the sexual relationship. Paradoxically, some women report feeling guilty if their partners rather than themselves are responsible for their difficulties in conception (Alder, 1984). Anger may also be directed at health professionals when treatment is unsuccessful. Infertility patients are extraordinarily compliant and clinicians find that they will often put up with the most invasive procedures and lengthy operations if there is even a small chance of success.

Sexuality may be adversely affected following the diagnosis of infertility and women and men may resent the constraints of timing of intercourse to optimise the chances of conception. Women may express more grief and distress about the lack of ability to conceive, and may feel that their femininity is threatened. There may be a greater adverse effect on male sexuality if the infertility problem is of male origin, and men are more likely to deny that there is a problem (Alder, 1984).

Donor insemination (DI) is used in couples where the man is infertile but the woman ovulates normally. Semen from an anonymous donor is inseminated into the vagina of the fertile woman. If she conceives she will have a child who carries half of her genes and half of those of the donor. The pregnancy proceeds normally and the couple need not tell anyone that the conception did not occur in the usual way. Until recently donors have remained anonymous, but Snowden and Snowden (1984) argued strongly that children should be told the full facts of their conception when they are considered old enough to understand. In an interview study we found that out of 20 couples receiving DI, seven wives and ten husbands would never tell a child that it was conceived by DI (Alder, 1984). However, a Swedish law in 1985 gave those born by DI the right to obtain information about the donor and the identity of the donor. Similar legislation was passed in 1992 in Austria and in Victoria, Australia. An open approach is also advocated in New Zealand, but by a voluntary code (Daniels & Lewis, 1996). A survey was carried out in Sweden to look at parents' views on informing their children. One hundred and forty-eight (80% response rate) parents of children born as a result of donor insemination at Umeå University Hospital and the Karolinksa Hospital in Sweden between 1995 and 1997 took part (Linblad, Gotlieb & Lalos, 2000). Fifty-two per cent had already told, or intended to tell, their child, but 19% had decided not to tell. Those who said that they would tell their child gave the following reasons: it was natural; they would avoid the risk of the child being told by the wrong person; to be open and honest; the child had a right to know; it would be more difficult later in life; there would be less tension if the child had been told and it would create respect for the decision. Those who did not intend to tell gave as their reasons: they were reluctant; it was unnecessary; it might harm the child; it might increase the risk of inequality between children and there was no relationship with the donor. The patterns of parental reasoning were complex and professionals may find it difficult to facilitate a couple's disclosure about telling. The authors suggested that a professional competent in behavioural science such as a counsellor or psychologist should be available within every team. Follow-up studies of DI couples and their children have been difficult to carry out because of the secrecy involved. No doubt part of this is because of the stigma surrounding male infertility and its association with virility. Many couples prefer to raise the children as their own and without any further contact with the medical team that carried out the insemination. Intra-cytoplasmic sperm injection (ICSI) is becoming more widely used and requires only one sperm so that it may be preferred by heterosexual couples where there is low sperm count.

Since the birth of the first "test tube baby" in 1978, in vitro fertilisation (IVF) has been used throughout the world and more than 40 000 babies are estimated to have been born as a result of IVF. Johnston (1987) found that couples entering an IVF programme overestimated their chances of success. At the time, the published success rate of having a live baby was as low as 8%, but over half the sample rated their chances as over 30%. Couples that take part in psychological studies may feel that they need to assert their suitability as parents (McMahon et al., 1995), but they appear well adjusted. They are likely to be older and highly motivated to become parents. They appear to have as good or better marital relationships than comparison groups. This may reflect a high level of commitment to marriage and the demands of infertility treatment and IVF may foster communication.

Overcoming infertility is stressful, possibly painful, time-consuming and expensive. Attempts have been made to understand the motivation for parenthood. A simple cost–benefit model has been used but listing the reasons may not reveal the complex motivation of infertile couples. Coplin, De Munter and Vandemeulebroecke (1998) found that the main reason for wanting a child was "happiness" followed by well-being, motherhood, identity continuity and social control. The parenthood motivation list (Van Balen & Trimbos-Kemper, 1995) showed few differences between IVF and non-IVF mothers, although it was a retrospective study. Langridge, Conolly and Sheeran (2000) used network analysis to investigate the reasons for parenthood among expectant couples and couples presenting for treatment by IVF or DI. The sample was small (10 expectant couples, 10 about to have IVF and 14 presenting for DI) although no recruitment response rate was reported. Like other studies they found that the most important reasons were the need to give and receive love and experience the enjoyment of children, and these were strongly interconnected. Pressures from family and friends were not given as reasons.

MISCARRIAGE AND ABORTION

Background

Miscarriage is defined as the spontaneous loss of a pregnancy within the first 24 weeks of gestation. Most miscarriages are caused by genetic malformation of the foetus, but they may also be caused by incompetence of the cervix, hormone deficiencies, uterine abnormalities or infections. The psychological effects of the loss of early pregnancy may be unrecognised. Clinicians may assume that the pregnancy is not thought of as a baby and that there is no need to mourn the loss (Iles, 1989). Women probably only stay in hospital for a short time, and medical and nursing staff may not be aware of later distress. Miscarriage carries the double social taboo of being both a gynaecological event and a death.

Women become aware that they are pregnant when they miss their first period and often use pregnancy kits in the privacy of their own home. They do not need to consult their general practitioner and may not confide in their partners or family, and so miscarriages may remain unacknowledged. Ultrasound scans mean that women may now become aware that they are pregnant at an earlier stage in pregnancy and at a time when there is a relatively high risk of miscarriage. It is seen as a minor, private event followed by full recovery and the expectation of a successful pregnancy shortly afterwards (Conway & Russell, 2000).

Psychological Consequences

Grief reactions after miscarriage similar to those following stillbirth have been found in retrospective interview studies (Friedman & Gath, 1989). Women may mourn the loss of self-esteem, question their female role and their status as a future mother. The literature on bereavement suggests that in any loss followed by grief and mourning, resolution may take some time (Parkes, 1985). In a prospective study to look at the support received after miscarriage, Conway and Russell (2000) followed up 39 women and their partners immediately after miscarriage and two to four months later. They used a shortened version of the Perinatal Grief Scale (Potvin, Lasker & Toedter, 1989). Immediately after miscarriage partners' scores were higher than those for women on Active Grief and Difficulty Coping. The majority were able to discuss their miscarriage with their partner and found the support from relatives and friends very helpful or helpful. The professional support was less adequate with less than a third reporting that they had been given an explanation as to why the miscarriage occurred, and only one-third reported that they had been asked by health professionals how they were coping with the miscarriage. Women who had had stressful events in the previous 12 months had higher active grief scores and higher overall scores.

There is some evidence of higher psychiatric morbidity following miscarriage but the evidence is conflicting. Jackman, McGee and Turner (1991) used semi-structured home interviews to assess 27 women who had had a previous miscarriage and attended hospital. Half were found to be "cases" measured by the GHQ-30 scale (Goldberg, 1972). In a study of 67 women admitted to hospital for spontaneous abortion (Friedman & Gath, 1989), 84% were diagnosed as being "cases" using the Present State Examination (PSE; Wing, Cooper & Satorius, 1974). Those who were more likely to show psychiatric morbidity were single, had a previous psychiatric history, were high on scores of neuroticism and had had previous obstetric problems.

Results based on retrospective accounts can be difficult to interpret, but of course prospective studies on miscarriage are difficult to do. Cuisinier et al. (1996) surveyed over 2000 women recruited from a Dutch magazine for expectant and new parents: 221 lost a singleton through miscarriage, stillbirth or neonatal death, and were followed up on four occasions at six-month intervals by postal questionnaire; 193 miscarried within the first 16 weeks of pregnancy and the women were assessed pre-loss and post-loss on a number of standardised questionnaires. Grief was assessed by the Perinatal Grief Scale (Potvin, Lasker & Toedter, 1989) but feelings about future pregnancies, contraceptive use and intentions to conceive were not reported. Most (86%) conceived again within 18 months. Of those who became pregnant within six months, only 3% reported that they saw the baby as a replacement child. The responses to the questionnaire were analysed by regression analysis and it was found that a new pregnancy and the birth of a new child significantly lessened grief, while grief significantly intensified following a new pregnancy loss. They also suggest that the speediness of the new pregnancy appears to reduce the grief to some extent. They found little indication of severe maternal psychopathology likely to interfere with a healthy mother–child relationship. However, they did not use a standardised psychiatric interview, the data was collected by post and the sample of readers may not be representative. These authors, and Davis, Stewart and Harmon (1989), suggest that the topic of a new pregnancy should be discussed with the couples, who should be helped to make their own informed decisions and given subsequent support.

Loss of pregnancy following IVF may be particularly problematic. If the eggs are fertilised and the embryo is successfully transferred women may feel that they are already pregnant. They may believe that they are pregnant early in gestation and be treated by others as being pregnant. Greenfield, Diamond and DeCherney (1988) describe the grief response following failure to become pregnant during an IVF cycle as being analogous to the reaction that women experience after miscarriage.

Abortion

Abortion (social termination of pregnancy) was legalised in the UK, for example, by the 1967 UK Abortion Act, but abortion is still controversial and open to legal disputes in different countries. The Abortion Act legalised termination of pregnancy "if the continuation of the pregnancy would involve risk to the life of, or injury to the physical or mental health of the pregnant woman or to any existing children of her family, greater than if the pregnancy were terminated". In the UK, the Human Fertilisation and Embryo Act in 1990 amended the 1967 Act to limit the gestation to 24 weeks, where formerly it had been limited to 26 weeks. Adler et al. (1990) reviewed abortion in the USA. Most descriptive studies found a low incidence of severe negative responses after abortion. Two studies (Athanasiou et al., 1973; Zabin, Hirsch & Emerson, 1989) compared those who had abortions with those who gave birth at term and neither found adverse effects of abortion. Distress was highest before abortion and decreased afterwards. Later levels of distress were related to difficulties in making the decision. However, Adler et al. (1990) point out that there are methodological problems of sample selection, no baseline data, short follow-up time and the lack of control for wantedness of the pregnancy.

The psychological effects of abortion have been much disputed. It has been suggested that women who have terminations before their first baby may resolve their feelings adequately at the time, but if they later have a baby they view the termination differently and may have resurgence of guilt (Riley, 1995). It is difficult to carry out research into the psychological effects of abortions because we do not know how women would have felt if they had not had the abortion and continued with the pregnancy.

PREGNANCY AND THE PUERPERIUM

Prenatal Screening

The implications of genetic testing in pregnancy are complex and the rapidly expanding range of genetic testing raises many issues that need to be addressed (Marteau & Richards, 1996).

Serum screening for Down's syndrome is offered to about 70% of pregnant women in the UK (Wald, Huttly & Hennessy, 1999). However, screening is not as sensitive as may be believed by parents. Parents expect that the lack of a positive result means that their child will not have Down's syndrome whereas the tests only have the ability to detect between 36 and 70% of foetuses affected by Down's syndrome. For this reason children may still be born with Down's syndrome. Other reasons are that not all parents are offered testing and some parents decline the test or pregnancy termination if an affected foetus is detected. Hall, Bobrow and Marteau (2000) compared the adjustment of parents who had received a false negative result with that of parents not offered a test and those who had declined a test. Parents of 179 children with Down's syndrome—obtained from the National Down's Syndrome Cytogenetic Register for England and Wales—were interviewed in their own homes. Anxiety, depression and parenting stress were measured using standardised scales. Mothers in the false negative group had higher parenting stress scores, had more negative attitudes towards their children and were more likely to blame others for the outcome compared with those who declined the test. Only a small adverse effect of the false negative result on parental adjustment was found, but blaming others was associated with poorer adjustment for mothers and fathers. There was no effect on anxiety or depression.

Chromosome abnormalities may be detected by amniocentesis and parents may expect to know that Down's syndrome has been detected. However, there are other sex chromosome anomalies that may or may not have phenotypic consequences for the child, and the understanding of these may be more problematic. Abramsky et al. (2001) interviewed health professionals and parents about the communication of sex chromosome anomalies in otherwise anatomically normal viable foetuses. They found great variation in what different health care professionals know, say and think about the same sex chromosome anomaly. The findings suggest that some counselling was inadequate and that this could introduce some long-term consequences.

A programme of maternal serum screening pregnancy offers a triple test of three bio-chemical markers: alpha feto protein (AFP), hCG and unconjugated estriol. These screen for neural tube defects and chromosome abnormalities such as Down's syndrome. The tests assess the relative risk, not the existence of the defect itself, and if risks are high then women are offered an amniocentesis test. The very offer of such a test may raise anxiety levels and the way in which information is presented is critical as even negative results may raise anxiety (Marteau, 1993). Women who have increased risk resulting from tests in pregnancy such as AFP screening for neural defects or amniocentesis for Down's syndrome may be faced with the decision to have a relatively late termination. Attitudes towards abortion may influence the uptake of prenatal screening (Marteau, van Duijn & Ellis, 1992). Green and Statham (1996) describe the experience of women undergoing an abortion for a foetal abnormality as a distressing event. Both parents may experience guilt about the decision, and loss of self-esteem because of the conception of a handicapped child.

Antenatal Preparation

Antenatal education or childbirth education programmes are found worldwide and have come about as traditional methods of information sharing has declined. They give an oppor-tunity for health professionals to intervene and are designed to reduce anxiety about labour and birth. This may be the main reason for women choosing to attend classes although the agenda of the professionals may go beyond this. In a systematic review, Gagnon (2001) reviewed randomised-controlled trials of the effectiveness of structured educational pro-grammes offered to parents. Outcomes included anxiety, sense of control, pain and psycho-logical adjustment. Only six trials met Cochrane criteria and they concluded that the effects of general antenatal education were unknown, and that differences were found in the above measures. There are methodological problems in randomly allocating women and Gagnon had previously found that only 10% of women were willing to be randomly allocated to either placebo or classes, so this may be one area in which randomised controlled trials are inappropriate.

Hillier and Slade (1989) compared women choosing to attend either hospital or commu-nity classes. They assessed the women at their first antenatal class and again after their last class. The antenatal classes consisted of eight weekly sessions, each lasting approximately two hours. They included one hour of teaching of relaxation and breathing and physical exercises to prepare for labour, and one hour for teaching and group discussion. Topics included self-care during pregnancy, labour, the first few weeks post-partum and a tour of the maternity unit and delivery suite. As expected, knowledge levels rose and anxiety levels fell but the changes were not significantly correlated at either the first or last assessment. Knowledge levels were related to social class at the initial assessment but not at the final assessment. This suggests that the effect of the classes was to reduce the differences related to social background. Michie, Marteau and Kidd (1992) tested the ability of the Theory of Reasoned Action (Ajzen & Fishbein, 1980) to predict antenatal attendance in a study of over 500 women. They found that the women's intentions to attend predicted their behaviour, and that perceptions of the fathers' attitudes were important.

Hayes, Muller and Bradley (2001) carried out a randomised-controlled trial of antenatal education to reduce postnatal depression. The intervention group was given an education package designed to inform them of mood changes that could occur in the prenatal and post-partum periods, consisting of a booklet, an audio tape of the experience of depression, and the guidance of an experienced midwife. The two groups were similar at the first interview during pregnancy and there were no statistically significant differences at post-partum. The women in this study were found to be more depressed antenatally than postnatally on total scores and subscales of the Profile of Mood States. Some evidence for the effectiveness of prevention in vulnerable women was shown in a study by Elliott et al. (2000). Women who were identified as vulnerable were allocated by their expected date of delivery to either a prevention programme or routine care. There were significant differences in the scores on the Edinburgh Postnatal Depression Scale (Cox, Holden & Sagovsky, 1987) and on the scores on the Present State Examination (Wing, Cooper & Satorius, 1974) for primiparae.

Pregnant women are seen as a captive audience by health professionals wanting to change behaviour and clinical health psychology may have a useful input here. For example, changing alcohol dependence or facilitating quitting smoking may present particular problems when a woman is pregnant. On the one hand, she may be highly motivated for the sake of the health of her unborn child and yet find it difficult to cope with changes in addition to the psychosocial changes described above. Smoking during pregnancy has health risks for the mother and the child and recent interventions have used social cognition models to try to effect change. In a review of 36 controlled intervention evaluation studies, Kelley, Bond and Abraham (2001) found that there was an overall effectiveness of OR = 1.93. Those that were effective included self-help leaflets or manuals specifically written, but there was less evidence for the effectiveness of one-to-one contacts.

Transition to Parenthood

Couples expecting their first child may reflect on their own experience as children and seek out the history of their own infancy. Unresolved issues in their childhood or their relationship with their parents may be highlighted. Many men become closely involved with the progress of the pregnancy, although young men tend to have had less experience of babies than young women, and are less likely to have been to classes on parenthood at school than women. Later in pregnancy the woman may give up work and this may change her social status. She may miss the social contacts, the structure and routine of work and feel isolated from her former colleagues. Changes in body image as she increases in size may reawaken fears of being fat. During the first trimester some women are nauseous and feel tired. They may be anxious about the implications of being pregnant and unsure of the future. Women who have had previous problems of infertility, previous miscarriages or who have delayed their child-bearing may be particularly anxious. By the second trimester most women will have had their pregnancy confirmed and become overtly "expecting". They begin to make plans about relationships, employment and housing. The foetus takes on an identity, and may even be given a nickname. The issues of antenatal screening become pertinent. They will be aware that their own health behaviour could affect the health of their baby and may stop or reduce their smoking and alcohol intake.

Pain in child birth may be understood by considering pain in general (Horn & Munafo, 1997) but it has unique characteristics. The development of the Gate Control Theory of Pain explained many previously complex phenomena of pain (Melzack & Wall, 1989). It allowed for differing theories of specificity and patterning to be unified and for consideration of psychological factors. Labour pain is expected and may be regarded as inseparable from motherhood. Its experience is dependent on culture (Mander, 1998). It occurs predictably and women have time to prepare for pain, often using psychological methods to control it. However, women often report that they do not remember their labour pain and memories of the intensity of pain immediately after birth are poorly related to memories several weeks later (Niven & Brodie, 1995). From the result of pain scales given to 18 women before and after delivery, Terry and Gijsbers (2000) suggest that memories of labour pain may be based on other aspects of the birth experience. Skills such as relaxation or distraction may be acquired in pregnancy and then used in other contexts in later life. Similarly, a negative experience of pain during labour may influence later coping strategies and attitudes towards pain or the threat of pain.

Postnatal Changes

Physical changes in the mother following the pregnancy and delivery, the effects of breast-feeding, lack of sleep, interrupted sleep and general fatigue are all physical factors that may affect mood and well-being. The psychological changes of role, the emotional experience of being parents for the first time and the altered dynamics in the family all make demands on the new couple. It has been suggested that maternal morbidity after delivery is extensive and under-recognised. Glazener et al. (1995) carried out a questionnaire survey of a 20% random sample of women delivering in 1 week ($n = 1249$), at 2 weeks, 8 weeks and 18 months after delivery, with a response rate of 90%. Psychological problems reported included tiredness (85, 87 and 76%), and tearfulness/depression (16, 21 and 17%). These were not related to parity or method of delivery.

Postnatal depression (a "morbid and persistent depressed mood, usually commencing six to twelve weeks after delivery"; Cox, 1989, p. 840) probably occurs in about 9–13% of women (O'Hara & Swain, 1996), and the more severe post-partum psychosis occurs in about two in 1000 deliveries (Kumar, 1989). If neither disorder is treated, it can result in a prolonged, deleterious effect on the relationship between the mother and baby and on the child's psychological, social and educational development. The relationship between the mother and her partner may also deteriorate.

The causes and treatment of postnatal depression have been reviewed in a meta-analysis of 59 studies (O'Hara & Swain, 1996). They included studies which (a) reported statistical relationships between post-partum depression and psychosocial variables, (b) assessed the variables during pregnancy or delivery, (c) recruited by random or quasi-random sampling and (d) assessed depression at least two weeks post-partum. Fifty-nine studies were included, although the method of searching was not described. They found an overall prevalence rate of 0.128 (95% CI, 0.123–0.134). Postnatal depression is not therefore a major problem in numerical terms and the incidence may not be much greater than that found in the general population. However, the context is very different. The presence of a new baby makes depression particularly significant not least because expectations of fulfilment and happiness are high.

The psychosocial argument for postnatal depression has focused on social and psychological risks and vulnerability factors. O'Hara and Swain (1996) in their meta-analysis found that postnatal depression was predicted by poor marital relationships, past psychiatric history, low levels of social support and stressful life events. They found no association with age, marital status, level of education or number of children. Mothers' mental health may also be affected by the health of the baby. In cohort studies, depression has been associated with neonatal risk (Bennett & Slade, 1991), stillbirth, neonatal death or Sudden Infant Death Syndrome (SIDS) (Boyle et al., 1996) and very low birth weight (less than 1500 g) (O'Brien, et al., 1999; Singer et al., 1999). There may still be a lack of knowledge or social stigma about postnatal depression. Whitton, Warner and Appleby (1996) recruited 78 mothers into a treatment trial for postnatal depression (Appleby et al., 1997), and asked them about their current symptoms and attitudes to treatment. Nearly all (97%) reported that they had been feeling worse than usual but only 25 (32%) believed that they were suffering from postnatal depression, even though they had reached Research Diagnostic Criteria (Spitzer, Endicott & Robins, 1978) for depression.

Counselling has been a major advance in treatment. In a randomised-controlled trial, Holden, Sagovsky and Cox (1989) showed that non-directive counselling given in up to eight visits of 30 minutes was effective in alleviating postnatal depression. Recovery took place in 69% of those counselled compared with 38% of those receiving routine care. This has led to the advocacy of listening visits that can be carried out by health visitors. In a major study, Murray and Cooper (1997), however, found no difference between non-directive counselling, psychotherapy and cognitive-behavioural therapy. Appleby et al. (1997) carried out a randomised-controlled trial of fluoxetine or placebo plus one or six sessions of cognitive-behavioural counselling. It could be argued that to offer cognitive-behavioural therapy in one session is a contradiction in terms but the results were very positive. There were highly significant improvements in all four treatment groups. Fluoxetine was significantly better than placebo and six sessions of counselling were better than one. There was no significant interaction between counselling and fluoxetine. Appleby et al. (1997) concluded that both drug therapy and counselling were effective but there was no advantage in receiving both. Thome and Alder (1999) found that those mothers scoring high on the Edinburgh Postnatal Depression Scale (Cox, Holden & Sagovsky, 1987) were also more likely to report infant difficulties. Having a difficult infant could also increase the likelihood of becoming depressed, or at least feeling fatigued and low in maternal self-efficacy.

Breast-feeding

Breast-feeding can be regarded as a health behaviour in the sense that it is a behaviour that has a direct effect on health. Antibodies from the mother are passed through the breast milk to the infant, and the composition of human breast milk may be superior to artificial formula feed. Infant feeding behaviour has been analysed using social cognition models but breast-feeding is a complex behavioural pattern involving relationships as well as health beliefs (Alder, 1989). It is difficult to separate out the beneficial effects of breast milk from breast-feeding. There may be many behavioural differences in parenting behaviour between parents who breast-feed (where feeding is exclusively by the mother) and those who bottle-feed (where feeds may be given by the father and other members of the family). Differences in attitudes towards feeding may persist into later feeding habits in the child's lifetime. Breast-feeding benefits the health of the baby (Howie et al., 1990) although it is unusual in that it may have positive benefits for the child but have some costs for the mother. Breast-feeding can be painful, physically tiring and emotionally demanding, nevertheless it is also very satisfying and fulfilling.

There have been many attempts to establish the reasons why women maintain breast-feeding and others give up (Renfrew, Woolridge & Ross-McGill, 2000). It is suggested that mothers' beliefs and attitudes may be predictive of early cessation of breast-feeding and if this is so then interventions should be directed at the mother rather than at early attachment or postnatal support. Changing behaviour by changing beliefs has been found to be very difficult in other areas of health behaviour (Conner & Norman, 1996) but attempts continue to be made to influence pregnant women. Typical results are illustrated by a recent study in the USA of 61 low-income mothers (Ertem, Votto & Leventhal, 2001). Half had enrolled into the study group and were compared with a non-participating control group, to control for the effects of participating in the study and data collection. Early discontinuation was associated with maternal age of less than 20, and lack of confidence about continuing to breast-feed until the infant was 2 months. It was not related to knowledge or breast-feeding problems. In addition, logistic regression showed that the belief that the baby enjoys bottle-feeding contributed significantly.

Being depressed may affect the progress of breast-feeding. Tamminen (1989), in a cross-sectional study in Finland, surveyed four groups of mothers: Group 1 in late pregnancy ($n = 10$), Group 2 just after delivery ($n = 17$), Group 3 with babies 2–4 months ($n = 30$) and Group 4 with babies 6–12 months ($n = 33$). Most of the delivered mothers were currently breast-feeding (Group 2, 90%; Group 3, 97%; Group 4, 50%). Eight per cent of mothers were depressed and reported more breast-feeding difficulties than non-depressed women. Successful breast-feeding can have a positive influence on mood whereas non-successful breast-feeding may have a negative influence. If breast-feeding and depression are interrelated then this could be an indirect route for the effect of breast-feeding on infant development.

Beale and Manstead (1991), in one of the few intervention studies in this area, used the Theory of Planned Behaviour in an intervention to influence parents' intention to let 5- to 6-month-old babies eat or drink sugar between meals. They followed babies up at 3–4 weeks and found that intention was not significantly affected, but they did not measure actual behaviour.

RESEARCH IN REPRODUCTIVE HEALTH PSYCHOLOGY

Theories make sense of related observations and help to focus the questions that will give meaningful answers. Theories about why people accept or reject prenatal screening must take into account what people think are the positive aspects of screening, as well as the risks. Theories are often based on models and these help us to predict behaviour. Models are representations of variables linked together that predict an outcome, and are often shown diagrammatically. Research into the psychology of health tests and extends existing psychological theories and also generates new theories. All the techniques of psychological research probably have some role in research into the psychology of reproductive health, and use well-established techniques of research methodology in health care (Altman, 1991; Crombie & Davies, 1996).

Methods

The effectiveness of a new treatment may be tested most effectively by a randomised double-blind controlled trial. However, this might mean random allocation of one group of patients to a treatment group and the other to no treatment. This might well be unethical, especially as there is some effective treatment for most problems. To test for a small effect, large numbers of participants may be needed. For example, a study of training of health professionals might need to have a hundred participants, which might involve several health providers. Some questions could be answered in a study in a large maternity hospital of 3000 deliveries per year, but not in a study of home deliveries.

Qualitative data is essentially descriptive. It gives us insight and may lead to new approaches or hypotheses. Data is often collected by interview on a relatively small number of subjects. Single case studies have traditionally been used to describe unusual medical or psychological conditions. In some cases a treatment is tried out and reported on an individual and the patient is followed up, sometimes over a period of years. It may be difficult to generalise from an individual to other populations, but the demonstration of success of a treatment in one individual may be enough to justify a larger study. Qualitative research based on a single person is also appropriate when a topic is new or particularly sensitive. For example, if little is known about the perception of miscarriage, then sensitive in-depth interviewing can identify issues that we would not get from written questionnaires or rating scales.

A quasi-experimental approach is often used in clinical health psychology, and in reproductive areas experimental manipulation is often neither practical nor ethical. In a true experiment participants are randomly allocated into two groups and the conditions in one of the groups is changed. In a quasi-experimental approach, the relevant variables are measured in two naturally occurring groups, often by collecting data from a cross-section of the population. A study of mood changes during the menstrual cycle could collect data from one group of women who were in their premenstrual phase, and another group of women who were in their postmenstrual phase. Mood would be recorded in the premenstrual phase and again in the postmenstrual phase. This is a more powerful design, but we might expect a time effect.

Double-blind randomised trials with crossover designs are very difficult to do in psychological research. Recruitment of participants into randomised-controlled trials is difficult and often research papers do not report on how many people were approached to get the required number. If the uptake is low then this limits the generalisability of the findings. Many people are reluctant to have a treatment that is determined by chance. If very few people are willing to take part then they may be so self-selected and the sample may be so biased that the results cannot be generalised to the original population. For example, the age range may be restricted.

Case studies are used extensively because of problems in carrying out randomised-controlled trials. The incidence of a health problem in parous women might be compared with the incidence in non-parous women of the same age and background. If a difference is found then some biological, psychological or social difference related to parity might explain it—for example, the effect of parity on post-partum incontinence.

Ethical Issues

Clinical trials are experiments and ethical principles are important. In research into reproductive health psychology there may be problems in obtaining consent of the mother for research that may affect her child, e.g. in a trial of a new intervention to increase quitting smoking in pregnancy. The new intervention may be poorer than the standard treatment in which case the child may be at risk. If the effect of a new treatment is to be tested we must be quite sure that one treatment is not more likely to be more beneficial than another for that particular individual. There are clearly ethical problems of withholding a treatment that might be effective.

CONCLUSION

Reproductive health affects everyone's life at some stage. The influence of reproduction continues throughout life and pervades all aspects of life. Reproductive issues have attracted attention from clinical health psychologists in individual clinical contexts or in attempts to explain and predict health behaviour. Similarly, in trying to understand psychological problems associated with "disease", reproductive issues are often relevant. Broome and Wallace (1984) made an early attempt to address the interrelationships of psychology and reproductive issues and focused on clinical psychology. Health psychology has developed since then, and more recently Niven and Walker (1996) have taken a broad approach to the psychological aspects of reproduction.

REFERENCES

Abraham, S. (1999). Disordered eating and pregnancy: Part 2. *Eating Disorders, Revision*, **10**, 1–3.

Abramsky, L., Hall, S., Levitan, J. & Marteau, T.M. (2001). What parents are told after prenatal diagnosis of a sex chromosome abnormality: interview and questionnaire study. *British Medical Journal*, **322**, 463–466.

Adler, N.E., David, H.P., Major, B.N., Roth, S.H., Ruddo, N.F. & Wyatt, G.E. (1990). Psychological responses after abortion. *Science*, **248**, 41–44.

Ajzen, I. & Fishbein, B. (1980). *Understanding Attitudes and Predicting Behaviour*. Englewood Cliffs: Prentice Hall.

Alder, E.M. (1984). Psychological aspects of AID. In A. Emery & I. Pullen (Eds), *Psychological Aspects of Genetic Counselling*. London: Academic Press.

Alder, E.M. (1989). Sexual behaviour in pregnancy, after childbirth and during breast-feeding. *Baillière's Clinical Obstetrics and Gynaecology*, **3**, 805–821.

Alder, E.M. & Templeton, A.A. (1985). Patient reaction to IVF treatment. *Lancet*, **1** (8421), 168.

Alder, E.M., Baird, D.T., Lees, M., Lincoln, D., Loudon, N. & Templeton, A.A. (1986). Attitudes of women of reproductive age to in vitro fertilisation (IVF) and embryo research. *Journal of Biosocial Science*, **18**, 155–167.

Altman, D.G. (1991). *Practical Statistics for Medical Research*. London: Chapman & Hall.

Appleby, L., Warner, R., Whitton, A. & Faragher, B. (1997). A controlled study of fluoxetine and cognitive behavioural counselling in the treatment of postnatal depression. *British Medical Journal*, **314**, 932–936.

Athanasiou, R., Oppel, W., Michaelson, L., Unger, T. & Yager, M. (1973). Psychiatric sequelae to term birth and induced early and late abortion: a longitudinal study. *Family Planning Perspective*, **5**, 227.

Beale, D.A. & Manstead, A.S. (1991). Predicting mothers' intentions to limit frequency of infants sugar intake: testing the theory of planned behaviour. *Journal of Applied Social Psychology*, **21**, 409–431.

Bell, J.S. & Alder, E. (1994). In T.M. Hargreaves (Ed.), *Male Infertility Second Edition*. Springer-Verlag.

Bem, S. (1974). The measurement of psychological androgyny. *Journal of Clinical and Consulting Psychology*, **42**, 155–162.

Bennett, D.E. & Slade, P. (1991). Infants born at risk consequences for maternal post-partum adjustment. *British Journal of Medical Psychology*, **64**, 159–172.

Berg, B.J. & Wilson, J.F. (1995). Patterns of psychological distress in infertile couples. *Journal of Psychosomatic Obstetrics and Gynaecology*, **16**, 65–78.

Boyle, F.M., Vance, J.C., Najman, J.M. & Thearle, M.J. (1996). The mental health of impact of still birth, neonatal death or SIDS: prevalence and patterns of distress among mothers. *Social Science and Medicine*, **43**, 1273–1282.

Broome, A. & Wallace, L. (1984). *Psychology and Gynaecological Problems*. London: Tavistock.

Burns, L.H. (1995). An overview of sexual dysfunction in the infertile couple. *Journal of Family Psychotherapy*, **6**, 25–46.

Churchill, D., Allen, J., Pringle, M., Hippisley-Cox, J., Ebdon, D., Macpherson, M. & Bradley, S. (2000). Consultation patterns and provision of contraception in general practice before teenage pregnancy: a case-control study. *British Medical Journal*, **321**, 486–489.

Conner, M. & Norman, P. (Eds) (1996). *Predicting Health Behaviour*. Buckingham: Open University Press.

Connolly, K.J., Edelmann, R.J. & Cooke, I.D. (1987). Distress and marital problems associated with infertility. *Journal of Reproductive and Infant Psychology*, **5**, 49–57.

Conway, K. & Russell, G. (2000). Couples' grief and experience of support in the aftermath of miscarriage. *British Journal of Medical Psychology*, **73**, 531–545.

Coplin, H., De Munter, A. & Vandemeulebroecke, L. (1998). Parenthood motives in IVF mothers. *Journal of Psychosomatic Obstetrics and Gynaecology*, **19**, 19–27.

Cox, J.L. (1989). Postnatal depression: a serious and neglected phenomenon. In M. Oates (Ed.), *Psychological Aspects of Obstetrics and Gynaecology. Baillière's Clinical Obstetrics and Gynaecology*, **3**, 839–955.

Cox, J.L., Holden, J.M. & Sagovsky, R. (1987). Development of the 10 item Edinburgh Postnatal Depression Scale. *British Journal of Psychiatry*, **150**, 782–786.

Crombie, I.K. & Davies, H.T.O. (1996). *Research in Health Care. Design, Conduct and Interpretation of Health Services Research*. Chichester: John Wiley & Sons.

Cuisinier, M.K., Janssen, H., de Graauw, C., Bakker, S. & Hoogduin, C. (1996). Pregnancy following miscarriage: course of grief and some determining factors. *Journal of Psychosomatic Obstetrics and Gynaecology*, **17**, 168–174.

Daniels, K. & Lewis, G.M. (1996). Openness of information in the use of donor gametes: developments in New Zealand. *Journal of Reproductive and Infant Psychology*, **14**, 57–68.

Davis, D.L., Stewart, M. & Harmon, R.J. (1989). Postponing pregnancy after perinatal death: perspectives on doctors' advice. *Journal of the American Academy of Child Psychiatry*, **28**, 481–487.

Demyttaenaere, K., Nijs, P., Steeno, O., Koninckx, P. & Evers-Kiebooms, G. (1988). Anxiety and conception rates in donor insemination. *Journal of Psychosomatic Obstetrics and Gynaecology*, **8**, 175–181.

Derogatis, L.R. (1977). The SCL-90-R Manual: a step in the validation of a new self-report scale. *British Journal of Psychiatry*, **128**, 280–289.

Edelmann, R.J. & Connolly, K.J. (1996). Sex role and emotional functioning in infertile couples: some further evidence. *Journal of Reproductive and Infant Psychology*, **14**, 113–119.

Elliott, S.A., Leverton, T.J., Sanjack, M., Turner, H., Cowmeadow, P.J., Hopkins, J. & Bushnell, D. (2000). Promoting mental health after childbirth: a controlled trial of primary prevention of postnatal depression. *British Journal of Clinical Psychology*, **39**, 223–241.

Ertem, I.O., Votto, N. & Leventhal, J.M. (2001). The timing and predictors of the early termination of breast-feeding. *Pediatrics*, **107**, 543–548.

Franko, D.L. & Spurrell, E.B. (2000). Detection and management of eating disorders during pregnancy. *Obstetrics and Gynaecology*, **95**, 942–946.

Franko, D.L. & Walton, B.E. (1993). Pregnancy and eating disorders: a review and clinical implications. *Journal of Eating Disorders*, **13**, 41–48.

Friedman, T. & Gath, D. (1989). The psychiatric consequences of spontaneous abortion. *British Journal of Psychiatry*, **146**, 55–61.

Gagnon, A.J. (2001). Individual or group antenatal education for childbirth/parenthood (Cochrane Review). In *The Cochrane Library Issue 4, 2001*. Oxford: Update Software.

Glazener, C.M., Abdalla, M., Stroud, P., Naji, S., Templeton, A. & Russell, I.T. (1995). Postnatal maternal morbidity: extent, causes, prevention and treatment. *British Journal of Obstetrics and Gynaecology*, **102**, 282–287.

Goldberg, D. (1972). *The Detection of Psychiatric Illness by Questionnaire*. Oxford: Oxford University Press.

Green, J. & Statham, H. (1996). Psychosocial aspects of prenatal screening and diagnosis. In T. Marteau & M. Richards (Eds), *The Troubled Helix Social and Psychological Implications of the New Human Genetics*. Cambridge: Cambridge University Press.

Greenfield, D.A., Diamond, M. & DeCherney, A.H. (1988). *Journal of Psychosomatic Obstetrics and Gynecology*, **8**, 169–174.

Hall, S., Bobrow, M. & Marteau, T.M. (2000). Psychological consequences for parents of false negative results on prenatal screening for Down's syndrome: retrospective interview study. *British Medical Journal*, **320**, 407–412.

Hayes, B.A., Muller, R. & Bradley, B.S. (2001). Perinatal depression: a randomized controlled trial of an antenatal education intervention for primiparas. *Birth*, **28** (1), 28–35.

Hillier, C.A. & Slade, P. (1989). The impact of antenatal classes on knowledge, anxiety and confidence in primiparous women. *Journal of Reproductive and Infant Psychology*, **7**, 3–13.

Holden, J. (1991). Postnatal depression: its nature, effects and identification using the Edinburgh Postnatal Depression Scale. *Birth*, **18**, 211–221.

Holden, J.M., Sagovsky, R. & Cox, J.L. (1989). Counselling in a general practice setting: controlled study of health visitor intervention in treatment of postnatal depression. *British Medical Journal*, **298**, 223–226.

Horn, S. & Munafo, M. (1997). *Pain Theory, Research and Intervention*. Buckingham: Open University Press.

Howie, P.W., Forsyth, J.G., Ogston, S.A., Clarke, A. & Florey, C. du V. (1990). Protective effect of breast-feeding against infection. *British Medical Journal*, **300**, 11–16.

Iles, S. (1989). The loss of early pregnancy. *Baillière's Clinical Obstetrics and Gynaecology*, **3–4**, 769–790.

Irvine, S., Cawood, E., Richardson, D., MacDonald, E. & Aitken, J. (1996). Evidence of deteriorating semen quality in the United Kingdom: birth cohort study in 577 men in Scotland over 11 years. *British Medical Journal*, **312**, 467.

Jackman, C., McGee, H.M. & Turner, M. (1991). The experience and psychological impact of early miscarriage. *The Irish Journal of Psychology*, **12**, 108–120.

Johnson, A., Wadsworth, J., Wellings, L. & Field, J. (1994). *Sexual Attitudes and Lifestyles*. London: Blackwell Scientific Publications.

Johnston, M. (1987). Emotional and cognitive aspects of anxiety in surgical patients. *Communication and Cognition*, **20**, 245–260.

Kelley, K., Bond, R. & Abraham, C. (2001). Effective approaches to persuading pregnant women to quit smoking: a meta analysis of intervention evaluation studies. *British Journal of Health Psychology*, **6**, 201–228.

Kubler Ross, E. (1969). *On Death and Dying*. New York: Macmillan Inc.

Kumar, R.F. (1989). Postpartum psychosis. *Clinical Obstetrics and Gynecology*, **3–4**, 823–838.

Kumar, R. & Brockington, I.F. (1988). *Motherhood and Mental Illness 2: Causes and Consequences*. London: Wright.

Lampman, C. & Dowling-Guyer, S. (1995). Attitudes towards voluntary and involuntary childlessness. *Basic and Applied Social Psychology*, **17**, 213–222.

Langridge, D., Conolly, K. & Sheeran, P. (2000). Reasons for wanting a child: a network analytic study. *Journal of Reproductive and Infant Psychology*, **18**, 321–338.

Lapane, K.L., Zeirler, S., Lasater, T.M., Stein, M. & Barbour, M.M. (1995). Is a history of depressive symptoms associated with an increase of infertility in women? *Psychosomatic Medicine*, **57**, 509–513.

Linblad, F., Gotlieb, C. & Lalos, O. (2000). To tell or not to tell—what parents think about telling their children that they were born following donor insemination. *Journal of Psychosomatic Obstetrics and Gynaecology*, **21**, 193–303.

Mander, R. (1998). *Pain in Childbearing and its Control*. Oxford: Blackwell Science Ltd.

Marteau, T. & Richards, M. (Eds) (1996). *The Troubled Helix Social and Psychological Implications of the New Human Genetics*. Cambridge: Cambridge University Press.

Marteau, T.M. (1993). Health related screening: psychological predictors of uptake and impact. In S. Maes, H. Leventhal & M. Johnston (Eds), *International Review of Health Psychology 2* (pp. 149–174). Chichester: John Wiley & Sons.

Marteau, T., van Duijn, M. & Ellis, I. (1992). Effects of genetic screening on perceptions of health: a pilot study. *Journal of Medical Genetics*, **29**, 24–26.

Matheson, J. & Babb, P. (Eds) (2002). *Social Trends, 32*. London: The Stationery Office.

McCluskey, S.E., Lacey, J.H. & Pearce, J.M. (1992). Binge eating and polycystic ovaries. *Lancet*, **340**, 723.

McMahon, C.A., Ungerer, J.A., Beaurepaire, J., Pennant, C. & Saunders, D. (1995). Psychosocial outcomes for parents and children after in vitro fertilisation: a review. *Journal of Reproductive and Infant Psychology*, **13**, 1–16.

Melzack, R. & Wall, P.D. (1989). *The Challenge of Pain* (2nd edn). Harmondsworth: Penguin.

Michie, S., Marteau, T.M. & Kidd, J. (1992). An evaluation of an intervention to increase antenatal class attendance. *Journal of Reproductive and Infant Psychology*, **10**, 183–185.

Miller, W.B. & Pasta, D. (1995). Behavioural intentions: which ones predict infertility behaviour in married couples. *Journal of Applied Social Psychology*, **25**, 530–555.

Morgan, J.F. (1999). Polycystic ovary syndrome, gestational diabetes and bulimia nervosa. *Journal of Clinical Endocrinology and Metabolism*, **84**, 4746.

Morse, C.A. (2000). Reproduction: a critical analysis. In J.M. Ussher (Ed.), *Women's Health Contemporary International Perspectives*. Leicester: BPS Books.

Murray, L. & Cooper, P.J. (1997). Effects of postnatal depression on infants development. *Archives of Disease in Childhood*, **77**, 99–101.

Niven, C.A. & Brodie, E.E. (1995). Memory for labour pain: context and quality. *Pain*, **64**, 387–393.

Niven, C. & Walker, A. (Eds) (1996). *The Psychology of Reproduction, Volume 2. Conception, Pregnancy and Birth*. Oxford: Butterworth Heinemann.

Norré, J., Vandereycken, W. & Gordts, S. (2001). The management of eating disorders in a fertility clinic: clinical guidelines. *Journal of Psychosomatic Obstetrics and Gynaecology*, **22**, 77–81.

Oates, M. (1989). Management of major mental illness in pregnancy and the puerperium. *Baillière's Clinical Obstetrics and Gynaecology*, **3–4**, 905–920.

O'Brien, M., Heron Asay, J. & McClusky-Fawcett, K. (1999). Family functioning and maternal depression following premature birth. *Journal of Reproductive and Infant Psychology*, **17**, 178–188.

O'Hara, M.W. & Swain, A.M. (1996). Rates and risks of postpartum depression—a meta-analysis. *International Review of Psychiatry*, **8**, 37–54.

O'Moore, M.A. & Harrison, R.F. (1991). Anxiety and reproductive failure: experiences from a Dublin infertility clinic. *The Irish Journal of Psychology*, **12**, 276–285.

Parkes, C.M. (1985). Bereavement. *British Journal of Psychiatry*, **146**, 11–17.

Pfeffer, N. & Woollett, A. (1988). *The Experience of Infertility*. London: Virago.

Potvin, L., Lasker, J. & Toedter, L. (1989). Measuring grief: a short version of the Perinatal Grief Scale. *J Psychosomatic Behavioural Assessment*, **11**, 29–45.

Read, J. (1999). ABC of sexual health: sexual problems associated with infertility, pregnancy, and ageing. *British Medical Journal*, **318**, 587–589.

Renfrew, M.J., Woolridge, M.W. & Ross-McGill, H. (2000). *Enabling Women to Breastfeed. A Review of Practices which Promote or Inhibit Breastfeeding—with Evidence Based Guidelines for Practice*. London: The Stationery Office.

Riley, D. (1995). *Perinatal Mental Health*. Oxford: Radcliffe Medical Press.

Schwartz, G.E. (1982). Testing the biopsychosocial model: the ultimate challenge facing behavioural medicine? *Journal of Consulting and Clinical Psychology*, **50**, 1040–1053.

Shaw, C. (2001). United Kingdom population trends. *Population Trends*, **103**, 37–46.

Singer, L.T., Salvator, A., Guo, S., Collin, M., Liffen, M. & Baley, J. (1999). Maternal psychological distress and parenting stress after the birth of a very low-birth-weight infant. *Journal of American Medical Association*, **281**, 799–805.

Snowden, R. & Snowden, E. (1984). *The Gift of a Child*. London: George Allen & Unwin.

Spitzer, R.L., Endicott J. & Robins, E. (1978). Research diagnostic criteria: rationale and reliability. *Archives of General Psychiatry*, **35**, 773–772.

Stewart, D.E., Robinson, G.E., Goldbloom, D.S. & Wright, C. (1990). Infertility and eating disorders. *American Journal of Obstetrics and Gynaecology*, **157**, 627–630.

Sutherland, C. (1997). Young people and sex. In G. Andrews (Ed.), *Women's Sexual Health*. London: Baillière Tindall.

Tamminen, T. (1989). The impact of mother's depression on her breast-feeding attitudes and experiences. *Journal of Psychosomatic Obstetrics and Gynaecology*, Supplement **10**, 69–70.

Terry, R. & Gijsbers, K. (2000). Memory for the quantitative and qualitative aspects of labour pain: a preliminary study. *Journal of Reproductive and Infant Psychology*, **18**, 143–152.

Thome, M. & Alder, B.A. (1999). Telephone intervention to reduce fatigue and symptom distress in mothers with difficult infants in the community. *Journal of Advanced Nursing*, **29** (1), 128–137.

Thommen, M., Vallach, L. & Kienke, S. (1995). Prevalence of eating disorders in a Swiss family planning clinic. *Eating Disorders*, **3**, 324–331.

Van Balen, F. & Trombos-Kemper, T.C.M. (1995). Involuntary childless couples, their desire to have children and their motives. *Journal of Psychosomatic Obstetrics and Gynaecology*, **16**, 137–144.

Wald, N.J., Huttly, W.J. & Hennessy, C.F. (1999). Down's syndrome screening in the UK in 1998. *Lancet*, **354**, 1264.

Whitton, A., Warner, R. & Appleby, L. (1996). The pathway to care in post-natal depression. Women's attitudes to postnatal depression and its treatment. *British Journal of General Practice*, **46**, 427–428.

Wing, J.K., Cooper, J.E. & Satorius, N. (1974). *Measurement of and Classification of Psychiatric Symptoms*. Cambridge: Cambridge University Press.

Woodward, V.M. (1995). Psychosocial factors influencing teenage sexual activity, use of contraception and unplanned pregnancy. *Midwifery*, **11**, 210–216.

Woollett, A. (1996). Reproductive decisions. In A. Walker & K. Niven (Eds), *Psychology of Reproduction, Volume 2: Conception, Pregnancy and Birth*. Oxford: Butterworth Heinemann.

Zabin, L.S., Hirsch, M.B. & Emerson, M.R. (1989). When urban adolescents choose abortion: effects on education, psychological status and subsequent pregnancy. *Family Planning Perspective*, **21**, 248.

CHAPTER 20

Appearance Anxiety

Gerry Kent
University of Sheffield, UK

INTRODUCTION

The aim of this chapter is to consider the processes involved in the development and mainte-nance of appearance anxiety in people whose appearance is noticeably different from others.

During the 1960s and 1970s Karen Dion and her colleagues made a significant contri-bution to our understanding of the importance of appearance for social relationships. Their contention that an attractive appearance can have implications for a variety of social per-ceptions has received repeated support (Eagly et al., 1991). In a more recent paper, Dion, Dion and Keelan (1990) developed the notion of "appearance anxiety"—apprehension con-cerning aspects of one's physical appearance and how others might evaluate it. They found evidence that people high in appearance anxiety were more likely to report a past history of others making disparaging remarks about their appearance, often since childhood. However, most of this research has been conducted with participants whose appearance has not been affected by medical conditions, accidents or surgery.

Differences in appearance can be due to congenital conditions (such as cleft lip and palate) or acquired injuries (such as amputations) and include skin diseases (such as eczema, psoriasis and vitiligo, which involves the loss of skin pigmentation leaving a patchy appear-ance), burns, craniofacial abnormalities and consequences of surgery for cancer and other diseases. Approximately 10% of the population can be said to possess some kind of bodily disfigurement, with 2–3% having a difference that is clearly visible to others (Rumsey, 1998). Several studies and recent reviews (Bull & Rumsey, 1988; Papadopolous & Bor, 1999; Papadopolous, Bor & Legg, 1999a; Thompson & Kent, 2001; Thompson, Kent & Smith, 2002) have demonstrated that people with a disfiguring condition are more likely to report higher levels of distress on emotional, behavioural and cognitive dimensions (Robinson, 1997; Walters, 1997). Although it is important not to stereotype people within this group, and there is considerable variation between individuals, emotional reactions can include heightened anxiety and depressed mood, low self-confidence and lowered self-esteem. Behaviourally, avoidance of social situations is common (Jowett & Ryan, 1985). People with disfigurements can also report a number of negative beliefs about themselves, associated with their appearance (Papadopolous & Bor, 1999). The important theoretical and practical question is why these consequences occur.

Handbook of Clinical Health Psychology. Edited by S. Llewelyn and P. Kennedy.
© 2003 John Wiley & Sons, Ltd.

This chapter is in two sections. The first outlines a general model of appearance anxiety, particularly as it applies to people with a disfigurement. Bringing together research in sociology, cognitive and social psychology, the model integrates previous research into a variety of disfiguring conditions. The second section of the chapter shows how the model can be used to understand the effects of medical, social and psychological interventions. Having a model helps the clinician to assess the most relevant aspects of a client's difficulties, develop a formulation and plan an appropriate intervention. Different types of medical, social and psychological interventions can improve quality of life by operating according to different aspects of the model's processes. While medical interventions can be effective because they alter the severity of the physical condition, psychological interventions such as cognitive behavioural therapy (CBT) or social skills training can operate on a schematic level or broaden the repertoire of impression management strategies. Thus, the purpose of this second section is to provide practical information that will be of use to a clinician working in this area.

A MODEL OF APPEARANCE ANXIETY

The aim of this section of the chapter is to describe a theoretical model which integrates existing findings, informs future research directions and provides guidance for clinical interventions. As illustrated by Figure 20.1, the model proposes an interaction between an appearance-altering condition and societal norms and beliefs associated with that condition. Together, they influence the likelihood that the condition will be considered socially unacceptable. Stigmatisation, understood here in terms of exclusion of the affected individual from a social grouping, can lead to the development of cognitive schema associated

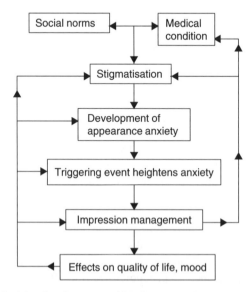

Figure 20.1 A model of the development of appearance anxiety
Source: Kent, G. (2002). Testing a model of disfigurement: effects of a skin camouflage service on well-being and appearance anxiety. *Psychology and Health,* **17** (3), 377–386. Reproduced with permission by Taylor & Francis Ltd, <http://www.tandf.co.uk>

with appearance anxiety. The individual can become vigilant to instances of possible exclusion from the social group, interpret others' behaviour (such as staring) as indicative of exclusion, and become anxious about rejection in the future. Because there are evolutionary reasons to be anxious about exclusion, this schema can be activated by triggering events that threaten exposure of the stigmatised condition. At such times, the main coping strategies involve impression management techniques, often avoidance of the anxiety-provoking setting. Avoidance can, in turn, lower quality of life and increase distress.

Medical Conditions and Social Norms

The model takes as its starting point the presence of a condition that in some way marks the individual as being different from the culture's expectations about appearance. Goffman (1968) used the term stigma to refer to the relationship between a characteristic possessed by an individual and the devaluation that society places on that characteristic. The psychological literature provides several illustrations of devaluation, avoidance and rejection of people with disfiguring attributes (Bull & David, 1986; Bull & Rumsey, 1988; Bull & Stevens, 1981; Finlay et al., 1990; Rumsey, Bull & Gahagan, 1982). These types of behaviour have apparently occurred throughout history, and across many cultures, suggesting to Kurzban and Leary (2001) that they have an evolutionary basis. The most clearly relevant biological threat in the case of dermatological conditions involves the notion of contagion; a condition becomes stigmatised when it is seen as a threat to physical well-being (Bull & David, 1986; Shackelford & Larsen, 1999). People with a skin disease can often cite instances when someone avoided making physical contact or touching any object that they have used.

However, there is also evidence that the extent of stigmatisation varies over time and across cultures and upbringing, so that social influences also play a part in determining the extent of rejection. Another approach to understanding rejection involves the potential effects of a different appearance on social interactions. One of the more important aspects of social interactions is that they flow smoothly, without undue disruption. It is crucial that when two individuals converse, shake hands, or pass each other in the street, each can make an accurate prediction of how the other will behave. Both Jones et al. (1984) and Goffman (1968) have argued that stigmatised conditions pose a threat to this orderly social interaction.

Development of Appearance-related Schema: Appearance Anxiety

Leary and his colleagues (Baumeister & Leary, 1995; Leary & Kowalski, 1995) argue that anxiety about rejection by others is both pervasive and innately based. Because humans are dependent on each other for their physical well-being, Leary contends that we are innately motivated to make and maintain connections with other people in the environment. Any threat to such connections endangered physical survival in our evolutionary past, so that as a species we have a preparedness to become socially anxious. Leary and Kowalski (1995) suggest that this innate concern about exclusion is responsible for the widespread prevalence of social anxiety.

Leary et al. (1998) have demonstrated the importance of social anxiety to adjustment with a disfigured appearance. They asked patients with psoriasis to rate the location and severity of their condition, to indicate the extent to which they were distressed by their condition, and to complete the Fear of Negative Evaluation (FNE) scale as a measure of social anxiety. Leary et al. found an interaction between FNE and distress. When disease severity was low, FNE was only weakly related to distress, but distress increased as severity increased for those high in FNE. Thus, it seemed that social anxiety was a factor moderating the strength of the relationship between the severity of a disfiguring condition and individuals' emotional reactions. Later, Kent and Keohane (2001) demonstrated that the visibility of psoriasis and FNE also interact when quality of life is measured.

Social Exclusion Theory (SET) provides a theoretical framework for understanding the impact of stigmatisation. SET holds that a primary source of anxiety is potential exclusion from important social groups. It is based on three propositions: (1) humans, as a species, possess a fundamental motive to avoid exclusion from social groupings; (2) much social behaviour reflects attempts to improve inclusion; and (3) negative affect (including lone-liness and depression) results when a person does not or cannot achieve a desired level of social inclusion. Instances of social exclusion through bullying and teasing can lead to lone-liness, depression and low self-esteem as well as increased anxiety (Leary, 1990). Although SET has not been applied to issues concerning exclusion due to appearance or disfigure-ment, there are indications that its propositions can be applied to this group. For example, Kent (2000) found that anxiety about rejection was a major determinant of why people with vitiligo often avoided situations where others would be able to see their depigmented skin.

Body Image Schema

One of the more important developments in theoretical psychology in recent decades has been the widespread acceptance of the notion of cognitive schema. This construct refers to a mental representation of the self and the environment that serves to organise and process incoming information. A robust finding has been the demonstration that there are significant biases in the way that information is processed, depending on schema and current emotional state. Markus (2000) applied the notion of schema to body image. Cash (1996) argues that a schema indicative of a disturbed body image can develop as a result of an interaction between cultural expectations, personality attributes and physical characteristics.

Recent extensions of Goffman's work on stigma parallel this work on schema. Jacoby (1994) has drawn a distinction between enacted stigma (actual incidents of rejection) and felt stigma (expectations of rejection). While instances of enacted stigma can be rare, felt stigma is extremely disabling, with constant attention being given to self-presentation and attempts to avoid disclosure (Scambler & Hopkins, 1986). In many respects, this sociological notion of felt stigma is identical to the psychological notion of schema. Kent (1999) showed that vitiligo patients who believed that their condition was stigmatised in our society were more likely to recall not only events of actual stigmatisation but also incidents of felt stigma. They were more likely to interpret ambiguous events as indicative of stigma.

Higgins's (Strauman & Higgins, 1987) discrepancy theory is also very relevant here. He draws attention to distinctions between ideal and actual selves, and how people imagine that others view them. From Higgins's point of view, it is not appearance per se that is important but rather the discrepancy between ideal and actual appearance. In support of this, using the Repertory Grid Technique, Ashworth, Davis and Spriggs (2000) found a significant convergence between the actual and ideal selves in their study on the effects of porcelain veneer treatment to improve the appearance of teeth. Similarly, Higgins's theory might be particularly relevant to understanding why cosmetic surgery and other medical interventions are often, but not always, successful in alleviating distress; cosmetic surgery might be viewed as successful depending on how successfully it reduces perceived discrepancies.

Triggering Events

In other types of emotional difficulty, the activation of schema depends on the presence of a triggering event. Emotional distress arising from disfiguring conditions varies over time and situations. This variation can be due to the wider context, such as a change in season from winter, when the skin is mainly covered, to summer, when there is a need to wear more revealing clothes. Times of transition, either in terms of physiological development as at puberty, or when meeting new people, as when changing school or jobs, may act as significant triggers.

More immediately, the activation of schema relating to disfigurement depends on the presence of a triggering social event. This could be an invitation to go swimming, the start of a new physically intimate relationship, or an instance of enacted stigma. In each example, appearance becomes more relevant to the self and to others. Kent (2000) asked patients with vitiligo to describe a situation when their skin condition affected their life in some way. The most common triggering events involved threatened (e.g. an invitation to go swimming) or actual (having to wear lighter clothing) exposure of the body, an instance of enacted stigma, or a sudden worsening of the condition.

Impression Management Strategies: Coping with the Possibility of Rejection

According to SET, the degree of social anxiety that people experience depends on their confidence that they can behave in a way that is acceptable to others. People become socially anxious when they believe they cannot make this desired impression. Anxiety about exclusion often leads to self-protective strategies and these strategies function in terms of impression management in order to avoid hurt and feelings of abandonment. The most obvious strategy is behavioural avoidance, as in declining an invitation to go swimming or not starting a new intimate relationship. Alternatives involve methods of concealment. For example, Lanigan and Cotterill (1989) found that 9% of their sample of women with port wine stains had never shown their birthmark to their partners, while Kent (2002) showed that the effective use of cosmetic creams to cover skin blemishes was associated with higher levels of confidence and lower avoidance of social settings.

Consequences of Avoidance and Concealment

These coping strategies appear to be useful to the individuals who use them. In the short term, they relieve anxiety by removing the person from the threatening setting or, in Goffman's

(1968) terms, assist in "passing". Given any experiences with enacted stigma, it is not surprising that such attempts at impression management are used frequently. However, they also have many negative consequences, including intrusiveness of cognitions, depressed mood, loss of intimacy and continuing anxiety about exposure. Such consequences have been shown in both quantitative and qualitative studies.

Quantitatively, the recent work on concealment and intrusive cognitions is relevant here. Smart and Wegner (1999), in their study on the effects of concealing an eating disorder from friends and family, found that keeping this stigmatised condition a secret resulted in highly intrusive thoughts. Similarly, Fortune et al. (2000) asked patients with psoriasis to complete the Penn State Worry Questionnaire—as a measure of pathological worrying—and also to indicate their beliefs about the causes and consequences of their disease. High levels of worry were related to beliefs about the social consequences of psoriasis, which an earlier study (Fortune et al., 1997) indicated centred about the use of avoidance and perceptions of being rejected on the basis of their skin condition. Thus, it seems that avoidance led to increased worry in this population.

These quantitative findings are mirrored in the qualitative literature. Kent (2000) found that many people with the skin disease vitiligo had many regrets about the use of avoidant strategies that left them ruminating on their condition, as the following quotations illustrate:

> Using camouflage for the first time has helped me to disguise the condition and therefore makes me feel better. However, it also leaves a feeling of inadequacy and self-embarrassment at having to resort to such measures.

> I am constantly feeling insecure about my body, which is quite good apart from the vitiligo, and I almost always feel hopeless about my situation and feel that this disease is ruining my life. My having vitiligo is constantly on my mind, day and night, and causes me huge amounts of depression and isolation.

Clinical Interventions

The model shown in Figure 20.1 indicates that there are feedback loops between appearance-related schema, coping strategies, and their emotional and behavioural consequences. Both the positive and negative consequences of chosen coping strategies feed back and affect higher level processes. The purpose of clinical interventions in this context is to maximise the likelihood that individuals will have positive and self-affirming means of dealing with their appearance anxiety. There are three topics of interest here: an understanding of why some individuals seek help with their appearance; assessment of appearance-related issues; and the types and efficacy of therapeutic intervention.

Help Seeking

There is a distinct paucity of research on the first of these issues. An exception is the research conducted by Fortune et al. (1998) with people with psoriasis. All patients who had been referred to a psoriasis clinic were asked to complete a battery of scales designed to assess the extent to which the psoriasis affected their social lives and caused them distress. At interview, 87 patients were invited to take part in a Symptom Management Programme, which was designed to assist in coping with the disease. However, only 10% of these patients actually took up the offer to participate. Apparently paradoxically, those who did *not* participate were more likely to believe that psoriasis had serious consequences on their life, were more anxious, were more likely to worry about their condition, and were more likely to feel stigmatised by their condition. These results suggest that those people who are most affected and disturbed by their condition are least likely to seek help.

Assessing Appearance-related Issues

As in any other instance where people are seeking assistance for psychological difficulties, a full history is essential. Identification of other issues relevant to well-being is needed. In this context two aspects may be particularly pertinent. The first is an assessment of symptoms of post-traumatic stress disorder (PTSD). Because disfigurement may be due to accidental injury (as in the case of burns) or surgery (as in the case of head and neck cancer or amputations), there may be emotional, cognitive and behavioural difficulties that can take precedence over treatment of appearance anxiety. The second is assessment of previous experiences of stigmatisation. Since stigmatisation may be a prime factor leading to appearance anxiety, an understanding of experiences of rejection, and what these experiences mean to the individual, may provide clues to the nature of the onset and maintenance of issues for individual clients.

Some scales provide observer-rated indicators of clinical severity; for example, the Katz Scale (Katz et al., 2000) for head and neck cancer, for obesity the Body Mass Index (Myers & Rosen, 1999), and a variety of scales for psoriasis (Ashcroft et al., 1999). But since severity is often weakly related to subjective distress, these need to be used in conjunction with self-report measures of well-being. The latter are of two types: global assessments and measures specific to the individual's condition. Some of these will be familiar to clinicians working in other areas of mental health, while some are quite specialised. It is also useful to consider measures in terms of their assessment of the emotional, cognitive and behavioural aspects of the difficulty. The scales outlined below have been shown to have good reliability and validity. More detailed reviews of some of these scales can be found in Cash and Grant (1996) and Thompson, Penner and Altabe (1990), while Cash (1977) presents several scales in a useful and accessible way.

Global Assessments

Global assessments of emotional issues could include the Hospital Anxiety and Depression Scale (Zigmond & Snaith, 1983) or the Brief Symptom Inventory. Measures of the cognitive component could include a measure of self-esteem such as the Rosenberg Scale (Rosenberg, 1965), social anxiety (Leary, 1983) and worry (e.g. the Penn State Worry Questionnaire; Molina & Borkovec, 1994). In the Situational Inventory of Body-Image Dysphoria (Cash, 1994a), respondents are asked to indicate their levels of negative emotions in 48 situations.

There are a large number of scales that are specific to appearance-related cognitions. These include the Derriford Scale (Carr, Harris & James, 2000), a 59-item scale that assesses the individual's level of distress and perceptions of difficulties; the Body-Image Automatic

Thoughts Questionnaire (Rucker & Cash, 1992), a measure of self-reported thoughts about appearance; the Multidimensional Body-Self Relations Questionnaire (Cash, 1994b), which provides a broad assessment of attitudes and appearance orientation; the Body-Image Ideals Questionnaire (Cash & Szymanski, 1995), which measures the discrepancy between actual and ideal selves; and the Appearance Schemas Inventory (Cash & Labarge, 1996), which assesses the extent of emotional investment in appearance.

The behavioural component involves an assessment of how appearance-related concerns impact on life, and could involve the administration of the Illness Intrusiveness Scale, which assesses the extent of disruption to everyday activities (Devins et al., 1997) or, for skin conditions, the Dermatology Life Quality Index (Finlay & Khan, 1994). The Body-Image Avoidance Questionnaire can be used to assess the extent to which an individual avoids situations and attempts to conceal appearance (Rosen et al., 1991).

Specific Assessments

A number of instruments designed to assess well-being for a range of medical conditions have appeared. They tend to concentrate on the cognitive and behavioural consequences of the condition. Because of their variety and because they are constantly being developed, only a small sample is provided here. Cognitively, Kopel et al. (1998) have developed the Body Image Instrument as a way of assessing body image concerns in childhood survivors of cancer; Sarwer, Wadden and Foster (1998) and Cooper et al. (1987) provide measures of body image dissatisfaction in obesity; Ryharczyk et al. (1995) describe a scale to measure body image disturbance resulting from a leg amputation; and Broder (2001) provides a review of assessments for people with craniofacial abnormalities. Ginsburg and Link (1989) have developed a scale to assess the extent to which people with psoriasis expected to be stigmatised because of their condition, while Kent (1999) has adapted this scale for use with vitiligo patients. Less commonly, researchers and clinicians have been interested in assessing the behavioural correlates of disfigurements, such as disorders of the facial neuromuscular system (Van Swearingen & Brach, 1996) and of head and neck cancer (Gilklich, Goldsmith & Funk, 1997).

Thus, there is a wide range and variety of assessment tools available in this area, several of which could be appropriate for a particular client. In terms of the model provided in Figure 20.1, some measures target schemata relevant to appearance anxiety, others concern coping and impression management strategies, while others assess general and specific outcomes. Many of these measures have been used in the assessment of therapeutic interventions, as described below.

INTERVENTIONS

This section of the chapter provides a review of the nature and efficacy of clinical interventions that have been used in this area. Following Figure 20.1, interventions that have aimed to change physical appearance are considered first, followed by those that alter the social environment. Programmes designed to change appearance-related schemata are then described, followed by attempts to help individuals to improve their impression management techniques in self-affirming and socially advantageous ways.

Reducing the Severity of Visible Differences

Changing appearance can have substantial beneficial effects. Medical interventions can include medication (as in the reduction of skin disorders such as acne, psoriasis and eczema), plastic and reconstructive surgery, gastroplasty for major obesity, dental interventions, steroid injections for torticollis and laser treatment for port wine stains (Thompson & Kent, 2001). There can be positive effects even when the visible difference seems relatively minor to an outside observer (Cole et al., 1994). Because the disfigurement may play a significant role in the development and maintenance of PTSD after traumatic injuries (Madianos et al., 2001), there may be secondary benefits to medical treatment; perhaps a change in appearance could also result in a lessening of PTSD symptoms.

However, such interventions can be insufficient in themselves. Levels of anxiety and social avoidance often remain high for people who have received plastic surgery (Newell, 2000), and in a survey of plastic surgery practices, Borah, Rankin and Way (1999) found that psychological complications were more common than physical problems such as infections. Most surgeons had encountered patients who were distressed after surgery: anxiety reactions and depression were reported by 95% of surgeons, sleep disorders by 89% and disappointment by 97%. Eighty-six per cent had diagnosed PTSD in their patients. Thus, it could be argued that medical interventions may help in a rather superficial way, not addressing more fundamental aspects of a person's difficulties.

Appearance can be changed on a more temporary basis. The use of camouflage creams is associated with improved quality of life as measured by self-reported confidence in social situations (Kent, 2002), but they do not address more fundamental issues of high investment in appearance or concerns about social exclusion. It is possible that difficulties persist because the use of such creams maintains the strategy of secrecy, or perhaps because they do not deal with pre-existing psychological difficulties unrelated to appearance per se (Bradbury, 1994).

Social Interventions

Given the critical role that experiences of stigmatisation appear to have on the development of social anxiety, it is surprising that there are very few reports of preventive interventions at a societal, group or family level. The aim of such interventions is to reduce the likelihood that people will encounter rejection and do not become self-conscious about their appearance.

There is relatively little research on interventions on an organisational or societal level. Because stigmatisation is related to the types of attributions made about the condition (Smart & Wegner, 1999), it seems possible that an educational approach might be effective in some instances. Working with 9- to 11-year-old children, Cline et al. (1998) developed an information pack that was designed to increase awareness and understanding of facial disfigurement. The children were interviewed before the study commenced and four months later. This approach had some success, with the children showing greater knowledge about disfigurement than those in the control group.

It may be that an individualised and intensive intervention is required to overcome the cultural stereotypes associated with some kinds of disfigurement. For example, it seems unlikely that a brief educational approach will be sufficient to change attitudes and behaviour if there is a strongly held cultural belief about the potentially harmful consequences of associating with people with a particular disease (Rozin & Fallon, 1987). Direct and prolonged contact with an affected individual may be required to effect change. Interventions at this level might be informed by the work on bullying in schools.

Lefebvre and Arndt (1988) outline the principles that could be involved in helping children on a family level. Based on their psychiatric input to a paediatric craniofacial team, they argue that a focus on prevention requires a significant shift of attitude from treating emotional difficulties to increasing competence. One principle concerns an accurate description of the condition with realistic information about the effects of surgery. Interventions with the family need to be aimed at promoting communication with the medical team, helping parents to find and develop their solutions to difficulties as they arise, modelling suitable attachment behaviours, and modelling frank and open communication between the parents to dispel any "conspiracy of silence" that might develop. They also argue that as the child grows he or she ought to be helped to develop suitable answers to questions and staring. Because times of transition can be particularly difficult for children, the move into school may require considerable preparation, as might preparation for surgery.

It might also be important for parents to reconsider any unhelpful attributions they make about the child's appearance. Cella et al. (1988) found that 25% of close relatives of children who had been hospitalised for burns reported intrusive and avoidant responses to the burn trauma. These stress responses could not be predicted by demographic information, severity of the burn or the presence of facial disfigurement; however, blaming themselves for the injury was a significant predictor of distress. Nixon and Singer (1993) describe how a group cognitive-behavioural session aimed at parents of children with severe developmental disabilities can have a significant effect on parental self-blaming; the same principles are likely to apply to parents of disfigured children. Thus, it seems that helping parents to examine and challenge their own attributions may be useful in aiding their children.

Cognitive-behavioural Interventions

Given the conceptual and empirical overlap between social anxiety and appearance anxiety, it seems likely that the CBT that has proved effective for social anxiety and social phobia (Rapee & Heimberg, 1997) would also be effective for appearance anxiety. CBT approaches for social anxiety include systematic exposure to the feared situations, relaxation procedures, video-taped feedback and cognitive restructuring.

Cash (1977, 1996; Cash & Grant, 1996) has concentrated his work with people whose appearance falls within the normal range but who are disturbed by their appearance. He has also shown that similar principles apply for people who have undergone surgery, such as a mastectomy. For his eight-step programme, he recommends a comprehensive body image assessment, to include a range of standardised assessments (such as those described above) as well as more informal information gathering. Step 2 involves diary keeping to help both the therapist and the client to identify problem areas. The third step aims to help clients to become desensitised to areas of the body and to situations that provoke distress. He uses a systematic desentisation approach; relaxation paired with items on a hierarchy. The identification and challenging of appearance-related assumptions constitute steps 4 and 5. Here, Cash draws on techniques used by Beck and Ellis to identify and alter maladaptive cognitive errors. As in other areas where CBT has been employed, the aim is to establish "a reasonable doubt" about these cognitions.

These cognitive interventions are supplemented by behavioural techniques (steps 6 and 7). He argues that defensive strategies such as avoidance, concealment and repeated checking of appearance used to gain temporary relief from anxiety, self-consciousness and embarrassment serve to maintain dysphoric mood in the longer term. Using Bandura's notion of self-efficacy, he asks clients to indicate their confidence that they would be able to avoid safety behaviours, such as repeated checking in the mirror, and to engage in positive behaviours, such as going swimming and trying on clothes in the shops. In order to develop a positive body image, Cash also encourages clients to undertake positive activities, such as playing sports, wearing attractive clothes, riding a bicycle, and so on. It seems that he uses many of the principles of motivational interviewing (Miller & Rollick, 1991) to encourage such activities. Finally, in step 8, Cash puts strategies in place that aim to maintain positive body image changes and high levels of social activity.

In a series of case studies, Bradbury (1996) describes the uses of CBT for people with clear visible differences. She argues that the first step in such interventions is to identify client needs (she recommends a SWOT—Strengths, Weaknesses, Opportunities, Threats—analysis to help this assessment), and then to set the aims of therapy. For example, she describes her work with "Maria", who was having difficulty in coping with social encounters. As a result of surgery, Maria was left with a pronounced droop on the left side of her face. She had become uncertain in social encounters, especially with acquaintances. In keeping with the CBT approach, Bradbury first asked her to keep a diary for two weeks. It indicated that one situation that Maria found particularly difficult was interacting with other mothers when she took her children to school or school outings. One particular setting was identified; Maria and the therapist discussed how she might handle it, and this strategy was rehearsed through a role-play beforehand. The actual encounter was very difficult for her, but Maria reported a greater sense of control and achievement. Maria and the therapist began to address other situations and ways in which they could be dealt with.

Some formal assessments of this type of intervention are now being published. In an analogue study, Butters and Cash (1987) offered a six-session individualised intervention to undergraduate psychology students. Compared to the waiting list controls, the 16 students reported improvements on a wide range of assessments, including appearance evaluation, appearance satisfaction and self-esteem. There were also significant reductions in cognitive errors.

There are also some studies with clients who are seeking help with their appearance. Rosen, Reiter and Orosan (1995) compared 16 hours of CBT with a no-treatment group for clients with Body Dysmorphic Disorder (BDD). The treatment group showed evidence of a reduction of symptoms, the disorder being eliminated in 82% of participants at the end of treatment and in 77% at the follow-up four to five months afterwards. There was also a significant reduction in psychological symptoms and an increase in self-esteem. Similar results were reported by Papadopoulos, Bor and Legg (1999b), who also found improvements after a seven-session CBT intervention for clients with vitiligo. The clients reported improvements on self-esteem, quality of life, body image distress and the Body-Image Automatic Thoughts Questionnaire.

The clear clinical significance of these various results suggests that the effects of CBT are robust for these populations. The effects may be sufficiently powerful to allow for the use of self-help guides. Cash's therapeutic steps are outlined in a client-friendly manner in his self-help workbook (Cash, 1977). A study by Newell and Clarke (2000) suggests that even a minimal self-help intervention can be beneficial. They gave half of a group with a facial disfigurement a self-help leaflet that offered cognitive-behavioural guidance. Compared to the non-intervention group, the intervention group reported lower anxiety and depressed mood and were engaging in more social leisure activities afterwards.

Impression Management Training

As described above, helping clients to develop strategies to cope with difficult events and situations forms an important component of the CBT approach. Social Skills Training (SST) has received attention in its own right. Several studies have indicated that people with disfiguring conditions can interact in ways that are not conducive to competent interactions and the development of supportive relationships (Kapp-Simon & McGuire, 1997).

It is clear that having behavioural strategies to deal with instances of stigmatisation and intrusive staring is of considerable benefit. Partridge (1994) takes the position that a person with a disfigurement needs to be able to present a social self that overrides his or her appearance. Especially on a first meeting, the non-disfigured person will be naturally interested in the appearance of the disfigured person, perhaps being hesitant to engage and almost certainly curious. Thus, in social settings it is important that the disfigured person be able to shift the listener's attention away from the blemish and towards their personality and abilities. Since there is a relationship between the presence of good social skills and social support (Cohen, Sherrod & Clark, 1986) assistance in these respects could potentially have many psychological benefits. Through the use of instruction, modelling, role-play and open discussion, the aim is to help participants learn more about the nature of social interactions, engender a sense of empowerment rather than shame, and provide practical skills that help them to influence the views of others. Robinson, Rumsey and Partridge (1996) have demonstrated that such a package can lead to reductions of social anxiety and distress and increase confidence, changes that were maintained at six-month follow-ups.

CONCLUDING REMARKS

Great strides have been made in understanding the experiences of those affected by disfiguring conditions. The field has moved from the initial findings that disfiguring conditions are associated with heightened levels of distress, through demonstrations that people with disfigurements encounter stigmatising and rejecting reactions from others, and more recent explorations of how the medical condition and experiences interact to affect cognitions, emotions, behaviour and quality of life. There is considerable support for the model outlined in Figure 20.1, which emphasises the roles of both societal and individual reactions to visible difference. Once appearance anxiety has developed, it seems likely that a combination of CBT and social skills training will be the most helpful types of intervention. Although exposure to feared situations to encourage habituation and cognitive restructuring is an important component of CBT, it may be damaging if used alone in this population. Stigmatisation does occur and people may well encounter rejection and other negative reactions. Here the social skills training component is needed to help people deal with such reactions.

There are many topics open to future research and developments in this area. Attention to societal and interpersonal factors seems crucial. Most of the above research on interventions operates on an individual level. CBT, for example, concentrates on the cognitions and behaviour of the individual, with the implication that the problem resides within the person. However, to the extent that distress is due to the reactions of others (Chang & Herzog, 1976), a thorough analysis of why rejection occurs is a central issue. By focusing on the effects of disfigurement on the individual, the wider societal issues have been ignored; a greater understanding of the causes of stigmatisation as well as the development of interventions at a social level are needed.

The psychological effects of stigmatisation also merit further attention. Although it is clear that rejection and social isolation of affected individuals have important psychological consequences, the theoretical basis for this is only now being developed. It seems likely that social exclusion theory (Leary, 1990) will prove to be heuristic in this respect. Baumeister and Leary (1995) argue that humans have an innate need to belong to social groups, due to their biological vulnerability. The kinds of consequences postulated to result from social exclusion—depressed mood, anxiety and loneliness—are very similar to those reported by those who have been stigmatised because of their appearance (Kent, 2000). Examining the cognitive schema of people who have been rejected on the basis of their appearance may indicate that there are many similarities between the research on social exclusion and the research on disfigurements. There is also much work to be done on the coping strategies used by people with a different appearance. In other areas of health psychology, avoidance and concealment are associated with higher levels of distress (Henderson et al., 2002; Smart & Wegner, 1999; Troster, 1997); similar processes might be operating here. In these ways, it may be possible to integrate the research on appearance anxiety with a wide variety of health-related topics.

ACKNOWLEDGEMENTS

I would like to thank Sophie Heason and Andrew Thompson for their discussions that have helped to shape the content of this chapter.

REFERENCES

Ashcroft, D., Po, A., Williams, H. & Griffiths, C. (1999). Clinical measures of disease severity and outcome in psoriasis: a critical appraisal of their quality. *British Journal of Dermatology*, **141**, 185–191.

Ashworth, P., Davis, L. & Spriggs, L. (1996). Personal change resulting from porcelain veneer treatment to improve the appearance of the teeth. *Psychology, Health and Medicine*, **1**, 57–69.

Baumeister, R. & Leary, M. (1995). The need to belong: desire for interpersonal attachments as a fundamental human motivation. *Psychological Bulletin*, **117**, 497–529.

Borah, G., Rankin, M. & Wey, P. (1999). Psychological complications in 281 plastic surgery practices. *Plastic and Reconstructive Surgery*, **104**, 1241–1246.

Bradbury, E. (1994). The psychology of aesthetic plastic surgery. *Aesthetic Plastic Surgery*, **18**, 301–305.

Bradbury, E. (1996). *Counselling People with Disfigurement*. Leicester: British Psychological Society.

Broder, H. (2001). Using psychological assessment and therapeutic strategies to enhance well-being. *Cleft Palate-Craniofacial Journal*, **38**, 248–254.

Bull, R. & David, I. (1986). The stigmatizing effect of facial disfigurement. *Journal of Cross-Cultural Psychology*, **17**, 99–108.

Bull, R. & Rumsey, N. (1988). *The Social Psychology of Facial Appearance*. New York: Springer-Verlag.

Bull, R. & Stevens, J. (1981). The effects of facial disfigurement on helping behaviour. *Italian Journal of Psychology*, **8**, 25–32.

Butters, J. & Cash, T.F. (1987). Cognitive-behavioral treatment of women's body-image dissatisfaction. *Journal of Consulting and Clinical Psychology*, **55**, 889–897.

Carr, T., Harris, D. & James, C. (2000). The Derriford Appearance Scale (DAS-59): a new scale to measure individual responses to living with problems of appearance. *British Journal of Health Psychology*, **5**, 201–215.

Cash, T.F. (1977). *The Body Image Workbook*. Oakland: New Harbinger Publications.

Cash, T.F. (1994a). The Situational Inventory of Body Image Dysphoria: contextual assessment of a negative body image. *The Behavior Therapist*, **17**, 133–134.

Cash, T.F. (1994b). Body-image attitudes: evaluation, investment and affect. *Perceptual and Motor Skills*, **78**, 1168–1170.

Cash, T.F. (1996). The treatment of body image disturbances. In K. Thompson (Ed.), *Body Image, Eating Disorders and Obesity* (pp. 83–107). Washington, DC: American Psychological Association.

Cash, T.F. & Grant, J. (1996). Cognitive-behavioral treatment of body-image disturbances. In V. van Hasselt & M. Hersen (Eds), *Sourcebook of Psychological Treatment Manuals for Adult Disorders* (pp. 567–614). New York: Plenum Press.

Cash, T.F. & Labarge, A. (1996). Development of the appearance schemas inventory: a new cognitive body-image assessment. *Cognitive Therapy and Research*, **20**, 37–50.

Cash, T.F. & Szymanski, M. (1995). The development and validation of the Body-Image Ideals Questionnaire. *Journal of Personality Assessment*, **64**, 466–477.

Cella, D., Perry, S., Kulchycky, S. & Goodwin, C. (1988). Stress and coping in relatives of burn patients: a longitudinal study. *Hospital and Community Psychiatry*, **39**, 159–166.

Chang, F. & Herzog, B. (1976). Burn morbidity: a follow-up study of physical and psychological disability. *Annals of Surgery*, **183**, 34–37.

Cline, T., Proto, A., Raval, P. & Di Paolo, T. (1998). The effects of brief exposure and of classroom teaching on attitudes children express towards facial disfigurement in peers. *Educational Research*, **40**, 55–68.

Cohen, S., Sherrod, D. & Clark, M. (1986). Social skills and the stress-protective role of social support. *Journal of Personality and Social Psychology*, **50**, 963–973.

Cole, R., Shakespeare, V., Shakespeare, P. & Hobby, J. (1994). Measuring outcome in low-priority plastic surgery patients using Quality of Life indices. *British Journal of Plastic Surgery*, **47**, 117–121.

Cooper, P., Taylor, M., Cooper, Z. & Fairburn, C. (1987). The development and validation of the Body Shape Questionnaire. *International Journal of Eating Disorders*, **6**, 485–494.

Devins, G., Beanlands, H., Mandin, H. & Paul, L. (1997). Psychosocial impact of illness intrusiveness moderated by self-concept and age in end-stage renal disease. *Health Psychology*, **16**, 529–538.

Dion, K.L., Dion, K.K. & Keelan, J.P. (1990). Appearance anxiety as a dimension of social-evaluative anxiety: exploring the ugly duckling syndrome. *Contemporary Social Psychology*, **14**, 220–224.

Eagly, A., Ashmore, R., Makhijani, M. & Longo, L. (1991). What is beautiful is good, but . . . . A meta-analytic review of research on the physical attractiveness stereotype. *Psychological Bulletin*, **110**, 109–128.

Finlay, A. & Khan, G. (1994). Dermatology Life Quality Index (DLQI): a simple practical measure for routine clinical use. *Clinical and Experimental Dermatology*, **19**, 210–216.

Finlay, A., Khan, G., Luscombe, D. & Salek, M. (1990). Validation of Sickness Impact Profile and Psoriasis Disability Index in psoriasis. *British Journal of Dermatology*, **123**, 751–756.

Fortune, D., Main, C., O'Sullivan, T. & Griffiths, C. (1997). Assessing illness-related stress in psoriasis: the psychometric properties of the Psoriasis Life Stress Inventory. *Journal of Psychosomatic Research*, **42**, 467–475.

Fortune, D., Richards, H., Main, C. & Griffiths, C. (2000). Pathological worrying, illness perceptions and disease severity in patients with psoriasis. *British Journal of Health Psychology*, **5**, 71–82.

Fortune, D., Richards, H., Main, C., O'Sullivan, T. & Griffiths, C. (1998). Developing clinical psychology services in an outpatient dermatology speciality clinic: what factors are associated with non-uptake of services? *Clinical Psychology Forum*, **115**, 34–36.

Gilklich, R., Goldsmith, T. & Funk, G. (1997). Are head and neck specific quality of life measures necessary? *Head and Neck*, **19**, 474–480.

Ginsburg, I. & Link, B. (1989). Feelings of stigmatization in patients with psoriasis. *Journal of the American Academy of Dermatology*, **20**, 53–63.

Goffman, E. (1968). *Stigma*. London: Penguin.

Henderson, B., Davison, K., Pennebaker, J., Gatchel, R. & Baum, A. (2002). Disease disclosure patterns among breast cancer patients. *Psychology and Health*, **17**, 51–62.

Jacoby, A. (1994). Felt versus enacted stigma: a concept revisited. *Social Science and Medicine*, **38**, 269–274.

Jones, E., Farina, A., Hastorf, A., Markus, H., Miller, D. & Scott, R. (1984). *Social Stigma. The Psychology of Marked Relationships*. New York: Freeman.

Jowett, S. & Ryan, T. (1985). Skin disease and handicap: an analysis of the impact of skin conditions. *Social Science and Medicine*, **20**, 425–429.

Kapp-Simon, K. & McGuire, D. (1997). Observed social interaction patterns in adolescents with and without craniofacial conditions. *Cleft Palate—Craniofacial Journal*, **34**, 380–384.

Katz, M., Irish, J., Devins, G., Rodin, G. & Gullane, P. (2000). Reliability and validity of an observer-rated disfigurement scale for head and neck cancer patients. *Head and Neck*, **22**, 132–141.

Kent, G. (1999). Correlates of perceived stigma in vitiligo. *Psychology and Health*, **14**, 241–252.

Kent, G. (2000). Understanding the experiences of people with disfigurements: an integration of four models of social and psychological functioning. *Psychology, Health and Medicine*, **5**, 117–129.

Kent, G. (2002). Testing a model of disfigurement: effects of a skin camouflage service on well-being and appearance anxiety. *Psychology and Health*, **17**, 377–386.

Kent, G. & Keohane, S. (2001). Social anxiety and disfigurement: the moderating effects of fear of negative evaluation and past experience. *British Journal of Clinical Psychology*, **40**, 23–34.

Kopel, S., Eiser, C., Cool, P., Grimer, R. & Carter, S. (1998). Assessment of body image in survivors of childhood cancer. *Journal of Pediatric Psychology*, **23**, 141–147.

Kurzban, R. & Leary, M. (2001). Evolutionary origins of stigmatization: the functions of social exclusion. *Psychological Bulletin*, **127**, 187–208.

Lanigan, S. & Cotterill, J. (1989). Psychological disabilities amongst patients with port wine stains. *British Journal of Dermatology*, **121**, 209–215.

Leary, M. (1983). A brief version of the Fear of Negative Evaluation Scale. *Personality and Social Psychology Bulletin*, **9**, 371–376.

Leary, M. (1990). Responses to social exclusion: social anxiety, jealousy, loneliness, depression, and low self-esteem. *Journal of Social and Clinical Psychology*, **9**, 221–229.

Leary, M. & Kowalski, R. (1995). *Social Anxiety*. London: Guilford Press.

Leary, M., Rapp, S., Herbst, K., Exum, M. & Feldman, S. (1998). Interpersonal concerns and psychological difficulties of psoriasis patients: effects of disease severity and fear of negative evaluation. *Health Psychology*, **17**, 1–7.

Lefebvre, A. & Arndt, E. (1988). Working with facially disfigured children: a challenge in prevention. *Canadian Journal of Psychiatry*, **33**, 453–458.

Madianos, M., Papaghelis, M., Ioannovich, J. & Dafni, R. (2001). Psychiatric disorders in burn patients: a follow-up study. *Psychotherapy and Psychosomatics*, **70**, 30–37.

Markus, H. (2000). Self-schemata and processing information about the self. *Journal of Personality and Social Psychology*, **35**, 63–78.

Miller, W. & Rollick, S. (1991). *Motivational Interviewing: Preparing People to Change Addictive Behavior*. New York: Guilford Press.

Molina, S. & Borkovec, T. (1994). The Penn State Worry Questionnaire: psychometric properties and associated characteristics. In G. Davey & F. Tallis (Eds), *Worrying. Perspectives on Theory, Assessment and Treatment* (pp. 265–283). Chichester: John Wiley & Sons.

Myers, A. & Rosen, J. (1999). Obesity stigmatization and coping: relation to mental health symptoms, body image, and self-esteem. *International Journal of Obesity*, **23**, 221–230.

Newell, R. (2000). Psychological difficulties amongst plastic surgery ex-patients following surgery to the face: a survey. *British Journal of Plastic Surgery*, **53**, 386–392.

Newell, R. & Clarke, M. (2000). Evaluation of a self-help leaflet in treatment of social difficulties following facial disfigurement. *International Journal of Nursing Studies*, **37**, 381–388.

Nixon, C. & Singer, G. (1993). Group cognitive-behavioral treatment for excessive parental self-blame and guilt. *American Journal of Mental Retardation*, **97**, 665–672.

Papadopoulos, L. & Bor, R. (1999). *Psychological Approaches to Dermatology*. Leicester: British Psychological Society.

Papadopoulos, L., Bor, R. & Legg, C. (1999a). Psychological factors in cutaneous disease: an overview of research. *Psychology, Health and Medicine*, **4**, 107–128.

Papadopoulos, L., Bor, R. & Legg, C. (1999b). Coping with the disfiguring effects of vitiligo: a preliminary investigation into the effects of Cognitive Behavioural Therapy. *British Journal of Medical Psychology*, **10**, 11–12.

Partridge, J. (1994). *Changing Faces. The Challenge of Facial Disfigurement*. London: Changing Faces.

Rapee, R. & Heimberg, R. (1997). A cognitive-behavioral model of anxiety in social phobia. *Behaviour Research and Therapy*, **35**, 741–756.

Robinson, E. (1997). Psychological research on visible differences in adults. In R. Lansdown, N. Rumsey, E. Bradbury, T. Carr & J. Partridge (Eds), *Visibly Different. Coping with Disfigurement* (pp. 102–111). Oxford: Butterworth Heinemann.

Robinson, E., Rumsey, N. & Partridge, J. (1996). An evaluation of the impact of social interaction skills training for facially disfigured people. *British Journal of Plastic Surgery*, **49**, 281–289.

Rosen, J., Reiter, J. & Orosan, P. (1995). Cognitive-behavioural body image therapy for Body Dysmorphic Disorder. *Journal of Consulting and Clinical Psychology*, **63**, 263–269.

Rosen, J., Srebnik, D., Saltzberg, E. & Wendt, S. (1991). Development of a body image avoidance questionnaire. *Psychological Assessment*, **3**, 32–37.

Rosenberg, M. (1965). *Society and the Adolescent Self-image*. Princeton: Princeton University Press.

Rozin, P. & Fallon, A. (1987). A perspective on disgust. *Psychological Review*, **94**, 23–41.

Rucker, C. & Cash, T.F. (1992). Body-images, body-size perceptions and eating behaviors among African-Americans and white college women. *International Journal of Eating Disorders*, **12**, 291–300.

Rumsey, N. (1998). Visible disfigurement. In M. Johnston & D. Johnston (Eds), *Comprehensive Clinical Psychology* (vol. 8; pp. 575–593). Amsterdam: Elsevier.

Rumsey, N., Bull, R. & Gahagan, D. (1982). The effect of facial disfigurement on the proxemic behaviour of the general public. *Journal of Applied Social Psychology*, **12**, 137–150.

Ryharczyk, B., Nyenhuis, D., Nicholas, J., Cash, T.F. & Kaiser, J. (1995). Body-image, perceived social stigma and the prediction of psychosocial adjustment to leg amputation. *Rehabilitation Psychology*, **40**, 95–110.

Sarwer, D., Wadden, T. & Foster, G. (1998). Assessment of body image dissatisfaction in obese women: specificity, severity and clinical significance. *Journal of Consulting and Clinical Psychology*, **66**, 651–654.

Scambler, G. & Hopkins, A. (1986). Being epileptic: coming to terms with stigma. *Sociology of Health and Illness*, **8**, 26–43.

Shackelford, T. & Larsen, R. (1999). Facial attractiveness and health. *Evolution and Human Behavior*, **20**, 71–76.

Smart, L. & Wegner, D. (1999). Covering up what can't be seen: concealable stigma and mental control. *Journal of Personality and Social Psychology*, **77**, 474–486.

Strauman, T. & Higgins, E.T. (1987). Automatic activation of self-discrepancies and emotional syndromes: when cognitive structures influence affect. *Journal of Personality and Social Psychology*, **53**, 1004–1014.

Thompson, A. & Kent, G. (2001). Adjusting to disfigurement: processes involved in dealing with being visibly different. *Clinical Psychology Review*, **21**, 663–682.

Thompson, A., Kent, G. & Smith, J. (2002). Living with vitiligo: dealing with difference. *British Journal of Health Psychology*, **7**, 213–225.

Thompson, J., Penner, L. & Altabe, M. (1990). Procedures, problems and progress in the assessment of body image. In T.F. Cash & T. Pruzinsky (Eds), *Body Images. Development Deviance and Change* (pp. 21–48). London: Guilford Press.

Troster, H. (1997). Disclose or conceal? Strategies of information management in persons with epilepsy. *Epilepsia*, **38**, 1227–1237.

Van Swearingen, J. & Brach, J. (1996). The facial disability index: reliability and validity of a disability assessment instrument for disorders of the facial neuromuscular system. *Physical Therapy*, **76**, 1288–1298.

Walters, E. (1997). Problems faced by children and families living with visible differences. In R. Lansdown, N. Rumsey, E. Bradbury, T. Carr & J. Partridge (Eds), *Visibly Different. Coping with Disfigurement* (pp. 112–120). Oxford: Butterworth Heinemann.

Zigmond, A. & Snaith, R. (1983). The Hospital Anxiety and Depression Scale. *Acta Psychiatrica Scandinavica*, **67**, 361–370.

CHAPTER 21

Psychological Management for Sexual Health and HIV

Barbara Hedge

University of Waikato, New Zealand

INTRODUCTION

Sexual health is a relatively new concept. Before the twentieth century, sexual behaviour was generally viewed in spiritual or biological terms. More recently, it has been studied as an activity with associated social and mental health implications as well as reproductive outcomes. The risks associated with sexual behaviours have become increasingly obvious since the 1980s as an increasing number of individuals became infected with herpes and with Human Immunodeficiency Virus (HIV). During the twentieth century we saw the metamorphosis of the venereal disease clinic into the sexual health centre. No longer is there simply a medical facility, discreetly located at the back of a hospital, for the treatment of sexually transmitted infections (STIs) such as syphilis and gonorrhoea. Sexual health centres continue to provide important medical assessments and interventions, but most also offer multidisciplinary input into a wider range of problems associated with sexual health, such as managing the psychological sequelae of STIs, sexual dysfunction, relationship difficulties and sexual assault.

In addition, many sexual health clinics manage the needs of people with HIV disease, particularly when they require outpatient services. As it is now well established that the transmission of HIV, which can lead to AIDS, is increased by the presence of untreated STIs (Cohen, 1998; Laga et al., 1993; Nkengasong et al., 2001; Schacker, 2001), we now see the maintenance of sexual health to be high on the international health agenda.

The value of psychological support in helping people to cope with unwelcome diagnoses, to live with chronic infections and to address sexual dysfunction and relationship difficulties is now well recognised. This chapter will introduce STIs, HIV and other problems frequently encountered in a sexual health centre, consider their psychological sequelae and discuss relevant psychological interventions. Finally, sexual assault and its consequences will be covered.

Handbook of Clinical Health Psychology. Edited by S. Llewelyn and P. Kennedy.
© 2003 John Wiley & Sons, Ltd.

SEXUALLY TRANSMITTED INFECTIONS

STIs are some of the most common infectious diseases in the world. Three hundred and thirty-three million new STI infections were reported in 1995 (WHO, 1995). In recent years there has been a change in the spectrum of STIs commonly seen. The prevalence of bacterial infections, e.g. gonorrhoea, which respond well to antibiotic treatments has decreased, while that of those caused by viral infection, e.g. genital warts, herpes simplex and HIV, has increased.

The symptoms of STIs frequently include localised, painful, burning or itching lesions or discharge in the genital, anal and oral regions. STIs may also give rise to systemic disease and can have significant serious consequences. For example, genital warts have been linked to cervical carcinoma (Ho et al., 1998), gonorrhoea can lead to sterility, syphilis can damage the cardiovascular and central nervous systems and chlamydia can cause pelvic inflammatory disease and subsequent ectopic pregnancy or infertility (Wasserheit, 1989).

PSYCHOLOGICAL DISTRESS AND DIFFICULTIES

A high incidence of psychiatric and psychological disturbance in genitourinary clinics has been reported (Catalan et al., 1981; Fitzpatrick, Frost & Ikkos, 1986; Ikos et al., 1987; Mayou, 1975; Pedder & Goldberg, 1970). These studies find between 20 and 45% of sexual health clinic attenders to be classifiable as psychiatric cases. The difference in case rates reported by Fitzpatrick, Frost and Ikkos (1986), who assessed psychiatric status before individuals saw the doctor (43%), and Pedder and Goldberg (1970), whose participants completed the ratings after the consultation (30%), and the finding of Bhanji and Mahony (1978), that less than 5% were referred for psychiatric assessment, suggest that the distress caused by the immediate presenting problem may result in an elevated but non-pathological level of anxiety. Alternatively, it is possible that psychological distress is not usually assessed during a routine sexual infection consultation and that many individuals are not receiving appropriate onward referrals.

An interesting question is whether some individuals are psychologically more vulnerable than others to acquiring an STI. Behaviours that are clearly linked to an increased risk of infection are high partner numbers, specific sexual practices, and the context in which the sex occurs (Ross, 1986). Early work (Hart, 1977) related sexual risk behaviours to an individual's personality. Extroverts, as measured by the Eysenck Personality Inventory, had higher levels of STIs. Supportive evidence is provided by Eysenck and Wilson (1979), who report that extroverts have their first sexual experience earlier, have more frequent sex, with more different partners.

Distress in genitourinary clinics does not appear to be limited to those with a diagnosable infection (Barczak et al., 1988; Catalan et al., 1981). For some, the psychological symptomatology appears to be related to abnormal concerns with illness (Ikkos et al., 1987).

Other common presentations in sexual health clinics are sexual dysfunction and relationship difficulties (Catalan et al., 1981). Although these may accompany an STI or the belief of an infection, presentation at the STI clinic is frequently a pragmatic choice. In many countries, including the UK, STI clinics have an open door policy to ensure easy access to STI treatment. The confidential, open access sexual health centre now proves popular for individuals with a diverse range of complaints.

Psychological Response to the Diagnosis of a Sexually Transmitted Infection

Most investigations into the psychological reactions associated with having an STI have studied individuals with genital herpes. Genital herpes is a common, often recurrent and frequently painful infection. Corey et al. (1983) reported that individuals with recurrent genital herpes experienced pain (67% men, 88% women) and itching (85% men, 87% women). Luby and Gillespie (1981) describe the reaction to a diagnosis of genital herpes to be akin to bereavement. They describe a series of reactions from denial, realisation that they have herpes, belief that there is a cure, loneliness, anger towards sexual partners, to the fear of sexual deprivation and the development of a poor self-image.

Not all individuals react similarly to the illness. Silver et al. (1986) found that those with frequent recurrences viewed their future as beyond their control, and attempted to deal with it by engaging in emotion-focused, avoidant, wishful thinking rather than trying to exert personal control over their illness-related thoughts or to use problem-focused coping strategies to shape their future. Similar findings by Manne, Sandler and Zautra (1986) suggest that attention to the beliefs associated with the diagnosis and to the coping strategies used by individuals with herpes might be useful points for therapeutic interventions.

The psychological impact of a first episode of herpes was investigated by Carney et al. (1993). A sample of individuals presenting with a first episode of genital herpes was compared with a sample without herpes presenting to the same genitourinary clinic, and a sample presenting with a chronic skin condition to the outpatient dermatology clinic. Significantly more individuals with a first episode of genital herpes (62%) were classified as psychiatric cases, as measured by the General Health Questionnaire (GHQ), than were in the genitourinary clinic control group (34%). The former were significantly more concerned about their infection than either of the control groups. Psychological well-being in the genital herpes sample, as measured by the Hospital Anxiety and Depression (HAD) scale, showed 52% to be anxious and 16% to be depressed at the first visit. These studies suggest that the psychological impact of a diagnosis of a genital herpes is high.

RESPONSE TO LIVING WITH A CHRONIC, TRANSMISSIBLE INFECTION

People with a diagnosis of genital herpes face the realisation that they will have to live with a potentially recurring, lifelong infection. This is particularly apparent if they experience frequent recurrences of symptoms. It would be reasonable to hypothesise that people with frequent recurrences would experience lower mood. Alternatively, low mood or high stress might directly reactivate the virus (Dalkvisk et al., 1995; Goldmeier & Johnson, 1982; Goldmeier et al., 1986, 1988; Kemeny et al., 1989; McLarnon & Kaloupek, 1988). A number of studies have investigated the causal link between psychological distress and recurrences. Reviewing the literature there is inconclusive support for either argument (Green & Kocsis, 1997; VanderPlate & Aral, 1987). Many studies are difficult to interpret because they are retrospective and susceptible to systematic biases in recall and perception; others suffer from sampling difficulties in that they only study those with frequent or severe recurrences and do not investigate the psychological impact on those (the majority) who have infrequent or mild recurrences. A prospective study by Rand et al. (1990) found no evidence for an increase in normal daily stress using the Daily Stress Questionnaire (Vuchinich & Tucker, 1988) before a recurrence of genital herpes. Cassidy et al. (1997) found no association between anxiety or depression and the number of recurrences.

An effective drug, Acyclovir, which, when taken prophylactically, reduces the probability of an occurrence, and when taken therapeutically reduces the severity of an attack (Mindel et al., 1988), is now widely available. Carney et al. (1993) found that the availability of Acyclovir reduced concern about the diagnosis and reported a lower rate of psychiatric caseness in those taking it. The sharp improvement seen in psychological functioning within three months of receiving Acyclovir suggests a causal link. It is possible, however, that the lower rate of psychiatric cases could be due to the effect of time—individuals having come to terms with having herpes.

Studies of those who have had multiple recurrences of genital herpes over a long period of time clearly report on those with most severe disease and are unlikely to be representative of the whole population. However, such studies (Drob, Loemer & Lifschutz, 1985; Keller, Jadack & Mims, 1991; Luby & Klinge, 1985) have identified a wide range of psychological problems including relationship difficulties, sexual difficulties, fears of transmitting the virus to others and feelings of sexual unattractiveness.

SEXUAL DYSFUNCTION CONSEQUENT ON THE INFECTION

It is not uncommon for sexual problems to be reported by individuals with STIs. These can be associated with pain from the infection, with fear of reinfection or fear of infecting a current sexual partner. There is little published research into how couples manage genital herpes. However, a qualitative study by Griffiths (1999) gives some insight into possible difficulties. Griffiths found discrepancies between the accounts of individuals with herpes and those of their sexual partners. The former reported no change in the frequency of sex, while the partners rated sex as less enjoyable due to the need for condoms and anxiety about infection. Sex was not usually negotiated explicitly, but a system of cues (both verbal and non-verbal) was developed within the couple to determine when and how sex would occur.

When there is a clear transient link between a sexual problem and an STI that will remit once the STI is cured, then education to clarify the temporary nature of the problem and information of what is possible in the meantime may well be sufficient. When this is not the explanation, it is important that sexual dysfunctions are not dismissed, as poor sexual functioning can be associated with low mood and perceived low quality of life (Catalan et al., 1981; Rosen, 1998).

STRESS, SOCIAL SUPPORT, COPING SKILLS AND SELF-EFFICACY

How well individuals adjust to chronic illness can partly be explained by the coping strategies they employ, the perceived availability of social support and the extent of their self-efficacy. A number of models have been proposed to explain how psychological and physical dysfunction are related to stress. One such model (Lazarus & Folkman, 1984) suggests that an individual's coping response is determined by his or her appraisal of both the extent of threat posed by the illness (primary appraisal), and the resources (including their possible coping strategies) perceived as available to help them to address the situation (secondary appraisal).

Coping strategies can be problem focused, i.e. intent on changing the problem aspects of the stressor, or emotion focused, i.e. intent on managing the emotional responses to the stressful situation. The choice of coping strategy is influenced by the extent to which the person appraises the situation as changeable or controllable and the extent to which they perceive each coping strategy as beneficial. Thus, individuals may employ a range of coping strategies, some of which are more adaptive than others. A number of questionnaires to measure coping strategies are available, including the Ways of Coping Questionnaire described in the *Manual of the Ways of Coping Questionnaire* (Folkman & Lazarus, 1988).

Coping with Genital Herpes

High scores on active coping (steps to remove the stressor), planning (devising action strategies before an event) and positive reinterpretation (managing the distressing emotions attached to the event) are generally found to be useful in managing recurrences (Manne & Sandler, 1984). Cassidy et al. (1997) found that those reporting frequent recurrences of genital herpes were less likely to use adaptive coping strategies. They suggest that if individuals are unable to plan how to deal with stressors, cope with the emotional distress that a recurrence arouses, or take an active role in minimising its impact, then the perceived link between stress and genital herpes may be strengthened. Stress can then be perceived as the cause of the recurrence.

Social Support

A factor frequently reported to be a buffer against stress is social support (Cohen & Wills, 1985). Thus, it might be expected that individuals with high levels of social support would cope more effectively with genital herpes. Interestingly, the findings are conflicting. For example, Silver et al. (1986) found that the number of recurrences was the same in those with and without good social support, but the psychopathology was less in those with good social support. Others, e.g. VanderPlate, Aral and Magder (1988) and Longo and Clum (1989), found that availability of social support did not predict the severity of an episode, while Hoon et al. (1991) reported individuals with greater social support to have more recurrences.

The social support hypothesis would suggest that membership of a self-help group might decrease psychological distress. However, studies looking at distress in members of self-help groups frequently find the opposite, i.e. that those in self-help groups show continuing distress and report worse adjustment than those who are not members (Manne, Sandler & Zautra, 1986). It is likely that this reflects a self-selection bias. It could be that those with more severe or frequent symptoms join a self-help group, or that the positive effects of the group for some are confounded by the unhelpful "reassurance" of others who provide an increase of attention to negative symptoms (Salkovskis & Warwick, 1986). Sometimes the coping strategies of a self-help group are directed towards a different problem, e.g. a search for a "cure", rather than to the adaptive problem of how to live with the infection.

SELF-EFFICACY

Self-efficacy describes an individual's confidence that he or she can perform a desired action (Bandura, Reese & Adams, 1982; Bandura et al., 1988). Lazarus and Folkman (1987) suggested that self-efficacy could be a powerful factor in mediating the stress response, i.e. a belief in one's ability to effect one's behaviour might relate to whether or not a potentially stressful event results in a stress response. This suggests that individuals with high self-efficacy might be better able to cope with a recurrence of genital herpes as they are more able to disclose their infection, and negotiate safer sex or sexual abstinence.

Summary

In summary, although the causative link between stress and recurrent episodes of genital herpes may be difficult to establish, it is clear that severe psychological distress can be associated with a first episode and continue in those who experience frequent recurrences. There is clearly a need for the psychological support of such individuals to be recognised and therapeutic support made available.

HUMAN PAPILLOMAVIRUS

Much less attention has been paid to the psychological impact of other STIs. Genital warts that are a consequence of human papillomavirus (HPV) are estimated to occur in 1% of sexually active adults (Koutsky & Kiviat, 1999). It has been widely publicised that HPV, which causes genital warts, is associated with the development of cervical cancer (Koutsky et al., 1992). Knowledge of this association between HPV and cancers can be disturbing.

A number of studies have investigated the psychological sequelae of a first episode of genital warts. Filiberti et al. (1993) found that 27% of individuals with a first episode of genital warts expressed a fear of cancer, and twice this number (55%) reported sexual dysfunctions and deteriorating emotional relationships with their partners. Clarke et al. (1996) found that more than 75% of a sample recruited from the readership of an HPV newsletter reported having experienced depression and anger at diagnosis, and although symptoms were less severe over time, more than 30% continued to experience some distress. Clarke et al. (1996) also found that sexual enjoyment and activity had been negatively affected by the diagnosis, but reported difficulties decreasing over time. Conaglen et al. (2001) report 68% of those with a first episode of genital warts to be classified as psychiatric cases, decreasing to 55% at a four-week follow-up. Twenty-nine per cent of men and 10% of women in their sample expressed sexual concerns at their first visit; concerns remained at the four-week follow-up. Discrepancies between studies could be a function of the sampling method adopted. Clarke et al. (1996) surveyed the readership of an HPV newsletter while Conaglen et al. (2001) studied a sexual health centre sample. Neither is likely to be a representative sample of all those with HPV.

INTERVENTION STRATEGIES FOR THE DEVELOPMENT OF ADAPTIVE COPING

Given the high levels of stress reported by individuals diagnosed with an STI, particularly those with recurring genital herpes, strategies are required to minimise the effects of the stressors. Managing an STI requires an individual successfully to:

- develop adaptive strategies for coping with infection
- disclose infection
- negotiate safer sex
- decrease sexual risk behaviours.

There is a substantial body of evidence that suggests that therapy based on a cognitive-behavioural model can be efficacious in reducing stress and disorders of mood such as anxiety and depression (Beck, 1976; Salkovskis, 1996). Cognitive-behavioural therapy aims to teach people methods of self-management. Cognitive therapy focuses on reappraising interpretations that give rise to mood and behavioural difficulties. It identifies cognitions that are linked to emotional states, then guides the reframing and decatastrophising of dysfunctional cognitions. The reframed cognitions are tested through behavioural experiments, both in the session and then in context (Beck, 1995; Greenberger & Padesky, 1995; Hawton et al., 1989). The following case study illustrates the method.

Case Study: Natalie

A young woman, Natalie, was distraught when diagnosed with genital herpes.

Initial beliefs:

- I am no longer sexually attractive
- I will never be able to marry and have children.

Reframing of negative beliefs and biases:

- I have many other positive attributes
- Everyone has some attributes that are less attractive than others
- A man who I would consider marrying would be interested in me as a whole person, and would not reject me on the basis of intermittent symptoms
- Given the number of individuals diagnosed with genital herpes and the number of new infections every year, it appears that many people with genital herpes must still be sexually attractive and sexually active.

In order to gain confidence in herself as sexually attractive, Natalie was then encouraged to explore the validity of her reframed cognitions:

- Keep a record of all the positive remarks made towards me
- Keep a record of all appreciative behaviours of others in social situations.

Natalie had no difficulty in reframing her cognitions but was still not confident of being able to cope with sexual rejection. She continued to avoid situations that might lead to sexual involvement.

Disclosure of Infection

Telling a sexual partner that one has an STI can be difficult, particularly if a possible consequence of disclosure is rejection. For individuals who hesitate to disclose, a problem-solving approach would be valuable (Hawton & Kirk, 1989).

In order to solve a problem successfully, a person must:

- identify the problem
- generate many possible solutions
- consider the advantages and disadvantages of each one
- weigh up the overall benefit of all
- choose the best possible solution
- decide how to live with the decision if it does not have the desired results
- implement that solution
- live with the decision made
- monitor the reaction of others when the solution is implemented.

Continuing with the example of Natalie, she was introduced to the problem-solving approach and asked to identify all the possible ways in which she could address sexual relationships now that she had genital herpes. Table 21.1 shows her generated solutions together with her assessment of the advantages and disadvantages associated with each.

When weighing up the advantages and disadvantages of each possible solution Natalie realised that none was perfect. Some solutions were easier in the short term, and some that seemed important were less so once she identified that a man who talked about her personal problems to others was not the type of man she wanted to associate with.

Natalie decided that the best solution was for her to get to know a potential partner well before she had sex with him or told him that she had herpes. This gave time for her to make a considered judgement about a potential sexual partner before putting it to the test, thus decreasing the chance of rejection.

Role-plays in sessions then helped Natalie to develop the communication skills of judging an appropriate time and place to tell, to develop an accurate but positive description of how sex with genital herpes could be managed successfully in a relationship, and to cope with both positive and negative responses from a potential sexual partner. Together with some information booklets to ensure that she understood the necessary constraints on sexual behaviour, Natalie resumed her social life. At follow-up she reported having coped successfully with one rejection following disclosure, and that she was now in a sexual relationship that she believed had good long-term prospects.

Although many people do not wish to make public their infection, there are some advantages to a group intervention for individuals with similar problems. Although role-play with the therapist in an individual session is always possible, a group enables each person to role-play all possible solutions with a number of different partners; all within a secure, safe setting. Additionally, it can be useful for group members to share their successful and unsuccessful approaches, providing peer support and aiding pre-event planning. However, some caution must be given. A number of studies of self-help groups have reported high levels of symptomatology. It could be that, in an unstructured group, members receive most reinforcement for presenting a worse case history, thus increasing their attention to and reporting of negative outcomes (Salkovskis & Warwick, 1986).

OUTCOME STUDIES

Although there are cognitive-behavioural strategies that seem appropriate to the psychological sequelae of STIs, very few studies investigate the efficacy of interventions to decrease its impact. McLarnon and Kaloupek (1988) compared the effectiveness of a

Table 21.1 Possible solutions to sexual relationships post-infection with genital herpes

Possible solutions	Advantages	Disadvantages
Decide never to have sex or a relationship again	Never be embarrassed by telling Never be rejected	Will miss sex Would like a relationship Would like to have children
Wait until I meet a man who tells me that he has genital herpes	I wouldn't have to worry about infecting him I wouldn't be embarrassed He wouldn't reject me	I might have to wait a long time People don't always tell you—that's how I became infected Just because we both have herpes doesn't mean we will make a good couple
Look for a man who already has genital herpes	Would actively seek someone who wouldn't reject me because of herpes I wouldn't have to worry about infecting him I wouldn't be embarrassed He wouldn't reject me	May have to tell a whole (self-help) group that I have herpes Would feel I belonged to a special odd class of people who couldn't have sex with who they wanted Just because we both have herpes doesn't mean we will make a good couple
Tell a person who I would like to have sex with that I have genital herpes	If he still wanted to have sex or a relationship with me I would know that he really liked me	I would be embarrassed by telling If he rejected me I would feel terrible He might tell others, then everyone would know
Tell only a man who I know well and would like to have sex and a long-term relationship with	If he still wanted to have sex or a relationship with me I would know that he really liked me I could judge that he wouldn't be nasty or tell everyone, before I told him If we've seen each other a number of times without having sex then he must like other things about me	If he rejects me I will know that I have poor judgement of men Or That he wasn't the right man for me anyway
Have sex without telling the person that I have herpes	I wouldn't be embarrassed He wouldn't reject me	I might infect him with herpes and he would know it was me If we got on well, at some time he would find out and then he might leave me for deceiving him

cognitive-therapy group and a discussion group. No differences in psychological distress were found but the cognitive-behavioural therapy group reported fewer recurrences. The number of recurrences has also been shown to decrease following relaxation training (Koehn, Burnett & Stark, 1993). These interventions are reasonably simple, time-limited and so relatively inexpensive and it would seem beneficial to offer these in a sexual health centre setting.

Although the evidence of effective interventions is minimal, the issues raised by individuals with herpes do give an insight into interventions that might be efficacious. The utilisation of a "problem-solving" approach (Hawton & Kirk, 1989) allows the issues of relevance for a particular individual to be analysed and tested and responses altered in a manner that builds support for negative consequences.

Anxiety reduction techniques can help people to lower stress between occurrences and during an occurrence. Training in anxiety management techniques, such as relaxation and breath control, can enable individuals to develop methods of reducing stress—for example, that associated with a recurrence of genital herpes—and thus minimise its negative impact on life.

Such techniques could be utilised either in an individual therapy or in group interventions. The latter would have an advantage of allowing social support to be incorporated in a controlled fashion, i.e. the possibility of a self-help group reinforcing non-adaptive coping strategies could be avoided.

REDUCING THE PROBABILITY OF FUTURE INFECTION

In order to prevent the spread of infection it is necessary that individuals can communicate their desire for sexual abstinence or for safer sex. For this they require not only the knowledge of what and when is safe, but also sufficient self-efficacy to communicate and maintain their desired behaviours. Training in social and assertiveness skills can increase the ability to cope with sexual situations.

It is important that any intervention is directed to the appropriate location on a stage of change model (Prochaska, DiClemente & Norcross, 1992). Fishbein et al. (1993) found women attending STD clinics in the USA to be more likely than men to consider using condoms. Although many of the sample attending the STD clinics had never used condoms and had no intention of using them consistently, others had formed long-range or short-range intentions to begin using condoms consistently. So, even within this select group it is apparent that any intervention that aims to change condom-use behaviour needs to focus on the individual's readiness for change.

HUMAN IMMUNODEFICIENCY VIRUS

In the early 1980s reports from the Centres for Disease Control (1981) first described Acquired Immune Deficiency Syndrome (AIDS), an acute illness in gay men which was usually fatal. In 1983 an infectious agent, the Human Immunodeficiency Virus (HIV), was identified as the causal factor of AIDS. It soon became clear that HIV is not only a disease of gay men, but also of heterosexuals.

The most frequent route of transmission is through penetrative sex between men, or between men and women. HIV can also be transmitted through blood and blood products. This may occur through the sharing of inadequately sterilised needles, syringes or other skin-piercing instruments while injecting drugs and occasionally through needle-stick injuries. The virus can also be passed from person to person via donated organs or semen, and from mother to child during pregnancy, at the time of delivery or postnatally through breast-feeding.

The global estimate of HIV infection is now more than 43 million individuals living with HIV (UN AIDS, 2002). In 2001 an estimated five million people became infected with HIV; over 800 000 of these were children and three million died from an HIV-related illness. The epidemic is now worldwide, with sub-Saharan Africa being the worst affected region of the world. Eastern Europe, Central, South and South East Asia including India and China are all experiencing fast-growing, widespread epidemics (De Cock & Weiss, 2000).

HIV disease is a chronic condition in which the asymptomatic phase, i.e. without symptoms, may last for many years. A diagnosis of AIDS is made when HIV has damaged the immune system to such an extent that certain opportunistic infections, tumours or encephalopathy are observed (Centres for Disease Control, 1992). Until 1996 most medical interventions were directed towards the control of diseases that occur as a result of the lowered immune function. In the late 1980s it was found that some benefit could be obtained by taking a single antiretroviral drug such as Zidovudine (AZT). Since then, an increasing number of antiretroviral drugs, including protease inhibitors, which inhibit the replication of HIV, have become available. When three or more of these are used in combination (Highly Active Antiretroviral Therapy or HAART) they effectively reduce the viral load and increase the CD4 count.[1] HAART is considered responsible for the increased survival times and decreased bouts of illness and decreased progression rates to AIDS (Hogg et al., 1998; Palella, Delaney & Moorman, 1998; Paredes, Mocroft & Kirk, 2000; Sepkowitz, 1998). However, HIV disease remains a life-threatening illness with no cure.

Psychological involvement commonly addresses four target areas: adjustment to HIV and stage of disease, managing the possibility of an extended life with a chronic disease, maintenance of adherence to antiretroviral medications, and decreasing risk behaviours. These will be considered first, followed by some particular difficulties which are frequently encountered by individuals with HIV disease.

Psychological Distress and HIV Disease

Many intense, negative psychological reactions including anxiety, depression and relationship difficulties have been reported in people with HIV disease (Hedge et al., 1992; King, 1989). Psychological symptoms have been reported at all stages of infection. The time of testing is frequently associated with high anxiety. For those who test negative this anxiety is soon dissipated. For those who test positive there frequently follows a period of gradual adjustment during which distress and psychological symptoms decrease (Perry et al., 1990). Other studies report psychological distress occurring during the asymptomatic phase (Egan, Brettle & Goodwin, 1992; Hedge et al., 1992; Pugh et al., 1994), with symptomatic infection (Catalan et al., 1992; Egan, Brettle & Goodwin, 1992; Hedge et al., 1992), and with a diagnosis of AIDS (Chuang et al., 1989; Hedge et al., 1992). Together, these studies suggest that all stages of HIV disease can be associated with severe psychological pathology.

Living with HIV is rarely uneventful. Circumstances such as a deterioration in health, indications that antiretroviral therapy should be started or changed, the need to tell parents the diagnosis, etc., can increase the psychological distress of living with HIV at any stage of

---

[1] A commonly used marker of immunosuppression is a count of CD4 cells. There is a trend for a decreasing CD4 count to be associated with increasing clinical symptoms of illness, with individuals becoming more vulnerable to particular infections and cancers. The viral load count is a measure of the amount of virus detected in the blood. The CD4 count together with the viral load count are good predictors of an individual's clinical disease pattern.

the disease. Individuals appear particularly vulnerable when a number of stressful events occur simultaneously (Hedge et al., 1992).

Most of the available antiretroviral medications do not penetrate the blood–brain barrier. It was therefore not immediately obvious whether the rate of cognitive disorders documented in the pre-HAART era would decrease. There is now some evidence that HAART does protect the central nervous system (Cohen et al., 2001; Stankoff et al., 2001; Suarez et al., 2001). However, not all individuals opt to take HAART and cases of organic brain disease still present.

The change in life expectancy seen in the mid-1990s, largely brought about by HAART, led some to consider HIV as a chronic disease, comparable to diabetes. As such, many assumed that the psychological distress of having HIV would fade away as it became an "ordinary" disease. However, for those infected, this is probably the time of most uncertainty since HIV's emergence in the early 1980s. Individuals are still faced with the reality that people continue to die from HIV-related illnesses. The length of remission that can be expected from HAART is uncertain. For some, drug resistance will require them to change their medication regimen and there is always concern as to whether they will be able to tolerate the side-effects of medications. Living with uncertainty remains a challenge for people with HIV.

Suicide and HIV

Individuals who have a chronic disease are frequently found to have an elevated risk of suicide. A meta-analysis of studies prior to 1992 (Harris & Barraclough, 1994) found the risk of suicide in HIV to be seven times the expected rate.

Reliable suicide rates can be difficult to obtain (Pugh, O'Donnell & Catalan, 1993) as there is frequently a reluctance to specify suicide as a cause of death. Consequently, reported numbers are frequently underestimates of actual rates (Kreitman, 1993). In addition, the HIV status of a person who has completed suicide is not always obtained.

Some early studies reported an elevated risk of suicide in persons with HIV (Marzuk et al., 1988), and, more recently, a wide range of rates of suicide in people with HIV have been reported (Cote, Biggar & Danneberg, 1992; Mitchell, 1999). However, it is difficult to compare studies or assess trends over time as not all studies adjust for sex, age, race or other relevant risk factors.

Individuals with HIV often have a number of general risk factors for increased suicide risk, such as a previous attempt, psychiatric morbidity, depression, substance misuse, homosexuality, gender (Beckett & Shenson, 1993; Guze & Robins, 1970). It appears that these factors mediate the association between HIV and suicide. It is not clear whether HIV with its particular stressors contributes an additional risk factor for suicide.

Suicide ideation, i.e. thoughts relating to behaviours directly harmful to life, is commonly reported by people with HIV (Hedge & Sherr, 1995; Kelly et al., 1998; Wood et al., 1997). There is little agreement for increased risk at any time point in the disease. A recent study (Goggin et al., 2000) found a 17% prevalence of gay men with HIV disease to have future plans to end their life. As the suicide ideation was not associated with other psychiatric diagnoses, the authors suggest that suicidal thoughts or plans may be an expression of control and independence in this time of uncertainty for those living with HIV.

It is not yet clear what impact HAART is having on suicide rates. The psychological impact of HAART may be complex. Although for many, improved physical health brings improved mental health and quality of life, for some the side-effects of the antiretroviral medications, or the required adherence to the medication regime, or the prospect of being a long-term survivor after most of one's colleagues and friends have died, can lower the quality of life experienced. An improvement in health may present some with a dilemma. Having prepared for a reduced length of life, and maybe prepared for death, they face the challenge of an extended life. For those who do not respond well to HAART there could be disappointment and guilt if it is surmised that their poor progress is associated with poor adherence. The changing impact of HIV since the introduction of HAART means that we may see a different profile of suicide risk emerging in this population.

Although many people with HIV disease have become infected in recent years, some have been living with the virus for more than 18 years. These individuals have seen the prognosis of those with HIV shift from a rapid death following an AIDS diagnosis to a long, but unpredictable future. Unfortunately, many have lost friends and companions who died before the advent of HAART. Many gave up employment in the belief that they were in the last years of their lives. Although well, they still require frequent hospital appointments and may have to take medications at inconvenient times with food restrictions that are difficult to manage in private or during work hours. For some, it is not clear what they have to live for: their chances of returning into employment are slim; their emotional losses have made it difficult to re-engage in intimate relationships; and they have lost their supportive network of friends.

MEDICATION ISSUES AND ADHERENCE

Adherence to HAART is vital if viral suppression is to be maintained. Unless viral replication is virtually eliminated any mutation that is resistant to the HAART regimen being taken can rapidly multiply. Drug-resistant viruses then render the individual susceptible to immune dysfunction illnesses. Unfortunately, the complex and demanding medication regimens required, and the unpleasant side-effects experienced by some people on HAART, have made adherence to drug regimens a problematic issue. Some medications must be taken at precise time intervals under strict nutritional conditions, and some have notable toxic effects. Incorporating them into a daily routine is no mean feat. Adherence requires considerable self-discipline.

As well as being an issue for affected individuals, who are then vulnerable to increased mortality (Hogg et al., 2002), non-adherence can also have a bearing on public health (Wainberg & Friedland, 1998). It is likely that those who are on HAART and whose viral load is low or undetectable[2] are less likely to transmit virus through unprotected sex; however, infection is still possible. Thus, non-adherence can increase the probability of transmission of drug-resistant virus. There is already evidence that a drug-resistant virus in newly infected persons has been found (Boden et al., 1999). Thus, people newly infected with HIV could find themselves unable to benefit from HAART.

---

[2] It is thought that virus is never completely eradicated (Blankson, Persaud & Siliciano, 2002). However, at their lower limit tests for virus are only able to detect a certain amount of virus. Below this level, a count of zero indicates that the test is unable to detect virus. It does not mean that HIV has been eradicated.

Lipodystrophy

One of the consequences of HAART can be a change in the deposition of body fat (lipodys-trophy). This leads to a distinctive change in a person's physical appearance with wasted muscles and an increase in central fat deposits around their body organs. This has become a distinguishing marker in some of those with HIV, much as the blue/black lesions of Karposi's sarcoma (a cancer frequently appearing as skin lesions) did before the advent of HAART. Testa and Lederking (1999) assessed the impact of HIV-associated wasting on quality of life through focus groups. They found wasting to have a negative impact that was associated with loss of energy, changes in appearance, physical, psychological social and sexual functioning.

Sex

When ill, for many individuals sex becomes the least of their concerns. While HAART has improved the physical health of many people, a number of these report sexual dysfunction. Difficulties with libido, erection maintenance or failure to ejaculate have all been noted (Lallemand et al., 2002). The cause of sexual difficulties is likely to be various. For some it seems probable that it is directly related to HIV, e.g. a loss of testosterone, for others a medication side-effect and for others that it is at least partly due to psychological factors (Catalan, Burgess & Klimes, 1995).

Psychological factors associated with sexual dysfunction in people with HIV disease have been found to include fear of rejection, fear of transmitting HIV to a sexual partner, fear of developing a relationship in order to prevent oneself from future trauma or loss if an HIV infected partner should become ill or die (Catalan, Burgess & Klimes, 1995). Thus, appropriate treatment can only follow a careful assessment of the formulation of the sexual problems in context. A shot of testosterone or a prescription for Viagra may be useful for some, but will not be the treatment of choice for many.

PROCREATION ISSUES

The vertical transmission of HIV from mother to her unborn child varies between 13 and 52% (Mok, 1994). The AIDS Clinical Trials Group study 076 (Conner et al., 1994) showed that when Zidovudine was administered orally to the mother after the first trimester of pregnancy, intravenously during labour and delivery, and orally to the infant for the first six weeks of life, then transmission rates fell from 22.6 to 7.6%. Other HAART regimens, delivery by caesarean section and an avoidance of breast-feeding, can lower the rate of transmission even further. Simpler, less expensive medication regimes that also reduce the rates of transmission are increasingly being used and found effective in developing countries such as Brazil.

The effect of discovering one's HIV status in pregnancy may be devastating. There is no evidence that the psychological effects of finding out one's HIV positive status do not apply to pregnant women. Indeed, an HIV diagnosis has significance for the mother, for the sexual partner and for the unborn child. It may reveal recent sexual infidelities, drug use or the past history of either partner. It is suggested that a woman needs to have considered such issues before testing. If mandatory testing for pregnant women is implemented, then it is possible that women who fear discovering their HIV positive status may fail to make appropriate use of available antenatal services and thus cause their babies harm in some other way.

Help with Conception

Now that people with HIV disease are living longer there is an increasing desire to "normalise" all aspects of life after infection. The ability to procreate and raise a family is generally seen as a basic human right. In some cultures the inability to have a child has implications for a couple's standing in the extended family. A man may lose his credibility if he is unable to produce an heir; a woman may not be perceived as adult until she has a child. Thus, if we are to perceive HIV as having a long chronic phase then entitlement to a "normal" life during this time has to be an objective of health and social services. Wesley et al. (2000) interviewed HIV-positive mothers who expressed joy at motherhood, found that it met their own needs, and showed that they had a life apart from HIV. Women expressed a desire for their whole lives to be considered meaningful, not just their HIV-positive status.

One of the requests seen increasingly frequently is for assistance with conception when natural methods have not brought the desired results. Once again, ethical questions have been raised (Englert et al., 2001). Is it fair to conceive a child when there is a chance that it will be infected with HIV? Reactions from gynaecologists and obstetricians have been mixed; some are happy to assist a couple while others make HIV a criteria for exclusion from assisted reproductive services. Others take a middle way, offering assessment of the conception difficulty and information that may help a person to increase the chances of natural conception, but not offering active treatment. The ethical standpoint of the "middle way" is not clear.

Managing HIV in Pregnant Women

Ideally, before conceiving, a woman (or a couple) would make an informed choice to test. If a woman is already pregnant, then counselling to ensure that an informed choice to test is being made is encouraged. However, some antenatal services do not make adequate counselling services available to all. Caution is expressed in the support for mandatory testing or for an "opt out" approach where the "informed" consent is easily and frequently omitted. A problem-solving approach, described earlier, can assist a woman to make an informed choice of whether to test and, if HIV positive, whether to continue with the pregnancy or to terminate it. In either case, the psychological trauma associated with decision-making may be great.

DEALING WITH DEATH AND DYING AND BEREAVEMENT

Although HAART has decreased the death rate, people still die from HIV-related illnesses. When death closely followed an AIDS diagnosis, many individuals with HIV prepared for death, sometimes seeking psychological support, sometimes spiritual (Hedge & Sherr, 1995). Now that the length of life with HAART has increased, attention to mortality appears to have decreased. Not only may the person with HIV not prepare for death, but people dear to them may also not prepare. The impact of death may now be greater for those bereaved through HIV.

Death from an HIV-related illness presents some unique features. Those who die are often young—the highest mortality being seen in those aged between 20 and 40 years. As HIV disease is sexually transmitted, it is not uncommon to find couples, heterosexual, bisexual or gay, where both partners are HIV positive. Consequently, those who are bereaved through an HIV-related illness are frequently also HIV positive.

In developed countries the typical caregiver is an older female relative. However, in couples where both have HIV the caregiver's role will usually be taken by one of the partners. It is not unusual for the role to alternate; whichever partner is most well at the time providing care. Caregiving by a partner rather than a relative appears to be a function of both the younger age of the couple and the failure of many to disclose their HIV status to relatives (McCann & Wadsworth, 1992). When there is no disclosure, social support and caregiving cannot be provided by others. Thus, many young gay men care for sick and dying partners in an absence of family support (Turner & Catania, 1997).

Folkman et al. (1994) described the distress experienced by partner caregivers during a person's HIV illnesses and after his or her death. Prior to the death, HIV-negative partners were more distressed than those who were positive. Following the death, the positive partners were more distressed. A possible explanation for these findings is that those who are HIV positive view the experience as a model of their own death. While their partner is still alive they empathise with him or her and deny the probability of death. After the partner's death they are unable to deny the possibility that the same event will happen to them, and the increased possibility that they will have to face death alone. Suicidal ideation is common in caregivers of individuals with HIV disease. Rosengard and Folkman (1997) found that 55% of caregivers reported suicide ideation at some point during a longitudinal two-year study. Lennon, Martin and Dean (1990) found suicidal ideation to be more common in those bereaved than in those not bereaved. The intensity of grief in bereavement was related to the extent of the caretaking during end-stage disease and to the adequacy of the emotional and practical support provided to the caregiver at this time. Stroebe and Stroebe (1993) report suicide ideation in the general population to be associated with bereavement, with young men being particularly vulnerable. Suicide ideation in those bereaved through HIV was related to increased caregiving burden, less perceived social support, less social integration and greater reliance on behavioural escape-avoidance coping strategies.

COPING STRATEGIES AND SOCIAL SUPPORT

Lazarus and Folkman's (1984) model of stress proposes that the costs and benefits of possible coping strategies are evaluated and that those perceived as most beneficial are employed. The appraisal of the threat of the stressor (HIV) can be buffered by the perceived availability and extent of social support (Cohen & Wills, 1985).

According to this model, the way that individuals deal with HIV will depend on their understanding and interpretation of it, the stresses that they experience and on mediating factors such as the coping strategies they adopt and the perceived availability of social support. Nilsson Schonnesson and Ross (1999) found that low levels of psychological distress were associated with the use of problem-solving, positive reappraisal and information-seeking coping strategies. The use of wishful thinking, avoidance, isolation and fatalism was associated with increased distress and lower levels of well-being. Antoni et al. (1995) attempted to relate the coping strategies of asymptomatic men to immunological markers, initially after they received notification of their antibody-positive status, and again one year later. Those who initially scored above the median on disengagement coping strategies, i.e. denial, behavioural disengagement and mental disengagement, had significantly lower concurrent immune responses. The use of disengagement predicted impairment on the immunological measures one year later.

The perceived availability of social support has been shown to be related to good psychological adjustment in individuals with HIV disease (Eckenrode, 1991). Hedge et al. (1993) found that while objective measures, such as a low CD4 count, were of little predictive value in identifying psychological morbidity, a self-rating of good social support contributed to a profile of psychological well-being. Lower levels of psychological distress were seen in those who reported a regular partner or a stable group of close friends; the total number of friends or family was not of predictive value. However, about one-third of the sample had no partner and 17% reported no close friends. Thus, the absence of social support is clearly an issue for many individuals.

Social support can be conceptualised as comprising components of practical, emotional and informational support. Zuckerman and Antoni (1995) proposed that the type of social support provided should be matched to the situational demands. However, the situational demands may not be immediately obvious. The medication regimens for those with long-term cytomegalovirus (CMV) eye disease includes a frequent, complex self-injecting procedure which suggests that practical support might be beneficial. A study by Hedge et al. (1994) showed that emotional support rather than practical support was beneficial in maintaining adherence to this regime. The authors found that people with CMV eye disease had to adjust to the knowledge that this is an end-stage HIV disease, i.e. increases the risk of mortality. Emotional support for this adjustment was more important than practical support in maintaining high levels of adherence. When available, it was associated with higher mood. It appears that emotional support can be beneficial in almost any situation, while informational or problem-solving support may also provide psychological buffers to stressors.

INTERVENTIONS

Although there are many reports of high levels of psychological distress and psychiatric morbidity in people with HIV disease, there is still a limited pool of intervention studies. Interventions can be targeted to address adjustment to HIV and stage of disease, managing the possibility of an extended life with a chronic disease, maintenance of adherence to antiretroviral medications and decreasing risk behaviours.

Adjustment to HIV and Stage of Disease

The majority of interventions to promote psychological adjustment in individuals with HIV disease have targeted the management of stress, increase of mood, promotion of self-efficacy and the use of adaptive coping strategies.

A number of group interventions have proved successful in reducing stress, improving mood, increasing self-efficacy and increasing the use of adaptive coping strategies. Kelly et al. (1998) found both a cognitive-behavioural group and a social support group to increase mood and decrease somatisation compared with a no-intervention group. Mulder et al. (1994) found both cognitive-behavioural and experiential group interventions to reduce distress and depressive symptoms compared with a wait-list control group. Chesney and Folkman (1994) designed a training package: Coping Effectiveness Training that was found to decrease stress, and increase self-efficacy significantly more than either an information group or a wait-list control group (Chesney, Folkman & Chambers, 1996). However, Hedge and Glover (1990) showed that an information plus discussion group not only provided information but could also be successful in relieving distress and enhancing mutual social support between group members.

It is probable that the vast majority of individuals with HIV who are receiving psychological support do so through individual therapy. However, literature highlights the success of groups in increasing adaptive coping for living with HIV. There appears to be much less evidence for the success or otherwise of individual psychological interventions. This probably reflects the difficulty in standardising and comparing what are essentially individualised treatments and the difficulties of matching individuals who receive interventions with non-intervention controls in the clinic setting.

However, there are some indications that individual psychological input is effective. George (1988) showed that individuals with HIV maintained sustained improvements in anxiety and depression six months or more after individual cognitive-behavioural therapy. Hedge, James and Green (1990) reported decreases in anxiety and depression and increased self-esteem after a ten-week individual cognitive-behavioural therapy designed to increase coping skills.

ADHERENCE

In the health care setting adherence can be understood as "the extent to which a person's behaviour . . . coincides with medical or health advice" (Haynes, Taylor & Sackett, 1979). This implies that adherence is more than just taking the medicine. It includes the entering into and continuing with a programme of treatment, keeping referral and follow-up appointments, correct consumption of prescribed medications, following appropriate lifestyle changes, the correct performance of therapeutic regimens in the home as well as in a health care setting and the avoidance of health-risk behaviours. Non-adherence can, therefore, take many forms, including both intentional and unintentional behaviour, and relate to both preventative and curative regimens.

The term adherence is used rather than that of compliance as the latter implies that one individual (the patient) is required to conform to the rules of another (the doctor or health carer). In reality, adherence in the health care setting is voluntary and under the control of the individual (see also Chapter 3, The Person's Experience of Health Care).

Associations have been found between level of adherence and the nature of the treatment recommendation. Highest rates of adherence are found for treatments that are short term, direct (e.g. pills or injections), with high levels of supervision and monitoring following an acute onset. Lowest rates occur when the disorder is chronic, when lifestyle changes are required, when there are no obvious symptoms, and when a treatment is preventative rather than curative (DiMatteo & DiNicola, 1982). A study by Dezii et al. (2002) describing adherence to HAART over a three-year period found a steep drop-off in adherence during the first six months followed by a gradual continued decline. An inverse relationship is found between rates of adherence and the degree and duration of behavioural change required by a regimen, its complexity and the extent to which it interferes with past life patterns (Haynes et al., 1976; Martlatt & Gordon, 1985; Turk & Spears, 1984).

Health care providers systematically overestimate rates of adherence (DiMatteo & DiNicola, 1982) and the probability of an individual's adherence (Becker & Rosenstock, 1984). Although many physicians believe that a patient's "uncooperative personality" is the primary cause of non-adherence (Davis, 1966), the concept of the chronic defaulting or uncooperative patient is unsubstantiated (Haynes, Taylor & Sackett, 1979). Neither is adherence consistently associated with demographic variables such as sex, age, social class or level of education (Eldred et al., 1998; Kleeberger et al., 2001).

Psychological factors that are associated with adherence to antiretroviral medications include depression and other psychiatric illnesses (Kleeberger et al., 2001; Singh et al., 1996; Stein et al., 2000), perceived social support (Eldred et al., 1998), self-efficacy (Chesney et al., 2000; Eldred et al., 1998; Tuldra et al., 2000), high levels of alcohol or drug use (Chesney et al., 2000) and body image concerns (Roberts & Mann, 2000).

Each of the above factors may influence adherence behaviours. In turn, adherence may affect mood, self-esteem, etc. Thus, the relationships between factors can be reciprocal and reinforcing (Ickovics & Meade, 2002). Interventions to increase adherence may need to target a number of factors simultaneously.

Strategies to Increase Adherence to Medication Regimens

Bringing about change is notoriously difficult. Health campaigns aiming to prevent smoking and increase exercise have had remarkably little effect. Failures can often be attributed to a lack of attention to the reasons why people fail to perform the necessary behaviours or to a lack of consideration of the processes necessary for an individual to make and maintain change (Prochaska & DiClemente, 1986).

Interventions to increase adherence have been successful in a number of medical settings (Haynes et al., 1976; Schafer, Glasgow & McCall, 1982). So far, few controlled studies have investigated the efficacy of interventions to increase adherence to antiretroviral medications. Many studies intervene in a number of ways simultaneously, which make it difficult to ascertain the useful interventions; others report only an intervention and no control. Those studies that appear to show some effect on adherence behaviours are now described. Also interventions that have some face validity, i.e. they address factors identified as being associated with non-adherence to antiretroviral treatments, are suggested.

If antiretroviral medication regimens could be reduced to a daily, single dose of a single pill, difficulties with adherence would be dramatically reduced. Likewise, if no drugs exhibited adverse side-effects, required precise timing or dietary restrictions, adherence would increase. Until such regimens are available, prescription of the simplest effective combination with the least perceived barriers may increase adherence. Unfortunately, given the number of other factors which influence the choice of medication regime and adherence behaviours, even thoughtful prescribing is unlikely to lead to full adherence.

Accurate knowledge and understanding about the required treatment regimen is clearly necessary for good adherence. For those who lack essential information or with erroneous beliefs (according to our current state of knowledge) about the efficacy of medication or their susceptibility to illness, provision of information may be vital. However, it may not be sufficient to ensure adherent behaviours. Tuldra et al. (2000) showed that individuals who received an psychoeducative intervention targeted at increasing self-efficacy maintained high levels of adherence over one year while those receiving routine medical follow-up showed a progressive decline in adherence.

Behavioural techniques of prompting, cuing, feedback of performance and reinforcement for success can all be used to promote medication-taking (Meichenbaum & Turk, 1987). Cuing may be a particularly useful technique. Intervention would involve the setting up of prompts to serve as reminders for medication-taking. Medication aids such as pill boxes with attached alarms can be useful. Rigsby et al. (2000) found that cue-dose training plus cash reinforcement increased adherence during the intervention period. However, at follow-up adherence had declined, suggesting that the improvement was consequent on the cash incentive rather than on newly learned skills. As pill boxes can be distinctive or bulky, pills are frequently decanted, stored inappropriately and sometimes lost. Cues that are part of the individual's everyday life may be more useful. For example, prompts can be developed for specific situations, e.g. at work, when travelling, socialising or staying with family members who are unaware of the HIV disease.

As mood disorder is strongly associated with avoidance coping, attention to mood and lack of social support, interventions to change these factors should indirectly increase adherence behaviours.

As so many factors may influence adherence behaviours, interventions need to be designed for individual lifestyles. Consequently, they are rarely simple or uni-focused.

SOMATIC SYMPTOMS

It is not uncommon for psychological distress to be reported in those who, following clinical and serological tests, are found to have no physical illness (Frost, 1985). High rates of hypochondriasis and veneroneurosis (a strong conviction of having a venereal disease) are found in sexual health clinics and are frequently associated with psychiatric morbidity (MacAlpine, 1957; Oates & Gomez, 1984). For some, distress can be related to intense concern about HIV that results in a persistent pursuit of medical care (Miller, Acton & Hedge, 1988).

For those convinced beyond the clinical or serological evidence that they are infected with HIV, an unfortunate name is frequently used, the "Worried Well". Although these individuals have no physical illness they usually have severe psychological distress and are far from being mentally "well". It can be more useful to consider their behaviours as obsessions and compulsions. Salkovskis (1989) suggests that severe health anxieties start with innocuous stimuli that are misinterpreted as a sign of a serious threat to illness. In certain circumstances normal variations in bodily appearance, sensations and bodily functions are brought to a person's attention, are misinterpreted, and are taken as evidence that they are suffering from a severe problem.

One factor which appears to lead to such misinterpretations is increased knowledge of a medical condition, either through personal or family history or by media attention. In the mid-1980s intensive media campaigns alerted the British public to the reality of AIDS and HIV. This resulted in an influx of persons without HIV, who remained convinced that they were infected, even after repeated testing for the virus, and after multiple consultations in which the absence of infection was discussed, confirmed and reassurance was provided (Miller, Acton & Hedge, 1988).

The cognitive-behavioural theory of obsessive-compulsive disorder (Salkovskis, 1985) proposes that intrusive thoughts are interpreted as an indication that the person may be responsible for harm or its prevention. This appraisal increases distress for which neutralising behaviours (compulsions) lead to a short-lived reduction. In order to maintain the reduction in distress the compulsion is repeatedly activated. A common reaction to those with obsessions and compulsions is to reassure them that the feared outcomes and their perceived responsibilities are unwarranted. The reassurance provides a temporary reduction in anxiety, but can increase their attention on their fears and beliefs, which leads them to seek further reassurance. Reassurance and repeated testing to confirm to them that they do not have the infection can then be a maintaining factor that increases rather than decreases their distress (Salkovskis & Warwick, 1986).

Interventions

Salkovskis' health preoccupation model (Salkovskis, 1989) suggests that rather than provide reassurance, therapy should address the patients' appraisal, assumptions and beliefs. By identifying and modifying assumptions that give rise to misinterpretations of mental activity and bodily phenomena, individuals can learn to reframe their interpretation of bodily sensations. This approach was successfully demonstrated by Miller, Acton and Hedge (1988) who report a series of cases all presenting with a conviction of being HIV positive. The important elements of treatment are shown in Table 21.2.

Table 21.2   Intervention with unsubstantiated beliefs of HIV infection

Elements of treatment	Examples of intervention
Contract (following medical examination to confirm the absence of physical pathology)	No reassurance to be sought from any medical or health professional, or from the therapist between sessions
Reassurance	After initial explanation of the psychological model linking behaviours and misinterpretations, no reassurance to be given during the therapy sessions
Reframing	Considering evidence for interpretation of beliefs. Reinterpreting evidence in terms of life stressors Changing attributions in view of evidence
Checking	Self-monitoring of body checking. Phasing out through cue exposure and response prevention
Introduction of adaptive behaviours	Behavioural experiments to produce evidence supporting alternative explanations for symptoms
Relapse prevention	Preparation for coping with future life stressors

It was found that the belief of infection reduced before the need for reassurance fell. This indicated how vulnerable persons are for relapse as they continue to need reassurance. If given, this can once more increase their attention to the initial stimuli and thus lead to a further episode of health anxiety. An important aspect of the treatment package is the inclusion of relapse prevention strategies—such as, e.g., guided self-dialogue, covert modelling, and role-playing—that are designed to enable people to cope with future situations that might trigger the misattributions.

SEXUAL ASSAULT

Lastly, this chapter centres on another sexual health issue. Following a reported sexual assault a medical examination is usually conducted. This is necessarily directed at those parts of the body involved in the assault, i.e. the oral, genital and anal areas. The examination has a number of functions, including forensic. Another is to gather evidence that relates to the potential physical consequences of the assault such as pregnancy or the acquisition of sexually transmitted infections including HIV. Consequently, assaulted people are frequently referred to sexual health centres even when an initial medical examination looking for circumstantial evidence has taken place in a police facility.

Petrak (2002) reviews the psychological impact of sexual assault. Research shows the impact to be wide-ranging and to extend beyond the stress disorders. Although not all people who have been assaulted develop psychological problems, high rates of acute stress immediately following the assault are commonly seen. With the exception of fear and anxiety, these generally dissipate over the first few months. Those whose symptoms do not dissipate are more likely to come to the attention of the health care system. Rape poses a great risk for the development of post-traumatic stress disorder (PTSD). Some studies suggest that up to 80% of individuals who have been raped develop PTSD at some time (Breslau et al., 1991; Kilpatrick et al., 1989). Less frequently considered is the psychological impact of the forensic and legal processes that follow the report of an assault.

To someone who has experienced a sexual assault, the medical investigations may bring further distress (Parrot, 1991). The negative experiences encountered while receiving services provided to help with the initial sexual assault have been described as "secondary victimisation" (Campbell & Raja, 1999; Williams & Holmes, 1981). Thus, the psychological effect of a sexual assault can be compounded by the medical and investigatory services.

Only in the 1970s did empirical studies of the psychological impact of sexual assault appear in the literature. Even now, the majority of studies refer to the US experience and few address the impact of sexual assault on men (Coxell & King, 2002). An increase in suicidal ideation has been reported in those with a history of sexual assault (Burgess, 1995; Resnick et al., 1989). Problems with social and sexual functioning have also been reported (Baker et al., 1991; Burgesss & Holstrom, 1979; Nadelson et al., 1982).

The incidence of STIs being acquired from a sexual assault is relatively low, typically in the range of 4 to 40% (Bottomley, Sadler & Welch, 1999; Forster, Estreich & Hooi, 1991; Forster et al., 1986). However, within a sexual health centre, a higher percentage of individuals will disclose that their STI was acquired through a sexual assault. People are also aware of HIV. Baker et al. (1990) reported that 26% of people who had been sexually assaulted expressed fears that they may have acquired HIV. A recent feature of rape is the assailant telling his victim that he or she will become infected with HIV consequent on the assault. Hillman et al. (1991) found that 57% of men who had been assaulted reported such threats.

Concern about the unpredictable outcomes of an assault can further increase the psychological burden of a sexual assault. Although the documented incidence of pregnancy following a sexual assault is low (1–5%) it cannot be discounted (Ledray, Lund & Kiresuk, 1979). Many women are concerned that the sexual assault may have resulted in a pregnancy. Bottomley, Sadler and Welch (1999) reported that 16% of women in a sexual assault clinical service requested emergency contraception.

Interventions

A number of treatments for the sequelae of sexual assault have been reviewed by Bennice and Resick (2002). They found few intervention studies to incorporate a control group or standardised treatment protocols. There is support for brief cognitive-behavioural treatment initiated shortly after the assault (Foa, Hearst-Ikeda & Perry, 1995; Foa, Rothbaum & Molnar, 1995). There is some evidence that stress inoculation training, and the exposure-based therapies (e.g. flooding), are more efficient and superior to systematic desensitisation in the treatment of post-trauma sequelae. Cognitive therapy has also proved effective (Frank et al., 1988; Marks et al., 1998; Tarrier et al., 1999). Frank et al. found the identification of automatic negative thoughts and cognitive distortions, core beliefs and the use of a daily activities schedule to be as effective as systematic desensitisation in reducing anxiety and fear.

Cognitive-behavioural therapy has been described for acute stress and PTSD (Naugle et al., 2002) for mood and behavioural problems (Kennerley, 2002).

Possible sequelae of a sexual assault require action to be taken by the assaulted person if adverse future outcomes are to be minimised, e.g. emergency contraception (Schein, 1999) or antiretroviral therapy to reduce the risk of HIV transmission (Myles et al., 2000). A problem-solving approach that enhances the probability of an individual being able to make an informed choice can be beneficial. Details of how this might be executed are described by Hedge (2002).

SUMMARY

This chapter has demonstrated the importance of recognising the risks attached to sexual behaviours and of providing appropriate interventions. It can be seen that psychological assessment and intervention plays an important role in maintaining and improving sexual health. In the absence of the perfect pill or vaccine to protect against infection, the clinical health psychologist will have a role to play in sexual health settings well into the future.

REFERENCES

Antoni, M., Goldstein, D., Ironson, G., LaPerriere, A., Fletcher, M. & Schneiderman, N. (1995). Coping responses to HIV-1 serostatus notification predict concurrent and prospective immunologic status. *Clinical Psychology and Psychotherapy*, **2**, 234–248.

Baker, T., Burgess, A., Brickman, E. & Davis, R. (1990). Rape victims' concerns about possible exposure to HIV infection. *Journal of Interpersonal Violence*, **5**, 49–60.

Baker, T., Skolnik, L., Davis, R. & Brickman, E. (1991). The social support of survivors of rape: the differences between rape survivors and survivors of other violent crimes and between husbands, boyfriends, and women friends. In A. Burgess (Ed.), *Rape and Sexual Assault, III*. New York: Garland Publishing.

Bandura, A., Reese, L. & Adams, N. (1982). Micro-analysis of action and fear arousal as a function of differential levels of perceived self-efficacy. *Journal of Personality and Social Psychology*, **43**, 5–21.

Bandura, A., Cioffi, D., Taylor, C. & Brouillard, M. (1988). Perceived self-efficacy in coping with cognitive stressors and opioid activation. *Journal of Personality and Social Psychology*, **55**, 479–488.

Barczak, P., Kane, N., Andrews, S. Congdon, A., Clay, J. & Betts, T. (1988). Patterns of psychiatric morbidity in a genito-urinary clinic: a validation of the Hospital Anxiety Depression Scale. *British Journal of Psychiatry*, **152**, 698–700.

Beck, A. (1976). *Cognitive Therapy and the Emotional Disorders*. New York: International Universities Press.

Beck, J. (1995). *Cognitive Therapy: Basics and Beyond*. New York: Guilford Press.

Becker, M. & Rosenstock, I. (1984). Compliance with medical advice. In A. Steptoe & A. Mathews (Eds), *Health Care and Human Behaviour*. New York: Academic Press.

Beckett, A. & Shenson, D. (1993). Suicide risk in patients with human immunodeficiency virus infection and acquired immunodeficiency syndrome. *Harvard Review of Psychiatry*, **1**, 27–35.

Bennice, J. & Resick, P. (2002). A review of treatment and outcome of post-trauma sequelae in sexual assault survivors. In J. Petrak & B. Hedge (Eds), *The Trauma of Sexual Assault: Treatment, Prevention and Practice*. Chichester: John Wiley & Sons.

Bhanji, S. & Mahony, J. (1978). The value of a psychiatric service within the venereal disease clinic. *British Journal of Venereal Diseases*, **54**, 566.

Blankson, J., Persaud, D. & Siliciano, R. (2002). The challenge of viral reservoirs in HIV-1 infection. *Annual Review of Medicine*, **53**, 557–593.

Boden, D., Hurley, A., Zhang, L., Cao, Y., Guo, Y., Jones, E., Tsay, J., Ip, J., Farthing, C., Limoli, K., Parkin, N. & Markowitz, M. (1999). HIV-1 drug resistance in newly infected individuals. *Journal of the American Medical Association*, **282**, 1135–1141.

Bottomley, C., Sadler, T. & Welch, J. (1999). Integrated clinical service for sexual assault victims in a genitourinary setting. *Sexually Transmitted Infections*, **75**, 116–119.

Breslau, N., Davis, G., Andreski, P. & Peterson, E. (1991). Traumatic events and posttraumatic stress disorder in an urban population of young adults. *Archives of General Psychiatry*, **131**, 981–986.

Burgess, A. (1995). Rape trauma syndrome. In P. Searles & R. Berger (Eds), *Rape and Society: Readings on the Problem of Sexual Assault*. Boulder, CO: Westview Press.

Burgess, A. & Holmstrom, L. (1979). Adaptive strategies and recovery from rape. *American Journal of Psychiatry*, **136**, 1278–1282.

Cambell, R. & Raja, S. (1999). Secondary victimization of rape victims: insights from mental health professionals who treat survivors of violence. *Violence and Victims*, **14**, 261–275.

Carney, O., Ross, E., Ikkos, G. & Mindel, A. (1993). The effect of suppressive oral acyclovir on the psychological morbidity associated with recurrent genital herpes. *Genitourinary Medicine*, **69**, 457–459.

Cassidy, L., Meadows, J., Catalan, J. & Barton, S. (1997). Are reported stress and coping style associated with frequent recurrences of genital herpes? *Genitourinary Medicine*, **73**, 263–266.

Catalan, J., Burgess, A. & Klimes, I. (1995). *Psychological Medicine of HIV Infection*. Oxford: Oxford University Press.

Catalan, J., Bradley, M., Gallwey, J. & Hawton, K. (1981). Sexual dysfunction and psychiatric morbidity in patients attending a clinic for sexually transmitted diseases. *British Journal of Psychiatry*, **138**, 292–296.

Catalan, J., Klimes, I., Bond, A., Day, A., Garrod, A. & Rizza, C. (1992). The psychological impact of HIV infection in men with haemophilia: controlled investigation and factors associated with psychiatric morbidity. *Journal of Psychosomatic Research*, **36**, 409–416.

Centres for Disease Control (1981). Pneumocystis pneumonia, *Morbidity and Mortality Weekly*, **30**, 250–252.

Centres for Disease Control (1992). CDC AIDS surveillance case definition for adolescents and adults: 1993. *Morbidity and Mortality Weekly*, **41**, 1–9.

Chesney, M. (2000). Factors affecting adherence to antiretroviral therapy. *Clinical Infectious Diseases*, **30**, S171–S176.

Chesney, M. & Folkman, S. (1994). Psychological impact of HIV disease and implications for intervention. *Psychiatric Clinics of North America*, **17**, 163–182.

Chesney, M., Folkman, S. & Chambers, D. (1996). Coping effectiveness training for men living with HIV: preliminary findings. *International Journal of STD and AIDS*, **7**, 75–82.

Chesney, M., Ickovics, J., Chambers, D., Gifford, A., Neidig, J., Zwickl, B. & Wu, A. (2000). Self-reported adherence to antiretroviral medications among participants in HIV clinical trials: the AACTG adherence instruments. *AIDS Care*, **12**, 255–266.

Chuang, H., Devins, G., Hunsley, J. & Gill, M. (1989). Psychosocial distress and well-being among gay and bisexual men with Human Immunodeficiency Syndrome. *American Journal of Psychiatry*, **146**, 876–880.

Clarke, P., Ebal, C., Catotti, D. & Stewart, S. (1996). The psychosocial impact of human papillomavirus infection: implications for health care providers. *International Journal of STD and AIDS*, **7**, 197–200.

Cohen, M. (1998). Sexually transmitted diseases enhance HIV transmission: no longer a hypothesis. *Lancet*, **351** (Supp. III), 5–7.

Cohen, R., Boland, R., Paul, R., Tashima, K.T., Schoenbaum, E., Celentano, D., Schuman, P., Smith, D. & Carpenter, C. (2001). Neurocognitive performance enhanced by highly active antiretroviral therapy in HIV-infected women. *AIDS*, **15**, 341–345.

Cohen, S. & Wills, T. (1985). Stress, social support and the buffering hypothesis: a critical review. *Psychological Bulletin*, **98**, 310–357.

Conaglen, H., Hughes, R., Conaglen, J. & Morgan, J. (2001). A prospective study of the psychological impact on patients of first diagnosis of human papillomavirus. *International Journal of STD and AIDS*, **12**, 651–658.

Conner, E., Sperling, R., Gelber, R., Kisley, P., Scott, G. & Sullivan, M. (1994). Reduction of maternal infant transmission of HIV type 1 with zidovudine treatment. *New England Journal of Medicine*, **331**, 1173–1180.

Corey, L., Adams, H., Brown, Z. & Holmes, K. (1983). Genital herpes simplex virus infections: clinical manifestations, course, and complications. *Annals of Internal Medicine*, **98**, 958–972.

Cote, T., Biggar, R. & Danneberg, A. (1992). Risk of suicide among persons with AIDS: a national assessment. *Journal of the American Medical Association*, **268**, 2066–2068.

Coxell, A. & King, M. (2002). Gender, sexual orientation and sexual assault. In J. Petrak & B. Hedge (Eds), *The Trauma of Sexual Assault: Treatment, Prevention and Practice*. Chichester: John Wiley & Sons.

Dalvisk, J., Wahlin, T., Bartsch, E. & Forsbeck, M. (1995). Herpes simplex and mood: a prospective study. *Psychosomatic Medicine*, **57**, 127–137.

Davis, M. (1966). Variations in patients' compliance with doctor's advice: analysis of congruence between survey responses and results of empirical observations. *Journal of Medical Education*, **41**, 1037–1048.

De Cock, K. & Weiss, H. (2000). The global epidemiology of HIV/AIDS. *Tropical Medicine and International Health*, **5**, A3–A5.

Dezii, C., Burtcel, B., Hodder, S., Grundy, S. & Kawabata, H. (2002). Long-term adherence with nucleoside reverse transcriptive inhibitor (NRTI) therapy. *XIV International AIDS Conference*, Barcelona. Abstract WPB 5842.

DiMatteo, M. & DiNicola, D. (1982). *Achieving Patient Adherence*. New York: Pergamon Press.

Drob, S., Loemer, M. & Lifschutz, H. (1985). Genital herpes: the psychological consequences. *British Journal of Medical Psychology*, **58**, 307–315.

Eckenrode, J. (Ed.) (1991). *The Social Context of Coping*. New York: Plenum Press.

Egan, V., Brettle, R. & Goodwin, G. (1992). The Edinburgh cohort of HIV positive drug users: patterns of cognitive impairment in relation to progression of disease. *British Journal of Psychiatry*, **161**, 522–531.

Eldred, L., Wu, A., Chaisson, R. & Moore, R. (1998). Adherence to antiretroviral and pneumocystis prophylaxis in HIV disease. *Journal of Acquired Immune Deficiency Syndrome and Human Retrovirology*, **18**, 117–125.

Englert, Y., van Vooren, J., Place, I., Liesnard, C., Laruelle, C. & Delbaere, A. (2001). ART in HIV-infected couples: has the time come for a change of attitude? *Human Reproduction*, **16**, 1309–1315.

Eysenck, H. & Wilson, G. (1979). *The Psychology of Sex*. London: Dent.

Filiberti, A., Tamburini, M., Stefano, B., Merola, M., Bandieramonte, G., Ventafridda, V. & De Palo, G. (1993). Psychological aspects of genital human papillomavirus infection: a preliminary report. *Journal of Psychosomatic Obstetrics and Gynaecology*, **14**, 145–152.

Fishbein, M., Douglas, J., Rhodes, F., Hananel, L. & Napolitano, E. (1993). Distribution of STD clinic patients along a stage of behavioural change continuum. *Current Trends*, **42**, 880–883.

Fitzpatrick, R., Frost, D. & Ikkos, G. (1986). Survey of psychological disturbance in patients attending a sexually transmitted diseases clinic. *Genitourinary Medicine*, **62**, 111–114.

Foa, E., Hearst-Ikeda, D. & Perry, K. (1995). Evaluation of a brief behavioral program for the prevention of chronic PTSD in recent assault victims. *Journal of Consulting and Clinical Psychology*, **63**, 948–955.

Foa, E., Rothbaum, B. & Molnar, C. (1995). Cognitive-behavioural therapy of post-traumatic stress disorder. In M. Friedman, D. Charney & A. Deutch (Eds), *Neurobiology and Clinical Consequences of Stress: From Normal Adaptation to Post-Traumatic Stress Disorder*. New York: Lippincott-Raven.

Folkman, S. & Lazarus, R. (1988). *Manual of the Ways of Coping Questionnaire*. Palo Alto, CA: Consulting Psychologists Press.

Folkman, S., Chesney, M., Cooke, M., Boccellari, A. & Collette, L. (1994). Caregiver burden in HIV-positive and HIV-negative partners of men with AIDS. *Journal of Personality and Social Psychology*, **70**, 336–348.

Forster, G., Estreich, S. & Hooi, Y. (1991). Screening for STDs (Letter to the editor). *Annals of Emergency Medicine*, **324**, 161–162.

Forster, G., Pritard, J., Munday, P. & Goldmeier, D. (1986). Incidence of sexually transmitted diseases in rape victims during 1984. *Genitourinary Medicine*, **62**, 267–269.

Frank, E., Anderson, B., Stewart, B., Dancu, C., Hughes, C. & West, D. (1988). Efficacy of cognitive behaviour therapy and systematic desensitization in the treatment of rape trauma. *Behaviour Therapy*, **19**, 403–420.

Frost, D. (1985). Recognition of hypochondriasis in a clinic for sexually transmitted disease. *Genitourinary Medicine*, **61**, 133–137.

George, H. (1988). AIDS: factors identified as helpful by patients. *IV International AIDS Conference*, Stockholm.

Goggin, K., Sewell, M., Ferrando, S., Evans, S., Fishman, B. & Rabkin, J. (2000). Plans to hasten death among gay men with HIV/AIDS: relationship to psychological adjustment. *AIDS Care*, **12**, 125–136.

Goldmeier, D. & Johnson, A. (1982). Does psychiatric illness affect the recurrence rate of genital herpes? *British Journal of Venereal Diseases*, **58**, 40–43.

Goldmeier, D., Johnson, A., Byrne, M. & Barton, S. (1988). Psychosocial implications of recurrent genital herpes simplex virus infection. *Genitourinary Medicine*, **64**, 327–330.

Goldmeier, D., Johnson, A., Jeffries, D., Walker, G., Underhill, G., Robinson, G. & Ribbans, H. (1986). Psychological aspects of recurrences of genital herpes. *Journal of Psychosomatic Research*, **30**, 601–608.

Green, J. & Kocsis, A. (1997). Psychological factors in recurrent genital herpes. *Genitourinary Medicine*, **73**, 253–258.

Greenberger, D. & Padesky, C. (1995). *Mind over Mood: Change How you Feel by Changing the Way you Think*. New York: Guilford Press.

Griffiths, S. (1999). *Discordant Couples with Genital Herpes*. HIV Special Interest Group Meeting. May, Sheffield.

Guze, S. & Robins, E. (1970). Suicide and primary affective disorders. *British Journal of Psychiatry*, **117**, 437–438.

Harris, E. & Barraclough, B. (1994). Suicide as an outcome for medical disorders. *Medicine*, **73**, 281–296.

Hart, G. (1977). *Sexual Maladjustment and Disease: An Introduction to Modern Venereology.* Chicago: Nelson-Hall.

Hawton, K. & Kirk, J. (1989). Problem-solving. In K. Hawton, P. Salkovskis, J. Kirk & D. Clark (Eds), *Cognitive Behaviour Therapy for Psychiatric Problems: A Practical Guide.* Oxford: Oxford University Press.

Hawton, K., Salkovskis, P., Kirk, J. & Clark, D. (Eds) (1989). *Cognitive Behaviour Therapy for Psychiatric Problems: A Practical Guide.* Oxford: Oxford University Press.

Haynes, R., Taylor, D. & Sackett, D. (Eds) (1979). *Compliance in Health Care.* Baltimore: Johns Hopkins University Press.

Haynes, R., Sackett, D., Gibson, E., Taylor, D., Hackett, B., Roberts, R. & Johnson, A. (1976). Improvement of medication compliance in uncontrolled hypertension. *Lancet*, **1**, 1265–1268.

Hedge, B. (2002). Coping with the physical impact of sexual assault. In J. Petrak & B. Hedge (Eds), *The Trauma of Sexual Assault: Treatment, Prevention and Practice.* Chichester: John Wiley & Sons.

Hedge, B. & Glover, L. (1990). Group intervention with HIV seropositive patients and their partners. *AIDS Care*, **2**, 147–154.

Hedge, B. & Sherr, L. (1995). Psychological needs and HIV/AIDS. *Clinical Psychology and Psychotherapy*, **2**, 203–209.

Hedge, B., James, S. & Green, J. (1990). Aspects of focused cognitive-behavioural intervention with HIV seropositive individuals. *VI International AIDS Conference, San Francisco.* Abstract SC 689.

Hedge, B., Clement, A., Hill, S., Evans, J. & Pinching, A. (1994). Psychosocial determinants of treatment compliance in CMV eye disease. *Second International Congress on Drug Therapy in HIV Infection, Glasgow.* Abstract PO-D22–4111.

Hedge, B., Petrak, J., Sherr, L., Sichel, T., Glover, L. & Slaughter, J. (1992). Psychological crises in HIV infection. *VIII International AIDS Conference, Amsterdam.* Abstract PoB3803.

Hedge, B., Slaughter, J., Flynn, R. & Green, J. (1993). Coping with HIV disease: successful attributes and strategies. *IX International AIDS Conference, Berlin.* Abstract PoB3803.

Hillman, R., O'Mara, N., Tomlinson, D. & Harris, J. (1991). Adult male victims of sexual assault: an undiagnosed condition. *International Journal of STD and AIDS*, **2**, 22–24.

Ho, G., Bierman, R., Beardsley, L., Chang, C. & Burk, R. (1998). Natural history of cervicovaginal papillomavirus infection in young women. *New England Journal of Medicine*, **338**, 423–428.

Hogg, R., Heath, K.V., Bangsberg, D., Yip, B., Press, N., O'Shaughnessy, M. & Montaner, J. (2002). Intermittent use of triple-combination therapy is predictive of mortality at baseline and after 1 year of follow-up. *AIDS*, **16**, 1051–1058.

Hogg, R.S., Heath, K.V., Yip, B., Kully, C., Craib, K.J., O'Shaughnessy, M.V., Schechter, M.T. & Montaner, J.S. (1998). Improved survival among HIV-infected individuals following initiation of antiretroviral therapy. *Journal of the American Medical Association*, **279**, 450–454.

Hoon, E., Hoon, P., Rand, K. & Johnson, J. (1991). Psycho-behavioural model of genital herpes recurrence. *Journal of Psychosomatic Research*, **35**, 25–36.

Ickovics, J. & Meade, C. (2002). Adherence to HAART among patients with HIV: breakthroughs and barriers. *AIDS Care*, **14**, 309–318.

Ikkos, G., Fitzpatrick, R., Frost, D. & Nazeer, S. (1987). Psychological disturbance and illness behaviour in a clinic for sexually transmitted disease. *British Journal of Medical Psychology*, **60**, 121.

Inskip, H., Harris, E. & Barraclough, B. (1998). Lifetime risk of suicide for affective disorder, alcoholism and schizophrenia. *British Journal of Psychiatry*, **172**, 35–37.

Keller, M., Jadack, R. & Mims, L. (1991). Perceived stressors and coping responses in persons with recurrent genital herpes. *Research and Nursing Health*, **14**, 421–430.

Kelly, B., Raphael, B., Judd, F., Perdices, M., Kernutt, G., Burnett, P., Dunne, M. & Burrows G. (1998). Suicide ideation, suicide attempts, and HIV infection. *Psychosomatics*, **39**, 405–415.

Kelly, J., Murphy, D., Bahr, G., Kalichman, L., Morgan, M. & Stevenson, Y. (1993). Outcome of cognitive-behavioural and support brief therapies for depressed HIV infected persons. *American Journal of Psychiatry*, **150**, 1679–1686.

Kemeny, M., Cohen, F., Zegans, L. & Conant, M. (1989). Psychological and immunological predictors of genital herpes recurrences. *Psychosomatic Medicine*, **51**, 195–208.

Kennerley, H. (2002). Cognitive-behavioural therapy for mood and behavioural problems. In J. Petrak & B. Hedge (Eds), *The Trauma of Sexual Assault: Treatment, Prevention and Practice*. Chichester: Jonn Wiley & Sons.

Kilpatrick, D., Saunders, B., Amick-McMullan, A., Best, C., Veronen, L. & Resnick, H. (1989). Victim and crime factors associated with the development of crime-related post-traumatic stress disorder. *Behaviour Therapy*, **20**, 199–214.

King, M. (1989). Psychological status of 192 out-patient with HIV infection and AIDS. *British Journal of Psychiatry*, **154**, 237–242.

Kleeberger, C., Phair, J., Strathdee, S., DEtels, R., Kingsley, L. & Jacobson, L. (2001). Determinants of heterogeneous adherence to HIV-antiretroviral therapies in the multicentre AIDS cohort study. *Journal of Acquired Immune Deficiency Syndrome*, **26**, 82–92.

Koehn, K., Burnette, M. & Stark, C. (1993). Applied relaxation training in the treatment of genital herpes. *Journal of Behaviour Therapy and Experimental Psychiatry*, **24**, 163–141.

Koutsky, L. & Kiviat, N. (1999). Genital human papillomavirus. In K. Holmes et al. (Eds), *Sexually Transmitted Diseases* (3rd edn). New York: McGraw-Hill.

Koutsky, L., Holmes, K., Critchlow, C., Stevens, C.E., Paavonen, J., Beckmann, A.M., DeRouen, T.A., Galloway, D.A., Vernon, D. & Kiviat, N.B. (1992). A cohort study of the risk of cervical intraepithelial neoplasia grade 2 or 3 in relation to papillomavirus infection. *New England Journal of Medicine*, **327**, 1272–1278.

Kreitman, N. (1993). Suicide and parasuicide. In R. Kendall & A. Zealley (Eds), *Companion to Psychiatric Studies* (5th edn). London: Longman.

Laga, M., Manoka, A., Kivuvu, M., Malele, B., Tuliza, M., Nzila, N., Goeman, J., Behets, F., Batter, V. & Alary, M. (1993). Non-ulcerative sexually transmitted diseases as risk factors for HIV-1 transmission in women. *AIDS*, **7**, 95–102.

Lallemand, F., Salhi, Y., Linard, F., Giami, A. & Rozenbaum, W. (2002). Sexual dysfunction in 156 ambulatory HIV-infected men receiving highly active antiretroviral therapy combinations with and without protease inhibitors. *Journal of Acquired Immune Deficiency Syndromes*, **30**, 187–190.

Lazarus, R. & Folkman, S. (1984). *Stress, Appraisal and Coping*. New York: Springer-Verlag.

Lazarus, R. & Folkman, S. (1987). Transactional theory and research on emotions and coping. *European Journal of Personality*, **1**, 141–170.

Ledray, L., Lund, H. & Kiresuk, T. (1979). Impact of rape on victims and families: treatment and research considerations. In D. Kjervik & I. Martinson (Eds), *Women in Stress: A Nursing Perspective*. New York: Appleton-Century-Crofts.

Lennon, M., Martin, J. & Dean, L. (1990). The influence of social support on AIDS related grief reactions among gay men. *Social Science and Medicine*, **31**, 477–484.

Longo, D. & Clum, G. (1989). Psychosocial factors affecting genital herpes recurrences: linear versus mediating models. *Journal of Psychosomatic Research*, **33**, 161–166.

Luby, E. & Gillespie, O. (1981). Psychological responses to genital herpes. *Helper*, **3**, 2–3.

Luby, E. & Klinge, V. (1985). Genital herpes. A pervasive psychosocial disorder. *Archives of Dermatology*, **121**, 494–497.

MacAlpine, I. (1957). Syphilophobia: a psychiatric study. *British Journal of Venereal Diseases*, **33**, 92.

Manne, S. & Sandler, I. (1984). Coping and adjustment to genital herpes. *Journal of Behaviour Medicine*, **7**, 391–410.

Manne, S., Sandler, I. & Zautra, A. (1986). Coping and adjustment to genital herpes: the effects of time and social support. *Journal of Behaviour Medicine*, **9**, 163–177.

Marks, I., Lovell, K., Noshirvani, H., Livanou, M. & Thrasher, S. (1998). Treatment of posttraumatic stress disorder by exposure and/or cognitive restructuring: a controlled study. *Archives of General Psychiatry*, **55**, 317–325.

Martlatt, G. & Gordon, J. (1985). *Relapse Prevention: Maintenance Strategies in the Treatment of Addictive Behaviours*. New York: Guilford Press.

Marzuk, P., Tierney, H., Tardiff, K., Gross, E., Morgan, E., Hsu, M.A. & Mann, J. (1988). Increased risk of suicide in persons with AIDS. *Journal of the American Medical Association*, **259**, 1333–1337.

Mayou, R. (1975). Psychological morbidity in a clinic for sexually transmitted disease. *British Journal of Venereal Diseases*, **51**, 57–60.

McCann, K. & Wadsworth, E. (1992). The role of informal carers in supporting gay men who have HIV related disease: what do they do and what are their needs? *AIDS Care*, **4**, 25–34.

McLarnon, L. & Kaloupek, D. (1988). Psychological investigation of genital herpes recurrence: prospective assessment and cognitive behavioural intervention for a chronic physical disorder. *Health Psychology*, **7**, 231–249.

Meichenbaum, D. & Turk, D. (1987). *Facilitating Treatment Adherence: A Practitioner's Guidebook*. New York: Plenum Press.

Miller, D., Acton, T. & Hedge, B. (1988). The worried well: their identification and management. *Journal of the Royal College of Physicians*, **22**, 158–165.

Mindel, A., Weller, I., Faherty, A., Sutherland, S., Hindley, D., Fiddian, A. & Adler, M. (1988). Prophylactic oral acyclovir in recurrent genital herpes. *Lancet*, **2**, 57–59.

Mitchell, C. (1999). Suicidal behaviour and HIV infection. In J. Catalan (Ed.), *Mental Health and HIV Infection*. London: UCL Press.

Mok, J. (1994). HIV transmission from mother to infant. *Quarterly Journal of Medicine*, **87**, 521–522.

Mulder, C., Emmelkamp, P., Antoni, M., Mulder, J., Sandford, T. & de Vries, M. (1994). Cognitive-behavioural and experiential group psychotherapy for HIV-infected homosexual men: a comparative study. *Psychosomatic Medicine*, **56**, 423–431.

Myles, J., Hirozawa, A., Katz, M., Kimmerling, R. & Bamberger, J. (2000). Post-exposure prophylaxis for HIV after sexual assault. *Journal of American Medical Association*, **284**, 1516–1518.

Nadelson, C., Notman, M., Zackson, H. & Gornick, J. (1982). A follow-up study of rape victims. *American Journal of Psychiatry*, **139**, 1266–1270.

Naugle, A., Resnick, H., Gray, M. & Acierno, R. (2002). Treatment for acute stress and PTSD following rape. In J. Petrak & B. Hedge (Eds), *The Trauma of Sexual Assault: Treatment, Prevention and Practice*. Chichester: John Wiley & Sons.

Nilsson Schonnesson, L. & Ross, M. (1999). *Coping with HIV Infection: Psychological and Existential Responses in Gay Men*. New York: Kluwer Academic/Plenum.

Nkengasong, J., Kestens, L., Ghys, P.D., Koblavi-Deme, S., Bile, C., Kalou, M., Ya, L.K., Traore-Ettiegne, V., Maurice, C., Laga, M., Wiktor, S.Z. & Greenberg, A.E. (2001). Human Immunodeficiency virus type 1 (HIV-1) plasma virus load and markers of immune activation among HIV-infected female sex workers with sexually transmitted diseases in Abidjan, Côte d'Ivoire. *Journal of Infectious Diseases*, **183**, 1405–1408.

Oates, J. & Gomez, J. (1984). Venerophobia. *British Journal of Hospital Medicine*, **32**, 266.

Palella, F.J., Delaney, K.M. & Moorman, A.C. (1998). Declining morbidity and mortality among patients with advanced human immunodeficiency virus infection. *New England Journal of Medicine*, **338**, 853–860.

Paredes, R., Mocroft, A. & Kirk, O. (2000). Predictors of virological success and ensuing failure in HIV positive patients starting highly active antiretroviral therapy in Europe. Results from the EuroSIDA Study. *Archives of Internal Medicine*, **160**, 1123–1132.

Parrot, A. (1991). Medical community response to acquaintance rape: recommendations. In L. Bechhofer & A. Parrot (Eds), *Acquaintance Rape: The Hidden Victims*. New York: John Wiley & Sons.

Pedder, J. & Goldberg, D. (1970). A survey by questionnaire of psychiatric disturbance in patients attending a venereal diseases clinic. *British Journal of Venereal Diseases*, **46**, 58–61.

Perry, S., Jacobsberg, L., Fishman, B., Weiler, P., Gold, J. & Frances, A. (1990). Psychological responses to serological testing for HIV. *AIDS*, **4**, 145–152.

Petrak, J. (2002). The psychological impact of sexual assault. In J. Petrak & B. Hedge (Eds), *The Trauma of Sexual Assault: Treatment, Prevention and Practice*. Chichester: John Wiley & Sons.

Prochaska, J. & DiClemente, C. (1986). Towards a comprehensive model of change. In W. Miller & N. Heather (Eds), *Treating Addictive Behaviours: Processes of Change*. New York: Plenum Press.

Prochaska, J., DiClemente, C. & Norcross, J. (1992). In search of how people change. *American Psychologist*, **47**, 1102–1114.

Pugh, K., O'Donnell, I. & Catalan, J. (1993). Suicide and HIV disease. *AIDS Care*, **4**, 391–339.

Pugh, K., Riccio, M., Jadresic, D., Burgess, A., Balderweg, T., Catalan, J., Lovett, E., Howbins, D., Gruzulier, J. & Thompson, C. (1994). A longitudinal study of the neuropsychiatric consequences of

HIV-1 infection in gay men: psychological and health status at baseline and 12 months follow-up. *Psychological Medicine*, **24**, 897–904.

Rand, E., Hoon, E., Massey, J. & Johnson, J. (1990). Daily stress and recurrence of genital herpes simplex. *Archives of Internal Medicine*, **150**, 1889–1893.

Resnick, P., Jordan, C., Girelli, S., Hutter, C. & Marhoefer-Dvorak, S. (1989). A comparative outcome study of behavioural group therapy for sexual assault victims. *Behaviour Therapy*, **19**, 385–401.

Rigsby, M., Rosen, M., Beauvais, J., Cramer, J., Rainey, P., O'Malley, S., Dieckhaus, K. & Round-saville, B. (2000). Cue-dose training with monetary reinforcement: pilot study of an antiretroviral adherence intervention. *Journal of General Internal Medicine*, **15**, 841–847.

Roberts, K. & Mann, T. (2000). Barriers to antiretroviral medication adherence in HIV-infected women. *AIDS Care*, **12**, 377–386.

Rosen, R. (1998). Quality of life assessment in sexual dysfunction trials. *International Journal of Impotence Research*, **10** (Suppl. 2), S21–S23.

Rosengard, C. & Folkman, S. (1997). Suicide ideation, bereavement, HIV serostatus and psychological variables in partners of men with AIDS. *AIDS Care*, **9**, 373–384.

Ross, M. (1986). *Psychovenereology: Personality and Lifestyle Factors in Sexually Transmitted Diseases in Homosexual Men*. New York: Praeger.

Salkovskis, P. (1985). Obsessional-compulsive problems: a cognitive-behavioural analysis, *Behaviour Research and Therapy*, **23**, 571–583.

Salkovskis, P. (1989). Somatic problems. In K. Hawton, P. Salkovskis, J. Kirk & D. Clark (Eds), *Cognitive Behaviour for Psychiatric Problems: A Practical Guide*. Oxford: Oxford University Press.

Salkovskis, P. (1996). The cognitive approach to anxiety: threat beliefs, safety-seeking behaviour, and the special case of health anxiety and obsessions. In P. Salkovskis (Ed.), *Frontiers of Cognitive Therapy*. New York: Guilford Press.

Salkovskis, P. & Warwick, H. (1986). Morbid preoccupations, health anxiety and reassurance: a cognitive-behavioural approach to hypochondriasis. *Behaviour Research and Therapy*, **24**, 597–602.

Schafer, L., Glasgow, R. & McCaul, K. (1982). Increasing the adherence of diabetic adolescents. *Journal of Behavioural Medicine*, **5**, 353–362.

Schacker, T. (2001). The role of HSV in the transmission and progression of HIV. *Herpes*, **8**, 46–49.

Schein, A. (1999). Pregnancy prevention using emergency contraception: efficacy, attitudes, and limitations to use. *Journal of Pediatric and Adolescent Gynaecology*, **12**, 3–9.

Sepkowitz, K.A. (1998). Effect of HAART on natural history of AIDS-related opportunistic disorders. *Lancet*, **351**, 228–230.

Silver, P., Auerbach, S., Vishniavsky, N. & Kaplowitz, L. (1986). Psychological factors in recurrent genital herpes infection: stress, coping style, social support, emotional dysfunction, and symptom recurrence. *Journal of Psychosomatic Research*, **30**, 163–171.

Singh, N., Squire, C., Sivek, M., Wagener, M., Hong-Nguyen, M. & Yu, V. (1996). Determinants of compliance with antiretroviral therapy in patients with human immunodeficiency virus: prospective assessment with implications for enhancing compliance. *AIDS Care*, **8**, 261–269.

Stankoff, B., Tourbah, A., Suarez, S., Turell, E., Stievenart, J.L., Payan, C., Coutellier, A., Herson, S., Baril, L., Bricaire, F., Calvez, V., Cabanis, E.A., Lacomblez, L. & Lubetzki, C. (2001). Clinical and spectroscopic improvement in HIV-associated cognitive impairment. *Neurology*, **56**, 112–115.

Stein, M., Rich, J., Maksad, J., Chen, M., Hu, P., Sobota, M. & Clarke, J. (2000). Adherence to antiretroviral therapy among HIV-infected methadone patients: effects of ongoing illicit drug use. *American Journal of Drug and Alcohol Abuse*, **26**, 195–205.

Stroebe, M. & Stroebe, W. (1993). Who suffers more? Sex differences in health risks of the widowed. *Psychological Bulletin*, **93**, 279–301.

Suarez, S., Baril, L., Stankoff, B., Khellaf, M., Dubois, B., Lubetzki, C., Bricaire, F. & Hauw, J.J. (2001). Outcome of patients with HIV-related cognitive impairment on highly active antiretroviral therapy. *AIDS*, **15**, 195–200.

Tarrier, N., Pilgrim, H., Sommerfield, C., Faragher, B., Reynold, M., Graham, E. & Barrowclough, C. (1999). A randomised trial of cognitive therapy and imaginal exposure in the treatment of chronic posttraumatic stress disorder. *Journal of Consulting and Clinical Psychology*, **67**, 13–18.

Testa, M. & Lederking, W. (1999). The impact of AIDS-associated wasting on quality of life: qualitative issues of measurement and evaluation. *The Journal of Nutrition*, **129**, 282–289.

Tuldra, A., Fumaz, C., Ferrer, M., Bayes, R., Arno, R., Balague, M., Bonjoch, A., Jou, A., Negredo, E., Paredes, R., Ruiz, L., Romeu, J., Sierra, G., Tural, C., Burger, D. & Clotet, B. (2000). Prospective randomized two-arm controlled study to determine the efficacy of a specific intervention to improve long-term adherence to highly active antiretroviral therapy. *Journal of Acquired Immune Deficiency Syndrome*, **25**, 221–228.

Turk, D. & Spears, M. (1984). Diabetes mellitus: stress and adherence. In T. Burish & L. Bradley (Eds), *Coping with Chronic Disease*. New York: Academic Press.

Turner, H. & Catania, J. (1997). Informal caregiving to persons with aids in the United States: caregiver burden among central cities residents eighteen to forty-nine years old. *American Journal of Community Psychology*, **25**, 35–59.

UN AIDS (2002). Report on the global HIV/AIDS epidemic 2002. *XIV International AIDS Conference, Barcelona*.

VanderPlate, C. & Aral, S. (1987). Psychological aspects of genital herpes virus infection. *Health Psychology*, **6**, 57–72.

VanderPlate, C., Aral, S. & Magder, L. (1988). The relationship among genital herpes simplex, stress and social support. *Health Psychology*, **7**, 159–168.

Vuchinich, R. & Tucker, J. (1988). Contributions from behavioural theories of science to an analysis of alcohol abuse. *Journal of Abnormal Psychology*, **97**, 181–195.

Wainberg, M. & Friedland, G. (1998). Public health implications of antiretroviral therapy and HIV drug resistance. *Journal of the American Medical Association*, **279**, 1977–1983.

Wasserheit, J. (1989). The significance and scope of reproductive tract infections among third world women. *International Journal of Gynaecology and Obstetrics*, **3**, 145–163.

Wesley, Y., Smeltzer, S., Redeker, N., Walker, S., Palumbo, P. & Whipple, B. (2000). Reproductive decision making in mothers with HIV-1. *Health Care for Women International*, **21**, 291–304.

WHO (1995). Global Programme on AIDS. Global prevalence and incidences of selected curable sexually transmitted diseases: overview and estimates. *WHO/GPA/STD*, **1**, 1–26.

Williams, J. & Holmes, K. (1981). *The Second Assault: Rape and Public Attitudes*. Westport, CT: Greenwood Press.

Wood, K., Nairn, R., Kraft, H. & Siegal, A. (1997). Suicidality among HIV-positive psychiatric patients. *AIDS Care*, **9**, 385–389.

Zuckerman, M. & Antoni, M. (1995). Social support and its relationship to psychological physical and immune variables in HIV infection. *Clinical Psychology and Psychotherapy*, **2**, 210–219.

CHAPTER 22

An Average Old Age: Associations between Ageing, Health and Behaviour

Mary Gilhooly

and

Eileen McDonach

University of Paisley, Scotland, UK

INTRODUCTION

Recent years have seen an increased interest in "successful ageing", along with other concepts such as "healthy ageing" and "healthy life expectancy". The term "successful ageing" has been around since the 1960s, but seems to have been revived in recent years (Baltes & Baltes, 1993; Havighurst, 1963). While longevity might be seen as a prime indicator of successful ageing, living to an advanced old age, disabled and in pain, is not seen as a desirable state. Thus, successful ageing, at least from a medical or public health perspective, "consists of optimising life expectancy, while at the same time minimising physical, psychological and social morbidity" (Fries, 1990). The increase in numbers of people surviving into advanced old age has led to considerable interest into compression of morbidity, i.e. shifting the onset of disease closer to the time of death. Interestingly, the debate about compression of morbidity does not assume that it is possible to live a long life completely free of disease.

Ageing and ageing populations are of relevance to the practice of clinical psychology for a number of reasons. Firstly, age is linked to many diseases, e.g. heart disease, cancers, arthritis, etc. Diseases such as these have a number of psychological consequences which are of interest to psychologists. Secondly, an increase in the numbers of old people in a society increases the number of people with dementia. Although dementia does not affect most older adults, the impact on families and society is disproportionate because the financial and psychological costs of caring for those with dementia are high. Health is also known to be the main determinant of life satisfaction and quality of life in old age (Bowling, 1996). Despite these obvious reasons why clinical health psychologists might be interested in ageing, few textbooks in clinical health psychology contain chapters on ageing.

Handbook of Clinical Health Psychology. Edited by S. Llewelyn and P. Kennedy.
© 2003 John Wiley & Sons, Ltd.

One aim of this chapter is to examine the extent to which it is possible to age without disease. Is an "average old age" one of increasing likelihood of one or more diseases, combined with declining cognitive functioning? If so, what, if anything, can delay the onset of disease, or minimise the impact of illness when it occurs? The chapter will begin with an overview of the association of age with disease. The section will then examine the literature on psychological changes with age, e.g. changes in intelligence, memory, perception, etc., with older people. Many cognitive functions show decline with age, forcing us to ask if such declines are normal or if they are related to the increased incidence of disease with age. The second part of the chapter will examine research on the role of age as a mediator between behaviour and health. To what extent does age mediate the relationships between behaviour and health and between health and behaviour? For example, can changes in health behaviours in mid- or late life have the same impact on mortality and morbidity as changes at a younger age? This section will also examine the question from the other direction and discuss research on the role of age as a mediator between health and behaviour. To what extent does the development of disease in advanced old age differ in its impact on adaptive behaviours, disability, and psychological well-being compared to younger ages?

The literature on these issues is large and growing and the debate is often acrimonious. Pathologising old age is viewed as gross ageism by some gerontologists, who note that most older people live independent lives and do not place enormous burdens on the health service, the State or their families. In addition, it is suggested that focusing on the relation between age and disease draws attention away from the well-established link between social class and health. On the other hand, suggesting that living a long life without disease can easily be achieved implies that those who develop disease may somehow be at fault. This chapter aims to familiarise clinical health psychologists with the outline of the debate.

NORMAL AND ABNORMAL AGEING

The increase in life expectancy and in the numbers of older people has raised the question of whether or not it is possible to live a normal life span without disease and disability. The average life span of humans is around 85 years, with an upper limit of around 125 years (Cristofalo et al., 1999). Elizabeth "Pampo" Israel, believed to be the world's oldest living person, celebrated her 127th birthday in January 2002. Israel's next-door neighbour, Rose Pere, is 118 years old. Both women are from Dominica, which is home to 22 documented centenarians. Ms Jeanne Calmet, the oldest person living in 1997, died at the age of 122. In 2001 the oldest person alive in the USA was Mary Thompson living in Arkansas; she was aged 119 years, 2 months and 2 days when she died in October 2001.

Large numbers of very old people with disease and chronic illness put special demands on health and social services, as well as family caregivers. Pain and suffering are also of concern to caring societies. A question which has taxed gerontologists is whether or not old age is synonymous with disease, i.e. will it be possible, some time in the future, to prevent or cure all disease, so that we merely die of "old age"? There are those who take the view that old age necessarily brings about disease, while others argue that life span/life expectancy will not increase dramatically and that morbidity can be compressed to a shorter period. These two positions will now be considered as they have important consequences for what could and should be done in relation to health promotion and the provision of medical care in the future. The key to the future well-being of an ageing global population may rest, to a large extent, on how tightly linked ageing rates are to ageing-dependent diseases.

The Ageing–Disease Relationship

An examination of the age–disease relationship is not as straightforward as one might expect. The definitions of both age and disease are problematic and, thus, create problems when researching the relationship between the two (Woodruff-Pak, 1997). Many diseases only manifest themselves at an advanced stage, making it difficult to know whether or not a disease is present. If a disease has not yet manifested itself, can we say that the individual is ageing normally? Many definitions of ageing include the manifestation of disease as a component part of the definition. As noted by Grimley Evans (1988), "to draw a distinction between disease and normal ageing is to attempt to separate the undefined from the indefinable". For our purposes, however, the definition favoured by Solomon (1999) and put forward by Miller (1994) is useful: "Aging is a process that converts healthy adults into frail ones, with diminished reserve in most physiological systems and an exponentially increasing vulnerability to most diseases and death."

Any examination of the incidence and prevalence of disease by age shows a stark pattern; almost all diseases show an increase with age (Manton, 1989; Wood & Bain, 2001). Some diseases peak in childhood (e.g. lymphocytic leukaemia) and mid-life (polycystic kidney disease, multiple sclerosis and systemic lupus), but most peak in old age. Brody (1990) has proposed that the term "age-related" be used for diseases that peak at younger ages and "age-dependent" for those that peak in old age. As noted by Solomon (1999), this does not mean that ageing is the *sole* aetiology, but that the ageing process is a potent predisposing factor for disease and conditions whose aetiology is multifactorial. Of interest is whether or not diseases are age-dependent because they are *time-related*; that is, time is required for the disease process to mature. Some genetic disorders are of this nature and, hence, are not really to do with ageing processes.

Mortality increases exponentially with age from a late childhood nadir to approximately age 85, with a doubling time of around 8.5 years. Ageing-dependent diseases also follow this same Gompertzian law of linear relationship between the log of age-specific incidence and chronological age (Gompertz, 1825). Interestingly, evidence is accumulating that Gompertzian dynamics disappear after the age of 85–90 years. From around 85 years the mortality rate is more or less consistent with age. There are five "model" ageing-dependent diseases, ischaemic heart disease, malignant neoplasms, diabetes mellitus, osteoarthritis and Alzheimer's disease, that demonstrate these relationships (Solomon, 1999). The epidemiology and pathogenesis of each will be briefly described. Due to their chronicity and psychological consequences, these are also among the diseases most studied by clinical health psychologists.

Atherosclerosis and Ischaemic Heart Disease

Atherosclerosis is the pathogenetic mechanism for all cardiovascular disease in older people. Age-specific incidence and mortality for ischaemic heart disease rise exponentially, with a doubling time of 8 years. Although mortality from cardiovascular disease has been decreasing, incidence has declined very little. Acquired conditions such as hypertension, diabetes, obesity, hypercholesterolaemia, plus smoking, a high-fat diet and lack of exercise, are important risk factors.

Cancer

All of the common cancers increase in frequency by age. For some cancers, e.g. prostate cancer, the rise is exponential; for others the rise is gradual and linear. Solomon (1999) notes that cancer could be viewed as age-related rather than ageing-dependent because incidence and mortality appear to plateau after age 75 and even to decline after age 85. Because the pathogenesis of the cancers is so complex, there has been considerable controversy as to whether the rise in incidence with age is due to ageing processes or simply to the passage of time, and consequent accumulation of damaging events and exposure to carcinogenic influences.

Diabetes Mellitus

Insulin-dependent diabetes (Type I) is a classical example of an age-related disease. Incidence peaks in youth and it rarely occurs de nova after the age of 50 years. Type II diabetes is an ageing-dependent disease, with age-specific incidence and mortality rising exponentially with age, starting at age 40, with a doubling time of 6–8 years. Incidence falls at very late ages. Type II diabetes is caused by a genetic predisposition and risk factors such as over-eating and lack of exercise. Type II diabetes might be time-related, but authors such as Solomon (1999) argue that it is more likely that the obligatory component in the pathogenesis of Type II diabetes is the effect of ageing on islet cells.

Osteoarthritis

Osteoarthritis is the most common disease of older people. Age-specific incidence rises exponentially with age, with a doubling time of 5–7 years. The pathogenesis of osteoarthritis is unclear. Alteration in the structure and function of collagen, as well as changes in the properties of chondrocytes which occur with age, may play a role.

Alzheimer's Disease

The annual incidence for Alzheimer's disease (AD) is 1.4 per 1000 in the seventh decade, 6.4 per 1000 in the eighth decade and 20.5 per 1000 in those 80 years and over. These figures describe a Gompertzian exponential with a doubling time of 5–6 years from age 60–90 years; there is some evidence of a decreasing slope after age 90. There has been a great deal of research on the genetics of AD, with at least three genes and one allele linked to familial clusters (Solomon, 1999). Head trauma appears to be a risk factor (Morris, 2001). A review of the literature has indicated that those with more years of education are less likely to develop AD (Gilleard, 1997), but it is unclear if education or higher intellectual capacity raises the threshold for the manifestation of cognitive decline, or if education is merely a proxy measure for social class (Mortimer, 2000). Given that almost all disease shows a class gradient, it would not be surprising if this were true for AD. The exact role of ageing in AD is unclear.

Connecting Ageing to Disease

It has been noted that one explanation for the link between ageing and disease is not ageing processes per se, but increased time for exposure to environmental damage. The fact that comorbidity rises with age is, however, viewed as evidence that it is not merely greater exposure to disease-specific risks that accounts for the link between age and disease. In addition, the effect of risk factors appears to decrease with age, suggesting that it is not just time that accounts for the increase in disease rates with age. The very fact that the incidence of so many diseases increases exponentially, rather than linearly, is viewed as suggesting that longer exposure to risk factors is not the best explanation. Finally, as noted by Solomon (1999), the very multiplicity of ageing-dependent diseases implies a common pathogenic mechanism.

Unsurprisingly, there are many theories that account for ageing and for the link between ageing and disease (Cristofalo et al., 1999; Pederson, 1996). It is, however, the stress theories of ageing that, in the authors' view, best fit with the thesis being developed in this chapter. The stress theories start with two fundamental premises: (1) genetic variants on life span and the many outcomes of ageing is smaller than the unexplained variance, which, by default, is environmental (Finch & Tanzi, 1997) and (2) neuroendocrine regulation is a central facet of human physiological competence and differential patterns of response to challenge contribute importantly to observed trajectories of ageing (McEwen & Stellar, 1983; Sapolsky, 1992; Seeman & Robbins, 1994). It is hypothesised that cumulative levels of "stress" have deleterious effects on health and longevity, in particular on the risks for hypertension and cardiovascular disease.

One of the two main regulatory systems for responding to external stressors and maintaining internal homeostasis integrity is the hypothalamic–pituitary–adrenal (HPA) axis. A leading hypothesis posits an age-related decline in the HPA axis in response to challenge and stress, with the time needed for resetting of the HPA axis increasing with age (Finch & Seeman, 1999). Stimulation of the HPA axis results in increased levels of glucocorticoids, hormones and cardiovascular tone, all of which have the potential for negative effects on mortality and morbidity. Animal research shows little difference between young and old organisms in initial HPA stress responses, but marked differences in the post-stress recovery period, with older rats showing prolonged elevations in corticosterone (Sapolsky, 1992; Seeman & Robbins, 1994). An interesting study by Seeman and her colleagues on HPA reactivity in response to a driving simulation challenge found age-related prolongation of cortisol response (Seeman, Singer & Charpentier, 1995). The research by Seeman has also found gender differences in HPA reactivity that might account for gender differences in mortality and morbidity, as well as the link between social support, personal control and Type A behaviour and healthy ageing (Henry, 1988). Finally, what is especially interesting for psychologists is the growing body of research showing that increased cortisol levels are related to poorer performance on memory tasks (Kirschbaum et al., 1996; Lupien et al., 1994; Seeman et al., 1997). These findings are consistent with the hypothesis that higher levels of cortisol may be associated with risk of damage to the hippocampus, a region of the brain involved in memory (Finch & Seeman, 1999).

For clinical health psychologists, these studies present interesting challenges. Several studies show that individual differences in HPA reactivity are associated with differences in diet and psychosocial characteristics (Seeman & McEwen, 1996). Although there may be age-related changes towards less efficient regulation of the HPA axis and associated increased risks for disease, patterns of endocrine reactivity and regulation are potentially modifiable. It is also worth keeping in mind that declines in physical health which accompany ageing may be the most severe stressor that people ever experience (Lieberman, 1982).

Age, Cognitive Functioning and Health

The most feared diseases of old age are those that impair memory, thinking, problem-solving, intelligence, perception and our personality. Although a great deal of research has been conducted on age changes in cognitive functioning, much still needs to be done to develop our understanding of the borderlands between normal and abnormal declines in functioning. At the moment there are two camps: those who argue that dementia is distinctly different, qualitatively and quantitatively from mild cognitive impairment, and those who argue that there is a continuum from benign cognitive impairment to dementia.

Memory

Older people frequently complain of a failing memory and many find these memory problems worrying. Although there is a tendency to dismiss such complaints as the concerns of the "worried well", there is a growing body of evidence demonstrating that a significant proportion of those worried enough to consult a doctor go on to develop mild cognitive impairment or a dementing disorder. In addition, significant correlations have been found between memory complaints and depression. The literature on age changes in memory is large and growing and only a flavour can be given here of the findings.

Primary memory, which involves passively holding a small amount of information for immediate recall, does not appear to show large age differences in storage or amount of information retained. Even memory span shows few age differences up to the age of about 80 years (Johansson & Berg, 1989). Because memory span tests are used to screen for dementia it is important to know about age changes in this aspect of primary memory.

However, a different picture of the impact of age on primary memory is found when examining studies of working memory. As the name implies, working memory involves both holding the memory in store and manipulating the information. Both cross-sectional and longitudinal studies indicate that there are age differences and age changes in working memory (Hultsch et al., 1992). There is an interesting debate as to why age deficits in working memory might occur. The problem may occur during storage, in relation to the demands of processing information, or the speed of working on information. Research suggests that processing speed is the most important determinant of age differences in working memory (Salthouse & Babcock, 1991).

Interestingly, although it is commonly believed that old people are better able to remember events in the distant past, the research evidence indicates that remote memory is not superior to the recall of recent events (Erber, 1981). The reason why older people may believe that remote events are remembered better is that they may be comparing a sharp and clear memory from the past, perhaps an event of special personal significance, with a vaguely encoded recent event. Some remote events may also have been rehearsed many times. The possibility of distortions in memory as we age is of importance clinically and in real-life situations. Credibility of eyewitness testimony in court is dependent on accurate recall of information in long-term memory (Loftus, 1991). Health surveys often depend on reporting events and decisions from the past (Loftus, Fienberg & Tanur, 1985).

Intelligence

When information about age changes in intelligence first began to emerge, the picture looked grim. Early cross-sectional studies comparing the performance on intelligence tests of young and older adults indicated that intelligence declined fairly dramatically with age. However, these studies could not disentangle cohort from ageing effects. The older cohorts in these studies had fewer years of education and many were unfamiliar with the types of problems in most intelligence tests. The more recent longitudinal studies, however, have painted a somewhat rosier picture. Crystallised abilities (e.g. verbal ability) peak between age 30 and 55 and remain stable until old age. Fluid abilities, those that represent on-the-spot thinking, with novel material, on the other hand decline from young adulthood to old age (Deary, 2001; Schaie, 1996).

Explanations for Declines in Cognitive Functioning with Age

Fortunately, most of life's tasks do not require a high level of cognitive functioning. Nevertheless, it is worth asking why fluid intelligence declines at such an early age, and why even performance on tests of crystallised intelligence appears to decline in very old age. A related but slightly different question is also worth asking. Why do some very old people maintain very high levels of cognitive functioning well into an advanced old age?

Salthouse (1996) has argued that the reason so many mental abilities decline with age is because there is a decline in "general" ability, and that the decline in "g" is due to a decline in speed of information processing. It must then be asked why speed of information processing declines with age. Is it because of underlying disease or is the effect due directly to ageing?

The age-dependent diseases described previously may affect cognitive functioning directly due to effects on the brain. Cardiovascular disease has a major impact on brain function. Decreased blood flow to the brain (cerebrovascular disease) and stroke are clear examples of diseases that directly affect cognitive functioning. Even mild cardiovascular disease has been found to be related to deficits in memory and lower scores on intelligence test performance (Elias, Elias & Elias, 1990). Intellectual decline has also been found to be associated with hypertension, though the relationship is complex and may be curvilinear. Several studies have suggested that the relationship is consistent only when blood pressure is elevated above a certain level (Elias, Elias & Elias, 1990; Gruber-Baldini, 1991).

Longitudinal studies that have retroactively examined performance changes related to dying and death suggest that intellectual decline related to chronological age is due to the presence of undetected illness (Cooney, Schaie & Willis, 1988; Riegel & Riegel, 1972). These studies found that performance is more or less stable, with dramatic changes occurring in the five years immediately preceding death.

Numerous studies document brain atrophy, changes in neurotransmitter systems and changes at the molecular level within cells in older people. Brain cell loss in normal ageing, however, has not been found to be entirely random. Deficits in the frontal lobes and the hippocampus have been found to be strongly associated with age-related declines in cognitive functioning and behavioural capacity (Woodruff-Pak, 1997).

Medications, of which the elderly are particularly high consumers, are also associated with memory loss. For example, Valium, a drug used by large numbers of older people as a sedative, has been found to impair performance on memory tests (Block et al., 1985). High consumption of alcohol over many years has also been shown to affect memory (Parker & Noble, 1977).

Apart from illnesses and medications that may directly affect the brain, what other factors impact on the likelihood of declines in cognitive functioning with age? The Seattle Longitudinal Study conducted by Schaie and his colleagues (Schaie, 1996) has found that the following factors help some people to maintain good mental functioning in old age (Deary, 2001):

- living in a favourable environment, mediated by high social class
- having a spouse with high mental ability
- possessing a flexible personality style in mid-life
- satisfaction with life in middle age
- maintaining a fast level of processing speed in the brain
- involvement in a complex and intellectually stimulating environment.

Research in the UK has also indicated that engaging in mental activities is related to better cognitive functioning (Gilhooly et al., 2002).

The last item on this list is of special interest because of possibilities for interventions by clinical health psychologists that would help to maintain cognitive functioning in old age. As noted by Schaie and Willis, "Studies indicate that moderate brain atrophy is compatible with normal intellectual functioning. In short, it seems that those who live by their wits, die with their wits" (Schaie & Willis, 1996, p. 400).

A Healthy Old Age?

The exponential rise in the incidence of many diseases with age strongly indicates that ageing processes create the conditions for disease, rather than disease in old age being due to long-term exposure to a toxic environment. Thus, a disease-free old age may be almost impossible. There is certainly little evidence for marked compression of morbidity. Data from the General Household Survey over the past 20 years show that for England and Wales, for example, there has been minimal change in the expectation of life without limiting longstanding illness. Furthermore, the expectation of life without moderate disability has increased in line with total life expectancy in men and has shown minimal change in women. Thus, as noted by Wood and Bain (2001), the absolute time spent with moderate disability has increased. However, the good news is that expectation without *severe* disability and dependency appears to have not increased, providing some, though limited, evidence for compression of morbidity. Although this is welcome news, as Wood and Bain (2001) note, it is possible that the trend reflects being able to perform activities of daily living because of the availability of new aids and equipment.

Research on changes in cognitive functioning with age also suggests that at least some decline is the norm. Younger people consistently outperform older people on tests that assess different types of memory, as well as nearly all the tests of fluid intelligence. Longitudinal research indicates that these are real age effects and not just cohort effects.

Thus, while most of us can expect to survive into old age, few will experience a disease-free old age, and, while dementia will not be the norm, at least mild cognitive decline will be part of a normal old age. Nevertheless, the research evidence suggests that behaviours impact on the likelihood of making it into old age, as well as impact on some of the variance in decline. In addition, age may act as a mediator between health and behaviour.

AGE AS A MEDIATOR BETWEEN HEALTH AND BEHAVIOUR

The main question to be addressed in this section is, "How does ageing affect the relation between health and behaviour?" If the health–behaviour relationship is weaker in advanced age than it is at a younger age, it could be argued that age moderates the relationship (Deeg, Kardaun & Fozard, 1996). Possible mediating factors include changes in resources, norms and priorities, as well as changes in perceptions of self. There are two perspectives on possible age-associated mediators, the health consequences of behaviour and the behavioural consequences of ill health.

Impact of Behaviour on Health

It is well established that before old age, behaviour has both beneficial and negative effects on health. Smoking, alcohol abuse, poor diet, obesity, lack of exercise, etc., all reduce the probability of surviving into old age. The debate in gerontology, however, is whether risk factors associated with mortality and morbidity in middle age have as strong an effect in old age. Several studies indicate that the risk factors known to influence mortality and morbidity at younger ages have weaker effects in old age. For example, high blood pressure, high cholesterol levels and obesity are weaker predictors in old age (Sorkin et al., 1992). This could be a "survivor effect", i.e. those with high risk factors die at an earlier age. Alternatively, it could be an "ageing effect", that is, in advanced age there is a natural decline in risk-factor levels (Wilson et al., 1994). It has also been suggested that multiple risk factors may interact in different ways in old age (Kane, Kane & Arnold, 1985). In addition, there is a possibility that these findings are due to a cohort effect (Deeg, Kardaun & Fozard, 1996). Nevertheless, there is evidence that behaviour change in old age has a beneficial

Figure 22.1 Age-associated mediators as explanatory variables of the association between health and behaviour and between behaviour and health. (After Deeg, Kardaun & Fozard, 1996.)

effect on health and psychological well-being (Walters et al., 1999). It may also be the case that the same levels of behaviour in old age are more harmful than at younger ages.

Smoking Cessation

US studies suggest that smoking cessation for lifetime smokers in their sixties increases chances of survival. Cardiovascular risk is reduced so rapidly that older smokers who quit have a reduced risk within one or two years of smoking cessation. Older quitters also have a reduced risk of influenza and pneumonia mortality (LaCroix & Owenn, 1992).

Physical Activity and Trajectories of Disability

The evidence for changes in physical activity is in line with smoking cessation. The Harvard Alumni Study, the Alameda County Study and the Aerobics Center Longitudinal Study suggest that previously inactive older women and men who take up regular exercise live longer than those who remain inactive (Blair, Kohl & Barlow, 1995; Paffenbarger et al., 1993). The British Regional Heart Study also found that it was beneficial for men to take up physical activity after the age of 50 (Wannamethee et al., 1998). Moreover, this study also revealed that light activity, rather than vigorous sporting activity, can bring cardiovascular benefits for men over 60 years. Besides adding years to life, there is a growing body of evidence that exercise delays decline in physical functioning and mobility in older people both with and without chronic disease. For example, a large US prospective study found that the risk of osteoporotic hip fracture was decreased by 36% in the most active old women (over age 65) compared with the least active women (Gregg et al., 1998). Apart from the impact on physical outcome there is evidence that lower levels of physical activity were associated with higher levels of service use eight years after interview (Bath & Morgan, 1998). Interestingly, it has been found that even a single dose of low-intensity exercise may benefit cognitive performance in the very old. In a study of nursing home residents, Diesfeldt and Diesfeldt-Groenendijk (1977) found that verbal memory improved by 35%. In another study, Stones and Dawe (1993) found that, although activity raised heartbeat by only two beats per minute, there was a gain of 20% on a test of semantic memory.

Physical experiences also impact on mental functioning in old age. Dustman et al. (1984) showed that brain function as assessed by evoked potentials was more efficient in an older group of runners compared to sedentary older people. Dustman and his colleagues also found that performance on neuropsychological test performance improved after a four-month exercise programme.

Alcohol Use

Alcohol use and abuse are generally seen as less prevalent in older people (Office for National Statistics, 2002). The proportion of heavy drinkers decreases from age 50 and still further after the age of 65 (McAneny, 1992). This may partly be a survivor effect; those who drink especially heavily will not make it into old age. Many elderly non-drinkers are also former heavy drinkers who have stopped drinking for health and social reasons. The lower levels of drinking among older people may, however, largely be a cohort effect. Today's generations of older people grew up in an era in which alcoholic beverages were relatively expensive and where drunkenness and even drinking in public by women was frowned upon. Although alcohol consumption is lower in older cohorts, there is growing evidence of potentially harmful drinking among older people (Office for National Statistics, 2002; Scottish Executive, 2000). Surveys are generally thought to result in under-reporting of alcohol use. What is unknown is whether older people are more or less likely to under-report alcohol use.

It is well established that heavy consumption of alcohol has negative effects on health over time. There is also a growing body of evidence showing that even quite moderate amounts of alcohol, especially for women, may impact negatively on the health of older people. Several studies have shown that the cognitive deficits associated with alcohol abuse are more severe in older compared to younger alcoholics with similar drinking histories (Brandt et al., 1983; Ryan & Butters, 1980). The most common explanation is that heavy alcohol consumption accelerates the normal deterioration of the central nervous function that occurs as we age. Research also indicates that recovered alcoholics who may not have had a drink for many years perform less well on tests of tactual-motor speed, psychomotor speed, abstraction and other abilities than non-alcoholics (Brandt et al., 1983; Parson & Leber, 1981).

Although research evidence suggests a strong case for reduced consumption of alcohol in old age, if not before, in Western cultures the consumption of alcohol is closely associated with social life. For many people in the UK, for example, socialising takes place in pubs. Family gatherings in the home are rarely alcohol free. Those who report moderate drinking have been found to be more sociable and socially active and to perceive themselves to be in better health than those who abstain completely. It has been suggested that even providing limited social drinking in nursing homes can have beneficial effects on mood and social interaction (Chien, Stotsky & Cole, 1973).

Impact of Health on Behaviour

The question to be asked here is how age affects psychological well-being, functional ability, service use and medication compliance.

Psychological Well-being

There is research evidence that illness associated distress is less in older compared to younger people (Cassileth et al., 1984; Leventhal, 1984). Cassileth et al. (1984) have offered the following explanations:

1. Illness offers social advantages.
2. Older people have or develop more effective skills with which to manage illness and stressful life events.
3. The expectations of older people are more commensurate with adaptation to illness.
4. There may be biologic advantage for older people that enables them to adapt to illnesses that are associated with old age.

Increased attention and involvement from caregiving relatives and friends might be an advantage of illness, but it is not clear why this should be more so for older compared to younger people. The second explanation also has some support (Cassileth et al., 1984; Leventhal,

1984). Current generations of older people might be more accepting of poor health because they have grown up with lower expectation levels. Illness is likely to be more disruptive if one is working, making adaptation easier for older retired people. Neugarten and Neugarten (1987) have suggested that negative events produce lower levels of stress when they are experienced at predictable points in the life course than when completely unanticipated. Neugarten (1968) originally proposed that adults construct a "social timetable" against which they compare their own development, judging the right time for marriage, the right age to have children and the predictable time for losses such as bereavement and poor health. Support for this notion comes from studies that show that older adults are more likely to confront cancer with less anger than younger adults (Mages & Mendelsohn, 1979). Studies of heart disease also show that age influences reactions to heart attacks. Men under the age of 40 have been found to have a need to demonstrate that their virility and vigour are intact post attack. Nurses describe those under 40 who have been admitted to hospital as jovial, cheerful, manic and flirtatious; those under 40 are also more likely to disobey their physicians' orders. Those over 60, on the other hand, seem to accept the heart attack, and follow doctors' orders to the letter (Schaie & Willis, 1996).

Research on depression and ill health has revealed some interesting findings in relation to age. Depression can be considered as both an outcome measure and as pathology. Research has indicated that the development of depression is predicted by increasing numbers of medical conditions and problems in activities of daily living (Kennedy, Kelman & Thomas, 1990; Ormel et al., 1993; Von Korff et al., 1992). Presumably the more adjustments older people need to make, the greater the risk of developing a depressive disorder. Research has also indicated that depressed chronically ill people, compared to non-depressed people, are more likely to be functionally impaired and to show higher rates of mortality (Sullivan, 1995). Possible explanations for these findings include: (1) depression decreases motivation to engage in behaviours that would be beneficial in relation to the illness; (2) depression alters perceptions of somatic symptoms which may lead to assumption of the sick role, thereby decreasing use of health services; and (3) depression may have physiological effects that impact directly on the illness (Deeg, Kardaun & Fozard, 1996). Given that depression is highly treatable, early recognition could both improve the older person's psychological well-being and postpone functional impairment. It is, however, worth keeping in mind that depression rates are lower in older compared to younger adults, i.e. depression is not a natural consequence of the ageing process (Blazer, 1994; Wolfe, Morrow & Fredrickson, 1996).

Consequences of Disability

Inability to care for oneself is associated with higher levels of mortality in older people (Deeg, 1989; Grand et al., 1990; Koyano et al., 1986). Changes in activities of daily living have been found to be a better predictor of death than changes in blood glucose level, vital capacity, heart rate and blood pressure (Manton et al., 1994). In a study of people who survived beyond 95 years, Manton et al. found that these very long-lived people had exhibited slower than expected declines in both physiological and functional ability.

Service Use

Unsurprisingly, disability and decline have been associated with greater use of services. More interestingly, Logan and Spitze (1994) found that those who thought of themselves as old were more likely to use formal services than those who had a younger age identity. Thus, age identity appears to be a mediator between health and behaviours such as service use.

Adherence to Medical Advice

Several US studies suggest that, compared to younger people, elderly people are more likely to fail to comply with doctors' recommendations regarding medications. North American studies indicate that people in their seventies, compared to those in their forties, are twice as likely to fail to follow instructions. Of the medication "mistakes" made, nearly half involve omitting medications (Schaie & Willis, 1996). On the other hand, studies on specific drugs, e.g. antihypertensive drugs, have found that adherence is better in older patients (Bloom, 2001). Mistakes, or failure to take medications, can have serious or fatal consequences. Furthermore, studies on non-attendance for appointments at hospital clinics suggest that it is younger people who are less likely to turn up for their outpatient appointments (Gilhooly et al., 1984).

Paying Attention to Age

There is a growing body of research demonstrating the role of age as a mediator between behaviour and health. Explanations as to how and why age changes might influence the relationship between health and behaviour are, however, less often provided. One possible mechanism might be changes in perceived self-efficacy or control over health with age. Perceived control is associated with beneficial health practices and better functional ability. There is some evidence that there are decreases in perceived self-efficacy with age (Bosscher, 1994), as well as evidence that the associations between perceived control and positive health practices are weaker in older people (Deeg, Kardaun & Fozard, 1996). However, it is important to keep in mind that these findings may represent a cohort, rather than an ageing, effect.

The paucity of longitudinal studies from which to draw conclusions about the impact of ageing on the relationship between health and behaviour is just one methodological problem facing researchers in this field. Another problem is the use of statistical methods that ignore heterogeneity. Heterogeneity in responses across a range of measures has been found to increase with age (Howse & Prophet, 1999). While it is commonly said that all old people are alike, the gerontological literature suggests that young people are more alike than old people. This heterogeneity, combined with the complexity of findings to date, mean that much still needs to be done to understand the role of age in the pathway from health to behaviour and vice versa.

SUMMARY AND CONCLUSIONS

A number of theorists argue that the ageing process creates the conditions for disease and, hence, a disease-free old age is almost impossible. If we accept the argument that ageing and disease are linked, the focus of policy-makers and health and social care professionals must be on how older people can be encouraged to minimise the other risk factors associated with disease, as well as how to help older people to cope psychologically with the common diseases of old age. The growing body of evidence, showing that exercise in old age can reduce ill health, reduce falls, and increase flexibility and psychological well-being, is a good starting point for interventions to increase the numbers of older people who age healthily. Reducing smoking and alcohol consumption among older people would also be beneficial at both a public health and individual level. Monitoring medication use and the negative impact of polypharmacy and alcohol use could also positively impact on the health of older people.

Although risk factors for disease appear to have a differential impact in old age, and although the evidence is that ageing creates the circumstances that produce disease, there is still considerable unexplained variance in healthy and successful ageing which is likely to be amenable to intervention. Of considerable importance to clinical health psychologists are the studies showing that engagement in intellectual activities is associated with better cognitive functioning in old age. Whether this is cause or effect is an important area for future research.

REFERENCES

Baltes, P.B. & Baltes, M.M. (1993). *Successful Ageing: Perspectives from the Behavioural Sciences*. Cambridge, England: Cambridge University Press.

Bath, P. & Morgan, K. (1998). Customary physical activity and physical health outcomes in later life. *Age and Ageing*, **27** (Suppl. 3), 29–34.

Blair, S., Kohl, H.W. & Barlow, C.E. (1995). Changes in physical fitness and all-cause mortality: a prospective study of health and unhealthy men. *Journal of the American Medical Association*, 273, 1093–1098.

Blazer, D.G. (1994). Epidemiology of late life depression. In L.S. Schneider, D.E. Reynolds, B.D. Lebowitz & A.J. Friedhoff (Eds), *Diagnosis and Treatment of Depression in Late Life* (pp. 9–19). Washington, DC: American Psychiatric Association.

Block, R., Devoe, M., Stanley, M. & Pomora, N. (1985). Memory performance in individuals with primary degenerative dementia: its similarity to diazepam-induced impairments. *Experimental Ageing Research*, **11**, 151–155.

Bloom, B.S. (2001). Editorial. Daily regimen and compliance with treatment. *British Medical Journal*, **323**, 647.

Bosscher, R.J. (1994). Self-efficacy expectations. In D.J.H. Deeg & M. Westendorde Seriere (Eds), *Autonomy and Well-being in the Aging Population I: Report from the Longitudinal Aging Study Amsterdam 1992–1993* (pp. 45–51). Amsterdam: VU University Press.

Bowling, A. (1996). The most important things in life for older people. Comparisons between older and younger population age groups by gender. Results from a national survey of the public's judgements. *International Journal of Health Sciences*, **6**, 169–175.

Brandt, J., Butters, N., Ryan, C. & Bayog, R. (1983). Cognitive loss and recovery in chronic alcohol abusers. *Archives of General Psychiatry*, **40**, 436–442.

Brody, J.A. (1990). Chronic diseases and disorders. In A.L. Goldstein (Ed.), *Biomedical Advances in Ageing* (pp. 137–142). New York: Plenum Press.

Cassileth, B.R., Lusk, E.J., Strouse, T.B., Miller, D.S., Brown, L.L., Cross, P.A. & Tenaglia, A.N. (1984). Psychological status in chronic illness. *New England Journal of Medicine*, **311**, 506–511.

Chien, C.P., Stotsky, B.A. & Cole, J.O. (1973). Psychiatric treatment for nursing home patients: drug, alcohol and milieu. *American Journal of Psychiatry*, **130**, 543–548.

Cooney, T.M., Schaie, K.W. & Willis, S.L. (1988). The relationship between prior functioning on cognitive and personality variables and subject attrition in longitudinal research. *Journal of Gerontology: Psychological Sciences*, **43**, 12–17.

Cristofalo, V.J., Tresini, M., Francis, M.K. & Volker, C. (1999). Biological therories of senescence. In V.L. Bengtson & K.W. Schaie (Eds), *Handbook of Theories of Aging* (chap. 6, pp. 98–112). New York: Springer.

Deary, I.J. (2001). *Intelligence: A Very Short Introduction*. Oxford. Oxford University Press.

Deeg, D.J.H. (1989). *Experiences from Longitudinal Studies of Aging: Conceptualization, Organization and Output*. NIG-Trend Studies No. 3, Nijmegen, The Netherlands: Netherlands Institute of Gerontology.

Deeg, D.J.H., Kardaun, J.W.P.F. & Fozard, J.L. (1996). Health, behaviour and aging. In J.E. Birren & K.W. Schaie (Eds), *Handbook of the Psychology of Aging* (4th edn; chap. 7, pp. 129–149). San Diego: Academic Press.

Diesfeldt, H.F.A. & Diesfeldt-Groenendijk, H. (1977). Improving cognitive performance in psychogeriatric patients: the influence of physical exercise. *Age and Ageing*, **6**, 58–64.

Dustman, R.E., Ruhling, R.O., Russell, E.M., Shearer, D.E., Bonekat, W., Shigeoka, J.W., Wood, J.S. & Bradford, D.C. (1984). Aerobic exercise training and improved neuropsychological function of older individuals. *Neurobiology of Aging*, **5**, 35–42.

Erber, J.T. (1981). Remote memory and age: a review. *Experimental Ageing Research*, **1**, 189–199.

Elias, M.F., Elias, J.W. & Elias, P.K. (1990). Biological and health influences on behaviour. In J.E. Birren & K.W. Schaie (Eds), *Handbook of the Psychology of Ageing* (3rd edn, pp. 80–102). New York: Academic Press.

Finch, C.E. & Seeman, T.E. (1999). Stress theories of aging. In V.L. Bengtson & K.W. Schaie (Eds), *Handbook of Theories of Aging* (chap. 5, pp. 81–97). New York: Springer.

Finch, C.E. & Tanzi, R.E. (1997). The genetics of aging. *Science*, **278**, 407–411.

Fries, J.F. (1990). Medical perspectives upon successful aging. In P.B. Baltes & M.M. Baltes (Eds), *Successful Ageing: Perspectives from the Behavioural Sciences*. Cambridge, England: Cambridge University Press.

Gilhooly, M.L., Phillips, L., Gilhooly, K. & Hanlon, P. (2002). *Quality of Life and Real Life Cognitive Functioning*. Final Report on Grant Number L480254029 to the Economic and Social Research Council, UK.

Gilhooly, M.L., Wall, J.P., Jones, R.B, Naven, L. & McGhee, S. (1984). Non-attendance at Scottish out-patient clinics: client characteristics count. *Health Bulletin*, **52** (6), 395–403.

Gilleard, C. (1997). Education and Alzheimer's Disease: a review of recent epidemiological studies. *Ageing and Mental Health*, **1** (1), 33–46.

Gompertz, S. (1825). On the expressive law of human mortality and a new mode of determining the value of life contingency. *Philosophical Transactions of the Royal Society of London*, **115**, 513–585.

Grand, A., Grosclaude, P., Bocquet, H., Pous, J. & Albarede, J.L. (1990). Disability, psychosocial factors and mortality among the elderly in a rural French population. *Journal of Clinical Epidemiology*, **43**, 773–782.

Gregg, E.W., Cauley, J.A., Seeley, D.G. et al. (1998). Physical activity and osteoporotic fracture risk in older women. Study of Osteoporotic Fractures Research Group. *Annals of Internal Medicine*, **129**, 81–88.

Grimley Evans, J. (1988). Ageing and disease. In *Research and the Ageing Population* (pp. 38–57). Ciba Symposium (No. 134). Chichester, UK: John Wiley & Sons.

Gruber-Baldini, A.L. (1991). *The impact of health and disease on cognitive ability in adulthood and old age in the Seattle Longitudinal Study*. Unpublished Doctoral Dissertation, The Pennsylvania State University.

Havighurst, R.J. (1963). Successful aging. In R.H. Willians, C. Tibbits & W. Donahue (Eds), *Processes of Aging* (vol 1, pp. 299–320). New York: Atherton Press.

Henry, J.P. (1988). The archetypes of power and intimacy. In J.E. Birren & V.L. Bengston (Eds), *Emergent Theories of Ageing* (pp. 269–298). New York: Springer.

Howse, K. & Prophet, H. (1999). A rapid review of the literature on the prospects of improving the health of older Londoners. Centre for Policy on Ageing: London. www.doh.gov.uk/pdfs/ageing.pdf

Hultsch, D.F., Hertzog, C., Small, B.J., McDonald-Miszczak, L. & Dixon, R.A. (1992). Short-term longitudinal change in cognitive performance in later life. *Psychology and Aging*, **7**, 571–584.

Johansson, B. & Berg, S. (1989). The robustness of the terminal decline phenomenon: longitudinal data from the digit-span test. *Journal of Gerontology: Psychological Sciences*, **44**, 184–186.

Kane, R., Kane, R. & Arnold, S.B. (1985). Prevention and the elderly: risk factors. *Health Services Research*, **19**, 945–1006.

Kennedy, G.J., Kelman, H.R. & Thomas, C. (1990). The emergence of depressive symptoms in late life: the importance of declining health and increasing disability. *Journal of Community Health*, **15**, 93–103.

Kirschbaum, C., Wolf, O.T., May, M., Wippich, W. & Hellhammer, D.H. (1996). Stress- and treatment-induced elevations of cortisol levels associated with impaired declarative memory in healthy adults. *Life Sciences*, **58**, 1475–1483.

Koyano, W., Shibata, H., Haga, H. & Suyama, Y. (1986). Prevalence and outcome of low ADL and incontinence among the elderly: five years follow-up in a Japanese urban community. *Archives of Gerontology and Geriatrics*, **5**, 197–206.

LaCroix, A. & Owenn, G.S. (1992). Older adults and smoking. *Clinics in Geriatric Medicine*, **8**, 69–87.

Leventhal, E.A. (1984). Aging and the perception of illness. *Research on Aging*, **6**, 119–135.

Lieberman, M.A. (1982). The effects of social support on responses to stress. In L. Goldberger & S. Breznitz (Eds), *Handbook of Stress: Theoretical and Clinical Aspects*. New York: Free Press.

Loftus, E.F. (1991). The Glitter of Everyday Memory . . . and the Gold. *American Psychologist*, **46**, 16–18.

Loftus, E.F., Fienberg, S. & Tanur, J. (1985). Cognitive psychology meets the national survey. *American Psychologist*, **40**, 175–180.

Logan, J.R. & Spitze, G. (1994). Informal support and use of formal services by older Americans. *Journal of Gerontology: Psychological Sciences*, **49**, P25–P34.

Lupien, S., Lecours, A.R., Lussier, I., Schwartz, G., Nair, N. & Meaney, M. (1994). Basal cortisol levels and cognitive deficits in human aging. *Journal of Neuroscience*, **14**, 2893–2903.

Mages, N.L. & Mendelsohn, G.A. (1979). Effects of cancer on patients' lives: a personalogical approach. In G.C. Stone, F. Cohen & N.E. Adler (Eds), *Health Psychology*. San Francisco: Jossey-Bass.

Manton, K. (1989). Epidemiological, demographic, and social correlates of disability among the elderly. *The Millbank Quarterly*, **67** (Suppl. 2, P1), 13–58.

Manton, K.G., Stallard, E., Woodbury, M.A. & Dowd, J.E. (1994). Time-varying covariates in models of human mortality and ageing: multi-dimensional generalisation of the Gompertz. *Journal of Gerontology: Biological Sciences*, **44**, 675–683.

McAneny, L. (1992). Number of drinkers on the rise again. *The Gallup Poll Monthly*, February, 43–46.

McEwen, B.S. & Stellar, E. (1983). Stress and the individual: mechanisms leading to disease. *Archives of Internal Medicine*, **153**, 2093–2101.

Miller, R.A. (1994). The biology of aging and longevity. In W.R. Hazzard, E.L. Bierman et al. (Eds), *Principle of Geriatric Medicine and Gerontology* (3rd edn, pp. 3–18). New York: McGraw-Hill.

Morris, P.G. (2001). *Head Injury and Alzheimer's Disease. A Review of the Literature*. Dementia Services Development Centre. University of Stirling.

Mortimer, J.A. (2000). What are the risk factors for dementia? In F.A. Huppert, C. Brayne & D.W. O'Conner (Eds), *Dementia and Normal Ageing*. Cambridge: Cambridge University Press.

Neugarten, B.L. (1968). Adult personality: toward a psychology of the life cycle. In B.L. Neugarten (Ed.), *Middle Age and Ageing*. Chicago: University of Chicago Press.

Neugarten, B.L. & Neugarten, D.A. (1987). The changing meanings of age. *Psychology Today*, **21**, 29–33.

Office for National Statistics (2002). *Living in Britain 2000: Results of the 2000/01 General Household Survey*. Social Survey Division.

Ormel, J., Von Korff, M., Van den Brink, W., Katon, W. & Oldehinkel, T. (1993). Depression, anxiety, and social disability show synchrony of change in primary care patients. *American Journal of Public Health*, **83**, 385–390.

Paffenbarger, R.S., Hyde, R.T., Wing, A.L., Lee, I.M., Jung, D.L. & Kampert, J.B. (1993). The association of changes in physical activity level and other lifestyle characteristics with mortality among men. *New England Journal of Medicine*, **328**, 538–545.

Parson, D.A. & Leber, W.R. (1981). The relationship between cognitive dysfunction and brain damage in alcoholics: causal, interactive or epiphenomenal? *Alcoholism: Clinical and Experimental Research*, **5**, 326–343.

Parker, E.S. & Noble, E.P. (1977). Alcohol consumption and cognitive functioning in social drinkers. *Journal of the Study of Alcoholism*, **38**, 1224–1232.

Pederson, N.L. (1996). Gerontological behaviour genetics. In J.E. Birren & K.W. Schaie (Eds), *Handbook of the Psychology of Aging* (4th edn, pp. 59–74). San Diego: Academic Press.

Riegel, K.F. & Riegel, R.M. (1972). Development, drop, and death. *Developmental Psychology*, **6**, 306–319.

Ryan, C. & Butters, N. (1980). Further evidence for a continuum of impairment encompassing male alcoholic Korsakoff patients and chronic alcoholic men. *Alcoholism: Clinical and Experimental Research*, **4**, 190–198.

Salthouse, T.A. (1996). The processing-speed theory of adult age differences in cognition. *Psychological Review*, **103**, 403–428.

Salthouse, T.A. & Babcock, R. L. (1991). Decomposing adult age differences in working memory. *Developmental Psychology*, **27**, 763–776.

Sapolsky, R.M. (1992). *Stress, the Aging Brain and the Mechanisms of Neuron Death*. Cambridge, MA: MIT Press.

Scottish Executive (2000). *Results from the 1998 Scottish Health Survey*. Joint Health Surveys Unit. The National Centre for Social Research. Department of Epidemiology & Public Health.

Schaie, K.W. (1996). *Intellectual Development in Adulthood*. Cambridge: Cambridge University Press.

Schaie, K.W. & Willis, S.L. (1996). *Adult Development and Aging*. (4th edn). New York: Harper Collins College Publishers.

Seeman, T.E & McEwen, B.S. (1996). Impact of social environment characteristics and neuroendocrine regulation. *Psychosomatic Medicine*, **58**, 459–471.

Seeman, T.E. & Robbins, B.E. (1994). Aging and hypothalamic–pituitary–adrenal axis response to challenge in humans. *Endocrine Reviews*, **15**, 233–260.

Seeman, T.E., Singer, B. & Charpentier, P.A. (1995). Gender differences in HPA response to challenge: MacArthur studies of successful aging. *Psychoneuroendocrinology*, **20**, 711–725.

Seeman, T.E., McEwen, B.S., Albert, M.S. & Rowe, J.W. (1997). Urinary cortisol and decline in memory performance of older adults: MacArthur studies of successful aging. *Journal of Clinical Endocrinology and Metabolism*, **82**, 2458–2465.

Solomon, D.H. (1999). The role of aging processes in aging-dependent diseases. In V.L. Bengtson & K.W. Schaie (Eds), *Handbook of Theories of Aging* (chap. 8, pp. 133–150). New York: Springer.

Sorkin, J.D., Andres, R., Muller, D.C., Baldwin, H.L. & Fleg, J.L. (1992). Cholesterol as a risk factor for coronary heart disease in elderly men: the Baltimore longitudinal study of aging. *Annals of Epidemiology*, **2**, 59–67.

Stones, M.J. & Dawe, D. (1993). Acute exercise facilitates semantically cued memory in nursing home residents. *Journal of the American Geriatrics Society*, **41**, 531–534.

Sullivan, M. (1995). Depression and disability from chronic medical illness. *European Journal of Public Health*, **5**, 40–45.

Von Korff, M., Ormel, J., Katon, W. & Lin, E.H.B. (1992). Disability and depression among high utilisers of health care: a longitudinal analyses. *Archives of General Psychiatry*, **49**, 91–100.

Walters, R., Cattan, M., Speller, V. & Stuckelberger, A. (1999). In M. Drury (Ed.), *Proven Strategies to Improve Older People's Health*. London: Eurolink Age.

Wannamethee, S.G., Shaper, A.G., Walker, M. & Ebrahim, S. (1998). Lifestyle and 15 year survival free of heart attack, stroke and diabetes in middle-aged British men. *Archives of Internal Medicine*, **158**, 2433–2440.

Wilson, P.W.F., Anderson, K.M., Harris, T., Kannel, W.B. & Castelli, W.P. (1994). Determinants of change in total cholesterol and HDL-C with age: the Framingham study. *Journal of Gerontology: Medical Sciences*, **49**, M252–M257.

Wolfe, R., Morrow, J. & Fredrickson, B.L. (1996). Mood disorders in older adults. In L.L. Carstensen, B.A. Edelstein & L. Dornbrand (Eds), *The Practical Handbook of Clinical Gerontology* (pp. 274–303). Thousand Oaks, CA: Sage.

Wood, R. & Bain, M. (2001). *The Health and Well-Being of Older People in Scotland: Insights from National Data*. Information and Statistics Division, Common Services Agency for NHS Scotland: Edinburgh.

Woodruff-Pak, D.S. (1997). *The Neuropsychology of Aging*. Oxford: Blackwell.

PART III

Research Issues, the Social Context and Future Challenges

CHAPTER 23

The Nature of Evidence in Clinical Health Psychology

Richard Glynn Owens
University of Auckland, New Zealand

INTRODUCTION

As with all other scientific endeavours, clinical health psychology can only ever be as good as the evidence on which it is based; moreover such evidence must be systematically gathered, with the researcher constantly being on guard against accepting the obvious. It has been remarked often that obviousness must not be confused with truth—hence Bertrand Russell's (1907) dictum that "obviousness is always the enemy to correctness". That the world is flat is "obvious" to any casual observer, but such an obvious "fact" is not necessarily a *true* fact.

THE ROLE OF EVIDENCE

It is worth reflecting briefly on the *role* of evidence in health psychology. The most obvious role, enabling us to tell if our ideas, hypotheses and theories are right, is probably not the best. Arguably a much more important role for evidence is to enable us to tell if we are *wrong*, not if we are right. Although the Popperian (e.g. Popper, 1963) notion that refutability is a sine qua non of scientific endeavour may be open to question (e.g. Kuhn, 1962), and although critical psychologists may challenge the very notion of scientific truth (e.g. Nicholson, 2001) there is nonetheless an *epistemological* imperative surrounding refutability. Put most simply, if our ideas about the world could never be shown to be wrong, then there would never be any incentive to change these ideas. Any model we had of the way the world works, because it was never challenged by evidence, would be one to which we could cling tenaciously whether or not it was right. By contrast, if we consistently seek out evidence that contradicts our ideas, then when such evidence arises we are compelled to reject, adapt or extend our theoretical notions.

Of course the picture is far from being so simple. In practice, evidence is rarely such that a theory can be shown to be unequivocally wrong, and of course in some instances data are gathered more to help in the *generation* than the *testing* of a theory. Furthermore, there

Handbook of Clinical Health Psychology. Edited by S. Llewelyn and P. Kennedy.
© 2003 John Wiley & Sons, Ltd.

has, particularly in recent years, been a concerted challenge from those proposing alternative methodological perspectives, particularly those subsumed under so-called "critical" or
"qualitative" perspectives. Such perspectives range from simply arguing that non-numerical
data also have a place, to arguing that fundamentally differing principles and reasoning underlie such approaches. The detailed role of qualitative approaches will be discussed in
Chapter 24, and at this stage it is perhaps only necessary to point out that in some instances,
at least, both qualitative and quantitative data may be complementary.

In particular, qualitative data may be of especial value in helping to generate research
hypotheses for subsequent testing. Such data may be important when approaching a new
field in which there is little or no pre-existing information on which to base ideas. Data
of this kind may be obtained in a variety of ways, including participant observation, direct
or indirect non-participant observation, interviews and so forth. Thus Thorp et al. (1900),
in investigating patient anxieties about MRI scans, preceded their quantitative survey of
concerns with both participant observation and patient interviews; on the basis of data
gathered this way an extensive questionnaire was developed (and later modified further)
which permitted the gathering of quantitative data to complement the qualitative (Mackenzie
et al., 1995).

Qualitative and quantitative methods may also interact when the former are used not to
suggest possible research questions but rather to clarify the interpretation of other findings.
Thus, in a study investigating attitudes towards organ donation, Kent and Owens (1995)
found a marked reluctance to donate corneas relative to other bodily organs. This could not
be accounted for in terms of the quantitative findings regarding perceived effectiveness of
various transplant procedures, but qualitative data revealed a number of themes including a
perception that eyes were reflective of personal identity, and even that retention of corneas
was important so that the person would be able to see during an afterlife. Such aspects of
motivation may have been difficult to anticipate but could be identified because of the use
of qualitative data to supplement the quantitative.

In many sciences, much use has been made of the laboratory for the generation and
testing of hypotheses about the world. The laboratory provides a setting which permits a
high level of control and helps the scientist to exclude alternative explanations of findings.
Such laboratory experimentation also has its place in clinical health psychology, but for a
number of reasons, including the practical and the ethical, not all clinical health psychology research can be of this form. The fictional character Sherlock Holmes once remarked
that "One's ideas must be as broad as nature if one is to interpret nature" and a similar
case could be argued for one's methods of investigation. Reflecting this, clinical health
psychologists have used a variety of methodologies, each with its own particular strengths
and weaknesses, some of which will be outlined and illustrated in this and the subsequent
chapter.

LABORATORY METHODS IN CLINICAL HEALTH PSYCHOLOGY; THE EXAMPLE OF PSYCHONEUROIMMUNOLOGY

The field of psychoneuroimmunology, or PNI, is one that has attracted a considerable
amount of attention in recent years. While much of this research has been conducted outside
the experimental laboratory, it also provides some clear examples of how such laboratory
research can contribute to clinical health psychology. In one study (Wang et al., 1998)

researchers presented healthy men with acute stressors in a laboratory at different times during the day (early morning, midday, late afternoon) and monitored the effect on Natural Killer Cell Activity (NKCA) using a series of blood samples. The researchers were able to demonstrate greatest change in NKCA during the afternoon, paralleling mood changes.

Such a study illustrates many of the strengths and weaknesses of laboratory research. The close control of variables enhances the researcher's confidence that the differences do indeed reflect temporal differences and not the effect of some uncontrolled of confounding variable. At the same time, such research carries the usual questions about laboratory studies. With 30 healthy male students as participants, there are the obvious questions about representativeness of the sample—would the same results be obtained with women, with people who had a different social or educational background, with people who were ill? Similar questions may be asked about such variables as the measures taken (not just NKCA but also blood pressure, heart rate) and how well these reflect both the degree of stress imposed and the overall functioning of the immune system. In the same way the kinds of stressful tasks used (a mental arithmetic task, a Stroop test, and a speech task) may or may not adequately reflect the kinds of acute stressors that affect people more generally.

Such concerns have generally been discussed in terms of the validity of laboratory procedures, adopting the language of classical psychometrics. Just as a psychological test's validity is evaluated in terms of the extent to which it measures what it's meant to measure, so the validity of the laboratory experiment is considered similarly. In discussing the validity of laboratory experimentation, it has been common to suggest that such approaches are high in *internal* validity but low in *external* validity. In terms of modern psychometric theory (Cronbach et al., 1972) the issues might better be considered in terms of *generalisability*— the problem of determining which variables, when changed, might alter the findings (and therefore across which they are not generalisable) and which have no effect (across which, therefore, they *are* generalisable).

It is important, however, not to become too obsessed with these issues. Firstly, it can be argued that generalisability is in essence a *scientific* problem, a function of our understanding of the functional relationships between variables. To the extent that we understand the process, we are able to indicate what the effect of any change in variables might be, and in that sense to predict the generalisability.

Secondly, it is worth remembering that the old question of "whether laboratory results can be generalised to the real world" may not always, if ever, be relevant. Looked at from another viewpoint, the fact that a scientific notion has its origins in the laboratory is not the prime issue. Rather the issue is the extent to which the notion can withstand empirical testing; where it originated is of no consequence. Scientists may obtain their theories and hypotheses from laboratory experiments, discussions with friends, rational analysis or even (in some cases) from the content of their dreams. How the scientist *got* the idea is irrelevant; what matters is whether the predictions of the theory stand up to rigorous testing. From this point of view the kind of theories which are laboratory-based may wish to claim a stronger epistemological base, with the notion that the laboratory is the most severe testing ground of all. A theory whose predictions fail to come about in the "real world" can always be defended in terms of some unknown factor, confound or variable. In the laboratory, where these can be much better controlled, it is harder to make excuses for results that do not match those predicted.

MOVING OUTSIDE THE LABORATORY: EXPERIMENTS IN OTHER SETTINGS

Of course, it is not essential to an experimental approach that it be conducted within a laboratory; much effort has been expended, in clinical health psychology as in other approaches, to conducting experimental research within ecologically natural settings, often using statistical as well as experimental methods to control extraneous variables.

For example, Deadman et al. (2001) used a simple experimental design to investigate the role of taking responsibility for treatment on psychological outcome in breast cancer. Although a considerable amount of research has been conducted on outcome in breast cancer patients who choose their own treatment (e.g. Deadman et al., 1989; Leinster et al., 1989; Morris & Royle, 1987) such research has always had a confound between *choice* and *preference*. To clarify, imagine a situation in which a group of women is subdivided randomly into two groups, one allowed to choose their own treatment, the other having their treatment determined by the surgeon. Leaving aside the practical and ethical problems of such a study, such a study might seem a reasonable way of assessing whether women who feel they have taken control of their treatment decision subsequently feel better or worse. However, there is a possibility that any resulting difference between the two groups may be a function not of taking control per se, but rather that women are likely to have an existing preference for one treatment over the other, and that those given a choice are all likely (unless choosing in a particularly perverse manner) to obtain their preferred treatment, while only some in the remaining group would do so. Thus the process of *choice* is confounded with patient *preference*. Deadman et al. (2001) circumvented this problem by means of an experimental procedure whereby all patients ($N = 80$) were interviewed by a psychologist and their preference determined. Patients were randomly allocated to a "patient choice" or "surgeon choice" group, and each individual patient's preference was communicated to the surgeon. Then according to the individual's group membership, the surgeon either told the patient that having discussed it *she* should choose, or that having discussed it *he* had chosen—in the latter instance, always specifying the patient's particular preference. The design was a "double-blind" procedure, whereby neither the patients nor the interviewing psychologist (who carried out follow-up assessments) were aware of any individual's group allocation.

The procedure therefore permitted all patients to receive their preferred treatment, but only a random subsample (51%) had the experience of making the choice themselves. By means of this procedure, the benefits later found in the patient choice group relative to the surgeon choice group could be ascribed specifically to the experience of choosing, since preference had been kept constant in both groups. The use of a tight experimental procedure, with patients randomly allocated and the use of "double-blind" procedures similarly helped to maintain the integrity of the design, and the use of the preliminary interview minimised ethical concerns by ensuring that, irrespective of group membership, patients all received their preferred treatment.

Such experimental designs have been used in a variety of settings, including evaluating the role of questioning style on screening decisions (Wroe & Salkovkis, 1999; Wroe, Salkovkis & Rimes, 2000), impact of leaflet provision in rheumatoid arthritis (Barlow, Pennington & Bishop, 1997), improving adjustment to renal dialysis regimes (Leake, Friend & Wadhwa, 1999) and social comparison processes in adjusting to a diagnosis of breast cancer (Stanton et al., 1999). These and other studies illustrate that, as in other areas of psychology, research in health can often draw on classic principles of experimental design.

Frequently, however, a variety of constraints may prevent studies from fulfilling all of the requirements of a strictly experimental design, especially as regards random allocation to groups. For example, it may not be practical to allocate, randomly, a problem encountered by Maes et al. (1993) who investigated the implementation of two different health promotion programmes in six Dutch nursing homes. Random allocation of each participant to one or other programme would not be possible, since within any nursing home different individuals would receive different information, participants would be likely to discuss these and there would thus be cross-contamination between the two groups. Instead, Maes et al. allocated their programme randomly to one or other home, minimising the risk of cross-contamination, but failing to provide strict random allocation of *participants*. Other problems which prevent random allocation always being achieved have been discussed by Owens, Slade and Fielding (1996) and include political, ethical and methodological requirements (e.g. the possibility that inviting people to take part in a randomised-controlled trial may bias the sample when only a small percentage agree to participate).

In circumstances such as these, where true random allocation is not possible, Campbell and Stanley (1963) have suggested the use of so-called "quasi-experimental" designs, which parallel conventional designs except in the inability to allocate subjects randomly. In circumstances where a cause is studied after it has exerted its effect (for example, in studying the impact of natural disasters) the terms "ex post facto" or "causal comparative" have been used to describe such designs (Owens, Slade & Fielding, 1996). In general, researchers using quasi-experimental designs will attempt to minimise the impact of possible confounding factors by procedures such as matching on relevant variables. Where such matching is not possible, or is achieved only imperfectly, subsequent statistical analyses may be used to identify characteristics (additional to the experimental condition), which distinguish the two groups. If such analyses reveal that the differences are minor, no further action may be necessary, but if substantial differences are found it may be necessary to partial out the effects of the variables concerned using procedures like partial correlations, analyses of covariance and so on. Such procedures effectively work by "adjusting" the scores in one group to the values predicted if the variables had been similar. Thus, if two groups differ substantially in age, knowledge of the relationship between age and the variable of interest permits estimation of what the latter would have been in one group if the ages had been similar to, rather than different from, the other. Such procedures of course are far from foolproof, and interpretation of the outputs of such analyses need to be carried out with caution. It is also perhaps worth remembering at this point that, when checking for unintended differences between experimental and control groups, the concept of "significance" may be misleading; failing to find any significant difference between the two groups is not the same as demonstrating that no such difference exists. The best that can be done is to calculate confidence intervals for any differences, and to use these to estimate the underlying "true" difference that exists between the two.

Quasi-experimental designs have been widely used in clinical health psychology to investigate a range of problems including patient decision-making (e.g. Ashcroft, Leinster & Slade, 1985), the relationship between ovarian hormones and stress reactivity (Stoney et al., 1997), impact of renal transplantation on depression (Christensen et al., 2000), impact of dental veneers (Ashworth, Davis & Spriggs, 1996), immune response to stress in carers of dementia sufferers (Cacioppo et al., 1998) and a host of other topics. In some contexts, of course, comparisons are not made between subjects but other variables such as occasion; here too quasi-experimental methods may be applied. Thus Szabo et al. (1998) examined the mood of runners on days when they did and did not run, reporting higher mood ratings on days when they ran, but cautioning that the effects could (as with other quasi-experimental designs) be an effect of some confounding variable that both prevented running on a particular day at the same time as lowering mood. Thus the same logical issues arise in the context of comparisons across *occasions* as comparisons between *participants* when these are not allocated randomly.

LONGITUDINAL STUDIES

One obvious feature of the types of research mentioned above is that they effectively provide a "snapshot" of the individual's experience. Often, however, the researcher may be interested in changes and developments over a period of time. This may be a relatively short period; for example, Joseph et al. (1987) studied changes in risky sexual behaviour over a period of six months in a cohort of homosexual men. In some cases, however, the time period may be considerably longer. In Australia, the Women's Health Australia project (Lee, 2001), initiated in 1995, is designed to run for 20 years or more, gathering data on a range of physical and mental health topics from three age groups of women (18–23, 45–50, 70–75). The study has recruited between 12 000 and 15 000 women in each age group, largely representative of Australian women within these age groups when comparisons are made with census returns. The design allows for sequential surveying of each age group every three years; thus as time goes by the ages of each group will increase such that by the year 2015 data will have been sampled from women at all ages between 18 and 93.

Longitudinal studies have also been conducted on cohorts from birth; in the United Kingdom, the Isle of Wight study (see, e.g., Rutter, Graham & Yule, 1970) monitored all children on the island at ages 10 and 14. Similarly in New Zealand, the Dunedin study (e.g. Waldie & Poulton, 2002) monitored all children ($N = 1037$) born over a one-year period from April 1972 to March 1973. Children are assessed at two-year intervals until they reach the age of 15, and subsequently at ages 18, 21 and 26. Assessments include a range of measures designed to monitor a range of behavioural and health-related variables.

Longitudinal studies of this nature have an especial strength in investigating such questions as identifying early correlates of health problems, although it must also be remembered that large-scale studies like these, where the same group is repeatedly sampled, also provide cross-sectional data which are valuable in their own right, alongside the longitudinal comparisons.

Methodologists have also argued that longitudinal studies are good for examining developmental processes, since changes over time within inviduals can be assessed. While this is undoubtedly true to some extent the interpretation of such change is not always straightforward. Studies like those from the Isle of Wight or Dunedin can, in the end, only either see change or no change in any particular variable. If the variable changes (e.g. the probability of some particular illness), then logically, at least, it remains impossible to say to what extent the change is a result of some concomitant external change over the period of the study (e.g. a change in the social, political or physical environment) or of some internal change (e.g. some in-built developmental aspect of biology). Similarly, if some variable does not change (e.g. the overweight child remains overweight as an adult) the question remains open as to whether this *would* change if certain external variables were modified (e.g. dietary or exercise practices). The claim often made for longitudinal studies that they are good for establishing and demonstrating causality is therefore not quite as simple as it may appear. Where longitudinal studies recruit several different cohorts, the problems are less, especially where changes are apparent. Thus, if, over time, a young cohort reaches the age at which a different cohort started, it is possible to make useful comparisons. For example, a 20-year study which starts with cohorts aged 20 and 40 will by the end have data on two groups of 40-year-olds separated by a 20-year period. If the two groups 20 years apart show similar characteristics, then it remains difficult to determine whether this represents some inevitable biological determinance or simply that some important external variable has remained unchanged over that period (although the longer the period, arguably, the more implausible it becomes that external factors would remain the same). Conversely, however, if 20 years later the 40-year-olds show different characteristics to the original 40-year-old group, this argues strongly against a biological inevitability of the developmental process and in favour of the notion that the changes reflect some external change (the possibility, of course, remains that the two groups were biologically different initially, a possibility that is not always implausible, for example, when variables like average family size change over time with consequent implications for gene distribution).

Other problems with longitudinal studies concern the difficulties of dealing with dropouts from the sample. It is almost inevitable that, over time, contact will be lost with many of the original participants, although sometimes this is less than one might expect; in the Dunedin study, for example, 96% of the original participants were still available for assessment after 26 years. In the substantially larger Women's Health Australia study, high mobility among the younger women has meant a drop to around 70% of the original compared with over 90% among the older women (Lee, 2001). The obvious problem with dropouts (especially in studies like the Dunedin one which have a single cohort) is that if these are not a random subset, then changes will occur in the summary statistics which may appear to reflect a trend but in fact are simply a reflection of differential dropout. Thus, if on reaching adulthood those who show high levels of time urgency, hostility and so forth (characteristics of the so-called "Type A Behaviour Pattern") are more likely to decide they are too busy to remain in the study, then the *average* level of Type A behaviour in the sample will reduce (all other things being equal). It would, however, be a mistake to claim that because the average level of Type A behaviour in the group decreased over time, that people became more mellow with age if the differences represented nothing more than an attrition effect. Longitudinal studies, therefore, while potentially of considerable value, need to be conducted with considerable care and with caution exercised in interpreting their results.

SMALL-N EXPERIMENTAL RESEARCH

At the opposite extreme to the kinds of longitudinal studies described above, but still gathering data over a time period, are the so-called "small-N" or "single-case" experimental studies. Most widely used within the field of applied behaviour analysis, experimental studies of single cases have a long history across a range of fields (see, e.g., Chassan, 1979; Davidson & Costello, 1969). To date, however, such approaches have had only a relatively small impact in clinical health psychology, perhaps because the use of single-case experiments works particularly well where a clear behavioural outcome can be specified and repeatedly measured.

In its simplest form, the single-case experiment follows what has been termed the ABAB structure, where the variable of interest is monitored for a period during a baseline phase (A), then an experimental intervention (B) is applied. For example, if it is believed that a particular problem behaviour is under the control of specific stimuli, then the behaviour may be monitored for a while without any action being taken, and when a clear picture is apparent of the "normal" pattern of the behaviour, the stimulus may be removed. If the behaviour is indeed under the control of the stimulus in question, then removing the stimulus should result in a reduction of the behaviour. Again the behaviour is monitored until a clear picture is apparent of its occurrence without the stimulus, after which there is a return to baseline conditions (return of the stimulus) to see if this reinstitutes the original pattern of behaviour, and an eventual return to the intervention (hence the term ABAB).

Such single-case experiments have also been used to investigate the effects of manipulating reinforcement contingencies, enhancing self-control strategies (e.g. by introducing response-prevention procedures, or self-monitoring approaches). The range of experimental designs, too, extends beyond the simple ABAB to more complex designs using the same principle (e.g. ABCABC designs where more than one intervention is being assessed) and to procedures using multiple baselines both within and between subjects (for a fuller discussion of the principles of single-case design, see Barlow & Hersen, 1984; Kratochwill, 1978; and Sidman, 1960). Although this type of approach has been used with respect to a range of health-related behaviours including smoking (Azrin & Powell, 1968), obesity (Stuart, 1967) and problem drinking (Morosko & Baer, 1970) such reports have generally been atypical of prevailing mainstream studies in these fields. In the field of eating disorders, however, such designs were, for a period of time, used extensively, reflecting the evaluation of operant-based strategies particularly for anorexia.

The problem of anorexia might at first glance appear well suited to the use of single-case experimental designs, since a crucial variable (body weight) can be precisely and frequently monitored, enabling the establishment of clear baselines and detection of therapeutic effects. Moreover, early attempts at increasing body weight through operant programmes appeared to show considerable promise (Agras et al., 1974; Kellerman, 1977; Leitenberg, Agras & Thompson, 1968). However, other therapists (e.g. Bruch, 1977), working from different perspectives, claimed that such procedures could lead to subsequent deterioration; although these claims were not backed with rigorous data, there has nonetheless been a weakening of enthusiasm for such procedures. Touyz et al. (1984) nevertheless argued that some of the problems might result from an excessively strict operant regime which appeared to produce no benefits but had clear disadvantages and, more recently, Touyz and Beumont (1997) have further developed their operant approaches producing a more sophisticated approach that may have clear benefits.

As far as the research design is concerned, the clear problem with the early studies was their emphasis on a single outcome measure—objective body weight—ignoring other measures both objective (actual eating behaviour) and subjective (patient mood and well-being). Yule and Hemsley (1977), in an early overview of the use of single-case research in clinical health psychology, drew attention to the need for such research to draw, where possible, on a range of outcome variables.

In practical terms the use of small-N experimental procedures can on occasion provide dramatic benefits; for example, Kohlenberg (1973) used such an approach to show how a reinforcement programme could avoid the need for surgery in a 13-year-old encopretic boy. Clearly many of the questions of interest to clinical health psychologists do not lend themselves to being answered in these terms, but it seems likely that some of the reluctance to use the methods widely stems from lack of expertise on the part of researchers (many of whom may still fail to understand the processes or logic of such approaches). A particular problem (shared by many qualitative researchers) is that researchers trained in more traditional approaches may not appreciate that concerns such as generalisability—normally seen as a statistical problem—are seen quite differently within these other perspectives. Those interested in pursuing the fundamental principles of single-case experimental methodology in more depth will find many of the issues discussed in Sidman (1960).

SURVEY RESEARCH

At the opposite extreme to the intensive study of single cases is the use of large-scale survey methods. Such procedures have a range of uses, in particular to obtain a broad picture of some characteristic or phenomenon in a specific population, or to draw comparisons between particular populations. Thus, Temoshok, Sweet and Zich (1987) gathered data from three different cities (San Francisco, New York and London) in order to compare knowledge and attitudes towards AIDS. Although their samples were relatively small (127, 98 and 149 respectively) they were nevertheless able to show significant differences between the groups in such areas as perceived risk, anti-gay attitudes and general fear.

Clearly designs such as this share many of the problems previously outlined in the context of quasi-experimental designs. In both cases it is important when differences are observed between groups to minimise the risk that these merely reflect confounding variables. Thus, if the samples from each city had been different in their socio-economic status, it might mean that the results were simply a function of this, rather than differences between the cities. It is important, therefore, for researchers to assess (as was done in this example) such variables as demographic characteristics of the samples (this is not always easy; for example, when assessing income, does one look for equivalent salaries, or equivalence in terms of population percentiles? The answers to questions such as this may be quite variable according to the problem being considered).

It is important also, of course, that samples be not only large enough, but also as far as possible unbiased, so that differences detected represent differences across the relevant populations, not just particular subgroups of these populations (as might happen if, for example, only male respondents were obtained; the results would tell us nothing about whether there were differences between women in the same cities). Sometimes the samples from different centres may vary in representativeness; for example, in a study of stress in general practitioners in the UK and Canada, Rout and Rout (1997) took pains to point out that their Canadian sample was not only smaller than the British one (a little over a third of the size) but also less representative, having been sampled entirely from one area. Such problems can make interpretation of survey studies difficult and indicate the need for caution in generalising.

Surveys may, of course, involve only a single population, as when an attempt is made to determine the prevalence of some particular problem or characteristic, or to identify variables of which some phenomenon is a function. Again it is clearly necessary in such circumstances to be clear about issues of generalisation, and sometimes it is possible to gain some sense of the representativeness of a sample by comparison with data collected for less specific purposes. Ebrahim and Rowland (1996), for example, in surveying correlates of activity levels in older women, cross-checked their data where possible with broader census data in order to assess representativeness levels. As a consequence they were able to determine that activity levels in their sample were broadly similar to those in the comparable population.

Although highly sophisticated statistical techniques have been developed for use in survey analysis (see, e.g., Rao, 1963) there is still considerable reliance on basic descriptive statistics, correlational methods and related procedures. With these, and with the more complex procedures derived from them, it is important to remember the fundamental limitations of the techniques, and especially to recognise that correlations between variables do not show the direction of causality or even, indeed, any direct causal link at all (since two variables which correlate may both be consequences of some unknown third variable). It is also important to recognise the serious limitations of significance testing in the context of correlational analysis; reference to a correlation being "significant" may be almost meaningless in large surveys, where a very weak relationship may nevertheless reach hallowed probability levels of "less than 0.05" or "less than 0.01". At best the significance of a correlation tells us nothing more than that it is probably not truly zero (and it is hard to imagine any two variables whose correlation *is* truly zero) and that the sign of the correlation is in the direction indicated by the sample (that is, a significant positive correlation indicates that the true correlation is unlikely to be negative, and vice versa). For the most part, in analysing large-scale survey data, the *magnitude* of a correlation is likely to be of considerably more interest than its statistical significance.

CAUSAL MODELLING AND PATH ANALYSIS

Despite the concerns expressed in the foregoing, correlational data from surveys and similar sources have been of considerable value and psychologists have exploited such data in the building of complex models (see, e.g., Sharrock & Gudjonsson, 1993). Clinical health psychologists, too, are beginning to make use of such procedures. By examining the patterns of intercorrelations between variables, it is possible to determine the extent to which each predicts the other. Moreover, by examining partial correlations and multiple regressions it is possible to determine the extent to which one variable influences another directly, and to what extent it is mediated by others. Such approaches are subsumed under various headings as "causal modelling", "structural modelling" or "path analysis". In these approaches, the experimenter will typically hypothesise a series of relationships and interrelationships between variables, and then examine the intercorrelations between these in the data, comparing them with those in the specified model. By using computer software such as LISREL (LInear Structural RELations) or AMOS (Analysis of MOment Structures) the extent to which the interrelationships between variables in the data correspond to those predicted can be identified. Not uncommonly, using such approaches, links expected to be significant may turn out not to be so, and other relationships may operate almost entirely via particular mediating variables.

Thus, Schofield et al. (2001) looked at the occurrence of depressive symptoms in Ironman triathletes. These athletes, whose event involves a swim (sea or lake) of 3.8 km, a cycle ride of 180 km and a run of 42.2 km, obviously need considerable dedication in order to train for an event which will last, even for the elite competitors, six hours or more, and for the mainstream competitor as much as 17 hours. The researchers examined two particular dimensions, "cognitive complexity" and "conditional goal-setting", each of which was hypothesised to impact upon the likelihood of depression. Cognitive complexity (Linville, 1985), the extent to which people's self-concept is complex rather than simple, has been hypothesised to act as a buffer against stress. Conditional goal-setting refers to the practice of deciding that some outcome may be achievable only if a particular goal is reached; for example, deciding that one can only have pride in one's physical condition if one can complete an Ironman triathlon. Administering measures of the various factors to competitors, they were able to demonstrate that conditional goal-setting influenced depression both directly (a regression beta value of 0.26) and via somatic anxiety and task confidence. Cognitive anxiety, however, played no part. Cognitive complexity influenced depression only through the mediation of conditional goal-setting. This latter observation suggests that the individuals who were lower in cognitive complexity would be more likely to set conditional goals and, as a result, both directly and through the mediation of other variables, experience depression.

To date, this type of modelling has not been widely applied within clinical health psychology, although there appears to be no compelling reason why it should not be applicable. To use such methods the researcher needs to have adequate measures of the different variables which are implicated in the model, and an appropriate sample (in terms of size, homogeneity, etc.) to permit meaningful analysis. As with any research of this kind, of course, it is important to be cautious in extrapolating beyond the data obtained. For example, although Schofield et al. (2001) found no role for cognitive anxiety in their triathletes in producing depression, generalisation to athletes from other sports may not be straightforward. The need for a triathlete to revise tactics in the light of an opponent's performance may be minimal (especially for most of the field) while in other sports (e.g. judo, boxing) there may be a considerable period of active analysis of an opponent's moves with the need to develop new strategies and moves during the contest itself. Conceivably such sports could be more influenced by cognitive anxiety than triathlon, with an impact on depression. Extrapolating to other health areas, outside a sporting context, may require even greater caution. Nevertheless, such methods have the potential to clarify substantially the role of variables hypothesised to play a part in behavioural systems.

MULTI-CENTRE TRIALS AND META-ANALYSIS

Whatever approach a researcher adopts in conducting a study, there are inevitably a host of practical difficulties which limit the value of the findings. For example, research commonly attracts participants from a more or less restricted geographical area. The extent of the restriction may vary considerably—some studies may recruit from a particular undergraduate class in a particular year in a particular university, others may recruit from a particular suburb, a particular city and so on. Rarely if ever are researchers in a position, from a practical point of view, to sample in any kind of truly representative way from the population to which ideally they would like to generalise.

In order to circumvent these problems, at least to a degree, researchers have devised a number of ways of combining several studies examining the same issue. At the simplest level, this may involve nothing more than running the same piece of research in different locations, in so-called multi-centre trials. Such trials may be initiated in order to broaden the sampling base or in some cases merely to increase the numbers available for analysis. In principle such an approach to research is relatively unproblematic; by operating the research programme in several centres, it is possible not only to obtain samples with potentially wider generalisability and greater sensitivity, but it is also possible to consider the centres themselves as predictor variables, with data analysis directed towards the detection of possible differences between the centres. Thus Steptoe and Wardle (1996) examined a wide range of health-related behaviours in countries across Europe, generating a database which permitted a number of questions to be addressed and international comparisons made, sometimes with striking results. For example, Wardle et al. (1997) reported on dietary practices of over 16 000 students showing marked variation between extremes, such as only 15% of women in Belgium limiting their consumption of red meat by comparison with 96% of women in Norway. Clearly such multi-centre studies have the potential to highlight international variation in health issues.

Such multi-centre studies are not, however, without their problems. From a practical point of view considerable care, and a high standard of communication, are necessary if the study is to be conducted consistently in the various centres. The choice of variables may not be straightforward; for example, attempting to compare such variables as suicide rates internationally might seem straightforward with the use of such measures as coroners' verdicts, but often these will be influenced by cultural factors. An ambiguous death may be recorded as a misadventure in England where suicide is frowned upon, but a similar death in Japan recorded as suicide where this has traditionally been a respected course of action. Problems such as these are compounded further by linguistic difficulties, with questionnaire measures and interview schedules requiring careful validation to ensure comparability across centres. Procedures such as "reverse translation", where a questionnaire is translated from language A into language B by one person, then back from language B to language A by another, permit evaluation of the extent to which the linguistic shift has produced variation in meaning. At times it may be necessary to repeat this cycle on a number of occasions before a suitable result is obtained.

An alternative approach to the combining of data from several centres is that of "meta-analysis". In meta-analysis, the various studies to be combined will not usually have been designed by the same researchers, and will normally involve a range of measures, designs, participants and so on. Meta-analytic procedures developed from the tradition of the review article, in which researchers would report broad conclusions to be drawn from a broad survey of existing literature in a topic. Going beyond this approach, the idea of meta-analysis was to combine the data from a range of studies in order to permit calculation of the extent to which different variables affect the phenomenon in question.

In health psychology, meta-analysis has been employed in a range of subject areas in an attempt to draw together an often diverse literature. In the field of coronary heart disease a number of meta-analyses have been conducted in an attempt to clarify the potential benefits of such procedures as health education and/or stress management. Dusseldorp et al. (1999) examined 37 studies reported over a period of nearly 25 years, concluding that psychological intervention could be associated with an estimated reduction of 34% in mortality and 29% reduction in recurrence. Similarly in breast cancer, Moyer (1997) performed a meta-analysis on 40 published studies concerned with the psychosocial outcome of breast-conserving surgery versus mastectomy. She found a relatively small but significant effect size indicating some possible benefits for the former relative to the latter, but noted that this should not be used to justify advocating one treatment over another, but rather that attention be paid to individual preferences.

While such meta-analyses can be of considerable value in drawing together the results of research, it is important to remember that they also have their problems. Perhaps the most obvious of these parallels the old computing axiom of "garbage in—garbage out". All meta-analyses are limited by the quality of the studies which are entered into them. Any design fault which biases the results of individual studies in any way will also (although usually to a lesser degree, as a result of the "diluting" effect of incorporating other studies) bias the results of the meta-analysis. Considerable care must therefore be paid to the details of experimental design of those studies incorporated into the meta-analysis. Commonly researchers publishing meta-analyses will specify precisely their inclusion and exclusion criteria for the study; any meta-analysis which fails to do so should be regarded with caution.

It is also important to assess such criteria carefully; any meta-analysis will involve considerable heterogeneity within its sample, such that there is a danger of, metaphorically, averaging apples and oranges. Clearly if any general conclusion is to be drawn from a meta-analysis it is important that the differences between the various studies (e.g. in sampling, measures, design, etc.) be sufficiently minimal that they can be justifiably discounted. Such an approach may be seen as problematic, and an alternative argument suggests that if the differences were indeed so minimal then the results of the studies would be expected to be broadly similar, and if the studies included do indeed vary considerably in their findings, this must reflect some important difference in their design or execution which renders them incomparable. From this perspective meta-analysis would be seen as a tool which should only be used with extreme caution, if at all.

Another serious problem with the inclusion of studies in meta-analyses is that in almost all cases such analyses can include only studies that have been published. If it is the case (as has from time to time been suggested) that journal editors are reluctant to publish studies which produce only negative results, then the consequence would be that any sample of publications would contain an unrepresentative proportion of those with positive findings, and the meta-analysis would overestimate the size of any effect. This problem has been termed the "file drawer" problem and carries the potential risk not only that meta-analyses will overestimate effect sizes but that, as Begg (1993) has pointed out, these may give a spurious impression of precision when presented as the outcome of standard statistical methods.

Despite these concerns, meta-analysis has become widely adopted as a convenient and systematic means of drawing together the results of studies in a particular area, and their problems and disadvantages will be seen by many as outweighed by the convenience and practicality when interpreted with sufficient caution. From this perspective, a major task for the future is to ensure that the consumers of such analyses are well prepared to adopt a cautionary approach and to avoid excessive reliance on the outcomes.

HEALTH AUDIT

Although the foregoing sections have encompassed a range of strategies for conducting what might broadly be thought of as academic research (even if with practical implications), such does not subsume all, or even the majority, of research that is conducted within health care settings. In particular, the drive towards rationalisation of management procedures has had the result that professionals in applied health care settings have come under increasing pressure to monitor the services they provide and to audit the outcomes of such services. Such health care audit will very often involve a number of elements of the research process even if only to be applied at a local level, and the same concerns and problems regarding design, measurement, etc., will often arise.

Typically the implementation of an audit process will involve a number of elements, and normally an attempt will be made to ensure that such audit can, once established, be continued indefinitely while being modified in the light of experience. Among these elements will be the establishment of appropriate targets—for example, the percentage of clinical cases who will be seen by a psychologist within two weeks of a referral being made—and the determination of appropriate procedures for monitoring whether or not these targets are being met. Clearly neither of these is entirely simple or straightforward. Targets can be thought of as *outcome* measures, and at a simple level may be considered the critical data, indicating the bottom line of whether or not the service is providing the standards it aims for. From this point of view, other measures of structure and process are subservient to outcome, in that it is of little value having what appear to be excellent systems if they do not produce the required results. In practice, while this point of view has much to commend it, there are usually additional complications. Careful assessment of structures and processes may also be important, if only to highlight potential strategies for further improvement. Commonly, therefore, those involved in audit will endeavour to gather good data in all three areas—structure, process and outcome.

In practice the implementation of an audit process is only likely to succeed if it involves close cooperation with both providers and consumers of health care services. The expertise of service providers is necessary from the earliest stages of implementation of health care audit, these providers almost inevitably being in the best position to foresee dangers, impracticalities, risks of negative impact, etc. Part of the problem of involving such professionals is that often they will already be overworked, with little time to devote to what may be seen as bureaucratic gathering of statistics which will either, at best, be left to gather dust in a filing cabinet or, at worst, be used to browbeat them for perceived inadequacies of the service they provide. Even when convinced of the value of audit, professionals may feel that the demands of the service leave them too little time to devote to cooperating with the establishment of audit procedures. It is important, therefore, that those concerned with the implementation of health care audit, firstly, determine for themselves what resources will be available to produce improvements in the service and, secondly, make efforts to persuade health care professionals that involvement in the audit process is for the long-term benefit of the service they provide.

Although clinical audit may appear somewhat distantly removed from mainstream research, it is important to remember that the implementation of audit procedures may not only provide data which are of value to other researchers (e.g. on treatment outcomes) but may also provide structures which facilitate the gathering of data for research. Thus an audit of a group of hospice providers in the UK was able to show that the majority of patients being treated by the hospice described their pain as "mild" or less (Owens, 1997). Such information is typical of the kind of measure seen as valuable in the auditing of palliative care services, but also provides valuable research data concerning the controllability of pain in cancer patients. There is therefore much to be said for researchers of all persuasions being alert to the implementation of clinical audit procedures and for the possibilities of collaboration. Such collaboration carries the potential for productive interaction between the activities of academic researchers and service providers with eventual benefits for the users of those services.

FAILINGS OF EXISTING RESEARCH

While there is little doubt that health psychology research is thriving and productive, this should not be regarded as grounds for complacency. Even in those areas where psychology has become most firmly grounded in health care, many questions remain unanswered. Thus, in the field of cardiovascular disease, the notion of the Type A Behaviour Pattern (TABP) has become firmly established in the folklore as a significant risk factor. Yet careful examination of the data relating to TABP on long-term follow-up suggests that any relation to coronary heart disease is slight (Ragland & Brand, 1988), and follow-up of the original Framingham study showed little difference between rates for those classed as Type A and those as Type B (Haynes & Feinleib, 1982). Allen (1998) has suggested that the original findings on TABP may apply only to middle-aged middle-class males within a particular historical period. Much of the research in health psychology carries a similar risk that the findings will apply only to particular groups at a particular historical time. If psychologists are to appreciate fully the limitations of their findings in this respect, it is necessary to know the specific temporal or other parameters that will affect the findings. To know that results may not apply in 5, 10 or 20 years' time is little more than guesswork unless the underlying processes are sufficiently well understood that we can identify *what* changes during these time periods would affect our findings.

Unfortunately this enthusiasm simply for identifying relevant variables carries its own risk. Feynman (1986), in commenting on the methods of psychology, has suggested that these methods typically reflect only a "cargo cult" science, a scientism characterised by going through the motions without actually appreciating scientific principles of investigation. Such accusations from a Nobel laureate cannot be dismissed out of hand, and it is certainly the case that psychologists have at times neglected some basic principles of scientific investigation. For example, a considerable amount of research has illustrated beneficial effects on the immune system of asking individuals to write about personal traumatic events. In the typical experiment in this area participants are asked to write for 20 minutes on each of four days about a traumatic or upsetting experience (Booth, Petrie & Pennebaker, 1997). Experimental programmes in this area have investigated a range of predictor variables (e.g. gender) and outcome variables (e.g. response to vaccines, circulating white cell counts). Such investigation of categorical variables, however, while assuredly important, has not generally been accompanied by even the simplest of parametric investigation. If a similar phenomenon were identified in an area such as physics or chemistry it is likely that one of the very first questions would concern the funtional relationships between variables. These would be changed, quantitatively, one at a time and the effect on the outcome variable determined. In the present example this might mean asking people to write for 5 minutes, 10 minutes, 20 minutes, 40 minutes and so on in order that the form of the relationship between time spent and immune response could be plotted. Similarly groups of participants could be asked to write for one day, two days, three days and so forth, the effects of this type of variation again being plotted. Such a pattern of investigation is rare in health psychology, leaving it open to accusations of scientism rather than science, and of adopting a Baconian approach where phenomena are accumulated in a largely unsystematic way leading to limited, if any, understanding.

PROSPECTS FOR THE FUTURE

Clearly there is no reason why, used intelligently, the kinds of approach to research described above should not continue to be important within the field of clinical health psychology. Similarly it is to be hoped that clinical health psychologists will guard against slipping into scientistic rather than scientific approaches to experimentation, as described in the preceding section. Health psychology's long-standing emphasis on research skills in the training of its practitioners can hopefully be relied upon to ensure that standards of scientific enquiry continue to improve.

It is, perhaps, also useful (or at least entertaining) to speculate on novel ways in which clinical health psychology research might advance. A resurgence of interest in the investigation of within-subject research, and particularly the development of regression-style approaches to handling such data (Judd, Kenny & McClelland, 2001), may encourage researchers to incorporate within-subject approaches as well as between-subject approaches into their research toolbox. Challenges to traditional Fisherian significance testing continue to be voiced within general psychology, and where these criticisms are valid in the general sense they will also be valid within the specific context of clinical health psychology. Such criticisms may lead to consideration of alternative orientations within the logic of statistical inference such as likelihood or Bayesian methods. Such methods have already begun to be developed and used; Wiggins et al. (1991) have illustrated how a Bayesian approach can be used to analyse data on social attitudes, and Bin Ibrahim and Metcalfe (1991) used Bayesian methods to evaluate the introduction of mini-roundabouts on road safety outcomes. Hutton and Owens (1991) and Pham-Gia and Turkhan (1992) have demonstrated ways in which Bayesian approaches can be used in the determination of sample sizes.

Stepping outside the specifics of experimental design and data analysis, it may also be instructive to speculate on other ways in which the field may develop. In particular it seems likely that the nature of evidence in clinical health psychology will continue to broaden and include not only outcomes like attitudes and intent, and physiological measures such as those used in studies of PNI, but also increasing use of direct behavioural measures—individuals who actually *attend* for screening after declaring an intent to do so, amounts of sunscreen actually *sold* (and possibly containers discarded!) after programmes to encourage its use. Evidence is also likely to be considered in a broader context, with increased emphasis given to cultural and other factors. The growth of the broader discipline of behavioural medicine means that the role of health psychology is being recognised by a wider range of professional disciplines, including cardiologists, oncologists, nurses, epidemiologists and others. Greater collaboration with such groups will bring useful cross-fertilisation not only of theoretical perspectives but also of methodological approaches, enabling psychologists to provide even greater improvements to society's health and well-being.

REFERENCES

Agras, W.S., Barlow, D.H., Chapin, H.N., Abel, C.G. & Leitenberg, H. (1974). Behaviour modification of anorexia nervosa. *Archives of General Psychiatry*, **30**, 279–286.

Allen, F. (1998). *Health Psychology*. St Leonards: Allen & Unwin.

Ashcroft, J.J., Leinster, S.J. & Slade, P.D. (1985). Breast cancer: patient choice of treatment. *Journal of the Royal Society of Medicine*, **78**, 43–46.

Ashworth, P., Davis, L.G. & Spriggs, L.S. (1996). Personal change resulting from porcelain veneer treatment to improve the appearance of the teeth. *Psychology, Health and Medicine*, **1**, 57–69.

Azrin, N.H. & Powell, J.R. (1968). Behavioural engineering: the reduction of smoking behavior by a conditioning apparatus and procedure. *Journal of Applied Behavior Analysis*, **1**, 193–200.

Barlow, D.H. & Hersen, M. (1984). *Single Case Experimental Designs*. New York and Oxford: Pergamon Press.

Barlow, J., Pennington, D.C. & Bishop, P.E. (1997). Patient education leaflets for people with rheumatoid arthritis: a controlled study. *Psychology, Health and Medicine*, **2**, 221–235.

Begg, C. (1993). Publication bias. In H. Cooper & L.V. Hedges (Eds), *The Handbook of Research Synthesis*. New York: Russell Sage Foundation.

Bin Ibrahim, K. & Metcalfe, A.V. (1991). Bayesian overview for evaluation of mini-roundabouts as a road safety measure. *The Statistician*, **42**, 525–540.

Booth, R., Petrie, K.J. & Pennebaker, J. (1997). Changes in circulating lymphocyte numbers following emotional disclosure: evidence of buffering? *Stress Medicine*, **13**, 23–29.

Bruch, H. (1977). Anorexia nervosa. In E.D. Wittkower & H. Warnes (Eds), *Psychosomatic Medicine*. New York, San Francisco, London: Harper & Row.

Cacioppo, J.T., Poehlmann, K.M., Kiecolt-Glaser, J.K., Malarkey, W.B., Burleson, M.H., Berntson, G.G. & Glaser, R. (1998). Cellular immune responses to acute stress in female caregivers of dementia patients and matched controls. *Health Psychology, 17,* 182–189.

Campbell, D.T. & Stanley, J.C. (1963). *Experimental and Quasi-Experimental Design for Research*. Boston: Houghton Mifflin.

Chassan, J.B. (1979). *Research Design in Clinical Psychology and Psychiatry*. New York: Wiley Irvington.

Christensen, A.J., Ehlers, S.L., Raichle, K.A., Bertolatus, J.A. & Lawton, W.J. (2000). Predicting change in depression following renal transplantation: effect of patient coping preferences. *Health Psychology*, **19**, 348–353.

Cronbach, L.J., Gleser, C.G., Nanda, H. & Rajaratnam, N. (1972). *The Dependability of Behavioural Measurements: Theory of Generalizability for Scores and Profiles*. New York and London: John Wiley & Sons.

Davidson, P.O. & Costello, C.G. (1969). *N = 1: Experimental Studies of Single Cases*. New York and London: Van Nostrand Rheinhold.

Deadman, J.M., Dewey, M.E., Owens, R.G., Leinster, S.J. & Slade, P.D. (1989). Threat and loss in breast cancer. *Psychological Medicine*, **19**, 677–681.

Deadman, J., Leinster, S.J., Owens, R.G., Dewey, M.E. & Slade, P.D. (2001). Taking responsibility for cancer treatment. *Social Science and Medicine, 53*, 669–677.

Dusseldorp, E., van Elderen, T., Maes, S., Meulman, J. & Kraaij, V. (1999). A meta-analysis of psychoeducational programs for coronary heart disease patients. *Health Psychology*, **18**, 506–519.

Ebrahim, S. & Rowland, L. (1996). Towards a new strategy for health promotion for older women: determinants of physical activity. *Psychology, Health and Medicine, 1*, 29–40.

Feynman, R.P. (1986). *Surely you're Joking Mr Feynman: Adventures of a Curious Character*. London: Unwin Paperbacks.

Haynes, S. & Feinleib, M. (1980). Women, work and coronary heart disease: prospective findings from the Framingham heart study. *American Journal of Public Health*, **70**, 133–141.

Hutton, J. & Owens, R.G. (1991). Bayesian sample size calculations and prior beliefs about child sexual abuse. *The Statistician*, **42**, 399–404.

Joseph, J.G., Montgomery, C.-A.E., Kessler, R.C., Ostrow, D.G., Wortman, C.B., O'Brien, K., Eller, M. & Eshleman, S. (1987). Magnitude and determinants of behavioral risk reduction: longitudinal analysis of a cohort at risk for AIDS. *Psychology and Health*, **1**, 73–96.

Judd, C.M., Kenny, D.A. & McClelland, G.H. (2001). Estimating and testing mediation and moderation in within-subject designs. *Psychological Methods*, **6**, 135–146.

Kellerman, J. (1977). Anorexia nervosa: the efficacy of behavior therapy. *Journal of Behavior Therapy and Experimental Psychiatry*, **8**, 387–390.

Kent, B. & Owens, R.G. (1995). Conflicting attitudes to corneal and organ donation: a study of nurses' attitudes to organ donation. *International Journal of Nursing Studies*, **22**, 484–492.

Kohlenberg, R.J. (1973). Operant conditioning of human anal sphincter pressure. *Journal of Applied Behavior Analysis*, **6**, 201–208.

Kratochwill, T.R. (1978). *Single Subject Research; Strategies for Evaluating Change*. New York and London: Academic Press.

Kuhn, T.S. (1962). *The Structure of Scientific Revolutions*. Chicago: University of Chicago Press.

Leake, R., Friend, R. & Wadhwa, N. (1999). Improving adjustment to chronic illness through strategic self-presentation: an experimental study on a renal dialysis unit. *Health Psychology*, **18**, 54–62.

Lee, C.E. (2001). *Women's Health Australia*. Brisbane: Australian Academic Press.

Leinster, S.J., Ashcroft, J.J., Slade, P.D. & Dewey, M.E. (1989). Mastectomy versus conservative surgery: psychological effects of the patient's choice of treatment. *Journal of Psychosocial Oncology*, **7**, 179–192.

Leitenberg, H., Agras, W.S. & Thompson, L. (1968). A sequential analysis of the effect of selective positive reinforcement in modifying anorexia nervosa. *Behavior Research and Therapy*, **6**, 211–218.

Linville, P.W. (1985). Self-complexity and affective extremity: don't put all of your eggs in one cognitive basket. *Social Cognition*, **3**, 94–120.

Mackenzie, R., Sims, C., Owens, R.G. & Dixon, A.K. (1995). Patients' perceptions of magnetic resonance imaging. *Clinical Radiology*, **50**, 137–143.

Maes, S., van der Gulden, J., van Elderen, T., Senden, T., Kittel, F., Hertog, C., Seegers, G., van der Doef, M., Engels, J. & Gebhardt, W. (1993). *Healthier work in nursing homes*. Presented to conference of the European Health Psychology Society, Brussels, Belgium.

Morosko, T.E. & Baer, P.E. (1970). Avoidance conditioning of alcoholics. In R. Ulrich, T. Stachnik & J. Mabry (Eds), *Control of Human Behavior* (vol. II). Illinois: Scott Foresman.

Morris, J. & Royle, G.T. (1987). Choice of surgery for early breast cancer: pre- and post-operative levels of clinical anxiety and depression in patients and their husbands. *British Journal of Surgery*, **74**, 1017–1019.

Moyer, A. (1997). Psychosocial outcomes of breast-conserving surgery versus mastectomy: a meta-analytic review. *Health Psychology*, **16**, 284–298.

Nicholson, P. (2001). Critical health psychology: a radical alternative to the "mainstream"? *Psychology, Health and Medicine*, **6**, 256–259.

Owens, R.G. (1997). Going gently into the good night: psychological contributions to palliative care. *New Ethicals*, **34**, 9–17.

Owens, R.G., Slade, P.D. & Fielding, D.M. (1996). Patient series and quasi-experimental designs. In G. Parry & F. Watts (Eds), *A Handbook of Skills and Methods in Mental Health Research* (pp. 229–251). Hove: Lawrence Erlbaum.

Pham-Gia, T. & Turkhan, N. (1992). Sample size determination in Bayesian analysis. *The Statistician*, **41**, 389–398.

Popper, K.R. (1963). *Conjectures and Refutations; the Growth of Scientific Knowledge*. London: Routledge & Kegan Paul.

Ragland, D. & Brand, R. (1988). Coronary heart disease in the Western Collaborative Group Study: follow-up experience of 22 years. *American Journal of Epidemiology*, **127**, 462–475.

Rao, C.R. (1963). In C.R. Rao (Ed.), *Contributions to Statistics*. Calcutta: Statistical Publishing Society and Oxford/New York: Pergamon.

Rout, U. & Rout, J.K. (1997). A comparative study on occupational stress, job satisfaction and mental health in British general practitioners and Canadian family physicians. *Psychology, Health and Medicine*, **2**, 181–190.

Russell, B. (1907). *Mysticism and Logic, and Other Essays*. London: Allen & Unwin.

Rutter, M., Graham, P. & Yule, W. (1970). *A Neuropsychiatric Study in Childhood*. Philadelphia: Lippincott.

Schofield, G., Dickson, G., Smith, A. & Mummery, K. (2001). *Psychological well-being in ironman triathletes*. Presented to Australian Conference of Science and Medicine in Sport, Perth, Australia.

Sharrock, R. & Gudjonsson, G.H. (1993). Intelligence, previous convictions and interrogative suggestibility: a path analysis of alleged false-confession cases. *British Journal of Clinical Psychology*, **32**, 169–176.

Sidman, M. (1960). *Tactics of Scientific Research*. New York: Basic Books.

Stanton, A.L., Danoff-Burg, S., Cameron, C.L., Snider, P.R. & Kirk, S.B. (1999). Social comparison and adjustment to breast cancer: an experimental examination of upward affiliation and downward evaluation. *Health Psychology*, **18**, 151–158.

Steptoe, A. & Wardle, J. (1996). The European health and behaviour survey: the development of an international study in health psychology. *Psychology and Health*, **11**, 49–73.

Stoney, C.M., Owens, J.F., Guzick, D.S. & Matthews, K.A. (1997). A natural experiment on the effects of ovarian hormones on cardiovascular risk factors and stress reactivity: bilateral salpingo oophorectomy versus hysterectomy only. *Health Psychology*, **16**, 349–358.

Stuart, R.B. (1967). Behavioral control of overeating. *Behavior Research and Therapy*, **5**, 357–365.

Szabo, A., Frenkl, R., Janek, G., Kálmán, L. & Lászay, D. (1998). Runners' anxiety and mood on running and non-running days: an in situ daily monitoring study. *Psychology, Health and Medicine*, **3**, 193–199.

Temoshok, L., Sweet, D.M. & Zich, J. (1987). A three city comparison of the public's knowledge and attitudes about AIDS. *Psychology and Health*, **1**, 43–60.

Thorp, D., Owens, R.G., Whitehouse, G.W. & Dewey, M.E. (1990). Subjective experiences of Magnetic Resonance Imaging. *Clinical Radiology*, **41**, 276–278.

Touyz, S.W. & Beumont, P.J.V. (1997). Behavioural treatment principles to promote weight gain. In D.M. Garner & D.M. Garfinkel (Eds), *Handbook of Psychotherapy for Eating Disorders*. New York: Guilford Press.

Touyz, S.W., Beumont, P.J.V., Glaun, D., Phillips, T. & Cowie, I. (1984). A comparison of lenient and strict operant conditioning programmes in refeeding patients with anorexia nervosa. *British Journal of Psychiatry*, **144**, 517–520.

Waldie, K.E. & Poulton, R. (2002). Physical and psychological correlates of primary headache in young adulthood: a 26 year longitudinal study. *Journal of Neurology, Neurosurgery and Psychiatry*, **72**, 86–92.

Wang, T., Delahanty, D.L., Dougall, A.L. & Baum, A. (1998). Responses of Natural Killer Cell Activity to acute laboratory stressors in healthy men at different times of day. *Health Psychology*, **17**, 428–435.

Wardle, J., Steptoe, A., Bellisle, F., Davou, B., Reschke, K., Lappalainen, R. & Fredrikson, M. (1997). Healthy dietary practices among European students. *Health Psychology*, **16**, 443–450.

Wiggins, R.D., Ashworth, K., O'Muircheartaigh, C.A. & Galbraith, J.I. (1991). Multilevel analysis of attitudes to abortion. *The Statistician*, **40**, 225–234.

Wroe, A.L. & Salkovkis, P.M. (1999). Factors influencing anticipated decisions about genetic testing: experimental studies. *British Journal of Health Psychology*, **4**, 19–40.

Wroe, A.L., Salkovkis, P.M. & Rimes, K.A. (2000). The effect of nondirective questioning on women's decisions whether to undergo bone density screening: an experimental study. *Health Psychology*, **19**, 181–191.

Yule, W. & Hemsley, D. (1977). Single case methodology in medical psychology. In S.J. Rachman (Ed.), *Contributions to Medical Psychology* (vol. 1). Oxford and New York: Pergamon Press.

Qualitative Research: Evaluating the Process and the Product

William B. Stiles
Miami University, Oxford, USA

INTRODUCTION

Qualitative research is a way for psychological science to encompass observations that are not adequately dealt with using traditional quantitative methods. Like all scientific research, qualitative research consists of comparing ideas with observations. In good research, the ideas are thereby changed—strengthened, weakened, qualified, or elaborated in some way. Evaluating qualitative research requires attending to both the process and the product of the research, that is, to the means by which the ideas are changed (the method) and to the changed ideas themselves (the interpretation).

As explained shortly, qualitative research characteristically (though not always) yields results in words rather than numbers, uses empathy and personal understanding rather than detached observation, places observations in context rather than in isolation, focuses on good examples and special cases rather than representative samples, and seeks to empower its participants rather than merely observe them. Partly because of these characteristics, qualitative methods are particularly well adapted for studying human experience and meaning, which are central to the concerns of clinical health psychology (see also Chamberlain, Stephens & Lyons, 1997). Maintaining health and dealing with illness are intensely personal and interpersonal activities that cannot reasonably be studied in ignorance of people's experience of them.

This chapter is a review of criteria for evaluating qualitative research on human experience in clinical health psychology and other fields (cf. Stiles, 1993, 1999) and an examination of some epistemological bases for this evaluation. It is not a review of qualitative methods. Methods of doing qualitative research are at least as varied and complex as quantitative methods; readers are referred to texts and collections (e.g., Barker, Pistrang & Elliott, 1994; Denzin & Lincoln, 2000; Murray & Chamberlain, 1999; Smith, Harré & Van Langenhove, 1995) and to published examples (some are cited later).

Handbook of Clinical Health Psychology. Edited by S. Llewelyn and P. Kennedy.
© 2003 John Wiley & Sons, Ltd.

The chapter begins by considering some limits to traditional quantitative approaches that pointed me and other psychologists toward qualitative approaches. Following this summary of critiques, the chapter lists some qualities that distinguish qualitative research from traditional quantitative approaches. Next, it offers a list of good practices that promote and reveal permeability, and hence trustworthy observations in qualitative research, followed by a list of types of validity that qualitative investigators have identified. These lists have been drawn from many sources, and readers are referred to overlapping lists that have been published elsewhere (e.g., Altheide & Johnson, 1994; Elliott, Fischer & Rennie, 1999; Guba & Lincoln, 1989; Kvale, 1996; Leininger, 1994; Mishler, 1990; Packer & Addison, 1989a, 1989b). Finally, the chapter considers the place of theory in qualitative research and describes forms of discourse that are alternatives to the usual theoretical-didactic discourse of science.

WHY IS QUALITATIVE RESEARCH NECESSARY?

The Process–Outcome Correlation Problem

My interest in qualitative research was stimulated—coerced, really—by the failure of a decade-long search for correlations between verbal processes, such as asking questions, and the outcomes of psychotherapy and medical interviews (Stiles, 1988, 1989). Originally, like many other researchers, my colleagues and I had reasoned more or less as follows: if a process component, such as physicians' question-asking or psychotherapists' interpretation, is important, then patients who received more of that component should tend to have better outcomes than those who received less, so process and outcome should be positively correlated across patients (McDaniel, Stiles & McGaughey, 1981; Stiles et al., 1979). We were unable to demonstrate the clear, consistent process–outcome relationships we expected (e.g., Stiles & Shapiro, 1994). Other researchers using their own measures failed just as badly. At first, we thought that we had been wrong about which components were important or had failed to measure the components accurately. However, I now think the main reason for this failure lay in our use of linear-model statistics, such as correlation and regression, to describe responsive—and hence nonlinear—processes of human interaction (Stiles, 1989; Stiles, Honos-Webb & Surko, 1998).

The problem can be illustrated with a constructed example of how process–outcome correlations can be reversed. Consider the effect of physician question-asking on making an accurate diagnosis for patients presenting with chest pain. Well-informed, forthcoming patients tend to provide good information in response to a few questions, whereas poorly informed, recalcitrant, or verbally unskilled patients tend to provide poorer information despite many questions. Suppose that doctors are responsive to patient differences, asking more or fewer questions depending on how forthcoming patients are. Then it is likely that the recalcitrant patients will be asked more questions but may still receive less accurate diagnoses, whereas forthcoming patients will be diagnosed more accurately despite having been asked fewer questions. That is, questioning and diagnostic accuracy may be *negatively* correlated despite the *positive* causal contribution of questioning to diagnosis. Reviewers seeing such correlations across several studies would be likely to conclude, erroneously, that questioning is useless or counterproductive.

One can construct parallel examples for virtually any process component or outcome index (Stiles, 1988, 1989; Stiles, Honos-Webb & Surko, 1998). The general problem is using linear models, which assume independent measurement of variables, to assess process–outcome relationships that are responsive and hence obviously not linear. Information about probable outcome—how the patient is responding—continually feeds back to influence process. That is the whole point of skillful interviewing. We cannot expect to find linear scientific laws such as, "questioning promotes accurate diagnosis", because the independent and dependent variables interact with each other.

This is *not* a measurement problem. The responsiveness problem would remain even if we had perfect measures of key process components and outcomes. This problem is one corner of a larger one that is more profound than a need for new measures or new statistics. The larger problem has been called the *received view*.

Critique of the *Received View*

Most psychological research in the twentieth century was premised by a loose set of assumptions that can be summarized by a nineteenth-century prescription by John Stuart Mill: "The backward state of the moral sciences [such as psychology] can be remedied by applying to them the methods of physical science, duly extended and generalised" (Mill, 1953).

This *received view* has been called scientific empiricism, which was formalized as logical positivism. The positivist goal was a hypothetico-deductive system, which was to be axiomatic, like mathematics, except that the terms were to refer explicitly to entities in the world. All scientific statements were to be tied directly or deductively to observations.

Unfortunately, this has not gone as well as expected, in clinical health psychology (e.g., Chamberlain, 2000) or elsewhere. My problem with process–outcome relationships was only one of many disappointments. MacIntyre (1984, p. 88) said: "The salient fact about [the social] sciences is the absence of the discovery of any law-like generalisations whatsoever." Packer and Addison (1989a) described this as the failure of the Enlightenment project—the idea of progress through the scientific accumulation of knowledge. This may have been overstated, but there was a chorus of objections to the received view.

1. *Facts are interpretations of events.* Consequently, facts reflect the observer's assumptions and values. Facts are statements, whereas events are not. Stating an observation represents an interpretation of the event. Any choice of words classifies an event as being of a particular kind (i.e., of being related to other events described using those words) and invokes a host of assumptions about such events. This core objection has been raised in various ways. Context is necessary for meaning, yet it affects meaning (Spence, 1982). Different assumptions made by investigators, participants, observers, and readers give an event different meanings. The inner–outer and subjective–objective dimensions are not the same (Harré, 1987). Nothing is objective, in the sense of viewed from outside. A psychologist observing behavior may be looking at the outside of one organism, but he or she is looking at it from the inside of another organism. Consequently, readers have to look inside of the scientist organism to understand the report of the research.

2. *The problem of induction.* Scientific theories can be falsified but not proven, a logical asymmetry usually associated with Popper (1959). Logically, if P implies Q, then the

negation of Q implies the negation of P. That is, contrary evidence should falsify the theory, a logical operation called *modus tolens*. If all birds are supposed to have feathers and this bird has none, then that theory of birds cannot be true. The converse doesn't hold; the affirmation of Q does not imply the affirmation of P. If this bird does have feathers, there may still be others that do not. Support for scientific theories is of the latter type, in effect, affirming the consequent (a classical logical fallacy). Thus, in the received view, theories are supposedly constructed to be falsified. However, this is not what happens. Generalizations in psychology and the social sciences often coexist with recognized counter-examples.

3. *Meehl's lament*. Meehl (1978) argued that the use of inferential statistics, particularly significance tests, is a barrier to progress in psychology. Conventionally, we construct a null hypothesis that is contrary to our theory and then use statistical tests to reject it, regarding such a result as indirect support for the theory. However, it is highly unlikely that the true correlation between any two or more psychological variables is exactly zero, so whether the null hypothesis is refuted depends on statistical power. One can never falsify a theory by accepting the null hypothesis, because one can always construct a more powerful test that will reject it. On the other hand, rejecting a null hypothesis is very weak support for a substantive theory, because there are always many plausible alternative explanations for why the relationship between the variables is not null.

4. *Pretheoretical knowledge*. Rosenwald (1986) argued that psychology fails to make progress because pretheoretical knowledge—common sense or intuitive beliefs about how people experience events—takes precedence over scientific theory and results. Results are criticized not because of failed predictions or conflicting findings, but because of beliefs that other events would have been observed if it had not been for situational artefacts. For example, Festinger and Carlsmith's (1959) classic demonstration of cognitive dissonance—showing that participants' attitudes changed more when they were paid 50 cents to make counterattitudinal statements than when they were paid 20 dollars—was subsequently criticized not on theoretical or methodological grounds but on the basis of other researchers' commonsense beliefs regarding the participants' experience. Critics suggested, for example, that 20 dollars might have been seen as unrealistically high or as an insulting bribe, or that participants might have experienced fear of social retaliation, threats to their self-esteem, or guilt about making misleading statements. The critiques were derived not from scientific investigations, but from background beliefs grounded in the critics' life experience outside the laboratory: "As one of your subjects I would have experienced such-and-such." The critics did not proceed to collect evidence in support of their new interpretation; instead they carried out new experiments testing the same hypothesis but free of the particular problem they had cited. So the new studies rarely shed any light on the alleged defectiveness of the previous ones (see Rosenwald, 1986, for a review).

Gergen (1982) suggested that psychologists obtain support for hypotheses because they are familiar with their culture. They can guess correctly how, when, and where to gather evidence for a hypothesis. But they could equally well find evidence against it.

5. *Ethical concerns*. Received view research has been criticized on social and ethical grounds as well. It has been described as alienating and mystifying to participants. Data-gathering has often been specifically designed to disguise its purpose from participants. Ironically, in research aimed at the elucidation of people's experience, it has been considered bad practice for research participants to participate in constructing the meanings to be attached to their behaviour.

Permeability and Understanding Replace Objectivity and Truth as Scientific Goals

Perhaps because qualitative research represents a departure from the received view, qualitative researchers have had to consider and address epistemological issues that scientists using traditional approaches could avoid. Central among these are the traditional scientific goals of objectivity and truth. Most qualitative investigators have concluded that it is impossible to attain either of these in any complete or absolute way, and they have identified replacements.

The goal of objectivity is replaced by the goal of *permeability*, the capacity of understanding to be changed by encounters with observations. Investigators argue that we cannot view reality from outside of our own frame of reference. Instead, good practice in research seeks to ensure that understanding is permeated by observation, and good practice in reporting seeks to show readers how the understanding has been changed.

The goal of truth in scientific statements is replaced by the goal of *understanding by people*. Thus, the validity of an interpretation is never absolute but always in relation to some person. Procedures and criteria for assessing validity depend on who that person is, for example, the investigator, research participant, or reader of the research report.

WHAT IS QUALITATIVE RESEARCH?

The term *qualitative research* defies comprehensive definition. Perhaps it is best characterized by pointing to examples. Qualitative research encompasses case studies (Bromley, 1986; Kotre, 1984; Moore, 1999; Radley & Chamberlain, 2001; Rosenwald, 1988; Wackerbarth, 1999; Weinholtz, Kacer & Rocklin, 1995; Wiersma, 1988; Williams, 1993), conversation analysis (du Pre & Beck, 1997; Frankel, 1984, 1989, 1990; Peräkylä, 1991, 1998; Poskiparta, Kettunen & Liimatainen, 1998), discourse analysis (Horton-Salway, 2001; Lupton, 1992, 1993, 1994; Parker, 1992; Potter & Wetherell, 1987; Radtke & Mens-Verhulst, 2001; Wiggins, Potter & Wildsmith, 2001; Willig, 2000; Yardley & Beech, 1998), ethnography (Banister, 1999; Barroso, 1997; Engebretson, 1996; Kleinman, 1992; McAllister & Silverman, 1999; Tourigny, 1994; Ventres & Frankel, 1996), focus groups (Barlow, Wright & Kroll, 2001; Gallagher & MacLachlan, 2001; Jirojanakul & Skevington, 2000; Skevington, MacArthur & Somerset, 1997; Wilkinson, 1998), grounded theory (Charmaz, 1990, 1994; Fitzsimmons et al., 1999; Glaser, 1992; Glaser & Strauss, 1967; Rennie, Phillips & Quartaro, 1988; Schou & Hewison, 1998; Strauss & Corbin, 1990; Weiss & Hutchinson, 2000; Yardley et al., 2001), narrative analysis (Baumeister & Newman, 1994; Elderkin-Thompson, Silver & Waitzkin, 1998; Garro, 1994; Good, 1994; Hunter, 1991; Kotre, 1984; Linde, 1983; Mishler, 1984, 1995; Murray, 2000; Viney & Bousfield, 1991), phenomenological analysis (Baillie et al., 2000; Barnard, McCosker & Gerber, 1999; Giorgi, 1970; Smith, 1996, 1999a, 1999b; Smith, Flowers & Osborne, 1997; Smith, Jarman & Osborne, 1999; Smith et al., 2000), and a variety of other approaches to analyzing and understanding interviews, conversations, and texts.

Despite the diversity, there appear to be some common features that distinguish qualitative from received-view research on human experience. The following characteristics of qualitative research are not mutually exclusive or exhaustive, nor are all of them characteristic of every piece of qualitative research.

Results Expressed in Words; Polydimensionality of Experience

In qualitative research, results tend to be expressed in words rather than primarily in numbers. Dialogues, narratives, and so forth are analyzed, presented, and summarized without being reduced to numbers (e.g., by coding or rating). It is argued that using words retains more of the richness and immediacy of human experience.

Qualitative results typically include many descriptive terms (Geertz, 1973), rather than being focused on a few targeted dimensions. Every descriptor of experience can be considered as a new dimension. Using the term *polydimensionality* rather than multidimensionality is meant to suggest that the difficulty will not yield to adding further terms to a multidimensional linear model.

It is possible, of course, to project a person's experience onto one or a few dimensions or rating scales, for example, characterizing one's position as "agree moderately" with some statement about satisfaction with service. However, such tactics oversimplify and thus distort the experience the person actually had. Psychologists do this to aggregate and compare results precisely, but only after professional socialization do they come to think it an adequate characterization human experience.

Empathy as an Observation Strategy

Qualitative research uses empathy as a legitimate observation strategy. Rather than counting only people's externally observable behavior as data, qualitative research additionally uses the investigator's understanding of their experience. For example, what a participant says and does in an interview is considered as conveying meanings and feelings. The participant's direct and indirect communications are experienced and understood by the interviewer (albeit imperfectly) and can inform the study's interpretations. Thus, qualitative research encompasses the meanings, purposes, and significance that people attach to what they say or do. This may be the most radical difference from received-view research. It explicitly makes use of information not available for objects in the universe that do not have experience like ours.

Looking inside people's heads reverses the behaviorist revolution. Of course, the radical version of the behaviorist project was abandoned long ago by most psychologists, who have constructed theories about people's experience and tested the theories by asking people to press buttons or mark forms. Even within the received view, psychologists use language to instruct research participants, implicitly assuming that the participants accurately understand the instructions. Such a procedure would not work with nonhuman objects of scientific study. Similarly, a shared understanding with readers is assumed in presenting hypotheses and interpretations in written results. In effect, even within the received view, scientists use empathy in their introduction, method, and discussion sections. The qualitative step was introducing empathy into the results section.

Contextual Interpretation

Events are understood and reported in their context, that is, in relation to specific times, places, and circumstances, rather than isolated or abstracted. This represents an acknowledgment that each event is unique; no two things in the world are exactly alike. Meanings of events depend on participants' and observers' cultural and personal histories as well as on the sequence of preceding and succeeding events.

Acknowledging the importance of context yields a more interpretive understanding of *replication*, a core concept of scientific inquiry: replication is always an interpretation, a human judgment that some set of unique events can be gathered under a common conceptual umbrella. Thus, the concept of generalizability of a scientific theory or interpretation is replaced with the concept of *transferability*—the extent to which an interpretation's meaning and applicability can be transferred to another setting, and the ways in which it must be adjusted.

Sample Composition Informed by Emerging Results; Focus on Exemplars

Materials or participants may be chosen because they are exemplars—good or informative examples—or because they offer distinct perspectives, rather than because they are representative of some larger population. For example, participants may be selected to be interviewed because they are good informants or because they seem likely to express an important or previously unrepresented viewpoint (Rosenwald, 1988). Cases may be considered in sequence, rather than independently, so that earlier observations inform later ones. Sample size and composition may be informed by emerging results. For example, cases may be chosen to fill gaps. Data-gathering may be continued until new cases seem redundant, rather than until a set quota is filled.

Nonlinear Causality

Research hypotheses in psychology are most often stated in linear terms—one thing causes another thing or a particular linear relationship holds under stated conditions. However, relationships among most experiential and behavioral variables are obviously nonlinear. That is, the variables interact with each other across time. In medical interviews, for example, doctors continually adjust their behavior in light of what seems to be working. If the patient does not give an intelligible answer, the doctor asks the question again or puts it a different way. In such a system, there can be great sensitivity to initial conditions; a seemingly minor event—the phrasing of some statement, perhaps—can initiate an unexpected cascade of reactions with unpredictable results.

As popularly described in chaos theory (Barton, 1994; Gleick, 1987), nonlinear systems often behave unpredictably. Even though a system is completely deterministic, predicting its behavior more than a few steps in advance may be impossible. Trivial differences in starting points can lead to enormous differences in outcomes, a phenomenon described as sensitive dependence on initial conditions. A standard example is the weather, which cannot be accurately predicted more than a few days in advance because temperature, pressure, wind, moisture, and so forth continually feed back to influence themselves and each other. It is said that a butterfly flapping its wings in China may determine whether or not there are tornadoes in Kansas months later. Most social and developmental processes are chaotic in this sense. In human development, early experiences may have profound effects that are unpredictable, though they can be traced historically in the lives of individuals. Qualitative approaches can accommodate the chaos by selecting exemplars or revealing cases rather than representative cases, by interpreting contextually, and by reporting results verbally and polydimensionally.

Empowering Participants as a Research Purpose

Many qualitative commentators have advocated empowerment or emancipation or enhancement of participants as a legitimate or even a central purpose of research (e.g., Freire, 1973; Gergen, 1982, 1985; Guba & Lincoln, 1989; Lather, 1986a, 1986b; Rosenwald, 1985; Sullivan, 1984). The imposition of an interpretation on participants' experiences can be seen as a political as well as a scientific act. Inevitably it has implications for the power relationships among the research's producers, consumers, and participants. Insofar as research is interpersonal and political, ethical issues are bound up with scientific ones. Taking this perspective directs attention to constructing interpretations that advance participants' interests rather than maintaining vested interests and to involving participants in the construction of the interpretations.

Results Are Always Tentative

Finally, because it is linguistic, polydimensional, empathic, contextual, and nonlinear, qualitative interpretations tend to be advanced more tentatively than those of received-view research. Qualitative investigators express varying degrees of confidence in their formulations, but they are typically not surprised by exceptions. The tentativeness of interpretations is a central aspect of the shift from seeking true statements to seeking people's understanding. Insofar as statements have meaning only as people understand them, and insofar as people's understanding is variable and evolving, no interpretation can be considered as final, ultimate, or immutable.

GOOD PRACTICE AND PERMEABILITY IN QUALITATIVE RESEARCH

How does one design, conduct, and report high-quality qualitative research? In many respects, good practice follows similar principles in all research. For example, like all research reports, qualitative research reports should clearly describe and justify the investigator's choices (e.g., of questions to address, of participants or materials to study, of methods for gathering and analyzing observations). However, there are some forms of reliability and validity that seem to distinguish qualitative from received-view research.

Reliability and validity concern trustworthiness. Reliability refers to the trustworthiness of observations or data. Validity refers to the trustworthiness of interpretations or conclusions.

In rejecting the possibility of objectivity—of standing outside one's personal frame of reference—qualitative investigators have also changed the concept of reliability. Different views of a phenomenon can be considered as not only inevitable but informative. The trustworthiness of observations is fostered, then, not so much by restricting the observations to aspects that different observers call by the same name as by enhancing permeability. That is, understanding is trustworthy to the extent that it can incorporate and be changed by observations. Investigator bias can be reframed as impermeability—understanding that cannot be changed by new observations. An emerging canon of good practice aims (a) to enhance permeability and (b) to help readers to assess how well observations have permeated investigators' understanding.

Practices that Enhance Permeability

Personal Engagement

In contrast to the traditional ideal of scientific detachment, qualitative research seems facilitated by immersion in the data. This may involve personal contact with participants or intimate familiarity with a text. It may include prolonged engagement, persistent observation, discussion of preliminary interpretations with other investigators, actively seeking disconfirming data, and repeatedly checking participants' reactions to interpretations. This does not deny the possibility of motivated distortions and biases, but it acknowledges the potential insights attendant on intimate familiarity with the material.

Iteration

In addition to engaging with the material, qualitative work seems to demand iterative cycling between observation and interpretation, repeatedly reformulating and examining revised interpretations in light of further observation or examination of evidence. Glaser and Strauss (1967), for example, formalized iteration in their method of constant comparison.

Grounding

Interpretations require grounding—systematic procedures for linking (relatively abstract) interpretations with (relatively concrete) observations. Qualitative researchers have developed procedures for linking their more abstract interpretations with their more concrete observations and for conveying the links to readers. For example, qualitative research reports often include substantial amounts of illustrative text, meant to make the meanings of the interpretations explicit and accessible.

Seeking Information that the Participants Have

In interviewing, qualitative researchers must be careful to ask questions that participants can answer. Normally, this involves asking them to report things they have actually done or perceived, as distinct from asking them to explain or interpret their actions or perceptions. There is a danger in assuming that because participants have more direct access to their own experience, their interpretations of it are likely to be more valid (Silverman, 1989). Research participants often have no better access than researchers to the causes of their behavior.

Inquiries seeking participants' interpretations often produce an impoverished amalgam of popular culture and socially acceptable reasoning (e.g., Linde, 1983) or accounts of causes that are demonstrably incorrect (Nisbett & Wilson, 1977). As a rule of thumb, ask "what", not "why". Just as patients may have limited explanations for biological aspects of illness (e.g., nature of tuberculosis infections; Ailinger & Dear, 1997), they may have limited explanations for psychological or behavioral aspects (e.g., resistance to lifestyle changes for preventing heart disease; Treloar, 1997).

Practices that Help Readers to Assess Permeability

Disclosing Investigators' Forestructure

Investigators should reveal their initial orientations, expectations, preconceptions, values, theories, and personal background. This collection of material is sometimes called the investigator's *forestructure*—the understanding that existed before the investigation began. Such disclosures help readers to understand the meaning the observations had to the investigator, and they indicate a starting position against which to gauge subsequent changes in interpretation.

Explicating the Social and Cultural Context

Similarly, the investigator should try to accurately represent the social, institutional, and cultural context of the investigation, including shared assumptions, relevant cultural values, circumstances of data-gathering, and the meaning of the research to the participants. Part of the investigator's responsibility is to reflect on implicit assumptions within the institutional and cultural context (both the participants' and the investigators') that may affect the interpretations.

Describing the Investigator's Internal Processes

Along the same lines, good practice reports the investigator's internal processes during the investigation and development of the interpretations. This might include the personal experience of conducting interviews, relationships with participants, and personal reactions to the observations and findings. It should particularly include descriptions of the impact of the process and product of the investigation on the investigators' forestructure, including what seemed expected or surprising and how expectations and preconceptions were affected. Qualitative investigators often address topics that are personally significant and thus involve them in self-examination, significant personal learning, and change. Good practice dictates that these processes should be shared with the readers, as a part of the study's context.

Bracketing versus Exposure: A Personal View

Some qualitative methodologists (e.g., Glaser & Strauss, 1967; Hill, Thomson & Williams, 1997) have recommended that, in trying to understand their material, qualitative investigators should try to set aside their biases and expectations and try to approach the material as blank slate, ready to let the material show itself in its own terms. This practice is sometimes called *bracketing*.

Qualitative research employing bracketing can be self-deceptive and self-defeating, however. It may be self-deceptive in the sense that all understanding must be based on past experience—both the investigator's and others'. Any use of language imports culturally shaped ways of understanding observations, based on the experience of personal and intellectual forebears. Bracketing can at most set aside expectations that are explicit in awareness—particularly those informed by formal theories. What remains is likely to be unarticulated conventional views—cultural preconceptions and common sense. It seems doubtful to me that these will promote more sophisticated, more useful, or more humane understandings than those informed by consciously articulated expectations, theory, and values.

Bracketing can be self-defeating in the sense that the point of scientific research is quality control on theory, or more broadly on concepts and interpretations. Systematically setting aside previous theory denies the possibility of improving it. Presumably, the observations of previous investigators have, to some extent, permeated their interpretations and theories. Starting with a blank slate makes every project a new beginning, failing to credit or use or dispute what previous investigators have observed. Interpersonally, bracketing cuts investigators off from the community of other investigators who share interests and whose understandings can, in principle, build on each other. Bracketed investigations must each stand alone—or be understood as a derivative of unarticulated common sense.

As noted earlier, the problem of bias can be addressed by practices likely to enhance and reveal permeability. Rather than denying expectations, investigators can state and explore them, reveal them to readers, and expose them systematically and intensively to new observations.

TYPES OF VALIDITY

Reframing the goal of research as fostering understanding by people, rather than making statements that are objectively true, changes the concept of validity. Validity still concerns the trustworthiness of interpretations, but this trustworthiness must be judged from the perspective of particular people, rather than according to some universal or absolute standard. The familiar received-view validity criteria (e.g., Cook & Campbell, 1979; Cronbach & Meehl, 1955; and see Chapter 25) are nevertheless still very important because they are convincing to people—to the research's readers, participants, or investigators. That is, reconstruing validity as impact on people affirms the importance of received-view criteria but places them in a broader context.

In principle, each person may evaluate the trustworthiness of an interpretation differently. Nevertheless, qualitative investigators and methodologists have come to distinguish several broad types of validity, which can be classified to reflect relationships of people to the research. In particular, types of validity can be classified according to whether the interpretation's impact is on (a) the readers of the research report, (b) the participants in the research, or (c) the investigators, particularly on the investigators' theoretical forestructure. Within each of these classes, validity criteria can be further subdivided according to whether the impact of the interpretation is one of (a) fit or agreement of the new observations or interpretations with prior understanding (forestructure) or (b) change or growth in understanding produced

Table 24.1 Types of validity in qualitative research

	Impact of interpretation on forestructure	
Group of people	Fit or agreement	Change or growth
Readers	Coherence	Uncovering; self-evidence
Participants	Testimonial validity	Catalytic validity
Investigators	Consensus; replication	Reflexive validity

by the new observations or interpretations (Stiles, 1993). The latter sort of impact under-
lines the importance accorded to permeability of understanding and the potential to empower
those who participate in and read about the research (Lather, 1986a, 1986b; Lincoln & Guba,
1990). This classification of types of validity is shown in Table 24.1. No single one of these
criteria by itself establishes an interpretation's validity, of course, but, other things being
equal, any interpretation can be considered as more trustworthy if it meets one of these
criteria than if it does not.

Readers' Judgments

Some types of validity can be judged by the readers of research reports—people who have
not been either participants or investigators in the research.

Coherence

A coherent interpretation gives a satisfactory account of the observations reported in the
research. Coherence includes internal consistency, comprehensiveness of the elements to
be interpreted and the relations between elements, and usefulness in encompassing new
elements as they come into view. A better interpretation encompasses its rivals, confirming,
supplementing, elaborating, simplifying, or superseding them (Lincoln & Guba, 1990;
Potter & Wetherell, 1987; Rosenwald, 1985; Taylor, 1979).

Uncovering; Self-evidence

The interpretation produces change or growth in the reader's perspective and yields action
(Packer & Addison, 1989b; Rosenwald, 1988). The interpretation feels right in the context of all of the reader's other knowledge and beliefs (hence, *self-evident*). That is, the
interpretation accounts not only for the observations reported in the research, but also for
additional observations by the reader. Often, this means that the interpretation is a solution
to the concern that motivated the reader's interest in the first place.

Participants' Reactions

Interpretations may be presented to research participants in some form. Some investigators systematically use such *member checks* as a way of confirming and refining their

interpretations. Interpretations may be negotiated with participants. When such procedures are used, the participants' reactions yield information about the interpretations' validity.

Testimonial Validity

In response to hearing an interpretation, participants may—or may not—indicate that it accurately describes their experience. This is evidence of testimonial validity. Others have called this *representational validity* (Folger & Poole, 1981), or *credibility* (Guba & Lincoln, 1989). Evidence of testimonial validity includes participants' direct agreement with interpretations, but it also may include direct or indirect allusions to feeling understood, or behavior consistent with the interpretation's motifs (in effect, exemplifying the interpretation), or revealing of fresh and deeper material, confirming the interpretation by elaborating upon it (Kotre, 1984).

Catalytic Validity

A catalytically valid interpretation produces change or growth in the people whose experience is being described. The research process reorients, focuses, and energizes participants. If participants are empowered by the interpretation, they will change by taking more control of their lives (Freire, 1973; Guba & Lincoln, 1989; Lather, 1986a, 1986b).

Impact on Investigators

Investigators are typically the people most familiar with the theory and observations. They are also often the people with the greatest personal stake in finding the research's results to be valid.

Consensus; Replication

Consensus suggests that the observations fit the theoretical forestructure of multiple investigators (Guba & Lincoln, 1989; Potter & Wetherell, 1987); for example, members of the research team or external reviewers or auditors (Hill, Thomson & Williams, 1997) or adversaries (Bromley, 1986; Levine, 1974) who were familiar with the observations and who found the proposed interpretation convincing. Consensus may be based on formal rules of evidence and validity criteria (e.g., Cook & Campbell, 1979; Cronbach & Meehl, 1955; see also Chapter 25), but also on fit with widely accepted exemplars.

Replication represents another form of fit between an investigator's forestructure and observation. It is important to recognize that no results are ever repeated exactly. Thus, successful replication reflects an investigator's judgment that an interpretation encompasses new observations as well as previous ones.

Reflexive Validity

Reflexive validity refers to whether the investigator's understanding, including formal theory, is changed by the observations. New ideas and goals emerge from a living theory, as it encounters new data and is acted upon by new minds. The converse of reflexivity is the tendency for an interpretation to lose its power and immediacy and become a slogan. Kuhn (1970) pointed out that scientific research is rarely designed to test a theory in Popper's sense of seeking to falsify it. Instead, scientists work within paradigms, which they seek to elaborate and extend. A theory that becomes rigid (impermeable) and can no longer support dialectical interaction and change is scientifically dead.

Triangulation

Many qualitative investigators emphasize the importance of *triangulation* in assessing validity—seeking information from multiple data sources, multiple methods, and multiple prior theories or interpretations, and applying multiple validity criteria. Interpretations supported by converging sources are generally more trustworthy than those that are not. The principle of triangulation is also incorporated into many of the validity categories just reviewed. For example, uncovering represents triangulation involving a reader's previous experiences as well as the current observations, and consensus represents triangulation among multiple investigators, auditors, or adversaries.

TRUTH AND THEORY IN QUALITATIVE RESEARCH

The usual language of science was called *didactic* discourse by Bruner (1986). In the received view, discourse of this type was considered as a search for general truth. If the possibility of general truth is denied, the understanding of this search must change, but it is still useful to distinguish didactic discourse from some alternative discourse forms, as described later.

Empirical Truth as Corresponding Experiences

Instead of being considered as general or absolute, empirical truth can be understood as match between theoretical understanding and observation, where both are considered as a person's experience (Stiles, 1981). The correspondence account of truth is nonsensical in its naïve form. A true statement is composed of spoken or written words, which are obviously not identical to the concrete objects or events they describe. But the correspondence account is more tenable in an experiential form. Both the words of a statement and events in the world are experienced, and these experiences, being composed of the same stuff, can be directly compared and judged as similar or different. In effect, this formulation transforms the epistemological question of what truth is into the classical *psychological* problem of stimulus equivalence.

What is lost in this understanding of truth is the assurance that it can be general or absolute, insofar as different people may experience the same words or events differently. Both the meanings of words and the experience of events in the world are affected by biological equipment, culture, and life history, which differ across people. This is not a problem for research, however, if its goal is not permanent truths but understanding by people. The core scientific goal of assessing, elaborating and refining scientific theory is retained.

How Qualitative Research Can Be Cumulative

A scientific theory can thus be understood not as a set of falsifiable statements but as an understanding that is shared to varying degrees by those who have propounded it or been exposed to it. The means of sharing understanding is the exchange of signs, such as words and stories (Stiles, 1997). The understanding is not fixed, but changes continually. An investigator's understanding changes as it encounters new observations or as it is framed in new ways (e.g., new words and stories). Similarly, a reader's understanding grows and changes as he or she reads research reports. Of course, no reader's understanding ever matches the author's understanding perfectly—though it is not unusual for some readers to understand more than the author did.

A scientific theory may thus be regarded as a living thing, resident in many people, growing and changing as it enters new minds. Paradoxically, observations have more value as evidence when they change a theory than when they leave it unchanged. Research is cumulative because each new observation that enters (permeates) a theory changes it in some way. The change may be manifested, for example, as a greater or lesser confidence in theoretical assertions, as the introduction or revised meanings of terms, or as differences in the way particular ideas are phrased or introduced.

Testing Theories in Interpretive Research

Theory can thus be considered as the principal product of science and the work of scientists as quality control—insuring that the theories are good ones by comparing them with observations (Stiles, 1981). If science is understood in this way, theory is just as central in interpretive (qualitative) research as it is in hypothesis-testing (received-view) research.

In a strict Popperian sense (Popper, 1959), interpretive research could disconfirm a theory merely by providing a negative instance. As noted earlier, few, if any, psychological theories make such firm predictions that they could be so simply disconfirmed.

Interpretive research can be confirmatory more generally, however. Consider the following argument. In all good research, investigators compare observations with theories (i.e., people's ways of understanding and talking about events). As a result of these comparisons, the theories are changed—strengthened, weakened, qualified, or elaborated, as the implications of the observations are incorporated into the theory. Theories are composed of statements (usually verbal statements in psychology, though they can be mathematical). In hypothesis-testing research, an investigator extracts or derives one statement (or a few statements) from a theory and attempts to compare this statement with observations. If the observations match the statement (that is, if the scientists' experience of the observed events resembles their experience of the statement), then people's confidence in the statement is substantially increased, and this, in turn, yields a small increment of confidence in the theory as a whole.

In interpretive research, instead of trying to assign a firm confidence level to a particular derived statement, an investigator tests many statements at once. A case study, for example, may simultaneously compare a large number of observations based on a particular individual with a correspondingly large number of theoretically based statements. Such studies ask, in effect, how well does the theory describe the details of a particular case. For a variety of familiar reasons (selective sampling, low power, potential biases, etc.), the increment or decrement in confidence in any one statement may be very small. Nevertheless, because many statements are examined, the increment (or decrement) in people's confidence in the whole clinical theory may be comparable to that stemming from a statistical hypothesis-testing study. Thus, a few systematically analyzed cases that match a theory in precise or unexpected detail may give people considerable confidence in the theory as a whole, even though each component assertion may remain tentative and uncertain when considered separately.

ALTERNATIVE DISCOURSE FORMS

Not all qualitative investigators see quality control on scientific theory as their main activity. What they do instead can be described in terms of alternative forms of discourse, including hermeneutics and narratives. In Hillman's (1983) colourful personification, didactic discourse, such as exposition of a theory, was called *senex*, a literary term for a wise old man (the same root as senator, senior, and senile). Hermeneutic discourse—Hillman would say *hermetic*—was traced to its namesake, Hermes, the messenger. Narrative discourse was called Apollonian, after Apollo, god of poetry and music. Hillman also distinguished a fourth discourse form, stream of consciousness or free association, which he called *Dionysian*, after Dionysius, god of wine. Although this is recognized as a literary form, it has not been much used as a final product in reports of empirical research. Hermeneutic and narrative discourse, however, are frequently used by qualitative researchers. Readers of reports of qualitative research should understand how these differ from didactic (senex) discourse, in order to recognize them when they are encountered.

Each alternative discourse form represents a distinct sort of intellectual activity, entails different goals and procedures, and yields distinct products. In particular, the products of hermeneutic and narrative discourse differ from didactic scientific research reports, qualitative or quantitative. With some adjustments, the principles of good practice and the validity criteria described earlier might apply to all of these activities.

Hermeneutic Discourse

Hermeneutic discourse focuses on interpretations. At first glance these interpretations may look like theoretical interpretations, as described in preceding sections, but the goal is different. The goal of hermeneutic discourse can be described as *deepening*. The activity consists in understanding what the target material, such as some text or concept, has meant or could mean to other people. Put another way, it is unpacking the experiences that have been or could be embodied in the words and other signs of the target material. Insofar as most words have very long histories, this process is potentially endless. Packer and Addison (1989a, 1989b) described this process of unpacking as the hermeneutic circle—observing, interpreting, reviewing through the new interpretation, revising, and so forth. The product is thus a series of reinterpretations, leading to ever-deeper understandings but not necessarily to a unified synthesis (Hillman, 1983; Woolfolk, Sass & Messer, 1988). The exploration of alternatives is itself the product of the activity rather than a means of developing a particular theory. The understanding achieved is valued for its depth—the richer appreciation—not necessarily because it is more simple or unified.

As in didactic studies, procedures for deepening understanding in a particular hermeneutic study can be evaluated for how well they promote and reveal permeability. And the understandings themselves can be evaluated for how well they fit or change the understanding of people, including readers, participants, and investigators, parallel to the categories shown in Table 24.1.

Narrative Discourse

Narrative discourse (i.e., stories) reflects a search for connections between specific events. Narrative discourse in a research report seeks to link the particular events described rather than to use those events to support an explicit theory. Nevertheless, a good story constructs reality according to some internal logic, though that logic may not be explicit or articulated by the storyteller. Elements of the events have to be sorted out and made intelligible. Details have to be sacrificed, selected, emphasized, sequenced. The emphasis on connections among a story's elements distinguishes stories from mere listings of events. In brief, a story has a point.

Stories can record the limits of what people may do and prepare them for a range of eventualities. For example, physicians can use stories about interviews to build a repertoire of demonstrated possibilities for how one may deal with difficult patients. Such stories can facilitate recognition of similar situations, along with actions that may be effective. "Here is the sort of case where I need to ask what's going on at home." "Here is a case where what looks like a disagreeable symptom to me is experienced as a valuable gift by the patient." This use of stories represents an epistemology of clinical wisdom rather than law-like generalizations.

In natural discourse, people tell stories when they have difficulty making a point in a didactic way. Conversely, stories may convey points that are beyond the teller's ability to articulate. Investigators may be able to tell you what happened in their study better than they can tell you why it happened. Consequently, narrative discourse in scientific reports can sometimes capture underlying causal mechanisms of human behavior better than didactic discourse, albeit implicitly. For example, anthropological ethnographies may be more useful than the explicit theories because they imply more subtle implicit theories.

Narrative discourse has some distinctive advantages for presenting qualitative research. Narratives are linguistic. Narratives facilitate empathy with the protagonist. Narratives supply the context as part of the story. And narratives can deal with chaos, in the technical sense, that is, with human behavior that is like the weather, deterministic but unpredictable in the long term. In this sense, narratives are particularly well suited to integrating unexpected or unusual events.

Mixing the Alternative Discourse Forms

The foregoing descriptions consider the discourse types as alternative kinds of research activity, with different goals and distinct sorts of products. Whereas didactic scientific research reports describe how observations fit or do not fit an interpretation or theory, hermeneutic reports deepen understanding by uncovering alternative meanings, and narrative reports put particular events into a coherent sequence and context.

In addition, however, the discourse forms can be used in service of each other. Discourse of one type can be used as a target for analysis or as a step in analysis for activity of another type. To illustrate:

1. Participants' stories can be used as data in didactic scientific studies. In testing a theory, one might first try to summarize observations in narrative form.
2. Hermeneutic unpacking can be used to reveal meanings, which might serve to strengthen or elaborate a theory. For example, iteration, listed earlier as a desirable way to foster permeability, may be regarded as a hermeneutic procedure that can be used to foster better and more flexible theories.
3. Case studies have used narratives (or, in some cases, Dionysian stream of consciousness data) to advance theory (e.g., psychoanalytic theory).

On the other hand:

4. Alternative theoretical accounts can be applied and explored as part of a hermeneutic analysis. Understanding alternative theoretical perspectives can deepen understanding of a phenomenon.
5. People's theories can be centrally important to understanding their actions, and hence may be integral to narrative accounts.

And so forth. The point here is that the alternative discourse forms do not represent a hierarchy. Each can be used in service of the others.

CONCLUDING COMMENTS

Qualitative research can be understood as offering a wider array of tools than is normally available in hypothesis-testing research in psychology. Many of these tools are not new, however. Linguistic, polydimensional, empathic, contextual, nonlinear approaches to human experience of health and illness often draw on analytic skills and practices that are familiar and used by people in everyday life—listening, understanding, storytelling.

Reintroducing qualitative approaches into psychological research entails some dangers and cautions, however. Many aspects of hypothesis-testing methodology and lore were constructed specifically to avoid fallacies, magical reasoning, superstition, and other problematic ways of thinking—aiming to promote the validity of scientific interpretations. These problems remain. For example, the problems of investigator bias, generalizing from unrepresentative samples, and mistaking correlation for causation, cannot be swept away merely by renaming anecdotal evidence as narrative analysis, or statements of impermeable belief as qualitative interpretations. Qualitative approaches offer greater scope and freedom but probably require more critical thought and more vigilance regarding rigor and quality than do formulaic hypothesis-testing approaches. This chapter has reviewed practices and concepts that qualitative investigators have developed to this end.

ACKNOWLEDGMENTS

I thank Meredith J. Glick, Carol L. Humphreys, James A. Lani, Katerine Osatuke, and D'Arcy Reynolds for comments on an earlier draft of this chapter. Special thanks to D'Arcy Reynolds for bibliographic assistance.

REFERENCES

Ailinger, R.L. & Dear, M.R. (1997). Latino immigrants' explanatory models of tuberculosis infection. *Qualitative Health Research*, **7**, 521–531.

Altheide, D.L. & Johnson, J.M. (1994). Criteria for assessing interpretive validity in qualitative research. In N.K. Denzin & Y.S. Lincoln (Eds), *Handbook of Qualitative Research* (pp. 485–499). Thousand Oaks, CA: Sage.

Baillie, C., Smith, J., Hewison, J. & Mason, G. (2000). Ultrasound screening for chromosomal abnormality: women's reactions to false positive results. *British Journal of Health Psychology*, **5**, 377–394.

Banister, E.M. (1999). Women's midlife experience of their changing bodies. *Qualitative Health Research*, **9**, 520–537.

Barker, C., Pistrang, N. & Elliott, R. (1994). *Research Methods in Clinical and Counseling Psychology*. Chichester: John Wiley & Sons.

Barlow, J., Wright, C. & Kroll, T. (2001). Overcoming perceived barriers to employment among people with arthritis. *Journal of Health Psychology*, **6**, 205–216.

Barroso, J. (1997). Reconstructing my life: becoming a long-term survivor of AIDS. *Qualitative Health Research*, **7**, 57–74.

Barnard, A., McCosker, H. & Gerber, R. (1999). Phenomenography: a qualitative research approach for exploring understanding in health care. *Qualitative Health Research*, **9**, 212–226.

Barton, S. (1994). Chaos, self-organization, and psychology. *American Psychologist*, **49**, 5–14.

Baumeister, R.F. & Newman, L.S. (1994). How stories make sense of personal experiences: motives that shape autobiographical narratives. *Personality and Social Psychology Bulletin*, **20**, 676–690.

Bromley, D. (1986). *The Case-Study Method in Psychology and Related Disciplines*. Chichester: John Wiley & Sons.

Bruner, J. (1986). *Actual Minds, Possible Worlds*. Cambridge, MA: Harvard University Press.

Chamberlain, K. (2000). Methodolatry and qualitative health research. *Journal of Health Psychology*, **5**, 285–296.

Chamberlain, K., Stephens, C. & Lyons, A.C. (1997). Encompassing experience: meanings and methods in health psychology. *Psychology and Health*, **12**, 691–709.

Charmaz, K. (1990). "Discovering" chronic illness: using grounded theory. *Social Science and Medicine*, **30**, 1161–1172.

Charmaz, K. (1994). Identity dilemmas of chronically ill men. *The Sociological Quarterly*, **35**, 269–288.

Cook, T.D. & Campbell, D.T. (1979). *Quasi-experimentation: Design and Analysis for Field Settings*. Boston: Houghton-Mifflin.

Cronbach, L.J. & Meehl, P.E. (1955). Construct validity in psychological tests. *Psychological Bulletin*, **52**, 281–302.

Denzin, N.K. & Lincoln, Y.S. (Eds) (2000). *Handbook of Qualitative Research* (2nd edn). London: Sage.

du Pre, A. & Beck, C.S. (1997). "How can I put this?" Exaggerated self-disparagement as alignment strategy during problematic disclosures by patients to doctors. *Qualitative Health Research*, **7**, 487–503.

Elderkin-Thompson, V., Silver, R.C. & Waitzkin, H. (1998). Narratives of somatizing and non-somatizing patients in a primary care setting. *Journal of Health Psychology*, **3**, 407–428.

Elliott, R., Fischer, C. & Rennie, D. (1999). Evolving guidelines for publication of qualitative research studies in psychology and related fields. *British Journal of Clinical Psychology*, **38**, 215–229.

Engebretson, J. (1996). Urban healers: an experiential description of American healing touch groups. *Qualitative Health Research*, **6**, 526–541.

Festinger, L. & Carlsmith, J. (1959). Cognitive consequences of forced compliance. *Journal of Abnormal and Social Psychology*, **58**, 203–210.

Fitzsimmons, D., George, S., Payne, S. & Johnson, C.D. (1999). Differences in perception of quality of life issues between health professionals and patients with pancreatic cancer. *Psycho-oncology*, **8**, 135–143.

Folger, J.P. & Poole, M.S. (1981). Relational coding schemes: the question of validity. In M.S. Burgoon (Ed.), *Communication Yearbook V*. New Brunswick, NJ: Transaction.

Frankel, R.M. (1984). From sentence to sequence: understanding the medical encounter through microinteractional analysis. *Discourse Processes*, **7**, 135–170.

Frankel, R.M. (1989). "I wz wondering—uhm could Raid uhm effect the brain permanently d'y know?": some observations on the intersection of speaking and writing in calls to a poison control center. *Western Journal of Speech Communication*, **53**, 195–226.

Frankel, R.M. (1990). Talking in interviews: a dispreference for patient-initiated questions in physician–patient encounters. In G. Psathas (Ed.), *Interaction Competence* (pp. 231–262). New York: Irvington Publishers.

Freire, P. (1973). *Pedagogy of the Oppressed*. New York: Seabury Press.

Gallagher, P. & MacLachlan, M. (2001). Adjustment to an artificial limb: a qualitative perspective. *Journal of Health Psychology*, **6**, 85–100.

Garro, L.C. (1994). Narrative representations of chronic illness experience: cultural models of illness, mind, and body in stories concerning the temporomandibular joint (TMJ). *Social Science and Medicine*, **38**, 775–788.

Geertz, C. (1973). Thick descriptions: toward an interpretive theory of culture. In C. Geertz (Ed.), *The Interpretation of Culture* (pp. 3–30). New York: Basic Books.

Gergen, K.J. (1982). *Toward Transformation in Social Knowledge*. New York: Springer-Verlag.

Gergen, K.J. (1985). The social constructionist movement in modern psychology. *American Psychologist*, **40**, 266–275.

Giorgi, A. (1970). *Psychology as a Human Science: A Phenomenologically based Approach*. New York: Harper & Row.

Glaser, B.G. (1992). *Basics of Grounded Theory Analysis: Emergence versus Forcing*. Mill Valley, CA: Sociology Press.

Glaser, B.G. & Strauss, A.L. (1967). *The Discovery of Grounded Theory: Strategies for Qualitative Research*. Chicago: Aldine.

Gleick, J. (1987). *Chaos: Making a New Science*. New York: Penguin.

Good, B.J. (1994). *Medicine, Rationality and Experience: An Anthropological Perspective*. Cambridge: Cambridge University Press.

Guba, E.G. & Lincoln, Y.S. (1989). *Fourth Generation Evaluation*. Newbury Park, CA: Sage.

Harré, R. (1987). Rights to display: the masking of competence. In S. Fairburn & G. Fairburn (Eds), *Psychology, Ethics and Change* (pp. 58–73). London: Routledge.

Hill, C.E., Thompson, B.J. & Williams, E.N. (1997). A guide to conducting consensual qualitative research. *The Counseling Psychologist*, **25**, 517–572.

Hillman, J. (1983). *Healing Fiction*. Barrytown, NY: Station Hill.

Horton-Salway, M. (2001). Narrative identities and the management of personal accountability in talk about ME: a discursive psychology approach to illness narrative. *Journal of Health Psychology*, **6**, 247–259.

Hunter, K.M. (1991). *Doctors' Stories: The Narrative Structure of Medical Knowledge*. Princeton, NJ: Princeton University Press.

Jirojanakul, P. & Skevington, S. (2000). Developing a quality of life measure for children aged 5–8 years. *British Journal of Health Psychology*, **5**, 299–321.

Kleinman, A. (1992). Local worlds of suffering: an interpersonal focus for ethnographies of illness experience. *Qualitative Health Research*, **2**, 127–134.

Kotre, J. (1984). *Outliving the Self: Generativity and the Interpretation of Lives*. Baltimore, MD: Johns Hopkins University Press.

Kuhn, T.S. (1970). *The Structure of Scientific Revolutions*. Chicago: University of Chicago Press.

Kvale, S. (1996). *InterViews: An Introduction to Qualitative Research Interviewing*. Thousand Oaks, CA: Sage.

Lather, P. (1986a). Issues of validity in openly ideological research: between a rock and soft place. *Interchange*, **17**, 63–84.

Lather, P. (1986b). Research as praxis. *Harvard Educational Review*, **56**, 257–277.

Leininger, M. (1994). Evaluation criteria and critique of qualitative research studies. In J.M. Morse (Ed.), *Critical Issues in Qualitative Research Methods* (pp. 95–115). London: Sage.

Levine, M. (1974). Scientific method and the adversary model. *American Psychologist*, **29**, 661–677.

Lincoln, Y.S. & Guba, E.G. (1990). Judging the quality of case study reports. *Qualitative Studies in Education*, **3**, 53–59.

Linde, C. (1983). *The Creation of Coherence in Life Stories*. Norwood, NJ: Ablex.

Lupton, D. (1992). Discourse analysis: a new methodology for understanding the ideologies of health and illness. *Australian Journal of Public Health*, **16**, 145–150.

Lupton, D. (1993). Risk as moral danger: the social and political functions of risk discourse in public health. *International Journal of Health Services*, **23**, 425–435.

Lupton, D. (1994). Femininity, responsibility, and the technological imperative: discourses on breast cancer in the Australian press. *International Journal of Health Services*, **24**, 73–89.

MacIntyre, A. (1984). *After Virtue: A Study in Moral Theory*. South Bend, IN: University of Notre Dame Press.

McAllister, C.L. & Silverman, M.A. (1999). Community formation and community roles among persons with Alzheimer's disease: a comparative study of experiences in a residential Alzheimer's facility and a traditional nursing home. *Qualitative Health Research*, **9**, 65–85.

McDaniel, S.H., Stiles, W.B. & McGaughey, K.J. (1981). Correlations of male college students' verbal response mode use in psychotherapy with measures of psychological disturbance and psychotherapy outcome. *Journal of Consulting and Clinical Psychology*, **49**, 571–582.

Meehl, P.E. (1978). Theoretical risks and tabular asterisks: Sir Karl, Sir Ronald, and the slow progress of soft psychology. *Journal of Consulting and Clinical Psychology*, **46**, 806–834.

Mill, J.S. (1953). A system of logic, Book VI. On the logic of the moral sciences. In P.P. Weiner (Ed.), *Readings in the Philosophy of Science* (pp. 255–281). New York: Scribner's. (Original work published 1843.)

Mishler, E.G. (1984). *The Discourse of Medicine: Dialectics of Medical Interviews*. Norwood, NJ: Ablex.

Mishler, E.G. (1995). Models of narrative analysis: a typology. *Journal of Narrative and Life History*, **5**, 87–123.

Mishler, E.G. (1990). Validation in inquiry-guided research: the role of exemplars in narrative studies. *Harvard Educational Review*, **60**, 415–442.

Moore, K.D. (1999). Dissonance in the dining room: a study of social interaction in a special care unit. *Qualitative Health Research*, **9**, 133–155.

Murray, M. (2000). Levels of narrative analysis in health psychology. *Journal of Health Psychology*, **5**, 337–347.

Murray, M. & Chamberlain, K. (Eds) (1999). *Qualitative Health Psychology: Theories and Methods*. London: Sage.

Nisbett, R.E. & Wilson, T.D. (1977). Telling more than we can know: verbal reports on mental processes. *Psychological Review*, **84**, 231–259.

Packer, M.J. & Addison, R.B. (1989a). Introduction. In M.J. Packer & R.B. Addison (Eds), *Entering the Circle: Hermeneutic Investigation in Psychology* (pp. 13–36). Albany, NY: State University of New York Press.

Packer, M.J. & Addison, R.B. (1989b). Evaluating an interpretive account. In M.J. Packer & R.B. Addison (Eds), *Entering the Circle: Hermeneutic Investigation in Psychology* (pp. 275–292). Albany, NY: State University of New York Press.

Parker, I. (1992). *Discourse Dynamics: Critical Analysis for Social and Individual Psychology.* London: Routledge.

Peräkylä, A. (1991). Hope work in the care of seriously ill patients. *Qualitative Health Research*, **1**, 407–433.

Peräkylä, A. (1998). Authority and accountability: the delivery of diagnosis in primary health care. *Social Psychology Quarterly*, **61**, 301–320.

Popper, K. (1959). *The Logic of Scientific Discovery*. New York: Basic Books. (Original work published 1934.)

Poskiparta, M., Kettunen, T. & Liimatainen, L. (1998). Reflective questions in health counseling. *Qualitative Health Research*, **8**, 682–693.

Potter, J. & Wetherell, M. (1987). *Discourse and Social Psychology: Beyond Attitudes and Behaviour*. London: Sage.

Radtke, H.L. & Mens-Verhulst, J. (2001). Being a mother and living with asthma: an exploratory analysis of discourse. *Journal of Health Psychology*, **6**, 379–391.

Radley, A. & Chamberlain K. (2001). Health psychology and the study of the case: from method to analytic concern. *Social Science and Medicine*, **53**, 321–332.

Rennie, D.L., Phillips, J.R. & Quartaro, G.K. (1988). Grounded theory: a promising approach to conceptualization in psychology? *Canadian Psychology*, **29**, 139–150.

Rosenwald, G.C. (1985). Hypocrisy, self-deception, and perplexity: the subject's enhancement as methodological criterion. *Journal of Personality and Social Psychology*, **49**, 682–703.

Rosenwald, G.C. (1986). Why operationism doesn't go away: extrascientific incentives of social-psychological research. *Philosophy of the Social Sciences*, **16**, 303–330.

Rosenwald, G.C. (1988). A theory of multiple case research. *Journal of Personality*, **56**, 239–264.

Schou, K.C. & Hewison, J. (1998). Health psychology and discourse: personal accounts as social texts in grounded theory. *Journal of Health Psychology*, **3**, 297–311.

Silverman, D. (1989). Six rules of qualitative research: a post-romantic argument. *Symbolic Interaction*, **12**, 215–230.

Skevington, S.M., MacArthur, P. & Somerset, M. (1997). Developing items for the WHOQOL: an investigation of contemporary beliefs about quality of life related to health in Britain. *British Journal of Health Psychology*, **2**, 55–72.

Smith, J.A. (1996). Beyond the divide between cognition and discourse: using interpretative phenomenological analysis in health psychology. *Psychology and Health*, **11**, 261–271.

Smith, J.A. (1999a). Identity development during the transition to motherhood: an interpretive phenomenological analysis. *Journal of Reproductive and Infant Psychology*, **17**, 281–299.

Smith, J.A. (1999b). Towards a relational self: social engagement during pregnancy and psychological preparation for motherhood. *British Journal of Social Psychology*, **38**, 409–426.

Smith, J.A., Flowers, P. & Osborne, M. (1997). Interpretive phenomenological analysis and the psychology of health and illness. In L. Yardley (Ed.), *Material Discourses of Health and Illness* (pp. 68–91). London: Routledge.

Smith, J.A., Harré, R. & Van Langenhove, L. (Eds) (1995). *Rethinking Methods in Psychology* (pp. 9–26). Thousand Oaks, CA: Sage.

Smith, J.A., Jarman, M. & Osborne, M. (1999). Doing interpretive phenomenological analysis. In M. Murray & K. Chamberlain (Eds), *Qualitative Health Psychology: Theories and Methods* (pp. 218–240). London: Sage.

Smith, J.A., Michie, S., Allanson, A. & Elwy, R. (2000). Certainty and uncertainty in genetic counselling: a qualitative case study. *Psychology and Health*, **15**, 1–12.

Spence, D.P. (1982). *Narrative Truth and Historical Truth: Meaning and Interpretation in Psychoanalysis*. New York: Norton.

Stiles, W.B. (1981). Science, experience, and truth: a conversation with myself. *Teaching of Psychology*, **8**, 227–230.

Stiles, W.B. (1988). Psychotherapy process–outcome correlations may be misleading. *Psychotherapy*, **25**, 27–35.

Stiles, W.B. (1989). Evaluating medical interview process components: null correlations with outcomes may be misleading. *Medical Care*, **27**, 212–220.

Stiles, W.B. (1993). Quality control in qualitative research. *Clinical Psychology Review*, **13**, 593–618.

Stiles, W.B. (1997). Signs and voices: joining a conversation in progress. *British Journal of Medical Psychology*, **70**, 169–176.

Stiles, W.B. (1999). Evaluating qualitative research. *Evidence-Based Mental Health*, **2**, 99–101.

Stiles, W.B. & Shapiro, D.A. (1994). Disabuse of the drug metaphor: psychotherapy process–outcome correlations. *Journal of Consulting and Clinical Psychology*, **62**, 942–948.

Stiles, W.B., Honos-Webb, L. & Surko, M. (1998). Responsiveness in psychotherapy. *Clinical Psychology: Science and Practice*, **5**, 439–458.

Stiles, W.B., Putnam, S.M., Wolf, M.H. & James, S.A. (1979). Interaction exchange structure and patient satisfaction with medical interviews. *Medical Care*, **17**, 667–681.

Strauss, A. & Corbin, J. (1990). *Basics of Qualitative Research: Grounded Theory Procedures and Techniques.* Newbury Park, CA: Sage.

Sullivan, E.V. (1984). *A Critical Psychology: Interpretation of the Personal World.* New York: Plenum Press.

Taylor, C. (1979). Interpretation and the science of man. In P. Rabinow & W. Sullivan (Eds), *Interpretive Social Science: A Reader* (pp. 25–71). Berkeley: University of California Press.

Tourigny, S.C. (1994). Integrating ethics with symbolic interactionism: the case of oncology. *Qualitative Health Research*, **4**, 163–185.

Treloar, C. (1997). Developing a multilevel understanding of heart disease: an interview study of MONICA participants in an Australian center. *Qualitative Health Research*, **7**, 468–486.

Ventres, W.B. & Frankel, R.M. (1996). Ethnography: a stepwise approach for primary care researchers. *Family Medicine*, **28**, 52–56.

Viney, L.L. & Bousfield, L. (1991). Narrative analysis: a method of psychosocial research for aids-affected people. *Social Science and Medicine*, **32**, 757–765.

Wackerbarth, S. (1999). Modeling a dynamic decision process: supporting the decisions of caregivers of family members with dementia. *Qualitative Health Research*, **9**, 294–314.

Weinholtz, D., Kacer, B. & Rocklin, T. (1995). Salvaging quantitative research with qualitative data. *Qualitative Health Research*, **5**, 388–397.

Weiss, J. & Hutchinson, S.A. (2000). Warnings about vulnerability in clients with diabetes and hypertension. *Qualitative Health Research*, **10**, 521–537.

Wiersma, J. (1988). The press release: symbolic communication in life history interviewing. *Journal of Personality*, **56**, 205–238.

Wiggins, S., Potter, J. & Wildsmith, A. (2001). Eating your words: discursive psychology and the reconstruction of eating practices. *Journal of Health Psychology*, **6**, 5–15.

Wilkinson, S. (1998). Focus groups in health research: exploring the meanings of health and illness. *Journal of Health Psychology*, **3**, 329–348.

Williams, G. (1993). Chronic illness and the pursuit of virtue in everyday life. In A. Radley (Ed.), *Worlds of Illness: Biographical and Cultural Perspectives on Health and Disease* (pp. 92–108). London: Routledge.

Willig, C. (2000). A discourse-dynamic approach to the study of subjectivity in health psychology. *Theory and Psychology*, **10**, 547–570.

Woolfolk, R.L., Sass, L.A. & Messer, S.B. (1988). Introduction to hermeneutics. In S.B. Messer, L.A. Sass & R.L. Woolfolk (Eds), *Hermeneutics and Psychological Theory: Interpretive Perspectives on Personality, Psychotherapy, and Psychopathology* (pp. 2–26). New Brunswick, NJ: Rutgers University Press.

Yardley, L. & Beech, S. (1998). "I'm not a doctor": deconstructing accounts of coping, causes and control of dizziness. *Journal of Health Psychology*, **3**, 313–327.

Yardley, L., Sharples, K., Beech, S. & Lewith, G. (2001). Developing a dynamic model of treatment perceptions. *Journal of Health Psychology*, **6**, 269–282.

CHAPTER 25

The Social Context of Health

Paul Bennett
Universities of Plymouth and Exeter, UK

INTRODUCTION

Our health is not only the result of how we live our lives. It is influenced by the type of job we hold, our income, and the social world we inhabit. Indeed, there is increasing evidence that apparently biologically mediated health differentials, in particular related to gender, are mediated by social as well as biological factors. These differences are not trivial. Men live, on average, five years less than women. The better-off live, on average, five years longer than the poor (Haberman & Bloomfield, 1988). These factors can override the risk attributable to any individual health behaviour, including smoking (Hein, Suadicani & Gyntelberg, 1992). If one's goal is to improve population health, changing the context in which people live may prove as powerful a force for change as programmes focusing on individual risk behaviours.

This chapter focuses on the health risks associated with a number of social contexts, including socio-economic status, gender, working conditions, and ethnicity. These factors are intertwined in a complex web of causality. So much so that one individual is likely to be at risk of illness, or protected against such risk, by a variety of related factors. Socio-economically deprived individuals are likely to face multiple stressors including economic and environmental pressures. They are also more likely to work under conditions related to the development of disease than the better off. Those who occupy minority status are more likely to be poorer than the majority, and combine the problems associated with economic deprivation with those resulting from their minority status. Accordingly, although this chapter attempts to identify the specific health risks or gains associated with different social contexts, it should be remembered that many individuals face disadvantage as a result of occupying several social contexts.

SOCIO-ECONOMIC STATUS AND HEALTH

There is strong evidence that the more affluent members of society have always lived longer than the less well off. In an imaginative study of nineteenth-century Scottish obelisks in Glasgow graveyards, for example, Davey Smith et al. (1992) measured their height as a proxy for the wealth of the individuals buried below them. They compared the height of each

Handbook of Clinical Health Psychology. Edited by S. Llewelyn and P. Kennedy.
© 2003 John Wiley & Sons, Ltd.

obelisk with the age of the first generation buried below and found a strong linear relationship between the two variables, suggesting that the more wealthy lived the longest. Of note is not just that this relationship existed, but that the families buried in them represented a small and relatively wealthy fraction of the Glasgow population. This is not evidence that the very poor did not live as long as the rich: rather, that the relatively rich did not live as long as the very rich.

Such a gradient still exists. It is progressive, and occurs throughout the social classes. It holds for women as well as men and is characteristic of all Western countries (Wilkinson, 1992). In simple terms, individuals situated in the lower socio-economic groups are more likely to be born with a low birth weight, die in infancy, childhood, or earlier in adulthood than the better off, and experience more illness when alive. That it is progressive and not a threshold effect is important. If there were a threshold above which all individuals fared well and below which they fared badly, this would suggest a simple effect of poverty on health. A gradient—in which those who are increasingly well off fare better than those who are less well off wherever in this gradient they lie—suggests a more complex causal process.

The explanations that have been proposed to account for these differences have typically focused on behavioural, environmental, and physical differences across the socio-economic groups.

Social Selection

The first explanation to be considered suggests that ill health leads to low socio-economic status. It suggests that those in poor health move down the social scale as a consequence of their illness: perhaps due to a reduced capacity to work or work overtime. Those in good health move up the social scale for the opposite reasons. While this hypothesis has a degree of face validity, there is little evidence to support it. Perhaps the most convincing evidence here is that a number of longitudinal studies that have identified individuals with no evidence of disease at baseline, and whose socio-economic status at this point is therefore highly unlikely to have been influenced by disease, still find the mortality gradient found within the general population at follow-up (e.g. Marmot, Shipley & Rose, 1984). Considering the issue from a different perspective, Goldblatt (1989) reported that mortality differentials among those who did not change social class were no different to those who did change social class. These data counter the social selection model, as this would predict that mortality differentials would be clustered among those who changed socio-economic status.

Differential Behaviours

One of the most frequently suggested explanations for the health differentials across the socio-economic groups is that less well off individuals engage in more health-damaging behaviours, such as smoking or excess alcohol consumption (e.g. Winkleby, Fortmann & Barrett, 1990). While both these explanations may account for some of the differences in some of the studies, they cannot explain them all. Marmot, Shipley and Rose (1984), for example, explored the impact of a number of these variables on the health of British civil servants working in London over a period of ten years. Their findings indicated that while those in the more deprived social groups did engage in more health-damaging behaviours, this did not fully explain the health–socio-economic status relationship. When variations in smoking, obesity, plasma cholesterol and blood pressure were statistically partialled out of the risk equation, occupational status-related differentials in health still remained. Mortality was still three times higher among men in the lowest grade than those in the highest.

What evidence there is suggests that socio-economic status may interact with risk be-haviour to predict morbidity, and that while people who occupy the lower socio-economic groups may engage in more health-damaging behaviours, the adverse health effects of these behaviours may be overwhelmed by factors associated with their economic position. Hein, Suadicani and Gyntelberg (1992), for example, reported data from a 17-year prospective study of coronary heart disease (CHD) in Danish men. Adjusting for a variety of con-founding factors, they found that men who smoked were three and half times more likely to develop CHD than non-smokers. However, when these data were analysed according to socio-economic status, white-collar smokers were six and half times more likely to experience a cardiac event than the equivalent non-smokers. Among blue-collar workers, smoking status conferred no additional risk for CHD. Less middle-class people may smoke, but those that do may be particularly vulnerable to the health-damaging effects of smoking. Conversely, the impact of smoking on the health of the less well off may be overwhelmed by social factors.

Access to Health Care

Access to health care is likely to differ according to both personal characteristics and the health care system with which the individual is attempting to interact. Most studies of this phenomenon have been conducted in the USA, where different health care systems operate for those with and without health insurance. Here, the less well off clearly receive poorer health care. Qureshi et al. (2000), for example, noted that while access to mammography screening in the USA did not vary according to ethnicity or education level, it was lower among those with "health care access or insurance problems". Even among those with some form of health insurance (Medicare), patients who live in poor neighbourhoods receive worse health care than those from better off areas, particularly in rural and non-teaching hospitals (Kahn et al., 1994).

This phenomenon is not confined to the USA. In Italy, where there is universal health care provision, Ancona et al. (2000) reported that while men in the lowest socio-economic group were more likely to suffer from CHD than those in the highest socio-economic status level, they were the least likely group to be offered coronary artery bypass surgery. In addition, those that did have surgery had double the risk of death in the following month than those in the higher socio-economic groups, even when initial illness severity was taken into account. For whatever reason, those in different socio-economic groups may also differentially attend for medical consultations. In the UK, Goyder, McNally and Botha (2000) reported that attenders at a routine diabetes clinic were more likely to be younger, have access to a car, and have a non-manual occupation than non-attenders.

Stress, Strain and Depression

Stress has been associated with both autonomic and immune dysregulation and the onset of a number of diseases including CHD and cancer (see Bennett, 2000). More recently, there is increasing evidence that depression also contributes strongly to the risk of CHD and, perhaps, other illnesses (e.g. Vaillant, 1998). Both risk factors are more prevalent among those in the lower socio-economic groups (Gallo & Matthews, 1999). In addition, such individuals have fewer resources through which the adverse effects of these stressors can be moderated. The lower individuals are within the social structure, the greater the reported exposure to stressful life events and the greater the emotional impact they have (House et al., 1991; McLeod & Kessler, 1990). Socio-economic position is also associated with lower levels of available social support. Ruberman et al. (1984), for example, found a strong negative association between years of education and measures of life stress and social isolation. These, in turn, were related to mortality in the year following myocardial infarction. Similarly, Marmot, Smith and Stansfield (1991) found that fewer male blue-collar workers than white-collar workers reported having a confidante whom they could trust with their problems or from whom they received practical social support. In addition, blue-collar workers reported more negative life events and hassles, such as paying bills and problems with money, than those in the higher socio-economic groups.

Environmental Insult

People in lower socio-economic groups are exposed to more environmental insults. Low-quality and damp accommodation and higher air pollution levels may each impact directly on health (Stokols, 1992). However, environment factors may also do so indirectly, through social and psychological pathways. One mechanism though which this may occur is through the stress associated with overcrowding (see Baum, Garofalo & Yali, 1999). However, more subtle processes may also be evident. One example of this can be found in the effect of the type of housing we occupy.

In Britain, age-standardised mortality rates are about 25% higher among social tenants than owner-occupiers (Filakti & Kox, 1995). Tenants also experience higher rates of long-term illness and psycho-social problems than owner-occupiers (e.g. Lewis et al., 1998). There are a number of explanations for these differentials: (1) renters may experience more damp, poor ventilation, overcrowding, and so on; (2) rented occupation may be further away from amenities, making access to leisure facilities or good-quality shops more difficult; and (3) the psychological consequences of living in differing types of accommodation may directly impact on health. Although the third pathway has received little attention, MacIntyre and Ellaway (1998) found that a range of mental and physical health measures were significantly associated with housing tenure even after controlling for the quality of housing, age, sex, income and self-esteem. They took these data to suggest that the type of tenure itself is associated directly with health, and is mediated by factors such as control over one's living environment and the social comparative process referred to below.

Socio-economic Status as a *Relative* Issue

Comparisons of life expectancy across different Western countries suggest some intriguing explanations of the relationship between social class and health. Wilkinson (1992) provided powerful evidence that it is not absolute wealth that determines health. He drew on evidence that showed only a weak relationship between the absolute wealth of the society and overall life expectancy. More predictive is the distribution of wealth within a society. The narrower the distribution, whatever its absolute level, the better the overall health of the nation. Wilkinson (1990) compared data on income distribution and life expectancy from nine Western countries and found that while the overall wealth of the country was not associated with life expectancy, income distribution (defined as the percentage of total post-tax income and benefit received by the least well off 70% of families) was. The correlation between the two variables was a substantial 0.86.

A further example of the role of wealth distribution is afforded by comparison of life expectancy in Japan and Cuba. Although both countries differ substantially on measures of economic wealth, both have relatively equitable distributions of income and long-life expectancies throughout their populations. Also of interest is evidence from Scotland, which tracked average age of mortality and income distribution over the life of the Conservative government (e.g. McCarron et al., 1994). As earning differentials rose over this period, so did premature mortality among the less well off, despite their access to material goods, food, clothing, and so on, remaining relatively constant over time. These and other similar data led Wilkinson (1992) to suggest that, for the majority of people in Western countries, health hinges on relatively more than absolute living standards. Wilkinson's explanation of health differentials suggests that we engage in some form of comparison of our living conditions with others in society, and that knowledge of a relative deprivation in some way increases the risk of disease.

MINORITY STATUS AND HEALTH

Ethnic Minorities

There is a strong association between ethnicity and health status. In the UK, rates of ill health and premature mortality among ethnic minorities are typically higher than those of the white population (Harding & Maxwell, 1997), although there are also differences in mortality patterns between ethnic minorities. Rates of CHD among British men from the Indian sub-continent are 36% higher than the national average and among young people are two to three times higher than that of whites. The Afro-Caribbean population has particularly high prevalence rates of hypertension and strokes, while levels of diabetes are high among Asians. In contrast, both groups have lower rates of cancer than the national average (Balarajan & Raleigh, 1993). A similar picture is found in the USA, where black people have higher age-adjusted mortality rates than whites for a number of diseases including various cancers, heart disease, liver disease, diabetes and pneumonia (Krieger, Quesenbery & Peng, 1999).

Consideration of the relationship between ethnicity and health is, however, a complex process as this tends to lump different ethnic groups together as one single group. Nazroo (1998) warns against such a mistake, noting that ethnicity encompasses a variety of issues: language, religion, experience of races and migration, culture, ancestry, and forms of identity. Each of these may individually or together contribute to differences between the health of different ethnic groups. It is important not to reify the concepts of ethnicity and to pathologise minority ethnic status itself.

It is also important to provide a second cautionary note. Measures of ethnicity are frequently confounded with other factors, perhaps the most important being socio-economic status. A significant proportion of, but not all, members of ethnic minorities occupy relatively low socio-economic groups. Accordingly, explanations of health or behavioural differences between ethnic groups have to take socio-economic factors into account. Using this approach, two studies from the USA that found higher mortality rates among blacks than whites (as large as a 30% difference) found no differences after partialling out the influence of socio-economic status (Haan & Kaplan, 1985). Other studies have found a diminution, but not negation of the effect of ethnicity (e.g. Sorlie, Backlund & Keller, 1995). Socio-economic gradients within ethnic groups follow that of society in general: those in the higher socio-economic groups generally live longer and have higher health-ratings throughout the life course (e.g. Davey Smith et al., 1996; Harding & Maxwell, 1997). However, again highlighting the dangers of placing ethnic minorities into a single heterogeneous group, there are some exceptions to this rule. In the UK, for example, there is no gradient of mortality as a result of CHD for men born in the Caribbean or West or South Africa (e.g. Harding & Maxwell, 1997).

Despite these cautionary notes, there is a general consensus that ethnicity does impact on health—although different factors may affect different ethnic groups. A number of explanations for these differences have been proposed. The behavioural hypothesis suggests that some variations in health outcomes may be explained by differences in behaviour across ethnic groups. In the UK, for example, alcohol-related morbidity is high among African Caribbean men and Asian males of Punjabi origin, while a high dietary fat intake is common among Asians. Ethnicity may also confer different sexual norms and behaviours that may impact on health. The most common exposure route for human immunodeficiency virus (HIV) infection among whites is through sexual intercourse between men: for blacks it is through heterosexual intercourse, while for Asians it is a mixture of both (see, for example, Nazroo, 1997; Rudat, 1994).

A second explanation focuses on the social impact of carrying minority status. Ethnic minorities generally experience wider sources of stress than the majority population as a consequence of discrimination, racial harassment and the demands of maintaining or shifting their culture. A particular issue faced by racial minorities is that of racism, and its associated stresses. This has been implicated in the development of a number of disease states. Of particular interest is that African Americans both have higher rates of hypertension and are exposed to disproportionate levels of chronic stressors, including racism (e.g. Klag et al., 1991). Much of the data relevant to this hypothesis is epidemiological. However, a number of laboratory studies have also explored this hypothesis. Clarke (2000), for example, found that among a sample of young African American women, the more they reported experiencing racism, the greater their rises in blood pressure during a task in which participants talked about their views and feelings about animal rights. They took this to suggest that they had developed a stronger emotional and physiological reaction to general stress as a result of their long-term responses to racism, which in turn was contributing to the long-term development of hypertension (Brosschot & Thayer, 1998).

A third explanation for the poorer health among ethnic minorities may be found in the problems some face in accessing health care. In addition, once within the hospital system, ethnic minority patients are less likely to receive expensive treatments than the equivalent white patient. Mitchell et al. (2000), for example, found that, even after adjusting for demographic factors, comorbidity, ability to pay, and provider characteristics, African American patients with transient ischaemic attacks were significantly less likely to receive non-invasive cerebrovascular testing, cerebral angiography, or carotid endarterectomy, or to have a specialist doctor as their attending physician, than white patients. Other studies have shown variations in doses of analgesics administered in emergency departments, that

Hispanics and blacks were substantially under-treated for pain from fractures of long bones, and that post-operative pain was inadequately managed in non-white patients (e.g. Todd et al., 2000).

There is convincing evidence that in the USA blacks are less likely than whites to receive curative surgery for early-stage lung, colon, or breast cancer (e.g. Brawley & Freeman, 1999) and that these differentials translate into higher mortality rates among black people. Furthermore, blacks with chronic renal failure are less likely to be referred for transplantation and are less likely to undergo transplantation than are whites. Ayanian et al. (1999), for example, reported that the rate of referral for evaluation at a transplantation centre was 50% for black women, compared with 70% for white women; and 54% for black men, compared with 76% for white men. These racial and gender differences remained significant after adjustments for patients' preferences, socio-demographic characteristics, the cause of renal failure, and the presence or absence of coexisting illness.

Other Minorities

Minority status may also be conferred by behaviour. A number of studies have shown that isolation experienced as a consequence of sexual orientation may impact significantly on health. Cole et al. (1996), for example, found that healthy gay men who concealed their sexual identity were three times more likely to develop cancer or infectious diseases than men who were able to express their sexuality. The same research group found that social rejection influenced disease progression in HIV-infected men. Those who experienced social rejection evidenced a significant acceleration towards a critically low CD4 + lymphocyte level and time to diagnosis of AIDS.

GENDER AND HEALTH

Women, on average, live longer than men. In the UK, life expectancy rates in 1996 were 75 years for men and 80 years for women. Men's age-adjusted death rate for heart disease in the USA is two times higher than women's, and men's cancer rate is one and a half times higher (Department of Health and Human Services, 1996). Nearly three-quarters of those who die of myocardial infarction (MI) before the age of 65 years are men (American Heart Association, 1995). The most obvious explanations for these differences are biological. Oestrogen, for example, delays the onset of CHD by reducing clotting tendency and blood cholesterol levels. Not only is there a marked increase in the prevalence of CHD in post-menopausal women, they also become affected by the same influences as men. Lahad et al. (1997), for example, found that hostility scores were linearly associated with increased risk for MI in post-menopausal women.

Physiological studies suggest that men typically evidence greater stress hormone, blood pressure, and cholesterol rises in response to stressors than women. However, while there may be some differences in the process of response between the sexes, these differences may not simply reflect biological differences. Work by Lundberg et al. (1981), for example, suggested that women in traditionally male occupations exhibit the same level of stress hormones as men. In addition, where women feel equally or more threatened by the stressor than men, their physiological response matches those of men. These findings suggest that social and cultural processes may drive some of these differences.

Further evidence that these gender differences in mortality are not purely biological stems from studies that show clear health-related behavioural differences between men and women. Men are more likely to smoke cigarettes, and smoke higher nicotine and tar cigarettes than women. They typically eat less healthily, and drink more alcohol than women (Reddy, Fleming & Adesso, 1992). More men than women engaged in all but 3 of the 14 non-gender- specific health-risk behaviours that were examined by Powell-Griner, Anderson and Murphy (1997), including smoking, drinking and driving, not using safety belts, and not attending health screening. Men may also encounter adverse working conditions more frequently than women. Not only do men engage in more health-risking behaviours, they are less likely to seek medical help when necessary. Men visit their doctor less frequently than women, even after excluding reproductive health care visits (Verbrugge & Steiner, 1985). Even when ill, men are significantly less likely to consult a doctor than women; socially disadvantaged men are twice as likely as their female counterparts not to have consulted a doctor, and high-income men 2.5 times more likely (Department of Health and Human Services, 1998). One of the few health-related behaviours that is conducted more frequently by men is regular exercise (Reddy, Fleming & Adesso, 1992), although even here more women than men are starting to exercise regularly (Caspersen & Merrit, 1995).

The reasons for these behavioural differences appear to be social in origin. Courtenay (2000) contended that they arise from different meanings ascribed to health-related behaviours by the different sexes. They reflect issues of masculinity, femininity, and power. Men show their masculinity and power by engaging in health-risking behaviours and not showing signs of weakness—even when ill. Societal norms endorse the belief that men are independent, self-reliant, strong, and tough. The health behaviours in which they engage reflect this norm. He contended that when men state "I haven't been to a doctor in years", they are simultaneously stating a health practice and endorsing their masculinity. Similar processes are at work when men refuse to take sick leave from work, insist they need little sleep or assert that their driving is better when they've had something to drink. By contrast, illness is threatening to masculinity. Jaffe (1997), for example, noted the advice given to a US senator not to "go public" about his prostate cancer as "some men might think his willingness to go public with his private struggle as a sign of weakness". Charmaz (1994) noted several examples of, sometimes quite extreme, health-risk behaviours that men would engage in to hide their disabilities. Examples included a wheelchair-bound diabetic man skipping lunch (and risking a coma) rather than embarrass himself by asking for help in the dining area, and a middle-aged man declining offers of easier jobs to prove he was still capable of strenuous work.

Together, these data suggest that while biological factors may contribute to some of the differentials in health status between men and women, others are behaviourally or societally mediated. Gender differentials in life expectancy arise, to a significant degree, from the cumulative effects of different social worlds that men and women experience from the moment of their birth.

WORK AND HEALTH

The environment in which we work can impact directly on our health. Although health and safety legislation has improved the working conditions of most workers, there are still environments, such as building sites, that carry a significant risk of injury or disability.

Work factors may also impact on health in a number of ways. Ames and Janes (1987), for example, found job alienation, job stress, inconsistent social controls and the evolution of a drinking culture to be associated with heavy drinking among blue-collar workers. Similarly, Westman, Eden and Shirom (1985) reported that high numbers of work hours and lack of control and support were each positively associated with smoking intensity. Karasek and Theorell (1990) found increased smoking to be associated with job change in women but not in men.

Work stress may also impact on health more directly. Karasek and Theorell's (1990) job strain model identified three key stress factors: the demands of the job, the latitude the workers have in dealing with these demands, and the support available to them. They suggested that these interact to predict stress and stress-related risk of disease. In contrast to previous theories of work stress, they noted that high job demands are not necessarily stressful; it is when these combine with low job autonomy and low levels of support that the individual is likely to experience stress. Their model suggests that rather than the stereotypical "stressed executive", those who experience stress are likely to hold blue-collar or supervisory level posts. In a review of studies examining the strength of the Karasek model, Kristensen (1995) considered 16 studies measuring the association between job strain and mental and physical health outcomes. Fourteen reported significant associations between conditions of high job strain and the incidence of either CHD or poor mental health. More recently, Nordstrom et al. (2001) measured the degree of arterial plaque development in 467 working men who had previously completed a job strain questionnaire. In an age-adjusted model, plaque was greatest among men scoring in the highest stress quintile. No such association was found among women. Evidence of an association between job strain and cancer is generally negative (e.g. Achat et al., 2000).

An alternative model of work stress has been proposed by Siegrist et al. (1990). This suggests that work stress is a consequence of an imbalance between perceived efforts and rewards. High effort and low reward are thought to result in emotional distress and adverse health effects. In a five-year longitudinal study tracking over 10 000 British civil servants (Stansfeld et al., 1998) both theories received some support. Age-adjusted analyses showed low decisional latitude, low work social support, and effort–reward imbalance to predict poor physical health. Most studies of this model (e.g. de Jong et al., 2000), however, have focused on well-being rather than physical health.

For men, it appears that job strain is generally a function of the working environment alone. For women, who may frequently have significant responsibilities beyond the work-place, work strain appears to combine with other areas of demand to confer risk for disease. Haynes and Feinleib (1980), for example, showed working women with three or more children to be more likely to develop CHD than those with no children. Alfredsson, Spetz and Theorell (1985) compared the risk conferred by work strain and working overtime on men and women in a sample of 100 000 Swedish men and women. As predicted by Karasek's model, higher rates of MI were associated with increased work strain in both sexes. However, working overtime *decreased* risk for MI among men, while it was associated with an *increased* risk in women. For women, working ten hours or more overtime per week was associated with a 30% increase in risk for CHD. One explanation for these contradictory findings is that men may compensate for their increase in working hours by a decrease in demands elsewhere in life. For women, such increases may not be so compensated and simply increase the total demands made on them. This increase in overall demands may constitute the main risk for stress and disease. Support for such a hypothesis can be found in the findings of Lundberg et al. (1981), who found that female managers' stress hormone levels remain raised following work, while those of male managers typically fell: this effect was particularly marked where the female managers had children. It seems that men relaxed once home, women continued their efforts—only the context changed.

Not having a job appears to have negative effects on both mental and physical health, at least in the short to medium term (e.g. West & Sweeting, 1996). Many of the studies investigating the impact of unemployment on long-term health have been confounded by the fact that some of those who were made unemployed were already in poor health: a fact that led to poor work performance and their unemployment (Dooley, Fielding & Levi, 1996). In addition, those who are ill when they become unemployed or become ill in the short term are unlikely to gain further employment, meaning that unless these factors are taken into account in any analysis, explanation of any association between long-term unemployment and ill health as causal may be spurious. This has led cautious commentators such as Weber and Lehnert (1997) to contend that the evidence of a direct causal link between long-term unemployment and CHD is, at present, unwarranted. Their concerns are further added to by findings that those who become unemployed increase levels of smoking and alcohol consumption, making any association potentially secondary to behavioural changes resulting from unemployment (Stronks et al., 1997).

Despite this cautionary note, there is some evidence of an increase in ill health among employees who are made redundant as the result of large-scale lay-offs not related to their own job performance. Financial strain and change in psychosocial measures and health-related behaviours accounted for little of the observed associations. Other studies (e.g. Janlert, Asplund & Weinehall, 1992) have reported links between unemployment and increases in cholesterol levels or systolic/diastolic blood pressure, but the clinical relevance of such slight changes is not great.

SOCIAL ISOLATION AND HEALTH

There is substantial evidence that both men and women who have a small number of social contacts are more likely to die earlier than those who have more extended networks. Data from the Alameda County Study (Berkman & Syme, 1979), for example, showed increased longevity to be associated with relatively high numbers of social ties as a consequence of marriage, contacts with close friends and relatives, church membership, and membership of other organisations. The most isolated were the most prone to death even after controlling for factors such as smoking, alcohol use, and levels of physical activity. In a later study, Reynolds and Kaplan (1990) found that women who had few social contacts and were socially isolated were at double the risk for the development of hormone-related cancers and evidenced an almost five-fold increase in risk of dying from them than less isolated women.

Similar results have been reported in European samples. Orth-Gomer and Johnsson (1987), for example, followed a cohort of 17 400 men and women for a period of six years and found that both men and women who scored within the lowest third of social network scores evidenced a 50% greater risk for CHD than those who were socially embedded. However, the relationship between social contact and health was not always linear: those with many social contacts did not always benefit in terms of health. Older women, for example, who had many social contacts, evidenced higher mortality than those with medium-sized networks. To explain these apparently anomalous findings, they analysed their data not according to the absolute number of contacts, but took into account the nature of these contacts. They then found that the strongest predictor of mortality was a lack of social integration, which the authors considered to provide guidance, practical help and a feeling of "belonging". They found only a low association between the provision of emotional support and CHD, although a later study by the same group found this to be an important protective factor. In an alternative interpretation of the Type A hypothesis, Orth-Gomer and Unden (1990) suggested that either Type A behaviour or hostility might confer risk for CHD as a consequence of an associated social isolation. In a longitudinal study, following a cohort of men for ten years, they found no differences in mortality between Type A and Type B men. However, over this period, 69% of the socially isolated Type A men in the cohort had experienced an MI, in contrast to the 17% incidence among those who were socially integrated. For further discussion on psychological aspects of CHD, see Chapter 6.

Further evidence of the impact of social isolation can be found in studies of populations already experiencing disease. Williams et al. (1992), for example, found that patients with CHD who were unmarried and without a confidant experienced a three-fold higher risk of mortality over a five-year follow-up period than those who were not so isolated. Reflecting the subjective nature of social support, some studies that have failed to find a relationship between marital status and mortality following diagnosis of illness have found the *quality* of these relationships and the emotional support within them to be associated with survival.

The mechanisms through which social isolation confers risk are yet to be fully understood. However, a number of potential mechanisms have been proposed. Firstly, social support may itself be protective. It may also reduce the incidence of depression—a factor both associated with lack of social support and ill health. Secondly, social networks may exert a controlling function, and discourage health-damaging behaviours such as smoking, excessive eating, and alcohol consumption (e.g. Broman, 1993). Finally, social networks may tie individuals into a range of resources supportive of health, including medical networks and support groups (Berkman & Glass, 2000).

IMPROVING HEALTH

Most clinical health psychology interventions focus on the individual. It is possible that many of the issues raised in the previous section can be addressed using such an approach. Worksite health promotion programmes have targeted stress at work through the use of stress management groups, with some success (see, e.g., Murphy, 1996). A number of interventions have focused on reducing social isolation and increasing social support, at least to individuals with identified disease, and have proved of some value in improving quality of life, although their impact on morbidity and mortality is less clear (Gellert, Maxwell & Siegel, 1984; Spiegel, Bloom & Yalom, 1981). The National Institutes for Health in the USA has recently funded a massive trial involving over 3000 participants looking at the effectiveness of treating depression and social isolation in individuals who have had an MI using a cognitive-behavioural approach (The ENRICHD Investigators, 2000). Unfortunately, at the time of writing, this large trial has yet to yield its results. Data are currently being analysed.

Despite the potential of such interventions, an increasing number of commentators are now arguing that the most compelling intervention strategies to reduce health inequalities are likely to be social, economic and environmental. A number of approaches can be considered under this rubric, including controlling factors such as: taxation of health-damaging products, including tobacco and alcohol; restricting advertising of such products; and restricting availability of cigarettes and alcohol.

These are discussed in some detail in Bennett and Murphy (1997). The discussion here will briefly focus on three approaches that address specific issues raised in the first part of this chapter: economic interventions designed to minimise socio-economic inequalities; worksite interventions targeted at entire workforces; and environmental interventions designed to encourage "healthy lifestyles".

Economic Interventions

From an economic perspective, effective strategies to reduce health inequalities must include measures to reduce unemployment to the lowest possible level. This clearly requires political and economic policies. The Swedish economic model, for example, identified a series of strategies that have proved effective in maintaining high levels of employment, including proactive employment exchange, high-quality training aimed at providing skills required by the employment market, recruitment incentives for employers, and the right to temporary public employment in the last resort. This could be applied in other economies. Davey Smith et al. (1999) called for a series of differing economic measures. They argued for the implementation of "affordable" basic income schemes as a means of ending poverty and improving health. Schemes could take the form of a payment received by every person or household to provide a minimal income, with the amount paid based on age and family status. In addition, they suggested that all benefits to families with children receiving income support should be increased to avoid the next generation being disadvantaged from birth. They noted that a quarter of all children are born to mothers under the age of 25 years, and that governments should ensure that those under this age receive no less benefits than older individuals (as they did at the time of their paper). It is beyond the scope of the present chapter to comment further on the strengths and weaknesses of various economic systems. However, they evidently have significant implications for health and should, therefore, form a legitimate area of influence for those involved in promoting health.

Worksite Interventions

As noted previously, initiatives that have addressed worksite stress have almost uniquely done so through the provision of programmes that teach stress management skills: that is, they help attenders to cope more effectively with the demands placed upon them. However, this approach has limited utility. Oldenburg and Harris (1996), for example, noted that on-site stress management programmes only attract between 10 and 40% of the workforce, and that many of those who attend have little to gain, while many anxious individuals refrain from attending such courses. However, they have a more fundamental weakness in that they fail to address directly issues relevant to work stress or the well-being of the majority of the workforce, and in particular those in blue-collar jobs.

One of the few programmes to address these more fundamental issues was reported by Maes et al. (1998). Their intervention focused both on lifestyle change and modifying key aspects of the working environment in order to foster mental and physical well-being throughout the workforce. The first year of the programme followed a conventional pattern, and focused on individual behavioural change through the provision of health education classes. In the second phase of the intervention, the programme became more innovative. It drew upon a substantial literature that has identified working conditions that enhance both the well-being of workers and work production levels, including individuals working within their capabilities, avoiding short and repetitive performance tasks, having some control over the organisation of work, and adequate social contact. With these factors in mind, they attempted, within the constraints of production, to change the nature of each worker's job to bring it closer to the ideal. In addition, they trained managers in communication and leadership skills and identified methods through which they could recognise, prevent and reduce individual stress within the workforce. These various approaches addressed at least two of the factors that the Karasek model (see above: Karesek & Theorell, 1990) considers central to the stress process: control and social support.

Evaluation of the intervention involved following four groups of workers: those working in the intervention worksite; those in control sites; and participants and non-participants in the individual lifestyle-change programme. Their results indicated highly specific effects of each intervention. By the end of the individual intervention phase, participants in the lifestyle programme evidenced greater reductions in risk for CHD than those in the control group. However, by the end of the third year of the project, these gains were no longer evident. In contrast, the wider intervention was associated with increased quality of work and lower absenteeism rates in comparison to the control sites over the duration of the intervention. No data on "stress" levels were taken by the research team. However, these data are at least indicative of positive changes in stress or job satisfaction levels.

Environmental Interventions

Unhealthy environments have been characterised as those that threaten safety, undermine the creation of social ties, and are conflictual, abusive, or violent. A healthy environment, in contrast, provides safety, opportunities for social integration, and the ability to predict and control aspects of that environment. These requirements present a significant challenge to future town and city planners and administrators. Issues relevant to health vary from the design and architecture of "safe" housing estates to the planning and geographical location of shopping or leisure centres. Such initiatives may occur at a national or city-wide level, for example, by protecting "green spaces" in urban areas so they are available for recreational exercise, or through transport policies that encourage bicycle users and pedestrians rather than the use of cars.

Not all environmental interventions need be permanent fixtures. An innovative approach carried out in Edinburgh, Scotland, for example, involved selling high-quality fresh fruit and vegetables from travelling vans in economically deprived areas where the shops did not provide such a service. On a larger scale, the Heartbeat Wales programme (Nutbeam et al., 1993) facilitated a number of environmental changes designed to reduce barriers and to cue appropriate behavioural change. Initiatives included encouraging food labelling and increasing the availability of "healthy foods" in major retailers and local butchers, facilitating the establishment of "healthy restaurants", and providing exercise trails in local parks.

Evaluation of large-scale programmes focusing solely on the physical environment has proved difficult. Evaluation of the Healthy Cities movement serves as an example. Participating cities across the world were concerned with monitoring and improving environmental indicators of quality of life including unemployment, housing quality, democratic participation, and education provision (Ashton, 1992). Unfortunately, environmental changes were not instituted in a controlled manner and were not monitored effectively, making it impossible to establish any relationship between environmental changes and any changes in behaviour or health. Nevertheless, smaller-scale controlled trials of environmental manipulation attest to their potential effectiveness. Linegar, Chesson and Nice (1991), for example, measured the impact of environmental changes on exercise levels within the general population. Taking advantage of the closed community provided by a naval base, they established cycle paths, exercise equipment, exercise clubs, and fitness competitions within the base. In addition, workers were given "release time" from other duties while they participated in some physical activities. In comparison to a control area, where no such changes were initiated, significant increases in activity and fitness were found among both existing exercisers and previous non-exercisers.

CONCLUDING REMARKS

The social, economic and physical environment in which we live matters. It impacts both directly and indirectly on our quality of life, and our mental and physical health. The fact that it affects both mental health and quality of life makes this an arena of relevance to psychology. The fact that some of the adverse impacts of our environment appear to be mediated by psychological factors adds to the need for psychologists to be involved in both understanding the processes by which social context influences health, and identifying both targets and strategies for change.

Psychologists typically work with individuals or small groups. The data documented in this chapter, in the author's opinion, demand that we begin to work in differing and less direct contexts—to work in areas related to public health and public health policy at both a local and national level. This may demand a change of perspective and that, at least, some clinical health psychologists work at a political level and develop the knowledge and skills for both identifying the need for change and influencing the key players in this arena. Until then, psychologists will remain observers of these powerful processes rather than a force for change.

REFERENCES

Achat, H., Kawachi, I., Byrne, C., Hankinson, S. & Colditz, G. (2000). A prospective study of job strain and risk of breast cancer. *International Journal of Epidemiology*, **29**, 622–628.

Alfredsson, L., Spetz, C.-L. & Theorell, T. (1985). Type of occupational and near-future hospitalization for myocardial infarction and some other diagnoses. *International Journal of Epidemiology*, **4**, 378–388.

American Heart Association (1995). *Heart and Stroke Facts: 1995 Statistical Supplement*. Dallas, TX: American Heart Association.

Ames, G.M. & Janes, C.R. (1987). Heavy and problem drinking in an American blue-collar population: implications for prevention. *Social Science and Medicine*, **25**, 949–960.

Ancona, C., Agabiti, N., Forastiere, F., Arcà, M., Fusco, D., Ferro, S. & Perucci, C.A. (2000). Coronary artery bypass graft surgery: socio-economic inequalities in access and in 30 day mortality. A population-based study in Rome, Italy. *Journal of Epidemiology and Community Health*, **54**, 930–935.

Ashton, J. (1992). *Healthy Cities*. Buckingham: Open University Press.

Ayanian, J.Z., Cleary, P.D., Weissman, J.S. & Epstein, A.M. (1999). The effect of patients' preferences on racial differences in access to renal transplantation. *New England Journal of Medicine*, **341**, 1661–1669.

Balarajan, R. & Raleigh, V. (1993). *Ethnicity and Health in England*. London: HMSO.

Baum, A., Garofalo, J.P. & Yali, A.M. (1999). Socioeconomic status and chronic stress. Does stress account for SES effects on health? *Annals of the New York Academy of Science*, **896**, 131–144.

Bennett, P.D. (2000). *Introduction to Clinical Health Psychology*. Buckingham: Open University Press.

Bennett, P.D. & Murphy, S. (1997). *Psychology and Health Promotion*. Buckingham: Open University Press.

Berkman, L.F. & Glass, T. (2000). Social integration, social networks, social support, and health. In L.F. Berkman & I. Kawachi (Eds), *Social Epidemiology*. New York: Oxford University Press.

Berkman, L.F. & Syme, S.L. (1979). Social networks host resistance, and mortality: a nine-year follow-up study of Alameda County residents. *American Journal of Epidemiology*, **109**, 186–204.

Brawley, O.W. & Freeman, H.P. (1999). Race and outcomes: is this the end of the beginning for minority health research? *Journal of the National Cancer Institute*, **91**, 1908–1909.

Broman, C.L. (1993). Social relationships and health-related behaviour. *Journal of Behavioral Medicine*, **16**, 335–350.

Brosschot, J.F. & Thayer, J.F. (1998). Anger inhibition, cardiovascular recovery, and vagal function: a model of the link between hostility and cardiovascular disease. *Annals of Behavioral Medicine*, **20**, 326–332.

Caspersen, C.J. & Merritt, R.K. (1995). Physical activity trends among 26 states, 1986–1990. *Medicine and Science in Sports and Exercise*, **27**, 713–720.

Charmaz, K. (1994). Identity dilemmas of chronically ill men. *Sociological Quarterly*, **35**, 269–288.

Clarke, R. (2000). Perceptions of interethnic group racism predict increased vascular reactivity to a laboratory challenge in college women. *Annals of Behavioral Medicine*, **22**, 214–222.

Cole, S.W., Kemeny, M.E., Taylor, S.E. & Visscher, B.R. (1996). Elevated physical health risk among gay men who conceal their homosexual identity. *Health Psychology*, **15**, 243–251.

Courtenay, W.H. (2000). Constructions of masculinity and their influence on men's well-being: a theory of gender and health. *Social Science and Medicine*, **50**, 1385–1401.

Davey Smith, G., Carroll, D., Rankin, S. & Rowan, D. (1992). Socio-economic differentials in mortality: evidence from Glasgow graveyards. *British Medical Journal*, **305**, 1554–1557.

Davey Smith, G., Dorling, D., Gordon, D. & Shaw, M. (1999). The widening health gap: what are the solutions? *Critical Public Health*, **9**, 151–170.

Davey Smith, G., Wentworth, D., Neaton, J.D., Stamler, R. & Stamler, J. (1996). Socio-economic differentials in mortality risk among men screened for the Multiple Risk Factor Intervention Trial, 2: black men. *American Journal of Public Health*, **86**, 497–504.

de Jong, J., Bosma, H., Peter, R. & Siegrist, J. (2000). Job strain, effort–reward imbalance and employee wellbeing: a large-scale cross-sectional study. *Social Science and Medicine*, **50**, 1317–1327.

Department of Health and Human Services (1996). *Report of Final Mortality Statistics, 1994. Monthly Vital Statistics Report*, **45** (3 Supplement). Hyattsville, MD: Public Health Service.

Department of Health and Human Services (1998). *Health, United States, 1998: Socio-economic Status and Health Chartbook*. Hyattsville, MD: National Center for Health Statistics.

Dooley, D., Fielding, J. & Levi, L. (1996). Health and unemployment. *Annual Review of Public Health*, **17**, 449–465.

The ENRICHD Investigators (2000). Enhancing recovery in coronary heart disease patients (ENRICHD): study design and methods. *American Heart Journal*, **139**, 1–9.

Filakti, H. & Fox, J. (1995). Differences in mortality by housing tenure and by car access from the OPCS Longitudinal Study. *Population Trends*, **81**, 27–30.

Gallo, L.C. & Matthews, K.A. (1999). Do negative emotions mediate the association between socio-economic status and health? *Annals of the New York Academy of Science*, **896**, 226–245.

Gellert., G.A., Maxwell, R.M. & Siegel, B.S. (1984). Survival of breast cancer patients receiving adjunctive psychosocial support therapy: a 10-year follow up study. *Journal of Clinical Oncology*, **11**, 66–69.

Goldblatt, P. (1989). Mortality by social class, 1971–85. *Population Trends*, **56**, 6–15.

Goyder, E.C., McNally, P.G. & Botha, J.L. (2000). Inequalities in access to diabetes care: evidence from a historical cohort study. *Quality in Health Care*, **9**, 85–89.

Haan, M.N. & Kaplan, G.A. (1985). The contribution of socio-economic position to minority health. In M. Heckler (Ed.), *Report of the Secretary's Task Force on Black and Minority Health: Crosscutting Issues in Health and Human Services*. Washington, DC: USDHHS.

Haberman, D. & Bloomfield, D.S.F. (1988). Social class differences in mortality in Great Britain around 1981. *Journal of the Institute of Actuaries*, **115**, 495–517.

Harding, S. & Maxwell, R. (1997). Differences in mortality of migrants. In F. Drever & M. Whitehead (Eds), *Health Inequalities: Decennial Supplement*. London: HMSO.

Haynes, G. & Feinleib, M. (1980). Women, work, and coronary heart disease: prospective findings from the Framingham heart study. *American Journal of Public Health*, **70**, 133–141.

Hein, H.O., Suadicani, P. & Gyntelberg, F. (1992). Ischaemic heart disease incidence by social class and form of smoking: the Copenhagen male study—17 years follow-up. *Journal of Internal Medicine*, **231**, 477–483.

House, J.S., Kessler, R., Herzog, A.R., Mero, R., Kinney, A. & Breslow, M. (1991). Social stratification, age, and health. In K.W. Scheie, D. Blazer & J.S. House (Eds), *Aging, Health Behaviours, and Health Outcomes*. Hillsdale, NJ: Lawrence Erlbaum.

Jaffe, H. (1997). Dying for dollars. *Men's Health*, **12**, 132–137.

Janlert, U., Asplund, K. & Weinehall, L. (1992). Unemployment and cardiovascular risk indicators. Data from the MONICA survey in northern Sweden. *Journal of Social Medicine*, **20**, 14–18.

Kahn, K.L., Pearson, M.L., Harrison, E.R., Desmond, K.A., Rogers, W.H., Rubenstein, L.V., Brook, R.H. & Keeler, E.B. (1994). Health care for black and poor hospitalized Medicare patients. *Journal of the American Medical Association*, **271**, 1169–1174.

Karasek, R. (1996). Lower health risk with increased job control among white collar workers. *Journal of Organizational Behavior*, **11**, 171–185.

Karasek, R. & Theorell, T. (1990). *Stress, Productivity and the Reconstruction of Working Life*. New York: Basic Books.

Klag, M.J., Whelton, P.K., Coresh, J., Grim, C.E. & Kuller, L.H. (1991). The association of skin color with blood pressure in US Blacks with low socio-economic status. *Journal of the American Medical Association*, **265**, 599–602.

Krieger, N., Quesenberry, C. & Peng, T. (1999). Social class, race/ethnicity, and incidence of breast cervix, colon, lung, and prostate cancer among Asian, black, Hispanic, and white residents of the San Francisco Bay Area. *Cancer Causes Control*, **10**, 525–537.

Kristensen, T.S. (1995). The demand–control–support model: methodological challenges for future research. *Stress Medicine*, **11**, 17–26.

Lahad, A., Heckbert, S.R., Koepsell, T.D., Psaty, B.M. & Patrick, D.L. (1997). Hostility, aggression and the risk of nonfatal myocardial infarction in postmenopausal women. *Journal of Psychosomatic Research*, **43**, 183–195.

Lewis, G., Bebbington, P., Brugha, T., Farrell, M., Gill, B., Jenkins, R. & Meltzer, H. (1998). Socio-economic status, standard of living, and neurotic disorder. *Lancet*, **352**, 605–609.

Linegar, J., Chesson, C. & Nice, D. (1991). Physical fitness gains following simple environmental change. *American Journal of Preventive Medicine*, **7**, 298–310.

Lundberg, U., de Chateau, P., Winberg, J. & Frankenhauser, M. (1981). Catecholamine and cortisol excretion patterns in three year old children and their parents. *Journal of Human Stress*, **7**, 3–11.

Macintyre, S. & Ellaway, A. (1998). *Ecological Approaches: Rediscovering the Role of the Physical and Social Environment*. Oxford: Oxford University Press.

Maes, S., Verhoeven, C., Kittel, F. & Scholten, H. (1998). Effects of the Brabantia-project, a Dutch wellness-health programme at the worksite. *American Journal of Public Health*, **88**, 1037–1041.

Marmot, M.G., Shipley, M.J. & Rose, G. (1984). Inequalities in health—specific explanations of a general pattern? *Lancet*, **i**, 1003–1006.

Marmot, M.G., Smith, G.D. & Stansfield, S. (1991). Health inequalities among British civil servants: the Whitehall study II. *Lancet*, **337**, 1387–1393.

McCarron, P., Davey Smith, G. & Wormsley, J. (1994). Deprivation and mortality in Glasgow: changes from 1980 to 1992. *British Medical Journal*, **309**, 1481–1482.

McLeod, J.D. & Kessler, R.C. (1990). Socio-economic status differences in vulnerability to undesirable life events. *Journal of Health and Social Behaviour*, **31**, 162–172.

Mitchell, J.B., Ballard, D.J., Matchar, D.B., Whisnant, J.P. & Samsa, G.P. (2000). Racial variation in treatment for transient ischemic attacks: impact of participation by neurologists. *Health Services Research*, **34**, 1413–1428.

Murphy, L.R. (1996). Stress management in work settings: a critical review of the health effects. *American Journal of Health Promotion*, **11**, 112–135.

Nazroo, J. (1997). *The Health of Britain's Ethnic Minorities: Findings from a National Survey*. London: Policy Studies Institute.

Nazroo, J.Y. (1998). *Genetic, Cultural or Socio-economic Vulnerability? Explaining Ethnic Inequalities in Health*. Oxford: Blackwell.

Nordstrom, C.K., Dwyer, K.M., Merz, C.N.B., Shircore, A. & Dwyer, J.H. (2001). Work-related stress and early atherosclerosis. *Epidemiology*, **12**, 180–185.

Nutbeam, D., Smith, C., Murphy, S. & Catford, J. (1993). Maintaining evaluation designs for long-term community-based health promotion programmes: Heartbeat Wales Case Study. *Journal of Epidemiology and Community Health*, **47**, 127–133.

Oldenburg, B. & Harris, D. (1996). The workplace as a setting for promoting health and preventing disease. *Homeostasis in Health and Disease*, **37**, 226–232.

Orth-Gomer, K. & Johnsson, J.V. (1987). Social network interaction and mortality: a six year follow-up study of a random sample of the Swedish population. *Journal of Chronic Diseases*, **40**, 949–957.

Orth-Gomer, K. & Unden, A.-L. (1990). Type A behaviour, social support, and coronary risk: interaction and significance for mortality in cardiac patients. *Psychosomatic Medicine*, **52**, 59–72.

Powell-Griner, E., Anderson, J.E. & Murphy, W. (1997). State and sex-specific prevalence of selected characteristics behavioural risk factor surveillance system, 1994 and 1995. *Morbidity and Mortality Weekly Report, Centres for Disease Control, Surveillance Summaries*, **46**, 1–31.

Qureshi, M., Thacker, H.L., Litaker, D.G. & Kippes, C. (2000). Differences in breast cancer screening rates: an issue of ethnicity or socioeconomics? *Journal of Women's Health and Gender Based Medicine*, **9**, 1025–1031.

Reddy, D.M., Fleming, R. & Adesso, V.J. (1992). Gender and health. In S. Maes, H. Leventhal & M. Johnston (Eds), *International Review of Health Psychology*. Volume 1. Chichester: John Wiley & Sons.

Reynolds, P. & Kaplan, G.A. (1990). Social connections and risk for cancer: prospective evidence from the Alameda County Study. *Behavioral Medicine*, **16**, 101–110.

Ruberman, W., Weinblatt, E., Goldberg, J.D. & Chaudhary, B.S. (1984). Psychosocial resilience and protective mechanisms. *American Journal of Orthopsychiatry*, **57**, 316–330.

Rudat, K. (1994). *Black and Minority Ethnic Groups in England: Health and Lifestyles*. London: Health Education Authority.

Siegrist, J., Peter, R., Junge, A., Cremer, P. & Seidel, D. (1990). Low status control, high effort at work and ischemic heart disease: prospective evidence from blue collar men. *Social Science and Medicine*, **35**, 1127–1134.

Sorlie, P.D., Backlund, E. & Keller, J.B. (1995). US mortality by economic, demographic, and social characteristics: the National Longitudinal Mortality Study. *American Journal of Public Health*, **85**, 949–956.

Spiegel, D., Bloom, J.R. & Yalom, I.D. (1981). Group support for patients with metastatic cancer: a randomised prospective outcome study. *Archives of General Psychiatry*, **38**, 527–533.

Stansfeld, S.A., Bosma, H., Hemingway, H. & Marmot, M.G. (1998). Psychosocial work characteristics and social support as predictors of SF-36 health functioning: the Whitehall II study. *Psychosomatic Medicine*, **60**, 247–255.

Stokols, D. (1992). Establishing and maintaining health environments. *American Psychologist*, **47**, 6–22.

Stronks, K., VandeMheen, H., VandenBos, J. & Mackenbach, J.P. (1997). The interrelationship between income, health and employment status. *International Journal of Epidemiology*, **16**, 592–600.

Todd, K.H., Deaton, C., D'Adamo, A.P. & Goe, L. (2000). Ethnicity and analgesic practice. *Annals of Emergency Medicine*, **35**, 11–16.

Vaillant, G.E. (1998). Natural history of male psychological health, XIV: relationship of mood disorder vulnerability and physical health. *American Journal of Psychiatry*, **155**, 184–191.

Verbrugge, L.M. & Steiner, R.P. (1985). Prescribing drugs to men and women. *Health Psychology*, **4**, 79–98.

Weber, A. & Lehnert, G. (1997). Unemployment and cardiovascular diseases: a causal relationship? *International Archives of Occupational and Environmental Health*, **70**, 153–160.

West, P. & Sweeting, H. (1996). Nae job, nae future: young people and health in a context of unemployment. *Health and Social Care in the Community*, **4**, 50–62.

Westman, M., Eden, D. & Shirom, A. (1985). Job stress, cigarette smoking and cessation: conditioning effects of peer support. *Social Science and Medicine*, **20**, 637–644.

Winkleby, M., Fortmann, S. & Barrett, D. (1990). Social class disparities in risk factors for disease: eight year prevalence patterns by level of education. *Preventive Medicine*, **19**, 1–12.

Wilkinson, M. (1992). Income distribution and life expectancy. *British Medical Journal*, **304**, 165–168.

Wilkinson, R.G. (1990). Income distribution and mortality: a "natural" experiment. *Social Health Illness*, **12**, 391–412.

Williams, R.B., Barefoot, J.C., Califf, R.M., Haney, T.L., Saunders, W.B., Pryor, D.B., Hlatky, M.A., Siegler, I.C. & Mark, D.B. (1992). Prognostic importance of social resources among patients with angiographically documented coronary artery disease. *Journal of the American Medical Association*, **267**, 520–524.

CHAPTER 26

Telehealth and Chronic Illness: Emerging Issues and Developments in Research and Practice

Robert L. Glueckauf,* Treven C. Pickett,
Timothy U. Ketterson, Jeffrey S. Loomis
University of Florida, USA

and

David W. Nickelson
American Psychological Association, Washington, DC, USA

INTRODUCTION

One of the most promising developments in health care today is the growing use of telecommunication technologies to provide information, assessment, and treatment to individuals with health concerns, particularly those with chronic medical conditions. This new field of health care communications, known as telehealth or e-health, has expanded greatly over the past decade in the USA, Canada, Europe, Australia, and the Pacific Rim. The promise of this technology is intuitive and straightforward: telehealth has the potential to expand access, increase the quality of health care, and reduce the spiraling costs of specialty services (Glueckauf, Whitton & Nickelson, 2002; Glueckauf et al., 1999; Nickelson, 1996, 1998).

The recent growth of telehealth has been quite remarkable, particularly in the public sector (e.g., the armed forces and correctional systems). According to a recent survey conducted by the Association of Telehealth Service Providers (Grigsby & Brown, 2000), there are now in excess of 170 telehealth programs in the USA alone. Furthermore, 40% or more of these programs have been in operation for fewer than five years (cf., Nickelson, 1998).

Telehealth has begun to replace traditional forms of providing health information and services, but a substantial gap remains between the widespread demand for this health delivery

---

* Please address all correspondence to Robert L. Glueckauf.

Handbook of Clinical Health Psychology. Edited by S. Llewelyn and P. Kennedy.
© 2003 John Wiley & Sons, Ltd.

mode and the scientific evidence supporting its efficacy and cost-effectiveness. There are only a small number of well-designed controlled studies across different telecommunication modalities (e.g., Internet and automated telephone) to provide guidance in determining how and under what conditions telehealth leads to positive health outcomes. Research on consumer perceptions about the desirability of telehealth interventions and cost-effectiveness has increased both in scope and quality over the past few years, but is still underdeveloped both in terms of theory and methodological rigor. Furthermore, quality assurance standards, ethical guidelines, and professional training curricula on the utilization of telehealth services have only recently captured the attention of health organizations and government entities (e.g., Jerome et al., 2000).

In the first portion of this chapter, we define the field of telehealth and outline the factors that have contributed to the growth of telehealth services. In the second section, we provide a framework for categorizing the technologies used to deliver telehealth services and describe commonly used equipment and transmission networks. In the third section, we review barriers to the growth of telehealth networks, followed by a discussion of reimbursement and regulatory developments across the USA and Europe. In the fourth section, we review outcome studies on the effects of telehealth interventions for individuals with chronic medical conditions, particularly their physiological and psychosocial functioning. Finally, we propose future directions for telehealth practice and research.

DEFINITION OF TELEHEALTH

Any definition of telehealth must be flexible enough to accommodate technological advances and acknowledge current clinical and political realities. This is why the authors have defined telehealth as

> the use of telecommunications and information technologies to provide access to health information and services across a geographical distance, including (but not limited to) consultation, assessment, intervention, and follow-up programs to ensure maintenance of treatment effects. (Glueckauf et al., in press)

This definition of telehealth acknowledges that telehealth applications must meet multiple clinical and education needs. It also recognizes the broad range of health care providers and educators who will use these applications. The definition clarifies the most significant way in which telehealth differs from face-to-face encounters: it overcomes geographic limitations.

The authors favor this definition because it does not frame telehealth as a new form of practice. Rather, telehealth is simply a tool with the potential for facilitating the practice of already established professional skills across distance. The definition emphasizes that telehealth also may serve as a vehicle for enhancing maintenance of treatment effects, as well as establishing positive health routines in home and community settings (Liss, Glueckauf & Ecklund-Johnson, 2002).

Factors Contributing to the Growth of Telehealth

Three pervasive problems in health care have contributed significantly to the growth of telehealth: (1) uneven geographic distribution of health care resources, including health care facilities and health manpower; (2) inadequate access to health care for certain segments of the population, such as individuals living in rural areas and those who are physically confined; and (3) the spiraling cost of health services, particularly specialty care.

First, most health services in the USA, Europe, and other developed countries are centralized in metropolitan areas, leaving a sizable segment of the population without adequate access to health services. Although a variety of outreach programs have been implemented, they have not succeeded in narrowing this resource gap. Persons living in rural areas represent one of the most underserved constituencies. For example, more than 60 million people—approximately 25% of the US population—live in rural areas (Office of Technology Assessment, 1990). For these individuals, travel to needed health services, particularly specialty services, may require several hours of travel and attendant financial loss.

Second, several populations have inadequate access to health care, primarily as a result of physical confinement and mobility limitations. Individuals who are homebound, such as geriatric populations with neurological and mobility disabilities, older persons living in high crime areas, and those with persistent mental illnesses, such as agoraphobia, may encounter difficulties in obtaining adequate health care as their medical problems make it difficult to travel even short distances. In all these cases, telehealth may offer an effective means for closing the gap between limited provider resources and the health care needs of the population.

Third, one of the most pressing problems in health care is the escalating cost of specialty services. This is particularly the case for persons in rural areas who may require treatment by specialists located in large metropolitan cities. Clients in rural areas frequently experience high transportation costs and concomitant loss of wages to obtain specialty health care that is unavailable in the rural areas. Telecommunication-mediated specialty services delivered in the home or at a local medical facility have the potential of reducing significantly the economic hardship of rural citizens. However, the key question is whether such services can be provided without significant reduction in quality of care. A recent study by Australian investigators Trott and Blignault (1998) offered preliminary support for the economic benefits of rural behavioral telehealth. They compared the costs of providing face-to-face vs. telehealth-based psychiatric and psychological services to a small mining town 900 kilometers from the regional hospital in Townsville, Queensland. The findings of the investigation showed substantial cost savings, primarily attributable to reduced travel expenditures by psychiatrists and by rural patients.

TELEHEALTH TECHNOLOGY AND TELECOMMUNICATION SYSTEMS

The communication technologies used to provide telehealth services fall into two broad categories: asynchronous and synchronous.

Asynchronous Transactions

Asynchronous communication refers to information transactions that occur among two or more persons at different points in time. Electronic mail (e-mail) is the most common form of asynchronous communication and has been used in the delivery of a variety of health care services (e.g., Gustafson et al., 1993).

Synchronous Transactions

Synchronous communication refers to information transactions that occur simultaneously among two or more persons. Synchronous telecommunications include computer synchronous *chat systems*, Telecommunication Display Devices, telephone, and videoconferencing. Chat systems permit users to communicate instantly with one another through typed messages. Users can "chat" in two different ways: (a) through channels or "chat rooms" in which several individuals communicate simultaneously, or (b) through a direct connection in which two persons hold a private conversation. During chat room discussions, each person's contribution is displayed on screen in the order of its receipt, and is read by all participants in the "room" (Howe, 1997).

Telecommunication Display Devices

Telecommunication Display Devices (TDD)—of particular benefit to those with impaired hearing—are instruments that facilitate text-based conversations through standard telephone lines. TDDs typically consist of a touch-typing keyboard, a single-line, moving-LED screen, text buffer, memory, and a signal light. The entire unit is approximately the size of a laptop computer (see Scherer, 2002).

Telephone

The most common form of synchronous communication is the telephone. The major advantage of the telephone is its widespread availability and ease of access. The telephone has become the standard mode of communication in psychological practice for conducting preliminary screening interviews, follow-up sessions, and crisis intervention (Haas, Benedict & Kobos, 1996). Over the past few years, innovative, low-cost automated telephone technologies have become an increasingly viable option in treating persons with chronic health conditions, such as hypertension (e.g., Friedman et al., 1996) and in providing support to their caregivers (e.g., Mahone, Tarlow & Sandaire, 1998).

Videoconferencing Technology

Although telephone is presently the most accessible form of communication technology, we anticipate that videoconferencing technology (VCT) will become the modality of choice for delivering telehealth services in the twenty-first century. Public demand for interactive VCT services is expected to grow exponentially over the next decade. This surge of popularity is fueled by the declining costs of VCT equipment and software, increased penetration of telecommunication services, the broadening appeal of the World Wide Web, as well as the anticipation of gigabit-speed Internet 2 (Mittman & Cain, 1999).

Three types of VCT equipment are currently used to deliver telehealth services: (a) room or roll-about, (b) desktop, and (c) plug-and-play videophone systems.

Roll-about VCT

Although room or roll-about systems (e.g., Tandberg, Polycom, and Sony) are available in several different configurations, the basic set-up consists of a roll-about cart, a single large-screen monitor, codec (i.e., specialized computer programs and hardware that compress the video signal by reducing the number of bytes consumed by large files), microphone or speakerphone, set-top camera and, frequently, an accompanying document camera. Many roll-abouts use a second large-screen monitor to exhibit documents. This enables users on each end to view simultaneously the document displays and each other. Room or roll-about systems are ideal for facilitating multi-point group (i.e., groups in various sites), as well as person-to-person videoconferencing. The cost of room or roll-about units varies from $14 000 to $50 000.[1]

Desktop VCT

Desktop systems (e.g., Polycom, VCon and Sony) offer a low-cost, high-quality alternative to room systems in a convenient smaller package. Desktop solutions can accommodate peripheral devices (e.g., document camera and large-screen monitors) and are portable. The typical desktop VCT unit consists of a standard desktop computer (e.g., 1 GHz processor with PCI bus, 128 MB RAM, 100 MB free drive space, PCI SVGA Card, and a current MS Windows operating system) with a 19-inch monitor, and a PC-based VCT kit (e.g., Polycom, VCon and Sony). These systems are typically outfitted with a digital camera, speakerphone, and digital network interface hardware. Transmission of simultaneous audio and video signals is accomplished through the use of Integrated Service Delivery Networks (ISDN), Internet Protocol (IP), and, in certain cases, Switch 56 service. The current cost of a desktop VCT system is $2000 and upward, varying with CPU speed, memory, monitor size, and the selection of peripheral devices.

Plug-and-play VCT

Plug-and-play systems (e.g., TeleVyou and Motion Media) are currently the cheapest solution among the VCT options. These devices generally use plain old telephone service (POTS), but newer models can accommodate ISDN or IP. Note, however, that the POTS-based videophones require a smaller signal size to send video and must rely on a codec to compress the video signal across the telephone network. As a result, images can frequently be jerky or grainy, and sound may be poor in quality. Furthermore, image-to-sound synchronization may be periodically inadequate, rendering verbal communications difficult to follow. The current costs of plug-and-play systems range between $500 and $2500.

POTS, IP and ISDN Networks

Next, three basic telecommunication networks are currently used for VCT-based telehealth applications: (a) POTS, (b) Internet Protocol (IP) networks [including Wide Area Network

---

[1] Current prices of telehealth equipment and telecommunication network services are quoted in US dollars.

Systems (WANS) and Local Area Network Systems (LANS)] and (c) ISDN point-to-point and multipoint connections.

POTS

First, the POTS network is a circuit-switched service offered to private homes and businesses from the local telephone company. A switched circuit is defined as a two-way connection that exists only for the time required to make a call. When the user completes a long-distance call, the circuit is broken and the individual is no longer charged for the service. This is contrasted with a permanent or "nailed-up" circuit, which is connected and usable at all times (e.g., a dedicated T1 line).

The major downfall of POTS is the local loop or the wire from the local telephone company's switch or pole to the user's facility. Transmissions within the local loop are analog in nature (i.e., electronic transmissions accomplished by adding signals of varying frequency to carrier waves of a given frequency of alternating electromagnetic current). Telephone has conventionally used analog technology. This is the reason why we use a modem (i.e., a device that converts a computer's digital signal to an analog transmission and vice versa) to connect with the Internet. This analog local loop is slowly being replaced with digital technology. As this happens, the bottleneck of slow connectivity from the home to the Internet will diminish significantly (Glueckauf et al., 1999).

To make a video call on the POTS network, the sender dials the telephone number of the recipient or end user the same way he or she would dial a regular phone call. Note that the end user must have a compatible videoconferencing device to establish a connection. Such interactions are termed "point-to-point" videoconferencing calls. Multipoint video transmissions are also possible on POTS and involve simultaneous interactions among three or more parties.

Internet Protocol

Second, the IP network is a packet, switched service where digital information (i.e., ones and zeros from the computer) is bundled into sets or groups called packets. These packets contain data in combination with transfer-formatting information to facilitate transmission from place to place on the Internet. Individuals typically gain access to the Internet at their work site (through their employer's LAN or WAN) or at home through a local Internet Service Provider (ISP).

ISPs connect the consumer to the Internet using a router-based network. Routers are very fast computers whose sole job is to route or transfer IP packets to their destination. These digital packets traverse the network directed by routers and bridges to the addresses contained in the packets. When the packets arrive at their destination, they are amalgamated and are then seen by the end user as files, images or text on the screen.

IP-based networks can experience transmission delays and sometimes lose information (i.e., data packets), particularly at times when the network is congested. This results in a degradation of image and sound quality, as well as image-to-sound synchronization.

ISDN

Third, ISDN is one of several switched digital services on the market that can support high-quality, point-to-point or multipoint videoconferencing. The user pays an initial installation charge ($100 to $200), a monthly service fee ($75 to $100), a per-minute usage charge from the local provider for the service, and, if applicable, long-distance charges. ISDN can be obtained in several different bandwidths ranging from 128 kilobits per second (kbps) to 1.56 megabits per second (mbps). Although ISDN is currently expensive, this telecommunication mode provides an attractive high-speed (e.g., 128 kbps) alternative to slower analog transmission (56 kbps), particularly in rural areas where broadband Internet service may not be available.

In our view, the future of Internet videoconferencing appears especially promising. With advancements in switched network technology, improved protocols, and low-cost, high-bandwidth Next Generation Internet, IP videoconferencing is likely to become the preferred mode of communication in telehealth transactions (Glueckauf, Whitton & Nickelson, 2002).

BARRIERS TO THE DEVELOPMENT OF TELEHEALTH SYSTEMS

Barriers to the development of telehealth networks have been discussed in detail in a number of publications (e.g., Council on Competitiveness, 1994, 1996; Glueckauf et al., in press; Nickelson, 1997, 2000). These barriers are long-standing, pervasive, and difficult to overcome, particularly in the context of complex and highly fractionated health care systems. Key obstacles to the future growth of telehealth are as follows:

- *Reimbursement:* Who will pay, how much, to whom, for what services?
- *Licensure and regulation:* How do we protect patients from substandard practice?
- *Standards, guidelines, and credentials:* Do we need them? If so, who will develop them?
- *Evaluation:* Are telehealth services "clinically appropriate" and "cost-effective"? Who decides?
- *Privacy and confidentiality:* What information should be protected, and under which conditions should the protection be waived?

Over the past decade, both the USA and Europe have made significant efforts to remove these barriers to the development of telehealth systems. These initiatives can be divided into two major domains: (a) reimbursement strategies, and (b) licensure and regulatory actions. US telehealth initiatives will be reviewed first, followed by recent developments among the European Union countries.

Developments in Telehealth Reimbursement

Several US federal agencies have been involved in the development of telehealth policy and programs, including the Department of Defense, National Aeronautics and Space Administration, Department of Veterans Affairs, and the Department of Health and Human Services (General Accounting Office, 1997).

Lobbying efforts by the American Telemedicine Association and the Association of Telehealth Service Providers, groups representing the industry, have strongly influenced changes in US federal telehealth reimbursement policy. The Balanced Budget Act (BBA) of 1997 (US Government Printing Office, 1997) is one such effort that merits special consideration. The BBA of 1997 mandated that the US Health Care Financing Administration (HCFA) pay for telehealth services to eligible Medicare beneficiaries in rural Health Provider Shortage Areas (HPSAs).

While the BBA of 1997 ultimately excluded clinical psychologists as a telehealth services provider group after organized psychiatry raised last-minute objections, the passage of the Medicare, Medicaid, and SCHIP Benefits Improvement and Protection Act of 2000 (HR 5661) removed this restriction. In addition to expanding the range of professionals who were eligible for reimbursement, this latter groundbreaking legislation nullified earlier HCFA regulations that required (a) telehealth providers to split fees with the referral source, and (b) the referring rural provider to be physically present during the teleconsultation interview.

Although HCFA has not established a formal telehealth reimbursement scheme for the State-based Medicaid program, 20 American States currently provide reimbursement for telehealth services. As expected, reimbursable Medicaid services must satisfy federal requirements of efficiency, economy, and quality of care. To encourage greater utilization of telehealth services, HCFA has encouraged individual States to be flexible in adapting federal law to create innovative payment methodologies for telehealth providers. For example, State-based Medicaid programs have the capacity to reimburse additional costs (e.g., technical support, line charges) associated with the delivery of a covered telehealth service (see HCFA, 2002).

Within the European Union, an influential Green Paper by the European Health Telematics Association's Thematic Working Group on Legal and Ethical Issues (EHTEL, 2001) asserted that the development of a unified reimbursement plan was critical to the widespread implementation of telehealth services in Europe. A recent market analysis prepared by Deloitte & Touche (2000) for the European Commission Directorate General for the Informational Society echoed this appeal. Their marketing report, *The Emerging European Health Telematics Industry*, suggested that the creation of reimbursement processes and regulatory controls was essential for the stimulation and growth of the telehealth marketplace. These authors asserted that leadership was lacking in the establishment of telehealth standards and practice guidelines from competent authorities of the member States or from professional groups. They noted that the "health telematics applications were not ... sufficiently integrated into mainstream healthcare delivery for a substantial body of medical opinion to have evolved, against which an allegedly negligent health professional can be assessed" (p. 21).

Health care reimbursement policies in the EU vary considerably across member countries. Certain countries, such as the United Kingdom and Denmark, have national health services funded by the State through general taxation. Health care in these countries is generally free to all citizens at the point of delivery, although a co-payment may be required for certain health services (e.g., prescription drugs).

Compulsory nationwide insurance is more common among health care systems in Europe. In such systems, payment for consultations and treatment is made directly to the health service provider by the insurance or, alternatively, the patient pays part or all of the cost up front and is later reimbursed. In the context of compulsory insurance, reimbursement for telehealth services may further complicate an already cumbersome system. Clearly, these complexities pose a major barrier to the wide-scale implementation and acceptance of telehealth services (EHTEL, 2001).

Licensure and Regulatory Developments

In the USA, individual States retain the legal right to regulate the provision of health services to their citizens (Geiger v. Jenkins, 1971). The majority of health care professionals in the

USA are licensed in a single State. If the provider desires to practice in a State other than his or her own, a second full and unrestricted license usually must be obtained from the State where he or she hopes to practice (Granade, 1996). Not surprisingly, multi-State licensure requirements are frequently cited as a major barrier to the development of telehealth systems (e.g., Nickelson, 1998).

Professional psychology has made significant strides in developing regulatory guidelines in the practice of telehealth across State lines. In 1998, the Association of State and Provincial Psychology Boards altered its Model Licensure Act to include a section on "telepractice". The revised Act would permit psychologists to engage in telehealth practice for up to 30 days across State lines without obtaining a license, provided that the licensure requirements of the State in which the consumer resides are equivalent to those of the provider's State. A number of States are currently reviewing the language of the revised Model Licensure Act for possible incorporation into their State's psychology licensing law (Association of State and Provincial Psychology Boards, 1998).

In Europe, supervision and control of the health professions rests with national or regional authorities and specialist colleges within each EU country. For a health service provider to practice in an EU member state, other than the state of original licensure, completion of formal registration procedures in all "host" countries is required, regardless of whether the provider intends to be physically present in that host country. In some EU countries (e.g., Germany) health professionals may also be required to register in the specific districts or regions where they intend to practice. Registration in a new host country is neither automatic nor guaranteed. Furthermore, because of the need to supply multiple certified documents and to manage bureaucratic complexities, the licensure application process may be long and demanding.

Increased utilization of telehealth consultation and intervention across European borders has created significant challenges for government agencies charged with the regulation of the health care services. Only a few nations (e.g., United Kingdom), to date, have offered guidance in standardizing and regulating telehealth licensure and practice requirements (Darling, 2000; Eysenbach, 1998).

A recent task force report by the Professional Affairs Board of the British Psychological Society (BPS, 1999) provided guidelines for licensure and standards for psychological practice over the Internet. The primary emphases of the BPS telehealth guidelines were the normalization of telehealth services, public licensure verification of "on-line" chartered psychologists and recommendations for quality assurance and security. First, the Professional Affairs Board Working Group asserted that psychological services delivered over the Internet or through the use of other telecommunication systems were in "no way different ethically to ordinary practice" and that normal standards articulated in the BPS Code of Conduct and Guidelines for Professional Practice could be applied and enforced (p. 2). Second, the Working Group also recommended that the BPS "offer links maintained by chartered psychologists, who in turn link to the Society's website" (p. 2). This would permit consumers to verify that the Internet provider was indeed a chartered psychologist. Third, the report recommended that the BPS require security and encryption of web-based psychological services transmissions over the Internet and that telehealth providers fully inform consumers about the rules of confidentiality and access to information. Finally, the Working Group recognized that each telecommunication mode (e.g., telephone and Internet-based videoconferencing) posed its own set of concerns or problems. Thus, some types of psychological problems would suit "distance media" better than others.

Overall, there is currently considerable agreement between the USA and the EU regarding the specific barriers to the growth of telehealth. Both the USA and the EU are in accord that more reliable reimbursement mechanisms and standardized licensure/regulatory practices are needed to ensure the success of this emerging alternative health care delivery system. The differences in reimbursement and regulatory approaches between the two entities are primarily a matter of emphasis. The USA has concentrated on the development of universal (i.e., federal) telehealth reimbursement strategies, and at the same time has encouraged individual States to develop their own licensure and regulatory practices. Conversely, the EU has focused on establishing standards of telehealth practice across member countries and has given little attention to the development of overarching reimbursement policies.

TELEHEALTH INTERVENTION STUDIES

Turning to telehealth outcome research, a major strength of clinical health psychology is its solid foundation in the scientific method, experimental design, and applied statistics. It is now the norm for psychologists, particularly those in health science and medical centers, to participate in telehealth program evaluation research. As a consequence, health care psychologists are well equipped to take advantage of emerging research opportunities in telehealth. Indeed, over the past decade or so, a small cadre of psychologist-researchers (along with researchers from other health disciplines) has made important empirical and scholarly contributions to the field. We highlight their contributions in the telehealth research review below. We have restricted our review of the telehealth literature to representative, controlled intervention studies involving persons at risk for, or currently with, disabling health conditions. These studies broadly fall into four categories: Internet, telephone, videoconferencing and comparative studies across telephone, videoconferencing and face-to-face modalities.

Internet Studies

David Gustafson and colleagues at the University of Wisconsin have conducted several investigations (e.g., Gustafson et al., 1993, 1999) of the effects of Internet-based interventions for adults with chronic illnesses. Their program of research has focused on the development and evaluation of the Comprehensive Health Enhancement Support System (CHESS), a home-based computer system that provides a variety of interactive services to individuals with life-threatening conditions, such as women with breast cancer and persons with HIV/AIDS. CHESS users are able to communicate with others via typed messages in a "discussion or chat group", type in questions for experts to answer, read articles about others with similar health concerns, monitor their health status, and gain information about coping techniques.

In their most recent investigation, Gustafson et al. (1999) randomly assigned 204 HIV-positive individuals to either CHESS plus routine medical care ($n = 107$) or routine medical care ($n = 97$). CHESS participants consisted of three separate cohorts from two Wisconsin communities. The first cohort was administered CHESS for six months; the second and third cohorts received CHESS for three months only. HIV-positive participants were predominantly male (90%) and Caucasian (84%). Ninety per cent of the sample completed all phases of the study.

Outcome measures included self-report inventories of quality of life (QOL) [i.e., a modified version of the Medical Outcomes Survey consisting of eight subscales (Stewart, Hays & Ware, 1989)] and medical service utilization. Participants completed these measures at pretreatment, and at two months, five months, and for the first cohort only, nine months after CHESS implementation.

At the two-month post-implementation phase, Gustafson et al. (1999) found that CHESS participants (all three cohorts) rated their perceptions of QOL significantly higher on four of eight QOL measures (e.g., higher cognitive functioning, lower negative emotions, more active lifestyle, and greater social support) than the 97 controls who did not receive CHESS services. At the five-month post-implementation phase, CHESS users reported significantly higher QOL on three of eight measures (e.g., increased participation in their own health care and more active life) than that of control participants.

In addition, Gustafson et al. (1999) assessed differences in maintenance of gains in QOL between the two cohorts that received CHESS for three months and the one cohort that had CHESS for six months. They found that duration of treatment conferred a substantial advantage in maintenance of gains. Participants who received CHESS for six months showed maintenance of gains on three of eight QOL measures (i.e., active participation in their own health care, less negative emotion, and more social support) at follow-up. In contrast, the three-month cohorts showed lasting improvement only on one of the QOL measures (i.e., cognitive functioning) at follow-up.

Gustafson et al. (1999) also compared efficiencies in the utilization of medical services between the two conditions. During the active treatment phase, experimental participants (all three cohorts) reported fewer and shorter hospitalizations than those of routine care controls. The authors attributed this positive effect to CHESS users' increased knowledge and vigilance in recognizing and treating opportunistic infections. Note, however, that after the removal of CHESS, no differences in hospitalization rates and length of stays were found between the experimental and control groups.

The investigators also examined the impact of CHESS on the utilization of ambulatory care services. Although the total number of ambulatory care visits was similar for both experimental and control groups during the active treatment phase, CHESS participants reported significantly less time in medical visits and higher rates of phone consultations than control participants. The authors attributed CHESS users' shorter visits to better preparation with questions, clearer expectations for treatment, and increased empowerment to raise questions. No group differences in duration of medical visits were evidenced following the removal of CHESS. However, rates of phone consultation with providers continued to differentiate between experimental and control participants at the follow-up phase.

Thus, the overall pattern of findings suggested that CHESS led to substantial health benefits for HIV-positive individuals, including higher perceptions of QOL, fewer hospitalizations, and less time in medical visits. However, maintenance of gains on the QOL measures was found mainly for participants who received CHESS services for six months. The authors argued that these positive effects were attributable to the increased duration of treatment.

In a related investigation, Flatley-Brennan (1998) assessed the effects of an Intranet-based, decision-making skills program (i.e., ComputerLink) on the social, psychological and physical functioning of persons with HIV. Fifty-seven community-dwelling, HIV-positive individuals were randomly assigned to either the ComputerLink program ($n = 26$) or standard medical care ($n = 31$). Ninety-three per cent of the participants were male and 61% were Caucasian. Their average age and mean years of education was 33 and 13.5, respectively. Thirty-five per cent of the sample was employed at the time of the study, and mean years of education was 13.5 years. The ComputerLink equipment consisted of a Wyse 30 terminal with a 1200-baud modem that was linked to a public access computer network. ComputerLink services consisted of an encyclopedia of information about AIDS, self-care, medications, and local services, e-mail, and a public message board. In addition, participants received instruction in the use of a decision support system that helped to clarify their values and preferences in selecting self-care strategies. The control condition received routine medical care at an outpatient immunology clinic as well as printed information and a monthly telephone call.

The primary objectives of the study were to assess the differential effects of the ComputerLink program versus routine medical care on participants': (a) self-confidence in decision-making and decision-making skills, (b) functional status, and (c) extent of social participation. In addition, the investigator examined the relationship between changes in health status and network use, as well as the extent of utilization of the ComputerLink system.

The dependent measures consisted of: (a) a modified version of the Saunders and Courtney (1985) scale of decision-making success, (b) a count of unique alternative solutions for participant-identified problems, (c) a seven-item activities of daily living subscale of Multidimensional Functional Assessment device (Duke University Center for the Study of Aging and Human Development, 1978), and (d) 26-item self-report questionnaire that measured the participants' perceptions of the adequacy of social support (Ensel & Woelfel, 1986). Both ComputerLink and control participants received two administrations of the dependent measures: the first at pretreatment and the second six months later.

Only the level of social support significantly differentiated between the ComputerLink and routine care control condition from pre- to the six-month post-testing.[2] No substantial post-treatment differences between ComputerLink and control participants were found among the measures of decision-making confidence and skill, as well as activities of daily living. Flatley-Brennan (1998) attributed the null findings across three of the four dependent measures to both the difficulty level of HIV-related information and decision-making materials as well as the use of weak measurement tools.

The investigator also examined the extent of utilization of the major components of the ComputerLink network. Of the five different user options, participants used the communication function (i.e., message board and e-mail) most often, with e-mail exceeding the rate of message board submissions (6086 hits for e-mail versus 4886 hits for the message board). Similar to Gustafson et al. (1999), electronic mail and message board, both of which involve social contact with peers, were used significantly more than the other user options.

Next, Gray and colleagues (2000) conducted a randomized clinical trial of the effects of an innovative Internet-based telehealth program, Baby CareLink, on the quality of care of high-risk infants at Beth Israel Deaconess Medical Center. Within ten days of birth, families of very low birth weight (VLBW) were randomly assigned to either Baby CareLink ($n = 26$) or routine neonatal intensive care ($n = 30$). The Baby CareLink program was

---

[2] Initial one-tailed t tests on the dependent measures showed no significant differences between the ComputerLink and control conditions from pre- to the six-month post-testing. However, a post-hoc analysis using CES-D depression scores as a covariate led to significant six-month post-treatment gains for ComputerLink participants on the social support measure only.

carried out in two phases: hospitalization and post-discharge. During hospitalization Baby CareLink provided virtual baby visits (i.e., "see your infant"), daily clinical reports, a confidential message center between parents and hospital staff, and distance learning for family members. Following discharge from the neonatal intensive care unit (NICU), the Baby Care-Link program offered virtual "house calls" from hospital and community-based providers, remote monitoring of the infant's health, a "family room" option that provided answers to common questions, information about services available to family members, links to web-based resources, and an on-line library for browsing available print and video resources. Control group families received standard treatment at the NICU, including specialized medical and nursing services, didactic information about the infant's medical condition and care, and emotional support from hospital staff.

The primary dependent measures of the study included family ratings of quality of care, the infant's length of hospital stay, frequency of family visitations, time spent interacting with infants in person, time spent interacting with staff, and disposition of discharge (e.g., home, transfer to a community hospital, or death). Standardized quality-of-care questionnaires [i.e., Picker Institute NICU Family Satisfaction Survey (Picker Institute, 2000)] were administered to all families after discharge from the hospital.

Gray et al. found that the average rating of quality of care was significantly higher for the Baby CareLink families than that for standard treatment controls. CareLink families also endorsed significantly fewer problems with hospital care, the neonatal care physical environment, and visitation policies than did control group participants. In contrast, no substantial differences were found between the two conditions on frequency of family visits, telephone calls to the neonatal care unit, and holding of the infant. Duration of hospital stay was also similar across Baby CareLink and standard treatment (M = 68.5 days, SD = 28.3 versus M = 70.6 days, SD = 35.6, respectively). Last, all infants in the CareLink program were discharged directly to home, whereas six of 30 control group infants were transferred to their referring Level II hospital facilities before they were finally discharged to their homes.

Gray et al. concluded that the Baby CareLink program significantly improved family satisfaction with VLBW patient care and reduced costs associated with hospital-to-hospital transfers. The investigators ascribed the differential effects of the Internet-based program on family satisfaction with quality of care to heightened perceptions of skill, knowledge, confidence, and comfort in assuming the primary caregiver role. They also suggested that lower rates of transfer to Level II facilities in the CareLink condition may have resulted from increased parental confidence and comfort in managing their infant's care. Transfer to Level II hospitals prior to discharge was standard practice at Beth Israel Deaconess unless families actively declined this option.

In a conceptually driven investigation, McKay et al. (2002) reported the initial outcomes of their randomized-controlled trial of the impact of Internet-based education and support for individuals with diabetes. One hundred and sixty adults with Type 2 diabetes (ages ranging from 40 to 75) who had no prior Internet experience were randomly assigned to one of four conditions: (a) Internet-based information (IO) only, (b) IO and personalized self-management coaching (I + PC), (c) IO and peer support (I + PS), and (d) a combination of all three conditions (I + PC + PS). The IO condition consisted of web-based readings on diabetes-related medical information, nutrition, and lifestyle management; the I + PC condition included information provided to the IO group, with the addition of an Internet-based professional who acted as a coach, helping participants work on their specific dietary goals; the I + PS included IO-group information, with the addition of peer interaction via Internet discussion groups, chat, and message boards; the I + PC + PS condition was an amalgamation of all three treatments (i.e., IO + PC + PS).

All participants received a computer that remained in their home over the ten-month duration of the study. The dependent measures consisted of reported eating behavior (Block Fat Screener; Block et al., 1989; Kristal Food and Fiber Behavior Questionnaire; Kristal, Shattuck & Henry, 1990), mental health status [Symptom Frequency-12 (SF-12); Stewart, Hays & Ware, 1989; Center for Epidemiological Studies-Depression scale (CES-D); Radloff, 1977], and physiological changes measured by blood level of HbA_{1c} and total cholesterol. All measures were administered at baseline and at three months after installation of the computer equipment.

McKay et al. (2002) found significant and equivalent reductions in reported fat intake and ineffective eating habits across all four treatment groups. In contrast, no significant improvements in HBA_{1c} and cholesterol levels were evidenced from pretreatment to the three-month post-implementation phase. The investigators had predicted that improvements in dietary habits would enhance physiological functioning of patients with diabetes over time, particularly HbA_{1c} and cholesterol levels. Such positive changes in eating habits, however, may require more than three months to have a measurable effect on physiological indicators such as HbA_{1c}. McKay et al. also expected improvements in mental health indices, such as depressive affect and psychological well-being. Note that only a trend for an interaction between condition and time ($p = 0.10$) was obtained. The personalized coaching and the combined condition showed substantial increases in psychological well-being from pretreatment to the three-month assessment phase, whereas the peer support and information-only conditions showed little or no change over time.

Turning to website utilization patterns, user activity varied considerably both between groups and within participants across time. Overall usage of the website, however, was modest. The investigators reported that the two support conditions (i.e., PS and PS + PC + IO) generated significantly more log-ons than the IO and the PC + IO conditions. This finding was consistent with those of Gustafson et al. (1999) and Flatley-Brennan (1998) who showed substantially increased utilization of services that provide social interaction. Thus, consumers with disabilities may tend to make greater use of web-based health care resources that involve substantial peer interaction than stand-alone information or professional instruction.

In summary, McKay et al.'s initial findings suggested that Internet-based information and support interventions exert a positive impact on health-promoting behaviors of patients with Type 2 diabetes. Improvements in health behaviors, however, were circumscribed to eating behavior, specifically reported reduction of fat intake and poor dietary practices. It is notable that the gains in reported dietary intake were found for participants who had no prior Internet experience, suggesting that this intervention could be helpful to a wide segment of the population and not simply those who are already comfortable with computers. Although the current study permitted comparisons of different types of Internet-based diabetes-related services, it also would have been beneficial to compare all four groups against a routine medical care group. Such a design would have tested whether the web-based interventions yielded gains beyond those typically obtained from standard care.

Overall, Internet-based technologies appear to be a promising vehicle for providing health care education and support to individuals coping with effects of chronic medical problems (e.g., HIV/AIDS, IDDM) and life-threatening medical conditions at birth (e.g., VLBW). Preliminary support for the efficacy of Internet-based interventions was found across three different populations using a combination of group chat, e-mail, message board, and stand-alone information modules. The studies showed self-reported improvements in health-related QOL and a reduction in the need for health care services. In addition, preliminary evidence from Gustafson and colleagues (1999) and Flatley-Brennan (1998) illustrates the potential value of offering both public and private modes of communication in Internet-based interventions as a means of enhancing communication among peers (e.g., patients), families, community, and health care professionals. These investigators also reported intriguing data suggesting that participants used the communication aspects (e.g., e-mail, message board, and group chat) of the intervention programs most often, particularly e-mail. Finally, caution should be exercised in interpreting the findings of these early Internet studies. Both Gustafson et al. (1999) and McKay et al.'s (2002) investigations are seminal efforts and require replication to ensure that the obtained effects are reliable.

Telephone Studies

Telephone-based telehealth research can be classified into two major categories: (a) "first-generation" evaluations of telephone counseling and assessment procedures using standard POTS equipment, and (b) "second-generation" studies of automated telephone systems that offer a variety of services, including access to health education modules, consultation with health care experts, and telephone support groups for peers with similar medical conditions or their caregivers.

Evans and colleagues have conducted the majority of first-generation, telephone counseling studies (e.g., Evans & Jaureguy, 1982; Evans et al., 1984, 1986). In one of the first controlled telephone studies, Evans and Jaureguy (1982) assigned veterans with visual disabilities to one of two groups: telephone group counseling ($n = 12$) or standard office-based treatment ($n = 12$). They found significantly lower levels of depression and loneliness and higher participation in social activities for counseling participants than for no-treatment controls who showed no change over time. The veterans' positive response to telephone-mediated counseling was consistent with findings from similar studies that relied on uncontrolled, single group designs (Evans et al., 1984, 1986; Stein, Rothman & Nakanishi, 1993).

Turning to second-generation studies, Follick et al. (1988) assessed the impact of transtelephonic electrocardiography (ECG) on the QOL of adults with a recent myocardial infarction (MI). Participants were randomly assigned to a transtelephonic monitoring system (TMS) plus standard medical care or to standard care only. TMS participants were encouraged to make regularly scheduled calls to a hospital hub site to transmit ECG readings. In the case of symptomatic chest pain or other heart-related symptoms (e.g., numbness or pain in the left arm), patients were instructed to contact the on-call nurse who subsequently downloaded and interpreted their ECG recordings. If necessary, the on-call nurse sent out a rescue team, instructed the participant to self-administer Lidocaine, or both.

The primary dependent variables of the study included psychological distress and functional status—Symptom Checklist-90 (SCL-90; Derogatis, Lipman & Covi, 1973); Sickness Impact Profile (Bergner et al., 1981)—as well as self-confidence in coping with symptoms (a Likert-type rating scale of an undisclosed number of items, designed for this study and based on a similar scale used by Taylor et al., 1985). These measures were administered at baseline, and at one, three and nine months following randomization to condition.

Although both groups showed initial improvement with treatment, TMS participants were significantly less preoccupied with their condition and showed significantly fewer depressive symptoms than controls at the nine-month post-implementation phase. Furthermore, subsequent nonparametric statistical analysis revealed a substantial discrepancy between the two groups in the proportion of participants falling within the clinically depressed range on the SCL-90. Although rates were similar in the two groups than baseline, clinical levels of depression were twice as likely to occur in the control group as in the TMS condition at the nine-month follow-up. No significant post-treatment group differences in reported functional status were found based on the Sickness Impact Profile. However, TMS users returned to work at a significantly higher rate (92%) than that controls (76%).

In a second innovative cardiology intervention, Robert Friedman and colleagues (1996) randomly assigned 267 individuals with hypertension to a Telephone-Linked Computer (TLC) system or to standard treatment over a period of six months. TLC interacted with home-based participants over the telephone via computer-controlled speech. The participants, in turn, communicated using the touch-tone keypad on their telephones. The primary functions of the TLC system were to inquire about the health status of users and to promote adherence to the treatment regimen. During TLC "conversations", patients reported self-measured blood pressures, data on adherence to antihypertensive medications and, if pertinent, medication side-effects. This information was stored in a database and was subsequently transmitted to each patient's physician in printed form. Standard treatment patients received usual care from their health care providers.

Friedman et al. found that TLC patients reported significantly greater average adherence to treatment and lower diastolic blood pressure as compared to controls who showed little change over time on these measures. Note, however, that these effects were largely attributable to gains made by nonadherent patients in the TLC condition. TLC participants who were nonadherent prior to treatment (i.e., those who took less than 80% of their antihypertensive medications) showed significant improvements in mean adherence at the six-month post-test, whereas nonadherent standard treatment controls showed no change over time. Furthermore, adherent TLC and adherent control participants showed no significant between- or within-group differences on both blood pressure and behavioral (i.e., adherence) outcomes. Cost-effectiveness ratios also were calculated for the TLC users. The cost per 1 mm Hg improvement in diastolic blood pressure across all TLC participants was approximately $5 and $1 in the nonadherent TLC group.

In a diabetes application of automated telephone technology, Piette, Weinberger and McPhee (2000) recently conducted a randomized-controlled trial of Automated Telephone Disease Management (ATDM) plus nurse follow-up for adults with diabetes (diabetes subtypes were not specified). The authors randomly assigned 248 primarily low-income, underinsured diabetic individuals from a multilingual population (approximately half of the population was Hispanic; approximately 75% of the total participants were primarily English-speaking, and 25% were Spanish-speaking) to either ATDM plus nurse follow-up or usual care. ATDM participants received biweekly automated calls for a period of 12 months, reminding them of the importance of diabetes care behaviors, providing them with diabetes care tips, and asking participants to enter blood glucose levels. Participants interacted with the ATDM system using their telephone keypads to enter blood glucose levels and other information and to access the diabetes care tips. Individuals who had additional questions were encouraged to call the study nurse. Controls received typical care (i.e., standard office-based care) and did not have access to the ATDM system. The investigators collected data from all participants at baseline and at 12-month follow-up on patient glycemic control (i.e., HbA_{1c} and fasting serum glucose) and psychosocial variables, including depression (CES-D; Radloff, 1977), anxiety (Rand Mental Health Inventory Anxiety subscale; Veit & Ware, 1993), diabetes-related self-efficacy (an 11-item rating scale developed by the authors for this study to measure patients' confidence about their ability to conduct diabetes self-care, i.e., medication-taking, blood glucose-monitoring, etc.), days of reduced activity or confinement to bed, and diabetes-specific QOL (Diabetes Quality of Life Scale; Diabetes Control and Complications Trial Research Group, 1988). Data were also collected at baseline and follow-up on satisfaction with care and general health-related QOL [Symptom Frequency-36 (SF-36); Ware & Sherbourne, 1992] for primarily English-speaking participants (no Spanish translations of these measures were available).

The overall pattern of findings suggested that the ATDM system had a positive impact on both diabetes management and psychosocial functioning. In regard to diabetes management, the ATDM group reported significantly lower mean blood glucose levels and were twice as likely to be within the normal range on this measure as compared with the control group. Piette, Weinberger and McPhee (2000) also examined the impact of ATDM on several areas of psychosocial functioning, including depressive symptoms, anxiety, health-related QOL, satisfaction with care, and self-efficacy in performing diabetes care behaviors. ATDM participants reported significantly fewer depressive symptoms, greater satisfaction with care (for the subgroup of participants whose primary language was English), greater self-efficacy, and fewer days of reduced activity than controls. No significant differences were observed between the treatment and control groups for anxiety or overall health-related QOL. No treatment effects were noted based on language spoken (English vs Spanish), and no analyses were reported on ethnic differences. One weakness of this study is that the ATDM intervention had two components: a telephone component and a home visitation component. It is unclear which aspects of the intervention had an impact on results because all participants in the experimental condition received both parts. Disaggregation studies need to be performed to assess the specific contributions of the telephone and home visit components to the success of the intervention.

In summary, there is mounting evidence that automated telephone systems may be efficacious in enhancing adherence to intervention and reducing depressive symptoms in persons with chronic disabling conditions. Automated telephone systems that couple medication or health care regimen reminders with access to condition-specific educational modules may be particularly powerful methods for enhancing adherence to treatment and emotional well-being. However, there continues to be a lack of basic information about the social-psychological mechanisms that link telephone-based communications (e.g., reminders) to changes in health behaviors and emotional functioning. Future studies need to elucidate the specific health-promoting processes that automated telephone care appears to trigger in consumers with disabilities and, in turn, the relationship between these health-promoting processes and positive health outcomes. In addition, disaggregation studies are needed to determine which elements (i.e., reminders vs. educational modules) of automated telephone systems account for improvements in health functioning.

Videoconferencing Studies

Two major types of controlled videoconferencing studies have been performed: (a) comparisons between VCT-based and face-to-face interviews, and (b) evaluations of the reliability (e.g., interrater agreement) of VCT-based mental status examinations (e.g., Ball et al., 1993;

Elford et al., 2000; Hubble et al., 1993). Although the latter represent an important domain of research (see Ball & McLaren, 1997), we will not review these studies because they are not in keeping with the telehealth intervention focus of the present chapter. Furthermore, these studies generally make no explicit linkages between assessment and rehabilitation treatment.

Using the well-established University of Missouri (UM) hub-and-spoke teleconferencing network, Schopp, Johnstone and Merrell (2000) assessed the impact of performing initial neuropsychological assessment interviews across two delivery modes: remote interactive videoconferencing vs. standard face-to-face interaction. The participants of the study were adults with a wide range of neuropsychological problems (e.g., learning disabilities, traumatic brain injuries, and vascular dementia) referred by the Missouri Division of Vocational Rehabilitation for evaluation to assist in developing comprehensive vocational plans. Forty-nine participants were randomly assigned to each condition for a total of 98 participants. The video-teleconferencing group included 27 men and 22 women; the control group had 30 men and 19 women. Ninety-two per cent of participants ($n = 90$) were White; 6% of the sample was African American ($n = 6$). The two groups were matched based on age and diagnosis. The mean age of participants and years of education was 33.8 and 12.8, respectively. The nine interviewers in the study included UM neuropsychologists ($n = 4$), neuropsychology postdoctoral fellows ($n = 3$), and neuropsychology interns ($n = 2$), each of whom performed both in-person and video interviews. The telehealth network used in the study included the UM medical center hub, and 18 rural hospital and clinic spoke sites. Dedicated T1 connections were used to conduct the videoconferencing interviews, thus ensuring good-quality video and audio transmission. A psychometrist, who later administered neuropsychological tests, also attended the videoconference at the rural locale. In-person interviews were carried out at the first two authors' neuropsychology laboratory located in the UM medical center. After each interview, clients and interviewers completed closed-ended questionnaires. Clients rated their global satisfaction with the interview, how relaxed or tense they felt during the interview, ease of communication, perceived caring by the examiner, and whether or not they would repeat the experience under the same condition (i.e., videoconference or in-person). The neuropsychology staff rated their level of satisfaction with the interview after each videoconference or in-person control session. No significant differences were found between the two conditions on client global satisfaction, ease of communication, level of relaxation during the interview, and psychologist caring. Also, between the video group and the control group, a significantly larger proportion of clients in the video condition reported that they would repeat their experience. In contrast, the neuropsychology staff expressed significantly less satisfaction with the VCT-based approach than the in-person interview approach. The authors attributed this discrepancy to interviewers' unrealistically high expectations for transmission speed and reliability. Apparently, they were frustrated by even small delays in establishing digital connections between UM and the rural spoke sites. Finally, the authors compared the cost of videoconferencing against two alternative scenarios: (a) client traveling to and from the hospital and (b) psychologist traveling to and from the rural site. In both cases, the composite cost of the VCT-based interview was significantly lower than that of the two travel scenarios.

Next, Johnston et al. (2000) have conducted the first multipopulation clinical trial of VCT-based home care. The overarching goal of the Tele-Home Health program was to assess the feasibility and desirability of replacing a portion of patient home care visits for adults with chronic illnesses with VCT-mediated intervention. The specific objectives of this quasi-experimental evaluation were to assess the differential effects of VCT-based home care plus routine care vs stand-alone traditional in-person home care on patients' perceptions of quality of care, program satisfaction, and cost-effectiveness. Johnston et al. (2000) assigned newly referred Kaiser-Permanente outpatients with chronic illnesses (e.g., congestive heart failure, pulmonary disease, stroke, and cancer) to one of two conditions: (a) ISDN-based Tele-Home Health ($n = 102$) plus routine home care or (b) routine home health care only ($n = 110$). The Tele-Home Health intervention included on-demand, 24 hours per day, VCT interaction between patients and nursing staff, as well as remote monitoring of vital signs and medication compliance. In addition, Tele-Home Health participants received routine home health care. Controls received only routine home health care, consisting of regularly scheduled home visits plus telephone contact. The mean duration of the Tele-Home Health and the standard home care interventions were 53 days (SD $= 38.4$) and 40 days (SD $= 51.1$), respectively.

Primary outcomes included three quality of care indicators (i.e., medication compliance, knowledge of disease, and ability or self-care); the 12-item Short-Form Health Survey (SF-12; Ware, Kosinski & Keller, 1996), a measure of health QOL; patient satisfaction; rates and duration of service utilization rates; and costs of VCT-based and routine home health care services. The average costs for both the Tele-Home Health and routine home care programs were based on the following calculations: (a) outpatient costs for physician and emergency visits as well as for laboratory and pharmacy tests, (b) inpatient hospital costs, and (c) home health care costs, including payroll, benefits, travel, and cellular phone expenses. In addition, the costs of the VCT equipment and telecommunication charges (e.g., ISDN fees) were included in estimating the mean cost for the Tele-Home Health condition.

The overall pattern of findings of the study were mixed. Tele-Home Health post-test ratings of quality of care and of program satisfaction were high and equivalent to those of standard home health care treatment. In addition, no significant differences in health quality of life (i.e., SF-12 mean scores) were found between the two treatment programs. Surprisingly, however, the frequency of in-person home health visits for Tele-Home Health ($n = 1003$) was similar to that of standard home care ($n = 1197$).

Johnston et al. (2000) conducted two separate cost analyses: (a) a cross-program comparison of outpatient and inpatient hospital costs, and (b) a cross-program comparison of total costs of health services. First, the mean cost of outpatient and inpatient hospital services was significantly lower for Tele-Home Care patients ($1948) than that for controls ($2674). The reduced cost of hospital-based services in the Tele-Home Care group was attributable primarily to lower rates of hospitalization. Note, however, that this pattern of findings was not replicated in the analysis of overall costs. The total cost of health services, including equipment and telecommunications expenses, was $1830 for the Tele-Home Health group versus $1167 for standard home health care group.

In explaining the findings of the cost analysis, Johnston and colleagues (2000) contended that the overall expense of Tele-Home Care would have been significantly lower (approximately $900 rather than $1830) had the telecommunications equipment been leased or amortized over several years rather than purchased at the outset of the study. Although this argument may be valid, one of the primary reasons for the lack of cost savings may be found in the study's design. Johnston et al. bundled telehealth and traditional home services in the Tele-Home Care condition rather than creating a stand-alone telehealth intervention. The effect of bundling these services into one treatment package may have been to decrease substantially the likelihood of detecting differences in overall costs between Tele-Home Care and routine home health services.

In summary, the overall results of the two studies suggested that consumer perceptions of the desirability and utility of VCT-based health services were high. Health professionals, on the other hand, may not share the same high levels of satisfaction. Schopp, Johnstone and Merrell (2000) noted that neuropsychology staff tended to express less satisfaction with VCT-based interviews compared with those performed in the clinic. This finding was consistent with the results of closed-circuit TV interview studies with mental health populations that showed substantial discrepancies in perceptions of satisfaction with VCT between professionals and psychiatric patients (e.g., Ball et al., 1995; Dongier et al., 1986).

Only partial support was obtained for cost reductions in the use of VCT-based clinical interventions. On the positive side, Schopp, Johnstone and Merrell (2000) provided preliminary evidence that remote neuropsychological assessment interviews led to significant cost savings as compared with traditional professional outreach methods. Johnston and colleagues (2000), however, reported equivocal results on cost savings in their home-based VCT evaluation. Further research is needed to determine the specific settings (e.g., home vs. outpatient clinic) and types of health services (clinic consultations vs. home care services) that result in substantial cost savings.

Comparative Studies of Telecommunication Technologies

Glueckauf and colleagues (e.g., Glueckauf et al., 1998a, 1998b, 2002b) have performed, to our knowledge, the only randomized-controlled trial of the differential effects of video vs. speakerphone vs. face-to-face counseling for individuals with chronic medical conditions. This multisite investigation is ongoing and ultimately will involve over 95 families of rural teens with seizure disorders across five Midwest and three Southeastern States.

Glueckauf and associates' most recent paper (Glueckauf et al., 2002b) highlighted the findings of Phase 1 (i.e., the Midwest phase) of the study. Thirty-nine teenagers with uncontrolled epileptic seizures and their parents from the rural Midwest were randomly assigned to one of three conditions following initial assessment: (a) home-based (HB), family video-counseling (or HB speakerphone counseling when digital services were not available in the community), (b) traditional, office-based family counseling, or (c) a waiting list control group (after three months these participants were reassessed, and randomly assigned to one of the first two conditions). The intervention consisted of six sessions of issue-specific family counseling, an integrative family therapy approach that matches the specific concerns of teens and their parents to specific intervention strategies (Glueckauf et al., 1992). The differential effects of the issue-specific counseling intervention on outcome were assessed one week post-treatment and six months later. Twenty-two families completed the six-session counseling program; 12 families dropped out before the first assessment session, and five families dropped out after the initial assessment session. Dropout was differentially associated with office counseling, which required long-distance travel.

The investigators (Glueckauf et al., 2002b) used a multimethod approach in assessing key intervention and process variables. Their outcome measures were (a) problem-specific rating scales derived from the Family and Disability Assessment System (FDAS; Glueckauf, 2001; Glueckauf et al., 1992) and (b) the Social Skills Rating System (SSRS; Gresham & Elliott, 1990). Process measures included the modified Working Alliance Inventory (Glueckauf et al., 2002b; Horvath & Greenberg, 1989) and Homework Completion Ratings and Missed Appointments (Glueckauf et al., 2002b).

On the FDAS measures, teenagers and parents reported significant reductions in both severity and frequency of identified family problems across all three modalities, from pretreatment to one-week post-treatment and from pretreatment to the six-month follow-up. On the SSRS scales, parents reported significant improvement in prosocial behaviors (e.g., agreeing to perform chores and avoiding arguments with siblings) from pretreatment to one-week post-treatment, whereas teachers reported no substantial changes in classroom behavior over time. Consistent with previous telehealth research, mode of transmission did not differentially influence the outcomes of treatment. Significant and equivalent treatment gains were found across HB desktop-video, HB speakerphone, and face-to-face office counseling for all measures except for teachers' ratings of prosocial and problem behavior.

Next, Glueckauf et al. (2002b) found that the overall level of therapeutic alliance was moderately high across treatment conditions and family members. However, teens' perceptions of the therapeutic alliance varied with the mode of transmission. Teens reported significantly higher levels of alliance with therapists in the office and speakerphone conditions as compared with the video condition. Parents, on the other hand, reported similar levels of therapeutic alliance across the three therapy modes.

Turning to treatment adherence, the researchers had anticipated that video and speakerphone families would show higher levels of homework completion and fewer missed appointments as a result of the placement of the intervention in the home environment. Contrary to prediction, no substantial differences were found across conditions on completion of therapy homework assignments and number of missed appointments. The investigators hypothesized that the convenience of the HB video and speakerphone sessions needed to be weighed against the ease with which appointments could be rescheduled. Parents and teens may have concluded that their therapists could reschedule sessions with only limited difficulties, similar to the experience of calling someone back on the telephone at a later hour of the day.

In summary, consistent with telehealth research on clinical interviews (e.g., Schopp, Johnstone & Merrell, 2000), Glueckauf et al. (2002b) found that mode of transmission of telehealth services did not substantially influence treatment outcomes. Additionally, therapeutic alliance was shown to be moderately high across all modalities. Although a preliminary finding, alliance was found to vary significantly with type of modality and family member. Glueckauf and colleagues noted that further research is needed to evaluate the potential interactions among modality attributes, client characteristics, and situational factors on user perception of the quality of the therapeutic relationship. There currently exists only limited information about the factors that both enhance and reduce the quality of therapeutic alliance across modalities and disability groups and, in turn, their relationship with treatment outcome. Last, Glueckauf and colleagues suggested that caution should be exercised in interpreting the findings of their study primarily as a result of the small sample size and the need for replication in their Southeastern sample.

FUTURE DIRECTIONS FOR RESEARCH AND PRACTICE IN TELEHEALTH

In summary, telehealth holds considerable promise for resolving the access barriers of persons in rural areas and to homebound populations who require psychological services.

However, we currently have limited information about how and under what conditions telecommunication-mediated services lead to positive psychological and health care outcomes. We also have only initial evidence of the cost utility of telehealth services. This is especially true for the cost-effectiveness of telehealth applications in health psychology. In a health care marketplace increasingly focused on both the cost and quality of care, this research will be important to payers and policy-makers, and will ensure that health psychology has a place in future technology-laden iterations of our health care system.

Outcome and Cost Utility Studies

It is imperative that large-scale evaluations of the differential effects of telecommunications-mediated interventions become a funding priority for health care agencies such as the US National Institutes of Health, Health Resources and Services Administration and comparable research programs elsewhere in the world. Although a substantial number of demonstration grants have been awarded over the past 15 years, funding for large-scale randomized, clinical trials of the benefits of telehealth with chronic medical populations (e.g., persons with traumatic brain injuries and progressive memory disorders) has been slow to emerge. We can no longer tout the benefits of telehealth services for persons with chronic medical conditions without solid empirical evidence for their effectiveness. If we are to advance as a responsible scientific enterprise, we must begin to subject our basic assumptions about "what works" in telecommunications with our clients to scientific scrutiny.

Cost-effectiveness studies are also an integral component of the acceptance of large-scale telehealth interventions. To become a viable health service option, telehealth networks must show that the costs of treatment are at least equal to or less than those of alternative approaches that produce similar outcomes. Although several studies have documented the cost-effectiveness of psychotherapeutic interventions for psychiatric, substance abuse and geriatric populations (see Glen et al., 1997; Krupnick & Pincus, 1992), there has been little published research on the cost-effectiveness of telecommunication-mediated psychological interventions for persons with chronic disabilities (e.g., Cheung et al., 1998; Trott & Blignault, 1998).

Process Studies

Although randomized-controlled field studies are the litmus test of the effectiveness of telehealth, it is essential to understand the social–psychological mechanisms that link intervention and outcome. We currently have limited information about the factors that both enhance and reduce the quality (e.g., clarity, ease of use, distractibility, and comfort) of telehealth communications across modalities, age groups, minorities, and ethnic groups, and, in turn, their relationship with treatment outcome. Furthermore, only a few studies (e.g., Glueckauf et al., 2002b) have examined the impact of different telecommunication modalities (e.g., HB videoconferencing vs. telephone) on intervention adherence, attendance, and attrition.

Practice Guidelines and Client Training Material

Practice guidelines are potentially powerful tools to enhance quality control. Guidelines provide a method of determining the most effective treatment of a disorder and establish accepted treatment approaches and duration of treatment modalities. They are likely to be critical to the broad-based acceptance of telehealth interventions and may help to establish the appropriate level of expertise of telehealth providers (cf., DeLeon, Frank & Wedding, 1995). The Joint Working Group on Telemedicine has outlined the critical questions that the health professions need to work together to answer in the development of practice guidelines for the delivery of telehealth services (Arent-Fox, 1998; Joint Working Group on Telemedicine, 1998; NTIA, 1997). The time is ripe for developing and evaluating the use of practice guidelines in the delivery of telecommunication-mediated psychological services to persons with chronic disabilities and their families. Furthermore, we also need to create training materials for consumers of telehealth services. At the present time, the lay public has little guidance about how to purchase, install, and effectively use HB telecommunications services.

FINAL NOTE

As computer technologies, telecommunication networks, and health care systems continue to evolve, specific developments are difficult to predict. However, the convergence of these evolutions—coupled with increasing consumer demand and investor interests—have increased substantially the likelihood that telehealth practice and evaluation will become integral elements of health care systems. To take full advantage of these opportunities, psychologists need to become knowledgeable about the legislative, legal, marketplace, and consumer education forces that are driving the telehealth revolution and our changing health care system.

ACKNOWLEDGMENT

This chapter has been supported partially by grants from the National Institutes of Health, State of Florida Department of Elder Affairs and the Department of Veterans Affairs to the first author. The opinions expressed in this chapter are solely those of the authors and do not reflect the policies of the University of Florida or the American Psychological Association.

REFERENCES

Arent-Fox (1998). *Report of the Interdisciplinary Telehealth Standards Working Group*. Retrieved from http://www.arentfox.com/

Association of State and Provincial Psychology Boards (1998). *Model Act for the Practice of Psychology*. Mobile, AL: Author.

Ball, C. & McLaren, P. (1997). The tele-assessment of cognitive state: a review. *Journal of Telemedicine and Telecare*, **3**, 126–131.

Ball, C.J., McLaren, P.M., Summerfield, A.B., Lipsedge, M.S. & Watson, J.P. (1995). A comparison of communication modes in adult psychiatry. *Journal of Telemedicine and Telecare*, **1**, 22–26.

Ball, C.J., Scott, N., McLaren, P.M. & Watson, J.P. (1993). Preliminary evaluation of a Low-Cost VideoConferencing (LCVC) system for remote cognitive testing of adult psychiatric patients. *British Journal of Clinical Psychology*, **32**, 303–307.

Bergner, M., Bobbitt, R.A., Carter, W.B. & Gilson, B.S. (1981). The Sickness Impact Profile: development and final revision of a health status measure. *Medical Care*, **19**, 787–805.

Block, G., Clifford, C., Naughton, M.D., Henderson, M. & McAdams, M. (1989). A brief dietary screen for high fat intake. *Journal of Nutrition Education*, **21**, 199–207.

BPS (1999). *The Provision of Psychological Services via the Internet and Other Non-direct Means.* Professional Affairs Board of the British Psychological Society. Retrieved April 19, 2002, from http://www.bps.org.uk/documents/Online_therapy.pdf.

Cheung, S., Davies, R.F., Smith, K., Marsh, R., Sherrard, H. & Keon, W.J. (1998). The Ottawa telehealth project. *Telemedicine Journal*, **4**, 259–266.

Council on Competitiveness (1994). *Breaking Barriers to the National Information Infrastructure.* Washington, DC: Author.

Council on Competitiveness (1996). *Highway to Health: Transforming US Health Care in the Information Age.* Washington, DC: Author.

Darling, K.E.A. (2000). *Guide to Working in Europe for Doctors.* London: Churchill Livingstone.

DeLeon, P.H., Frank, R.G. & Wedding, D. (1995). Health psychology and public policy: the political press. *Health Psychology*, **14**, 493–499.

Deloitte & Touche (2000, February). *The Emerging European Health Telematics Industry: Market Analysis (Version 1.1).* European Commission Directorate General for the Information Society (p. 190). Retrieved April 19, 2002, from http://www.ehtel.org/

Derogatis, L.R., Lipman, R.S. & Covi, L. (1973, January). Symptom Checklist List-90: an outpatient psychiatric rating scale—preliminary report. *Psychopharmacology Bulletin*, **9**, 13–28.

Diabetes Control and Complications Trial Research Group (1988). Reliability and validity of a diabetes quality-of-life measure for the diabetes control and complications trial (DCCT). *Diabetes Care*, **11**, 725–732.

Dongier, M., Tempier, R., Lalinec-Michaud, M. & Meuneir, D. (1986). Telepsychiatry: psychiatric consultation through two-way television: a controlled study. *Canadian Journal of Psychiatry*, **31**, 32–34.

Duke University Center for the Study of Aging and Human Development (1978). *Multidimensional Functional Assessment: The OARS Methodology.* Durham, NC: Duke University.

EHTEL (2001). *Legal Aspects of Health Telematics. Green Paper 5.0.* European Health Telematics Association. Retrieved April 19, 2002, from http://www.ehtel.org/SHWebClass.asp?WCI= ShowDoc&DocId=3895

Elford, R., White, H., Bowering, R., Ghandi, A., Maddiggan, B., St John, K., House, M., Harnett, J., West, R. & Battcock, A. (2000). A randomized, controlled trial of child psychiatric assessments conducted using videoconferencing. *Journal of Telemedicine and Telecare*, **6**, 73–82.

Ensel, W. & Woelfel, M. (1986). Measuring the instrumental and expressive functions of social support. In N. Lin & A. Dean (Eds), *Social Support, Life Events, and Depression.* Orlando, FL: Academic Press.

Evans, R.L. & Jaureguy, B.M. (1982). Group therapy by phone: a cognitive behavioral program for visually impaired elderly. *Social Work in Health Care*, **7** (2), 79–90.

Evans, R.L., Fox, H.R., Pritzl, D.O. & Halar, E.M. (1984). Group treatment of physically disabled adults by telephone. *Social Work in Health Care*, **9** (3), 77–84.

Evans, R.L., Smith, K.M., Werkhoven, W.S., Fox, H.R. & Pritzl, D.O. (1986). Cognitive telephone group therapy with physically disabled elderly persons. *The Gerontologist*, **26** (1), 8–10.

Eysenbach, G. (Ed.) (1998). *Medicine and Medical Education in Europe: The Eurodoctor.* New York: Georg Thieme Verlag Stuttgart.

Flatley-Brennan, P. (1998). Computer network home care demonstration: a randomized trial in persons living with AIDS. *Computers in Biology and Medicine*, **28**, 489–508.

Follick, M.J., Gorkin, L., Smith, T.W. & Capone, R.J. (1988). Quality of life post-myocardial infarction: effects of a transtelephonic coronary intervention system. *Health Psychology*, **7**, 169–182.

Friedman, R.H., Kazis, L.E., Jette, A., Smith, M.B., Stollerman, J., Torgerson, J. & Carey, K. (1996). A telecommunications system for monitoring and counseling patients with hypertension: impact on medication adherence and blood pressure control. *American Journal of Hypertension*, **9**, 285–292.

General Accounting Office (1997). *Telemedicine: Federal Strategy is Needed to Guide Investments* (GAO Publication No. GAO/NCIAD/HEHS-97-67). Gaithersburg, MD: Author.

Geiger v. Jenkins 316 F. Supp. 370 (ND Ga., 1970), aff'd 401 US 985.

Glen, G.O., Lazar, S.G., Hornberger, J. & Spiegel, D. (1997). The economic impact of psychotherapy: a review. *American Journal of Psychiatry*, **154**, 147–155.

Glueckauf, R.L. (1990). Program evaluation guidelines for the rehabilitation professional. In M.G. Eisenberg & R.C. Grzesiak (Eds), *Advances in Clinical Rehabilitation* (vol. 3; pp. 250–266). New York: Springer.

Glueckauf, R.L. (2000). Doctoral education in rehabilitation and health care psychology: principles and strategies for unifying subspecialty training. In R.G. Frank & T.R. Elliott (Eds), *Handbook of Rehabilitation Psychology* (pp. 621–624). Washington, DC: American Psychological Association.

Glueckauf, R.L. (2001). The Family and Disability Assessment System. In J. Touliatos, B.F. Perlmutter & G.W. Holden (Eds), *Handbook of Family Measurement Techniques* (vol. 2). Newbury Park, CA: Sage.

Glueckauf, R.L., Whitton, J.D. & Nickelson, D.W. (2002). Telehealth: the new frontier in rehabilitation and health care. In M.J. Scherer (Ed.), *Assistive Technology: Matching Device and Consumer for Successful Rehabilitation* (pp. 197–213). Washington, DC: American Psychological Association.

Glueckauf, R.L., Fritz, S.P., Ecklund-Johnson, E.P., Liss, H.J., Dages, P. & Carney, P. (2002a). Videoconferencing-based family counseling for rural teenagers with epilepsy: Phase 1 findings. *Rehabilitation Psychology*, **47**, 8–30.

Glueckauf, R.L., Hufford, B., Whitton, J., Baxter, J., Schneider, P., Kain, J. & Vogelgesang, S. (1999). Telehealth: emerging technology in rehabilitation and health care. In M.G. Eisenberg, R.L. Glueckauf & H.H. Zaretsky (Eds), *Medical Aspects of Disability: A Handbook for the Rehabilitation Professional* (2nd edn, pp. 625–639). New York: Springer.

Glueckauf, R.L., Liss, H.J., McQuillen, D.E., Webb, P.M., Dairaghi, J. & Carter, C.B. (2002b). Therapeutic alliance in family therapy for adolescents with epilepsy: an exploratory study. *The American Journal of Family Therapy*, **30**, 125–139.

Glueckauf, R.L., Nickelson, D.W., Whitton, J. & Loomis, J.S. (in press). Telehealth and healthcare psychology: current developments in telecommunications, regulatory practices and research. In T. Boll, A. Baum & R.G. Frank (Eds), *Handbook of Clinical Health Psychology* (vol. 3). Washington, DC: American Psychological Association.

Glueckauf, R.L., Webb, P. , Papandria-Long, M., Rasmussen, J.L., Markand, O. & Farlow, M. (1992). The Family and Disability Assessment System: consistency and accuracy of judgments across coders and measures. *Rehabilitation Psychology*, **37**, 291–304.

Glueckauf, R.L., Whitton, J., Baxter, J., Kain, J., Vogelgesang, S., Hudson, M. et al. (1998a). Videocounseling for families of rural teens with epilepsy—project update. *TeleHealthNews*, **2** (2). Retrieved April 19, 2002, from http://www.telehealth.net/subscribe/newslettr_4a.html - 1

Glueckauf, R., Whitton, J., Kain, J., Vogelgesang, S., Hudson, M., Hufford, B. et al. (1998b). Home-based, videocounseling for families of rural teens with epilepsy: program rationale and objectives. *Telehealth News*, **2** (1), 3–5. Retrieved April 19, 2002, from http://www.telehealth.net/subscribe/newslettr_3.html

Granade, P. (1996). Implementing telemedicine on a national basis—a legal analysis of licensure issues. *Federation Bulletin*, **83**, 7–17.

Gray, J.E., Safran, C., Davis, R.B., Pompilio-Weitzner, G., Stewart, J.E., Zaccagnini, L. & Pursley, D. (2000). Baby CareLink: using the internet and telemedicine to improve care for high-risk infants. *Pediatrics*, **106** (6), 1318–1324.

Gresham, F.M. & Elliott, S.N. (1990). *Social Skills Rating System Manual*. Circle Pines, MN: American Guidance Service.

Grigsby, B. & Brown, N. (2000). *The 1999 ATSP Report on US Telemedicine Activity*. Portland, OR: Association of Telehealth Service Providers.

Gustafson, D.H., Hawkins, R., Boberg, E., Pingree, S., Serlin, R.E., Graziano, F. & Chan, C.L. (1999). Impact of a patient-centered, computer-based health information/support system. *American Journal of Preventive Medicine*, **16** (1), 1–9.

Gustafson, D.H., Wise, M., McTavish, F., Taylor, J.O., Wolberg, W., Stewart, J., Smalley, R.V. & Bosworth, K. (1993). Development and pilot evaluation of a computer-based support system for women with breast cancer. *Journal of Psychosocial Oncology*, **11** (4), 69–93.

Haas, L.J., Benedict, J.G. & Kobos, J.C. (1996). Psychotherapy by telephone: risks and benefits for psychologists and consumers. *Professional Psychology: Research and Practice*, **27**, 154–160.

H.B. 2953, 5th Leg. (1999).

HCFA (2002). *Medicaid and Telemedicine*. Health Care Financing Administration. Retrieved April 19, 2002, from http://www.hcfa.gov/medicaid/telemed.htm

Horvath, A.O. & Greenberg, L.S. (1989). Development and validation of the Working Alliance Inventory. *Journal of Counseling Psychology*, **36**, 223–233.

Howe, D. (1997). *Free On-line Dictionary of Computing*. Retrieved April 19, 2002, from http://wombat.doc.ic.ac.uk

H.R. 5661 Medicare, Medicaid and SCHIP Improvement Act of 2000. 106th Congress, 2nd session (2000).

Hubble, J.P., Pahwa, R., Michalek, D.K., Thomas, C. & Koller, W.C. (1993). Interactive video conferencing: a means of providing interim care to Parkinson's Disease patients. *Movement Disorders*, **8**, 380–382.

Jerome, L.W., DeLeon, P.H., James, L.C., Folen, R., Earles, J. & Gedney, J.J. (2000). The coming of age of telecommunications in psychological research and practice. *Professional Psychology: Research and Practice*, **55**, 407–421.

Johnston, B., Wheeler, L., Deuser, J. & Sousa, K.H. (2000). Outcomes of the Kaiser Permanente Tele-Home Health Research Project. *Archives of Family Medicine*, **9** (1), 40–45.

Joint Working Group on Telemedicine (1998, January 6). *Report of the Interdisciplinary Telehealth Standards Working Group*. Retrieved April 19, 2002, from http://telehealth.hrsa.gov/jwgt/jwgt.htm

Kristal, A.R., Shattuck, A.L. & Henry, H.J. (1990). Patterns of dietary behavior associated with selecting diets low in fat: reliability and validity of a behavioral approach to dietary assessment. *Journal of the American Dietetic Association*, **90**, 214–220.

Krupnick, J.L. & Pincus, H.A. (1992). The cost-effectiveness of psychotherapy: a plan for research. *American Journal of Psychiatry*, **149**, 1295–1305.

Liss, H.J., Glueckauf, R.L. & Ecklund-Johnson, E.P. (2002). Research on telehealth and chronic medical conditions: critical review, key issues and future directions. *Rehabilitation Psychology*, **47**, 8–30.

Mahone, D.F., Tarlow, B. & Sandaire, J. (1998). A computer-mediated intervention for Alzheimer's caregivers. *Computers in Nursing*, **16** (4), 208–216.

McKay, H.G., Glasgow, R.E., Feil, E.G., Boles, S.M. & Barrera, M.M. (2002). Internet-based diabetes self-management and support: initial outcomes from the Diabetes Network Project. *Rehabilitation Psychology*, **47**, 31–48.

Medicare, Medicaid, and SCHIP Improvement Act of 2000, HR 5661, 106th Cong., 2nd Sess. (2000).

Mittman, R. & Cain, M. (1999). *The Future of the Internet in Health Care: Five-Year Forecast*. California Health Care Foundation.

Nickelson, D.W. (1996). Behavioral telehealth: emerging practice, research and policy opportunities. *Behavioral Sciences and the Law*, **14**, 443–457.

Nickelson, D.W. (1997). Wired on capitol hill. In *Telemedicine Source Book: 1998* (pp. 99–104). New York: Faulkner & Gray, Inc.

Nickelson, D.W. (1998). Telehealth and the evolving health care system: strategic opportunities for professional psychology. *Professional Psychology: Research and Practice*, **29**, 527–535.

Nickelson, D.W. (2000). Telehealth, healthcare services and healthcare policy: a plan of action in the new millennium. *New Jersey Psychologist*, **50** (1), 24–27.

NTIA (1997, January 31). *Telemedicine Report to Congress*. National Telecommunications and Information Administration. Retrieved April 19, 2002, from http://www.ntia.doc.gov/reports/telemed/

Office for the Advancement of Telehealth (OAT) (1998). *Federal Telemedicine Directory*. Washington, DC: Author.

Office of Technology Assessment (1990). *Health Care in Rural America* (OTA-H-434). Washington, DC: US Government Printing Office.

Picker Institute (2000). Improving the quality of health care through the eyes of patients: surveys 2000. Retrieved April 19, 2002, from http://www.pickereurope.ac.uk/research/default.htm

Piette, J.D., Weinberger, M. & McPhee, S.J. (2000). The effect of automated calls with telephone nurse follow-up on patient centered outcomes of diabetes care: a randomized, controlled trial. *Medical Care*, **38**, 218–230.

Radloff, L.S. (1977). The Center for Epidemiological Studies-Depression (CES-D) Scale: a self-report depression scale for research in the general population. *Applied Psychological Measurement*, **1** (3), 385.

Reed, G.M., McLaughlin, C.J. & Milholland, K. (2000). Ten interdisciplinary principles for professional practice in telehealth: implications for psychology. *Professional Psychology: Research and Practice*, **31** (2), 170–178.

Saunders, G. & Courtney, J. (1985). A field study of the organizational factors influencing DDS success. *MIS Quarterly*, **9**, 77.

Scherer, M.J. (Ed.) (2002). *Assistive Technology: Matching Device and Consumer for Successful Rehabilitation*. Washington, DC: American Psychological Association.

Schopp, L., Johnstone, B. & Merrell, D. (2000). Telehealth and neuropsychological assessment new opportunities for psychologists. *Professional Psychology: Research and Practice*, **31**, 179–183.

Stein, L., Rothman, B. & Nakanishi, M. (1993). The telephone group: accessing group service to the homebound. *Social Work with Groups*, **16** (1–2), 203–215.

Stewart, A.L., Hays, R.D. & Ware, J.E. (1989). The MOS short-form general health survey: reliability and validity in a patient population. *Medical Care*, **26**, 724–735.

Taylor, C.B., Bandura, A., Ewart, C.K., Miller, N.H. & DeBusk, R.F. (1985). Exercise testing to enhance wives' confidence in their husbands' cardiac capability soon after clinically uncomplicated acute myocardial infarction. *American Journal of Cardiology*, **55** (6), 635–638.

Trott, P. & Blignault, I. (1998). Cost evaluation of a telepsychiatry service in northern Queensland. *Journal of Telemedicine and Telecare*, **4** (Suppl. 1), 66–68.

US Department of Commerce (1997). *Telemedicine Report to Congress*. Washington, DC: Author.

US Government Printing Office (1997). *Balanced Budget Act of 1997* (Pub. L. No. 105-33). Washington, DC: Author.

Veit, C.T. & Ware, J.E. (1993). The structure of psychological distress and well-being in general populations. *Journal of Consulting and Clinical Psychology*, **51**, 730–742.

Ware, J.E. & Sherbourne, C.D. (1992). The MOS 36-item short-form health survey (SF-36). *Medical Care*, **30**, 473–483.

Ware, J.E., Kosinski, M. & Keller, S.D. (1996). A 12-item short-form health survey: construction of scales and preliminary tests of reliability and validity. *Medical Care*, **34**, 220–233.

CHAPTER 27

The Relevance of Health Policy to the Future of Clinical Health Psychology

Robert G. Frank
University of Florida, USA
Janet E. Farmer
University of Missouri-Columbia, USA
and
Joshua C. Klapow
University of Alabama at Birmingham, USA

INTRODUCTION

The diversity of psychological science and practice has mirrored the rapid growth of the profession. Psychology is now incorporated into an astounding array of disciplines and topics. Psychology has been shaped by events within the sciences as well as social systems. So broad are the applications of psychology that any attempt to succinctly describe the boundaries or unify the panoply of interests affected by the discipline is likely to struggle. While the applications of psychology have expanded and defy simple description, the professional skills inherent to training in the discipline are easier to describe. Fundamental to all psychology-training programs is an emphasis upon rigorous training in the scientific method, the development of critical thinking skills including the ability to analyze problems and develop response alternatives, and the ability to present succinct options. As a discipline, psychology tends to draw individuals with strong verbal and writing skills. Analytic ability, both verbally and non-verbally mediated, is a fundamental skill. Training in methodology and statistics is also fundamental. Consequently, many psychologists are proficient in an array of statistical procedures ranging from single subject to small sample non-parametric analyses to the analysis of large data sets.

These skills are necessary for the practice of psychology as defined by the scientist-practitioner model (Stone, 1983). The intellectual skills common among individuals attracted to psychology, and the skills acquired in training in the scientist-practitioner model,

Handbook of Clinical Health Psychology. Edited by S. Llewelyn and P. Kennedy.
© 2003 John Wiley & Sons, Ltd.

are also useful in an array of other disciplines. In this chapter we propose that training in clinical health psychology can provide an effective platform facilitating the development of skills and knowledge in the analysis of health policy.

The delivery of health services has become a global industry. World wide, health care accounts for a surprising portion of the world's economy. More than 23 of every 1000 employed individuals work in the health sector (Reinhardt, Hussey & Anderson, 2002). In the health database of the Organization for Economic Cooperation and Development (OECD), almost 8% of the gross domestic product of participating countries is spent on health services.

Reinhardt, Hussey and Anderson (2002, p. 169) noted:

> Increasingly health care and health policy have become global enterprises for they respond to a common set of human problems and with the aid of modern information technology, rely on a globally shared body of clinical and health services research.

Health policy has grown to encompass a range of human problems from poverty to medical compliance. As frequently noted in the psychology literature, many of these problems have psychological underpinnings (e.g., Orleans, Ulmer & Gruman, in press). Despite the magnitude of the health economy, psychologists have not routinely viewed health policy as germane to the field. While there is increasing recognition that psychology is a health specialty, this recognition has often been applied only to the clinical aspects of the field. In this chapter we argue that psychologists have the requisite skills to participate in health policy. In addition, we will show that international trends in health policy—emphasizing a shift away from "acute" health systems, efforts to eliminate or reduce health system fragmentation, alignment of different health care system sectors, and emphasis upon coordinated, integrated health systems—are integral to training in psychology (WHO, 2002). Psychologists have not, however, recognized the contributions they are prepared to make to health policy and health services research.

This chapter considers international and national issues affecting psychology and the development and implementation of health policy. We start with consideration of what defines health policy. Next, we review the most pressing health issues and the changing health care utilization patterns that will affect these issues. We then consider if psychology can offer any insight into these issues. Next, we turn to the evolution of psychology and consider if the natural direction of the field will intersect with health policy. We conclude with consideration of future opportunities for psychology in the area of health policy.

HEALTH POLICY

Frank and Callen (1996, p. 23) stated that

> Public policy refers to the total of all laws, regulations, court rulings, and administrative procedures that guided this nation in solving socially agreed upon problems. Subgroupings of public policy might include educational policy, welfare policy, defense policy, economic policy.

Over the last 50 years health policy has become increasingly important. As will be discussed below, the ascendance of health policy reflects the ever-increasing economic power of the sector. The importance of health policy reflects more than the impact of the economics. As life expectancy has increased secondary to improvements in the diagnosis, treatment, and prevention of disease, the definition of health has broadened. Health now encompasses human biology, brain and body functioning. Health includes "the human mind, its thoughts and feelings, human actions and behavior as well as the nature of social ties, friendships, family and community life" (Singer & Ryff, 2001). Although less recognized, behavioral factors contribute significantly to mortality. In the USA, for example, it has been estimated that behavioral and environmental factors account for 50% of all US mortality. Although the contribution of psychology to illness and good health is only poorly understood, there is widespread recognition that the discipline has essential contributions to understanding the multifaceted relationships (Singer & Ryff, 2001). The broadened definition of health resulting in the integration of psychology has occurred as economic resources devoted to health have increased. We next examine the relevance of increased health spending to the importance of health policy.

INTERNATIONAL HEALTH SPENDING

The USA leads the world in health care spending, with $4358 per capita. Switzerland spends 33% less ($2853 per capita), followed closely by Luxembourg ($2543), Canada ($2463) and Germany ($2361) (Reinhardt et al., 2002). Overall, national spending ranges from a low of 5.3% of the gross domestic product (GDP) to a high of 12.9% in the USA. For all countries, national health care spending is associated with per capita GDP, which serves as a proxy for the "ability to purchase". When GDP is considered and the cost of local goods are included, a 1990 microanalyses found that Americans used slightly less health care (hospital days, physician visits, drugs, etc.) than German counterparts. The primary issue for health care spending is not the overall growth of health care spending, but the willingness of consumers to sacrifice goods and services for higher health care costs. If, however, the USA spent comparable per capita amounts as the second most expensive country, US health care spending would have declined by $400 billion in 1998 (Anderson & Hussey, 2001). Most comparisons of health care spending have focused on national health care spending as a proxy measure describing the quality of national health care systems. Such comparisons, though common, yield relatively little information regarding the quality of national health care systems at the national or consumer level. The long asked question "which country has the best health care system?" is not answered by simple summaries of national health care spending. Instead, more narrowly focused questions on particular facets of the health care system are more informative—for example, payment methods, gatekeeping on health care spending and outcomes.

   Overall, comparisons of health care spending have found that as countries become wealthier and spend more on health care, the citizens become healthier. Wealthier countries tend to be healthier. Increases in health care spending, and health outcomes, have occurred as governments have become more involved in health policy. During the last century spectacular improvements in health outcomes have occurred as governments became more involved in health (Feachem, 2001).

ROLE OF GOVERNMENT

The government's role, both in the direct public financing of health care and through economic programs that increase national wealth, demonstrates the centrality of that entity in determining health policy (see Feachem, 2001, for more detail on the ideas described in this section). Government assumes the central role in the determination of national health policy. Government directly or indirectly affects health policy through regulation of health financing systems, including health insurance markets or payment systems that subsidize payments for the poor.

Government oversees the level of annual expenditure. It is generally recognized that spending must exceed 5–7% of the GDP to achieve a viable health care system. As noted earlier, there is considerable variation in national health care spending levels. Governments can increase spending through central mechanisms or direct others to spend more through private or semi-private markets (Feachem, 2001). Governments can develop policies designed to minimize health expenditures by establishing spending caps for health spending or decreasing incentives that encourage spending.

In less-developed countries, individuals pay for health services out-of-pocket. Thus, the risk pool, or number of individuals who share the costs of health care, is small and includes the individual, his or her family and occasionally the village unit. As countries develop, they tend to develop more advanced risk pools or nationalized payment systems that alleviate individual payment burdens. Larger risk pools provide more protection and lessen financial risk to the individual. Nationalized health systems such as Great Britain or Canada constitute large risk pools.

Creation of risk pools can lead to organized health insurance markets. Whether privatized, as is the case in the USA, or hybridized, as in Germany, health insurance products can create larger risk pools. At the same time, insurance markets can be manipulated to allow sicker or healthier groups to be aggregated in ways that are counter-productive. For example, if healthier individuals are included in one health plan, costs will be reduced. In contrast, if less healthy individuals can be identified and excluded through adverse selection, the plan saves money. Consumers can also manipulate the insurance market through "moral hazard" in which consumers or providers chose insurance products because they recognize that additional benefits will be available.

Governments must address the role of subsidies for the poor. They can provide undirected subsidies for all citizens, including the poor. Alternatively, they can target certain individuals, such as the poor and near poor. Government can target locales where citizens with special needs reside. Last, government can designate certain populations, such as individuals suffering from specified conditions, as targets for coverage.

In addition to supporting access to health services, most governments sponsor the delivery of health services. Government activity in health services can range from direct sponsorship of services, as occurs in Canada, to management, through laws and regulations of the health care systems.

INTERNATIONAL ISSUES IN HEALTH POLICY

All nations encounter similar problems providing health care to their citizens. Common to all health policy conversations are considerations of how to finance health care, how to assure access to health care, quality of health care and the dissemination of new technology.

While the USA spends more on health services than any other nation and has uniquely failed to provide routine access to health services, the dimensions of the challenges faced by the USA do not differ greatly from the other highly developed nations.

In the USA, the vast majority of health expenditures provide services to a small number of persons. For example, health services to individuals with mood disorder, diabetes, heart disease, hypertension, and asthma cost $62.3 billion in 1996. When total spending for individuals with one or more of these conditions is considered, it accounted for 49% of all spending documented in the 1996 Medical Expenditure Survey. Only one-quarter of this amount was spent on direct treatment of the conditions. The majority of spending was directed to coexistent conditions (Druss et al., 2001).

The high cost of chronic illness impacts all developed nations. Unfortunately, developing nations are emulating the lifestyles of the richer nations. Consequently, the globalization of the world's economy includes the transmission of deadly health behaviors. For example, four million people die from smoking-related causes each year. It is estimated that this number will increase to ten million by 2020, making tobacco the leading cause of death throughout the world (Frenk & Gómez-Dantés, 2002).

ROLE OF PSYCHOLOGY IN NATIONAL HEALTH OUTCOMES

The daily manifestations of psychology in the form of health behaviors have increasingly been recognized to be a major determinant of national health outcomes. Health-affecting behaviors such as smoking, substance abuse, sedentary lifestyle, and risky sexual behaviors are linked to the most pressing health problems. In the USA, these links have been recognized in the latest national health objectives established by the Surgeon General in *Healthy People 2010*.

Understanding of how to modify health behaviors has improved dramatically over the last 20 years. Starting with Bandura's Social Learning Model and progressing to Prochaska's Stages of Change Model, the factors that lead to maintained change are now better understood (Bandura, 1986; Prochaska & DiClemente, 1983). The importance of prevention and the effectiveness of prevention models are increasingly appreciated. These prevention models are best applied in population-based interventions.

During the last two decades, clinical health psychologists have recognized the limitations of focusing exclusively on individual interventions. Individualized interventions to modify health behaviors are costly and are, by definition, limited to the individual, or possibly a small group. Intervention sites are limited to professional medical or psychological clinics. In contrast, community interventions, utilizing a model akin to the public health perspective, have the potential for greater reach and higher cost-effectiveness (Schneiderman & Speers, 2001). Such interventions can be provided in worksites, communities, and primary care settings. Often these interventions can target high-risk groups who may not be ready to engage actively in health behavior change (Lichtenstein & Glasgow, 1992; Orleans, Ulmer & Gruman, in press).

In the next two sections, we discuss two roles that psychologists can take to advance the quality of health outcomes and influence health policy: (1) evaluation of health outcomes and (2) improving health outcomes, particularly through large-scale public health interventions.

PSYCHOLOGY AND HEALTH OUTCOMES RESEARCH

While it is clear that behavior is a primary determinant of health status, the evaluation of health outcomes presents a formidable challenge for clinicians, researchers and policy-makers. The process of defining, quantifying and evaluating health outcomes offers an important opportunity for clinical heath psychology.

Health outcome has typically referred to the endpoint of a health service that accounts for patient experiences, preferences and values (Clancy & Eisenberg, 1998). Donabedian (1966) referred to outcome as "A change in patients' current and future health status that can be attributed to antecedent health care". While it is convention to consider an outcome as the endpoint of a particular intervention or service, outcome may also refer to an endpoint of any number of factors, including disease progression, environmental changes or psychological processes (Klapow et al., 1993). In the end, outcomes measurement within a health care context functions to provide empirical evidence for decisions made by all those involved in the health care setting (Clancy & Eisenberg, 1998).

In order to measure health outcomes, there must be some consensus on the definition of health and illness. Different definitions emphasize related, but divergent, concepts. Some terms used to describe health are positive concepts, such as wellness or normality. Other definitions emphasize negative concepts, such as disability and illness. Much of the debate has centered on whether health is a continuum. Are disability and illness distinct from health, or are they opposite ends of the same continuum (Patrick & Erickson, 1993)?

Because the concept of health lacked conceptual clarity, the World Health Organization (WHO) proposed a comprehensive definition of health in 1948 in their charter document. Health was defined as, ". . . a state of complete physical, mental, and social well-being and not merely the absence of infirmity". In the 50 years since the introduction of this definition, there has been some convergence of thought. It is now widely recognized that health has multiple dimensions. Further, it is now accepted that measures of mortality alone cannot summarize the health status of populations (Field & Gold, 1998). However, there is still considerable debate about what constitutes health and health status when measuring health outcomes.

From the medical perspective, people are healthy if they are free of disease. A disease is recognized in a human organism through the manifestation of clinical signs and symptoms. These signs and symptoms are associated with underlying lesions or pathology. Diagnostic tests are used to identify pathology and interventions are designed to repair the lesion or stop the pathological process. Thus underlying pathology is the ultimate target of assessment and treatment. The traditional biomedical model is predicated on finding a specific biologic problem and repairing the problem (Klapow, Kaplan & Doctor, 2000).

A patient-centered outcomes model of health is defined from the patient's perspective, and measurement of health outcome is focused on those endpoints that have direct meaning to the patient. Typically these outcomes include two broad categories: length of life and quality of life. In an outcomes model of health, biochemical measures do not have meaning as endpoints in and of themselves; rather, they are important to the extent that they are associated with length and quality of life (Klapow, Kaplan & Doctor, 2000).

Nearly all definitions of health recognize that health is multidimensional. Spilker (1996) argued that there are five major domains of life quality: (1) physical status and functional abilities; (2) psychological status and well-being; (3) social interactions; (4) economic and/or vocational status and factors; and (5) religious and/or spiritual status. Various approaches to the measurement of health outcome typically attempt to assess different dimensions, although the exact dimensions vary considerably.

An emerging consensus suggests that the concept of "health" must integrate the concept of mortality with multiple dimensions of life quality. By themselves, measures of mortality and morbidity are incomplete indicators of health. Combined indices of morbidity and mortality may more accurately represent the level of wellness. In most attempts to define health, the measurable components include behavioral functioning and both physical and mental symptoms. Symptoms might be pain, cough, anxiety, or depressed mood. Physical functioning is usually measured in terms of limitations in ambulating, or disruptions in functioning due to restrictions of mobility, confinement to home, or bed. Social functioning might be represented by limitations in performance of usual social role; and this would include attendance at school, ability to work, or participation in recreational activities. The concept of health-related quality of life usually attaches value to combinations of these attributes (Erickson, Wilson & Shannon, 1995; Patrick & Erickson, 1993). Health-related quality-of-life measures are now common in clinical trials, epidemiological studies, and other clinical investigations (Spilker, 1996). Many different compendia of quality-of-life measures are now available (e.g., Schumaker & Berzon, 1995; Spilker, 1996; Walker & Rosser, 1993).

The challenges associated with evaluating such concepts as health status and health-related quality of life lend themselves to the skills and training of clinical health psychologists. The process of defining and operationalizing a construct (e.g., health, anger, pain hostility), quantifying it through instrument development, validating the instrument to assure both reliability and accuracy in measurement, and interpreting data obtained from such an instrument is common practice (Klapow, Kaplan & Doctor, 2000). Unfortunately, the field of clinical health psychology has played a relatively limited role in this area of inquiry. By applying their unique combination of expertise in psychometric theory and behavioral science, psychologists can improve the evaluation of health outcomes and facilitate the process of health care decision-making. The results from quality health outcomes measures will also inform health policy-makers and contribute to the development of effective health policy.

PSYCHOLOGY AND THE PUBLIC HEALTH MODEL

Most psychologists work in small practices, clinics or hospitals. In these settings, clinical care focuses upon individuals who manifest problems requiring immediate attention. Treatment of these conditions requires relatively significant effort and cost. The reach and impact of clinical interventions is less than broadly based programs that target non-symptomatic individuals in the population at large. The conditions treated in individual or small group treatments tend to be more advanced than cases that have not met the threshold for treatment that may exist among the larger population. Broader community interventions may address less-developed conditions, preventing the need for individual treatment with associated higher costs and difficulty (see Tucker et al., in press). Interventions aimed at larger populations have typically been viewed as falling within the realm of public health.

In the public health venue, interventions are generally provided in non-specialty settings by trained non-professionals. Interventions are not dependent upon personal contact and may utilize a variety of modalities including advertising, the phone, Internet, and large groups. Interventions delivered in this manner tend to cost less, but are less effective than individual interventions (Tucker et al., in press). These large-scale interventions frequently rely upon psychological models, but rarely utilize psychologists in their design or implementation. Over the last two decades the new subspecialty of behavioral epidemiology has developed. Behavioral epidemiology is dedicated to the study of behavioral determinants of disease (Tucker et al., in press). Behavioral epidemiology provides a link between large population studies and the individual study characteristic of psychology.

More evidence for the importance of this link is provided by emergence of chronic conditions as a significant health threat (Frank, Hagglund & Farmer, in press; Tucker et al., in press). Chronic conditions include chronic diseases and impairments that involve recurrent exacerbations and risk of long-term limitations and disabilities (Frank, Hagglund & Farmer, in press). "Chronic conditions, defined as illnesses that last longer than 3 months and are not self-limiting, are now the leading cause of disability and death (in the United States)" (Institute of Medicine, 2001, p. 27). More than half the population of the USA is affected by chronic health conditions, yet the American health care system, and the health care systems of most other countries, are designed to treat acute illnesses (Institute of Medicine, 2001). Many of the chronic conditions are co-morbid. In the USA, 44% of those with chronic conditions have more than one condition.

Chronic conditions require a new approach to health delivery. Patients will become more "consumer" like in their approach to health services, seeking information through new channels such as the Internet (Frank, Hagglund & Farmer, in press). Consumer exchange of information and knowledge will enhance their role in the development of new interventions and the dissemination of research findings. Health care delivery systems will become less medically driven, using team models focusing on the primary or "cardinal symptoms" that patients experience as most debilitating (Frank, Hagglund & Farmer, in press). Because of its focus on consumer needs and integrated service delivery teams, the cardinal symptom model of care will bridge current approaches to primary care with specialty models focusing on single systems (e.g., cardiac hospitals). More coordinated care, sensitive to the patient's perceptions of disabling symptoms and the contributions of co-morbid conditions, will result from these changes in the delivery and structure of health care systems.

Recently, the World Health Organization (WHO, 2002) focused on the threat of chronic health conditions to the world's population. WHO (2002) noted:

> Growing evidence from around the world suggests that when patients receive effective treatments, self-management support and regular follow-up, they do better. Evidence also suggests that organized systems of care, not just individual health care workers, are essential in producing positive outcomes.

The WHO report also suggests that the most pressing health problems, manifested in chronic conditions, require extended and regular health contact (see also Frank, Hagglund & Farmer, in press).

The WHO report also states that health policy is made within a political context. Political leaders, community members, and health care leaders all influence decisions. Changing the acute-care-driven health systems that characterize the delivery systems for most nations requires recognition of the need to influence political and health care systems. As noted by the WHO report, "for transformation toward care for chronic conditions to be successful, it is crucial to initiate bi-directional information sharing and to build consensus and political commitment among stakeholders at each stage" (WHO, 2002). Other issues addressed by the WHO report include:

- The need to reduce fragmentation in acute health care systems (see also Frank, Hagglund & Farmer, in press), and increase integration between sectors such as child labor laws, agriculture, education and health care financing.
- Development of health teams using evidence-based models that focus on managing chronic health conditions.

- Increasing emphasis upon the role of patients in the self-management of their conditions, focusing upon the patient and family in active disease management.
- Health care must extend beyond clinics into communities.
- Prevention is essential to the management of chronic conditions including patient and community education.

Challenges associated with understanding, describing and treating chronic health conditions provide clinical health psychologists with an important avenue by which to utilize the public health model and influence the development of national health policy. Throughout the world, the cost of treating chronic health conditions threatens each nation's ability to provide health services. Chronic health conditions evolve through multiple pathways including genetic, biological and behavioral factors. Some of these risk factors, such as genetic and demographic factors, are not currently modifiable. Other risk factors, such as medical predictors like hypertension, can be modified through a combination of pharmacological interventions mediated by behavioral factors. Most chronic conditions straddle behavioral risk factors mediated by lifestyle choices: dieting, smoking, inactivity, mood, personality style, and social support can all modify the course and outcome of chronic conditions (Tucker et al., in press). Psychologists have the knowledge and skills to understand, describe and predict the relationships among these factors, to design individual treatments and large-scale preventive interventions, to assess the impact of such interventions on health outcomes, and to utilize these data to drive national and international health policies.

POLICY AND THE TRANSLATION OF PSYCHOLOGICAL SCIENCE

National health policy is derived from the interaction between analyses of research, the exchange of information and the consequent development of informed decisions regarding the best course of action given the perceived benefits and costs of the options. More simply put, "policy analysis is client-oriented advice relevant to public decisions and informed by social values" (Weimer & Vining, 1999, p. 27). Policy analyses differ from academic research. In the academy, research is directed to developing theoretical or empirical models aimed at establishing scientific truths. The process utilizes rigorous experimental and statistical methods and is designed to resist time pressures and proceed at a pace enhancing confidence in the outcome and conclusions. Immediate applicability of the information is of little concern; the focus is instead on answering the question: "What do we know?"

Policy research, in contrast, focuses on factors that can be modified through public policy. The product of the analyses is directed toward individuals creating policy in answer to the primary question: "What should we do?" Experimental methods and measurement recognizes the demand for information. Compromises in experimental design may yield "quick and dirty" studies with known threats to validity or reliability. Data for policy studies is often drawn from huge samples with less control in the integrity of the data; missing data is a common problem. Analyses tend to focus on independent variables such as the structure of health care financing or the organization of health service delivery systems, in contrast to psychology's focus on dependent measures. The value of policy studies is the ability to translate the findings into effective policy. Findings that have no translation applications are of much less value.

All psychologists, regardless of area of expertise, share common skills and knowledge. Training at the doctoral level provides psychologists with the ability to critically analyze information and interpret the findings while appreciating the limitations of the conclusions. These skills are fundamental to training at the doctoral level and are also essential to effective translation of research into policy.

Much of the work of government, particularly in the area of health, focuses on behavioral issues. For example, how will changes in payment affect professional behaviors, such as the quality or geographical availability of the services provided? Or how should health care delivery systems be organized to encourage consumers to use primary care services? How do we create comprehensive health services for all aspects of human functioning? Many psychologists have not considered these issues. Yet, a small, consistently increasing number of psychologists recognize the importance of pairing large-scale interventions and outcome measurement skills with the traditional emphasis of psychology upon the individual. There is also an increasing appreciation of the need to analyze current health policies, evaluate the impact on consumers, and translate findings into more effective health policy and practice. Perusal of the faculty roles of schools of public health reveals a surprising number of psychologists. In a similar vein, were a single source available to describe the education of individuals in health services research and policy positions, again, a surprising number of psychologists would be evident. These individuals have utilized their training in psychology programs to establish successful careers in health policy and health services research. Because these areas are not seen as germane to psychology, most of these individuals have little contact with organized psychology or education programs, preventing recognition of the applicability of their training to practice in health policy and health services research.

TRAINING HEALTH PSYCHOLOGISTS

The delivery of health care services is a complex and dynamic process. As illustrated in the WHO report, *Innovative Care for Chronic Conditions: Building Blocks for Action* (2002), health care systems can be divided into three levels (see Figure 27.1). The micro level of

Figure 27.1 The three levels of health care systems

health care represents services that involve direct patient interaction; for clinical health psychologists, this is the foundation of our training. The meso level represents the organization of health care services and the associations with community resources. The macro level represents policies that create the parameters within which health care organizations, communities, and providers function. As noted in the WHO report, the delineation between these levels is not always clear. However, when health care policies, organizations, communities and interventions align, the quality of health care services is likely to improve. As a profession comprising behavioral scientists, clinical health psychology is potentially capable of functioning at any of these levels; however, current training models can be enhanced by offering the necessary expertise at the meso and macro levels.

Preparing clinical health psychologists to work across the dimensions of the health care system necessitates several conceptual shifts in current training programs. Training programs have been understandably hesitant about requiring more coursework and expanding the core curriculum (Elliott & Klapow, 1997). However, failure to provide psychologists with these skills will tend to limit clinical health psychology to the micro level within health care systems.

At the foundation of health psychology is rigorous training, the scientific method, research methodology, statistics, psychometric theory, personality theory, learning theory, and behavior change interventions. These skills are unfortunately applied primarily at the micro level of the health care system. A general training model which focuses on a blend of these core skills applied across the levels of the health care system may enable trainees to learn how to apply basic skills in a dynamic system and remain current with whatever the market forces happen to be (Elliott & Klapow, 1997).

TRAINING MODELS

While it is necessary for clinical health psychologists to have an understanding of the health care system from the micro to macro levels, the mode of training can take several forms. Integration of coursework and areas of concentration into doctoral training programs, continuing education opportunities, and additional post-graduate degrees are all possible depending on the depth of understanding desired.

The possibilities for content are virtually endless when considering the study of the health care system. There are several core content areas necessary for a basic level of expertise. While not exhaustive, these content areas may include: Health Economics, Health Insurance, Health Policy, Quality Improvement, Program Evaluation, Patient Based Outcomes Evaluation, Cost-Effectiveness Analysis, Design and Evaluation of Clinical Trials. It is important to note that these content areas are in addition to the foundation of training clinical health psychologists receive. Thus it is assumed that a clinical health psychologist who explores these content areas has requisite skills in statistics, psychometric theory, instrument development and validation, and research methods. With a clinical health psychology foundation and these additional content areas, an individual is poised to pursue opportunities across the spectrum of health care. As stated earlier, without knowledge in these content areas, clinical health psychologists are more limited in their ability to work within the meso (health care organization) or macro (health policy) levels.

One example of a program to prepare psychologists to work at the meso and macro levels of health care has been developed in the USA at the University of Alabama at Birmingham

(UAB). UAB is a large urban institute offering undergraduate, graduate and professional degrees. Among the variety of schools, departments and centers are the School of Social and Behavioral Sciences, the School of Public Health, and the School of Medicine. These three schools provide several opportunities for psychologists to gain expertise in health services and outcomes research, at the pre-doctoral, post-doctoral and professional levels.

The joint PhD/Masters in Public Health (MSPH) in Medical Clinical Psychology and Health Outcomes and Policy Research is the most comprehensive program. This program was designed specifically to provide psychology doctoral trainees with coursework and re-search experiences in outcomes and policy research that complement their existing training. Students enrolling in this program complete basic coursework in clinical health psychology and then are permitted to enroll in the Outcomes and Policy Research MSPH program in the School of Public Health. The curriculum for the program is presented in Table 27.1. Students complete the core content areas and two elective courses. The elective course choices enable students to concentrate efforts in health policy, advanced analytics, or clin-ical outcome evaluation. Because of their foundation of skills in statistics and research design, the biostatistics requirements are waived. Upon completion of coursework, students conduct an independent research project under the mentorship of School of Public Health faculty. The program is typically completed in one year and thus adds an additional year to their doctoral training (see Table 27.1).

For those who have already completed a PhD, the UAB Center for Outcomes and Effectiveness Research and Education (COERE) post-doctoral fellowship is a one- to two-year training program that provides research experiences in outcomes and health services research. During the fellowship, psychologists are exposed to a wide variety of outcomes and health services research projects. While the content of the projects varies from year to year, they all address core Outcomes and Health Services Research topics such as: quality improvement, cost-effectiveness analyses, patient-centered outcome evaluation, program evaluation, and clinical trials. Fellows attend weekly research discussion groups and jour-nal clubs, attend health services methods workshops, and have the opportunity to enroll in the

Table 27.1   Required courses for the coordinated Master of Science of Public Health (MSPH) and Doctor of Philosophy in Psychology

MSPH Core	Approved Electives
Biostatistics I: 3 hours	Regression Analysis
Biostatistics II: 3 hours	Health Program Evaluation
Principles of Epidemiologic Research: 4 hours	Applied Logistic Regression
Principles of Epidemiologic Research Lab	Clinical Trials and Survival Analysis
Outcomes Research	Survey Research Methods
Design of Clinical Trials	Public Health Policy
Health Economics	Public Health Law
Patient Based Outcomes Measurement	Improving Health Care Quality Outcomes
Social and Ethical Issues in Public Health	Aging Policy
Health Insurance and Managed Care	Policy Analysis: Modeling and Simulation
Cost-Effectiveness Analysis for Public Health and Medicine	Special Problems in Policy Analysis
Decision Analysis for Public Health and Medicine	Research Experience
	Master's-Level Research Project

courses listed above. The COERE fellowship further affords psychologists the opportunity to collaborate with other fellows from a diverse training background, including medicine, economics, and health administration. Psychology fellows are jointly supervised by the Center directors and by a clinical psychologist who serves as a division director within the COERE.

While comprehensive health services and outcomes training programs may not be available at some academic institutions or feasible for all clinical health psychologists, it is useful for clinical health psychologists with an interest in these fields to gain some level of understanding in the core content areas that are essential for working within the macro (health policy) and meso (health care organization) levels of health care. Individual courses, independent reading, and continuing education seminars are all possible avenues for exposure to these content areas. In addition, acquiring knowledge of health policy and the political environment has gained salience among psychologists through fellowships aimed at introducing psychologists to national governance. In the USA, the Robert Wood Johnson Foundation sponsors a health policy fellowship in which psychologists have learned about and participated in national health policy. Programs are also offered by the American Psychological Association and the Public Health Service in the US Department of Health and Human Services (DeLeon et al., in press).

SUMMARY

Clinical health psychology and, to a large degree, clinical psychology have focused upon individual interventions. The results of more than three decades of involvement in the interaction between health care issues and psychological factors have yielded a large body of research and practice whose influence goes much beyond the discipline. At the same time, within psychology there are a number of efforts to develop new knowledge and interventions that coincide with demands encountered by evolving health systems throughout the world. Foremost among these demands is the need to effectively treat and prevent chronic health conditions. With few exceptions, these long-term health conditions provide the greatest threats to world health. Few nations have been able to wean their delivery systems from the focus upon acute health threats.

Recognition of the subtle change of those utilizing health care services from passive patients to active consumers is fundamental to the changing health care paradigm. These consumers will use knowledge derived from multiple sources to become active participants in their health care treatment. The development of new models of health care using coordinated teams providing services and education is fundamental to this new paradigm. These teams will rely less upon single leaders such as physicians and more upon an array of individuals with many levels of training. Fundamental to this model will be an emphasis upon evidence-based practice. Increased emphasis upon prevention will also be important.

Psychologists possess many skills relevant to the needs of these emerging international systems. Traditional emphasis within the discipline upon individual interventions and research models must be augmented by education on large-scale samples and interventions common to public health models. With such enhanced training, psychologists will be prepared to become full partners in the shaping of health care policy and practice.

REFERENCES

Anderson, G. & Hussey, P.S. (2001). Comparing health system performance in OECD countries. *Health Affairs*, **20** (3), 219–232.

Bandura, A. (1986). *Social Foundations of Thought and Action: A Social Cognitive Theory.* Washington, DC: American Psychological Association.

Clancy, C.M. & Eisenberg, J.M. (1998). Outcomes research: measuring the end results of health care. *Science*, **282**, 245–236.

DeLeon, P.H., Hagglund, K.J., Ragusea, S.A. & Sammons, M. (in press). Expanding roles for psychologists: the 21st century. In I.B. Weiner, G. Stricker & T.A. Widiger (Eds), *Clinical Psychology: Vol. 8: Comprehensive Handbook of Psychology* (edn, pp. 00). New York: John Wiley & Sons.

Donabedian, A. (1966). Evaluating the quality of medical care. *Milbank Memorial Fund Quarterly*, **44**, 166–206.

Druss, B.G., Marcus, S.C., Olfson, M., Tanielian, T., Elinson, L. & Pincus, H.A. (2001). Comparing the national economic burden of five chronic conditions. *Health Affairs*, **20** (6), 233–241.

Elliott, T.E. & Klapow, J.C. (1997). Training psychologists for a future in evolving health care delivery systems: building a better Boulder model. *Journal of Clinical Psychology in Medical Settings*, **4**, 255–269.

Erickson, P., Wilson, R. & Shannon, I. (1995). *Years of Health Life. Healthy People 2000*. Statistical Notes Number 7. USDHHS, Public Health Service, Centers for Disease Control and Prevention, NCHS, April.

Feachem, R.G.A. (2001). The role of governments. In C.E. Koop, C.E. Pearson & M.R. Schwarz (Eds), *Critical Issues in Global Health*. San Francisco, CA: Jossey-Bass.

Field, M.J. & Gold, M.R. (1998). *Summarizing Population Health*. Washington, DC: Institute of Medicine.

Frank, R.G. & Callan, J.E. (1996). Public policy—a process with a purpose. In R.P. Lorion, I. Iscoe, P.H. DeLeon & G.R. Vandenbos (Eds), *Psychology and Public Policy: Balancing Public Service and Professional Need*. Washington, DC: American Psychological Association.

Frank, R.G., Hagglund, K.J. & Farmer, J. (in press). Chronic illness management in primary care: cardinal symptom model. In R.G. Frank, S. McDaniel, J. Bray & M. Heldring (Eds), *Primary Care Psychology*. Washington, DC: American Psychological Association.

Frenk, J. & Gómez-Dantés, O. (2002). Globalisation and the challenges to health systems. *Health Affairs*, **21** (3), 160–165.

Institute of Medicine (2001). Crossing the quality chasm: a new health system for the 21st century. *Institute of Medicine Committee on Quality Health Care in America*. Washington, DC: National Academy Press.

Klapow, J.C., Kaplan, R. & Doctor, J. (2000). *Outcomes Measurement: The Role of Health Psychology*. Under editorial review for T. Boll (Ed.), *Health and Behavior Handbook*. Washington, DC: American Psychological Association.

Klapow, J.C., Slater, M.A., Patterson, T., Atkinson, J.H., Doctor, J.N. & Garfin, S. (1993). An empirical evaluation of multidimensional clinical outcome in chronic low back pain patients. *Pain*, **55**, 107–118.

Lichtenstein, E. & Glasgow, R.E. (1992). Smoking cessation: what have we learned over the past decade? *Journal of Consulting and Clinical Psychology*, **60** (4), 518–527.

Orleans, C.T., Ulmer, C. & Gruman, J. (in press). The role of behavioral factors in achieving national health outcomes. In R.G. Frank, A. Baum & J. Wallender (Eds), *Models and Perspectives in Health Psychology*. Washington, DC: American Psychological Association.

Patrick, D.L. & Erickson, P. (1993). *Health Status and Health Policy: Allocating Resources to Health Care*. New York: Oxford University Press.

Prochaska, J.O. & DiClemente, C.C. (1983). Stages and processes in self-change in smoking: towards an integrative model of change. *Journal of Consulting and Clinical Psychology*, **51**, 390–395.

Reinhardt, U.E., Hussey, P.S. & Anderson, G.F. (2002). Cross-national comparisons of health systems using OECD data, 1999. *Health Affairs* **21** (3), 169–181.

Schneiderman, N. & Speers, M.A. (2001). Behavioral science, social science, and public health in the 21st century. In N. Schneiderman, M.A. Speers, J.M. Silva, H. Tomes & J.H. Gentry (Eds),

Integrating Behavioral and Social Sciences with Public Health (pp. 3–28). Washington, DC: American Psychological Association.

Singer, B.H. & Ryff, C.D. (2001). *New Horizons in Health: An Integrative Approach*. Washington, DC: National Academy Press.

Shumaker, S.A. & Berzon, R. (1995). *The Assessment of Health-Related Quality of Life*. Oxford, UK: Rapid Scientific Communications.

Singer, B.H. & Ryff, C.D. (2001). *New Horizons in Health: An Integrative Approach*. Washington, DC: National Academy Press.

Spilker, B. (Ed.) (1996). *Quality of Life and Pharmacoeconomics in Clinical Trials* (2nd edn). Philadelphia, PA: Lippincott-Raven.

Stone, G. (Ed.) (1983). National working conference on education and training in health psychology. *Health Psychology*, **2** (5, Suppl.).

Tucker, J., Phillips, M., Murphy, J.G. & Raczynski, J. (in press). Behavioral epidemiology and health psychology. In R.G. Frank, A. Baum & J. Wallender (Eds), *Models and Perspectives in Health Psychology*. Washington, DC: American Psychological Association.

Walker, S.R. & Rosser, R.M. (1993). *Quality of Life Assessment: Key Issues for the 1990s*. Dordrecht: Kluwer Academic Publishers.

Weimer, D.L. & Vining, A.R. (1999). *Policy Analysis: Concepts and Practice* (3rd edn). Upper Saddle River, NJ: Prentice Hall.

WHO (2002). *Innovative Care for Chronic Conditions: Building Blocks for Action*. Annual report of the World Health Organization.

CHAPTER 28

Convergence, Integration and Priorities

Paul Kennedy
and
Susan Llewelyn
University of Oxford, UK

This book has provided an overview of much that is known in clinical health psychology today. What is now needed is further growth of the broad portfolio of applied research, so that findings can be put into practice and integrated within the health care context. We also need to increase the awareness of the contribution of psychological factors to service providers and consumers. Smith, Kendall and Keefe (2002) note that one of the greatest opportunities and challenges for researchers and clinicians is translating the wealth of basic behavioural and medical science research into clinical research and practice. This book echoes this concern. The contributors to this Handbook have all highlighted a number of themes, challenges, future directions and trends for the future.

The first challenge is conceptual. The exact mechanisms of the interplay of many of our models and theoretical frameworks remain unclear and require further research and exploration. We need to maintain our commitment to the scientific basis of practice, which should also include replications of existing studies and the construction of more conclusive knowledge frameworks. Much of our research is non-cumulative. We need to be cautious about our more exciting and provocative findings—for example, Miller and Cohen (2001) reviewed the evidence that psychological interventions modulate the human immune response, and found that only modest evidence existed to support successful immune modulation. However, with further conceptual and methodological refinement, definitive conclusions are achievable. Greater integration is required between the practice of clinical health psychology and its theoretical underpinnings.

Clinical health psychology exemplifies the scientist-practitioner model. Much has been achieved, utilising traditional behavioural and social cognition models, and further integration is required with models of organisational behaviour, the new biogenetics and health economics. Glanz, Lewis and Rimer (1997) examined the theoretical frameworks in the health behaviour literature and reviewed all issues of 24 journals in health education, medicine and behavioural sciences from mid-1992 to mid-1994. Two-thirds of the total instances of theory

Handbook of Clinical Health Psychology. Edited by S. Llewelyn and P. Kennedy.
© 2003 John Wiley & Sons, Ltd.

use accounted for the following eight theories or models: the Health Belief model (20%); Social Cognitive Theory (15%); Self-Efficacy (15%); Theory of Reasoned Action/Theory of Planned Behaviour (13%); Community Organisation (10%); Transtheoretical Model (10%); Social Marketing (9%) and Social Support (8%). While there is a value in maintaining the distinctness of some of these models, there is also merit in recognising the need for parsimony, convergence and synthesis. A challenge for theoreticians is to consolidate, refine and integrate existing models, yet ensure that they are comprehensible to our health care colleagues and communities. Theory-driven intervention research will help us to improve our models and enhance our methods in managing health-related problems.

Second, research has demonstrated that it is possible to reduce risk factors associated with the main causes of morbidity and mortality. Much is known, much has changed, and more should be done. In future we need to consider ways of integrating behavioural change factors into society at a broader level. This will include focusing on community level interventions in the workplace and places of education. Also, prevention strategies need to be targeted to younger people and integrated within social structures with a greater focus on a reduction of morbidity.

Third, demographic shifts have highlighted that fewer and fewer people will be available as service providers. In the longer-term future, we require different methods of interventions outside traditional health care services. Wren and Michie, in this Handbook, have highlighted the importance of investing in staff, promoting wellness and increasing support. We also need to consider the position and conditions of informal health care providers and the health impact of the largely female carers of working age that provide support to those with chronic conditions as they move through the life span. We need to identify psychological and social factors associated with effective functioning in providing health care, of both a formal and informal nature. The wider issue of deteriorating female health needs to be explored, as well as a greater focus on community social facilitation of health care with respect to knowledge, intervention and management.

A related issue is that clinical health psychologists also need to continue to focus more on the wider social context of health. Historically, it has focused on the individual and less on the family, school, work, community and governmental context. Socially isolated people have two to five times higher death rates than those who maintain close ties to family, friends and the community (Berkman & Glass, 2000). We have already discussed the impact of caregiving, but we also know that involving spouses and family caregivers in health interventions in people with debilitating chronic diseases maximises positive health outcomes (Keefe et al., 2002; Lehrer et al., 2002).

A further challenge relates to the more dangerous environments we are creating with respect to pollution, toxicity and materialism. Wadden, Brownell and Foster (2002) suggest that the frequent junk food advertisements and the greater availability of poor-quality food in schools has combined to create a toxic environment that fosters unhealthy eating patterns very early in children's lives. Perri and Corsica, in this Handbook, highlight not only how prevalent worldwide obesity has become, but that effective interventions are expensive and require continuous life-long approaches.

We also need to promote a more integrated perspective with respect to research on aetiological factors and treatment of conditions. Greater collaboration is required between the disciplines of psychology, which also needs to include other health disciplines, such as biostatistics, health economics and epidemiology. There has been a tremendous growth in research expenditure on medication and in biogenetics. We need to ensure that appropriate attention is placed on behavioural factors associated with these issues. Two per cent of deaths are directly attributable to purely genetic diseases and 60% of late-onset disorders (such as diabetes, strokes and some cancers) have some genetic component. However, as with most predispositions, risk is expressed only with exposure to behavioural lifestyle factors that are controllable (Rowe & Kahn, 1998). The best treatments are rendered ineffective by non-adherence, yet biomedical practitioners largely ignore the extensive evidence supporting behavioural interventions (see Chapter 3). Much research is focused on disease categories, and what is required is the creation of funding mechanisms that support research efforts across a broad range of behavioural and social risks, rather than risk reductions for specific diseases. The "cardinal symptom" health care delivery system described by Frank and his colleagues in Chapter 27 of this Handbook exemplifies a bridge between primary care and hospital specialties. Behavioural science is not as expensive as much of the biomedical research undertaken and, arguably, the potential payoff is greater. We need to refocus, refine and increase the accessibility of measures of behavioural outcomes.

Most health economies (except for the USA) spend less than 10% of their gross national product on health care. It is unlikely that this will change, and yet there is a growing call on these resources. Clinical health psychologists, therefore, also need to demonstrate both the cost-effectiveness and improved outcomes of their interventions. The research by Lorig, Mazonson and Holman (1993) remains one of the very few studies to demonstrate both, in that their Arthritis Self Help Group course resulted in significant reductions in the use of health services and better patient functioning. Kaplan and Groessl (2002) reviewed the evidence for cost-effectiveness of behavioural and psychological interventions, and concluded that while the literature consistently shows a reduction in the utilisation of health care services following intervention across a wide range, few studies met the criteria for high-quality cost-effective evaluations. The methodological standards on cost-effectiveness, as outlined by Gold et al. (1996), offer several suggestions for the conduct of such studies. They reported on the results of a panel on cost-effectiveness and produced guidelines, which address many of the limitations of previous designs and analysis. Clinical health psychology researchers need to focus more on cost-effectiveness and cost–benefit analysis and should incorporate into their designs the recent methodological advances in this area. Kaplan and Groessl (2002), in their review, found that many studies presented no formal cost accounting and were difficult to evaluate in relation to other changes in current medical care (for example, length of stay for most surgery has decreased considerably in the past few years).

The next issue to be considered is the need to work more closely with others. In particular, closer partnerships need to be established with consumers and users of health care. There are tremendous complexities and potential political difficulties here, as there is a potential for conflict between groups with respect to resource allocation and making policy decisions with respect to research priorities and need. Clinical health psychologists also need to build up partnerships with consumer groups and the public to increase their awareness and responsivity to supporting clinical research and services.

Another major challenge to be addressed is the changing nature of ill health. Shewchuk and Elliott (2000) report that over 100 million Americans of all ages have at least one chronic physical condition. Such chronic conditions are positively related to levels of morbidity, mortality and disability. They also place individuals at risk for secondary complications, further disability and increased health care expenditure. Individuals are surviving longer and many terminal conditions have become chronic diseases, such as HIV/Aids, many cancers, Alzheimer's disease and even strokes. Increased survival will require attention to the management of such chronic conditions with a need to apply rehabilitation strategies to those older persons with concurrent chronic diseases. We need more research that longitudinally examines disability pathways in such chronic conditions, as well as highlighting factors that mediate or mitigate morbidity. In recent years, patients and their families are recognised as the primary caregivers to chronic illness (Holman & Lorig, 2000). Collaborative self-management strategies have been found to be effective in improving medical, emotional and functional outcomes (Andersen, 1992; Glasgow, Toobert & Hampson, 1996; Turner, 1996). More research needs to be encouraged to develop such intervention models, identifying key therapeutic strategies and linking with user groups, voluntary groups and local services. The British National Health Service has utilised the essential elements of self-management as the basis for its *Expert Patient: The New Approach to Chronic Disease Management in the Twenty-First Century*, a policy framework document (NHS, 2001) (see Chapter 3 of this volume). Holman and Lorig (2000) highlight how self-management, group involvement and remote management of chronic diseases reduce costs and improve health status across a range of conditions. The ascendancy of chronic over acute conditions requires a change in the delivery of health care. We propose that clinical health psychology is central to primary care, and that we have a challenge ahead.

Other related issues are those of cultural, social and ethnic differences. Recently, research attention has focused on the relationship and impact of race/ethnicity, gender, and social economic status on health disease and health behaviours. Cross-cultural studies are also needed to delineate biological, psychological, behavioural and social correlates of health among persons and societies with varying degrees of social and economic orderings (Whitfield et al., 2002). We have growing expectations of what health care can provide. There are fewer people employed to support the infrastructure of health care regardless of source of funding, i.e. private health insurance, state funding or corporate providers. With greater demands, some of the more contentious areas of health care will require careful thought and examination. These include issues associated with personal responsibility for health problems, such as smoking and obesity, and issues associated with rationing and end-of-life decision-making with respect to assisted suicide and euthanasia. In many ways we have yet to develop an integrated, coherent, moral, scientific and philosophical framework for exploring these issues. This is a challenge for the twenty-first century.

Another related issue is the growth of differential health care provision. In many developed economies, a four-tier health care system appears to be developing, i.e. the unprovided, the underprovided, the provided and the overprovided. The broader costs of a more concierge or "boutique" health care system needs to be fully accounted for with respect to training, provision and support. Effective clinical health psychology training provides a rigorous foundation in psychological science, research design, formulation, psychological theory and a range of psychotherapeutic interventions. Providers of services will require greater flexibility, increased multidisciplinary models of training and more focus on population needs. The major health improvements of the industrial era came more from changes in food production, sanitary conditions and family size than from medical interventions.

We also need to be prepared to adopt different paradigms for clinical practice, research and policy-making. We may not know what these paradigms are at the moment, but challenges ahead include: integrating clinical health psychology with the new biogenetics; managing primary care; moving away from more traditional one-to-one intervention models to include group interventions; adopting models such as Lorig's programme in Stanford based on a cascading system involving volunteers and users of health care; and refining our formulation and assessment methods to match the limited resources and high demand in health care.

Further challenges include integrating with new technologies in the areas of communication, physiological assessment and neuro-imaging. Future pandemics need to be considered. There is a need to consider many other factors, such as: lifelong support and intervention systems; research in integrating newer psychological models, e.g. positive psychology; the issue of adherence, costs of transplants; costs of prolonging life; multi-centre longitudinal meta-analyses; role of self-examination; technologies integrated into domestic environments; pushing findings from the West into the developing world; improving our assessment of outcome; increasing our focus on quality-of-life outcomes; the issue of corporate responsibilities, e.g. fast food manufacturers, the tobacco and alcohol industries; consequences of recent research concerning psychological interventions in the immune system. There are many other challenges that we have yet to predict.

To conclude, the agenda for clinical health psychology is enormous. The demands are high, and will increase, as our competencies, expectations and aspirations also increase. Our resources are diminishing with respect to changes in demography and possible economic recession. The costs could be considerable, but so can the benefits in terms of increasing the quality and value of life. We hope that this volume will contribute to this venture, and will prove to be of use to researchers, students, policy-makers and practitioners of clinical health psychology in taking this enormous agenda into the future.

REFERENCES

Andersen, B.L. (1992). Psychological interventions for cancer patients to enhance the quality of life. *Journal of Consulting and Clinical Psychology*, **60**, 552–568.

Berkman, L.F. & Glass, T. (2000). Social integration, social networks, social support and health. In L.F. Berkman & I. Kawachi (Eds), *Social Epidemeology* (pp. 137–173). New York: Oxford University Press.

Glanz, K., Lewis, F.M. & Rimer, B.K. (1997). *Health Behavior and Health Education: Theory, Research and Practice* (2nd edn). San Francisco: Jossey-Bass.

Glasgow, R.E., Toobert, D.J. & Hampson, S.E. (1996). Effects of a brief office based intervention to facilitate diabetes dietary self-management. *Diabetes Care*, **19**, 835–842.

Gold, N.R., Siegel, J.E., Russell, L.B. & Weinstein, M.C. (1996). *Cost Effectiveness in Health and Medicine*. New York: Oxford University Press.

Holman, H.R. & Lorig, K. (2000). Patients as partners in managing chronic disease. *British Medical Journal*, **320**, 526–527.

Kaplan, R.M. & Groessl, E.J. (2002). Applications of cost-effectiveness methodologies in behavioural medicine. *Journal of Consulting and Clinical Psychology*, **70**, 482–493.

Keefe, F.J., Smith, S.J., Buffington, A.L.H., Gibson, J., Studts, J. & Caldwell, D. (2002). Recent advances and future directions in the biopsychosocial assessment and treatment of arthritis. *Journal of Consulting and Clinical Psychology*, **70**, 640–655.

Lehrer, P., Feldman, J., Giardino, N., Song, H. & Schmaling, K. (2002). Psychological aspects of asthma. *Journal of Consulting and Clinical Psychology*, **70**, 691–711.

Lorig, K.R., Mazonson, P.D. & Holman, H.R. (1993). Evidence suggesting that health education for self-management in patients with chronic arthritis has sustained health benefits while reducing healthcare costs. *Arthritis and Rheumatology*, **36**, 439–446.

Miller, G.E. & Cohen, S. (2001). Psychological interventions in the immune system: a meta-analytic review and critique. *Health Psychology*, **20**, 47–63.

Rowe, J.W. & Kahn, R. (1998). *Successful Ageing*. New York: Pantheon Books.

Shewchuk, R. & Elliott, T.R. (2000). Family care-giving in chronic disease and disability. In *Handbook of Rehabilitation Psychology* (pp. 553–563). Washington, DC: American Psychological Association.

Smith, T.W., Kendall, P.C. & Keefe, F.J. (2002). Behavioral medicine and clinical health psychology: introduction to the special issue, a view from the decade of behavior. *Journal of Consulting and Clinical Psychology*, **70**, 459–462.

Turner, J.A. (1996). Educational and behavioural interventions for back pain in primary care. *Spine*, **21**, 2851–2857.

Wadden, T.A., Brownell, K.D. & Foster, G.D. (2002). Obesity: responding to the global epidemic. *Journal of Consulting and Clinical Psychology*, **70**, 510–525.

Whitfield, K.E., Clark, R., Weidner, G. & Anderson, N. (2002). Social demographic diversity and behavioural medicine. *Journal of Consulting and Clinical Psychology*, **70**, 463–481.

Author Index

Abbey, S. 294
Abiodun, O.A. 331
Abraham, C. 377
Abraham, S. 335, 338, 370
Abramsky, L. 375
Achat, H. 509
Acton, T. 424, 425
Adams, N. 410
Adams, P.C. 278
Adams, P.F. 160
Addison, R.B. 478, 479, 488, 492
Adesso, V.J. 508
Adetoro, O.O. 331
Adler, N.E. 374, 375
Adlis, S.A. 185
Afari, N. 318
Agius, R.M. 42
Agle, D.P. 170
Agras, W.S. 464
Ahles, T.A. 294
Aikens, J.E. 288
Ailinger, R.L. 486
Ainsleigh, H.G. 106
Ajzen, I. 376
Albert, H. 343
Albrecht, G.L. 267, 269
Albrecht, R.J. 188
Alder, B.A. 379
Alder, E.M. 370, 371, 372, 379
Alexander, C.J. 259
Alfredsson, L. 509
Allen, E.V. 304
Allen, F. 471
Allen, S. 110
Allen, S.M. 120
Allen, T.D. 46
Allison, D.B. 183
Allshouse, J.E. 184
Altabe, M. 393
Altheide, D.L. 478
Altman, B.A. 70
Altman, D.G. 380
Alvarez, W. 114, 361
Ames, G.M. 509

Ancona, C. 503
Andersen, B.L. 110, 114, 115, 117, 119, 120, 566
Andersen, T. 186, 190, 194
Anderson, B. 207
Anderson, B.J. 69
Anderson, G.F. 548, 549
Anderson, J.E. 508
Anderson, J.G. 43
Anderson, K.O. 138
Anderson, R. 212
Anderson, S. 240
Andersson, G. 234, 237, 238, 241, 242, 244
Andersson, T. 323
Anderton, K.J. 331, 332
Andrykowski, M.A. 110, 120
Anllo, L.M. 120
Annesi, J.J. 32
Annis, H.M. 285
Anthonisen, N.R. 158
Antó, J.M. 157
Antoni, M.H. 109, 110, 116, 117, 119, 120, 318, 421
Antonucci, T. 65
Apfelbaum, M. 187
Appels, A. 82, 83, 95
Appleby, L. 307, 379
Aral, S. 407, 409
Aranda, M.P. 65, 66
Arendt, H. 172
Armstrong, B.K. 106
Arndt, E. 396
Arndt, L.A. 114
Arnetz, B. 52
Arnold, P. 236
Arnold, S.B. 445
Arsenault, A. 46
Arthur, H.M. 87
Artis, J.E. 64
Ashcroft, D. 393
Ashcroft, J.J. 461
Ashton, J. 514
Ashutosh, K. 160
Ashworth, P. 390, 461

Subject Index

Note: Page references in *italic* refer to Figures and Tables